LANGUAGE DEVELOPMENT

VOLUME 1
Syntax and Semantics

CHILD PSYCHOLOGY

A series of volumes edited by **David S. Palermo**

*This book is lovingly dedicated to Abe and Ben Kuczaj,
who have learned more about language in the past ten and five
years, respectively, than I have.*

Contents

PREFACE

There is almost no scientific theory which was held to be funda-mental in 1867 which is thought to be true in that form today.
(Bronowski, 1978, p. 56)

Science is not quite the objective enterprise envisioned by most laymen and popularized by many B-movies. To the contrary, science is a largely subjective enterprise subjected to the biases of its participants (i.e., scientists). This is not to say that scientists are intentionally non-objective in their formation of hypotheses and interpretation of data. Nonetheless, their unconscious biases may color their interpretation of data (and perhaps even the data themselves, see Rosenthal, 1966). One of the factors which contributes most to a biased interpretation of data is *theoretical stance*. It is not always the case that believers in a theory objectively interpret data relevant to the theory (Kuhn, 1962). If the data contradict predictions made by the theory, believers in the theory need not abandon the theory as an incorrect guess. Instead they may attack the data, so that by putting the data into question, it no longer becomes necessary to abandon the theory, since the data which cast the theory into doubt are themselves cast into doubt. Or, advocates of a theory might attempt to interpret the data such that it accords with the theory. Thus, the simple collection of data will not necessarily resolve theoretical disputes, given the typical unwillingness of theorists to abandon their views in the face of bothersome data.

The study of language acquisition is a science, albeit a relatively young one. As such, it possesses a number of important questions which direct research in the field. However, given that developmental psycholinguists are scientists and human beings (not always in that order), the types of answers a particular developmental psycholinguist gives to these questions depends on his or her assumptions about the nature of language and the nature of the language acquisition process. If they believe that language is primarily a surface structure phenomenon [i.e., syntactic/semantic relations are specified in the surface structure (or level of spoken speech)], then they will probably argue that language acquisition is primarily an experiential phenomenon, i.e., one in which the child's linguistic environment (input) plays a crucial role (see Braine, 1976; Derwing, 1973; Starosta, 1976). If on the other hand they believe that language involves both abstract deep structures which differ significantly from their corresponding surface structures and mechanisms (transformational rules) for relating deep structures to surface structures, then they will be led to posit innate tacit knowledge of deep structures and transformational rules (although the innate knowledge need not specify particular individual deep structures nor particular transformational rules), a position having been taken by Chomsky (1957, 1965) and McNeill (1970). If language involves deep structures and transformational rules (if it involves one, it necessarily involves the other) such as those specified by Chomsky (1957, 1965), innate tacit knowledge of deep structures and transformational rules is necessary for language acquisition because the child experiences only surface structures and there is no viable account of how the child could abstract deep structures and transformational rules from experience with surface structures unless the child possesses innate means for such acquisition. However, the fewer distinctions made between deep structure and surface structure, the less necessary it becomes to posit innate linguistic knowledge and the more likely an empirical account of syntactic development becomes (see Derwing, 1973).

Thus, there are different theoretical camps in the study of language acquisition which may lead to different accounts of the same data. As one might expect, differing interpretations have occurred. For example, errors such as *What's that is?, Whose is that is?, What did you did?* and *What did I told?* have been interpreted as support for theories of language development which emphasize the development of deep structures and transformational rules (Hurford, 1975; Fay, 1978; Mayer, Erreich & Valign, 1978; Goodluck & Solan, 1979) and as support for more surface-structure based accounts of language development (Kuczaj, 1976; Prideaux, 1976; Maratsos & Kuczaj, 1978). The ambiguity of data (though each of us attempt to disambiguate the data as best we can) is not only a problem for different investigators interpreting the same data, for individual investigators have also noted the difficulty of unequivocally interpreting their data. For example, in his discussion of Adam, Eve, and Sarah's acquisition of the fourteen morphemes studied by he and his colleagues, Brown (1973) noted that

> there is evidence that transformational complexity is a determinant of the order of acquisition but that except for simple plurals and the predicate nominative plurals,

this evidence can be alternatively interpreted as demonstrating that sematic complexity is a determinant of the order of acquisition. Whether it will some day be
possible to separate the two kinds of complexity remains to be seen. [p. 379].

All of the above is not intended to imply that theoretical disputes and questions about language acquisition cannot be resolved empirically. Answers to such
questions certainly rest heavily on empirical findings. However, straightforward
solutions to the problems and straight-forward resolutions of the disputes will not
readily appear from consideration of data concerning how children learn to talk,
given the ambiguity of many data. In fact, theoretical biases not only affect
interpretation of data but also may affect the data that is collected since different
theoretical positions may lend themselves to varying sorts of empirical tests. If
one is a proponent of a transformationally based account of language acquisition,
then one will tend to collect data which *may* be interpreted as support for such an
account. If one advocates a more surface-structure oriented account of language
learning, then one will tend to gather data which *may* be interpreted as supporting such an account (the italization of *may* in both of the preceding sentences is
meant to emphasize the usual ambiguity of the data cited to support given
theoretical positions).

The above may have given the reader the impression that one's view of
language governs one's view of the language acquisition process. In fact, such
has typically been the case–e.g., Chomsky (1957, 1965) and McNeill (1970) attempted to account for language structure and relations in terms of an abstract linguistic system (Chomsky, 1957, 1965). An account of language was formulated
that led to certain assumptions about the language acquisition process and the
amount and type of innate knowledge the child brings to the language acquisition task. It seems likely that this approach to the study of language acquisition
is overly one-sided in the emphasis on theories of language qua language, accounts of language acquisition then being molded so that they accord with the
preferred theory of language. Although it is true that any theory of language
places constraints on corresponding accounts of language acquisition (i.e., one's
account of language acquisition should be consistent with one's account of language as a productive communicative system), accounts of language development
also place constraints on corresponding accounts of language in the sense that
what develops determines what it is that is supposed to be accounted for by
theories of language per se. Thus the theoretical constraints are bidirectional
rather than unidirectional and developmental psycholinguists can provide insights
about the nature of language as well as the nature of language acquisition.

The chapters that follow concern themselves with both theoretical and empirical accounts of language development. The chapters fall into two broad
categories; those concerned with syntactic development and those concerned
with semantic development. Those chapters focusing on syntactic development
address issues about the nature of syntactic categories and rules, and the factors

that contribute to the acquisition of such categories and rules. Those chapters focusing on semantic development are concerned with the nature of word meaning and its acquisition. The author(s) of the chapters attempt to specify the important questions for their area of concern and then attempt to answer these questions. There is no doubt that the chapters reflect the individual biases of the author(s). Nonetheless, even though the answers may be incomplete (or perhaps even wrong), it seems more important at this stage of the study of language acquisition to specify the questions—the right questions must be asked before the right answers can be found. The Bronowski quote that began this preface was not intended to cast a pessimistic note on the contents of this book in particular and the study of language acquisition in general. Instead, it was intended to place the current state of the art in proper perspective. The study of language acquisition is an exciting and dynamic area. For the area to continue to progress along these lines, questions must be asked and answered, to be replaced by new questions and new answers, etc. If the chapters which follow spur such advancement, this book will have been successful.

Stan A. Kuczaj II
Dallas, Texas

REFERENCES

Braine, M. Children's first word combinations. Monographs of the Society for Research in Child Development, Vol. 41, *1*, No. 164, 1976.

Bronowski, J. *The origins of knowledge and imagination.* New Haven, Conn.: Yale University Press, 1978.

Brown, R. *A first language.* Cambridge, Mass.: Harvard University Press, 1973.

Chomsky, N. *Syntactic structures.* The Hague: Mouton, 1957.

Chomsky, N. *Aspects of the theory of syntax.* Cambridge, Mass.: M.I.T. Press, 1965.

Derwing, B. *Transformational grammar as a theory of language acquisition.* New York: Cambridge University Press, 1973.

Fay, D. Reply to Kuczaj (1976). *Journal of Child Language,* 1978, *5,* 143–149.

Goodluck, H., & Solan, L. A reevaluation of the basic-operations hypothesis. *Cognition,* 1979, *7,* 85–91.

Hurford, J. A child and the English question formation rule. *Journal of Child Language,* 1975, *2,* 299–301.

Kuczaj, S. Arguments against Hurford's 'Aux copying rule. *Journal of Child Language,* 1976, *3,* 423–427.

Kuhn, T. *The structure of scientific revolutions.* Chicago: University of Chicago Press, 1962.

Maratsos, M., & Kuczaj, S. Against the transformationalist account: a simpler analysis of auxiliary overmaskings. *Journal of Child Language,* 1978, *5,* 337–346.

Mayer, J., Erreich, A., & Valian, V. Transformations, basic operations and language acquisition. *Cognition,* 1978, *6,* 1–13.

McNeill, D. *The acquisition of language.* New York: Harper & Row, 1970.

Prideaux, G. A functional analysis of English question acquisition: A response to Hurford. *Journal of Child Language,* 1976, *3,* 417–422.

Rosenthal, R. *Experimental effects in behavioral research.* New York: Appleton, 1966.

Starosta, S. A place for case, *Language Learning,* 1976, *26,* 1–36.

LANGUAGE DEVELOPMENT

VOLUME 1
Syntax and Semantics

1

Theory and Method in Child-Language Research: Are We Assuming Too Much?

Ruth Clark
Queen Margaret College

INTRODUCTION

Simplification is necessary in science. Indeed, regarding a phenomenon as too complex is likely to lead to paralysis in the researcher. On the other hand, simplification has its risks. If one approaches a problem with simple assumptions, one is likely to contrive methods of measuring behavior that will confirm these assumptions. Borger and Seaborne (1966) commented about Thorndike's experiments on trial-and-error learning by cats in cages that they were more like studies of *cages with cats in them*. The behavior of the cat was so constrained by the limitations of the situation that the cat had no choice but to behave in a trial-and-error fashion, thereby confirming Thorndike's expectations.

It seems to me that in language-acquisition research, we are in some danger of studying *cages with children in them,* the cages being constructed of simplistic assumptions and inadequate research techniques. If you study children inside cages, you do not learn much about the children.

In this chapter, I plan to trace in very broad terms the development in the last 10 to 15 years of research into the acquisition of syntax, highlighting what I believe are some of the simplifications, of theory and method, that once may have been necessary to avoid paralysis, but should now be dispensed with.

The chapter consists of three main parts. In the first part, I look at some simplifications of theory, influenced mainly by the transformationalist approach. I explore the way that these simplifications have encouraged the researcher to view the child's output and the interrelationships between different language processes and different aspects of linguistic knowledge. I suggest that the concept of "ideal speaker-hearer" has not been properly exploited by these

1

simplified approaches, that they fail to capture either individual differences or the complex and many-faceted nature of language as a skilled performance, and that their stress on comprehension as the major vehicle of linguistic progress may be one-sided.

In the second part, I explore the role of production, with situational support, as a stepping stone towards the acquisition of knowledge about linguistic structure. I also examine claims that structured speech in the course of language development can be described as rule governed.

In the third part, I consider some simplistic assumptions underlying traditional research methods. In this discussion, I draw on points made earlier about the dependence of language on situation, the concept of ideal speaker–hearer, and differences between individual language learners.

SIMPLIFICATIONS OF THEORY

Relationships Between Processes

I am not drawn to the transformational approach to language acquisition (Chomsky, 1965), but there is one aspect of that theory that I believe has not been taken seriously enough: the concept of ideal speaker–hearer. In this section, I argue that the proper application of the concept has been avoided, but that it has been used in a distorted way to explain away evidence against the main tenets of the theory.

If rearchers had taken the idea of the ideal speaker–hearer seriously, they would have been at pains to create ideal conditions in which the child's performance would be at its best. In fact, the conditions in which studies have been made have often been far from ideal. In particular, insufficient allowance has been made for observer effects, a point I return to in the third section of this chapter.

Despite Chomsky's warning that not all speech is an ideal reflection of competence, all utterances in a corpus have been treated as relevant fodder for syntactic analysis (barring, of course, utterances judged to be imitations, which were held by followers of this approach to be irrelevant to the process of language learning). What was in fact assumed was that *all* the speech was produced in less than ideal conditions, rather than that some utterances were less ideal than others.

The concept of performance restrictions was abused to account for the inadequacies of the speech corpus, and assumptions were being made about what an adequate performance ought to be like. It was as if one were driving with a misty windscreen along a familiar road, assuming that the landmarks were there, although they could not actually be seen; in fact they had never been seen but were assumed to be there, according to a map drawn of another place, (i.e. adult competence). A typical example of this approach was Bellugi's (1968) appeal to a constraint on the joint operation of two rules to account for the immature structure of children's *wh* questions. Another was Bloom's (1970) use of 'reduction transformations' to explain the multiple ambiguity of children's utterances. An example relating to phonological development was Smith's (1973) formulation of 'incompetence rules' to elucidate the gap between children's receptive and productive capacities.

The 'common sense' view that comprehension is in advance of production was widely expressed at that time by professional, as well as lay, observers (Bellugi & Brown, 1964, p. 41). Although doubts were sometimes raised, it was a simplification that fit well with this theoretical approach, because it provided both an explanation of how children came to have more knowledge of language than they could express, and a field where the researcher's assumptions about superior knowledge could potentially be confirmed. Thus, it was assumed that there were fewer performance restrictions in comprehension than in the production of speech (an assumption that I have always regarded as counterintuitive, as I explain later). This alleviation of performance restrictions in comprehension explained children's apparent superior performance in comprehension over production. What could not be acknowledged without endangering the theory was that there are many cues to meaning in comprehension over and above the verbal input.

Nor could it be acknowledged that imitative utterances can be more complex in structure than spontaneous ones, unless it was also upheld that such imitations occurred with full comprehension by the child of what he or she was reproducing. Blind mimicry as a source of novel forms was incompatible with a theory based on complex processing abilities. Thus, the occurrence of imitations more elaborate in structure than spontaneous speech was explained in a similar way to the superiority of comprehension over production—by appeal to a lightening of performance restrictions. I take up this issue again in the second part of this chapter.

So, instead of the concept of the ideal speaker-hearer being used as it ought to be, to remind us that children are not always performing at their own current best in any activity, it was used to construct explanations for differences between the different types of performance—production, comprehension, and imitation. Performance restrictions were used as a sort of air valve, which could be operated to adjust the buoyancy in different parts of the structure, and keep it on an even keel. One grammar could account for all three performances, and variations between them could readily be dismissed. Thus, a simplified theory maintained a standard relationship between the three aspects of linguistic activity, a relationship consistent with the basic orientation of transformationalist theory.

But, there is a further aspect of the "ideal" nature of the ideal speaker-hearer that should have been kept in mind: that one can only be an ideal speaker-hearer when one has mastery of the language, which is precisely what the learner does not have. It is, therefore, important to keep in mind that all aspects of linguistic skill and conceptual, as well as social, understanding are in the process of development.

The Description of Data

Problematically, it is not easy to handle the description of a process in which the values of all the relevant variables are unknown. Thus, many researchers into child language have made simplifying assumptions that one aspect of linguistic skill develops in advance of others. In this section, I consider some of these simplifications, challenging each of them in turn. I try to show that it is very easy to find counterevidence against any categorical assumption about the priority of one aspect of conceptual or linguistic skill over another. My conclusion is that as a complex skill, language involves a number of functions, interwoven with each other, and that the relative order of their mastery need not be equivalent for all children. The three main proposals I discuss are: (1) that children have syntactic knowledge long before they can express it in structured speech (McNeill, 1970); (2) that children's use of certain formal devices is evidence of their intentions to express newly attained meanings (Bloom, 1973); and (3) that children's grasp of semantic relations is well ahead of their ability to express them verbally (Greenfield & Smith, 1976).

Syntactic Knowledge Prior to Structured Speech.   One way of simplifying is to attribute to children the ability to have intentions some time before they can be expressed by conventional linguistic means. For example, McNeill (1970) upheld that basic syntactic structures were known to children long before they could express them in speech. One source of evidence offered was the contrastive use of intonation to convey distinctions between different sentence types during the one-word stage. In other words, it was assumed that children are in command of expression at one level of linguistic structure before they have even begun to demonstrate tentative control at another level. This assumption allows the researcher to interpret word combinations fully when they do begin to occur, arguing that the underlying syntactic relations have been known to the child for some time.

But Halliday (1975) has shown that a child able to reproduce features of adult intonation does not necessarily use them for the same purposes as adults do, so the mere occurrence of forms in one-word speech that correspond to adult contrasts does not prove that they function to distinguish sentence types. A major problem in identifying the function *for the child* of an intonation pattern such as the one *we* might use for questioning is that there is often no clear correlate in the situation of the meaning distinction concerned. An attitude of questioning is in the speaker's mind, not outside where we can observe it. It is all too easy to assume that the child intended the question intonation to express a question, for, just as there is nothing to substantiate that in the situation, there may very well be nothing to contradict it either.

Another argument against McNeill's early theory that children beginning to put words together already know the rudiments of syntax is that in their word combinations, children do not always appear to be using phrase-structure rules. For example, a number of researchers have pointed out that semantic factors, such as "animacy," rather than syntactic factors, such as "subject," may determine word order (Bowerman, 1973; de Villiers & de Villiers, 1974).

Treating syntactic structures as known has not, it seems, proved a satisfactory way of reducing the complexity of our model of early childhood communication. What of the other simplifications I mentioned?

Formal Devices Signal Newly Acquired Meanings. Another simplification in interpreting early child speech is to identify on the basis of formal criteria a specific point at which syntax emerges and to deny that the child may intend to convey relational meanings prior to that point (Bloom, 1973). Bloom's claim was that before the two-word stage, children are unable to hold in their minds, in one unified thought, more than one aspect of the situation. Successive one-word utterances reflect a child's need to concentrate on one aspect of the situation at a time. Subsequently, a child achieves a conceptual grasp of the situation as a whole, but is still unable to express that grasp linguistically. Later, the newly achieved ability to do so becomes manifest in the earliest of genuine two-word utterances. These are characterized first by stable word order, and the child gradually achieves mastery of sentence prosody. Should sentence prosody occur in the absence of stable word order, Bloom concedes that the child has shown he or she can hold two concepts in the mind at the same time, without having yet learned the linguistic code for expressing the relationship between them.

Bloom's aim in making these proposals was a conservative one. She wanted to resist what she saw in theories such as McNeill's as the attribution of too much linguistic sophistication to children in the one-word stage. However, the identification of intention with systematic formal expression embodies two simplistic assumptions. In the first place, it assumes that children cannot conceive of, let alone communicate about, relations between people, objects, and activities in their world until they have command of the conventional formal means for doing so. In the second place, it assumes that systematic use of formal linguistic devices is foolproof evidence that children understand the way these devices function to communicate meanings.

Greenfield and Smith (1976) have rightly criticized Bloom for failing to distinguish between linguistic form and semantic content, in taking joint expression of two elements to be the only evidence for meaning. Their criticisms gain force from a consideration of Goldin-Meadow's (1979) findings regarding deaf children of hearing parents. If we deny that hearing children can express relational meanings before the two-word stage, and explain their inability in terms of lack of conceptual maturity, what sense can we make of the gesture sequences produced by these deaf children at a much younger age? Are deaf children developing conceptually at a greater rate? Surely not! Furthermore, how would we interpret cases of hearing children, like my second son Ivan, who began to produce gesture sequences at 14 months, several months earlier than he produced sequences of spoken words? Would one count him as a deaf child who had developed rapidly conceptually, or a hearing child with some early gesture sequences that had no relational meaning?

Perhaps we should resist attributing relational meaning to the gesture sequences, and only attribute it to the word sequences? But this seems a trifle arbitrary. A more reasonable interpretation, in my view, is that it is easier to express concepts by some means than by others—for example, by sequences of iconic gestures rather than sequences of conventional words, each with an internal phonological structure. Why deny or attribute the status of expression to one and not to the other?

Bloom, then , may have been wrong to deny intention to communicate relational meanings before the two-word stage. She may also have been wrong to treat certain formal characteristics of utterances as reliable evidence for the emergence of relational meaning. To cling to word order and prosodic contour as objective criteria for meaning is to treat these phenomena as given in the way that McNeill treated syntactic structures as given. It is to overlook the fact that the function of these devices is another thing that children must learn about their language. As soon as the formal devices appear, it is assumed that they are being used appropriately. The researcher ought rather to be tracing the child's gradual development towards mastery of these devices and their linguistic functions. In fact, Bloom herself presents some fascinating evidence that the transition to syntax is far less abrupt than her theory predicts. Yet, she seems to have felt the need to explain it away. (For a fuller discussion, see Clark, 1975b).

Similar evidence is also available from other sources. For example, there is evidence that a unified intonation contour is not an infallible sign in all children of semantic cohesion between the elements of an utterance. My colleagues and I found many examples of unified contours in the speech of my older son Adam, without any semantic cohesion between the words spoken (Clark, Hutcheson, & Van Buren, 1974). I have observed other children using successive one-word utterances with every appearance of an insistent intention to state something about the relationships between the components—for example, "hold, hand, hold, hand, hold, hand etc.,'' reaching out for his father's hand (Clark et al., 1974). At a later stage, we recorded phrases in Adam's speech that were related to separate aspects of a situation, but were integrated in one intonation contour. This in itself casts suspicion on the idea that there are sudden transitions in language development from one stage to the next. Far from being available at the outset as a reliable signal of semantic cohesion, a unified prosodic contour gradually brought to the service of meaning in two-word utterances may need to be worked at again before it can serve cohesive meaning in longer utterances.

Dore, Franklin, Miller, and Ramer (1976) cast further doubt on the view that an integrated prosodic contour signals the onset of relational meaning. They describe "presyntactic devices" that "serve a bridging function in the development of speech production [p. 24]." The child includes dummy elements in two-word utterances so that he or she can work at the prosody of two-word utterances independently of semantic relations. Dore et al. were concerned with the transition from one-word to two-word utterances, but there is evidence that children may practice producing longer prosodic units that are not correspondingly complex semantically at other phases in their development (Clark & Van Buren, 1973). When he was nearly 28 months old, my older son Adam prefaced a number of his utterances with his nickname "weasel" over the course of a few days—for example when he was 27 months, 29 days, he said "weasel rain gone" on a dry day that followed a rainy day on which he frequently commented on the rain. (Even if "weasel" were not semantically empty, but was the overt marker of the performative "I say," as some readers might be tempted to claim, this need not detract from its function as an aid to mastering the prosody of a longer utterance. After all, under this interpretation, "weasel" would derive from a different underlying sentence, so it would not be in direct semantic relationship with the other elements.) Peters (1977), too, has noted the use of "filler syllables" in the speech of a 17-month-old child, which she interpreted as "place holders to fill out not yet analyzed parts of a phrase [p. 564]."

An integrated prosodic contour seems to be neither a necessary nor a sufficient condition for the expression of a meaning relation. The same seems to be true of Bloom's other formal criterion, standard word order, which she saw as the expression not merely of relational meaning, but also as evidence for the mastery of the relevant linguistic code. Not only can meanings be expressed without the aid of standard word order, even well beyond the first word combinations, but standard word order may occur without being fully intended.

In my own data, word order went through a variety of highly idiosyncratic stages. For example, at one stage in my older son's development, two-word utterances seemed to reverse standard word order, apparently a result of the child's repeating the final word of the immediately preceding adult utterance as a preliminary to elaborating the idea by adding a word of his own. A little later, he placed nouns immediately after the verb regardless of their semantic function, yielding, for example, "clean floor up" and also "clean brush up." Certain words seemed to have preferred positions; for example, "Daddy" usually came at the beginning, regardless of its function: "Daddy post a letter" when we had just posted a letter *for* Daddy (Clark & Van Buren, 1973). Here is one child, at least, who appears to have expressed quite complex relational meanings over the course of many months with scant reference to standard word order.

In cases in which word order is standard, the problem is determining whether the standard form is the product of imitation, without full understanding of the semantic function of the word order, or whether the child grasps the potential function of the word order and is using it deliberately to convey meaning. I do not believe, as Bloom claimed in 1973, that we can take this for granted.

Furthermore, I suggest later in this chapter that for some children, orthodox, consistent forms may be more characteristic of formal observation sessions and idiosyncratic forms more characteristic of everyday interaction with familiar people (though this is apparently not true of Bloom's daughter).

Treating certain formal devices as available to subserve semantic intentions has apparently proved no more successful than McNeill's endeavor to simplify our view of language development. I have one more attempt at simplification to consider.

Semantic Knowledge Prior to Word Combinations.   The interest of Greenfield and Smith (1976) lay in describing one-word utterances, and tracing linguistic progress within the one-word stage. They therefore needed a principled basis for interpreting isolated words. Their argument is that children begin from a very early age to develop an understanding of their environment. They are aware of people performing actions, the effects these actions have on objects and on other people, the locations of objects and people, and so on. Greenfield and Smith are also impressed by the fact that mothers and their children appear able to communicate even before children can put two words together. They therefore adopt C. Fillmore's (1968) linguistic framework, which enables them to assign a semantic role, or case relation, to a word, whether or not any other word relating to the action is expressed. When a child utters a single word, they believe that child to be aware of the total event, or state of affairs, in which the named object, person, action, location, and so on, participates. The rest of the meaning is carried by the situation, or may be partly conveyed by the child's using gestures. The event, or state of affairs, is known to us from the situation, which can be interpreted by an adult observer. Thus, semantic roles can be assigned to the child's single words, and changes in the use of language can be traced during the one-word stage.

This, of course, contrasts sharply with Bloom's approach, for she only credits the child with a grasp of relational meaning once he or she can express it syntactically. Greenfield and Smith criticize Bloom for failing to distinguish form from content. They argue, quite properly, that there is a difference between being aware of a semantic relation and being able to encode it in the conventional way. They believe that a child may be holding a total situation in his or her head even though able to express only one word. Later, when more of the child's meaning is expressed overtly, by the addition of further words to utterances, the child is credited with appreciating the roles in the action of all the entities referred to, even though the word order may not conform to a conventional standard.

Sachs and Truswell (1978) make the same useful distinction between grasping an idea and grasping the means of its expression when they examine "nonsyntactic comprehension." Their study explores children's ability to respond to instructions by integrating words into a semantic relationship with one another.

The authors are not concerned with whether the children can decode word-order cues.

I find it an attractive feature of Greenfield and Smith's framework that it deemphasises the role of word order in the expression of early meanings by comparison with many other theories. Their justification for treating adult expansions as bona fide interpretations of a child's meaning is that a wide variety of specific wordings of expansions can be neutral with respect to the semantic relation encoded—for example (Greenfield & Smith, 1976), "break" in the appropriate circumstances might be expanded with impunity as either "the eggs break" or "Mummy breaks the eggs [p. 46]." Greenfield and Smith believe that the outline utterance that the child holds in his or her mind during the one-word stage is filled out with more linguistic elements, to substitute for nonlinguistic elements, by the child's taking additional words from the mother's expansion of his or her utterance. Because word order in the mother's expansions will be variable, it follows that word order cannot be crucial in interpreting the child's intentions.

Despite some of its advantages, I believe that there are crucial difficulties with this approach in the assumptions it makes regarding correspondence of meanings in child and adult speech and mutual comprehension between mother and child.

Greenfield and Smith criticize Bloom for not distinguishing between knowledge of concepts and knowledge of the linguistic elements that encode those concepts. But, in fact, they are guilty of the same confusion themselves. One of the key assumptions behind their interpretations is that when a child uses a single word he or she means by that word what an adult would mean. Greenfield and Smith (1976) say: "We assume that an element that phonetically resembles an adult vocabulary item also semantically resembles it [p. 45]." They criticize a number of previous commentators on one-word utterances for confusing "referential" with "combinatorial" meaning. A single word used in a variety of situations retains, they claim, its precise referential meaning. In combination with a variety of different situational elements, it assumes different combinatorial meanings. By this reasoning, they deny that the meaning of early words is as fluid as has been supposed. They also reject the concept of a "holophrase" with a single word standing for a whole sentence. For them, the word has its conventional meaning and the meaning of other elements of the sentence is supplied by aspects of the situation, or gestures by the child.

I fail to see how one can be quite so sure of the scope of early words. To assume that from their initial use, words mean what they will always mean is to ignore the need for learning about lexis, just as Bloom ignored the need for learning about formal linguistic features. Indeed, Greenfield and Smith accept evidence of certain clear-cut mismatches between child and adult meanings—for example, the child's use of "up" to mean both "up" and "down." It seems to me unreasonable to be so confident that when no evidence of mismatch occurs, meanings must necessarily correspond precisely. There are two questions involved here. One is: "Does the child always have the relevant concept before acquiring its linguistic exponent?" Greenfield and Smith (1976) take a categorical view on this issue, going so far as to accuse Halliday of taking "the untenable position that the child uses language to construct his conceptual framework [p. 209]." Not everyone finds this view totally untenable (e.g., Blank, 1974, Schlesinger, 1977; Vygotsky, 1962). Why must standpoints on this issue be either "untenable" or "incontravertably true"? May one not judge language to be helpful in developing and refining concepts without being committed to the view that understanding is impossible without it?

The second question is: "In a particular instance, if a child does have the relevant concept, will that child always identify the conventional exponent and match it up with his or her concept with unfailing accuracy?" A categorical assent to this view seems to me to be even less reasonable. Let us take a single example. A child says "leave" while lifting up the lid of the mother's sewing box (Clark, 1975a). We might well have doubts about the child's understanding of the word. If the child had said "lid," would we have been right to take understanding for granted? As Peters (1980) points out in a working paper: "Since the child does not know the language, it is unreasonable to assume that the first units s/he extracts will coincide exactly with the words and morphemes of the system [p. 6]."

This brings me to Greenfield and Smith's views about mutual comprehension between mother and child. Their description of how a child extends an utterance by filling out an outline from elements in the mother's expansion presupposes that the child can identify the component of the mother's expansion that fulfills the relevant function allowed for in the outline. Greenfield and Smith, quite properly, reason that all communication, even in adults, relies heavily on cues beyond the verbal formulations themselves. To view communication between mother and child in terms of the filling out of meanings from context is therefore to do justice to the broad nature of communication. What I feel they fail to acknowledge, however, is that a great deal of adult communication is, in fact, miscommunication, simply because preconceptions of the participants and the total social and conceptual frame of reference actually override the literal meanings of the words themselves, even for speakers who know the language. We all experience instances every day. Recently, for instance, I wrote "primitive" at the end of a students essay, assuming that the student was familiar with my habit of listing at the end words spelled wrong in the text. Unfortunately, the student took it as a criticism of her work. Also, a few days ago, I bought a bookcase; on leaving the store, I asked the antique dealer for a card. I was puzzled when he said, "Have you got a card?" There was stress on "card," which I took to be given information, and I could not see why he expected me to have a card in any case. It was some time later that I realized he had been inquiring whether I had a car.

As for a child's own involvement in communication, clearly not all imitations of expansions would need to be accurate for this process to play a part in language learning. But, for it to be the major mechanism of such learning, the child would need to be fairly competent at intuiting the meanings of elements of expansions. I find this proposal implausible as a general account of language learning, because my own research into my sons' speech abounds with examples of misconstrued copies of elements of adult utterances (Clark, 1977, 1980), as does Ferrier's data (1978). Furthermore, Bloom, Rocissano, and Hood (1976) have demonstrated that even for children beyond the one-word stage, it is difficult to adopt the perspective of the other participant in a dialogue. Greenfield and Smith are dispensing with this difficulty by assuming a natural correspondence between the perspectives of the participants, with what I feel to be undue optimism.

As for the adult's interpretations of the child's speech, the justification for Greenfield and Smith's approach was that mothers understand their children, yet when Greenfield and Smith (1976) describe how they checked the reliability of interpretations in their study [p. 60], we learn that training is necessary to make interpretations. Furthermore, in the case of some semantic relations, the correspondence between judges' interpretations was unsatisfactorily low. It seems to me that it would have been worth exploring why some situations were more difficult to interpret reliably than others, but the authors' aim was rather to achieve reliable interpretations, and so another judge was trained to this end. It is worth bearing in mind that these independent judgments were made on descriptions of the situation already provided by an observer. These descriptions could hardly fail to be influenced to some degree by the observer's own interpretation of the utterance when it occurred.

Another feature of the interpretations of the child's speech in Greenfield and Smith's study (1976) is that verbal context is used to invest the child's single word with a fuller meaning. "Dialogue in general is treated as a semantic structure created by two people together [p. 43]." But, we know from the work of Ervin-Tripp (1970), Steffenson (1978), and others that children's participation in a dialogue need not imply that they comprehend their partner's contribution.

To assume full awareness of the potential meanings implicit in situations before speech is used, and to take the use of early words at their face value are simplifications that I cannot accept, any more than the simplifications introduced by McNeill and Bloom. To quote Ryan (1974): "We cannot assume when a child starts to produce one-word utterances, that the possible meanings of her utterances are as clearly delimited for her as they are for the adults who interpret them [p. 205]."

Each of the aforementioned theories had a particular aim in view, associated with a particular stage of language acquisition. Is any theory comfortable with child speech at all ages, one wonders? Will any theory ever be so without making a clear-cut distinction between understanding of concepts and control over the linguistic forms that express them. Insofar as the previously discussed theories recognize such a distinction, they all assign priority to concepts. They all resist the idea that forms could be used without the corresponding concepts being grasped, and even the more moderate idea that preexisting concepts may be married to the wrong forms in the first place (see Clark, 1978).

The other feature that all these approaches have in common is that each makes some assertion about the order of development of different facets of linguistic knowledge. Are we justified in assuming that any particular aspect of skill in communication necessarily develops before other aspects for all children, and that a universal theory can be hinged on this assumption? Further counterexamples to claims of this nature can easily be offered, such as Blank, Gessner, and Esposito's (1979) finding that it is possible to develop syntax without a prior mastery of pragmatics, which contradicts some recent proposals (e.g., Cook-Gumperz, 1977).

Some General Features of Simplification and a Corrective

In the uncharted complexity of a child's growing ability to communicate, certain anchors have apparently been taken entirely for granted. Indeed, their firmness has hardly been questioned.

A Uniform System.   One basis of research has been the assumption that the bulk of a child's verbal output can be accounted for by a uniform set of principles. It has been the occasional utterance that has been discarded as irrelevant, because it seems to be an imitation, or idiosyncratic or unintelligible, but the idea that the main body of the corpus might not be referrable to a general descriptive framework is rarely, if ever, considered.

Perhaps this approach has unwittingly been adopted by analogy with linguistic studies of exotic languages, where the researcher had no need to consider whether or not the informant was operating one system of grammatical rules consistently. One can see, too, that it satisfies a need. In an area in which it has been so difficult to apply the traditional canons of scientific investigation, the emphasis on taking account of the fullest possible range of observations in a generalization lends some sense of academic respectability to the activity.

But is this assumption reasonable? Why should one suppose a child to have an interest in using consistent grammatical rules at all? Presumably, the child's main aim is to communicate. In justifying the interpretation of children's incomplete utterances, many researchers have drawn attention to the fact that the total communicational setting carries a great deal of the meaning. Furthermore, implicit in collocations of words is meaning, waiting to be drawn out by the hearer. These circumstances may absolve the child from being concerned with linguistic devices for conveying meaning much of the time.

Imagine studying the emergence of a complex skill, like driving, or playing the piano, in which a number of perceptual and motor skills are gradually being mastered and integrated into a smooth performance. Would one be tempted to explain the learner's performances at a particular stage in terms of a uniform set of rules deriving from one aspect of the performance only? For example, would one account for all errors in handling a car in terms of an inadequate grasp of rules of the road? On the contrary, it is recognized that in these instances, we are dealing with a complex interplay between a number of strands of performance, none of which is operating to perfection at all times.

Language, too, is a complex skill, and in the young child, no single aspect of the skill is automatic. Levels of performance in any one aspect of the skill will be subject to decline under the stress of grappling with some other novel aspects of performance.

If we think about an adult learning a foreign language, it seems fairly clear that in the effort of searching for an elusive word, or expressing a complex or emotionally threatening thought, the control of grammar may deteriorate. It would therefore be inappropriate to formulate grammatical rules to account for performance on the basis of the total output. In the case of the young child, it is even more inappropriate; at least the adult learner knows to strive for grammatical consistency, and has probably had some formal instruction in it.

I therefore think it would be fruitful to pursue alternative plans of action, rather than attempting to subsume the maximum number of utterances in a corpus under a general framework of rules. Cannot we consider the child as inventing a variety of means for communicating, using the limited resources at his or her command? On any one day, or in any one hour, all a child's output need not be explicable in terms of a single unified system of operations.

Investigators of thinking, such as Bruner, Goodnow, and Austin (1965), have given us accounts of problem solving viewed in terms of a repertoire of strategies, with varying strengths and weaknesses, called into play by different pressures of circumstance, not necessarily brought ready-made to the problem-solving situation, but perhaps evolving in the process of grappling with the problem itself. Such a model seems consistent with the view of language as a skill, and could therefore perhaps be a more fruitful framework than that deriving from the study, with the help of a native informant, of a fully developed language in a static state.

When looking at emergent language in children, we are concerned with processes over a longer term than in problem-solving studies, such as that of Bruner et al. Perhaps a helpful analogy might be of a river, flowing down a number of parallel channels that represent different aspects of linguistic skill—phonology, intonation, syntax, semantics, and so on. At any stage, the flow might be diverted into other channels to overcome obstacles to progress in some other aspect of performance, diverting effort from some areas towards others. Children will vary in the order in which they grapple with different aspects of the skill, and the same child will vary from time to time in what he or she is concentrating on, leading to periodic reversals in performance of some aspects of skill. Some individual differences in style of language learning may come to be understood in these terms—for example, the difference between macro- and microdevelopment described by Cazden (1968) and the unusual character of the speech of a hearing child of deaf parents (Sachs & Johnson, 1976).

Such an analogy dispenses with the implausible assumption, previously discussed, that some aspects of skill are fully developed before others begin to be attended to. It may suggest a rather ragged picture of children's performance, inconsistent with the tidy statement of rules we are accustomed to, but I have already hinted that I believe the data to be less tidy than they appear to be in formal recording sessions.

Comprehension and Production. I believe that thinking regarding the relationship between comprehension and production may have been influenced by the need for firm anchors to hold onto in language-acquisition research. Before comprehension can be discussed coherently, some clear distinctions need to be made between aspects that have often been blurred in the past. I refer to a child's grasp of concepts as "understanding." This is independent of an ability either to recognize or utter the linguistic form that conventionally represents that concept. I call the child's ability to make sense of an utterance spoken to him or her "interpretation." Such interpretation is based on a variety of cues. Facial expressions, gestures, and other nonverbal cues may be involved. The situation, with all the expectations it has come to evoke for the child, will contribute. The child may recognize certain words and be able to achieve what Sachs and Truswell (1978) called a "non-syntactic" interpretation, by integrating more than one word into a meaningful semantic relationship. I reserve the term "decoding" for that aspect of interpretation concerned with identifying grammatical markers in the input and making one's interpretation dependent on these.

Hypotheses about children's mastery of these various aspects of comprehension may in part be motivated by the investigators' need to treat the child's output as interpretable. It has been widely held that understanding precedes the discovery of linguistic forms, or, more specifically, whatever linguistic form a given investigator is anxious to study (e.g., one-word utterances in Greenfield & Smith's case [1976], two-word utterances of standard word order in Bloom's case [1973]). It has also been widely believed that once the child understands a concept, the ability to interpret the mother's speech enables the child to discover the appropriate linguistic form to express that concept. The form will not emerge in the child's speech until its appropriate function has been identified through interpretation. Investigators vary in the extent to which they need to believe children capable of analyzing fully the relationship between form and meaning in their mothers' speech, depending on what the investigators see to be the critical attributes of the children's output (e.g., the use of words in a context for Green-field & Smith [1976], the systematic use of word order to convey relational meaning for Bloom [1973]). But, each agrees that the use of the feature regarded as critical is mastered in interpretation before it occurs in production. Some only need to postulate the ability to make non-syntactic interpretations. Some need to postulate the ability to decode grammatical markers in the input. Each resists the possibility that forms will enter the child's speech before the child is fully cognizant of their meanings. Thus, the interpretation of children's output is facilitated, for all forms that occur in a corpus may legitimately be assigned the meaning they have in adult language.

Some researchers adopt a more moderate view. Although they accept the position just described, that new forms can be interpreted before they are produced, they allow that there may not be a one-to-one correspondence between the meaning of a form for the child and its meaning in the adult language. This discrepancy comes about as a result of the child's acquiring understanding of new concepts and adapting his or her existing forms to convey this understanding in an unconventional way, before searching the input for the conventional means of expression. This point of view is expressed by the adage in Slobin, (1973): "New forms first express old functions and new functions are first expressed by old forms [p. 184]." This approach, like the other, regards all the child's utterances as fully interpretable, though the forms may not always correspond to adult usage.

But, this more moderate claim does not differ from the other in its attitude to the order of emergence of different facets of comprehension. Understanding still comes first and interpretation precedes expression. All that has been changed is that another possible means of forging expressions has been interposed between understanding and learning the conventional means through interpretation. Neither approach allows that forms can ever occur without a clear-cut function, that the discovery of function may be facilitated by the use of a form in speech, or that an existing concept may be married to the wrong form in error in the first place.

Examples of all these phenomena occur in the literature. Slobin (1973), having just proposed that "New forms first express old functions and new functions are first expressed by old forms [p. 184]" presents counter evidence in claiming that plurals, masculine and feminine adjectives, and other parts of speech are used in free variation before they begin to be used appropriately. Here apparently are new forms with no clearly defined functions. Blank (1974) suggests that the function of why questions at a certain stage is not to seek information about the causes of events but to explore the meaning of the word "why," which the child has not yet grasped. Ferrier (1978) and Clark (1974, 1977, and elsewhere) report numerous mismatches between forms and concepts in developing speech. The previously discussed categorical claims about the order of emergence of understanding, interpretation, and expression are clearly false and could only have been adhered to in the face of the evidence because they are extremely convenient.

Recognition that children do not grasp the full meaning of the words that they use is legitimate, and widespread, in the study of comprehension by experimental means, where its acceptance does not undermine the methodology of the research, as it would if accepted by people seeking to describe a corpus of utterances. Thus, by a pleasing irony, studies of comprehension, which it was anticipated would demonstrate the child's superior understanding, have in fact been a major source of evidence for limitations in that understanding (e.g., E. V. Clark, 1973; Donaldson & McGarrigle, 1974; Ferreiro & Sinclair, 1971). And, these limitations underline the lack of correspondence between the conventional meanings of words and the meanings with which children invest them.

PRODUCTION AS A STEPPING STONE

In this section of the chapter, I explore an alternative approach to child-language development: one that sees production as the leading edge of development. The first section argues that children produce a great deal of speech that is only globally structured and whose potential meaning they do not fully understand. The second section explores some of the means whereby this material enters the child's repertoire. The third section challenges the view that child speech is rule governed, according to the accepted meaning of that term.

Talking to Learn

One unifying theme behind all the comments I have made so far is that there is no simple correspondence between what children say and what they mean. Intention is in the mind, where it cannot be directly observed. Linguistic forms in adult speech are overt, and can be copied as forms, within the limits of the child's perceptual and articulatory abilities. It would be difficult for anyone to deny that if a child can copy elements of adult speech, he or she can in principle copy them without understanding their full meaning. To claim that even though they can do so, they never in fact do, one would need to postulate some sort of embargo on copying without full understanding. Being a claim that the child *can* do more than he or she *does* do, such a hypothesis is analogous to claims that children have more phonological and syntactic knowledge than they put to use in their speech (Bellugi, 1968; Smith, 1973). It would amount to suggesting that there is a kind of "incompetence rule" preventing the reproduction of incompletely interpreted forms. But, such a theory regarding imitation would be even less plausible than its counterparts, because the implication is that children who can do something more difficult—namely, copy with full understanding—never, or very rarely, do the easier thing of copying something that they do not completely understand.

In an elegant study, Kuczaj and Maratsos (1975) have shown that children may delay using a form until they are confident that they understand its use in adult speech. But to carry that idea further, and to say that all children always delay using a form until they fully grasp its function would be to ignore a great deal of other research evidence. I would argue, therefore, that not all children's utterances mean what they ostensibly mean. Furthermore, the very arbitrary nature of words itself makes it more difficult to infer their meaning reliably than is the case for iconic gestures. Indeed, even in the case of gestures with an iconic component, there may be a mismatch between the accepted meaning and the purpose that the child puts them to (Karmiloff-Smith, 1979).

I am not claiming here that children generally produce utterances without meaning anything by them. That would indeed be an implausible claim, as Lenneberg (1962) noted when he used it to discredit the general thesis that comprehension need not precede production. But, this is just one of the many examples of confusion that arise through the multiple ambiguity of the term "comprehension" previously alluded to. I think we can take it as common ground among most researchers that the normal child does not utter countless meaningless forms, but speaks because he or she has something to say.

The less extreme claim that I am making is that there may be a great deal of meaning implicit in a child's utterances that the child has not fully unraveled before adopting the forms into his or her repertoire. The child processes both the form and the meaning of the input in terms of his or her own current conceptual and linguistic capacities, and this will lead to a different match than that of an adult between elements of an utterance and elements of a situation (Clark, 1978).

We may all carry around with us information without drawing out the full implications that are implicit in it. Some examples are of elementary cases, such as words that may be used for years without their inner structure being noticed. How many teachers in British educational establishments, for example, are aware of anomoly when they refer to their green chalk boards as "blackboards"? Other examples are much more elaborate. A number of operations functioning independently are eventually seen as part of a total system. This must be very common, for example, in the learning of mathematics. One may make use of logarithm tables for years, before eventually realizing that there is a relationship between their operation and what one learned in algebra about adding to multiply, and subtracting to divide when dealing with powers. Having material available for use allows one to gradually extract the knowledge that may be implicit in that material. Such a process is exemplified by the discovery of infinity by my son, when he had just turned 5. Having learned to count, and thus having the numbers as material to exercise and reflect on, he was able to arrive at the insightful query, "Do numbers ever stop, Mummy?"

Lock (1979) has formulated what to me is an exciting theory: Having language with which to describe experience enables a child to reach a self-consciousness about that experience that would not otherwise be possible, and is indeed not possible for creatures lacking language. Knowledge about the meaning relations implicit in verbal formulations, according to Lock, emerges over a period of time as the language is in use. There is a qualitative change in the manner in which the same utterances are used as the child gradually gains a fuller grasp of their implicit meaning.

Procedures for Acquiring Forms

If what I have been claiming is correct, however inconvenient it may be for the researcher, a child at any one time will be using a number of forms without a full grasp of their meaning. The question arises: From where does the child get these forms? Not always, I submit, by having a concept and searching the input for a means to express it, but often by much less abstract, lower-level procedures.

Ferrier (1978) has eloquently testified to the personal way children invest adult forms with their own individual meanings. "Maternal utterances," she remarks, "do not come labelled as to either their function or their referents [p. 305]." One might add that children do not necessarily withhold their use until they are fully satisfied that they have discovered their functions and referents, though Kuczaj and Maratsos have shown that they may sometimes do so (1975). Braine (1974), in a paper that seems to have been widely and unjustly ignored in the literature, proposes that early two-word utterances are produced by "holophrastic processes." "It seems to me," he says, "that what is probably happening in these utterances is that the child, lacking complete command of the English rules for making action phrases, is constructing such phrases simply by seizing on some salient feature of the action for which he has a word readily available [p. 454]." Examples are "Betty head"—Betty was moving a tractor along the top of the speaker's head; "Odi hallo"—said by Odi in response to the question, "What are you doing?" when she was telephoning. Clark and Van Buren (1973) made a similar proposal. One of our examples was "Mummy roof moff," in which Adam, aged 27 months, pointed out that Mummy had repaired the roof of the motor caravan (trailer) that had blown off in a gale.

I have outlined a number of simple procedures, observed in action in my own children's speech, for getting by without a great deal of syntactic knowledge. These are reported extensively in Clark 1974, 1977, and 1980, but here are some examples: "Plagiarism" is the borrowing of unanalyzed sequences from previous adult utterances to fill out the child's own utterance. An example is: "It's upside down," followed by Adam's "I want to upside down," snatching a coat from his mother, wanting to turn it the right way up himself (Clark, 1974). "Coupling" is the sandwiching of two units together, without internal modification. An example is: "That's mine—jam" (Clark, 1977). A "person shift" is an utterance imitated and used by the new speaker without modification. An example is: "Sit my knee," copied by Adam from "Do you want to sit on my knee?" and used subsequently as a request to be sat on someone's knee.

Peters (1977) contrasts "gestalt" with "analytic" speech. Gestalt utterances are those that she claims elsewhere (Peters, 1980) have traditionally been "relegated to the linguistic trash heap [p. 2]." They are global representations of adult utterances that will eventually yield knowledge of linguistic structure through being analyzed. In the 1980 paper, which purports to be a preliminary working document, but seems nevertheless to be fairly polished, Peters makes proposals regarding the way this analysis proceeds. One process is "fission," whereby phonological comparison of identical elements in different sequences helps the child to break utterances down into what Peters calls, following L. W. Fillmore (1976), a "formulaic sentence frame with analyzed slot (Peters, 1980)." Among the heuristic devices that Peters formulates to account for children's learning is H1.3: "When you know some markers that tend to introduce labels, separate off what comes after the introducer [p. 26]." It is worth noticing that Thorne and his associates incorporated the same heuristic into a machine analogue of human parsing over 10 years ago (Thorne, Bratley, & Dewar, 1968). This seems to be an unusual case of artificial intelligence being less artificial than the contemporary direct models of human behavior.

Peters' 1980 paper draws extensively on work by Fillmore about second-language acquisition by children, reported in a doctoral dissertation (1976). Unfortunately, I only know this work second hand, but L. W. Fillmore seems to have found substantial evidence for the use of formulae by such learners. Furthermore, other researchers into second-language acquisition have made similar proposals. Several papers in Hatch's collection *Second Language Acquisition* (1978) describe procedures for taking over incompletely understood forms, used by children learning a second language. For example, Burling (1959, reprinted in Hatch, 1978) states: "What from an adult point of view are multimorphemic words, or multiword sentences, were used before their complex nature was recognized by Stephen [p. 72]." Itoh and Hatch (1978) report that a Japanese child learning English used the phrase "This is a" as an unanalyzed routine from 2 years, 9 months until 3 years old. Huang and Hatch (1978) present evidence that a 5-year-old Chinese child first used "where's" as a routine, without appreciating the function of the copula. Wagner-Gough (1978) reports that a Persian child who began learning English at 5 years, 11 month of age extensively used the strategy of "incorporation" of undigested sequences from the previous adult utterance in constructing his own utterance, a procedure Wagner-Gough associates with my previously mentioned examples of "plagiarism."

Perhaps these "gestalt" or "formulaic" processes also have some role to play in adults' learning of second languages in informal situations. Perhaps they are a natural product of features of the human communication setting; the approach by one participant via his or her own interpretation of the context to the other participant's message, and the interaction between human-processing mechanisms and the dynamic flow of speech.

I am not claiming that these imitated fragments remain unanalyzed indefinitely, or that all children necessarily use such strategies, or that any child uses them exclusively. Much of the literature on second-language acquisition by children suggests that simple constructed sequences coexist with a repertoire of imitated, unanalyzed wholes. Eventually, the internal structure of these sequences will be unraveled and the knowledge of language the child has been hoarding in unopened packages will gradually be unpacked and integrated with the knowledge expressed in his or her simple constructions. Then, the child's whole language output will become more uniform and more systematic. But, the relative contributions of the language that is first used without being understood, and the language that is understood before being used, need to be evaluated without the prejudice born of preconceptions that has usually clouded this issue in the past.

Regularities or Rules

When can the child's constructions begin to be regarded as truly rule governed? This is not such a simple question. Regularities are not the same as rules. Considering what some philosophers have said about rules may not fully resolve the question, but can perhaps clarify some of its aspects, and reveal its complexity.

In philosophical discussions about the nature of rules, one point frequently made is that being able to state rules explicitly is not a necessary condition for having rules (Kenny, 1973; Searle, 1970; Snyder, 1971). On the other hand, mere regularity of behavior is not enough to warrant the ascription of a rule. A rule is more than a law of nature. To count as a rule follower, the person needs to be able to apply the behavior to new instances (Searle, 1970), and to recognize exceptions (Kenny, 1973; Searle, 1970).

Emphasis in these discussions is always on the understanding by the users of the agreed functions of the rules. For Searle, the essence is that users have to be capable of giving meaning to the forms. The essence of linguistic rules (in this case, rules governing speech acts) is that the performance only has its effect because the hearer knows the rules. Things "count as" instances of a particular act because this is agreed between the participants. This is what distinguishes "institutional" from "brute" facts. For Snyder (1971), there is an understanding that, even if the rules are frequently violated, a standard, which may be independent of what actually goes on between speakers, is recognized. Also, for Bennett (1976), following Lewis (1969), the emphasis is on the role of the community in *maintaining* a regularity of behavior because they *mutually know* that they have maintained it in the past. There is always, then, the emphasis on some shared knowledge that the behavior has a socially agreed significance, not just that it displays regularities.

Can the regularities in children's speech meet these criteria?

Slobin (1973) has made the stimulating suggestion that "at the beginning levels it could be that there is little difference between short-term processing strategies and linguistic rules [p. 196]." I have tried to demonstrate that such processing strategies may be implicated in language learning well beyond the beginning levels, and may explain such phenomena as errors in the use of pronouns, and the structure of *wh* questions (Clark, 1977). Structures that are regular because they reflect the operation of a processing mechanism, rather than conforming to an agreed convention, do not meet the criteria set by philosophers. If we call such structures rules, we are in danger of forgetting their special character.

Gradually, the child will become increasingly self-conscious about the structure of his or her utterances, and may succeed in ironing out inconsistencies of structure within his or her repertoire that have arisen through the independent operation of different procedures. An example that came to my notice occurred when my son Ivan was nearly 3 years old. As he watched me running water for a bath, he said, "You want to have a bath"—a sequence that could have originated as an "extract" (Clark, 1977) from "Do you want to have a bath?" A moment later, he picked up his teddy bear and produced, apparently through "coupling" (Clark, 1974), "I want teddy—have a bath." Having by chance produced the alternative structures successively, he seems to have reflected on the differences between them, and as a result, shortly afterwards, he produced, "I want teddy to have a bath." That children do reflect on and modify their patterns of behavior, even though they may be achieving results, has been demonstrated in a memory task by Karmiloff-Smith (1979).

But, by these modifications, and by this self-awareness, do the structures become rule based? Can the children judge new instances in terms of the structures? Sinclair (1979) has observed that children 4 1/2 years old and upwards, presented with sentences equivalent in structure to those they are themselves producing, will often say they "sound funny." Their judgment seems to depend on semantic and pragmatic factors rather than syntactic ones. A number of studies have shown that the particular words used may affect the facility of a child with a structure. For example, Sinclair, Sinclair, and De Marcellus (1971) found as much as two years difference between children's ability to handle the passive structure, depending on the particular verb used. "Knock down" was easier than "push," then "wash," then "overtake," and most difficult, "follow." Furthermore, the ease with which the children could produce and interpret passives using the word "wash" varied with the dirtiness of the clothes used as experimental props.

Can children recognize exceptions to the rules that they are following? More than one study has cast doubt on the ability of children, and even adults for that matter, to judge grammaticality. One example is the study by de Villiers and de Villiers (1974) in which they showed a lag between the production, comprehension, judgment, and correction of the same structure, and provided a useful clarification of the issues in their discussion.

But what of the dominant idea in the philosophical discussions of awareness of shared conventions? It seems that, in early child language, utterances "count as" expressions of particular linguistic functions because mothers so count them, not because of shared knowledge of a set of conventions. Snow (1976), Newson (1978), and others stress the importance to development of mothers' treating their children's noises and gestures as having meaning, even before they begin to do so. It is indeed very likely that by filtering the child's fragmentary utterances through her own linguistic framework, a mother may misperceive the child's actual intentions, always distorting them in the direction of the more conventional. More generally, having language, with the conclusions it encourages us to leap to, may blunt our sensitivity to other sources of information, through other senses.

Mutual communication can only be sustained in the face of the participants' very unequal competencies because language is a system that represents experience. A mother and child's common experience mediates their communication, helping them to overcome the disadvantage that, in effect, they speak different languages. This process is comparable to recognizing the subjects in damaged photographs, or interpreting schematic drawings, because we know what they are intended to depict and we fill in the debased representation from that knowledge. Indeed, in some circumstances, language may not readily outgrow this dependence on shared situations, as has been suggested regarding sign language for the deaf (Schlesinger, 1971).

Children begin by producing very personal symbols (Piaget, 1962), but gradually their language comes to approximate adult language more closely, ultimately sharing its forms and its meanings. It is as if mothers begin by bearing most of the burden of communication (Shugar, 1978), but gradually children come to be able to take responsibility for their own share in it—like being helped to swim by a pair of water wings, from which the air is let out by degrees as the child gains more confidence and more skill to support him- or herself.

Nor is communication between adults largely a question of decoding verbal messages. One tends rather to intuit what another person is saying from the personal construction one puts on the situation, and may even mishear the message to fit one's expectation. To give an example, I signaled to give right of way to an oncoming car one evening recently, and when the driver leaned out of the window to say something to me as she passed, I was convinced she was thanking me. Only when I subsequently noticed that I did not have my lights on did I realize what she had, in fact, been saying.

The shared knowledge on which mutual understanding rests embraces far more than a shared knowledge of linguistic rules. For example, in our household, if I say "How about scrambled eggs for breakfast?", the clear understanding is that I expect my husband to cook them, because part of the shared knowledge on which communication within our family depends is that he cooks scrambled eggs superbly. Communication depends to a considerable extent on knowledge that transcends the verbal message, and when we are compelled to rely on syntax alone, in interpreting ambiguous sentences out of context, for example, we do not do startlingly well. The importance of background knowledge for communication with young children should, therefore, not be underestimated. The fact that words are spoken between the participants in dialogues in child-language data should not mislead us into exaggerating the prominence of their role in the communication.

At one time, it was fashionable to advocate that the best way to approach the study of child language was to keep in mind the end product—that is, adult competence. Such strategies are misleading because they encourage overestimation of the child's current capacities. However, if we are to bear in mind adult competence at all, then I think it will have to be the kind of competence described by Bransford and his colleagues (e.g., Bransford & McCarrell, 1974), the competence to perceive verbal messages in a total meaningful context, dependent on previous knowledge and broader experience.

Returning for a moment to the Chomskyan model of language acquisition, we see that there is another major respect in which it was mistaken. It saw situation and experience as merely incidental to the process, whereas they are actually all important.

SIMPLIFICATIONS IN RESEARCH METHOD

In this final section, I present some criticisms of traditional research procedures in the area of child language. First, I consider the experimental approach, and second, naturalistic observation. Some of the issues previously discussed are raised again here, and the two methods are compared in terms of them. These issues include the concept of ideal speaker–hearer, the relationship between comprehension and production, and differences between individual learners.

The Experimental Approach

If the picture of language learning I have painted bears any resemblance to reality, then it is not merely a sketch whose details need to be filled in by further research. This knowledge about language learning must influence the manner in which research is conducted. Paradoxically, our study of an organism must be based on what we know about it already. As Gregory (1961) put it, talking about the study of the brain: "If we have no idea of the sort of system we are dealing with, controlled experiment becomes impossible, for we cannot know what to control [p. 330]." But, what if what we know about the sort of system we are dealing with causes us to doubt the possibility of controlled experiment at all?

In the preceding section, I stressed the strong dependence of language on situation, and the fact that the child has his or her own perspective on that situation and on the speech produced within it. The implications of both these points for research method need to be explored. The key methodological question is this: If communication is so heavily dependent on situation, is it meaningful to abstract children from familiar situations and test their ability to communicate without any of the habitual props?

Traditional experimental philosophy supports such a procedure because its aim is to simplify situations, isolating single variables and examining their effects, uncontaminated by other factors. Interestingly enough, in this area of study, the canonical procedures are underpinned by the concept of an ideal speaker–hearer, rather than undermined by it, as in the case of data-description procedures. But, is this experimental philosophy beyond criticism? It is not only researchers into language development who have been led to challenge its validity. Let me just mention three sceptical discussions, from widely diverse areas of study. Neisser (1976a) has questioned the relevance of studies focusing on one sensory channel (i.e., practically all existing studies) to an understanding of normal perception on the grounds that we normally receive our information through more than one receptor at a time. Bateson (1979) stresses that studies of animals reared under artificial conditions can give little information about normal patterns of development, Davies (1979) maintains that studies of the perception of tunes using artificially simplified inputs are misleading about the normal processes of identification.

We know that experiments are very peculiar social situations. We know this is true of social-psychology experiments with adult subjects (Orne, 1973); we know this is true of experiments on cognitive development (Donaldson, 1978); and we are beginning to know this is true of experiments on linguistic competence in children (Warden, in press). If the psychology experiment has "demand characteristics" (Orne, 1973), who is less capable of adapting to these demands than the young child with limited language capacity? By putting a creature into an artificial situation, feeding it with controlled stimulation, what can we learn that will illuminate our understanding of normal learning processes? Such a research strategy presupposes a creature with a fixed set of procedures that can be elicited on demand and manipulated to order—procedures that, like physical laws, cannot choose but to function. But the human brain is not like that. People can choose not to operate procedures available to them (Neisser, 1976b); instead, they can manufacture fresh procedures.

Experiments may tell us, then, what children do under unusual circumstances, not what they normally do. That may, of course, be what the researcher wants to find out. But, will what they can do in experiments be their ideal performance? To explore this issue further, we must turn to the second point previously mentioned: the child's individual perspective on the situation.

Cognitive explanations of language acquisition have generally drawn on the achievements of children at various stages in their development, as elaborated in Piaget's theory. In other words, it is the contents of the mind, the cognitive structures and schemas, that have been invoked, rather than the functional invariants (but see Herriot, 1970, and Clark, 1975a). This is paradoxical, because Piagetian claims regarding the stages at which various abilities emerge in childhood have come under considerable attack (e.g., Bower, 1971; Bryant, 1974), whereas the concepts of assimilation and accommodation have not. The relative immunity of these concepts from criticism may be due to a vagueness that makes them difficult to refute. However, I find them helpful in understanding the role of the child in the communication partnership.

The trouble with the language experiment as a technique for studying children is that it makes considerable demands on the children to accommodate to a perspective that is not naturally theirs. As I have already mentioned, Bloom et al. (1976) have produced evidence that children find such an adjustment difficult to make. These authors were well aware of the implications of their finding for research procedures, and also its relevance to the issue of comprehension as compared to production. Kuczaj and Daly's finding (1979) that accuracy in self-initiated hypothetical reference is better than in other-initiated hypothetical reference accords with this general approach.

It is instructive to compare the processes of comprehension and production with respect to the degree of accommodation that is demanded (Clark et al., 1974). In order to comprehend what an adult is saying, the child must accommodate to that adult's point of view, whereas this is not necessary in production. This is one of the factors that to my mind makes comprehension inherently more difficult than production. (Another is the fact that in comprehension, the child's performance is paced; he or she cannot stop the input periodically to listen to it more effectively.) But, the effect of the controlled experiment is to neutralize this difference between the two tasks, by requiring accommodation in both of them.

These points have been particularly well put by L. W. Fillmore (1976) in the unpublished doctoral dissertation already referred to earlier. I quote second hand from Peters (1980): Fillmore (1976) argues that children analyze structure as it occurs in their own output, with which they are thoroughly familiar. "How much more reasonable this seems," she rightly claims, "than to assume that the language learner can somehow apprehend the fast-fading message produced by someone else, figure out what it means and how it is put together, and then relate it to similar utterances he has heard [p. 301]."

Another factor about experiments that ought not to be ignored is the stress that children may be subject to when unusual demands are placed upon them by strange people in a strange place. There is evidence that stress can have a disruptive effect on performance (e.g., Watson, 1972). Such effects are rarely considered in relation to young children, and have certainly not been explored systematically, but this is just part of a general failure in psychology to adequately integrate affective and cognitive frames of reference. It is also well attested that under stressful conditions, simple tasks may be performed more effectively, but complex tasks are disrupted (Broadbent, 1964). This, too, has implications for the experimental method. Children's most elaborate utterances, in which they attempt to express the most complex thoughts, are most likely to occur when they are at their most relaxed, and in a natural and familiar setting. Furthermore, there may be a discrepancy between semantic complexity and formal tidiness that compels another choice on the part of the researcher. Which utterances is the researcher to consider more significant for an understanding of language development—the grammatically correct ones, or those in which the child pushes beyond his or her current level of grammatical competence, perhaps forging new tools of expression in the process? The formal study is likely to be tapping old learning rather than the process of discovery.

I find a complete correspondence between my own thinking on this issue and that of Iwamura (1979; cited by Peters, p. 42 1980). Iwamura speaks of situations in which children are under communicative stress: "In such situations they felt an urgent need to express certain ideas. This need forced them to strain their linguistic resources to their current limits. . . . The development of new analyses may occur at such moments of great communicative need (pp. 10–11)." One must not be misled by our different uses of the word "stress" here. Iwamura is not talking about the emotional stress that I have been discussing, but the strong desire to communicate. This "communicative stress" belongs in the natural environment, where the child's interest is engaged, not in the formal context, where what we have is, rather, the experimenter's desire that the child communicate, whether or not the task is meaningful to the child.

No doubt readjustments in conceptual development are sometimes provoked by unusual demands that overload current strategies and force more efficient ones to evolve, but a fair degree of basic competence is probably necessary before this becomes possible.

What implications does this have for the concept of ideal speaker–hearer? Will the researcher who, with Chomsky, is more interested in the best performance that the child can produce be more likely to find it in a contrived situation or in the natural setting? I indicated previously that an implicit rationale for experimentation was that naturalness was unnecessary because the "best" performance was required rather than the "normal" one. But, does the best performance occur in experiments? That depends on one's definition of the word "best"—either the grammatical patterns that have become routine, which may occur in experiments, or the patterns in the process of construction, which very likely will not. The answer to that question must also depend on whether one believes that production is the vehicle of learning, or whether one believes that it is the product of prior learning done via interpretation of other people's speech. The innovative utterances could be dismissed as performance errors if they are bizarre, as they well might be if one or other previously described strategy is at work. At any rate, they will be atypical, being new discoveries, and therefore may be dismissed on the principle of the need for general statements, alluded to earlier.

Many researchers feel that there is more to be learned from the study of behavior as it occurs in natural settings than the study of behavior that can be made to happen in contrived circumstances (e.g., Bridges, 1979). I now turn to a consideration of naturalistic observation.

Naturalistic Observation

The preceding discussion reflects my own preference for naturalistic rather than experimental data—a point of view that is even beginning to encroach on that stronghold of formal techniques, the measurement of intelligence (Charlesworth, 1976). But, it would appear that some types of naturalistic data are more naturalistic than others, and that the experience of stress is not exclusive to the experimental context.

A great deal of our information about children's speech production depends on recordings of mother–child dialogue in the presence of one or more observers. I recall vividly one such recording session at which I was present. The child sat for most of the period pointing at pictures in a book, but with her lips tightly sealed, stolidly refusing to interact with us at all. Children do not always give such obvious signs of unease, but can we be sure that they ever perform at their best under such conditions? We have little direct evidence, but we do have related evidence. For example, Ainsworth and Wittig (1969) showed that the presence of a stranger has an inhibiting effect on infants' exploratory behavior. Have such inhibitions on the performance of tasks in the process of mastery been overcome by the time the children are old enough to be the subjects of language acquisition research? Are they ever overcome? Social psychologists tell us that they are not (Edwards, 1974). It is also worth considering the sociolinguistic perspective. Silence can be a valued form of communication in many situations, and among them is the meeting of strangers (Basso, 1972). We know little of its role in children's social development. We need to know more.

One way of avoiding the presence of a stranger is to bring the child to a laboratory where he or she can be observed unawares through a one-way-vision screen. But, this introduces the influence of unfamiliar surroundings. At nursery-school age, large discrepancies may exist between what the child is capable of in the home setting and in a setting outside the home, even when he or she goes there every day. Tizard, Carmichael, Hughes, and Pinkerton (1980) demonstrated that the linguistic performance of working-class children, which compared favorably with that of middle-class children at home, was severely depressed in the nursery school. Have we any reason to deny the possibility of similar effects on younger children, whatever their social class, of settings outside the home? What would be gained in research contexts from having fewer people present would surely be lost by the experience's being atypical.

Even if an observation is not formally structured like an experiment, there may be more or less deliberate attempts to get the child to talk. But, the more obvious techniques for eliciting speech that adults often use in such situations may, in fact, be inhibiting rather than facilitating (Hubbell, 1977). Often, unfamiliar toys are introduced, on the assumption that their novelty will make them interesting. But, if the hope is that the operations that the child will perform with the material will be of a high level, it may be important that the material be familiar. Familiar material has been found to be significant in memory tasks with children (Bryant, 1974), in cross-cultural comparisons of cognitive development (Okonji, 1971), and in studies of adolescent thinking (Peel, 1978). Ferrier (1978) has made a convincing case for the importance of frequent exposure to stereotyped utterances in recurrent contexts in the very early stages of language development.

I argued earlier that mental resources have to be shared between different aspects of linguistic skill. They also have to be shared between language and other activities, so that the introduction of novel and challenging materials is likely to diminish rather than stimulate verbal activity. We have already seen that there is an interaction between stress and level of difficulty of a task. Under stress, simple tasks may be performed more effectively, but difficult tasks are disrupted. Exposure to unfamiliar materials can be a form of stress; the presence of strangers certainly is. Theoretical considerations, then, suggest that children will set themselves their most difficult linguistic tasks in natural situations in relation to familiar experiences.

I have a very limited amount of data to support these suggestions. Specially designed equipment (Clark, 1976) enabled me to record everyday linguistic interaction in my home, just within the family. Some samples were "monitored." With the help of a loop, I could select for retention utterances that I judged to be novel, after they occurred, together with the preceding speech. "Validation" samples were obtained by a research assistant setting the equipment to remain on without my knowledge for periods determined by a random schedule. "Continuous" samples were also collected in the traditional way—at first weekly, and later fortnightly—in the presence of a visiting phonetician, Sandy Hutcheson. So far, very little of the data has been compared, but a detailed comparison of samples of each type collected within 2 days, between 30 months, 12 days old and 30 months, 14 days old, about 15 months after the start of the study, showed quite startling differences (Clark, in press). The data from the continuous sample was far less advanced in function and far less elaborate in structure than the data in the family setting. The speech was "regulatory" rather than "heuristic" (Halliday, 1975), the child asked no questions, the only examples of complex sentences were joined by "and," and the ideas the child attempted to express were far more limited. Of interest in relation to the theme of this chapter is the comparative regularity of the speech in the sample with an observer present, and its idiosyncratic nature in the family setting.

Further samples need to be compared, but these findings accord with my strong impression that the speech within the family context is markedly different to that of the formal recording sessions at every stage. But in addition, incidents occur in the everyday contexts that throw light on the origins of particular usages. Considerable ingenuity would have been required to arrive at the correct explanations of these errors if the original contexts in which they were learned had not been observed. Following are two examples:

1. The misuse of the modal "mustn't" to mean "needn't" originated when Adam "converted" (Clark, 1977) an injunction of his father's that he "must finish his food" into "No, I mustn't."

2. The use of a comparative form in an absolute sense originated as a result of the child's failing to infer a part of the meaning not explicitly expressed in the adult utterance. Moving the child "nearer" the table without saying "nearer than you are now" led him to treat "nearer" as "near enough." "I am nearer," he would frequently say.

In reporting the findings of a study of adverbs of time, Kuczaj (1975) emphasized contextual information as "a prime determinant of the child's interpretation," which "determines what meaning he initially grants a word (p. 354)." Such an emphasis further underlines the value of naturalistic data.

Naturalistic recordings aim to collect representative samples of behavior, however problematic this may turn out to be in practice. This does not make such settings immune from the simplifications that occur in controlled experiments, because simplification can and does affect the way the data is analyzed. For example, all the verbal input may be ignored when accounting for the child's speech patterns. Equally simplistic is the procedure of analyzing *all* the input and seeking relationships with output when not all of it may be significant for learning. This is comparable to the analysis of the entire output, that I have questioned earlier. However, the use of naturalistic data has incidentally, if not by design, had one valuable consequence; this is considered in the next section.

Individual Differences

Studies using naturalistic data typically collect far more information about each individual child than is usual in the experimental situation, in which only a small sample of behavior is tapped. This has led to the discovery of individual differences in style of language learning (e.g., Bloom, 1973; Nelson, 1973). If the increased regularity of speech in recording with an observer present is a widespread phenomenon, and if I am right that the more formal the situation, the more the child depends on patterns that are already fully learned, which are more likely to be standard, it would follow that even the degree of individual variation in strategy that has been brought to light so far in naturalistic studies may be an underestimate.

It would not be true to say that experimental studies need to ignore individual variation. Donaldson and McGarrigle (1974), for example, identify detailed patterns that small groups of children share in their responses. Such an approach is to be applauded, especially when the patterns are not automatically assumed to reflect sequential stages in the development of mastery.

The traditional experimental technique of collecting samples of behavior from a large group of individuals and getting a statistical measure of group performance can seem illogical. If one were faced with a room full of unfamiliar machines, whose function one wanted to discover, even if they looked identical, one would not sample the behavior of all of them and generalize about them. One would study one machine in considerable detail. If one suspected that the machines varied, the sampling procedure would be even less likely to be effective.

CONCLUSION

To summarize, I have been challenging simplified assumptions and simplified procedures in language-acquisition research and I have been trying to promote the picture of an unruly, rather than a rule-governed process.

I am assuming, then, that the whole of a child's output is not necessarily governed by a uniform set of rules; the relationships between imitation, production, and comprehension are not necessarily standard for all children at all stages of their language learning; different children may develop the various aspects of linguistic skill in different orders to each other; some forms may be understood before they are uttered and others uttered before they are understood.

A respect for individual differences may save us from the fate of cognitive psychology, where for decades, two research streams have investigated general processes and individual differences independently. Emlen (1975) writes of bird migration: "In all probability, a differential weighting of several directional cues occurs. These weightings should be expected to vary not only between species but, for any individual bird, with changing meteorological conditions and at different points along the migratory path [p. 131]." If research on bird migration has forced the acceptance of multiple processes and individual variation, can it be unscientific to approach child language with these expectations?

I have also suggested that the traditional procedures for investigating child language may have contributed to our impression of uniformity being stronger than is justified. Experiments provide pigeon holes into which the behavior must fit, and any formal research method may induce conservatism in the responses of the children by fostering stress and perplexity.

I have further proposed that the use of a variety of simple strategies for taking over partially processed material from adult input may provide the child with a repertoire of linguistic forms whose implicit meaning is gradually unraveled in use over an extended period of time. Meanwhile, communication is carried not by a shared set of linguistic conventions, but by shared access to a common experience, which may nevertheless be differently construed by the two participants.

I have claimed that many of the simplifications that have guided research have been motivated by considerations of scientific accuracy. But precision of measurement is not enough. It is important to measure the right things (Miller, 1966). For example, you can measure one side of a solid object with commendable precision without realizing that it has extension in a third dimension.

It seems to me that in exploring language development further, far from being an essential tool, a theory may be a handicap. To borrow more words from Gregory (1961): "a too fixed and particular model tends to blinker the mental eye, making us blind to surprising results and ideas without which advance is impossible [p. 330]." The literature on language acquisition is full of valuable observations that are set aside because they are irrelevant to the argument that the author is presenting—observations that might have been given considerable prominence within a different framework. If we are to allow our viewpoint to be severely restricted by a theoretical framework, we may just as well be in the cage with Thorndike's cats. I believe the growth of knowledge would be well served by researchers having an open mind and a lively interest in the wide range of phenomena that could emerge from a closer observation of what children actually do in naturalistic settings.

Of more value than an elaborate theoretical framework, embodying simplistic assumptions, is an awareness of findings in a broad range of related research areas. Research into child-language development ought not to be divorced from the insights of adult comprehension studies (Bransford & McCarrell, 1974). The role of long-term memory in relation to the forms of early utterances could fruitfully be explored, whereas the role of short-term memory has been exaggerated. The concept of "episodic memory" (Tulving, 1972) needs to be related to Rosch's (1973) views about the development of early word meaning. We need more treatments, like Peters' (1977), that integrate first- with second-language acquisition and both with the development of the brain.

Furthermore, many significant advances in science come about by accident, rather than in pursuance of a theory. As Hubel and Wiesel report (1980), the finding of receptors in the brains of cats sensitive to vertical lines occurred when they were investigating patterns with dots, and happened to notice a response as the vertical edge of the slide was withdrawn from the apparatus. Penicillin was discovered when a preparation was accidentally contaminated by a spore blown in through an open window. Indeed, according to a letter in the Sunday newspaper (Somerville, 1979), the principle was known in the early 1900's to an unsung district nurse, Nurse Exelby, who had discovered for herself the healing properties of the mold on top of rasberry jam.

And, if theories are helpful in research, then the more theories there are, the more we can expect to find out, so that we are eventually equipped to devise an adequately complex theory. There is more than one way to crack an egg. We do not all have to be big enders or little enders. According to Sameroff and Harris (1979): "Simplicity is a pleasant ideal, but understanding can result only from models that approximate the complexity of the real world [p. 368]."

REFERENCES

Ainsworth, M. D. S., & Wittig, B. A. Attachment and exploratory behavior of one-year olds in a strange situation. In B. M. Foss (Ed.), *Determinants of infant behaviour* (Vol. 4). London: Methuen, 1969.

Basso K. H. To give up on words: Silence in Apache culture. In P. P. Giglioli (Ed.), *Language and social context.* Harmondsworth: Penguin, 1972.

Bateson, P. *The origins of behaviour.* Seminar at the School of Epistemics, University of Edinburgh, November 6, 1979.

Bellugi, U. Linguistic mechanisms underlying child speech. In G. M. Zale (Ed.), *Proceedings of the conference on language and language behavior.* New York: Appleton-Century-Crofts, 1968.

Bellugi, U., & Brown, R. (Eds.). *The acquisition of language. Monograph of the Society for Research in Child Development,* 1964, *29* (92, No. 1).

Bennett, J. *Linguistic behaviour.* Cambridge, Eng.: Cambridge University Press, 1976.

Blank, M. Cognitive functions of language in the pre-school years. *Developmental Psychology,* 1974, *10,* 229-245.

Blank, M., Gessner, M., & Esposito, A. Language without communication: A case study. *Journal of Child Language,* 1979, *6,* 329-352.

Bloom, L. *Language development: Form and function in emerging grammars.* Cambridge, Mass.: M. I. T. Press, 1970.

Bloom, L. *One word at a time.* The Hague: Mouton, 1973.

Bloom, L., Rocissano, L., & Hood, L. Adult-child discourse: Developmental interaction between information processing and linguistic knowledge. *Cognitive Psychology,* 1976, *8,* 521-552.

Borger, R., & Seaborne, A. E. M. *The psychology of learning.* Harmondsworth: Penguin, 1966.

Bower, T. G. R. The object in the world of the infant. *Scientific American,* 1971, *225*(4) 3-38.

Bowerman, M. *Early syntactic development: a Cross-linguistic study with special reference to Finnish.* Cambridge, Eng.: Cambridge University Press, 1973.

Braine, M. D. S. Length constraints, reduction rules and holophrastic processes in children's word combinations. *Journal of Verbal Learning and Verbal Behavior,* 1974, *13,* 448-457.

Bransford, J. B., & McCarrell, N. S. A sketch of a cognitive approach to comprehension: Some thoughts about understanding what it means to comprehend. In B. Weimer & D. S. Palermo (Eds.), *Cognition and the symbolic processes.* Hillsdale, N.J.: Lawrence Erlbaum Associates, 1974.

Bridges, A. Directing two year olds' attention; some clues to understanding. *Journal of Child Language*, 1979, *6*, 211-226.

Broadbent, D. E. *Behaviour*. London: Methuen, 1964.

Bruner, J. S., Goodnow, J. J., & Austin, G. A. *A study of thinking*. New York: Science Editions, 1965.

Bryant, P. *Perception and understanding in young children: An experimental approach*. London: Methuen, 1974.

Burling, R. Language development of a Garo and English speaking child. *Word*, 1959, *15*, 45-68. (Reprinted in E. Hatch (Ed.), *Second language acquisition. A book of readings*. Rowley, Mass.: Newbury House, 1978.)

Cazden, C. The acquisition of noun and verb inflections. *Child Development*, 1968, *39*, 433-438.

Charlesworth, W. R. Human intelligence as adaptation: An ethological approach. In L. B. Resnick (Ed.), *The nature of intelligence*. Hillsdale, N.J.: Lawrence Erlbaum Associates, 1976.

Chomsky, N. *Aspects of a theory of syntax*. Cambridge, Mass.: M.I.T. Press, 1965.

Clark, E. V. Non-linguistic strategies and the acquisition of word meaning. *Cognition*, 1973, *2*, 161-182.

Clark, R. Performing without competence. *Journal of Child Language*, 1974, *1*, 1-10.

Clark, R. Adult theories, child strategies and their implications for the language teacher. In J. P. B. Allen & S. P. Corder (Eds.), *Edinburgh course in applied linguistics*, (Vol. 2). London: Oxford University Press, 1975. (a)

Clark, R. Review of L. Bloom, *One word at a time. Journal of Child Language*, 1975, *2*, 169-193. (b)

Clark, R. A report on methods of longitudinal data collection. *Journal of Child Language*, 1976, *3*, 457-459.

Clark, R. What's the use of imitation? *Journal of Child Language*, 1977, *4*, 341-358.

Clark, R. Some even simpler ways to learn to talk. In N. Waterson & C. Snow (Eds.), *The development of communication*. London: Wiley, 1978.

Clark, R. Errors in talking to learn. *First Language*, 1980, *1*, 7-32.

Clark, R. Assessing language in the home. In A. Davies (Ed.), *Language and learning in the home and the school*. London: Heinemann, in press.

Clark, R., Hutcheson, S., & Van Buren, P. Comprehension and production in language acquisition. *Journal of Linguistics*, 1974, *10*, 39-54.

Clark, R., & Van Buren, P. How a two year old orders words about. *Edinburgh Working Papers in Linguistics*, 1973, *2*.

Cook-Gumperz, J. Situated instructions: Language socialization of school age children. In S. Ervin-Tripp & C. Mitchell-Kernan (Eds.), *Child Discourse*. New York: Academic Press, 1977.

Davies, J. Memory for melodies and tonal sequences: A theoretical note. *British Journal of Psychology*, 1979, *70*, 205-210.

de Villiers, J., & de Villiers, P. Competence and performance in child language: Are children really competent to judge? *Journal of Child Language*, 1974, *1*, 11-22.

Donaldson, M. *Children's minds*. Glasgow: Fontana, 1978.

Donaldson, M., & McGarrigle, J. Some clues to the nature of semantic development. *Journal of Child Language*, 1974, *1*, 185-194.

Dore, J., Franklin, M. B., Miller, R. T., & Ramer, A. L. H. Transitional phenomena in early language acquisition. *Journal of Child Language*, 1976, *3*, 13-28.

Edwards, W. T. *Social psychology: Theories and discussions*. Harlow, Essex: Longmans, 1974.

Emlen, S. T. Migration: Orientation and navigation. In D. S. Franer & J. R. King (Eds.), *Avian biology* (Vol. 5). London: Academic Press, 1975.

Ervin-Tripp, S. Discourse agreement: How children answer questions. In J. R. Hayes (Ed.), *Cognition and the development of language*. New York: Wiley, 1970.

Ferreiro, E., & Sinclair, H. Temporal relations in language. *Journal International de Psychologie,* 1971, *6*, 39–47.

Ferrier, J. L. Some observations of error in context. In N. Waterson & C. Snow (Eds.), *The development of communication.* London: Wiley, 1978.

Fillmore, C. The case for case. In E. Bach & R. T. Harms (Eds.), *Universals in linguistic theory.* New York: Holt Rinehart, & Winston, 1968.

Fillmore, L. W. *The second time around: Cognitive and social strategies in second language acquisition.* Unpublished doctoral thesis, Stanford University 1976.

Goldin-Meadow, S. Structure in a manual communication system developed without a conventional language model: Language without a helping hand. In H. Whittaker & H. A. Whittaker (Eds.), *Studies in neurolinguistics* (Vol. 4). New York: Academic Press, 1979.

Greenfield, P. M., & Smith, J. H. *The structure of communication in early language development.* New York: Academic Press, 1976.

Gregory, R. L. The brain as an engineering problem. In W. H. Thorpe & O. L. Zangwill (Eds.), *Current problems in animal behavior.* Cambridge, Eng.: Cambridge University Press, 1961.

Halliday, M. A. K. *Learning how to mean. Explorations in the development of language.* London: Edward Arnold, 1975.

Hatch, E. (Ed.) *Second language acquisition. A book of readings.* Rowley, Mass.: Newbury House, 1978.

Herriot, P. *An introduction to the psychology of language.* London: Methuen, 1970.

Huang, J., & Hatch, E. A Chinese child's acquisition of English. In E. Hatch (Ed.), *Second language acquisition. A book of readings.* Rowley, Mass.: Newbury House, 1978.

Hubbell, R. D. On facilitating spontaneous talking in young children. *Journal of Speech and Hearing Disorders,* 1977, *42,* 216–231.

Hubel, D. H., & Wiesel, T. N. Interview on *Horizon: The mind's eye.* London: British Broadcasting Corporation, January 28, 1980.

Itoh, H., & Hatch E. Second language acquisition, a case study. In E. Hatch (Ed.), *Second language acquisition. A book of readings.* Rowley, Mass.: Newbury House, 1978.

Iwamura, S. G. "I don't wanna don' throw": Speech formulas in first language acquisition. Unpublished manuscript, 1979.

Karmiloff-Smith, A. *Language as a formal problem-space for children.* Paper prepared for the MPG/NIAS conference, *"Beyond description in child language,"* Nijmegen, Holland, June 11–16, 1979.

Kenny, A. The origin of language. In A. J. P. Kenny, H. C. Longuet-Higgins, J. R. Lucas, & C. H. Waddington *Development of mind.* Edinburgh: Edinburgh University Press, 1973.

Kuczaj, S. A. On the acquisition of a semantic system. *Journal of Verbal Learning and Verbal Behavior.* 1975, *14,* 340–358.

Kuczaj, S. A., & Daly, M. J. The development of hypothetical reference in the speech of young children. *Jornal of Child Language,* 1979, *6,* 563–579.

Kuczaj, S. A., & Maratsos, M. P. What children *can* say before they *will. Merrill Palmer Quarterly,* 1975, *21,* 89–111.

Lenneberg, E. H. Understanding language without ability to speak: A case report. *Journal of Abnormal and Social Psychology,* 1962, *65,* 419–425.

Lewis, D. K. *Convention: A philosophical study.* Cambridge, Mass.: Harvard University Press, 1969.

Lock, A. *The early stages of communicative and linguistic development: Underlying process.* Paper presented at the NIAS International Conference on knowledge and representation. Wassenar, Holland, March 8–10, 1979.

McNeill, D. *The acquisition of language: The study of developmental psycholinguistics.* New York: Harper & Row, 1970.

Miller, G. *Psychology, the study of mental life.* Harmondsworth: Penguin Books, 1966.

Neisser, U. *Cognition and reality*. San Francisco: Freeman, 1976. (a)

Neisser, U. General, academic, and artificial intelligence. In L. B. Resnick (Ed.), *The nature of intelligence*. Hillsdale, N.J.: Lawrence Erlbaum Associates, 1976. (b)

Nelson, K. Structure and strategy in learning to talk. *Monograph for the Society for Research in Child Development*, 1973, *38*, 149 Nos. 1 and 2).

Newson, J. Dialogue and development. In A. Lock (Ed.), *Action, gesture and symbol*. London: Academic Press, 1978.

Okonji, O. M. The effects of familiarity on classification. *Journal of Cross-Cultural Psychology*, 1971, *2*, 39–49.

Orne, M. T. Communication in the total experimental situation, why it is important, how it is evaluated, and its significance for the ecological validity of findings. In P. Pliner, L. Krames, & T. Alloway (Eds.), *Communication and affect, language and thought*. New York: Academic Press, 1973.

Peel, E. Generalising through the verbal medium. *British Journal of Educational Psychology*, 1978, *48*, 36–46.

Peters, A. M. Language learning strategies: Does the whole equal the sum of the parts? *Language*, 1977, *53*, 560–573.

Peters, A. M. *The units of language acquisition*. (Working Papers in Linguistics, (*12*, 1) Jan.–Apr. 1980). Department of Linguistics, University of Hawaii at Manoa.

Piaget, J. *Play dreams and imitation in childhood*. New York: Norton, 1962.

Rosch, E. On the internal structure of perceptual and semantic categories. In T. Moore (Ed.), *Cognitive development and the acquisition of language*. New York: Academic Press, 1973.

Ryan, J. Early language development: Towards a communicational analysis. In M. P. M. Richards (Ed.), *The integration of a child into a social world*. Cambridge, Eng.: Cambridge University Press, 1974.

Sachs, J., & Johnson, M. Language development in a hearing child of deaf parents. In W. Von Raffler-Engel & Y. Lebrun (Eds.), *Baby talk and infant speech*. Lisse: Swets & Zeitlinger, 1976.

Sachs J. & Truswell, L. Comprehension of two word instructions by children in the one word stage. *Journal of Child Language*, 1978, *5*, 17–24.

Sameroff, A. J., & Harris, A. E. Dialectical approaches to development. In M. H. Bornstein & W. Kessen (Eds.), *Psychological development from infancy. Image to intention*. Hillsdale, N.J.: Lawrence Erlbaum Associates, 1979.

Schlesinger, I. M. The grammar of sign language and the problems of language universals. In J. Morton (Ed.), *Biological and social factors in psycholinguistics*. London: Logos Press, 1971.

Schlesinger, I. M. The role of cognitive development and linguistic input in language acquisition. *Journal of Child Language*, 1977, *4*, 153–168.

Searle, J. R. *Speech acts. An essay in the philosophy of language*. Cambridge, Eng.: Cambridge University Press, 1970.

Shugar, G. W. Text analysis as an approach to the study of early linguistic operations. In N. Waterson & C. Snow (Eds.), *The development of communication*. London: Wiley, 1978.

Sinclair, H. Personal communication, 1979.

Sinclair, A., Sinclair, H., & De Marcellus, O. Young children's comprehension and production of passive sentences. *Archives de Psychologie*, 1971, *49* (161), 1–22.

Slobin, D. I. Cognitive prerequisites for the development of grammar. In C. Ferguson & D. Slobin (Eds.), *Studies in child language development*. New York: Holt, Rinehart, & Winston, 1973.

Smith, N. *The acquisition of phonology: A case study*. Cambridge, Eng.: Cambridge University Press, 1973.

Snow, C. The language of the mother–child relationship. In S. Rogers (Ed.), *They don't speak our language*. London: Edward Arnold, 1976.

Snyder, A. Rules of language. *Mind*, 1971, *80*(318), 161–178.

Somerville, A. W. Jampot cure. Letter to (London) Sunday Telegraph, August 26, 1979.

Steffenson, M. S. Satisfying inquisitive adults: Some simple methods of answering yes/no questions. *Journal of Child Language,* 1978, *5,* 221–236.

Thorne, J., Bratley, P., & Dewar, H. The syntactic analysis of English by machine. In D. Michie (Ed.), *Machine intelligence 3.* Edinburgh: Edinburgh University Press, 1968.

Tizard, B., Carmichael, H., Hughes, M., & Pinkerton, G. Four year olds talking to mothers and teachers. *Journal of Child Psychology and Psychiatry, Book Supplement,* 1980.

Tulving, E. Episodic and semantic memory. In E. Tulving & W. Donaldson (Eds.), *Organization of memory.* New York: Academic Press, 1972.

Vygotsky, L. *Thought and language.* Cambridge, Mass.: M. I. T. Press, 1962.

Wagner-Gough, J. Excerpts from comparative studies in second language learning. In E. Hatch (Ed.), *Second language acquisition. A book of readings.* Rowley, Mass.: Newbury House, 1978.

Warden, D. Children's understanding of *ask* and *tell:* A reappraisal. *Journal of Child Language,* in press.

Watson, P. Can racial discrimination affect I. Q.? In K. Richardson & D. Spears (Eds.), *Race, culture and intelligence.* Harmondsworth: Penguin, 1972.

2 On the Nature of Syntactic Development

Stan A. Kuczaj II
Southern Methodist University

WHAT A THEORY OF LANGUAGE ACQUISITION MUST EXPLAIN

During the course of normal language acquisition, young children somehow acquire a *complex, abstract, productive rule-governed* conceptual system that allows them to produce and comprehend grammatical and semigrammatical sentences in communicative contexts and a number of noncommunicative contexts, the latter including both those situations in which the children engage in various forms of play with language and the various types of experimental settings frequently employed by developmental psycholinguists. Thus, the general problem with which developmental psycholinguists are confronted may be stated as follows: How do young and relatively cognitively immature children acquire the complex, abstract, productive rule-governed conceptual system that underlies their use of their mother tongue?

The answer(s) to this broad question depends, of course, on answers to a number of more specific (but still fairly general) questions that arise upon consideration of what is meant by the claim that children learning their first language learn a complex, abstract, productive rule-governed conceptual system. Although the meanings one grants the modifying terms *complex, abstract, productive,* and *rule-governed* will determine, to a large extent, one's assumptions about and explanations of language acquisition, the following discussion is not an attempt to specify unequivocal definitions of these terms insofar as their use in the study of language acquisition is concerned.

Complexity

Language is a *complex* system. Although the complexity of the system is inherent in that it is abstract, productive, and rule governed (given that the terms are not mutually exclusive), the complexity of language can also be demonstrated by the amount of dispute that has been generated concerning its nature. Skinner (1957) has suggested that language reflects basic and/or mediating stimulus–response associations whereas Lashley (1951) and N. Chomsky (1959) have argued that language is unexplainable in terms of stimulus–response associations. The rules of language have been argued to operate on deep-structure (i.e., underlying) syntactic categories (Chomsky, 1957, 1965), deep-structure semantic categories (Fillmore, 1968), and surface-structure semantic/syntactic categories (Starosta, 1976). The difficulty in describing and explaining language is itself a tribute to the complexity of the phenomenon of language. Language is a complex phenomenon that presupposes a complex conceptual system on the part of its users. The question for the developmental psycholinguist is how young children learn the complex system underlying their use of language during a developmental period in which children are thought to be lacking in many cognitive skills and processes.

Abstractness

The conceptual system underlying the use of language is *abstract* in that it is thought to go beyond associations of individual words (see Lashley, 1951) and instead involve the manipulation of abstract form classes, which linguists and psycholinguists characterize as nouns, verbs, agents, actions, etc., depending on their predispositions. However, it is very important to remember that the language-learning child never experiences the abstract form classes themselves, but instead only experiences particular instances (words and morphemes). Thus, two key questions about the conceptual system underlying language and its development arise. First, what is the nature of the abstract form classes employed by language users when they produce and comprehend utterances? This is certainly an important question, because one's view of the abstract form classes involved in language production and comprehension will undoubtedly lead one to posit certain types of developmental processes. The degree of abstractness one grants the form classes is quite important, because the more abstract the form classes are thought to be, the more removed the acquisition process becomes from the environment; that is, the actual speech the child hears is relatively unimportant if one views form classes as highly abstract. Whether one views the form classes as being primarily syntactic phenomenon—that is, nouns, verbs, etc. (N. Chomsky, 1957, 1965)—or semantic phenomenon—that is, agents, actions, etc. (Fillmore, 1968)—is also important. The theoretical stance emphasizing the syntactic aspect of form-class acquisition assumes that the child attends to, stores, and organizes in memory form classes based on distributional characteristics of words—that is, on what sentential positions and in what sentential contexts particular words and word-types can occur. The semantically based explanation(s) of form-class acquisition assumes that the child acquires form classes by attending to semantic relations that sentences and parts of sentences can express and by correlating these semantic relations with corresponding conceptual and/or real-world relations among objects and events. Attempts to explain form-class acquisition that emphasize both syntactic (structural) and semantic variables seem much more reasonable than those that ignore either set of variables. Recent work in this area shows promise for providing viable explanations of form-class acquisition (see Maratsos & Chalkley, in press).

The second key question facing scholars of language acquisition concerns how the child acquires abstract form classes given experience solely with individual instances. Regardless of the assumptions one makes about form classes, one must somehow account for the acquisition of abstract classes of linguistic units in the absence of any direct experience with the classes per se; the child has only experience with class instances. It should be noted that this is a general problem in studies of conceptual development. How does the child (and adult) form concepts of classes of objects and events given experience with individual instances rather than classes per se?

Productivity

The conceptual system underlying use of language is thought to be productive (creative) because it involves a finite (though large) number of individual morphemes, words, form classes, and rules, yet at the same time allows for the production and comprehension of an infinite (or indefinitely large) number of grammatical and semigrammatical sentences.[1] Other key questions that thus arise about the development of the conceptual system of concern include the following:

1. How does the child acquire a productive/creative system given his or her experience with a limited number of utterances? In other words, given a limited input, how does the child acquire the capacity to produce and comprehend an unlimited (or at least relatively unlimited) output?

2. How can we best characterize the notion of a "productive rule"? Are such rules categorical (N. Chomsky, 1957) or variable (Bloom, 1976; Brown, 1973; Cedergren & Sankoff, 1974; Labov, 1969) in nature?

---

[1]A theory of language must account for semigrammatical and ungrammatical utterances as well as for grammatical utterances, because the semigrammatical and ungrammatical utterances are produced and (sometimes) comprehended.

3. What evidence can we use to determine whether the child has learned/ created a productive rule? When can we say that the child has created a productive rule system? Perfect use of a form cannot be a criterion, given that even adult speakers produce ungrammatical utterances (and view them as ungrammatical as well). Because the rules of concern are *rules* rather than *laws*,[2] violations of the rules may occur without necessarily violating the status of the rules qua rules. The fact that the rules of concern need not be invariably applied (particularly if they are variable rather than categorical rules) causes extreme difficulty in pinpointing the exact point at which any given rule is acquired during the course of language acquisition (disagreements about exactly what is meant by the term *acquired* also cause difficulty in this regard).

Cognitive Capabilities of the Child

Young and supposedly cognitively immature children somehow succeed at the enormous task of acquiring their mother tongue. Consider for a moment what is involved in such a task. The acquisition of a first language involves acquiring a conceptual system consisting of (1) individual units (sounds, words, and nonword morphemes, such as the *un* in *unlikely* and the *ed* in *walked*); (2) phonological, syntactic, and semantic classes and subclasses (e.g., phonemes, nouns, agents, verbs, verbs that take *ed* to express pastness, and so on); and (3) information about the relational properties of the individual units, subclasses and classes—namely, information about what units may occur together and in what sorts of relationships. One cannot sensibly say sentences such as *boy the angry fell lady off, the rock ate a lettuce soup,* and *the green idea dreamed furiously;* there are restrictions on the relational properties of units, subclasses, and classes.

Thus, the conceptual system underlying the use of words and nonword morphemes involves the following mental representations: (1) phonological representations; (2) semantic representations, including information about the meaning(s) of individual words and the relation of such meaning to that of other words; and (3) syntactic representations, including information about the syntactic class(es) of which an individual word is a member and the syntactic/semantic relations in which individual words may engage (e.g., the phrase *hard dream* is peculiar at best, whereas *hard book* and *hard rock* are permissible, although the meaning of *hard* is different in the two phrases; examples such as these demonstrate that the representations are necessarily independent of one another).

---

[2]It is worth noting that rules are not laws. Rules describe tendencies that may be preferable to other possibilities, but do not exclude these other alternatives. Thus, although it is correct to say "that person may have been shopping" in English, it is possible, though incorrect, to say "that person may been shopping" (this error is common in the speech of 5- and 6-year-old children). Laws, on the other hand, may not be violated (otherwise, they are not laws). For example, the statement "for every action there is an equal and opposite reaction" must hold in all instances for the statement to have status as a law. Syntax clearly does not involve laws, but instead utilizes a system of probabalistic rules.

There can be little doubt that the development of the conceptual system underlying the use of language involves a significant amount of information acquisition and organization on the part of the young child during a time at which the child's cognitive prowess is usually described as lacking in some respect or another (see Flavell, 1963, 1977). Moreover, this acquisition takes place with apparent ease and rapidity (this has been recognized for some time; see Stern, 1924) and without any significant amount of direct tutorial assistance. Thus, to account for the language learning of the young child, one must assume that the child is not as cognitively unsophisticated as we have been led to believe, that language acquisition involves the use of cognitive processes and capacities restricted to the language-learning task, or that the child brings significant amounts of innately specified information about language and its characteristics to the task (of course, some combination of these three possibilities may also be correct). Obviously, though, the paradox of a cognitively unsophisticated organism learning with apparent ease a complex system the nature of which has baffled theorists throughout history must be resolved.

LANGUAGE ACQUISITION AS AN EXPERIENTIALLY BASED PHENOMENON

In the following discussion, an attempt is made to provide the basis for an account of syntactic development that emphasizes the child's experiences. This is *not* to say that the role of the child is minimized and that language acquisition is viewed as an externally based phenomenon that happens to a passive but absorbent organism. The role of the child is emphasized, but not in terms of innate knowledge of language that the child brings to the language-learning task. Instead, the child's *active*[3] attempts to interpret and organize his or her linguistic experiences are stressed.

By stressing the child's experiences (i.e., the linguistic and nonlinguistic environment) and by assuming that the child is not equipped with innate knowledge of language, an account of language acquisition that emphasizes surface-structure relations and surface-structure–based acquisitions is mandated. If parsimony between acquisition of language structure during the preschool years and the adult linguistic system is desired, this in turn necessitates a surface-structure–based account of language per se. In other words, if the preschool child is learning a system of surface-structure relations, and if one wishes what the preschool child is learning to be incorporated into the adult system (i.e., what the child learns becomes the adult system), then the adult linguistic system should also be one based on surface-structure relations. (Ingram, 1975, has argued that

---

[3]Piaget emphasizes the active role of the child in his theory of cognitive development. The activity of the child should also be recognized and emphasized in theories of language development.

the preschool child's language system differs qualitatively from that of the adult, the transition from child system [one based on phrase-structure rules] to adult system [one based on abstract linguistic deep structures and transformational rules to relate deep structures and surface structures] occurring during the school years. In an approach such as that of Ingram, it is not crucial for the language system of the preschool child to closely correspond to that of the adult.) Although it is not clear that an adequate surface-structure account of adult language has been formulated (see Starosta, 1976, for one attempt), a viable surface-structure–based account of syntactic development would argue for such an explanation of the adult system. In the following discussion, there is little concern with formulating a surface-structure account of language. Instead, the goal is to formulate a surface-structure–based account of language acquisition. This goal is predicated upon the assumption that the rules and form classes involved in syntax should be "learnable"—that is, capable of being abstracted from the examples that the child hears (Derwing, 1973; Paul, 1891). This in turn assumes that the child does not bring innate knowledge of linguistic rules and form classes to the language-learning task, and that input to the language-learning child is important.

The Nature of Form Classes and Syntactic Rules

The nature of form classes and syntactic rules has long been a subject of substantial debate. Obviously, decisions about the nature of form classes will affect one's decisions about the nature of syntactic rules, and vice versa. If one believes that form classes are best considered as deep-structure grammatical categories, then one must devise a system of syntactic rules that operate on these categories and transform deep-structure representations into surface-structure manifestations. If one believes that form classes are grammatical categories defined by surface-structure relations, then a corresponding system of rules is needed to operate on such categories and thus produce grammatical and sometimes novel grammatical (and semigrammatical) utterances. If one believes that syntactic form classes are best construed as semantically based categories, then rules to manipulate such categories and so produce and comprehend utterances are necessitated. The next section specifies the characteristics of form classes and syntactic rules with which a theory of syntactic development must accord.

FORM CLASSES

It is becoming increasingly clear that form classes are not self-defined, though it is too easy to view them as self-defined and self-apparent categories. Ross (1974) has suggested that the categories *noun* and *verb* might best be considered as nondiscrete dimensions of "nouniness" and "verbiness," such that grammatical categories may have degrees of membership (see de Villiers, 1979). According to this view, some members of a form classes are better than others (de Villiers, 1979) "in the grammatical sense of how they behave in the rule system [p. 3]." For example, some verbs are well behaved and enter into every rule, whereas others are unacceptable for many constructions. Thus, *eat* is a better instance of *verb* than is *belong,* as is illustrated below:

1. Generic construction:
   a. The child eats beans.
   b. The bike belongs to the monkey.
2. Progressive construction:
   a. The child is eating beans.
   b. The bike is belonging to the monkey. (?)
3. Imperative construction:
   a. Eat your beans!
   b. Belong to the monkey! (?)
4. Passive construction:
   a. The beans were eaten by the boy.
   b. The monkey is belonged to by the bike. (?)

Thus, not all verbs are equally "verbey," not all nouns are equally "nouney," not all adjectives are equally adjectival, and so on. But what does it mean to be "verbey," "nouney," and so on, at all? Lenneberg (1975) has suggested that it is a mistake to view categories such as *noun* and *verb* as absolute constructs. In Lenneberg's view, terms such as *noun* and *verb* are the names of relations between concatenated words. Moreover, in his view (Lenneberg, 1975): "words are not irrevocably born into fixed form classes. Form classes can be defined only by the particular formal relationship that one word has to others in a sentence [p. 28]."

This notion of form classes has also been suggested by de Villiers and de Villiers (1978): "Parts of speech are best defined in terms of their priviliges of occurrence, the positions they can occupy in sentences and the roles they play in them [p. 55]." Maratsos and Chalkley (in press) have also strongly advocated this idea: "What members of a form class share, in varying degree, that motivates our classifying them together, is a common set of diverse combinatorial-semantic properties [p. 9]."

Form classes, then, are *not* self-defined. Nor are members of form classes self-evidently members of the form class. That is, simply to say that a word is a noun (verb, adjective, etc.) is not particularly meaningful unless one knows what a noun is and therefore what it means for a word to be a noun. As Maratsos and Chalkley (in press) have noted, claiming that a word has particular combinatorial properties because it is a member of a given form class is making the causal implication in the wrong direction. Instead, words are members of particular form classes *because the words have certain particular combinatorial properties,* rather than vice versa.

It seems likely that the child uses *both* semantic information and syntactic information to form syntactic categories. The child learning language must attempt to ascertain the meaning(s) of the linguistic items he or she encounters and so meaning is implicated in all language learning. However, in order to learn syntax and syntactic categories, the child must also attend to the positional privileges of the linguistic items he or she encounters and group individual items according to shared semantic characteristics and shared syntactic characteristics (the two types of characteristics frequently overlapping with one another). As Maratsos and Chalkley (in press) suggest:

> the essential information a child needs about a new relational term in order to predict appropriate grammatical usage is not the meaning of the term but at least one semantic-distributional pattern in which it can occur. . . However, that is not the only analysis the child must make in order to build up this system. The child must be able to encode the semantic-distributional patterns and the connections among them which are a function of their application to overlapping sets of relational terms . . . Encoding and representing the correspondence of the uses of terms in *different* patterns is crucial; the child cannot just analyze the individual patterns [pp. 28–29, authors italics].

The child, then, must continually attend to, analyze, organize, and store for future comparisons the grammatical contexts in which an individual term has occurred. This does not occur in a semantic vacuum but syntactic (positional) analyses are crucial. By attending to both the semantic and syntactic characteristics of items, the child eventually is able to form abstract syntactic classes, which are determined by the items that the child has grouped together, the shared privileges of occurrence the members of a given class possess, and the interrelations of various syntactic classes.

Combinatorial Rules

The rules used to combine items may be characterized in a number of ways, depending on one's assumptions about the nature of the units and classes being combined and the number of rules (if any) needed to go from deep structure to surface structure. For example, linguistic rules may be viewed as categorical or variable. Categorical rules apply invariably and, as Brown (1973) notes, "ought to be acquired abruptly and manifested very generally in performance [p. 385]." Variable rules operate with different probabilities in different sentential contexts (Cedergren & Sankoff, 1974; Labov, 1969; Labov & Labov, 1978). Of the choice between categorical and variable rules, it appears that language acquisition is characterized by the acquisition of variable rules (Bloom, 1976; Brown, 1973; Labov & Labov, 1978), such rules perhaps becoming categorical with increasing development (see Brown, 1973). If so, this is another way of saying that the acquisition of linguistic rules follows a specific-to-general developmental path (see Kuczaj & Brannick, 1979).

THE ROLE OF INPUT IN SYNTACTIC DEVELOPMENT

N. Chomsky (1972) and McNeill (1970) advocated an account of language acquisition based on innate knowledge of language. One reason for this approach was the hypothesized poor input with which the child had to deal during the course of language acquisition (N. Chomsky, 1959). The language the child was thought to hear was hypothesized to be overly complex and irregular, as well as occasionally ungrammatical. Thus, the child was thought to have a poor set of data from which to form linguistic generalizations, an assumption leading to an account of language that presumed the child learned language *in spite of* the input to which he or she was exposed.

Obviously, an account of language acquisition that emphasizes the child's linguistic experiences must assume that language acquisition occurs *because* of linguistic input rather than in spite of linguistic input. Recent research has suggested that linguistic input may, in fact, be crucial to the language-acquisition process. First, the speech the child hears does not provide such a poor set of data as was once believed. It should be noted that it is not simply speech in the child's environment that is important. It is speech directed *to* the child that has the most effect on language development. Importantly, adult speech directed to the young child has been shown to possess the following characteristics:

1. The adult talking to a young child tends to speak in short and relatively uncomplex sentences (Farwell, 1975; Gleasen & Weintraub, 1978; Slobin, 1975).

2. The sentences produced by adults talking to young children are almost always grammatical. Newport, Gleitman & Gleitman (1975) found only one ungrammatical utterance per 1500 utterances produced by mothers speaking to their young children, a ratio that our records of early parent–child speech support.

3. Adult speech directed to young children is highly repetitive (Farwell, 1975; Newport et al. 1975; Slobin, 1975). Newport et al. (1975) found that up to 34% of the utterances produced by adults and directed towards young children consisted of full or partial repetitions of a previous utterance.

4. Adult speech directed towards young children is closely tied to present on-going events (Slobin, 1975).

These characteristics of adult speech directed towards the young language-learning child have been found to hold for different races (Drach,1969; Snow, 1974), different social classes (Snow Arlman-Rupp, Hassing, Jobse, Jooksen, & Vorster, 1974), and different cultures (Blount, 1972). Interestingly, these characteristics of adult speech are true of nonparents as well as parents (Sachs, Brown, & Salerno, 1972). Equally interesting, children modify their speech to younger children in much the same way that adults do (Shatz & Gelman, 1973). The fact that linguistic input from older children to younger children is similar to linguistic input from adults to young children may explain why children learning language in cultures in which the major linguistic input is from children rather than from adults do not seem to differ in terms of the course or rate of acquisition from children learning language from adult input (Blount, 1969; Kernan, 1969; Slobin, 1975).

Thus, it seems clear that the speech children hear does not provide as poor a data base for language acquisition as was once thought. Although it is not clear why adults and older children modify their speech to young children[4] (see Gleasen & Weintraub, 1978), it seems likely that such input could facilitate the rate of language acquisition or even determine the rate and/or course of language development. The following sections briefly examine research that has focused on the role of input in language development.

Frequency

One aspect of linguistic input that has been investigated is *frequency* of forms and constructions, the primary concern being the relation of frequency to acquisition. Typically, however, frequency of forms in adult speech around children has not been found to bear any significant relation to acquisition patterns (Brown, 1973; Cazden & Brown, 1975; Farwell, 1975; Maratsos, Kuczaj, Fox, & Chalkley, 1979, Slobin, 1975; Szajun, 1978). Cazden and Brown (1975) concluded that there is "no evidence that frequency of any sort is a significant determinant of acquisition [p. 303]," a conclusion shared by Farwell (1975). However, Newport, Gleitman, and Gleitman (1977) found that children whose mothers more frequently asked yes–no questions (and thereby used auxiliary form terms in sentence initial position) acquired the auxiliary verb system more quickly than did children whose others asked yes–no questions less frequently. Thus, frequency of forms in input may play a role in the acquisition of certain forms.

---

[4]The *reasons* that parents modify their speech to their children have yet to be clearly formulated. However, as Gleasen and Weintraub (1978) note, the fact that parental speech to children younger than 10 months of age differs from that to children older than 10 months of age has important implications for such formulations.

Frequency of certain functions in adult speech may also affect development and contribute to individual differences. Folger and Chapman (1978) found that the relative frequency with which children imitated their mothers reflected the relative frequency with which the mothers imitated the children. This led Folger and Chapman to suggest that individual differences in children's spontaneous imitations may result from the degree to which parents provide a model of imitation as a speech act.

Although it is not yet clear what role(s) frequency of forms in the child's language input plays in the language-acquisition process, it is obvious that some minimally sufficient amount of experience to a linguistic form must occur in order for the child to acquire the form. It does *not* seem to be the case that more frequent forms are acquired prior to less frequent forms. Thus, once the minimally sufficient amount of exposure to a form that is necessary for acquisition of the form has occurred (whatever this amount of exposure happens to be), it does not seem to be the case that increased exposure to the form facilitates its acquisition. Nelson, Denninger, Kaplan, and Bonvillian (1979) have suggested that higher frequency of a form in input might result in the child more quickly obtaining the minimally sufficient amount of experience necessary for acquisition. However, if this is so, then more frequent forms should be acquired prior to less frequent forms. Such an impact on rate of acquisition due to frequency has proven difficult to demonstrate in general, though Nelson et al. report data to suggest such an effect in terms of acquisition of past-tense verb forms. Thus, except for the necessity of some minimally sufficient amount of experience, frequency of forms in input may not *significantly* impact on the acquisition of the forms, though frequency of forms and functions in the speech the child hears may affect development of particular syntactic forms and systems (Nelson et al., 1979; Newport et al., 1977) and certain speech-interaction styles (Folger & Chapman, 1978). The importance of frequency of forms and/or functions in input, then, is likely to depend on the particular forms and/or functions being acquired.

Negative Feedback

It seems intuitively obvious that direct feedback to the child about the grammaticality of his or her utterances should facilitate the child's development of syntax. However, Brown and Hanlon (1970) found that parents rarely correct the ungrammatical utterances of their children, but instead focus on the "truthfulness" of their children's utterances, an interaction pattern between parents and child that I have also observed in the spontaneous speech samples I have studied. Children, then, do not receive much direct negative feedback about the grammatical well formedness of their utterances. Moreover, Braine (1971) has suggested that children are insensitive to negative feedback and explicit corrections, so that even when they are corrected, the correction does not necessarily facilitate syntactic development. The following exchange suggests how futile negative feedback may be:

Adult	Chlid
	I like these candy. I like they.
You like them?	Yes. I like they.
Say *them*.	Them.
Say "I like *them*."	I like them.
Good.	I'm good. These candy good too.
Are they good?	Yes. I like they. You like they? (Ben, 2 years, 2 months)

The likelihood that negative feedback plays a facilitative role in syntactic development diminishes even further if one considers recent work on the role of negative feedback in the acquisition of lexical items (Bowerman, 1976). Although parents may be more likely to correct erroneous word choice by their children than to correct ungrammatical utterances (Brown, 1958, Cazden, 1968), it is not clear that such negative feedback facilitates vocabulary growth (Bruner, 1975; Nelson, 1973). In fact, Nelson (1973) and Bruner (1975) have suggested that parental negative feedback about children's word use may impede lexical acquisition. Thus, negative feedback may play a negative role in language development, impeding rather than facilitating both vocabulary and syntactic development (see Bowerman, 1976).

Expansions and Recasts

Adults frequently expand their children's utterances, adding linguistic forms that were lacking in the child's utterance (Brown, Cazden, & Bellugi, 1969; Cazden, 1965). Adults apparently expand children's utterances in order to check if their interpretation of the child's utterance is correct (Cazden, 1965). Following are some examples of expansions:

Adult	Child
	That Clancy brush.
That is Clancy's brush. Do you want to brush him?	

Older Child	Younger Child
	Me push Abe. Ben push Abe.
Ben pushed me in the wagon. You're a big boy.	
	Abe push Ben.
Abe pushed Ben too.	
	Abe boy. Big boy.
Abe is a big boy. So is Ben.	

These examples demonstrate that expansions of children's utterances (regardless of whether the expansion is given by an adult or older child) build up the child's utterance by adding syntactic and semantic units. Brown and Bellugi (1964) pointed out that expansions should provide the child with a valuable kind of feedback. Because expansions immediately follow the child's utterance, their timing is optimal for the child to contrast them with a preceding utterance. Moreover, because expansions build up the child's own utterance, they should provide moderately discrepant information to the child and so facilitate development. However, expansions have not proven to be valuable for increasing the rate or changing the course of syntactic development (Cazden, 1965). Sarah, one of the three children in the longitudinal study of language acquisition by Brown and his collegues, received the *lowest* rate of parental expansions, yet was the *most* advanced in the development of her inflections, which are among the forms that are omitted in early child speech, but are included and supposedly modeled in adult expansions (Brown, Cazden, & Bellugi, 1969).

Although the significance of expansions for syntactic development has been difficult to demonstrate, Keith Nelson and his colleagues have been able to demonstrate that a slightly different type of response to a child's utterance may facilitate grammatical development. Nelson has termed this type of response a *recast;* the child's utterance is recast by the adult into a sentence with a different syntactic form but similar semantic content. Nelson, Carskaddon, and Bonvillian (1973) found that children who were exposed to recast replies by adult experimenters developed syntax more rapidly than did children who were not given an increased amount of recasts. Nelson (1978) and Nelson et al. (1979) found that the type of recast also influences development. In these studies, simple recasts were distinguished from complex recasts. Simple recasts are those in which the adult's reply maintains reference to the same basic meaning in the child's preceding utterance, with structural change limited to only one of three complex units (subject, verb, object). Complex recasts involve structural change to two or more of the three components. Simple recasts seem to facilitate the child's syntactic development, whereas complex recasts impede the rate of syntactic growth, most likely due to the moderately discrepant nature of the simple recasts. In Piagetian terms, the child is more likely to be able to successfully assimilate and accommodate simple recasts than complex recasts.

Why Is It Difficult to Demonstrate the Influence of Input on Syntactic Development?

Although certain of the studies previously mentioned lend credence to the notion that variations in input lead to corresponding variations in development, there are other studies (some also previously mentioned) that reflect the apparent insignificance of input variation on the rate and course of language development. It is my firm belief that input is crucial to the language-learning process and that future research will demonstrate exactly how crucial input is for language development. However, it should be emphasized that input per se is *not* important. What is important is the child's use of the input—whether he or she notices it at all, what interpretations he or she places on it, and how he or she organizes the information he or she has gained for subsequent interpretation. Thus, *intake* must be distinguished from *input*. *Input* refers to the linguistic information to which the child is exposed, whereas *intake* refers to the child's selective use of input (de Villiers & de Villiers, 1978). Children rarely attend to input in its entirety (Bever, 1970; R. Clark, 1978; Kuczaj, 1979; Shipley, Smith, & Gleitman, 1969; Slobin, 1973). Thus, not only may different inputs lead to different acquisition patterns (or have no effect on acquisition patterns in the case of invariant developmental sequences), but the same input (or experiences) may lead to different acquisition patterns for different children, depending on each child's interpretation and use of the input. In order to determine how children use input (i.e., what they intake from the input), three factors must be considered—strategies, past experience, and context.

Strategies.   Numerous theorists have suggested that the language-learning child may employ strategies to simplify the language-learning task; some strategies involve comprehension (Bever, 1970; Brown, 1973; C. Chomsky, 1969; E. Clark, 1977; Kuczaj, 1979; Slobin, 1973) and some involve production (R. Clark, 1974; Hakuta, 1974). Language-learning strategies are thought to assist the child in both the interpretation and organization of input, although particular strategies might occasionally mislead a child, as in the child's erroneous interpretations of passive sentences as active (Bever, 1970, Maratsos, 1974). It should be noted that strategies are not invariant across development. Comprehension strategies have been found to change with age (Kuczaj, 1979; Strohner & Nelson, 1974), and individual differences have been found in regard to strategy use by language-learning children (Bloom, 1970; Kuczaj, 1975).

The most comprehensive list of possible strategies the language-learning child might employ has been provided by Slobin (1973). The possible strategies (which Slobin terms operating principles) include the following:

1. Pay attention to the ends of words.
2. The phonological forms of words can be systematically modified.
3. Pay attention to the order of words and morphemes.
4. Avoid exceptions.
5. Avoid interruption or rearrangement of linguistic units.
6. Underlying semantic relations should be marked overtly and clearly.

Slobin suggests that strategies such as these are related to universal characteristics of language and that the strategies comprise innate predispositions for interpreting, organizing, and categorizing linguistic input (a view shared by Derwing, 1973, and Segalowitz & Galang, 1978). As Derwing (1973) notes, inborn predispositions designed for dealing with linguistic information are not the same as inborn knowledge about the content (i.e., the structures and rules) of language. Thus, the notion of innate language-learning strategies is independent of the notion of innate knowledge of language, the difference being that between process and content. Moreover, although the study of language has revealed a fair number of possible universals (Greenberg, 1963), the role of such universals differs in the language-acquisition process depending on whether one advocates innate language-processing capacities or innate knowledge of language (see Derwing, 1973). If innate knowledge of language exists, then linguistic universals might comprise the core or the entirety of this innate content. On the other hand, if innate processing skills exist, then linguistic universals are the *result* of innate cognitive predispositions rather than the *content* of such predispositions. Of course, it is possible that there are both innate content universals and innate processing universals. It is also possible that there are neither innate content universals nor innate processing universals. However, it seems most likely that linguistic universals result from the interaction of processing and organizing predispositions (some of which may be innate, others of which may be learned) and environmental factors.

The view that not all strategies need be innate is not unique. Bowerman (1974) suggested that children may make use of either the characteristics of their existing cognitive structures or the developmental process they went through in acquiring them in *deriving* strategies for the interpretation of linguistic data. This is an important claim for two reasons. First, the strategies used by children in the course of acquiring their mother tongue may result from children's earlier acquisitions and interactions with their environment as well as from innate predispositions. Second, if children derive strategies based on their past experiences, then different experiences could result in individual differences in strategy formation and use. Such individual differences have been reported in the literature (Bloom, 1970; Kuczaj, 1975; Ramer, 1976).[5]

---

[5]Ramer (1976) has suggested that *strategy* be distinguished from *style*. In this view, strategies are intentional whereas style is unintentional. This is an awkward and incorrect dichotomy. Although cognitive strategies and cognitive style are not isomorphic (though individual differences in the two may be related and cognitive strategies and cognitive style may covary from individual to individual), it would seem that both cognitive strategies and cognitive style are largely unintentional. Although many children appear to pay attention to word order (Bever, 1970; Segalowitz & Galang, 1978) and to the endings of words (Kuczaj, 1979; Miyahara, 1974; Slobin, 1973), it is not clear that these strategies are intentionally employed by the child. In fact, it would appear that they are not intentional processes, consciously directed by the child. In pilot testing for a recent study dealing with the relative ease of acquisition of suffixes and prefixes (Kuczaj, 1979), we asked children who exhibited a strong tendency to attend to and thus learn suffixes how they had learned the suffixes. None of the children we queried were able to state how they had learned what they had. Moreover, no child made any mention of attending to the ends of words.

Past Experience.   As alluded to previously, past experience may contribute to the types and number of strategies the child employs during the course of language acquisition. Experience might also contribute to the frequency with which children use strategies. If a strategy is successful, the child may frequently employ it, perhaps even erroneously. For example, children learning English fare quite well by attending to the ends of words. The use of this strategy makes it easier for the child to learn the progressive *-ing,* the regular past tense *-ed,* the possessive *-s,* and the third-person singular present *-s.* All of these forms are suffixes and are learned in the early periods of language acquisition (Brown, 1973; Cazden, 1968, Kuczaj, 1977,1978). Thus, children learning English have a fair amount of success by using a strategy that biases their processing of input in favor of suffixes. Because of this, they also come to employ this strategy too broadly. They not only pay more attention to suffixes, but they also occasionally interpret prefixes as suffixes (Kuczaj, 1979). Thus, at the level of initial processing, children pay too much attention to suffixes and even erroneously interpret information about nonsuffixes as suffixes. There is also evidence that older children who can attend to prefixes as well as suffixes during initial processing of input nonetheless learn suffixes more readily than prefixes, implicating a postinitial processing bias in favor of suffixes (Kuczaj, 1979). Thus, past experience is doubly important. If the child has been rewarded (by being successful) by use of innate strategies, then the child will continue to use these strategies in both the initial and postinitial processing of linguistic information. If a strategy has been unsuccessful, then the child will likely abandon the strategy (I do not mean to imply that the use or nonuse of a strategy is consciously manipulated by the child). Experience can also lead to the creation of new strategies and to the continued use or abandonment of these strategies.

Past experience can also play a role in how one interprets linguistic information by providing a context in which one interprets the information.

Context.   There are two types of context that must be distinguished from one another even though they are not necessarily mutually exclusive. These are *external context* and *internal context,* and the necessity for distinguishing them is made clear in the following quote from Kuczaj and Lederberg (1977):

What exactly . . . is meant by *context* and *interpretation of context?* Let O designate entities in the real world, and f designate an individual's focus on a particular entity or event. If f is on A (fA), then everything except A in O is context. If f is on B (fB), then everything except B in O is context. So anything in O is potentially f (i.e., that to which one is attending) and/or potentially context. The organism determines what is f and what is context . . . Given the same O, people may differ in what they attend to (f), and different fs necessarily result in different contexts simply because a particular entity (e.g., A) cannot be both that which is focused on *and* part of the context which the organism uses to better understand that on which he is focusing. Moreover, even given the same O, the same f and the same context, two people could end up with different interpretations of that which they have focused on. Why? Because the more or less identical context which is available to the two interpreters is *external context,* and each interpreter must use the information he obtains from the external context to construct an *internal context* (a mental construct), the internal context being important for the interpretation of the entity on which one's attention is focused. Thus, not only does one have to use the available context to interpret certain phenomenon, but one must also interpret the available external context to arrive at the internal context which one uses to interpret the more central phenomenon in which one is interested. Differentiating between external and internal context is necessary not only because it explains why interpretations of the same event are idiosyncratic from person to person, but also because it is able to account for the same person differently interpreting the same or similar events in the same or similar contexts at different times [p. 411].

The notion that *internal context* is what is important in the interpretation of a given experience emphasizes the active role of the child in the interpretation process. In a sense, the child determines the information that he or she obtains from a given experience. Thus, once again, we see that it is not only experience (input) that determines development. Experience contributes to development, but so does the child. It is the interaction of the child and experience that determines development.

A FRAMEWORK FOR A THEORY OF SYNTACTIC DEVELOPMENT

In this section, I outline a theoretical approach to syntactic development that emphasizes the interaction of input and the child's interpretation of input. I also emphasize the active role of the child in interpreting input. Even simplified speech containing many regularities will not help the child learning language unless the child pays attention to and utilizes the regularities. The view offered here, then, is one that assumes that child *creates* language within the limits set by his or her processing and organizing predispositions and the input. Thus, although input constrains the form of language a child learns, the child's processing of the input is more important than the input per se. As noted earlier, it is *intake* that is important, rather than input per se. However, what determines intake? The answer to this question depends on the period of development with which one is concerned. Early on in the acquisition of language, the child's intake is likely to be largely dependent on innate processing and organizing tendencies. Later in the acquisition sequence, the child's earlier intake will affect the current intake. In fact, previous experience can affect postinitial processing of intake as well as initial processing of input (Kuczaj, 1979). The child's interpretation of past experiences provides an internal context that assists (and perhaps biases) the child's interpretation of later experiences. Although input may be considered as external context, what the child extracts from this external context is what is important and internal context influences interpretation of external context (Kuczaj & Lederberg, 1977). This is certainly true of adult processing of novel sentences, as noted by Winograd (1973):

> People are able to interpret sentences syntactically even when they do not know the meanings of the individual words. Most of our vocabulary (beyond a certain age) is learned by hearing sentences in which unfamiliar words appear in syntactically well-defined positions. We process the sentence without knowing any category information for the words, and in fact use the results of that processing to discover the semantic meaning . . . What really seems to be going on is a coordinated process in which a variety of syntactic and semantic information can be relevant, and in which the hearer takes advantage of whatever is more useful in understanding a given part of a sentence [p. 84].

Young children also have the capability to create and comprehend novel lexical/syntactic items (Bogoyavlenskiy, 1973, Bowerman, 1974; Brown, 1957; Bushnell, 1977; Chukovsky, 1968; Kuczaj, 1977, 1978). For example, Brown (1957) found that 3-year-old children could guess something about the meaning of a new word by using information that implicated the form class of which the novel term was a member. It seems that even young children can create an internal semantic/syntactic context with which to interpret novel items within a known syntactic frame. Moreover, children must also use internally constructed semantic/syntactic frames to interpret novel syntactic constructions.

In addition to linguistic context, the child's interpretation of linguistic input is also dependent on the nonlinguistic context (Bloom, 1974; Kuczaj, 1975). According to Bloom (1974), however, "it is important to emphasize that it is not the immediate context **per se** that supports the child's message or that enables him to decode messages, but, rather, it is the child's mental representation of the circumstances and events in nonlinguistic context [p. 302]." It seems likely that the immediate context is more crucial during the early periods of language development than in later periods of development (Chapman & Miller, 1973; Wells, 1974). Bloom (1974) suggests that "the major task for the child in the course of language development is the ability to speak and understand messages that are independent of external situations or internal affectual and need states [p. 304]."

The interaction of internal context (both linguistic and nonlinguistic) and external context (both linguistic and nonlinguistic) is not always straightforward. As Wells (1974) notes: "learning situations are *not* always clear cut, and it will frequently happen that the child hears several different linguistic expressions in relation to the particular situation that he is engaged in, each focusing on different aspects of the situation [p. 267]." Any given situation may be described in a number of ways (see Russell, 1940) and the same verbal expression (e.g., *the red one*) may be used in many different situations. Thus, there is no one-to-one correspondence between a linguistic expression and an external context. To further complicate matters, the input to the child during the course of development will not consist solely of grammatical utterances. Children also hear ungrammatical utterances, so they cannot use all of the utterances they hear as equally good instances of correct syntactic constructions. Thus, all of the utterances input to a child may not be used as a basis for constructing a grammar. An explanation of syntactic development must account for the apparent unimportance of the ungrammatical utterances children hear, because children do not appear to be greatly affected by such ungrammatical utterances. Perhaps frequency plays a significant role in this phenomenon. Ungrammatical constructions that are frequent in the child's environment (perhaps due to another child's misanalysis of a given syntactic construction) might lead the child to mistakenly view the ungrammatical construction as a correct one. Ungrammatical constructions that are infrequent are less likely to become part of the child's syntactic repertoire if sufficient competing information about the correct syntactic forms is available to the child.

Although it seems clear that the child's interpretation of the input is more crucial than input per se, input is obviously important in the language-learning process. For example, Savic' and Mikes' (1974) report that children learning Serbo-Croation make word-order mistakes with qualifying adjectives but not with quantifying adjectives. This can be attributed to the input about such adjectives to the child—that is, the permissible uses of the forms in adult speech. In Serbo Croation, qualifying adjectives may occur in a prenoun phrase position or predicatively. However, quantifying adjectives may occur only in prenoun phrase positions, so the input to the child concerning quantifiers is structurally unambiguous whereas that concerning qualifiers is not as structurally straightforward and can thus lead to errors on the part of the language-learning child.

Following is an outline for an acquisition model of syntax. The model emphasizes the interaction of input, a data processor (which determines intake), a data organizer, and past experience. A first approximation of this interaction is given in Fig 2.1.

One can see that in this model, the data organizer may affect data processing by contributing relevant aspects of past experience to the data processor. Experience can also affect processing capabilities and strategies. The model assumes that the analysis and storage of surface-structure syntactic relations is a central concern, a notion that it shares with acquisition models proposed by Braine (1971) and Maratsos and Chalkley (in press). Like Braine, I assume that the input is scanned in order to ascertain the syntactic relations and that the ascertained syntactic properties are stored in memory. I also agree with Braine that the syntactic relations picked up by the input scanner may be recorded as deviations from previously learned patterns, or as special cases of these already learned

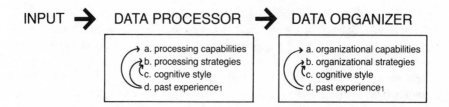

FIG. 20.1.   An acquisition model for syntax. The arrows indicate directional influence patterns.

Note: The interpretative variables of past experience include routines, probabilistic combinatorial rules, syntactic categories, and semantic categories. These variables change with development.

patterns. Unlike Braine, however, I am not assuming that there is an ordered series of memory stores, the last of which is the permanent store that contains the syntactic relations that are finally learned. Nor am I assuming that the syntactic acquisition system has *built-in* decay characteristics and rapidity of learning based on probability. As discussed earlier, there is little evidence to suggest that frequency of syntactic forms contributes more than marginally to the acquisition of such forms. The present model emphasizes the discovery of the corresponding use of forms in different syntactic relations. As argued by Maratsos and Chalkley (in press), the development of syntax depends on the encoding and representing of the uses of forms in different positional patterns. Simply analyzing the individual patterns is insufficient. The individual patterns must be related to one another in order for the child to learn a productive syntactic system.

It is assumed that the data processor and the data organizer operate on both semantic and syntactic information. The interpretation and organization of such information is influenced by processing and organizing strategies, some innate and others learned. Innate and learned strategies might possibly be distinguished in terms of the universality of a strategy. If a strategy is universal, then it is possibly innately specified. If a strategy is not universal (see Akiyama, 1979, for a discussion of a nonuniversal strategy), then it is more likely to be a learned strategy rather than one that is innately determined. However, the interaction of input, intake, and strategies may make these straightforward predictions somewhat less straightforward. Although nonuniversal strategies are quite likely to be learned, universal strategies need not be innate. Because strategies may be learned, and because languages may have universal characteristics (Greenberg, 1963), it is possible that universal strategies (or at least some universal strategies) result from the universal characteristics of language or, alternatively, that the universal strategies result in the universal characteristics of language. Thus, the universality of a strategy need not implicate innate characteristics. A strategy could be universal because all languages reward the use (and thereby the learning) of such a strategy. (It should be kept in mind that innate and learned strategies may be affected by experience; see Kuczaj, 1979). Moreover, it is possible that language universals result from limitations of the processing system even in the absence of innate language-learning strategies. Kiparsky (1971) and Slobin (1977) have suggested that historical loss of linguistic forms and/or rules may be facilitated by difficulty of learning. According to Slobin (1977): "Forms which are late to be acquired by children are presumably also relatively difficult for adults to process, and should be especially vulnerable to (historical) change [p. 194]." Kiparsky (1971) writes: "Basically, we can say that rules are susceptible to (historical) loss if they are hard to learn [p. 627]."

This brings us to consider once again the child's active role in the language-learning process. Input is important only to the extent that the child is able to put the input to use. Forms and rules that are hard to learn and thus subject to historical loss are hard to learn not because of low frequency (though this could be a factor), but because the child's processing and organizing skills are not designed to deal with such forms and rules. Thus, there is a significant interaction between cognitive capacities and input and it is likely that there are also significant interactions between cognitive development and processing of linguistic input, as well as between previous language development and the processing of input. Schlesinger (1977) has noted that:

> a modicum of cognitive development must precede any learning of language, because language remains meaningless unless referring to some already interpreted aspect of the environment. However, once some structuring of the environment has occurred and some primitive utterances can be understood in accordance with this structure, there is room for an influence of the form of these utterances on the child's cognitive development. They may direct him towards further interpreting events and states referred to [p. 166].

It is not the case, then, that cognitive development invariably provides the foundation for subsequent language development. Novel linguistic forms (de Villiers & de Villiers, 1978) "may serve to draw attention to events and categorizations that the child would *not* otherwise heed [p. 222]. (See also Schlesinger, 1977.) This notion is important, for it shows that there is no simple invariant unidirectional mapping from cognition to language, because language may lead to new cognitive categories. Schlesinger (1977) suggests that there may even be individual differences in whether cognitive development or linguistic input determines some particular development.

Children do not all receive the same input, nor do individual children necessarily interpret the same input in the same fashion. Also, individual children process input differently at different points in development. A given set of input may facilitate the syntactic development of some 3 year olds, but may either fail to influence or perhaps even impede the syntactic development of less linguistically sophisticated children. (Nelson, 1978, has suggested that particular kinds of input [adult replies to the child] at certain developmental points are crucial for syntactic development.) In the following discussion, I attempt to demonstrate how children's interpretation of input leads to specific-to-general development patterns.

Specific-to-General Development

The notion of specific-to-general syntactic developmental patterns would not appear to accord well with the notion that development typically results from the dual processes of differentiation and reintegration rather than integration per se (Bower, 1974; Lenneberg, 1975; Werner & Kaplan, 1963). The notion of differentiation in development assumes that initially overly broad classes, concepts, and so on, become more specialized and specific with development.

If differentiation characterizes the development of syntactic classes, the notion of specific-to-general developmental patterns is wrong. However, I should like to suggest that differentiation is not a characteristic of *syntactic* development per se (particularly in the early stages of syntactic development). It is true that differentiation characterizes the development of many concepts, but this does not entail that differentiation also characterizes the development of syntactic classes, a view that Lenneberg (1975) also seems to have held:

> The differentiation of the field of semantics leads necessarily and organically to the first and most basic aspect of syntax, predication. Because of differentiation, a single word no longer refers coarsely to entire physical or social situations . . . Progress in semantic differentiation leads to syntactic development because the reduction of the semantic field of one word naturally leads to the addition of specifiers, and this leads to topic–comment constructions by means of modifying words . . . The proliferation of syntactic processes is . . . a consequence of semantic differentiation [p. 27].

Although it is far from clear how semantic differentiation "necessarily," "organically," or "naturally" leads to syntactic development, it seems that the conceptual representations that may be expressed in speech as a result of syntactic development may follow the developmental course of differentiation. However, form classes and rules need not be developed via differentiation. Thus, differentiation may characterize the development of many concepts, but integration and thus specific-to-general developmental patterns characterize the acquisition of syntactic form classes and rules. Theoretical disputes about whether *syntactic* classes and rules are acquired in a differentiated fashion or an integrative fashion rest on more basic disagreements about the nature of form classes. If one assumes that children begin to formulate utterances by combining classes like noun and verb into simple combinations (which could be represented in phrase structure symbolization as S → N + V), then syntactic development could be characterized as the progressive differentiation of form classes and the corresponding expansion of combinatorial properties. However, if one believes that the child's initial attempts to construct multiword utterances consists of conjoining individual words qua individual words rather than qua members of form classes, then the child may *eventually* construct form classes by heeding the related semantic–distributional characteristics of related terms. The latter view implies a specific-to-general developmental pattern. In fact, the available data strongly suggest that a specific-to-general developmental pattern characterizes most, and perhaps all, syntactic developments (see following discussion).

An acquisition model that assumes specific-to-general developmental patterns also assumes that language development takes time—that is, that language development occurs gradually. Moreover, I am assuming that the specific-to-general developmental pattern holds for both early and late syntactic developments. Specific-to-general developments have been found in the rules for word order (Braine, 1976), the use of inflections (Tanouye, Lifter, & Bloom, 1977), and the passive construction. Consider the passive construction for a moment. Although it can be described in very general terms, the child fails to initially apprehend the scope of the structure. The result is that children do not learn the passive construction for all appropriate verbs simultaneously, but instead appear to initially learn a small set of verbs that may appear in the passive, and then gradually add verbs to the passive repetoire (Maratsos et al., 1979). This pattern has also been observed in children's acquisition of the progressive inflection (Brown, 1973; Kuczaj, 1978), of *wh* words in *wh* questions, and in the placement of auxiliary verbs in *wh* questions (Ervin-Tripp, 1970; Kuczaj & Brannick, 1979; Labov & Labov, 1978). (Also along these lines, Bowerman [1973] has cited the case of a child learning Russian who initially marked only certain direct objects; this is another example of a specific-to-general acquisition pattern.)

This is not to say that all syntactic development will appear to proceed specifically, on an item-to-item basis. Children do appear to acquire some linguistic forms and constructions quite generally, as has been found in the development of certain aspects of the English verb auxiliary system (Bellugi, 1971; Klima & Bellugi, 1966; Kuczaj & Maratsos, 1979, in preparation). In fact, some peculiar combinations of generality and specificity have been observed in syntactic development (Kuczaj & Brannick, 1979; Kuczaj & Maratsos, 1979). However, the argument here is that general developments such as those just described (and all other general syntactic developments) result from the integration of previous specific acquisitions.

The notion that syntactic development can best be characterized as occurring in a specific-to-general fashion assumes that form classes and syntactic rules (combinatorial rules) also develop in such a fashion. Form classes and combinatorial rules develop interdependently rather than independently. Initially, rules operate on individual words, leading to limited productivity. With development, form classes evolve and so the simultaneously evolving rules come to manipulate form classes as well as, and in some cases instead of, individual items. (It should be kept in mind that this pattern holds for developments throughout the language-acquisition process, so that at any period in development following the initial period, there will be a combination of specific and general developments, or more specifically, specific and general form classes and combinatorial rules.)

The specific-to-general developmental sequence hypothesis does not entail that children begin to produce multiword utterances only by combining individual words, though this is often the case (see Braine, 1976). Children may also begin to produce multiword utterances by using rote or routine processes (R. Clark, 1974, 1977, 1978; MacWhinney, 1978). Rote is accurately defined by MacWhinney (1978) as follows: "The central characteristic of rote processing is the absence of any form of analysis. Forms that are learned by rote and applied by rote are never broken up into their component pieces or decomposed in any way [p. 1]."

MacWhinney (1975, 1976) has shown that young children initially use rote to correctly produce regular forms like *horses* and irregular forms like *went* (see also Cazden, 1968; Kuczaj, 1977). Related to the notion of rote processes in syntactic development is the notion of routines. R. Clark (1977) has suggested that the young child has a "plagiarism" strategy, which means that he or she pads an utterance with undigested (unanalyzed) portions of the previous adult utterance. In fact, R. Clark (1974) suggests two strategies the young language-learning child may employ in early syntactic development. One is the plagiarism strategy, in which the child immediately incorporates some prior heard utterance, or some portion of it, into an utterance as if to avoid structuring the entire utterance from scratch. The second strategy might be labeled the juxtaposition strategy, whereby the child combines two known structures without reordering any of the elements to match adult syntax. For example, the child might combine the segment *I want* and the setment *we going store* to yield *I want we going store*. Eventually, of course, routines and unanalyzed segments come to be analyzed by the child and so become more productive and less routine-like. This occurs because syntactic development depends on the comparison and relation of known forms, rules, and structures (including rote forms and routines) with new input. This leads to forms, rules, and structures becoming more general with increasing development and rote forms and routines becoming less underanalyzed. At the same time, however, the appropriate scope of the forms and rules must be learned so that they do not become too general. Restricting the scope of rules and form classes is as much a part of development as is learning generality. Thus, the notion of specific-to-general developmental patterns does not mean that specific acquisitions become less important with development. Specific acquisitions are quite important throughout the course of syntactic development (Kuczaj, 1977, 1978).

It should be noted that the specific-to-general pattern proposed here for syntactic development is not an invariant consequence of the young child's cognitive processing predispositions. Young children who are specifically learning to combine individual words with one another also grant some object words overgeneral meanings. It appears that whether the child exhibits specific acquisition or general acquisition depends on the nature of the material being acquired and the relation the material has to the child's conceptual categories. At least some of the child's early word meanings and concepts may be too general and thus develop through the dual processes of differentiation and reintegration. However, the combinatorial rules with which the child learns to convey sentential meaning develop specifically, as do the form classes that the rules manipulate. Nelson and Nelson (1978) have recently proposed a general theory of development that assumes that an undifferentiated stage exists initially, followed by three successive periods: (1) a period of specific rule learning; (2) a period of general rule learning; and (3) a period of integration and consolidation. This theory accords well with the one proposed here in that it assumes specific-to-general developmental sequences. However, I should like to emphasize that even in the period of general rule learning proposed by Nelson and Nelson, the child continues to learn specific rules and items. Again, specific learning remains important throughout the course of syntactic development. The relation between specific and general developments may best be explained in terms of the relation between "vertical" development and "horizontal" development (Bloom, 1976):

> Language development is synergistic, integrative and multilateral—rather than simply additive, and proceeds vertically, through different 'levels of knowing', as well as horizontally, in that virtually all aspects of the linguistic system the child is learning figure in what he is learning. This is not to say that language development does not proceed sequentially. But children do not add one bit of information to another bit of information, rather, there is a progressive transformation of old information in relation to new information [p. 2].

Thus, vertical development consists of changes in the way in which what the child learns changes over time. For syntax, such development reflects changes from specific knowledge to general knowledge. Horizontal development reflects how different aspects of what the child knows interact with one another. Thus, a child who has learned some general form classes and combinatorial rules will need to relate newly acquired terms to these form classes and rules, as well as learn which forms are exceptions to the general rules. Failure to learn exceptions will lead to overgeneralization errors. Overgeneralization errors may be morphological, such as the addition of the regular past-tense marker to an irregular verb form—for example, *eated* (Cazden, 1968; Kuczaj, 1977, 1978). Such errors may also be syntactic, such as the placement of auxiliary verbs in standard *wh* question position in questions beginning with *how come*—for example, *How come will we go at the movie?* (Kuczaj & Brannick, 1979). There are over-generalization errors of different types, and these occur throughout the course of language development. Thus, there are two problems to be dealt with. First, how does the child learn regular rules? Second, how does the child learn exceptions to these rules? In other words, how does the child learn both regular forms and irregular forms? Also, why does the child correct overgeneralization errors (why does reanalysis occur?)?

These questions are best answered by considering what is meant by the notion of a syntactic rule. Instead of viewing rules as regular or irregular, it may be best to abandon the notion of regular and irregular rules and substitute the notion of probabilistic rules. Brown (1973) argued against the view that children initially acquire categorical rules on the basis that categorical rules should be acquired abruptly and manifested very generally in performance, although this does not prove to be the case. According to Brown (1973), syntactic rule learning "must be conceived as generally gradual change in a set of probabilities rather than as the sudden acquisition of quite general rules [p. 399]." This view is in line with the view posited here, although Brown believes that the child eventually formu-lates categorical rules, a point with which I disagree. Instead, I should like to suggest that grammatical rules be viewed as probabilistic rules rather than categorical rules (a notion that fits well with that of variable rules; see Bloom, 1976; Labov, 1969; Labov & Labov, 1978). According to this view, "regular" rules have a higher probability of applying to instances of a particular form class than do "irregular" rules. Although frequency does not seem to directly contrib-ute to the probability of various syntactic rules, it probably does significantly contribute to the probabilities of the "irregular rules," because these exceptions to the general, more probable rules must be learned by attending to their relative occurrence in the input. Thus, frequency may be more important in the estab-lishment of "irregular" rules (e.g., *went* is the past-tense form of *go*) than in the establishment of "regular rules," perhaps because of a predisposition of the child to generalize on the basis of a relatively limited amount of data. Thus, the child learns specific combinatorial information about particular forms, then comes to form generalizations based on sets of information about the individual items, and then must learn the exceptions to these generalizations (see Maratsos & Chalkley, in press).

The child, then, must not only learn the generality of forms and rules, but must also learn to limit the generality of the forms and rules—that is, the child must learn the appropriate scope of application of the forms and rules. Although it is far from clear exactly how much information is needed for the child to form generalizations and then to subsequently correctly limit the generalizations, the young, beginning language-learning child may need more information to form generalizations than he or she will later in development, because experience leads readily to the formation of generalizations. This developmental tendency may be affected by cognitive style, and "impulsive" children may form general-

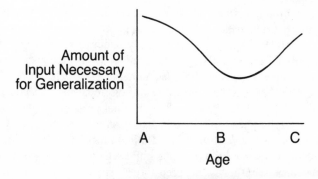

FIG. 20.2. The hypothesized development relation between age and amount of
input necessary for generalization to occur. During period *A*, the child requires
significant amounts of information in order to form generalizations. During period
B, the child requires significantly less information in order to form generalizations.
During period *C*, the child is more cautious about generalizing because he or she
realizes that overgeneralization errors have been made. Thus, the child now requires more information in order to generalize.

izations on less data than "reflective" children at all stages of development.
However, the hypothesized developmental tendency may reflect a developmental
trend in which the child becomes more prone to generalize (at least partially
because of past intake) and then must later learn to limit these generalizations.
This pattern can be schematized as shown in Fig. 2.2.

The overall picture of syntactic development that has been presented here is a
cyclic view that emphasizes the child's processing of input and the influence of
past intake on subsequent processing of input. This view emphasizes the interaction of processing and organizing predispositions (some innate and others
learned) and environmental factors, and at the same time acknowledges the
importance of intrinsic motivation in the language-learning processes (it would
be interesting to know how individual differences in intrinsic motivation relate to
individual differences in language acquisition). Thus, I am attributing great
importance to the child's experiences, and even greater importance to the child's
interpretation of these experiences, because the interpretation depends on the
internal context the child creates in an attempt to assimilate the external context
(differences in internal contexts lead to different children's interpreting the same
input in varying ways).

It seems likely that two main types of intake serve to facilitate syntactic
development. First, experience with the same item in different contexts and
different items in similar contexts leads the child to formulate and later differentiate form classes (the differentiation occurs because the child limits the
generality of earlier acquisitions). Thus, the specific-to-general developmental
pattern advocated here does not assume that differentiation does not occur.

Instead, the assumption is that differentiation occurs late in the acquisition process, after specific acquisitions have become general.

Second, resolvable conflict between early acquisitions and current intake, which seem crucial for cognitive growth (Piaget, 1972), are also important for language development (Nelson, 1978, accurately terms such conflicts "codable discrepancies"). I suspect that most codable discrepancies are noticed by the child in postinitial processing rather than in initial processing, though metalinguistic awareness may lead to the coding of discrepancies between the current input and previous analyses at the level of initial processing. Postinitial processing of intake may also contribute to the child's learning to express previously acquired meanings with newly acquired forms. The complimentary hypotheses that new forms are first used to express old functions and new functions are first expressed by old forms (Cassirer, 1955; Slobin, 1973; Werner & Kaplan, 1963) may reflect the differences between initial and postinitial processing. Children may initially store new forms and new functions and then compare these new acquisitions with previous ones in postinitial processing; the assimilation of the new acquisitions to the old may result in the initial dominance of earlier acquisitions over newer ones. Thus, there is an interaction between early and subsequent syntactic and semantic developments, as well as between language and cognitive development.

Individual Differences

Syntactic development involves both variant and invariant sequential-acquisition patterns. Attempts to explain invariant acquisition patterns have focused on variables such as cognitive complexity and linguistic complexity (Brown, 1973). Explanations of variant acquisition patterns have involved variables such as differences in cognitive style and/or strategy and differences in experience. Thus, an account of syntactic development that emphasizes the child's active interpretation of input should expect to observe individual differences in development.

One of the most readily observed development differences involves rate of acquisition. Children vary greatly in the speed with which they acquire their native tongue (Brown, 1973; Nelson, 1975), though all "normal" children acquire language at a remarkably quick pace.

There have also been a fair number of findings of individual differences in order of acquisition of various forms. These findings include the following:

1. Bates and Rankin (1979) studied the acquisition of adjectives and inflections by two children learning Italian. Even with this small sample, individual differences in development were found. One child acquired both adjectival and inflectional expressions for reference to size simultaneously. The other child used adjectives for size and value several months prior to acquiring the corresponding inflections.

2. Savic' & Mikes' (1974) observed that children learning Serbocroation differ in how they first express the possessive relation. Some children first express the possessive by placing the possessive attributive in a prenoun phrase position—that is, these children use word order to express the possessive. Other children first express the possessive relation by adding suffixes that denote the possessive relation to the appropriate noun.

3. Some children frequently make pronominal case errors such as *her curl my hair, me a good boy,* and *him bad dog* (Brown, 1973; Gruber, 1967; Menyuk, 1969) Tanz (1974) has suggested that such errors are almost always in the direction of substituting an objective form, such as *me, him, her, us,* or *them,* for a nominative form, such as *I, he, she, we,* and *they,* and almost never in the opposite direction. Tanz argues that this unidirectional error pattern can be accounted for in terms of general cognitive processing predispositions: (1) avoid exceptions—in English, the nominative form can be viewed as the exception; and (2) pay attention to the ends of sentences—in English, objective forms appear quite frequently at the ends of sentences. Although the reported evidence for young children learning English tends to support this generalization (Hatch, 1969; Huxley, 1970), my youngest son Ben very frequently produced erroneous forms such as *can we go with they?* and *This is for she* (these errors will be reported in more detail in a forthcoming paper). Moreover, Kaper (1976) has reported that two children acquiring Dutch as their native tongue repeatedly substituted the nominative form of the personal pronoun of the first person singular for the objective one, particularly after prepositions (other children learning Dutch use only the objective form after prepositions). Thus, what appeared to be an invariant developmental pattern is, in fact, a variant pattern. I suspect that other invariant patterns will also be found to be variant as more children are studied and more data are collected.

4. Maratsos and Kuczaj (1976) investigated children's knowledge of negative particle placement in multiple auxiliary sentences. Children frequently hear negative sentences containing a single modal auxiliary, such as *you may not eat that* and *he is not sad.* Sentences such as these may be interpreted as containing *not* in the sentential position following the first (and in these uses, only) auxiliary verb or as containing *not* in a sentential position immediately before the main verb or remaining predicate (in the case of sentences such as *she is not in the bus*). If children make the first interpretation, then they should place *not* in the correct post first auxiliary verb position in multiple auxiliary construction (as in *the boy should not have been eating jello*). If children make the second interpretation, then they should place *not* after all of the auxiliary verbs, producing sentences such as *she could have been not sleeping in bed* and *the dog might have been not in the living room.* Maratsos and Kuczaj found evidence for both types of interpretation, demonstrating that children interpret similar input in different ways.

In addition to individual differences in developmental patterns of syntactic development (see also Bloom, Lightbown, & Hood, 1975; Braine, 1976), there may also be substantial individual differences in language-learning strategies (Bloom, 1970; Bowerman, 1974) and in whether cognitive development or linguistic input determines some particular syntactic development (Schlesinger, 1977). Further work should be concerned with specifying important individual differences in syntactic development and the variables (such as the interaction of cognitive style and input) that contribute to these differences. The following quote from Braine (1976) concerning early syntactic development should also prove to be apt for later syntactic development:

> The possibilities for variation among children are limited, on the one hand, by the range of semantic content talked about, and, on the other hand, by the kind of positional structure used to express it. *Within these limits, children are about as different from one another as they could be* [p. 92, italics added].

SUMMARY

In this chapter, I have argued for an account of syntactic development that assumes that the interaction of the child and the environment is of primary importance. (It is also assumed that syntactic structures can eventually be accounted for in terms of surface-structure relations.) The hypothesized account assumes that how the child actively extracts and organizes information from the environment that depends on both past experience and learned (and possibly innate) language-learning strategies. The account also predicts specific-to-general developmental patterns, as well as considerable individual differences.

ACKNOWLEDGMENTS

I would like to thank Rick Boston and Ann Kuczaj for their comments on earlier versions of this chapter.

REFERENCES

Akiyama, M. *Language acquisition strategies may not be universal: Statement verification in English and Japanese.* Paper presented at the biennial meeting of the Society for Research in Child Development, San Francisco, March 15–18, 1979.

Bates, E., & Rankin, J. Morphological development in Italian: Connotation and denotation. *Journal of Child Language,* 1979, *6,* 29–52.

Bellugi, U. Simplication in children's language. In R. Huxley & E. Ingram (Eds.), *Language acquisition: Models and methods.* New York: Academic Press, 1971.

Bever, T. The cognitive basis for linguistic structures. In J. Hayes (Ed.), *Cognition and the development of language.* New York: Wiley, 1970.

Bloom, L. *Language development: Form and function in emerging grammars.* Cambridge, Mass.: M.I.T. Press, 1970.

Bloom, L. Talking, understanding, and thinking. In R. Schiefelbusch & L. Lloyd (Eds.), *Language perspectives—acquisition, retardation, and intervention.* Baltimore, University Park Press, 1974.

Bloom, L. An intergrative perspective on language development. *Papers and Reports on Child Language Development* (Stanford University), 1976, *12*, 1–22.

Bloom, L., Lightbown, P., & Hood, L. Structure and variation in child language. *Monographs of the Society for Research in Child Development,* 1975, *40*.

Blount, B. Acquisition of language by Luo children. Doctoral dissertation, University of California, Berkeley, 1969.

Blount, B. Parental speech and language acquisition: Some Luo and Samoan examples. *Anthropological Linguistics,* 1972, *14*, 119–130.

Bogoyavlenskiy, D. The acquisition of Russian inflections. In C. Fergusan & D. Slobin (Eds.), *Studies of child language development.* New York: Holt, Rinehart, & Winston, 1973.

Bower, T. *Development in infancy.* San Francisco: W. H. Freeman, 1974.

Bowerman, M. *Early syntactic development: A cross-linguistic study with special reference to Finnish.* Cambridge, Mass.: Harvard University Press, 1973.

Bowerman, M. Discussion summary—development of concepts underlying language. In R. Schiefelbusch & L. Lloyd (Eds.), *Language perspectives—acquisition, retardation, and intervention.* Baltimore: University Park Press, 1974.

Bowerman, M. Semantic factors in the acquisition of rules for word use and sentence constructions. In D. Morehead & A. Morehead (eds.), *Directions in normal and deficient child language.* Baltimore: University Park Press, 1976.

Braine, M. On two types of models of the internalization of grammars. In D. Slobin (Ed.), *The ontogenesis of grammar: a theoretical symposium.* New York: Academic Press, 1971.

Braine, M. Children's first word combinations. *Monographs of the Society for Research in Child Development,* 1976, *41*, serial no. 164.

Brown, R. Linguistic determinism and the part of speech. *Journal of Abnormal and Social Psychology,* 1957, *55*, 1–5.

Brown, R. How shall a thing be called? *Psychological Review,* 1958, *65*, 14–21.

Brown, R., & Bellugi, U. Three processes in the child's acquisition of syntax. *Harvard Educational Review,* 1964, *34*, 133–151.

Brown, R., Cazden, C., & Bellugi, U. The child's grammar from I to III. In J. Hill (Ed.), *Minnesota symposia on child psychology* (Vol. 2). Minneapolis: University of Minnesota Press, 1969.

Brown, R., & Hanlon, C. Derivational complexity and the order of acquisition in child speech. In J. Hayes (Ed.), *Cognition and the development of language.* New York: Wiley, 1970.

Brown, R. *A first language.* Cambridge, MA: Harvard University Press, 1973.

Bruner, J. The ontogenesis of speech acts. *Journal of Child Language,* 1975, *2*, 1–19.

Bushnell, E. *Children's dealing with accidental gaps in the lexicon.* Paper presented at the biennial meeting of the Society for Research in Child Development, New Orleans, March 17–20, 1977.

Cassirer, E. *The philosophy of symbolic forms* (Vol. 1). New Haven, Conn.: Yale University Press, 1955.

Cazden, C. Environmental assistance to the child's acquisition of grammar. Unpublished doctoral dissertation, Graduate School of Education, Harvard University, 1965.

Cazden, C. The acquisition of noun and verb inflections. *Child Development,* 1968, *39*, 433–438.

Cazden, C., & Brown, R. The development of the mother tongue. In E. Lenneberg & E. Lenneberg (Eds.), *Foundations of language development* (Vol. 1). New York: Academic Press, 1975.

Cedergren, H., & Sankoff, D. Variable rules: Performance as a statistical reflection of competence. *Language,* 1974, *50*, 333–355.

Chapman, R., & Miller, J. *Word order in early two- and three-word utterances: Does production precede comprehension?* Paper presented at Fifth Annual Child Language Research Forum, Stanford University, April 1973.

Chomsky, C. *The acquisition of syntax in children from 5 to 10.* Cambridge, Mass.: M.I.T. Press, 1969.

Chomsky, N. *Syntactic structures.* The Hague: Mouton, 1957.

Chomsky, N. Review of Skinner's *Verbal behavior. Language,* 1959, *3,* 26-58.

Chomsky, N. *Aspects of the theory of syntax.* Cambridge, Mass.: M.I.T. Press, 1965.

Chomsky, N. *Language and mind.* New York: Harcourt, Brace, Jovanovich, 1972.

Chukovsky, K. *From two to five.* Berkeley: University of California Press, 1968.

Clark, E. Strategies and the mapping problem in first language acquisition. In J. MacNamara (Ed.), *Language learning and thought.* New York: Academic Press, 1977.

Clark, R. Performing without competence. *Journal of Child Language,* 1974, *1,* 1-10.

Clark, R. What's the use of imitation? *Journal of Child Language,* 1977, *4,* 341-358.

Clark, R. Some even simpler ways to learn to talk. In N. Waterson & C. Snow (Eds.), *The development of communication.* New York: Wiley, 1978.

Derwing, B. *Transformational grammar as a theory of language acquisition.* Cambridge, Mass.: Harvard University Press, 1973.

de Villiers, J. *Prototypes in grammatical rule learning.* Paper presented at the biennial meeting of the Society for Research in Child Development, San Francisco, March 1979.

de Villiers, J., & de Villiers, P. *Language acquisition.* Cambridge, Mass.: Harvard University Press, 1978.

Drach, K. *The language of the parent: A pilot study* (Working Paper No. 14). Berkeley: University of California, 1969.

Ervin-Tripp, S. Discourse agreement: How children answer questions. In J. Hayes (Ed.), *Cognition and the development of language.* New York: Wiley, 1970.

Farwell, C. The language spoken to children. *Human Development,* 1975, *18,* 288-309.

Fillmore, C. The case for case. In E. Bach & R. Harms (Eds.), *Universals in linguistic theory.* New York: Holt, Rinehart, & Winston, 1968.

Flavell, J. *The development psychology of Jean Piaget.* Princeton, N.J.: Van Nostrand, 1963.

Flavell, J. *Cognitive development.* Englewood Cliffs, N.J.: Prentice-Hall, 1977.

Folger, J., & Chapman, R. A pragmatic analysis of spontaneous imitations. *Journal of Child Language,* 1978, *5,* 25-38.

Gleasen, J., & Weintraub, S. Input language and the acquisition of communicative competence. In K. Nelson (Ed.), *Language development.* New York: Wiley, 1978.

Greenberg, J. Some universals of grammar with particular reference to the order of meaningful elements. In J. Greenberg (Ed.), *Universals of language.* Cambridge, Mass.: M.I.T. Press, 1963.

Gruber, J. Topicalization in child language. *Foundations of Language,* 1967, *3,* 37-65.

Hakuta, K. Prefabricated patterns and the emergence of structure in second language acquisition. *Language Learning,* 1974, *24,* 287-298.

Hatch, E. *Pronoun case preference of young children. Four experimental studies in syntax of young children.* Los Angeles: Southwest Regional Laboratory for Educational Research and Development (TR 11). 1969.

Huxley, R. The development of the correct use of subject personal pronouns in two children. In G. Flores d'Arcais & W. Levelt (Eds.), *Advances in psycholinguistics.* New York: American Elsevier, 1970.

Ingram, D. If and when transformations are acquired by children. In D. Dato (Ed.), *Developmental psycholinguistics: Theory and applications.* Georgetown University Rount Table on Languages and Linguistics, 1975.

Kaper, W. Pronominal case-errors. *Journal of Child Language,* 1976, *3,* 439-442.

Kernan, K. *The acquisition of language by Samaon children.* Doctoral dissertation, University of California, Berkeley, 1969.
Kiparsky, P. Historical linguistics. In W. Dingwall (Ed.), *A survey of linguistic science.* College Park, Md.: University of Maryland Linguistics Program, 1971.
Klima, E., & Bellugi, U. Syntactic regularities in the speech of children. In J. Lyons & R. Wales (Eds.), *Psycholinguistics papers.* Edinburgh: Edinburgh University Press, 1966.
Kuczaj, S. On the acquisition of a semantic system. *Journal of Verbal Learning and Verbal Behavior,* 1975, *14,* 340-358.
Kuczaj, S. The acquisition of regular and irregular past tense forms. *Journal of Verbal Learning and Verbal Behavior,* 1977, *16,* 589-600.
Kuczaj, S. Why do children fail to overgeneralize the progressive inflection? *Journal of Child Language,* 1978, *5,* 167-171.
Kuczaj, S. Evidence for a language learning strategy: On the relative ease of acquisition of prefixes and suffixes. *Child Development,* 1979, *50,* 1-13.
Kuczaj, S., & Brannick, N. Children's use of the *wh* question modal auxiliary placement rule. *Journal of Experimental Child Psychology,* 1979, *28,* 43-67.
Kuczaj, S., & Lederberg, A. Height, age, and function: Differing influences on children's comprehension of *younger* and *older. Journal of Child Language,* 1977, *4,* 395-416.
Kuczaj, S., & Maratsos, M. *The initial verbs of yes-no questions: A different kind of general grammatical category.* Paper presented at the biennial meeting of the Society for Research in Child Development, San Francisco, March 1979.
Kuczaj, S., & Maratsos, M. *The development of the English verb auxiliary system,* manuscript in preparation.
Labov, W. Contraction, deletion, and inherent variability of the English copula. *Language,* 1969, *45,* 715-762.
Labov, W., & Labov, T. Learning the syntax of questions. In R. Campbell & P. Smith (Eds.), *Recent advances in the psychology of language.* New York: Plenum Press, 1978.
Lashley, K. The problem of serial order in behavior. In S. Jeffress (Ed.), *Cerebral mechanisms in behavior.* New York: Wiley, 1951.
Lenneberg, E. The concept of language differentation. In E. Lenneberg & E. Lenneberg (Eds.), *Foundations of language development* (Vol. 1). New York: Academic Press, 1975.
MacWhinney, B. Rules, rote, and analogy in morphological formations by Hungarian children. *Journal of Child Language,* 1975, *2,* 65-78.
MacWhinney, B. Hungarian research on the acquisition of morphology and syntax. *Journal of Child Language,* 1976, *3,* 397-410.
MacWhinney, B. The acquisition of morphophonology. *Monographs of the Society for Research in Child Development,* 1978, *43*(No. 174).
Maratsos, M. Children who get worse at understanding the passive: A replication of Bever. *Journal of Psycholinguistic Research,* 1974, *3,* 65-74.
Maratsos, M., & Chalkley, M. The internal language of children's syntax: The ontogenesis and representation of syntactic categories. In K. Nelson (Ed.), *Child language (Vol. 2).* Somerset, N.J.: John Wiley & Sons in press.
Maratsos, M., & Kuczaj, S. Preschool children's use of *not* and *n't: Not* is not (isn't *n't. Papers and Reports in Child Language Research* (Stanford University), 1976, *12,* 157-168.
Maratsos, M., Kuczaj, S., Fox, D., & Chalkley, M. Some empirical studies in the acquisition of transformational relations. In W. Collins (Ed.), *Children's language and communication, the Minnesota symposia on child psychology* (Vol. 12). Hillsdale, N.J.: Lawrence Erlbaum Associates, 1979.
McNeill, D. *The acquisition of language: The study of developmental psycholinguistics.* New York: Harper & Row, 1970.
Menyuk, P. *Sentences children use.* Cambridge, Mass.: M.I.T. Press, 1969.

Miyahara, K. The acquisition of Japanese particles. *Journal of Child Language*, 1974, *1*, 283–286.

Nelson, K. Structure and strategy in learning to talk. *Monographs of the Society for Research in Child Development*, 1973, *38* (Nos. 1–2), 1–135.

Nelson, K. Individual differences in early semantic and syntactic development. *Annuals of New York Academy of Science*, 1975, *263*, 132–139.

Nelson, K. E. *Toward a rare-event cognitive comparison theory of syntax acquisition*. Paper presented at the First International Congress for the Study of Child Language, Tokyo, August 1978.

Nelson, K. E., Carskaddon, G., & Bonvillian, J. Syntax acquisition: Impact of experimental variation in adult verbal interaction with the child. *Child Development*, 1973, *44*, 497–504.

Nelson, K. E., Denninger, M., Kaplan, B., & Bonvillian, J. *Varied angles on how children progress in syntax*. Paper presented at the biennial meeting of the Society for Research in Child Development, San Francisco, March 1979.

Nelson, K. E., & Nelson, K. Cognitive pendulums and their linguistic realization. In K. Nelson (Ed.), *Language development*. New York: Wiley, 1978.

Newport, E., Gleitman, L., & Gleitman, H. A study of mother's speech and child language acquisition. *Papers and Reports on Child Language Development* (Stanford University), 1975, *10*, 111–116.

Newport, E., Gleitman, H. R., & Gleitman, L. Mother, I'd rather do it myself: Some effects and non-effects of maternal speech style. In C. Snow & C. Ferguson (Eds.), *Talking to children: Language input and acquisition*. Cambridge, Mass.: Harvard University Press, 1977.

Paul, H. *Principles of the history of language*. London: Longmans, Green, 1891.

Piaget, J. *Psychology of intelligence*. Totowa, N.J.: Littlefield, Adams, 1972.

Ramer, A. Syntactic styles in emerging language. *Journal of Child Language*, 1976, *3*, 49–62.

Ross, J. Three batons for cognitive psychology. In W. Weimer & D. Palermo (Eds.), *Cognition and the symbolic processes*. Hillsdale, N.J.: Lawrence Erlbaum Associates, 1974.

Russell, B. *An inquiry into meaning and truth*. London: George Allen and Unwin, 1940.

Sachs, J., Brown, R., & Salerno, R. *Adult speech to children*. Paper given at the International Symposium on First Language Acquisition, Florence, Italy, 1972.

Savić, S., & Mikes, M. Noun phrase expansion in child language. *Journal of Child Language*, 1974, *1*, 107–110.

Schlesinger, I. The roles of cognitive development and linguistic input in language acquisition. *Journal of Child Language*, 1977, *4*, 153–170.

Segalowitz, N., & Galang, R. Agent-patient word-order preference in the acquisition of Tagalong. *Journal of Child Language*, 1978, *5*, 47–64.

Shatz, M., & Gelman, R. The development of communication skills: Modifications in the speech of young children as a function of listener. *Monographs of the Society for Research in Child Development*, 1973, *38*.

Shipley, E., Smith, C., & Gleitman, L. A study in the acquisition of language: Free responses to commands. *Language*, 1969, *45*, 322–342.

Skinner, B. *Verbal behavior*. New York: Appleton-Century-Crofts, 1957.

Slobin, D. Cognitive prerequisites for the development of grammar. In C. Ferguson & D. Slobin (Eds.), *Studies of child language development*. New York: Holt, Rinehart, & Winston, 1973.

Slobin, D. On the nature of talk to children. In E. Lenneberg & E. Lenneberg (Eds.), *Foundations of language development* (Vol. 1). New York: Academic Press, 1975.

Slobin, D. Language change in childhood and history. In J. MacNamara (Ed.), *Language learning and thought*. New York: Academic Press, 1977.

Snow, C. *Mother's speech research: An overview*. Paper presented at the Conference on Language Input and Acquisition, Boston, September 1974.

Snow, C., Arlman-Rupp, A., Hassing, Y., Jobse, J., Jooksen, J., & Vorster, J. *Mother's speech in three social classes*. Unpublished paper, University of Amsterdam, 1974.

Starosta, S. A place for case. *Language Learning*, 1976, *26*, 1–36.

Stern, W. *Psychology of early childhood*. New York: Harry Holt, 1924.

Stronher, H., & Nelson, K. The young child's development of sentence comprehension: Influence of event probability, nonverbal context, syntactic form, and strategies. *Child Development*, 1974, *45*, 567–576.

Szajun, G. On the frequency of use of tenses in English and German children's spontaneous speech. *Child Development*, 1978, *49*, 898–901.

Tanouye, E., Lifter, K., & Bloom, L. *Verb semantics and grammatical morphemes*. Paper presented at the biennial meeting of the Society for Research in Child Development, New Orleans, 1977.

Tanz, C. Cognitive principles underlying children's errors in pro-nominal case-making. *Journal of Child Language*, 1974, *1*, 271–276.

Wells, G. Learning to code experience through language. *Journal of Child Language*, 1974, *1*, 243–270.

Werner, H., & Kaplan, B. *Symbol formation*. New York: Wiley, 1963.

Winograd, T. A procedural model of language understanding. In R. Schank & K. Colby (Eds.), *Computer models of thought and language*. San Francisco: Freeman, 1973.

3 Basic Syntactic Processes

Brian MacWhinney
Carnegie-Mellon University

MacWhinney (1978) presented a computational model of the acquisition of morphophonology. The present chapter attempts to extend the model presented in that earlier paper to the acquisition of word-order patterns. This extension is supported by an examination of the previous research on syntactic acquisition. In the final section of the chapter, further possible extensions to phonology and semantics are considered.

The crucial claim underlying the basic approach to both morphophonology and syntax is that use of a given rule system is governed by a system of alternative strategies. Within such a multileveled model, alternative strategies can be compared in terms of their relative complexity. In the present chapter, these alternative strategies are evaluated through application of the following analytic technique:

1. A relatively simple strategy that can account for at least some of the observed data is presented.
2. It is shown that there are at least some data that are best explained by this strategy.
3. It is shown that, at some point in development, the child produces forms that cannot be explained by this simple strategy alone.
4. A strategy of somewhat greater complexity and power is introduced and it is shown that this strategy can account for at least some of the data not explained by the simpler (and weaker) strategy.

This line of argumentation proceeds until evidence has been presented for six alternative strategies in word-order processing.

The six strategies examined are: (1) rote; (2) analogy; (3) predispositions; (4) bound patterns; (5) free patterns; and (6) class-bound patterns. The last four strategies constitute four levels of the general strategy of combination. Thus, the three basic strategies considered are: rote, analogy, and combination. These are the same three strategies proposed by MacWhinney (1978) for morphophonological processing. Moreover, as we see in this chapter, the four strategies within combination correspond to the four strategies for morphophonological combination suggested by MacWhinney (1978). In accord with this division of syntactic processing into strategy types, the chapter has the following organization. The first three sections examine the strategies of rote, analogy, and combination. Within the four subsections of the third section, the four types of combinatorial strategies are discussed. Then, the fourth and final section compares the results of the analysis of word-order mechanisms with the analysis of the morphophonological system proposed by MacWhinney (1978). In that section, it is shown how the six ways of governing word order stand in a one-to-one relation with the six ways of controlling morphophonological alterations noted in MacWhinney (1978).

ROTE

The first of the three processing mechanisms proposed by MacWhinney (1978) is *rote*. The simplest way of controlling the order of a string of words is to memorize the string as a single rote unit. In word learning, it is generally the case that the articulatory gestures constituting the word are learned as a fixed rote string. This is because, in the word, articulatory gestures occur in sequence, and their order is fully specified. The word is, in effect, a finite state process in which all states have one entry and one exit. The initial state enters from the higher-level program and the final state returns control to the higher-level program.

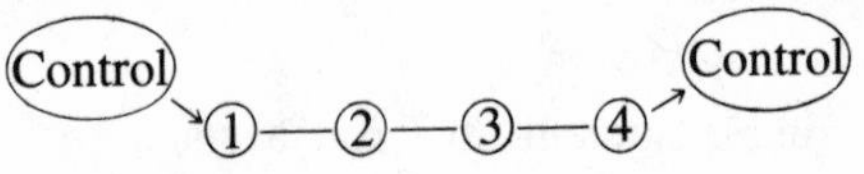

FIG. 3.1.

This definition of rote in terms of unitization (Hayes-Roth, 1977) is deceptively simple. In practice, it is useful to clarify this definition in five additional ways. First, it is important to relate the notion of rote to the notion of structural levels. For an item to be learned by rote, all that is necessary is that it not be analyzed on the next lower structural level. Thus, if a word is not analyzed into its morphs, it functions as a rote item on the morphophonological level. If a word is not analyzed into its lexes (meaning components), it functions as a rote item on the level of lexical analysis (MacWhinney, in press (a)). And, if a phrase is not analyzed into its component words, it functions as a rote item on the syntactic level. It is also possible that an item could remain unanalyzed for several structural levels down. For example, in the extreme case, a Fulani who speaks no Arabic could still memorize large sections of the Koran as single articulatory gestures.

Second, it must be recognized that items whose pieces are ordered by rote may still be susceptible to occasional errors in linear order. Thus, Shattuck-Hufnagel (1979) argues that the order of phonemes within a word must be actively controlled during speech production. However, it is possible for the production mechanism to generate errors in segment order such as *psghetti* for *spaghetti* even though the basic order of the segments in morphemes is controlled by rote. A similar argument applies on the syntactic level. Thus, having learned a string of words as an unanalyzed item, a speaker could still make an occasional production error in ordering the phonological pieces of that item. This suggests that rote memorization of a string actually involves two types of knowledge. The first is a coding of the presence of an element that occurs in a string and the second is a coding of the position of that element in relation to the other elements in the string.

A third qualification on rote is that a rote item may be analyzed semantically before it is analyzed morphologically. For example, as R. Brown (1973) and MacWhinney (1975b) have noted, a child may know that *shoes* refers to a plural although he or she does not know which piece of *shoes* encodes plurality. In such cases, the item still functions as a rote unit on the morphological level. Eventually, semantic analysis serves as a stimulus to morphological analysis (Mac-Whinney, 1978).

A fourth qualification on rote is that it is important not to confuse rote memorization with imitation. "Imitation" is a general mode of linguistic processing much like expression, reception, or play. "Rote," on the other hand, is being used here to refer to a strategy in string formation. Thus, imitation contrasts with expression, reception, and play, whereas rote contrasts with analogy and combination. Of course, the identification of rote with imitation espoused by some writers (R. Clark, 1977; Skinner, 1957 is not entirely without basis. It is certainly true that rote implies imitation, because all strings that are produced by rote can ultimately be viewed as deferred imitations. However, it is not true that imitation necessarily implies rote, because material can be imitated and not learned. In any case, the main point is that if we believe that a string has been learned by rote, we should be able to specify some actual input of which it could conceivable be an imitation. For example, the string *allgone sticky* could conceivably be derived from the child's (deferred) imitation of the sentence *say 'all-gone' to the sticky stuff*. Note that the reduction of the larger sentence to *allgone sticky* is based only on intonational prominence (du Preez, 1974) and not on grammatical processing (Slobin & Welsh, 1973). Such examples indicate that it will be exceedingly difficult in a given case to prove that a string of real words was not produced by rote.

Fifth, it is important to remember that rote can function in either short-term or long-term memory (Atkinson & Shiffrin, 1968). Unanalyzed items in short-term memory may also become unanalyzed lexical items in long-term memory. However, it may also happen that short-term rote items are not entered into long-term memory. In the next two sections, we examine evidence for the use of rote in both types of memory. We begin with a consideration of rote items in the long-term or lexical store.

Evidence for Long-Term Syntactic Rote

When a series of words functions as a single word, then we can say that it has been learned by rote. Such rote strings would be, in effect, single lexical items. If all syntactic productions were controlled in this way, then there would be no syntax, and syntax would, in effect, be replaced by the lexicon. This would amount to an extremely simple and parsimonious account of word order. Therefore, following the logic presented in the introduction to this chapter, we consider how far one can push an account of word order based on rote.

Researchers have offered 14 different arguments in support of the analysis of certain word strings as rote items. These 14 arguments are based on the use of three types of evidence: (1) evidence relating to the form of the interaction during which the item was presumably acquired; (2) evidence on the sequence in which forms emerge in production; and (3) evidence on the structure of forms in production. In a given case, any number of these arguments may or may not apply, and some of the arguments are inherently stronger than others. However, even when none of the 14 arguments apply, we cannot be sure that a word string is not being used as an unanalyzed whole. Thus, the 14 arguments tell us when rote should be suspected. They tell us nothing about when to reject a rote analysis of a given word string. It is also important to note that the 14 lines of evidence bear only on the issue of the use of rote in production. At present, the issue of the use of rote in comprehension by children is essentially unexplored.

Intonation as Evidence for Rote

Of the 14 lines of evidence that have been offered to support role analyses, four are based on aspects of the input. The first of these is one offered by Brown, Cazden, and Bellugi (1968, p. 51) to support a rote analysis for *I'm, that-a, drop-it, put-it, get-it, want-to, have-to, going-to, another-one, what-that* and *let-me*. Brown et al. argue that, because the source of these items was a single intonational unit, they may have been acquired as wholes. A similar argument is offered by MacWhinney (1978). The assumption in both cases is that the intonational unit represents a perceptual unit or package and that it is often easiest to pick up this package as a whole. Experimental support for this hypothesis has been provided by du Preez (1974). Although the exact shape of the process that MacWhinney (1978) calls "intonational packaging" remains to be specified, some further data constraining this specification can be found in MacWhinney (in press (a)) and Peters (1980).

Incorrect Imitation as Evidence for Rote

The second line of evidence in support of a rote analysis has been suggested by R. Brown (1973, p. 99), and R. Clark (1977, pp. 344,349). This line of argumentation can best be illustrated by an example. R. Clark (1977, p. 349) found that her son used *intit* to refer to an elephant. Evidently, this was an imitation of the last part of the sentence *that's an elephant, isn't it?* Similarly, R. Brown (1973, p. 99) reports that the child's item *put b'long* from the adult sentence *put it where it belongs* was used in a "noncomprehending way."

Rituals as Evidence for Rote

A third type of evidence for rote has been offered by a variety of writers over the years (R. Brown, 1973, p. 99; R. Clark, 1974, p. 4,6; R. Clark, 1977, p. 350; Fillmore, 1979; Gruber, 1973, p. 442; Kenyeres, 1938; Leopold, 1949b, p. 56; Nelson, 1973, p. 25; Peters, 1977, pp. 564, 566). According to this analysis, word strings that are used as parts of stereotyped rituals or games are probably rote items. For example, *off with shirt* was one of my son Ross's phrases during his bathing ritual. Because of its frequent repetition in a constant context, it appeared to be a single item. However, this analysis is supported largely by an impressionistic judgment. Although the relation between ritual and rote is undoubtedly of great importance (Fillmore, 1979; Ratner & Bruner, 1978), it would be a mistake to consider ritual as a sufficient condition for rote. Certainly, adults participate in a wide variety of social rituals. However, this is not usually taken as prima facie evidence for a rote characterization of adult speech.

Prizant (1978, pp. 39–42, 90–92) reports a number of rote-memorized ritual-oriented statements from the speech of 5- and 6-year-old autistic children. These rote items differ from those of younger normal children in that they tend to use long rote strings where normal younger children would use single words. Examples of such rote strings include *comb your hair* for "comb," *brush your teeth* for "toothbrush," *rest is over* for "all finished," *let's go for a walk* for "I want to get out," and *I hope you're feeling better* for "I feel sick."

Pronoun Errors as Evidence for Rote

The fourth line of evidence is related to the third, although it is somewhat more powerful. Evidence of this fourth type occurs when the child repeats a sentence that had been said to him or her as a part of a ritual. However, in the child's sentence, pronominal reference is incorrectly reversed. Phrases of this type have been reported by R. Clark (1974, pp. 4, 6), Gruber (1973, p. 442), Prizant (1978, p. 42) and van der Geest (1977, p. 98). For example, Clark's son used the phrase *I carry you* to request that the adult carry him. The incorrect pronominal references suggest that this phrase is a direct imitation of an adult sentence. However, one can never be sure in such cases that the child does not mean to call himself or herself *you* and the adult *I* (see MacWhinney, 1974, pp. 562–5, 584–5).

Production of the Whole Before its Parts

Three further types of evidence for a rote analysis of certain phrases are based on the fact that larger units often appear in production before their component pieces emerge. In the first argument of this type, writers have noted that certain phrases, contractions, and conjunctions appear before their parts. Brown, Cazden, and Bellugi (1968, p. 41) report use of *can't, won't,* and *don't* at a time when *can, will,* and *do* were absent; Hatch, Peck, and Wagner-Gough (1979, p. 278) report *it's* when *is* is absent; Leopold (1949a, p. 8) reports use of *sandbox* when *sand* was absent; and R. Clark (1977) reports use of *I could easily do that* when *could* was absent. MacWhinney (1974, 1978) presents a similar analysis for morphological underanalysis in Hungarian. *Eldobott* is considered to be a rote item, because the child does not use the suffix *-ott* with new verbs and makes no errors in its use, although errors would be unavoidable if the suffix were being used productively.

Brown (1973), Burling (1959), MacWhinney (1975b), and Ingram (1979) have noted that there is often evidence for preservation of a unit intact without substitution of parts. R. Clark (1974, p. 4) provides an example of a long phrase with parts that are not yet analyzed. Thus, her subject said *wait for it to cool* for several weeks before any element became free. Finally, the child said *wait for it to dry,* demonstrating at least some morphemic analysis of the phrase.

Production of Contractions Before Expansions

A related argument can be used to interpret contractions as rote items. Menyuk (1969, p. 82) reported use of *I'm* before *I am* had ever been used. Similarly, Brown, Cazden, and Bellugi (1968, p. 49) report *he's, can't,* and *don't* before *he is, cannot,* and *do not* appear. If *I'm* is formed by combination of *I* and *am,* one would expect *I am* to appear before *I'm.* Thus, when the analytic form fails to emerge before the contraction, one suspects that the contraction is an unanalyzed whole.

Precocious Strings

A third type of evidence based on acquisitional sequence was offered by Peters (1977, p. 564). Peters noted that when her 14-month-old subject had control of only six to 10 words, he said quite clearly *open the door*. Nelson (1973), makes a similar analysis for her four "expressive" children. In my own child Ross, I observed the strings *No, Mommy, I don't want to go bed* and *I like it; I love it* at a time when the first types of productive pivot-type two-word combinations had not yet emerged. However, one cannot necessarily assume that precocious sentences of this type are produced by rote. Quite to the contrary, at that time, Ross had never heard a sentence of exactly the form of *no, Mommy, I don't want to go to bed* and it is clear that, in this case, the precocious utterance was not produced by rote.

One possible way of understanding precocious control of this type is to claim that comprehension abilities develop far in advance of production abilities and that, under certain circumstances, knowledge may be transferred directly from comprehension to production. However, in most cases, production strategies must be constructed without intense reliance on comprehension. Thus, even though a child may produce a few surrendipitous forms in this way, the main thrust of development must focus on the construction of a more reliable set of techniques for controlling sentence production.

The remaining seven lines of evidence for the rote analysis of word strings are based on various aspects of the use of linguistic structure. These seven arguments can be divided into one that relates to phonological structure, two that relate to grammatical structure, and four that relate to semantic structure.

Phonological Structure as Evidence for Rote

Guillaume (1927) was the first to suggest that prosodic integration may be taken as evidence for the rote use of strings. More recently, Peters (1977, p. 563) has claimed that some children "learn the tune before the words." Peters claims that these children are in fact using gestalt speech rather than analytic speech. However, it is difficult to use prosodic data in this way as clear proof that a phrase has been learned by rote. Certainly, adult speech has good prosodic integration, and we do not conclude on this fact alone that adults speak sentences by rote. On the other hand, even in adult speech, we would expect that highly preplanned phrases would receive a stereotypic, unit-like intonation. Thus, it may be possible to use prosody as evidence for rote, but exactly how this evidence should be developed remains unclear.

Order Errors as Evidence for Rote

Order errors provide one line of evidence for underanalysis of word strings. Menyuk (1969, p. 94) reports these errors: *You pick up it, he took out her, Joanne took off them,* and *he beat up him.* Along a similar vein, Labov and Labov (1978) have noted that their daughter omitted the auxiliary in the phrases *what that means* and *why not.* In other structures, auxiliaries were often inserted. Thus, the omission of the auxiliary in these small phrases may be taken as evidence for rote. MacWhinney (1974, 1978) reports a large number of similar order errors for German and Hungarian. However, these errors only provide evidence for fairly small rote chunks. For example, *you pick up it* is evidence that *pick up* may be *a rote* unit.

Positional Frames as Evidence for Rote

A second line of evidence from word-order patterns emphasizes the ways in which small strings of words can serve as positional frames. For example, Bellugi (1965, p. 129) noted that, at Stage 2, Adam produced sentences like *why not me sleeping, why not . . . cracker can't talk, why not . . . we can't dance,* and *why not me break dat one.* The combination of *why not* with these various additional phrases suggests that it may be a positional frame. In these sentences, this analysis is further supported by the redundant negatives and the erroneous word order. In most cases, however, the proposal is based simply on the fact that certain word strings tend to be used together.[1]

The last five lines of evidence relate to five types of errors in semantic structure. The five types include errors involving contradiction and four types of errors involving superfluity.

Contradictions as Evidence for Rote

Semantic contradictions seem to constitute fairly good evidence for rote. Some of the reported contradictions involve locatives. R. Clark (1977, p. 350), for example, reports *hat on off* and Ferrier (1978, p. 306) reports *shoes on off.* The other reported semantic contradictions involve articles. Gruber (1967, p. 40) reports the error *where's the a truck* in which either *where's the* or *a truck* could be units. Similarly, Leopold (1949a) reports the error *I want a my shoes* in which *want a* seems to function as a unit.

Contradictions also arise when agreement is violated. Kuczaj (1976, pp. 424, 426) has reported several sentences in which the tense of the auxiliary disagrees with the tense or number of the main verb. They are as follows: *this don't had a map, don't he wanted to help somebody, what's was that, I'm want some dinner, that's are pretty ladies aren't they, it's have two,* and *it's went.* Similarly, R. Brown (1973, p. 263) reports the sentence *it's will go,* and Menyuk (1969, p. 76) reports the error *what's these things* in which it appears that *what's* is a rote item. A variety of parallel errors in Hungarian can be found in MacWhinney (1974). In these sentences, the contractions seem to be used even when their tense is incorrect, possibly because no other devices are available. Although such examples do not prove that the contractions are rote units in this case, they do suggest a rote interpretation.

Superfluity in Context

Semantic superfluity has also been used as evidence for underanalysis. We can distinguish at least three types of superfluity in which there is some evidence for rote. In the first type, an element is not clearly redundant, but seems to be unnecessary in the particular context. For example, Ferrier (1978, p. 306) reports the utterances *say bye-bye* and *there's Ursie* in which *say* and *there's* were apparently superfluous. The child used *say bye-bye* to simply say "goodbye" and *there's Ursie* when she meant to say simply "Ursie." Such phrases seem to

---

[1]Other multiword frames that have been suggested include: *where NP go?* and *what NP doing?* from Bellugi (1965, p. 128); *that's mine NP* and *wait for S* from R. Clark (1977, pp. 344–345); and *look what NP Ving* and *see what NP Ving* from Francis (1969, p. 298).

involve the same type of inaccurate imitation previously discussed. R. Clark (1977, p. 350) reports *cat name* and *picture of* in which *name* and *of* were superfluous in a similar way. And Leopold (1949b, p. 16) reports that *away* was superfluous in *my go away* and that *is* was superfluous in *my mommy is*. In each of these cases, the superfluity is evident not so much in the surface structure as in the use of the utterance in context. Thus, it seems strange to say *my mommy is* when what is meant is only *my mommy*. According to this analysis, we would then say that *say bye-bye, there's Ursie, go away,* and *mommy is* are all functioning as single units.

Presence of an Unusual Element

In the second type of superfluity, one of the elements, although not actually redundant, is clearly strange. For example, R. Clark (1977, p. 350) reports the utterance *hat on gone now* in which *hat on* is apparently a unit. Similarly, Ferrier (1978, p. 306) reports *bye-bye shoes on* in which *shoes on* seems to be a unit. Note that there is no contradiction here between, say, *shoes* and *on,* but there is something unusual about the use of the locative after the direct object *shoes*.

Redundancy as Evidence for Rote

In the third type of superfluity, a redundancy on the surface makes it entirely clear that at least one item is not needed, and that it may have been included as a part of a rote item. There seem to be at least nine constructions in which superfluity gives evidence for rote:

1. *The direct object.* Menyuk (1969, p. 48) reports *she took it away the hat;* Brown and Bellugi (1964, p. 151) report *saw it ball, mommy get it ladder, mommy get it my ladder, miss it garage,* and *I miss it cowboy boot;* and Braine (1976, p. 36) reports *have it egg, have it milk,* and *have it fork.* In these sentences, *took it, saw it, get it, miss it,* and *have it* seem to be rote units.

2. *Verbal particles.* Menyuk (1969, pp. 49, 56) reports *she put on the dress on, the barber cut off his hair off,* and *put on some rouge on.* Similarly, Leopold (1949b, p. 52) cites *zubinde mir meine Schuhe zu (on-tie me my shoes on).* In these sentences *put on, cut off,* and *zubinde* seem to be rote units.

3. *Quantifiers.* Menyuk (1969, p. 48) reports *I want some lots of flour* in which *lots of flour* seems to be a rote unit.

4. *Contractions.* Kuczaj (1976, p. 424) reports *I like to listen to who's is on this tape, that's makes a truck, it's don't have any oil in here, it's look like a bus, I think it's have a pile, that's means "get hawks,"* and *that what's the witch says to her brother.* Hurford (1975, p. 300) reports *what's that is?* and *what's this is?* Maratsos and Kuczaj (1978, p. 342) report *know what's this is;* and Menyuk (1969, pp. 49, 108) reports *he's go there everyday, he'll might get in jail, he's already's in the house,* and *he's now is copying him.* In these sentences, the contractions appear to be units. In a related set of errors, it may be that the

"excess" auxiliary is in fact a marker of the progressive and that the error is due to an omission of -ing. Some examples of this type of error are as follows: Menyuk (1969, p. 73, 75): *he's make it?* and *what's this plays?;* Mayer, Erreich, and Valian (1978, p. 12): *I'm feed the baby meat;* Gruber (1967, p. 41): *he's put* and *I'm go;* R. Brown (1973, p. 86): *it's go;* and Kuczaj (1976, p. 424): *he's do take his clean pants off* and *what's happen with Santa Claus?*

5. *Negatives.* Bellugi (1965, p. 117) reports *why not . . . me can't dance* and *why not . . . cracker can't talk* in which *why not* seems to be a rote unit, because there is a double negative.

6. *Modals.* Two redundant uses of modals have been reported in the literature. Bellugi (1971, p. 100) cites *what shall we shall have?* and Menyuk (1969, p. 76) cites *how can he can look?* In these errors, *shall have* and *can look* appear to be rote units.

7. *Copula.* Three redundant uses of the copula as both uncontracted auxiliary and as main verb have been reported. Menyuk (1969, p. 73) cites *is this is the powder?;* Hurford (1975, p. 300) cites *whose is this is?;* and Hatch et al., (1979, p. 242) cite *what is this is?* Hatch et al. believe that *what is this* could be a rote unit. In the other examples, *is this* and *whose is this* may also be rote units.

8. *Past tense.* There are four types of errors in which past tense is redundantly marked on the main verb. Double past-tense marking errors in questions such as *what did you found?* and *did I caught it?* are frequent. Hurford (1975, p. 300) reports five errors of this type; Kuczaj (1976, p. 423–424) reports eight; Klima and Bellugi (1966, p. 205) report one; Maratsos and Kuczaj (1978, p. 341) report 12; and Bellugi (1965, p. 122) reports four. In this first type of past-tense error, the main verb is almost always an irregular verb. A second type of past-tense redundancy involves negative declaratives such as *she didn't goed.* These errors are somewhat less frequent than those of the first type. Kuczaj (1976, p. 426) reports eight such errors and Klima and Bellugi (1966, p. 196) report three. Still less common is redundancy in affirmative declaratives such as *I did broke it.* Kuczaj (1976, p. 426) reports one such error and Mayer et al. (1978, p. 2) report three. The fourth type of error involves redundant marking of tense on the main verb, accompanied by incorrect tense on the auxiliary. Kuczaj (1976, p. 424,426), for example, reports *don't he wanted to help somebody, can you broke these,* and *this don't had a map.* In many of these past-tense redundancies, the redundant unit is a piece of an irregular verb. Because we know that *caught* and *took* are units in any case, we learn fairly little about rote from these redundancies.

9. *Present tense.* Present-tense redundancies occur only in the third person singular. And they appear mostly in yes–no questions such as *does it rolls?* Maratsos and Kuczaj (1978, p. 341) report nine errors of this type, Bellugi (1965, p. 122) reports two, and Menyuk (1969, pp. 73, 76) also reports two. Kuczaj (1976, p. 426) also reports the related error *it don't hurts* in which redundancy is accompanied by an error in agreement, and the error *it didn't has*

any in which the redundant present tense cooccurs with an error in the tense of the auxiliary.

For each of these nine types of redundancies, we have noted how the presence of rote units can explain at least some aspects of the error. For example, in *she put on the dress on,* one could argue that the child wanted to say *she put the dress on,* but that *put on* was the only way the child has to say *put.* However, this is often not the case. Children who use *put on, why not,* or *shall have* may also use *put, why,* and *have* in other sentences. If this is true, why do we find both *put on* as a main verb and *on* as a separable particle? The question seems to be parallel to the question of why children produce forms like *duckses* and *footses.* Menn and MacWhinney (1980) have argued that, in *duckses,* the plural *ducks* is a rote item and that *-es* is added to it as part of the productive plural rule. The point is that, although the child knows that *ducks* is plural, he or she still has difficulty suppressing the productive plural. In general, redundancy can occur whenever the child has two ways of saying the same thing. In the case of *she put on the dress on,* the verb *put on* is a rote unit and the particle *on* is a productive device. The child must learn to suppress *on* when using *put on* and to use *put* when saying *on.*

In addition to these 14 basic types of evidence for rote, there is a further type of evidence that is only relevant to the detection of the use of rote in second-language acquisition. This type of evidence occurs when a child refers to a sentence as a whole entity. For example, Kenyeres (1938) noted that his six-year-old Hungarian-speaking daughter would ask the meanings of whole French sentences. For instance, she would ask her parents to explain the meaning of school rituals such as *tout le monde à sa place* ("everyone to his seat") and song titles such as *feuille d'ou viens-tu?* ("leaf, where do you come from?"). Such items have only a generalized meaning attached to them for the young second-language learner. Rather than preserve these longish items as rote forms, the child tries to enlist the adult's help in breaking these items down into their component pieces.

Evidence for Short-Term Syntactic Rote

For an item to be used by rote, it is not necessary that it be stored in long-term memory. All that is necessary for syntactic rote is that an item not be fully analyzed into its component words. Thus, one important alternative to long-term rote is the rote use of strings that occur in immediately preceding discourse and that have not yet faded from short-term memory. We can distinguish two types of evidence for short-term rote: replacement sequences and discourse borrowing.

Replacement sequences, also known as build-ups and elaborations, have been studied by Braine (1973, p. 422), R. Clark (1974, p. 2), Francis (1969, p. 299), Gvozdev (1961), Iwamura (1980), MacWhinney and Osser (1977), and Weir

(1962). To illustrate the phenomena, consider this sequence from R. Clark (1974, p. 2): *Baby Ivan have a bath, let's go see Baby Ivan have a bath.* In this sequence, the child produces the chunk *Baby Ivan have a bath* and then stores it in short-term memory. He then adds *let's go see* to this item in short-term memory and produces the final sentence. By breaking the problem down into its pieces and by remembering the solution to a piece of the problem by rote (Jacoby, 1978), the child may be able to produce strings that go just beyond his or her normal processing span. This basic strategy may be extended over several utterances, as in these sequences cited by Iwamura (1980, pp. 61, 88):

1. Are you come to our house, Suzy?
   Do you come to our house?
   Does Suzy come to our house, Mommy?
   Is Suzy come to our house?
2. I don wan she.
   I don wan she to talk to me.
   I don wan him, she to talk to me.
   Don wan Suzy to talk to me.
   I don wan you to talk to me.
   Don wan.
   Don talk to me.

The second type of short-term memory rote involves the borrowing of a piece of the previous adult utterance to be used in the child's own utterance. For example, Clark (1974), pp. 3–4) cites these sequences.

3. Adult: We're all very mucky.
   Child: I all very mucky too.
4. Adult: Do you want to get off?
   Child: No, I want to get on.
5. Adult: That's upside down.
   Child: No, I want to upside down.

Clark (1977, p. 356) cites this sequence:

6. Adult: You want to have a bath?
   Child: I want Teddy have a bath.

Hatch et al. (1979, p. 272) cite these sequences from young second-language learners:

7. Adult: Come here.
   Child: No come here.

8. Adult: Don't do that.
   Child: Okay don't do that.
9. Adult: Where are you going?
   Child: Where are you going is house.

R. Brown (1968, p. 282) cites these:

10. Mother: He was playing a little tune.
    Adam: Why he play little tune?
11. Mother: I see a seal.
    Adam: Why you see a seal?
12. Mother: You bent that game.
    Adam: Why me bent that game?
13. Mother: Well, because she wanted to.
    Adam: Why she want to?
14. Mother: I think it's resting now.
    Adam: Why it's resting now?
15. Mother: I guess I'm not looking in the right place.
    Adam: Why not you looking right place?
16. Mother: Because you weren't careful.
    Adam: Why not me careful?
17. Mother: I don't see any.
    Adam: Why not you see any?
18. Mother: You can't dance.
    Adam: Why not me can't dance?
19. Mother: ... you're breaking that one.
    Adam: Why not me break that one?

Finally, Iwamura (1979, p. 3) cites this sequence:

20. Child A: Don't throw. Don't throw.
    Child B: I don wanna don throw.

Before concluding this section on evidence for rote, we should note, at least in passing, the important role of rote phrasal items in the adult lexicon. For example, Becker (1975) estimates that at least half of the items in the average adult lexicon are polymorphemic. Included in this count are ritual phrases (*what do you know?*), extended syntactic frames (*X gives Y a piece of X's mind*), frozen metaphors (*dead as a door nail*), and phrases with words that are no longer productive as individual items (*arms akimbo, short shrift, run amok*). Many of these adult items are used in ways that closely resemble the more primitive rote items used by children.

Evidence Against Rote

Whenever there is no evidence supporting any of these 14 lines of evidence, one begins to suspect that a string is not being produced by rote. However, there are also four more positive lines of evidence that can be used to limit the importance assigned to rote. First, it can be shown that rote is not being used when a string contains an error that could not be derived from imitation. The error may be one in word order, affix choice, or morphophonology. For example, if a child says *I didn't want to get uped,* we may assume that *get up* is a rote substring. However, the larger string could not be a rote formation, because it could not be a (nonaltered) imitation of an adult sentence. Formal errors of this type are reported quite widely (R. Brown, 1973, p. 98; Brown & Bellugi, 1964; p. 149; MacWhinney, 1974) and constitute the most widely used evidence that children's sentences cannot be produced by rote alone.

However, recently, Platt and MacWhinney (1980) have demonstrated how formal errors of this type could occur in items that had been learned by rote. A child could produce a word like *foots* as a productive combination of *foot* and *-s.* Having produced this word, the child could then learn his or her own error. Subsequent uses of *foots* could then be simple rote uses. Moreover, this process can also operate to produce correct rote items; *cats* may be initially produced by combination and subsequently controlled by rote. In general, this kind of learning follows the principle of unitization or redintegration discussed by Horowitz and Prytulak (1969), Hayes-Roth (1977), Shiffrin and Schneider (1977), and many others. As Jacoby (1978) puts it, after a learner has solved a problem once, he or she can then simply remember the solution, instead of actually solving the problem again from scratch. Note that such learning by rote can occur without any imitation of another speaker. All that is required is that the child listen to him- or herself. Clark (1977, p. 353) cites examples that indicate that learning one's own productions may be an important mechanism even for sentence-length strings. Her child Adam, for instance, used to say *Adam turn a light on* and would receive the answer *soon.* Eventually, he came to say *Adam turn a light on soon.* Or, having said *where's Adam? . . . upstairs* many times, he came to say *where's Adam upstairs?*

A second, more powerful, line of evidence against rote is based on the child's use of nonce words (Braine, 1963). Strings that contain nonce words whose meaning is arbitrarily assigned by the experimenter cannot possibly be produced by rote, unless the experimenter presented them. Thus, if the experimenter keeps an accurate record of the use of each nonce word, he or she can determine with some certainty whether a given string with the nonce word could conceivably have been produced by rote. In practice, this technique has not been extensively applied. This is unfortunate, because it means that when children do not make errors, we have little evidence demonstrating that the sentences they form could not be produced by rote. Moreover, even when they do make errors, those errors could be rote repetitions of forms that had once been productive.

Researchers have often devoted more attention to two somewhat more general lines of argumentation. In the third line of argumentation, it is claimed that rote is, in principle, incapable of accounting for all the sentences of a language. N. Chomsky (1957), G. Miller (1965), and Postal (1964) argue that the number of possible grammatical sentences for a given language far exceeds the capabilities of rote-based production. Although these arguments clearly prove that all of the utterances produced by an adult community cannot be based on rote alone, they place no important limits on the use of rote in the speech of preschoolers.

The fourth line of argumentation emphasizes the ways in which mnemonic processing limits the size of what can be learned by rote. Short-term memory is certainly capable of storing full sentences in their complete surface form. However, some studies (Sachs, 1967) have suggested that, after a few minutes, recognition memory for surface structure declines sharply. Recall is even more sharply affected. On the other hand, more recent data (Keenan, MacWhinney, & Mayhew, 1977) indicate that, under certain conditions, recognition memory for surface structure may be present even several days after the initial exposure. In any case, it is generally recognized that, for school-age children and adults, rehearsal (Conrad, 1972) can allow speakers to commit huge texts (Rubin, 1978) to memory. Thus, the question is not so much what the mnemonic system can commit to rote. Rather, the question is what does it commit to rote, and how much of this is available in production as opposed to comprehension.

So far, we have considered one very simple strategy for ordering words into strings, and it has been shown that there are at least some strings that are probably produced or comprehended through use of this strategy. However, there is also evidence that at least some other strings are *not* produced by rote, but by some more complex strategy or strategies. Although there are clear upper limits on the role of rote in language acquisition, these limits are not yet well understood. It would be a mistake to offer a more complex account for phenomena that can be accurately described as instances of rote application. This is to say that, when a given phenomenon can be explained equally well either by rote or by some more complex mechanism, the rote account is preferrable because it is simpler.

How Much Rote Do Children Use?

It is important to distinguish three formulations of this question:

1. How much rote do we know that children use?
2. How much rote might children be using?
3. How much rote might children know but not use expressively?

The data previously cited provide an answer to the first question only. They show that small word strings such as *put on,* or *say goodbye,* may be learned by rote and that contractions and complex words are often rote units. However, we have almost no evidence for rote units that extend beyond the level of the kinds of prosodic units that can be perceived as if they are words.

On the other hand, it may well be that we have not found large rote units because the kinds of evidence we have tended to accept are not suitable for longer strings. Or, it may be that we have not found large rote units because we have not been looking for them. Data from second-language acquisition (Fillmore, 1979; Hakuta, 1977) suggest that older children may have longer rote units. However, the answer to the second question is not simply that children may form all sentences by rote. In the next section, we show why rote must have limits.

A third possibility is that large rote chunks are used in comprehension but not production. Certainly, we know that recognition far surpasses recall. Thus, there is good reason to suspect that rote should play an important role in comprehension. However, no tests of this possibility have yet been conducted.

ANALOGY

We noted in the preceding section that the rote account for syntax fails on four grounds: (1) it cannot explain neologisms and errors; (2) it cannot explain the use of nonce forms; (3) too many sentences would have to be memorized; and (4) these sentences would be too long. In this section, we examine a simple strategy for producing sentences that meets the first two objections. However, as we see, this strategy also fails to meet the last two objections.

The strategy we consider is *analogy,* the second of the three processing mechanisms proposed by MacWhinney (1978). Analogy is defined as a process that operates on one or more items in memory to extract a pattern that can then be used to control a new formation. The crucial characteristic of analogy that distinguishes it from the system of rules or *combination* is that in analogy, the pattern is implicit in a set of lexical items, but is not available apart from an analysis of those items. For example, a neologism like *leadsel* could be produced on analogy with *tinsel.* In such a case, no one would argue that *-sel* is a productive suffix denoting "an object made from a metal." Thus, the pattern isolated by analogy in such cases is essentially ad hoc. In combination, on the other hand, the pattern or rule has developed a life of its own apart from the lexical items from which it developed. However, no sharp line should be drawn between analogy and combination, and it may be best to view analogy as one aspect of the first stages of rule development.

Occasionally, there are clear cases of analogical processing in syntax. Most of these examples involve operation on rote strings by the processes of replacement or conversion that were discussed earlier. For example, R. Clark (1974, p. 1) reports the production of *wait for it to dry*, on apparent analogy with *wait for it to cool*. In this particular case, it was reasonable to imagine that the rote item *wait for it to cool* was stored in short-term memory and that the *wait for it to* section was analyzed out and subsequently added to *dry* to produce *wait for it to dry*. Reporting on the acquisition of French by his 6-year-old Hungarian-speaking daughter, Kenyeres (1938) notes that the sentence *óu sont les mamans?* ("where are the mothers?") for "where is my mother?" must have been derived from the sentence *óu sont les oiseaux?* ("where are the birds?"), which she had learned at school. To cite another example, Peters (1980) reports that at 1;8 Satoshi Hayasaka learned the sentence *what a nice bicycle you have* and soon after produced *what a nice elbow you have* and *what a nice daddy you have*. Similarly, Clark (1977, p. 354) and MacWhinney (1974, p. 584) report sequences such as the adult's *are you?* followed by the child's *I are* in which the child produces a sentence on analogy to the sentence of the adult but in which the pronoun is converted. Further examples of this type of analogy were given previously. An analogic mechanism of this type can also be used to explain certain types of strings containing errors. For example, *you pick up it* (Menyuk, 1969, p. 94) could be formed on analogy with *you pick up John*, and *did I caught it* could be based on analogy with *did I take it*. Furthermore, sentences with nonce words such as *this is my wug* could be produced by analogy with rote items such as *this is my bear*.

In general, one can argue that analogy has occurred when there is reason to believe that a model sentence is available in either short- or long-term memory. It is also necessary to specify how the child uses the information in this stored rote chunk to produce the current utterance. In the case of build-ups, the chunk is used as a whole and one cannot speak of the result as an analogy. Analogy requires replacement rather than build-up. At least one element in the rote string must be analyzed out and replaced by some other semantically similar element.

In the area of morphophonology, it is often possible to get positive evidence for the use of analogy in the production of at least some forms. This is done by "priming" the child with the basis of an analogy. A child is asked first for the plural of *scarf* and then for the plural of *narf*. The production of *scarves* would serve as a prime for the plural *narves*. The evidence suggests that, in systems where the structure of the patterns to be learned is complex and irregular, it will take a long time to perfect the full set of combinatorial rules. In such systems, there is evidence that analogy continues for a long time to play a major role in producing new forms. One example of a system that encourages the use of analogy is the complex and arbitrary system of gender, case, and number in German (MacWhinney, 1978). In other systems, in which rules are less subject to exceptions and idiosyncrasies, we would expect that analogy should quickly give way to combination. For example, many of the basic rules that govern both the order of morphemes in words and the ordering of words in strings are fairly consistent. Therefore, we should expect analogy to play a fairly minor role in the control of word order. To see why this is true, consider this example: A child learns the item *my book* by rote and uses it frequently. Later, the child wants to say that a certain toy is his, or hers. Taking *my book* as the basis of the analogy, the child then produces *my toy*. However, having done this once, the child immediately sets up the sequence *my + X* as a combinatorial pattern. Because *my* always appears before the noun it possesses, the pattern rapidly grows in strength and becomes a full-fledged rule (MacWhinney, 1978). Analogy was important only at first and later it was overtaken by the rule itself. Because of this, we do not expect to find much evidence for analogy in early syntax.

In fact, there is good evidence that analogy alone cannot explain a variety of error types both in morphophonology (MacWhinney, 1978) and syntax. Some sentential error types for which it is difficult to imagine correct analogues are: *allgone sticky, why not me sleeping, shoes on off, where's the a truck, it's have two, saw it ball, put on some rouge on, some lots of flour, does it rolls?, I'm go,* and many others. However, if we assume that these errors are produced by analogic operation upon rote chunks, they can be explained fairly easily. For example, *shoes on off* is based on analogy with *pants off,* and *shoes on* is considered to be a rote item meaning something like "shoes." Similarly *some lots of flour* could be an analogy with *some bread,* and *lots of flour* could be taken to be a rote unit.

Thus, although both analogy and rote are fairly weak accounts when taken alone, when they are taken together, they are much more powerful. Although this combined model is quite powerful, there are still three major objections that can be raised against such a simple rote-plus-analogy model. First, the number of rote sentence types to be memorized would still be fairly large. However, by combining rote with analogy, it is possible to limit this total number to some finite set. Second, there is no way of knowing in a given case just what the basis of a purported analogy might have been. Thus, the rote-plus-analogy model is really highly unconstrained. Third, and most important, we have very little evidence that either children or adults spend much time memorizing sentence-length sentence patterns. Nor do we have any evidence that such long rote forms have any impact on either the production or the comprehension of word strings. Until such evidence becomes available, we must assume that rote and analogy, by themselves, cannot explain word-string production in either children or adults. This does not mean that rote and analogy have no role in word-string formation. In fact, there is evidence that many short strings are learned by rote and that analogy can work on strings held in short-term memory. However, until evidence for long rote units becomes available, we must attempt to explain the production and comprehension of long strings of novel combinations by some more complex mechanism.[2]

---

[2]Maratsos and Chalkley (1980) argue that analogy also fails to deal with the fact that the use of certain grammatical markers, like tense in the third person singular, is obligatory. Although this

COMBINATION

The third mechanism that we consider is *combination*. Combination is defined as the set of principles that serves to transform an unordered string of lexical items into an ordered string. When defined this way, combination presupposes that lexical items are initially unordered, because a preordered string of items would be governed by rote and, when rote operates, combination is precluded.

Combination must begin, then, with a search for a series of lexical items or morphemes. When this search yields more than one item, combination is called into play. Combination itself involves two major subsystems. One is the system of morphophonological rules that alter the phonological shapes of morphemes; this system was discussed in MacWhinney (1978). The second major subsystem of lexical combination is linearization. This system comprises the set of principles that govern the ordering of morphemes into strings, and it is the major focus of the present section. The four principles or strategies that we consider here are: (1) predispositions; (2) bound rules; (3) free rules; and (4) class-bound rules. In this section, we examine the evidence for and against each of these four strategies.

Predispositions

In order to formulate the notion of combinatorial predispositions in a maximally simple way, we must make two assumptions. The first is that, for a given item, the process of lexicalization precedes the process of linearization. This assumption is accepted by some linguists (Chafe, 1971) and psycholinguists (Clark & Clark, 1977), and rejected by others (N. Chomsky, 1965; Schlesinger, 1977). However, for our present purposes, it is useful to make this assumption, because it permits a simple formulation of the notion of predispositions.

Assuming, then, that lexicalization precedes linearization, we must also make a second simplifying assumption: When linearization rules do not apply, the order of lexical items in a sentence is a function of the order in which those items are lexicalized. This could be referred to as the "first come–first served" principle. In fact, some of the child's earliest utterances seem to provide good evidence for this hypothesized principle. In particular, a number of writers (Bloom, 1973, p. 53, Brown, 1973, p. 148, Greenfield & Zukow, 1978; Guillaume, 1927;

---

observation is entirely true, it is not necessarily the case that all obligatory elements must be inserted by the syntactic component. In fact, it is quite reasonable to argue that obligatory intentions are inserted, in certain cases, by the semantic component. For example, in English, the child would learn that he or she would always have to specify the tense of any action or process in semantic structure. Once this decision is made, the lexicalization of the semantic intention can proceed by either rote, analogy, or combination. This solution to the problem raised by Maratsos and Chalkley does not negate the importance of the issue. Rather, it suggests that the child will attempt to solve this problem not by setting up word-order rules, but by coordinating semantic intentions.

Shipley, Smith, & Gleitman, 1969; Smith, 1970; Weisenburger, 1976) have argued that the order of items in successive single-word utterances is not governed by principles of semantic relation. Rather, the child seems to say words, one by one, as they come to his or her mind.

Given the assumption that lexicalization precedes linearization and that linearization orders items on a first come–first served basis, we must consider what principles might be involved in predicting the order in which items will be lexicalized. If we can discover such principles, and if they hold uniformly, we will have succeeded in accounting for syntax. Of course, this solution will not exclude rote and analogy as alternative strategies. However, it would provide us with a combinatorial mechanism that would be so powerful that we would have no need to consider any additional combinatorial strategies.

The notion of a predisposition is being used here in a very nonspecific way to refer to any strategy whose origin has not yet been traced and whose consequences appear to be universal. It may be that some predispositions rest upon a set of epigenetically canalized abilities (Waddington, 1957). What is important for the present analysis is not the source of the predispositions, but the fact that they govern operations on the information-processing level that constrains the level being examined. In the case of word order, predispositions work on lexicalization, because the order of lexicalization can constrain the order of linearization. In the case of morphophonology, predispositions operate on the phonological level, constraining the shape of morphological productions.

There are at least seven predispositional principles that have been suggested at various points by various writers. These items tend to be lexicalized and/or ordered in terms of decreasing: (1) informativeness (Greenfield & Zukow, 1978; MacWhinney, 1977; Sgall, Hajičova, & Benešova, 1973); (2) grammatical complexity or size (Bloom, Miller, & Hood, 1975, p. 45, Dik, 1978); (3) agency (Osgood & Bock, 1977, p. 93); (4) salience (Horgan, 1976); (5) perspective (MacWhinney, 1977, Osgood & Bock, 1977, p. 94); (6) order of occurrence (E. Clark, 1971); and (7) relatedness (Clark & Clark, 1977; Slobin, 1973). Let us briefly examine evidence for each of these seven principles.

Informativeness

The predisposition that has received the most attention is the informativeness. Studies by Braine (1973, p. 425), deLaguna (1927, 1963), Greenfield and Zukow (1978), Sechehaye (1926), Snyder (1976), and Vygotsky (1934/1962) have suggested that, in early one-word utterances, the child vocalizes the most-informative or newest item and suppresses less-informative or given items. Similarly, in early two-word utterances, children seem to place the most-informative word first (Guillaume, 1927; Leonard & Schwartz, 1977; Lindner, 1898; Menyuk, 1969; O'Shea, 1907; also see MacWhinney & Bates, 1978, p. 546 for additional references).

It is probably impossible to distinguish between informativeness and newness (MacWhinney, 1977) as determinants of early word order. However, whether we speak of informativeness or newness, the tendency to order the new before the given runs exactly counter to the tendency in many adult languages to order the given before the new (Bock, 1977; also see MacWhinney, 1977, pp. 159-161 for details). In this regard, it is important to realize that no one has ever claimed that this particular predisposition is a rule. Eventually, the child will have to learn to overcome this hypothesized predisposition in order to produce grammatical utterances. Moreover, even in the early periods, the child begins to order the given before the new (Gruber, 1967; MacWhinney, 1975a; Menyuk, 1969, p. 49). However, we do not know whether the child actually has to try to overcome the predisposition in order to do this or whether she or he relies on some opposing predisposition towards saying the given first. Nor do we know what it would mean to have two predispositions working in opposite directions.

Complexity

Dik (1978, pp. 189-211) has suggested that there is a universal tendency to order constituents by size. According to this principle, short, simple phrases or words come early and long, complex strings come late. In other words, we prefer to say *it amazed me that he arrived late* rather than *that he arrived late amazed me* because the latter begins with the relatively complex phrase *that he arrived late* whereas the former begins simply with *it*. Similarly, other things being equal, pronouns occur earlier than nouns. Dik's proposed ordering by complexity seems to be closely related to the idea of an ordering by degrees of givenness suggested by Prague School functionalism (Sgall et al., 1973). In any case, there are no investigations of complexity as a determinant of early child word orderings.

The next three predispositions we consider were proposed in slightly different formats by MacWhinney (1977) and Osgood and Bock (1977). In the terms of Osgood and Bock, the predispositions are: naturalness, vividness, and motivation of speaker. In the terms of MacWhinney (1977), the choice of the starting point for English is influenced by agency, salience, perspective, and givenness. In MacWhinney's account, agency expresses one aspect of Osgood and Bock's naturalness. However, Osgood and Bock make the broader claim that our cognitions utilize agent–action–recipient order and that our language reflects this underlying natural cognitive order. MacWhinney's salience corresponds to Osgood and Bock's vividness and MacWhinney's perspective corresponds to Osgood and Bock's motivation of speaker. Thus, the overall fit between these proposals is fairly close (see also Ertel, 1977).

Osgood and Sridhar (1979) have assembled a variety of experimental data supporting a role for perspective, salience, and agency in the speech of adults from 14 language communities. However, as Osgood himself admits (1971), claims regarding predispositions must eventually be tested on young children. Although Osgood has not yet conducted such tests, a variety of other studies do suggest that agency, salience, and perspective may in fact function as predispositions for young children.

Agency

First let us consider agency. The strategy of choosing the first noun phrase (NP) as the agent was proposed by Bever in 1970. Studies of the comprehension of alternative word orders by children in Japanese (Hakuta, 1979; Hayashibe, 1975) and Tagalog (Segalowitz & Galang, 1976) have provided evidence for a fairly weak tendency to take the first NP as the agent, although no such rule is present in the adult language. Unfortunately, the exact status of word-order variations in Tagalog is a matter of controversy. Moreover, in Hungarian (Mac-Whinney, 1976) and Turkish (Slobin, and Aksu, in press), which also allow object–agent ordering, no such tendency emerges. Of course, in English, which heavily disfavors object–agent ordering, children tend to take the first noun as the agent (see the section *Free Rules* later in this chapter) and to initialize agents even in the period of successive single-word utterances (Horgan, 1976, p. 120). However, English is hardly a useful test case. Rather, what we need is further data on both comprehension and production in Verb–Object–Subject (VOS) languages like Tagalog.

Salience

The fourth of the six predispositions we are considering is salience or vividness. Although there are a variety of studies of the effects of perceptual salience on adult production and comprehension (see MacWhinney, 1977), there are no clear-cut experimental demonstrations of its effects on word ordering in children. Horgan (1976) reports that some of her child subjects began their picture descriptions by mentioning what first "caught their eye [p. 122]." However, it is not clear how this definition of salience serves to distinguish it from informativeness and newness.

Perspective

The fifth predisposition that has been suggested is that children might tend to initialize the element with which they most closely identify. This is what Mac-Whinney (1977) calls the perspective. Of course, in many cases, the perspective is also the agent. However, in the passive or in nontransitive sentences, the perspective is not the agent. Here, again, English provides a very poor test of the hypothesized predisposition, because the initialization of the perspective is a central rule of English grammar. The kinds of tests we need could be made, say, in Navajo, where the order of nouns is governed by animacy and not perspective.

If children were to initialize a perspective that was low in animacy, there would be evidence for the hypothesized predisposition, because they would be running directly counter to a basic word-order rule of the language.

Order of Occurrence

The five predispositions already mentioned all serve to constrain the order of constituents in a clause. However, there may also be predispositions that constrain the order of clauses in a sentence. One such predisposition would be the tendency to mention events in the order of their actual occurrence. Clark and Clark (1968), E. Clark (1971), and Ferreiro and Sinclair (1971) have shown that subjects tend to assume that the first clause mentioned in a complex temporal sentence (i.e., a sentence with either "before" or "after") also occurred first. However, studies by Amidon and Carey (1972), Amidon (1976), and Johnson (1975) have failed to detect an effect for order of mention. Amidon (1976) attributes these differences in results to task variables.

This hypothesized preference for the first action as the first clause is not necessarily supported by linguistic analysis. For example, Talmy (1978, p. 638) argues that the main predisposition in complex sentences is to place the figure before the ground. In temporal sentences, the earlier event is usually the reference point. Thus, as the reference point, it is the conceptual ground and should occur in a second (subordinate) clause, whereas the later event, which functions as the figure, will appear first in a main (asserted) clause.

A somewhat different, but closely related, predisposition for interclausal ordering might be the putative universal tendency to order the cause before the result. In fact, Bebout, Segalowitz, and White (1980) have found that children prefer to interpret causal conjunctions such as "because" and "so" in terms of a cause followed by a result. Here again, the hypothesized universal order is opposite to that suggested by Talmy (1978) on the basis of his linguistic analysis. According to Talmy, the result functions as the figure and the cause functions as the ground. Thus, the basic order in causal conjunctions should be result before cause.

Relatedness

In general, it seems that words that are most closely related in the sense of semantic constituency are ordered closest to each other. This tendency has been called Behaghel's Law (Clark & Clark, 1977, pp. 80–84) and it seems to have surprisingly universal results both for word order (Bolinger, 1952) and affix order (Chafe, 1974). To some degree, we can say that this law functions as a predisposition regarding the order in which items may be lexicalized.

In order to comply with Behaghel's Law, speakers must optimize the relatedness of neighboring items. Thus, both Bever (1970) and Slobin (1973, pp. 199–201) have cited evidence indicating that both speakers and listeners tend to avoid interruption of related items. Although this principle seems generally quite reasonable, its exact importance in specific cases has been the subject of some dispute (Sheldon, 1974). Later, we examine this dispute in regard to the impact of relatedness and interruption on the processing of relative clauses.

It should be clear from the preceding discussion that the evidence for these seven predispositions in early combinations is far from overwhelming. This does not mean that predispositions are not there. Rather, it means that if we want to demonstrate their existence, we need to devise more convincing experiments that can be used with younger children. However, there is no need for us to suspend other lines of inquiry until such experiments are conducted, for it is likely, in any case, that predispositions are not the only mechanism underlying combinations. As evidence for this, consider that there is no universally valid rule of surface syntactic order. In some languages, the adjective follows the noun. In others it precedes the noun. If the first come–first served principle were operative, we would have to argue that in some cultures, adjectives are more important than nouns, whereas in other cultures, nouns are more important than adjectives. Such extreme linguistic relativism seems fairly unlikely. Therefore, we are left with the fact that surface syntax exists and must be explained. Moreover, even those who support the importance of predispositions (Bates & MacWhinney, in press; Dik, 1978) recognize that language-specific fixed word orders constitute the bulk of syntactic structure even in so-called "free word-order" languages. And, it is clear that any theory of syntactic acquisition must include mechanisms that can account for these language-specific fixed word orders. Such mechanisms must also be able to account for the basic phenomenon mentioned earlier—that we have no evidence for widespread rote encoding of long strings of words and that, therefore, rote and analogy are insufficient as accounts of the production and comprehension of long strings of words.

Bound Rules

We now turn to the consideration of a simple, rule-governed way for combining lexical items. This strategy makes use of a set of lexically bound rules, which we call item-based patterns.[3] These patterns are designed to place two strings into a linear order when one of these strings is a single item. However, as we note later, such simple binary patterns can be combined to produce large structures. We see that such patterns are able to overcome the chief inadequacies of rote, analogy, and predispositions—that is, they can produce long strings of words without relying on rote templates and they can account for the systematic control of patterns that are language specific rather than universal.

---

[3]This analysis relies heavily on Braine (1976). However, it differs from Braine's analysis in that it distinguishes more sharply between item-based patterns and feature-based patterns. Also, it attempts to locate semantic relations within the lexical specifications of the operator and the nucleus.

Each item-based pattern is an ordering procedure that is bound to (i.e., stored on) a single lexical item. The item on which the procedure is stored is called the operator. The procedure allows an operator to either precede or follow some other string, which is called the nucleus. Whereas, by definition, an item-based pattern specifies a single, unique lexical item as the operator, it may specify either a single item or some set of items as the nucleus. Thus, one can imagine two types of item-based patterns: (1) item–item patterns; and (2) item–set patterns. However, the first type of pattern is uninteresting, because it is equivalent to a rote item. For example, we might know about the item *shrift* that it follows the item *short* in the sequence *short shrift*. However, this is equivalent to saying that we have *short shrift* as a rote item (Becker, 1975).[4] It is clear, then, that item–item patterns are of little explanatory value, although they may be of importance in talking about the emergence of item–set patterns from rote items (see Braine, 1976, p. 9, Maratsos & Chalkley, 1980). Therefore, we use the term "item-based pattern" to refer to item–set patterns rather than to item–item patterns.

The shape of the nucleus of an item-based pattern could be defined in a variety of ways. In the present section, we consider a characterization of the nucleus in terms of a single semantic feature. Thus, we talk about item-based patterns like *my + entity* and *action + -ed*. In the *Nonsemantic Class-Bound Positional Patterns* section later in this chapter, we see why this characterization is inappropriate. However, for the moment, we explore the potential applicability of this initial simple formulation of the item-based pattern.

Evidence for Item-Based Patterns

The notion of an item-based pattern just given is so simple that one immediately wonders whether such a mechanism could really be of any value in analyzing even the most primitive utterances of young children. Thus, in order to lend credibility to the notion, we would need to see that it actually worked to explain some important phenomena. In this section, we first examine the kinds of data that seem to be satisfactorily explained by item-based patterns and then consider the kinds of data that are not well explained by this account. We can distinguish at least seven lines of evidence that argue for the usefulness of item-based patterns. These include their ability to explain: (1) ordering in short strings; (2) children's failure to generalize; (3) the control of discontinuous morphemes; (4) item–phrase orderings; (5) competitive orderings; (6) strings not attributable to analogy; and (7) the nonoccurrence of certain types of errors. Let us consider each of these seven lines of evidence in sequence.

Ordering in Short Strings.   Item-based patterns have received the widest attention in regard to their ability to account for early multiword utterances.

---

[4]As explained in MacWhinney (in press (a)), items like *short shrift, cranberry,* and *phone up* can be viewed as lexical entries with one lex and two morphs.

Braine (1976) proposed two criteria for full positional patterns in early grammars. The first is that such patterns should be consistent and the second is that they should be productive. For example, if we find that the word *too* occurs after the nucleus nine times out of 10, then by calculating binomial probabilities, we have evidence for a positional pattern (Braine, 1976) for the item *too*. This pattern can be represented as: $X + too$. Productivity for the $X + too$ pattern would be indicated if *too* occurred with more than just two or three words. Using these criteria, MacWhinney (1975a) examined the word order of 11,077 utterances produced by two Hungarian children during the ages of 1;5,2 to 2;2,3 and 1;11,18 to 2;5,23. He found that between 85 and 100% of the utterances in these large samples could be generated by a set of 42 item-based patterns. Some examples of these patterns in English translation are: $X + too$, $no + X$, $where + X$, $dirty + X$, and $see + X$. For the full list of patterns, see MacWhinney (1975a, pp. 155-158).

More recently, Ingram (1979) presented an analytic framework that extended that of Braine (1976) and MacWhinney (1975a) in certain ways. Ingram first attempted to determine whether or not a given lexical item was syntactically free or bound by examining the extent to which it combined with other words. Once it was determined that an item was free, Ingram examined the words with which it cooccurred to determine if it was placed in a consistent position. In fact, most of the sentences in his two corpora seemed to utilize some form of item-based pattern. Thus, his two 1-year-olds used the words *here, my, hi, a, that, want, its*, and *what* as operators before object words. The words *this* and *it* were used after action words and the word *I* was used before action words.

It is important to recognize that a fair test of the power of the item-based pattern concept requires a sample density that at least approaches that of Ingram (1979) and MacWhinney (1975a). There is a very simple reason for this: If an observer records only a small set of sentences, the less frequent item-set patterns may occur only once or twice. For example, in a sample of 100 sentences, the pattern $X + walk$ may occur twice. However, in a sample of 1000 sentences, the same pattern may occur 20 times. On the basis of the first sample, one would not conclude that an item-based pattern was operative. However, in a larger sample, it will be clear that the $X + walk$ pattern is consistent and productive.

In fact, many of the most widely cited and influential corpora in the literature (Blount, 1969; Bowerman, 1976; Braine, 1963, 1976; Gruber, 1967; Kernan, 1969; Lange & Larsson, 1973; Miller & Ervin, 1964) contain less than 300 multiword utterances per child grammar. Bloom (1970) and Brown (1973) have somewhat larger corpora, but they remain unpublished and have not been analyzed in terms of item-based patterns. Given this, it is quite remarkable that there is, in fact, much evidence at all for item-based patterns. Much of this evidence is displayed in Braine (1976) and the interested reader may wish to examine the data published there. Additional support for the importance of item-based patterns can also be found in Francis (1969) and Smoczyńska (1976). However, it should be remembered that a full appraisal of the explanatory power of the item-based pattern requires very large corpora, and that in the only large corpora that have been analyzed this way, item-based patterns can account for from 85 to 100% of the multiword utterances.

Failure to Generalize. It has often been noted that, when a child acquires a new combinatorial pattern, that pattern fails to generalize immediately to all elements of a given type. Kuczaj and Brannick (1979) note that auxiliary attachment applies to *what* before it applies to *how long;* children say *what are you doing?* at a time when they also say *how long you (are) staying?* Similarly, Bowerman (1976, p. 157) noted that at 17½ months, her daughter Eva used the patterns *want* + *X* and *more* + *X* fairly productively. However, these patterns did not generalize to other words like "open," "close," "bite," "no more," or "all gone." That is, she did not form sentences according to the pattern *open* + *X*. Eva's failure to produce combinations for words for which she had not yet formulated item-based patterns can be understood by viewing the item-based pattern as a way of bringing words together. Item-based patterns can facilitate not only the concatenation of morphemes, but also their integration into an overall intonational contour (Bloom, 1970; Branigan, 1979; Fónagy, 1972; Scollon, 1976).

Discontinuous Morphemes. Item-based patterns can also be used to explain the child's control of so-called discontinuous morphemes. Such "morphemes" seem to be better understood as two separate lexical items each with its own item-based positional pattern. During the process of lexicalization, which precedes linearization, these two items each facilitate the lexicalization of the other. Having been lexicalized, each is ordered in terms of its own positional patterns. For instance, in the French negative *ne pas, ne* would be placed according to the pattern *ne* + *verb* and *pas* would be placed according to the pattern *verb* + *pas*. Francis (1969, p. 298) suggests that children may have learned forms such as *look what NP Ving* (as in look what John is eating) as discontinuous units. Similarly, Bellugi (1965, pp. 128–130) and Klima and Bellugi (1966, p. 200) report a number of sentences in which these discontinuous frames appear: where _____go?, where_____ going?, what_____doing?, and what_____name? Of course, these frames need not be analyzed as discontinuous morphemes. One could simply argue that they are morphemes that happen to cooccur because of natural aspects of the things children talk about.

It is important to remember that many idioms can be controlled as discontinuous morphemes; the idiom *give five* (i.e., give a slapping handshake) can be realized as *give me five, give your little brother five,* and so on. Similarly, the combination of *think* and *over* is best treated as a discontinuous morpheme, because it has the frozen meaning of "consider," but can appear in frames like *think it over* and *think all my problems over once again.* A large array of adult items of this type is discussed by Becker (1975).

Item-Phrase Orderings.   The fourth major class of phenomena that can be explained by item-bound patterns are item–phrase orderings. As Block, Moulton, and Robinson (1975), Braine (1976), and Schlesinger (1977) have noted, the concept of an item-based pattern is in no way limited to explanations of two-word utterances, because the nucleus for an item-based pattern may be a phrase. For example, in the string *my big chair,* we can say that *my* is being ordered vis a vis the phrase *big chair.* In this way, we can account not only for the generation of noun phrases and verb phrases, but also for certain interesting aspects of the ordering of interrogatives, negatives, and auxiliaries. Klima and Bellugi (1966, pp. 192, 201) and Brown, Cazden, and Bellugi (1968, p. 58) argue that in one fairly early period in the acquisition of English, all the child knows is that certain interrogatives and negatives are often ordered as operators in front of some nucleus. This nucleus may be a noun phrase, a verb phrase, or a whole clause. To relate this ordering to the notion of item-based patterns, an NP nucleus may be characterized as having the semantic feature (+ entity) (see Miller & Johnson-Laird, 1976); a VP nucleus may be said to have the feature (+ state/process/action) (Chafe, 1971); and a clause may be said to have the feature (+ predication) (MacWhinney, 1980). Abbreviating these features as *ent, spa,* and *pred,* we can formulate these item-based patterns quite simply. For the word *where,* we would have *where + ent, where + spa,* and *where + pred.* In fact, there is evidence that children use each of these patterns. Bellugi (1965, pp. 128–130) cites these examples of the *where + ent* patterns from Adam, Eve, and Sarah: *where Ann pencil?, where Mama boot?, where kitty?, where string?, where boot?, where Donna?, where my mitten?, where crayons?, where Fraser elbow?, where you coffee?, where Baby Sarah rattle?, where Mommy?, where Fraser and Cromer?,* and *where big round clock?* As these examples show, the *ent* in these cases may be either an item or a phrase. Similar patterns for *who + ent, what + ent, what color + ent, where's + ent,* and *what's + ent* from Bellugi (1965, pp. 128–130) are *who that?, what that?, what train?, what dat needle?, what color dis?, where's the wheel?,* and *what's this thing?* The reported combinations of *no* with NP's are *no cowboy* (Menyuk, 1969, p. 73), *there no squirrels, no Rusty hat, that no fish school, no money, no mitten, no a boy bed,* and *that no Mommy* (Klima & Bellugi, 1966, pp. 192, 194). The reported combinations of *not* with NP's are *not a Teddy bear* (Klima & Bellugi, 1966, p. 192), *that not "O" that blue* (Klima & Bellugi, 1966, p. 194), and *that not cowboy* (Menyuk, 1969, p. 73). Of course, formulas such as *where's + ent, there's + ent,* and *not + ent* do not necessarily lead to errors, and wherever the use of a pattern leads mostly to correct productions, we tend to see it mentioned less frequently in the literature.

There is also evidence that children formulate at least some of these interrogative and negative item-based patterns so that the nucleus is a verb phrase. In the case of *not* and contractions with *not (can't, don't, didn't, won't,* etc.), this formulation is correct. Klima and Bellugi (1966, pp. 193–194) report correct use of *can't* and *don't* even before *can* and *do* are learned. As we noted earlier, this suggests that *can't* and *don't* are single rote items and not productive combinations. Thus, it is possible to speak of *can't* + *spa* and *don't* + *spa* as item-based patterns. Errors such as *I not touch* (Menyuk, 1969, p. 73), *I not hurt him, I not see you anymore*, and *ask me if I not made mistake* (Klima & Bellugi, 1966, p. 196) show that the positioning of *not* is not controlled simply by rote.

Children also seem to extend the permissible *not* + *spa* pattern to create an incorrect *no* + *spa* pattern. Some errors illustrating this incorrect overextension are: *no do this, I no do this, no touch,* and *no write dis* (Menyuk, 1969, pp. 71, 73); *no wipe finger, no fall, no singing song, no sit there, no play that, he no bite you, I no want envelope, I no taste them,* and *no pinch me* (Klima & Bellugi, 1966, pp. 192, 194); and *no fall* and *no put* (Brown, Cazden & Bellugi, 1968, p. 41).

There is no similarly confusing model for interrogatives that would lead to *where* + *spa, what* + *spa,* and *why* + *spa.* Because of this, errors of this type are quite rare, although Bellugi (1965, pp. 128–129) reports *where go?, what happen?, where put him on a chair?, what happen me?,* and *why need them more?* Some of these errors may be reduced imitations. For example, *what happen?* may come from *what's happening?* and *where go?* may come from *wherezit go?* Of course, *who* + *spa* is a perfectly correct pattern and forms like *who bought that?* are correctly produced at an early age (Klima & Bellugi, 1966). Eventually, the positioning of all the *wh* words may be correctly controlled by patterns such as *what* + *tense* and *why* + *tense,* because the word that follows the interrogative is always the main tense marker for the sentence.

Perhaps the most widespread error in the positioning of interrogatives is their use in patterns such as *where* + *pred, why* + *pred, why* + *pred, why not* + *pred, how* + *pred,* and *what* + *pred* without auxiliary attachment. Such patterns lead to errors such as *what they are doing?* and *where he's going?* (Menyuk, 1969, p. 76), in which the auxiliary follows the subject rather than the interrogative. There are so many reports of this type of error that a full listing would be prohibitively lengthy. Menyuk (1969, pp. 71–76) cites nine such errors; R. Brown (1968) cites about two dozen such errors throughout his article; Bellugi (1971) cites 15 errors of the *why* + *pred* variety; Klima and Bellugi (1966, p. 205) cite about 18 interrogative plus predication errors; Bellugi (1965, p. 129–130) cites several dozen; Brown, Cazden, and Bellugi (1968, pp. 57–60) cite 17 errors; Gruber (1967) cites four and Hatch et al. (1979, p. 273) cite one.

As Brown (1968) notes, there are at least three possible sources for these errors. One is the adult subordinate clause. Another is a reduction of full adult questions. For example, *what you do?* (Menyuk, 1969, p. 76) could be a reduction of *what are you doing?* Finally, as illustrated by examples 3, 4, and 10–19 the section *Evidence for Short-Term Syntactic Rote,* the nucleus of these combinations could be a rote item in short-term memory, with a pronoun or auxiliary possibly altered by what Clark (1977) calls conversion (see the section *Analogy*).

The examples cited by Brown (1968) suggest that this last influence may be the most important source of this error type. However, a fuller account of this phenomenon will need to be based on the use of discourse data such as that cited by Brown (1968).

Although there are many errors involving interrogatives and misplaced auxiliaries, there are no reports of incorrect placement of interrogatives. Labov and Labov (1978) report that, in the huge collection of questions produced by their daughter, there are no errors such as *he can't do it why*. Although such errors would seem to be predicted by transformational–generative grammar, their nonoccurrence is correctly predicted by the notion of the item-based pattern.

Of course, the use of item-based patterns with whole predicates as nuclei such as *does + pred* or *can't + pred* in yes–no questions is perfectly correct. In fact, Brown, Cazden, and Bellugi (1968) report early correct positioning of these forms. Erroneous use of *no + pred* is fairly rare. The reported errors are *no picture in there* (Brown, Cazden, & Bellugi, 1968, p. 41), *no the sun shining, no square is clown* (Klima & Bellugi, 1966, pp. 192, 194) and *no books in* (Menyuk, 1969, p. 71 and 73).

Competitive Orderings.   The fifth major class of phenomena that can be explained by item-based patterns are competitive orderings. So far, we have treated item-based patterns as if they were never in competition. Such a restriction is not at all necessary and there is no reason that any number of item-based patterns cannot be operative in a single utterance. However, when more than one item-based pattern is operating on a string of lexical items, there must be a way of resolving potential conflicts between patterns. Two types of conflicts can arise: reversal conflicts and precedence conflicts. Reversal conflicts occur when one pattern or group of patterns leads to the order $A + B$ and the other produces the order $B + A$. An example of an ordering in which a reversal conflict must be resolved is the ordering of the set of items *why, did,* and *she*. Here, the item *why* has the positional pattern *why + tense* that places it before the subject of the sentence—in this case *she*. However, *did* has one pattern that places it after interrogatives (*int + did*) and another that places it after the sentence subject.

The most primitive way of improving performance is to give the *int + did* pattern a stronger vectorial weight (MacWhinney 1978, 1981b) than the *ent + did* pattern. If this is done, then *why did she?* will be the maximally satisfactory ordering and *why she did?* will be avoided. This type of solution to competition in word order is parallel developmentally to the use of allomorph strength to govern morphophonological variation (MacWhinney, 1978). A more advanced solution to this type of competition involves the formation of specific lexical links. When an interrogative occurs, the *ent + did* pattern is specifically inhibited. Such specific inhibitions and facilitations are particularly important in the area of lexicalization (MacWhinney, in press (a)).

Evidently, there is a time during the development of English when patterns of the type just discussed have either not yet been acquired or are insufficiently strong. Apart from the huge number of errors like *where he's going?* that were previously noted, there are also errors in which the auxiliary is misplaced within the nucleus. Reported errors of this type, include *what you did eat?* (Kuczaj, 1976, p. 427) and *where the wheel do go?* (Menyuk, 1969, p. 90). It is clear, however, that at some later time, patterns like *where + tense* become productive. Overgeneralization errors attesting this productivity are: *where goes the wheel?* (Menyuk, 1969, p. 73), *where could be the shopping place?*, and *where's going to be the school?* (Menyuk, 1969, p. 76); *what do wheel?*, *what does the truck?*, and *where went the wheel?* (Gruber, 1967, p. 41). Kuczaj and Brannick (1979) show that, in fact, the interrogatives *what* and *where* show stronger attraction of the auxiliary than do interrogatives like *how long* or *when*. Thus, it may well be that the child eventually learns to rely on patterns like *where + tense* rather than patterns like *int + did*. However, the details of this competition still need to be worked out. In any case, it is important to realize that the acquisition of auxiliary ordering can be explained in terms of item-based patterns and that it is not necessary to invoke a transformational account (Hurford, 1975; W. R. Miller, 1973) for this ordering.

The second type of conflict that may arise between item-based patterns, or any set of independent patterns, is a precedence conflict. This occurs when one pattern specifies the order *A + B* and the other specifies the order *A + C*. If the first takes precedence, then the result will be *ABC*. If the second takes precedence, then the result will be *ACB*. For example, if the words *big, ball,* and *rubber* are lexicalized, the pattern *rubber + ent* will take precedence over the pattern *big + ent* and the result will be *big rubber ball*. In fact, as we see later, control of modifier ordering takes many years to learn. The problem is that modifier ordering is variable and the number of different modifiers is very large.

When item-based patterns are strong and simple, their precedence can be controlled without much error. One area in which item-based patterns would be particularly useful is affix ordering. In fact, affix ordering is so consistent that the morphology of the word can be reasonably well described in terms of a series of fixed positions or plots, each of which contains certain affixes (Pike, 1967). Evidently, children find this very easy to learn. We know that in English (Braine, 1963), Garo (Burling, 1959), Hungarian (MacWhinney, 1974, 1977, 1978), Japanese (Hakuta, 1979, p. 18), and Turkish (Slobin, 1973, p. 197) the ordering of affixes vis a vis the base is almost always correct, even at the youngest ages. A series of item-based patterns with affixes as operators and the base as the nucleus might well be controlling this ordering.

The control of precedence between words seems to be a far more difficult matter. It seems that for young children, the relative position of words in the sentence cannot always be determined at a single pass. Often, children need to determine the order of a nucleus of two or more words and then add on words to this nucleus. Evidence for this type of analysis comes from word-string repetition phenomena. Thus, at age 1;11,3, my child Ross said *hot water # nice hot water,* whereas at 1;11,5, he said simply *nice hot water* without joining *hot water* as a separate element. At the earlier date, it is almost as if he had spent so much energy saying *hot water* that he decided to say it aloud and then try to use it as a short-term memory rote basis for his next production.

As the child continues to work with these patterns, their use becomes more automatic (Shiffrin & Schneider, 1977) and unitized (Hayes-Roth, 1977). As a result, longer strings can be produced before there is any need for emptying the contents of the processor. However, studies by Jarvella (1971) and Rubin (1976) indicate that adult production and comprehension are still influenced by the clustering of operators about a nucleus. Thus, a noun with its operators constitutes a noun phrase, a verb with its auxiliaries constitutes a verb phrase, and the verb serves as a center about which the various phrases constellate (C. Fillmore, 1968). Although adult processing is fairly smooth and automatic, it still appears that precedence decisions must be made in a sequential fashion.

Strings not Attributable to Analogy. A sixth line of support for item-based patterns involves their ability to account for strings that cannot be attributed to rote or analogy. For example, an error like *no down* can be understood as an application of the pattern *no + X*. Of course, *no* cannot be combined indiscriminately and the child must learn to prune the nucleus (*X*) into something more like (+ entity). Similarly, *where Tim go* can be viewed as a combination of *where* and a phrasal nucleus. Note that neither *no down* nor *where Tim go* could be based on either rote or analogy. We have noted that productive use of a nonce word cannot be based on rote, although it can be based on analogy. For instance, the string *this my wug* could be based on analogy with *this my shoe*. But, then, it would be difficult to specify how *this my shoe* could be an analogy. On the other hand, both *this my shoe* and *this my wug* could be based on use of *this + ent* and *my + ent.*

Nonoccurrences. A seventh line of evidence for item-based patterns involves their ability to account for the absence of certain error types. For example, Kuczaj and Maratsos (1979) note that the errors like *gonna he go?* have never been reported, although children say *he's gonna go, he will go* and *will he go?* If analogy were an important process in syntax, we would expect to find *gonna he go* on analogy with *will he go?* However, if we attribute the placement of *will* before *he go* to an item-based pattern with *will* as its operator, it is not surprising to see that the pattern does not generalize to *gonna*, because by definition item-based patterns do not generalize to new operators. A further example of this type is cited by Bellugi (1971, p. 99). She notes that errors like *I should put it where* do not occur, although they could be produced by analogy with *I should put it here*. However, the availability of the *where* + *pred* pattern serves to block this possible error type.

Evidence Limiting the Generality of the Item-Based Pattern Concept

There are at least five major problems with the item-based pattern concept. These are that it fails to deal with (1) productive use of nonce operators; (2) pattern overgeneralization; (3) the semantics of the nucleus; (4) synchrony in development; and (5) the ability to operate on structures. Let us consider each of these five limitations in order.

Productive Use of Nonce Operators. This phenomenon has not yet been demonstrated empirically. But, for the sake of our analysis, we assume that it could be demonstrated. For example, given a new nonce item such as *narf* with the meaning "smelly and ugly," presented in the frame of the sentence *this is really narf*, we assume that the child will be able to produce the utterance *that's a narf apple?* If this were possible (and it seems reasonable to imagine that it could be), then we would have to say that the child had formed an item-based pattern for *narf* + *ent*. But note that, in order to formulate such a pattern, the child would have to know that positional patterns could be related to each other in terms of a system of implications (MacWhinney, 1978; Maratsos & Chalkley, 1980). Moreover, control of such a system goes far beyond the simple combinatorial strategy of the item-based pattern.

However, there is at least one other way to generate *that's a narf apple* without use of the pattern *narf* + *ent*. This is to use an analogy with a pattern such as *smelly* + *ent*. If item-based patterns are supplemented by analogy in this way, they become an extremely powerful explanatory device. Of course, such an account still begs the basic question of how the child decides what other item to choose as the basis for the analogy.

Pattern Overgeneralization. If syntax were entirely governed by item-based patterns, the acquisition of a given pattern would not be influenced by the variety or frequency of patterns of a similar structure. However, there is a variety of evidence indicating that there are item-based patterns that are in competition with certain more general patterns. For example, up to about age eight, children have trouble with the interpretation of sentences with *easy* (Cambon & Sinclair, 1974; p. 135; C. Chomsky, 1969; Cromer, 1970; pp. 401–402; Kessel, 1970, pp. 38, 49 but see Morsbach & Steel, 1976, p. 445). *Easy* requires that the patient be initialized. This goes against the prevailing *actor* + *action* pattern in English that is discussed in the next section. Similarly, the verb *promise* specifies that the actor of the main clause will also be the actor in the complement clause (Maratsos, 1974b). However, most verbs that take complements stipulate that the patient of the main clause will be the actor in the complement clause. In this case, the generality of the primary pattern delays full control of *promise* until adolescence (see C. Chomsky, 1969; Goldman, 1976; Kramer, Kopf, & Luria, 1972, p. 126 and compare with C. Chomsky, 1972, and Kelleher, 1973).

Synchrony in Development.   A third problem with the item-based pattern is its inability to account for across-the-board changes in uses of a group of lexical items. Bellugi (1971), Klima and Bellugi (1966), and Miller and Ervin (1964) report that movement of the auxiliary to sentence initial position in yes–no questions comes in at about the same time for all auxiliaries. If initialization were learned item by item, we would not expect such simultaneity. To the degree that simultaneity occurs, we must imagine that some principle stronger than the item-based pattern is at work.

The Semantics of the Nucleus.   The fourth major problem with the item-based pattern as formulated in this section is that it relies on the use of a single semantic feature to characterize the nucleus. For example, the pattern *my + entity* relies on the feature "entity" as a characterization of the nucleus. In nonsemantic terms, this nucleus would be called a noun or a noun phrase. In many cases, it is clear that nouns are in fact entities. However, if the nucleus is one like *arriving late on Saturday night,* then the "entity" quality of the nucleus is far less transparent (Ross, 1972). In the next section, we see how the notion of meaning as a set of vectors can be used to increase the explanatory power of the feature-based pattern. We see then how the expanded semantic account can also be applied to the item-based pattern.

The Ability to Operate on Structures.   Perhaps the most interesting but elusive of our grammatical abilities is that of forming paraphrases (Gleitman & Gleitman, 1970). Closely related to this are the abilities to rewrite passages (Hunt, 1969), reinterpret sentences (Lashley, 1951), detect grammaticality (Gleitman, Gleitman, & Shipley, 1972), and monitor contradiction (Markman, 1979). All of these abilities seem to depend on use of a representation of the structure of the sentence that far transcends the level of the item-based pattern. Later, we discuss these abilities in greater detail.

One further type of objection that may be raised against the notion of an item-based pattern is that it requires excessive learning of individual lexical frames, and that it therefore fails to capture a series of "significant generalizations" regarding syntactic classes. However, if such generalizations are real, we should be able to detect their influence, and establish these influences as separate limitations on the power of item-based patterns.

Free Rules

The next level of complexity that must be added to our theory is the level of the free rule or feature-based pattern. The feature-based pattern differs from the item-based pattern in that both the operator and the nucleus are characterized in terms of a set of semantic features or vectors. As a result, the feature-based pattern does not depend on lexical information; rather it is lexically free.

Our discussion of feature-based patterns is in five sections. First, we consider data on the general role of an *actor + action* pattern in early English child language. Second, we consider data on a variety of other feature-based patterns in several languages. Third, we consider in detail the internal structure of the *actor + action* pattern and then the internal structures of other feature-based patterns. On the basis of this discussion, we propose a more complex account for the semantics of both item-based and feature-based patterns. Fourth, we compare the revised notions of item-based and feature-based patterns in terms of explanatory power. Finally, we consider certain problems with all semantically based positional patterns in English.

Evidence for the Actor + Action Pattern

In English, it is usually the case that, if a noun plays the role of the actor, then it usually appears before the verb. Of course, this pattern is reversed in the passive. However, the correlation seems to be good enough to induce children to formulate an *actor + action* feature-based pattern. Evidence for the reality of this pattern can be found in (1) early spontaneous productions; (2) elicited production; (3) comprehension as measured by enactment; and (4) comprehension as measured by verification. In early spontaneous productions in English (Bloom, 1970; Bowerman, 1973; Braine, 1976; Brown, Cazden, & Bellugi, 1968; Greenfield & Smith, 1976; Leonard, 1976), many children exhibit a consistent placement of the agent/actor before the action. Similar results have been reported for Finnish (Bowerman, 1973) and Swedish (Lange & Larsson, 1973). In Samoan, which has VSO order, Kernan (1969) found evidence for consistent use of an *action + agent* pattern. Throughout the preschool years, children continue to rely on this pattern and, as a result, spontaneous use of the passive is a fairly late development (Harwood, 1959; Leopold, 1953; Slobin, 1966). When called upon to describe pictures in which the object is focused and salient, even older children resist use of the passive (Turner & Rommetveit, 1967) and use the *actor + action* order. When asked to enact reversible passive sentences, children tend to choose the noun before the verb as the actor (Beilin, 1975; Bever, 1970; Braine & Wells, 1978; Chapman & Miller, 1975, p. 365; de Villiers & de Villiers, 1974; Dewart, 1972, Huttenlocher, Eisenberg, & Strauss, 1968; Maratsos, 1974a; p. 570, Sinclair & Bronckart, 1972, p. 337, Strohner & Nelson, 1974). When asked to enact NNV sentences, children choose the noun before the verb as the actor (Bates, McNew, MacWhinney, & Smith, 1980; Lempert & Kinsbourne, 1980). And, when children are asked to judge whether sentences are true or false, they seem to assume that the noun preceding the verb is the actor (Beilin, 1975; Gaer, 1969; Slobin, 1966; Suci & Hamacher, 1972, p. 44; and Turner & Rommetveit, 1967, p. 657).

A variety of evidence suggests that this pattern is not fully stable in comprehension until after the third year. Thus, for nonreversible sentences like *the door pushes the cat,* it has been found that 2 year olds fail to take the first noun as actor. This has been demonstrated both by the use of enactment (Chapman & Kohn, 1977, p. 27, Chapman & Miller, 1975, p. 365; Strohner & Nelson, 1974, p. 570) and by various acceptability response measures (de Villiers & de Villiers, 1972, p. 307; Kramer, 1977; Petretic & Tweney, 1976, p. 205; Shipley et al., 1969; Wetstone & Friedlander, 1973, p. 738). Using the enactment technique, de Villiers and de Villiers (1972, p. 335) and Sinclair and Bronckart (1972, p. 339) have shown that 2 year olds also fail to uniformly apply the *actor + action* pattern to reversible sentences. Thus, it appears that use of the *actor + action* pattern in comprehension is fairly unstable in 2 year olds. Moreover, cross-sectional data suggest that young children rely very little on word order as a cue to the actor role, depending instead on relative potency and activity. As a result, they often enact passives correctly. However, around age 3;8, many children start to apply the *actor + action* pattern more strictly. As a result, their comprehension of passive sentences actually declines in accuracy (Bever, 1970; de Villiers & de Villiers, 1974, p. 336; Maratsos, 1974a; Sinclair & Bronckart, 1972, p. 335; and Strohner & Nelson, 1974, p. 570). Eventually the child learns to rely on both word order and semantic cues such as potency as cues to the actor role. Word order is overridden only when the morphemes associated with the passive are also present.

Evidence for Early Use of Other Feature-Based Patterns

Braine (1976) reviews much of the diary evidence for early use of feature-based patterns. In English, he reviews data for six children. We have already noted that many of these children use an *actor + action* pattern. In addition, there is evidence for several other feature-based patterns. Thus, Kendall I (Bowerman, 1973) seems to have acquired a *possessor + possessed* pattern and a *located + location* pattern; Kendall II seems to have these patterns together with an *action + location* pattern and an *identified + identification* pattern; and Jonathan II (Braine, 1976, p. 34) seems to use the *possessor + possessed, modifier + modified,* and *located + location* patterns productively. Braine notes that the *modifier + modified* pattern is not fully congealed in Jonathan II and that Jonathan may have more specific patterns such as *size + entity.* David II (Braine, 1976, p. 44) has some evidence for use of an *action + object* pattern. In Samoan, Tofi (Kernan, 1969) uses both an *action + object* pattern and an *action + location* pattern and Sipili uses a *possessed + possessor* pattern. In English,

Bates et al. (1980) have shown that children interpret VNN strings as VOS sentences, thus evidencing use of an *action* and *object* pattern.

The Internal Structure of Grammatical Concepts

Up to this point, we have treated the notion of the actor as a single unified concept. In this section, we see why this simple formulation is untenable. We examine an alternative formulation that treats grammatical categories in terms of clusters of vectors rather than single semantic features. For our present purposes, all we need to assume is that the decision to place an item into a given semantic role is influenced by a variety of converging data sources rather than some single criterial attribute. Following MacWhinney (in press b), each of these data sources is called a "vector." There are many consequences of this analysis for language history and linguistic analysis (Bates & MacWhinney, in press). However, in this section and the next we confine our attention to the internal structure of grammatical concepts as they are reflected in positional patterns.

There is evidence that the decision to treat an item as an actor in English is influenced by at least four semantic vectors: potency, mobility, causation, and perspective. Of course, there are a variety of syntactic vectors promoting the choice of a noun as an actor. These include preverbal positioning (i.e., *actor + action* patterning), placement in an agential by-clause, and postcopula placement in clefts when no other noun occurs in preverbal position. The control of these vectors is discussed later. For the present, however, we focus on the four semantic vectors. Tests of these vectors usually require manipulation of the positional pattern so that the actor does not always appear in preverbal position.

Potency.   There is a fair amount of evidence that potency and/or animacy is a major attribute of the actor in English. In tests of comprehension with nonreversible sentences, it is possible to obtain evidence for use of potency as an evidential vector (MacWhinney, in press b) for the actor role. For example, given a sentence like *the ball bit the dog,* children will assume that it was the dog who did the biting. We refer to this as the "potency strategy." Very young children seem to be quite dependent on this strategy. Strohner and Nelson (1974) and Chapman and Miller (1975, p. 365) found a high reliance on the potency strategy in their 1- to 3-year-old subjects. Although Strohner and Nelson found this strategy to be strong for both 2 and 3 year olds, Chapman and Miller found some decrease in use of potency from 1;11 to 2;8.

There then follows a slow but continual decline in the use of the potency strategy from 1;11 to 12;0. During the period from 3 to 5 years, Grimm, Scholer, and Wintermantel (1975, p. 88) working in German and Strohner and Nelson (1974, p. 569) working in English found that there was a decrease in use of the strategy for both actives and passives. However, Strohner and Nelson (1974) found that this decrease was faster for actives than for passives. Throughout the period from 6 to 12 years, children show a minimal use of the potency strategy for actives. For passives, however, the strategy has some importance at age 6, but declines in importance throughout the period (Beilin, 1975, p. 48; Grimm et al., 1975, p. 88; Powers & Gowie, 1977; and Slobin, 1966, p. 226).

The role of the potency strategy in production is more difficult to assess. In early productions, the first of two nouns is usually the most potent. Of course, it is also most often the mover, the causer, the topic, and so forth. Because these roles are confounded in spontaneous production, researchers have relied on preference judgments and sentence completion tasks as indices of possible production biases. Sentence completion studies by H. Clark (1965), Jarvella and Sinnott (1972), and Kail and Segui (1978) show that older children and adults prefer sentences that begin with potent nouns. Dewart (1975) asked children to choose referents for nonsense words in NVN sentences. She found that 3 year olds had a very strong bias towards choice of an animate referent for the first noun but that this preference was somewhat less in 5 year olds. This decline in reliance on the dimension of animacy or potency parallels the decline found in the studies of sentence comprehension.

Mobility.   In a series of studies, Huttenlocher and her associates (Huttenlocher et al., 1968; Huttenlocher & Strauss, 1968; Huttenlocher & Weiner, 1971) have shown that 9- and 10-year-old children comprehend sentences most readily when the noun that is placed in the role of actor by the syntax is also mobile. Dewart (1972, p. 201) replicated the results of Huttenlocher et al (1968) and found that 5 and 6 year olds made more errors in understanding sentences when the actor was immobile than when no context was given.

The importance of motion as an aspect of the actor role can also be assessed by comparing treatment of moving and nonmoving participants. Braine and Wells (1978) have shown that children's judgments regarding semantic roles are more consistent for actors than for experiencers. And Leonard (1976) has shown that very young children assimilate new terms to the actor role before they assimilate them to the experiencer role.

Causation.   Anderson (1976) has argued that the prototypical actor is the causal agent of the transitive clause—that is, the ergative. In fact, Schieffelin (1979) reports that children learning Kaluli, an ergative language, almost never overgeneralize the ergative to the noncausal actor—that is, the absolutive in intransitive clauses. This suggests that the notion of causality is particularly clear to at least some very young children, and that they find it easy to relate this concept to specific surface devices.

Perspective.   Dewart (1975, cited in Cromer, 1976, p. 307) found that 3 and 4 year olds who did not know the passive could be induced into a correct interpretation of passive sentences by setting up a prior perspective. For example, given the sequence *bad duck # the cat was bitten by the duck,* children would choose the "duck" as the ator in the enactment task. Alternatively, given the sequence *poor cat # the cat was bitten by the duck,* children would still choose the duck as the actor. However, these same children were unable to correctly enact passive sentences without this perspective cue.

In the Dewart experiment, the preamble serves to establish either an active perspective (*bad duck*) or a passive perspective (*poor cat*). This perspective is then maintained into the next clause. MacWhinney (1977) suggested that the starting point of a sentence establishes a perspective that is then maintained until it is overtly canceled by some new perspective. At each juncture, the perspective will be assumed to be the actor unless otherwise marked. In a sentence like *Bill was told by Tom that his picture was hanging in the Post Office,* neither "Bill" nor "he" are actors. However, the perspective of "Bill" seems to be maintained enough for most speakers to establish its identity with "he." As we note later, perspective maintenance is one aspect of a general parallel-function strategy (Sheldon, 1974). This effect of perspective maintenance seems to be of particular importance between clauses within a sentence. In particular, perspective maintenance seems to be involved in the interpretation and production of relatives, complements, and conjoined clauses. Of course, perspective maintenance is not the only factor involved in the processing of complex sentences. However, as we see later, there is reason to believe that English-speaking children often attempt to process complex sentences by assuming the perspective of the first preverbal noun.

The first major area where perspective maintenance has been studied is in the interpretation of relative clauses. In a variety of experiments, children have been asked to enact sentences like these:

21. SS: The dog that chased the cat kicked the horse.
22. SO: The dog that the cat chased kicked the horse.
23. OO: The dog chased the cat that the horse kicked.
24. OS: The dog chased the cat that kicked the horse.

The perspective maintenance hypothesis holds that, in terms of ease of enactment, the sentences should be ordered in this way: SS > OO~OS > SO. The explanation for this ordering is as follows: Sentences of the SS type can be correctly interpreted without conducting any perspective shift. Both OO and OS sentences require a single perspective shift. Thus, in the OO type, the shift occurs once the NN sequence is encountered. In the OS type, the shift occurs when the object noun (i.e., "the cat") is followed by a relative pronoun. In both cases, there is a surface syntactic cue signaling a perspective shift. Both OO and OS are, therefore, predicted to be harder to understand than SS. However, SO sentences should be the hardest of all because they require a double perspective shift. The first shift, from "the dog" to "the cat," occurs upon detection of an NN sequence. Then, following "chased," the child must return perspective to the dog. Because of this double perspective shift, SO is predicted to be harder than OO, OS, or SS. Thus, the five specific predictions are: SS > OS, SS > OO, SS > SO, OS > SO, and OO > SO. Some of these predictions are also generated by alternative hypotheses such as the parallel-function hypothesis (Sheldon, 1974), the adjacency principle (Sheldon, 1977b), the "bird-in-the-hand" approach (Legum, 1975), the avoid-interruptions principle (Slobin, 1973), the first-NP-as-agent strategy (Bever, 1970), the conjoined-clause hypothesis (Tavakolian, 1978), and others. However, the particular set of five predictions just given is unique to the perspective-shift hypothesis.

The data from the various enactment studies support these predictions quite strongly: (1) the superiority of SS over OS is supported by Aller, Aller, and Trover (1979), H. Brown (1971), Ferreiro, Othenin-Girard, Chipman, and Sinclair (1976, p. 237), Fluck (1977, p. 62; 1978, p. 195), Lahey (1974, p. 665), Legum (1975, cited by Sheldon, 1977 , p. 54), Sheldon (1974a), and Tavakolian (1978); (2) the superiority of SS over OO is supported by Brown (1971), Ferreiro et al. (1976, p. 237), Grimm et al. (1975, p. 124), Legum (1975), and Tavakolian (1978); (3) the superiority of SS over SO is supported by Aller et al. (1979), Brown (1971), de Villiers, Tager-Flusberg, and Hakuta (1977), Ferreiro et al. (1976), Grimm et al. (1975, p. 124), Legum (1975), Sheldon (1974, 1977a), and Tavakolian (1978); (4) the superiority of OS over SO is supported by Brown (1971), de Villiers et al. (1977), Ferreiro et al. (1976), Legum (1975), Sheldon (1974, 1977a), and Tavakolian (1978); and (5) the superiority of OO over SO is supported by Aller et al. (1979), Brown (1971), de Villiers et al. (1977), Ferreiro et al. (1976), Legum (1975), Sheldon (1974, 1977a), and Tavakolian (1978).

The only exceptions to the five predictions of the perspective-maintenance hypothesis are failures to find significant differences. There are no significant reversals. Aller et al. failed to find SS superior to OS or OS superior to SO; de Villiers et al. failed to find SS superior to OS or SS superior to OO; and Sheldon failed to find SS superior to OO. In each case, the failure to find the predicted relations could be interpreted as the result of a ceiling effect. Therefore, no true counterinstance to the perspective-maintenance hypothesis for the enactment of sentences with relative clauses has yet been detected.

However, using a task that measured latency to comprehension, Foss, Bias, and Starkey (1977) were able to show that OO sentences could be processed faster and with fewer mistakes than SS sentences. Given sentences like examples 21 or 24, children were asked "Who kicked the horse?" Latency to response was taken as a direct measure of comprehension. Foss et al. interpreted their results as supporting Slobin's (1973) proposal regarding the listener's tendency to avoid interruptions. The longer latency in SS sentences is then attributed to the separation of the subject of the main clause from its verb. One way of reconciling the results of Foss et al. with the results of the enactment studies is to view relatedness as previously discussed as of greater importance during the initial processing of a sentence and perspective (another predisposition) as of greatest importance during the imitation and/or subsequent reenactment of the sentence.

By way of an aside, it is important to recognize that these results regarding perspective maintenance are limited to the comprehension of sentences when no context is provided. Ferreiro et al. (1976, p. 250) have found that comprehension can be greatly facilitated by providing a motivation for use of the relative clause. For example, if the child is shown two people, one who paints self-portraits and one who is chased by a dog, it is reasonable to ask the child to act out the sentence *the person the dog chased climbs a ladder*. In such a framework, comprehension is greatly facilitated. This distinguishing or specifying function of the relative clause is also evident in production. There, Limber (1976, p. 315) and Menyuk (1969, p. 16) find that OO and OS relatives emerge before SO and SS types. Limber argues that this is because the object of the matrix sentence is more foregrounded than the subject and more in need of specification. Thus, although SS seems to be easily processed, sentences of the OS type seem to fit in more closely with overall discourse patterns.

The second area in which perspective maintenance seems to be important is in the interpretation of the actor in complement clauses. Some of the structures involved are as follows:

25. The lion wanted to go.
26. The lion wanted the pig to bump into the horse.
27. John promised Bill to go.
28. John criticized Bill for leaving too soon.
29. John apologized to Bill for leaving too soon.
30. John hit Bill standing on the platform.
31. John saw Bill standing on the platform.
32. Standing on the platform, John hit Bill.
33. The lion jumped over the pig to stand on the horse.

As a number of writers have discovered (C. Chomsky, 1969; Garvey, Caramazza, & Yates, 1975; Goodluck & Roeper, 1978; Grober, Beardsley, & Caramazza, 1978), the choice of an actor for the complement clause in these sentences is largely dependent on the identity of the main verb. As we noted earlier, it is reasonable to imagine that each verb has associated with it a set of expectations for various roles—for example, *promise* has a frame for a person who received the promise. This role follows the verb according to the positional pattern *promise + promissee*. The verb also determines whether or not the actor of the main clause will be maintained into the complement clause. The verb *criticize*, on the other hand, works to shift perspective to the person being criticized. The verb *want* shifts perspective, but only if another perspective is available. Verbs like *jump* and *hit,* as in examples 31 and 32, do not seem to have any such frames.

The perspective-maintenance hypothesis suggests that, in English, children assume that the perspective of the main clause is also the perspective and actor of the subordinate clause unless the perspective is expressly shifted to another noun. In fact, Tavakolian (1978, pp. 77,80) has found that 3 year olds interpret sentences like numbers 26 and 33 according to the perspective-maintenance principle. However, after this early period, children begin to learn that perspective maintenance is violated for the complements of many verbs. Goodluck and Roeper (1978) argue that this learning occurs verb by verb even when general semantic principles are available. Of course, perspective maintenance is never challenged in structures like numbers 25 and 32 and errors seldom arise for these forms. In the adult grammar, perspective maintenance is only challenged in the cases of sentences like numbers 26, 28, and 31. However, because number 27 is like 26, and because number 29 is like 28, and because number 30 is like 31, the weight of syntactic analogy seems to draw the perspective-maintenance principle into doubt in all but numbers 25 and 33. In any case, the child must eventually come to rely on word-by-word learning of complement restrictions, except for structures like numbers 25 and 33.

The third major area in which perspective maintenance seems important is the processing of gaps in conjoined clauses. Conjoined clauses have been studied in terms of imitation, production, and comprehension. There is evidence (Lust, 1977) that children find sentences like numbers 34 and 35 easier to imitate than sentences like numbers 36 and 37:

34. Kittens hop and ϕ run.
35. Mary cooked the meal and ϕ ate the bread.
36. The kittens ϕ and the dogs hide.
37. John baked ϕ and Mary ate the bread.

In these sentences, the phi symbol indicates where there is missing information. In numbers 34 and 35, this missing information can be filled in by looking back in the sentence; these are anaphoric gaps. In numbers 36 and 37, the gaps must be filled by looking forward in the sentences; these are cataphoric gaps. In particular, the gaps in sentences 34 and 35 can be filled by maintaining the initial perspective without any shift. The perspective-maintenance hypothesis holds that sentences 34 and 35 should be easier to imitate than 36 and 37. Moreover, children should simplify the dual perspectives in 36 and 37 by expanding them to 38 and 39, respectively:

38. The kittens hide and the dogs hide.
39. John baked the bread and Mary ate the bread.

No such expansion is predicted for sentence 40, because there is no split in perspective. In fact, sentence 41 will likely be reduced to 40:

40. Give me the oranges and ϕ the apples.
41. Give me the oranges and give me the apples.

These predictions of the perspective-maintenance hypothesis have been supported in studies of elicited imitation by Beilin (1975), Lust (1977), and Slobin and Welsh (1973). A study by de Villiers et al. (1977) also examines imitations of coordinate structures. However, the data are not reported by individual sentence type and the relative ease of sentences like numbers 34 to 41 cannot be directly determined.

In the area of the production of conjoined clauses, there are three recent studies. Lust and Mervis (1978) analyzed a corpus of 435 spontaneously produced coordinate structures. They found that 84% of the phrasal coordinations reflected the anaphoric reduction pattern. In a study of elicited production, Ardery (1979) found that children's coordinations were mostly of the types found in sentences 34, 35, and 40. In another elicited production study, Greenfield and Dent (1979) found that children used virtually no cataphoric gapping at all. Greenfield and Dent interpret this finding in terms of the fact that only anaphoric deletion serves to decrease redundancy. This account seems quite reasonable. Thus, it seems necessary to view redundancy elimination as complementary to the role of perspective maintenance in the processing of coordination. In general, the data gathered by these three studies of production seem to be congruent with the data gathered by studies of elicited imitation.

In the area of comprehension, coordinate structures have been examined principally in terms of the choice of a referent for the pronoun in the second clause of sentences like numbers 42 to 47:

42. The camel hit the lion, and then he hit the elephant.
43. The camel hit the lion, and then HE hit the elephant.
44. The camel hit the lion, and then the elephant hit him.
45. The camel hit the lion, and then the elephant hit HIM.
46. The camel hit the lion, and then he kicked him.
47. The camel hit the lion, and then HE kicked HIM.

The interpretation of sentences 42, 44, and 46 by adults is governed by the parallel-function principle, which can be stated as a generalization of the perspective-maintenance principle. The perspective-maintenance principle holds that the perspective of the main or first clause will also be the perspective of the subordinate or conjoined clause, unless perspective is expressly shifted. The parallel-function hypothesis (Akmajian, 1979; Grober et al., 1978, Sheldon,

1974) holds that the pronominal or missing referent in a second or subordinate clause will be identified with the noun that serves a parallel function in the main clause. This principle works to establish referents in sentences 42, 44, and 46. Tavakolian (1978) has shown that children do not care whether the second referent in a sentence like number 42 is pronominalized or ellipsed. In both cases, they interpret the sentence through perspective maintenance. N. Chomsky (1971) and Maratsos (1973) have shown that the parallel-function strategy is widely used by 3 and 4 year olds for sentences 42 to 47. By age 5, Maratsos (1973) found that some children could use contrastive stress, as in 43 and 45, to correctly shift reference. However, these children did better with sentences like numbers 45 than 43. This suggests that perspective maintenance as a particular type of parallel-function strategy may be a stronger than parallel function in general. Recently, Solan (1979) has examined the comprehension of sentences like 42 to 47 in 5 to 7 year olds. In this age group, parallel function seems to have lost its clear force and children actually do better on stressed sentences like numbers 43, 45, and 47 than on unstressed sentences like 42, 44, and 46. These surprising findings suggest that children may be engaged in the acquisition of some general sentence-processing strategies during this period that operate on the structure of the sentence as a whole. One possibility is that children develop a means of representing the sentence as a formal object in working memory. Having done this, they can then acquire transformations that operate on the sentence as a whole.

Interaction of Vectors.   To summarize this section, up to this point, we can say that there is evidence that children's use of the actor concept involves a vectorial convergence of syntactic and semantic data sources. Prototypically, the element chosen as the actor is supported by a strong combination of the vectors for potency, mobility, causation, and perspective. In production, such an element will be placed before the verb. Conversely, in comprehension, the children generally assume that the element before the verb is the one that has potency, mobility, causation, and perspective. Eventually, children also learn to counterbalance the word-order vector by a vector for the passive morphemes when those morphemes occur.

Other Grammatical Categories.   Bates and MacWhinney (in press) have suggested that this type of analysis can be extended to grammatical concepts in general. Thus, one could speak of the vectors present for a prototypical verb (Bloom, Lightbown, & Hood, 1975; Bowerman, 1973, p. 210; Leonard, 1976); those for a prototypical direct object (Bowerman, 1973, p. 208, 1978; Braine & Wells, 1978); a prototypical instrument (Duchan & Lund, 1979, p. 243); a prototypical locative (Braine & Wells, 1978); a prototypical past tense (Antinucci & Miller, 1976; Bronckart & Sinclair, 1963); and a prototypical modifier (Richards, 1979, p. 225).

However, in English, for these particular concepts, only the *action + object* and *modifier + modified* patterns are conventionalized word-order patterns. The acquisition of modifier ordering before the noun in English is particularly interesting, because nouns may be preceded by long strings of adjectives. Several writers have noted that adjectives seem to be ordered along some general semantic dimension. Sweet (1898) called this "denotativeness"; Martin (1969) called it "definiteness"; Bever (1970) called it "nouniness"; and Danks and Glucksberg (1972) called it "intrinsicalness." These dimensions are clearly related to the tendency for some modifiers to be placed closer to the noun. However, it is doubtful that full adult control of adjective ordering can rely on this predisposition. Quirk, Greenbaum, Leech, and Svartvik (1972, p. 267) have suggested that adjective ordering could be controlled by something like a set of feature-based patterns that place adjectives in this order: (1) intensification; (2) number; (3) subjective measure; (4) size or shape; (5) age; (6) color; (7) material; and (8) provenance, or material. For example, ordering of *big, rubber,* and *ball* would rely on use of the pattern *size + material,* as well as the general *modifier + modified* pattern. In fact, Richards (1979) presents data suggesting that 4 and 5 year olds may not yet be in control of the full set of particular patterns like *size + material* and *numeral + age.* Both Richards (1979) and Scheffelin (1971) show that the most basic patterns begin to emerge after age 5, but Martin and Molfese (1972) show that even by age 14 adolescents had not mastered the full adult system. The general pattern that seems to emerge from these studies is one of the slow acquisition of a series of particular feature-based patterns for the different types of adjectives.

However, some of the data presented by Bever (1970) and Richards (1979) seem, at first, to contradict this interpretation. Bever (1970) found that 3 year olds had essentially adult-like preferences for adjective-order retention in imitation. However, Bever's methodology has been strongly criticized by Martin and Molfese (1972) and Richards (1979), both of whom also present data contradicting Bever's findings. At the same time, Richards (1979) reports that 3 year olds are more like adults in their production of adjective strings than are 4 and 5 year olds. Although Richards presents few examples of 3-year-old adjective strings, it may well be that they include many rote orderings such as *big fat, little round,* and *nice clean.* By using rote, 3 year olds could appear to have adult-like rules, whereas 5 year olds might be attempting to string adjectives together without knowing the various feature-based rules that govern their combination.

Reformulation of the Notion of a "Feature." In the preceding section, we examined in detail the internal structure of the actor category and considered briefly several other categories that figure in free rules. These facts suggest that a fundamental revision be made in the way that both item-based and feature-based patterns were previously defined. For the item-based pattern, the revision is that the semantics of the nucleus should be represented by a set of semantic vectors.

For the feature-based pattern, both the operator and the nucleus are defined as a set of semantic features that interact in a vectorial fashion.

Item-Based Patterns Versus Feature-Based Patterns

We are now in a position to compare the relative generative power of item-based and feature-based patterns. The main point to observe is that, if we allow analogy to operate on item-based patterns, they start to resemble feature-based patterns. Thus, a child could produce *narf apple* on analogy with *red apple*. But, as King (1969), MacWhinney (1975b), and many others have argued, the problem with analogy is that it fails to tell us how the speaker selects the form to serve as the basis of the analogy. The power of the feature-based pattern is that it can account for productivity and error without ad hoc recourse to analogy.

However, in the case of certain pseudopassive verbs like *receive* and *belong*, there is some reason to prefer an item-based account of word ordering to a feature-based account. For example in sentences like numbers 48 and 49, the word before the verb is not as much an actor as the word following the verb:

48. Mary received a letter from Jane.
49. The tree belongs to Tim.

For such verbs, item-based patterns like *recipient + receive* and *object owned + belong* could successfully control word ordering. Because fairly young children are able to successfully control the syntax of *please, like, own, belong, take*, and *receive* (Maratsos & Chalkley, 1980), it is likely that at least some item-based patterns are being used.

Inadequacies of All Semantically Based Positional Patterns

Both the item-based pattern and the feature-based pattern involve the prediction and control of word order on the basis of the semantic properties of the words being ordered. Item-based patterns are bound to specific lexical items, whereas feature-based patterns are lexically free. It is also possible to imagine a type of rule that is bound not to a single lexical item, but to a whole network or class of lexical items. Such a rule type is involved in the control of systems such as the marking of gender (i.e., declension) on the German article (MacWhinney, 1978). In fact, many morphophonological systems make extensive use of rules with different degrees of binding to lexical structures. However, it remains to be seen whether syntax also shows nonsemantic lexical classes of this type. If there exist word classes that have no consistent or usable semantic bases, then it is clear that no combination of predispositions, item-based patterns, and feature-based patterns can be fully sufficient as an account of syntactic combination. Rather, we need to consider a way in which arbitrary cooccurrence classes can be acquired and utilized. What evidence is there, then, for the reality of nonsemantic classes in syntax?

Nonsemantic Class-Bound Positional Patterns

There seem to be at least four types of evidence that can be cited in support of the inadequacy of semantic classes and the need for nonsemantic classes. These four are: (1) category interpenetration; (2) lack of privileges for the prototype; (3) deduction of class membership; and (4) the ability to operate on surface structure. Let us examine each of these four types of evidence.

Category Interpenetration

Maratsos and Chalkley (1980) argue that there is a class of "process" adjectives like *variable, fond, nice, noisy,* and *aware* that are semantically indistinguishable from process verbs like *vary, like, treat well, make noise,* and *know.* Given this extreme overlap of categories, one would expect to find errors like *he fonds the dog* and *I am like of him.* Maratsos and Chalkley argue that, because such errors are vanishingly rare, there must be a firmer basis for the separation of adjectives from verbs than the semantic features (+ state) and (+ process). Following Braine (1963, 1971), they suggest that this firmer basis is a reliance on the network of semantic-distributional patterns that constitutes a class. Adjectives can occur in the frames: be_____, is_____, _____NP, and so on, whereas verbs can occur in the frames: _____ed, am _____ing, and will_____. According to Maratsos and Chalkley, the basis for the separation between classes is not some semantic feature or set of features, but the facts of correlated distributional uses.

Before considering Maratsos and Chalkley's basic argument regarding category interpenetration, we should note some facts about the behavior of these borderline "process" adjectives. When words like *fond, nice,* and *aware* stand alone as prenominal modifiers or predicate adjectives, they act as states. However, when they are combined with particles, they act more nearly like processes. For example, we can say that *Mary is a fond mother* or we can say *Mary is fond of Mark.* In the former case, the stative qualities of *fond* are emphasized, whereas in the latter case, the processual qualities are focused. Formally and semantically, these adjectives seem to form a third class at the border between states (adjectives) and processes (verbs). In general, adjectives of this type indicate a state that arises from and gives rise to a process—for instance, a noisy door often makes noises and nice parents often treat their children well. Furthermore, note that verbs like *consist* (*of*) and *compare* (*with*) also require particles and also have a similar process/state ambiguity.

This ambiguity in the stative quality of certain adjectives is important to the interpretation of a further supporting argument offerred by Maratsos and Chalkley. They note that one can say *be obnoxious* and *be nice to Bill.* They reason that the use of *be* in such phrases cannot be governed by the feature (+ process), because that would mean that a process was being treated as a state by the copula. However, a somewhat different semantic analysis of the adjectives suggests a different interpretation of these phrases. According to this account, adjectives like obnoxious and nice involve a process that characteristically places the actor into a state. Thus, by committing certain disagreeable acts, a person enters into the state of being obnoxious. If we say to someone *be obnoxious,* we mean for that person to commence those actions that will lead towards entry into the state of obnoxiousness. Thus, the copula is in fact referring to a process, even though the adjective itself refers, at least in part, to a state.

Returning now to the basic argument regarding category interpenetration, it is important to recognize that, on some level, the semantics of *fond* and *like* show a real overlap. However, speakers seem to be able to deal with this problem by "stativizing" *fond* and "processualizing" *like*. In the next section, we discuss how this might be achieved.

Deduction of Class Membership

There is reason to believe that acquisition of the semantics of lexical items depends heavily on their appearance in specific syntactic contexts. When adults hear the sentence *this is narf,* they know that *narf* must be a modifier. That is, they know that *narf* describes some characteristic of certain entities. Thus, it is clear that adults can use semantic–distributional frames such as *this is +* X to infer aspects of the semantics of lexical items. Moreover, there is good evidence that young children can make similar inferences. For example, at age 1;11, my son Ross referred to his sleeper as a *warm;* he would say *no warm, want warm,* and *my warm.* In these utterances, the word *warm* occurs in an item-based pattern that requires an entity as a nucleus. It seems, then, that Ross assumed that *warm* was the name for a sleeper. This is not surprising, because he learned the word at 1;10,16 from my utterance *this is warm.* Although an adult would recognize that the absence of an article meant that the word was an adjective or a mass noun, Ross failed to detect the missing article and ended up treating *warm* as a count noun. Errors of this type are quite frequent (MacWhinney, 1974) for very young children, because the exact shape of the major syntactic frames has not yet been fully determined. These errors underscore the importance of this deductive process at even the youngest ages. However, it is important to distinguish the deduction of semantic features from the deduction of arbitrary formal class. MacWhinney (1978, p. 48) found that the ability to deduce arbitrary formal class may not emerge until age 5. The ability to deduce semantic content, on the other hand, is evidenced even before 2;0.

Lack of Privileges for the Prototype

Prototype theory, according to Maratsos and Chalkley (1980), predicts that central instances of a category will enjoy more privileges of occurrence than noncentral instances. However, in English, peripheral adjectives like *obnoxious* can occur in even more frames than core adjectives like *red*. Thus, according to Maratsos and Chalkley, prototype theory seems to be violated. The problem with this argument is that prototype theory is not committed to this particular identification of the operative prototypes with the traditional parts of speech. Rather, it is necessary to talk about prototypes as they relate to specific positional patterns in specific languages. Thus, as previously noted, English syntax tends to distinguish process-initiating statives like *noisy* from pure statives like *red*. Moreover, in the case of modifiers, syntax makes fine distinctions between provenance, shape, quality, etc. (Quirk et al., 1972). In general, then, one must know what syntactic rules are involved with what semantic structures in order to state how prototypes should operate for a given language.

A somewhat different version of this same argument has been advanced by Kuczaj, Maratsos, Fox & Chalkley (1979) in regard to the acquisition of the English past tense. If the past suffix had the frame *verb + ed,* Kuczaj argues, then we should expect that this rule should apply earlier to verbs that are more prototypically "verbal" than to verbs that are less prototypically verbal. Following this line of reasoning, we would expect errors like *breaked* and *hitted* to appear earlier than *thoughted* or *knowed.* However, no such difference between action verbs and mental-process verbs actually appears in Kuczaj's data. Thus, this version of prototype theory fails to receive support.

The problem with this line of analysis is the same as the problem with Maratsos and Chalkley's analysis of adjectives' privileges of occurrence. In both cases, prototype theory is assumed to relate only to the traditional parts of speech. However, the version of prototype theory that was presented in the section *Free Rules* assumes no such relation. Rather, each item-based or feature-based pattern stipulates its own set of semantic vectors. The past-tense positional pattern stipulates a feature set like (+ process, + mental activity), whereas the present progressive *be + ing* stipulates (+ action) and excludes (+ mental activity). For example, we can say *I wanted,* but not *I am wanting.*

The arguments presented by Maratsos and Chalkley and Kuczaj on this issue are of real importance. They show that one very simple version of prototype theory will fail to account for certain aspects of even the earliest stages of language acquisition. However, these arguments seem to be reasonably well addressed by the notions of item-based and feature-based patterns, as they have been presented in this chapter. Moreover, syntactic devices that operate on standard categories should be sensitive to the prototype structure of those categories. For example, Sinclair, Sinclair, and deMarcellus (1971), and Turner and Rommetveit (1968) have found that passives are first acquired for active verbs and causal subjects.

The Ability to Operate upon Surface Structure

Eventually, all school children learn to perform operations upon sentences. They learn to parse sentences into phrases and clauses, to rewrite according to specifications, to perform specific transformations, and to make judgments regarding synonymity, ambiguity, and acceptability. These skills could conceivably operate on semantic classes. However, it seems likely that, at some point, the child uses his or her knowledge of formal classes to achieve a full structural representation of the sentence. The control of contrastively stressed pronouns (Solan, 1978), clefts, dislocations, adjective reorderings (Schwenk & Danks, 1974), passives (Olson & Nickerson, 1977), and raising transformations may require the child to represent the sentence as a whole and then to operate on this representation. It seems likely that this representation would make use of information about formal classes. However, an examination of this possibility lies outside of the scope of the present chapter.

SYNTAX AND MORPHOPHONOLOGY: AN ANALOGY

Application

In MacWhinney (1978), the language-acquisition device was interpreted in terms of three types of processing: application, monitoring, and acquisition. The present chapter has focused on the system of application. We have examined a set of six strategies in string formation and have found that none is sufficient to account for syntactic development, but that each is necessary. The six strategies are rote, analogy, predispositions, simple bound rules, free rules, and class-bound rules. Each of these six strategies corresponds to one of the six strategies in morphophonological application that were proposed in MacWhinney (1978).

In both systems, rote involves the use of a multimorphemic string as a single unit. Morphophonological rote involves single complex words whereas syntactic rote involves word strings. However, from the child's point of view, this distinction is moot. In morphophonology, analogy uses the sound structure of some rote form as a guide to the sound structure of some new form. In syntax, analogy uses the morpheme order in some rote unit as a guide to the placement of some new material into a similar string.

In combination, both morphophonology and syntax are subject to predispositions. In morphophonology, predispositions derive from phonology. They include both phonotactic rules (i.e., morpheme-structure conditions) and segment-structure conditions. In syntax, predispositions relate to the sequencing of lexicalization decisions. Both morphophonology and syntax also make use of free rules. In morphophonology, these rules change segments or features without regard to lexical information. MacWhinney (1978) speaks of these free rules as "modifications." In syntax, free rules are the feature-based positional patterns previously discussed. Both morphophonology and syntax also make use of bound patterns. In syntax, the item-based pattern is bound to a lexical item. It specifies a choice between prepositioning and postpositioning in a given context. In morphophonology, selections are bound to specific lexical items. They specify a choice between allomorphs of a morph in a given context. The fourth class of combinatorial pattern, the class-bound rule, corresponds to the paradigmatic

TABLE 3.1
Levels of Application in Morphophonology and Linearization

	Morphophonology		Linearization	
Process	Level-Specific Term	Example	Level-Specific Term	Example
Rote	Amalgam	*jumped*	Amalgam, idiom, phrase	*short shrift*
Analogy	Analogy	*narves* (on *scarves*)	Replacement, analogy	*gonna he go*
Predisposition	Phonotactic constraints	voicing assimilation	Lexicalization order	"informativeness"
Free rule	Modification	vowel harmony	Feature-based pattern	*actor + action*
Bound rule	Selection	*wife, wives*	Item-set pattern	my ____
Class-bound rule	Paradigmatic selection	*den Mann*	Formal phrase structure	"part of speech"

selection in morphophonology. In syntax, class-bound rules are governed by the classes traditionally known as the "parts of speech." In morphophonology, class-bound rules are governed by membership in declensional and conjugational classes. Table 3.1 summarizes the analogy between morphophonology and syntax. For a fuller characterization of rule types in morphophonology, the reader should consult MacWhinney (1978). For additional discussion of the consequences of the analogy, consult MacWhinney (in press a).

We see, then, that each of the six basic strategies in syntax corresponds to a basic strategy in morphophonology. On the basis of this analogy, we might risk the following speculations: In any given problem domain (at least in language and related domains), solutions can be formulated by rote, analogy, or combination. Within combination, predispositions will operate between structural/ information-processing levels. They will force more abstract levels to adapt to the constraints of processing more concrete levels. All domains will also make use of free rules and bound rules. Finally, in many domains, we should expect to encounter class-bound rules that operate on formally defined classes of items. These six levels and their interactions should be operative in a wide variety of domains, including spelling, phonology, composition, drawing, semantics, and mathematics.

If we were to extend the analogy given in Table 3.1 to phonology and lexical semantics (what MacWhinney, in press a, calls "lexology"), we might expect to find something like the analysis that is presented in Table 3.2. In the case of phonology, rote would lead to the use of phonological idioms, such as those first reported by Leopold (1949). Analogy would rely on some well-learned word or canonical form to serve as the basis for other productions. Predispositions would impose articulatory constraints on segmental structures. The various levels of

TABLE 3.2
Levels of Application in Phonology and Lexology

	Phonology		Lexology	
Process	Level-Specific Term	Example	Level-Specific Term	Example
Rote	Phonological idions	pretty	Amalgams, portmanteaus	"dogs"
Analogy	Extension by canonical forms	spoon → pu	Semantically based analogy	deer, fish
Predispositions	Phonetic constraints	segment structure	Natural construal	under → in
Free rules	Target modifications	VOT	General construal, agreement, conflation	subject–verb agreement
Bound rules	Feature assimilations, allophony	nasal assimilation	Selections, homonymy	red→ Communist

combinatorial rules would affect either segments, features, or the target values of the motor movements underlying features.

In lexology (i.e., the semantics of lexical combinations), rote would select a lexical amalgam to refer to an exactly matching referent (Carey, 1978, p. 289). Analogy would produce a combination on the basis of a complex amalgam with a similar meaning. Predispositions would be natural tendencies towards specific construals (E. Clark, 1973; G. Miller, 1978). On the various levels of combinatorial rules, construal patterns would select between alternative readings of specific lexes. Further ideas regarding the application of rote, analogy, and combination in lexical semantics can be found in MacWhinney (in press a).

Acquisition

This section outlines the central processes in form acquisition and sketches out informally the major predictions that arise from the hypothesized analogy between morphophonology and syntax. These processes and predictions are discussed in relation to the three major strategies in application: rote, analogy, and combination. For details regarding the specific predictions, see MacWhinney (in press, a).

In syntax, as in morphology, the child will acquire items that: (1) are intonationally salient; (2) comprise entire intonation units; (3) refer to aspects of activities or perceptions that are important to the child; (4) are produced in the context of a clear referent within the situation; (5) are not too long; and (6) do not involve too many phonological structures outside of the child's control. Once a rote phrasal unit is acquired, the child may begin to subject it to semantic analysis. If this analysis is successful, an attempt at lexical/morphemic analysis may soon follow. In particular, children will attempt to analyze rote strings when they contain embedded semantic clusters that they want to use.

The continued use of an unanalyzed rote string will be promoted by several factors. If the item is semantically unanalyzable or opaque (i.e., *short shrift*), there will be a tendency to preserve the unit as a whole. If it is used frequently, it will be maintained and its latency to lexicalization will decrease to a certain floor value. In general, rote items will be able to preserve all sorts of phonological, semantic, and syntactic irregularities against the pressures of analysis and regularization.

Children may also acquire rote forms out of their own combinatorial productions. This will occur when a given combination is used so frequently that its unitization facilitates processing in both comprehension and production.

Analogy

When children do not have rote forms to express certain meanings, they may produce word strings by analogy. However, in English syntax, most analogies will lead directly to the emergence of new combinatorial rules. In a few areas of irregular syntax, such as the use of archaisms and idioms, analogy may continue to be important. In general, analogies that rely on long-term storage will involve only a few words. However, analogies that work on items in short-term memory may be somewhat longer.

Combination

Combinatorial patterns will be acquired both receptively and expressively. The basic data for expressive acquisition will be the use of order information in parsing. Patterns that are initially formulated for reception will soon be transferred to expression. However, this transfer is not automatic. Frequent, highly consistent patterns that are central to parsing will transfer most quickly. Thus, the ordering of high-frequency affixes and closed-class operators (*the, to*) will seldom be incorrect. A secondary source of acquisitional data will be the order errors produced by the child (Type 1 correction, MacWhinney, 1978). Errors such as *bottle Mark's* will be useful if the child also has stored rote forms such as *Mark's bottle* that indicate the nature of the error in the combination. Finally, some learning may occur when the child attempts to match the input by generating his or her own alternative productions (Type 4 correction, MacWhinney, 1978).

Rules will be either free, bound, or class-bound. Free rules are the most applicable and also the most easily disconfirmed. The least general rules are those that are bound to lexical classes. For a given piece of data, the child will formulate alternative patterns on each of these three levels. As long as a free rule remains correct, it will dominate over the other rules because its greater applicability leads to rapid growth in its strength. However, once a free rule starts to falter, bound rules will move to the fore. In general, the pattern that wins out in the end is the one that maximizes applicability without sacrificing correctness.

This final section has been sketchy and speculative. However, it may serve to suggest to the reader useful tests of the model underlying this approach. These tests are crucial to further elaboration of this type of account. If the analogy between morphophonology and linearization that was presented in this chapter is to be of any use, it must serve not only to account for existing data but also to predict the shape of new data. If this goal can be achieved, then it may be possible to go beyond the analogy and begin to think about the fundamental patterns that govern the acquisition of cognitive systems. However, in any such extension, we must be eventually willing to abandon applicability for correctness.

ACKNOWLEDGMENTS

My thanks to Morgan Allsup, Dan Bullock, Roberta Carrigan, Suzanne Gendreau, Stan Kuczaj, Svenka Savic, Judith Schlesinger, Jeremy Smith, and Lynn Snyder for their comments on an earlier draft of this chapter. Research connected with this chapter was supported by grant #MH3116002 from the National Institute of Mental Health and grant #BNS7905755 from the National Science Foundation.

REFERENCES

Akmajian, A. *Aspects of the grammar of focus in English*. New York: Garland, 1979.

Aller, S., Aller, W., & Trover, M. *The role of parallel function in children's comprehension of coordinate and relative constructions*. Paper presented at the Midwestern Psychological Association Meetings, 1979.

Amidon, A. Children's understanding of sentences with contingent relations: Why are temporal and conditional connectives so difficult? *Journal of Experimental Child Psychology*, 1976, *22*, 423-437.

Amidon, A., & Carey, P. Why five-year-olds cannot understand before and after. *Journal of Verbal Learning and Verbal Behavior*, 1972, *11*, 417-423.

Anderson, S. On the notion of subject in ergative language. In C. Li (Ed.), *Subject and topic*. New York: Academic Press, 1976.

Antinucci, F., & Miller, R. How children talk about what happened. *Journal of Child Language*, 1976, *3*(2), 167-189.

Ardery, G. The development of coordinations in child language. *Journal of Verbal Learning and Verbal Behavior*, 1979, *18*, 745-756.

Atkinson, R. C., & Shiffrin, R. Human memory: A proposed system and its control processes. In K. Spence & J. Spence (Eds.), *The psychology of learning and motivation* (Vol. 2). New York: Academic Press, 1968.

Bates, E., and MacWhinney, B. Functionalist approaches to grammar. In E. Wanner and L. Gleitman (Eds.), *Child language: The state of the art*. New York: Cambridge University Press (in press).

Bates, E., McNew, S., MacWhinney, B., & Smith, S. The comprehension of basic word order by Italian- and English-speaking adults. Unpublished manuscript, University of Colorado, 1980.

Bebout, L., Segalowitz, S., & White, G. Children's comprehension of causal constructions with "because" and "so." *Child Development*, 1980, *51*, 565-568.

Becker, J. *The phrasal lexicon* (AI Report No. 78). Bolt, Beranek, and Newman, 1975.

Beilin, H. *Studies in the cognitive basis of language development*. New York: Academic Press, 1975.

Bellugi, U. The development of interrogative structures in children's speech. In K. Riegel (Ed.), *The development of language functions* (Report No. 8). University of Michigan Center for Human Growth and Development, 1965.

Bellugi, U. Simplification in children's language. In R. Huxley & E. Ingram (Eds.), *Methods and models in language acquisition*. New York: Academic Press, 1971.

Bever, T. G. The cognitive basis for linguistic structures. In J. R. Hayes (Ed.), *Cognition and the development of language*. New York: Wiley, 1970.

Block, H., Moulton, J., & Robinson, G. Natural language acquisition by a robot. *International Journal of Man-Machine Studies*, 1975, *7*, 571-608.

Bloom, L. *Language development: Form and functions in emerging grammars*. Cambridge, Mass.: M.I.T. Press, 1970.

Bloom, L. *One word at a time*. The Hague: Mouton, 1973.

Bloom, L., Lightbown, P., & Hood, L. Structure and variation in child language. *Monographs of the Society for Research in Child Development*, 1975, *40*(Whole No. 2).

Bloom, L., Miller, P., & Hood, L. Variation and reduction as aspects of competence in language development. In A. Pick (Ed.), *Minnesota symposia on child psychology* (Vol. 9). Minneapolis: University of Minnesota Press, 1975.

Blount, B. *Acquisition of language by Luo children.* Unpublished doctoral dissertation, University of California, Berkeley, 1969.

Bock, K. The effect of a pragmatic presupposition on syntactic structure in question answering. *Journal of Verbal Learning and Verbal Behavior,* 1977, *16,* 723–734.

Bolinger, D. Linear modification. *Publications of the Modern Language Association of America,* 1952, *67,* 1117–1144.

Bowerman, M. *Early syntactic development: A cross-linguistic study with special reference to Finnish.* Cambridge, Eng.: Cambridge University Press, 1973.

Bowerman, M. Semantic factors in the acquisition of rules for word use and sentence construction. In D. M. Morehead & A. E. Morehead (Eds.), *Normal and deficient child language.* Baltimore, University Park Press, 1976.

Bowerman, M. The acquisition of word meaning: An investigation into some current conflicts. In N. Waterson & C. Snow (Eds.), *The development of communication.* New York: Wiley, 1978.

Braine, M. D. S. On learning the grammatical order of words. *Psychological Review,* 1963, *70,* 323–348.

Braine, M. D. S. The acquisition of language in infant and child. In C. Reed (Ed.), *The learning of language.* New York: Appleton-Century-Crofts, 1971.

Braine, M. D. S. Three suggestions regarding grammatical analyses of children's language. In C. A. Ferguson & D. I. Slobin (Eds.), *Studies of child language development.* New York: Holt, Rinehart, & Winston, 1973.

Braine, M. D. S. Children's first word combinations. *Monographs of the Society for Research in Child Development,* 1976, *41*(Whole No. 1).

Braine, M. D. S., & Wells, R. S. Case-like categories in children: The actor and some related categories. *Cognitive Psychology,* 1978, *10,* 100–122.

Branigan, G. Some reasons why successive single word utterances are not. *Journal of Child Language,* 1979, *6,* 411–421.

Bronckart, J., & Sinclair, H. Time, tense and aspect. *Cognition,* 1963, *2,* 107–130.

Brown, H. Children's comprehension of relativized English sentences. *Child Development,* 1971, *42,* 1923–1936.

Brown, R. The development of Wh acquisition in child speech. *Journal of Verbal Learning and Verbal Behavior,* 1968, *7,* 279–290.

Brown, R. *A first language: The early stages.* Cambridge, Mass.: Harvard University Press, 1973.

Brown, R., & Bellugi, U. Three processes in the child's acquisition of syntax. In E. H. Lenneberg (Ed.), *New directions in the study of language.* Cambridge, Mass.: M.I.T. Press, 1964.

Brown, R., Cazden, C., & Bellugi, U. The child's grammar from I to III. In J. P. Hill (Ed.), *Minnesota Symposia on Child Development.* Minneapolis: University of Minnesota Press, 1968.

Burling, R. Language development of a Garo and English speaking child. *Word,* 1959, *15,* 45–68.

Cambon, J., & Sinclair, H. Relations between syntax and semantics: Are they "easy to see?" *British Journal of Psychology,* 1974, *65,* 133–140.

Carey, S. The child as word learner. In M. Halle, J. Bresnan, & G. Miller (Eds.), *Linguistic theory and psychological reality,* Cambridge, Mass.: M.I.T. Press, 1978.

Chafe, W. *Meaning and the structure of language.* Chicago: University of Chicago Press, 1971.

Chafe, W. Language and consciousness. *Language,* 1974, *50,* 111–132.

Chapman, R. S., & Kohn, L. Comprehension strategies in two- and three-year-olds: Animate agents or probable events. *Papers and Reports on Child Language Development,* 1977, *13,* 22–29.

Chapman, R. S., & Miller, J. F. Word order in early two and three word utterances: Does production precede comprehension? *Journal of Speech and Hearing Research,* 1975, *18,* 355–371.

Chomsky, C. *The acquisition of syntax in children from 5 to 10.* Cambridge, Mass.: M.I.T. Press, 1969.

Chomsky, C. Stages in language development and reading exposure. *Harvard Educational Review,* 1972, *42,* 1–33.

Chomsky, N. *Syntactic structures*. The Hague: Mouton, 1957.

Chomsky, N. *Aspects of the theory of syntax*. Cambridge, Mass.: M.I.T. Press, 1965.

Chomsky, N. Deep structure, surface structure, and semantic interpretation. In D. Steinberg & L. Jakobovits (Eds.), *Semantics*. Cambridge, Eng.: Cambridge University Press, 1971.

Clark, E. On the acquisition of the meaning of before and after. *Journal of Verbal Learning and Verbal Behavior*, 1971, *10*, 266-275.

Clark, E. Non-linguistic strategies and the acquisition of word meanings. *Cognition*, 1973, *2*, 161-182.

Clark, H. Some structural properties of simple active and passive sentences. *Journal of Verbal Learning and Verbal Behavior*, 1965, *4*, 365-370.

Clark, H., & Clark, E. Semantic distinctions and memory for complex sentences. *Quarterly Journal of Experimental Psychology*, 1968, *20*, 129-138.

Clark, H., & Clark, E. *Psychology and language*. New York: Harcourt, Brace, Jovanovich, 1977.

Clark, R. Performing without competence. *Journal of Child Language*, 1974, *1*, 1-10.

Clark, R. What's the use of imitation? *Journal of Child Language*, 1977, *4*, 341-358.

Conrad, C. Cognitive economy in semantic memory. *Journal of Experimental Psychology*, 1972, *92*, 149-154.

Cromer, R. F. "Children are nice to understand": Surface structure clues for the recovery of a deep structure. *British Journal of Psychology*, 1970, *61*, 397-408.

Cromer, R. F. Developmental strategies for language. In V. Hamilton & M. Vernon (Eds.), *The development of cognitive processes*. New York: Academic Press, 1976.

Danks, J. H., & Glucksberg, S. Psychological scaling of adjective orders. *Journal of Verbal Learning and Verbal Behavior*, 1972, *11*.

deLaguna, G. A. *Speech: Its function and development*. Bloomington, Indiana: Indiana University Press, 1963. (Originally published, 1927.)

de Villiers, J., & de Villiers, P. Competence and performance in child language: Are children really competent to judge? *Journal of Child Language*, 1974, *1*, 11-22.

de Villiers, J., Tager-Flusberg, H., & Hakuta, K. Deciding among theories of the development of coordination in child speech. *Papers and Reports on Child Language Development*, 1977, *13*, 118-125.

de Villiers, P., & de Villiers, J. Early judgments of semantic and syntactic acceptability by children. *Journal of Psycholinguistic Research*, 1972, *1*, 299-310.

Dewart, M. H. Social class and children's understanding of deep structure in sentences. *British Journal of Educational Psychology*, 1972, *42*, 198-203.

Dewart, M. *Children's preferences for animate and inanimate actor and object nouns*. Unpublished manuscript, Medical Research Council, London, England, 1975.

Dik, T. *Functional grammar*. New York: North-Holland, 1978.

Duchan, J., & Lund, N. Why not semantic relations? *Journal of Child Language*, 1979, *6*, 243-252.

du Preez, P. Units of information in the acquisition of language. *Language and Speech*, 1974, *17*, 369-376.

Ertel, S. Where do the subjects of sentences come from? In S. Rosenberg (Ed.), *Sentence production: Developments in research and theory*. Hillsdale, N.J.: Lawrence Erlbaum Associates, 1977.

Ferreiro, E., Othenin-Girard, C., Chipman, H., & Sinclair, H. How do children handle relative clauses? *Archives de Psychologie*, 1976, *44*, 229-266.

Ferreiro, E., & Sinclair, H. Temporal relationships in language. *International Journal of Psychology*, 1971, *6*, 39-47.

Ferrier, L. Some observations of error in context. In N. Waterson & C. Snow (Eds.), *The development of communication*. New York: Wiley, 1978.

Fillmore, C. The case for case. In E. Bach & R. Harms (Eds.), *Universals in linguistic theory*. New York: Holt, Rinehart, & Winston, 1968.

Fillmore, L. W. Individual differences in second language acquisition. In C. Fillmore, D. Kempler, & W. Wang (Eds.), *Individual differences in language behavior*. New York: Academic Press, 1979.

Fluck, M. J. Young children's comprehension of complex sentences. *Language and Speech*, 1977, *20*, 48-66.

Fluck, M. J. Comprehension of relative clauses by children five to nine years. *Language and Speech*, 1978, *21*, 190-201.

Fónagy, I. A propós de la genése de la phrase enfantine. *Lingua*, 1972, *30*, 31-71.

Foss, D., Bias, R., and Starkey, P. Sentence comprehension processes in the pre-schooler. In R. Campbell & P. Smith (Eds.), *Recent advances in the psychology of language*. New York: Plenum Press, 1977.

Francis, H. Structure in the speech of a 2½-year old. *British Journal of Educational Psychology*, 1969, *39*, 291-302.

Gaer, E. Children's understanding and production of sentences. *Journal of Verbal Learning and Verbal Behavior*, 1969, *8*, 289-294.

Garvey, C., Caramazza, A., & Yates, J. Factors influencing assignment of pronoun antecedents. *Cognition*, 1975, *3*(3), 227-243.

Gleitman, L., & Gleitman, H. *Phrase & paraphrase*. New York: Norton, 1970.

Gleitman, L., Gleitman, H., & Shipley, E. F. The emergence of the child as grammarian. *Cognition*, 1972, *1*, 137-164.

Goldman, S. Reading skill and the minimum distance principle: A comparison of listening and reading comprehension. *Journal of Experimental Child Psychology*, 1976, *22*, 123-142.

Goodluck, H., & Roeper, T. The acquisition of perception verb complements. In H. Goodluck & L. Solan (Eds.), *Papers in the structure and development of child language* (*Occasional Papers in Linguistics* [Vol. 4]). University of Massachusetts, 1978.

Greenfield, P. M., & Dent, C. Syntax vs. pragmatics: A psychological account of coordinate structures in child language. *Papers and Reports on Child Language Development*, 1979, *17*, 65-72.

Greenfield, P. M., & Smith, J. *The structure of communication in early language development*. New York: Academic Press, 1976.

Greenfield, P. M., & Zukow, P. G. Why do children say what they say when they say it?: An experimental approach to the psychogenesis of presupposition. In K. E. Nelson (Ed.), *Children's language* (Vol. 1). New York: Gardner Press, 1978.

Grimm, H., Scholer, H., & Wintermantel, M. *Zur Entwicklung sprachlicher Strukturformen bei Kindern*. Weinheim: Beltz, 1975.

Grober, E., Beardsley, W., & Caramazza, A. Parallel function strategy in pronoun assignment. *Cognition*, 1978, *6*, 117-133.

Gruber, J. S. Topicalization in child language. *Foundations of Language*, 1967, *3*, 37-65.

Gruber, J. S. Correlations between the syntactic constructions of the child and of the adult. In C. A. Ferguson & D. I. Slobin (Eds.), *Studies of child language development*. New York: Holt, Rinehart, & Winston, 1973.

Guillaume, P. Les débuts de la phrase dans le langage de l'enfant. *Journal de Psychologie*, 1927, *24*, 1-25.

Gvozdev, A. N. *Voprosy izucheniya detskoy rechi*. Moscow: Akademija Pedagogika Nauk RSFSR, 1961.

Hakuta, K. Word order and particles in the acquisition of Japanese. *Papers and Reports on Child Language Development*, 1977, *13*, 110-117.

Hakuta, K. *Comprehension and production of simple and complex sentences by Japanese children*. Doctoral dissertation, Harvard University, 1979.

Harwood, F. W. Quantitative study of the speech of Australian children. *Language and Speech*, 1959, *2*, 236-270.

Hatch, E., Peck, S., & Wagner-Gough, J. A look at process in child second-language acquisition. In E. Ochs & B. Schieffelin (Eds.), *Developmental pragmatics*. New York: Academic Press, 1979.

Hayashibe, H. Word order and particles: A developmental study in Japanese. *Descriptive and Applied Linguistics*, 1975, *8*, 1-9.

Hayes-Roth, B. Evolution of cognitive structures and processes. *Psychological Review*, 1977, *84*, 260-278.

Horgan, D. Linguistic knowledge at early stage I: Evidence from successive single word utterances. *Papers and Reports on Child Language Development*, 1976, *12*, 116-126.

Horowitz, L., & Prytulak, L. Redintegrative memory. *Psychological Review*, 1969, *76*, 519-531.

Hunt, K. Syntactic maturity in schoolchildren and adults. *Monographs of the Society for Research in Child Development*, 1969 (Serial No. 134).

Hurford, J. R. A child and the English question formation rule. *Journal of Child Language*, 1975, *2*, 299-301.

Huttenlocher, J., Eisenberg, K., & Strauss, S. Comprehension: Relation between perceived actor and logical subject. *Journal of Verbal Learning and Verbal Behavior*, 1968, *7*, 527-530.

Huttenlocher, J., & Strauss, S. Comprehension and a statement's relation to the situation it describes. *Journal of Verbal Learning and Verbal Behavior*, 1968, *7*, 300-304.

Huttenlocher, J., & Weiner, S. Comprehension of instructions in varying contexts. *Cognitive Psychology*, 1971, *2*, 369-385.

Ingram, D. *Early patterns of grammatical development*. Paper prepared for the conference "Language behavior in infancy and early childhood," Santa Barbara, October 1979.

Iwamura, S. *I don't wanna don't throw: Speech formulas in first language acquisition*. Unpublished manuscript, 1979.

Iwamura, S. *The verbal games of pre-school children*. London: Croom Helm, 1980.

Jacoby, L. On interpreting the effects of repetition: Solving a problem versus remembering a solution. *Journal of Verbal Learning and Verbal Behavior*, 1978, *17*, 649-668.

Jarvella, R. Syntactic processing of connected speech. *Journal of Verbal Learning and Verbal Behavior*, 1971, *10*, 409-416.

Jarvella, R., & Sinnott, J. Contextual constraints on noun distribution to some English verbs by children and adults. *Journal of Verbal Learning and Verbal Behavior*, 1972, *11*, 47-53.

Johnson, H. L. The meaning of *before* and *after* for preschool children. *Journal of Experimental Child Psychology*, 1975, *19*, 88-99.

Kail, M., & Segui, J. Developmental production of utterances from a series of lexemes. *Journal of Child Language*, 1978, *5*, 251-260.

Keenan, J., MacWhinney, B., & Mayhew, D. Pragmatics in memory: A study of natural conversation. *Journal of Verbal Learning and Verbal Behavior*, 1977, *16*, 549-560.

Kelleher, T. Testing, teaching, and retesting syntactic structures in children from 5 to 10. *Linguistics*, 1973, *115*, 15-38.

Kenyeres, E. Comment une petite hongroise de sept ans apprend le français. *Archives de Psychologie*, 1938, *26*, 521-566.

Kernan, K. *The acquisition of language by Samoan children*. Doctoral dissertation, University of California, Berkeley, 1969.

Kessel, F. The role of syntax in children's comprehension from ages six to twelve. *Monographs of the Society for Research in Child Development*, 1970, *35*(6, Serial No. 139).

King, R. *Historical linguistics and generative grammar*. Englewood Cliffs, N.J.: Prentice-Hall, 1969.

Klima, E., & Bellugi, U. Syntactic regularities in the speech of children. In J. Lyons & R. J. Wales (Eds.), *Psycholinguistics papers*. Edinburgh: Edinburgh University Press, 1966.

Kramer, P. Young children's free responses to anomalous commands. *Journal of Experimental Child Psychology*, 1977, *24*, 219-234.

Kramer, P., Kopf E., & Luria, Z. The development of competence in an exceptional language structure in older children and adults. *Child Development*, 1972, *43*, 121–130.

Kuczaj, S. A. Arguments against Hurford's 'Aux copying rule.' *Journal of Child Language*, 1976, *3*, 423–427.

Kuczaj, S. A., & Brannick, N. Children's use of the Wh question model auxiliary placement rule. *Journal of Experimental Child Psychology*, 1979, *28*, 43–67.

Kuczaj, S. A., & Maratsos, M. *The initial verbs of yes–no questions: A different kind of general grammatical category.* Paper presented at the meeting of the Society for Research in Child Development, San Francisco, 1979.

Lahey, M. Use of prosody and syntactic markers in children's comprehension of spoken sentences. *Journal of Speech and Hearing Research*, 1974, *17*, 656–668.

Lange, S., & Larsson, K. *Syntactical development of a Swedish girl Embla, between 20 and 42 months of age, I: Age 20–25 months* (Report No. 1, Project Child Language Syntax). Institutionen for nordiska sprak, Stockholms Universitet, 1973.

Labov, W., & Labov, T. Learning the syntax of questions. In R. Campbell & P. Smith (Eds.), *Recent advances in the psychology of language: Formal and experimental approaches.* New York: Plenum Press, 1978.

Lashley, K. The problem of serial order in behavior. In L. A. Jeffress (Ed.), *Cerebral mechanisms in behavior.* New York: Wiley, 1951.

Legum, S. *Strategies in the acquisition of relative clauses.* Proceedings of the Fifth Annual California Linguistics Association Conference, 1975.

Lempert, H., & Kinsbourne, M. Preschool children's sentence comprehension: Strategies with respect to word order. *Journal of Child Language*, 1980, *7*, 371–379.

Leonard, L. *Meaning in child language.* New York: Grune and Stratton, 1976.

Leonard, L., & Schwartz, R. Focus characteristics of single-word utterances after syntax. *Journal of Child Language*, 1977, *5*, 151–158.

Leopold, W. F. *Speech development of a bilingual child: A linguist's record* (Vol. 1) Evanston: Northwestern University Press, 1949.(a)

Leopold, W. F. *Speech development of a bilingual child: A linguist's record,* Vol. 2. Evanston: Northwestern University Press, 1949.(b)

Leopold, W. F. Patterning in children's language learning. *Language in Learning*, 1953, *5*, 1–14.

Limber, J. Unravelling competence, performance and pragmatics in the speech of young children. *Journal of Child Language*, 1976, *3*, 309–318.

Lindner, G. *Aus dem Naturgarten der Kindersprache.* Leipzig: Grieben, 1898.

Lust, B. Conjunction reduction in child language. *Journal of Child Language*, 1977, *4*, 257–288.

Lust, B., & Mervis, C. *Development of coordination in the natural speech of young children.* Unpublished manuscript, Cornell University, 1978.

MacWhinney, B. *How Hungarian children learn to speak.* Unpublished doctoral dissertation, University of California, Berkeley, 1974.

MacWhinney, B. Pragmatics patterns in child syntax. *Papers and Reports on Child Language Development*, 1975, *10*, 153–165. (a)

MacWhinney, B. Rules, rote, and analogy in morphological formations by Hungarian children. *Journal of Child Language*, 1975, *2*, 65–77. (b)

MacWhinney, B. Hungarian research on the acquisition of morphology and syntax. *Journal of Child Language*, 1976, *3*, 397–410.

MacWhinney, B. Starting points. *Language*, 1977, *53*, 152–168.

MacWhinney, B. The acquisition of morphophonology. *Monographs of the Society for Research in Child Development*, 1978, *43*(Nos. 1–2).

MacWhinney, B. *Miniature linguistic systems as tests of language processing universals.* Unpublished manuscript, University of Denver, 1980.

MacWhinney, B. The acquisition of Hungarian grammar. In D. Slobin (Ed.), *The cross-cultural study of language acquisition.* Hillsdale, N.J.: Lawrence Erlbaum (in press). (a)

MacWhinney, B. Point-sharing. In R. Schiefelbuch (Ed.), *Communicative competence: Acquisition and intervention*. Baltimore, Md.: University Park Press, (in press). (b)

MacWhinney, B., & Bates, E. Sentential devices for conveying givenness and newness: A cross-cultural developmental study. *Journal of Verbal Learning and Verbal Behavior*, 1978, *17*, 539-558.

MacWhinney, B., & Osser, H. Verbal planning functions in children's speech. *Child Development*, 1977, *48*, 978-985.

Maratsos, M. The effects of stress on the understanding of pronominal co-reference in children. *Journal of Psycholinguistic Research*, 1973, *2*, 1-8.

Maratsos, M. P. Children who get worse at understanding the passive: A replication of Bever. *Journal of Psycholinguistic Research*, 1974, *3*, 65-74. (a)

Maratsos, M. P. How preschool children understand missing complement subjects. *Child Development*, 1974, *45*, 700-706. (b)

Maratsos, M., & Abramovitch, R. How children understand full, truncated, and anomalous passives. *Journal of Verbal Learning and Verbal Behavior*, 1975, *14*, 145-157.

Maratsos, M., & Chalkley, M. The internal language of children's syntax: The ontogenesis and representation of syntactic categories. In K. Nelson (Ed.), *Children's language* (Vol. 2). New York: Gardner Press, 1980.

Maratsos, M., & Kuczaj, S. Is not n't? A study in syntactic generalization. *Papers and Reports on Child Language Development*, 1976, *12*, 157-168.

Maratsos, M., & Kuczaj, S. A., II. Against the tranformationalist account: A simpler analysis of auxiliary overmarkings. *Journal of Child Language*, 1978, *5*, 337-345.

Maratsos, M., Kuczaj, S. A., II, Fox, D. E. C., & Chalkley, M. A. Some empirical studies in the acquisition of transformational relations: Passives, negatives, and the past tense. In W. A. Collins (Ed.), *Children's language and communication*. Hillsdale, N.J.: Lawrence Erlbaum Associates, 1979.

Markman, E. Realizing that you don't understand: Elementary school children's awareness of inconsistencies. *Child Development*, 1979, *50*, 643-655.

Martin, J. Semantic determinants of preferred adjective order. *Journal of Verbal Learning and Verbal Behavior*, 1969, *8*, 697-704.

Martin, J., & Molfese, D. Preferred adjective ordering in very young children. *Journal of Verbal Learning and Verbal Behavior*, 1972, *11*, 287-292.

Mayer, J., Erreich, A., & Valian, V. Transformation, basic operations and language acquisition. *Cognition*, 1978, *6*, 1-14.

Menn, L., & MacWhinney, B. *Towards a psychology of morphological marking: Evidence from linguistic structure, child language, and language dysfunction.* Unpublished manuscript, University of Denver, 1980.

Menyuk, P. *Sentences children use.* Cambridge, Mass.: M.I.T. Press, 1969.

Miller, G. Some preliminaries to psycholinguistics. *American Psychologist*, 1965, *20*, 15-20.

Miller, G. Semantic relations among words. In M. Halle, J. Bresnan, & G. Miller (Eds.), *Linguistic theory and psychological reality*, Cambridge, Mass.: M.I.T. Press, 1978.

Miller, G., & Johnson-Laird, P. *Language and perception*. Cambridge, Mass.: Harvard University Press, 1976.

Miller, W. R. The acquisition of grammatical rules by children. In C. A. Ferguson & D. I. Slobin (Ed.), *Studies of child language development*. New York: Holt, Rinehart, & Winston, 1973.

Miller, W. R., & Ervin, S. M. The development of grammar in child language. *Monographs of the Society for Research in Child Development*, 1964, *29*(Serial No. 92).

Morsbach, G., & Steel, P. M. 'John is easy to see' re-investigated. *Journal of Child Language*, 1976, *3*, 443-447.

Nelson, K. Structure and strategy in learning how to talk. *Monographs of the Society for Research in Child Development*, 1973, *38* (Serial No. 149).

Olson, D., & Nickerson, N. The contexts of comprehension: On children's understanding of the relations between active and passive sentences. *Journal of Experimental Child Psychology*, 1977, *23*, 402–414.

Osgood, C. E. Where do sentences come from? In D. D. Steinberg & L. A. Jakobovits (Eds.), *Semantics*. Cambridge, Eng.: Cambridge University Press, 1971.

Osgood, C. E., & Bock, K. J. Salience and sentencing: Some production principles. In S. Rosenberg (Ed.), *Sentence production: Developments in research and theory*. Hillsdale, N.J.: Lawrence Erlbaum Associates, 1977.

Osgood, C. E., & Sridhar, S. *Cognitive bases of structural equivalents: A 10-language comparative study*. Paper presented at the winter meetings of the Linguistics Society of America, Los Angeles 1979.

O'Shea, M. *Linguistic development and education*. London: MacMillan, 1907.

Peters, A. Language learning strategies. *Language*, 1977, *53*, 560–573.

Peters, A. The units of language acquisition: Unpublished manuscript, University of Hawaii, 1980.

Petretic, P., & Tweney, R. Does comprehension precede production? The development of children's responses to telegraphic sentences of varying grammatical adequacy. *Journal of Child Language*, 1976, *4*, 201–209.

Pike, K. *Language in relation to a unified theory of human behavior*. The Hague: Mouton, 1967.

Platt, C., & MacWhinney, B. *Solving a problem vs. remembering the solution: Error assimilation as a strategy in language acquisition*. Unpublished manuscript, University of Denver, 1980.

Postal, P. Limitations of phase structure grammars. In J. A. Fodor & J. J. Katz (Eds.), *The structure of language: Readings in the philosophy of language*. Englewood Cliffs, N.J.: Prentice-Hall, 1964.

Powers, J., & Gowie, C. Children's strategies in processing active- and passive-voice sentences: Use of semantic and syntactic information. *Genetic Psychology Monographs*, 1977, *96*, 337–355.

Prizant, B. *An analysis of the functions of immediate echolalia in autistic children*. Unpublished doctoral dissertation, SUNY Buffalo, 1978.

Quirk, R., Greenbaum, S., Leech, G., & Svartvik, J. *A grammar of contemporary English*. London: Longman, 1972.

Ratner, N., & Bruner, J. Games, social exchange and the acquisition of language. *Journal of Child Language*, 1978, *5*, 391–401.

Richards, M. Adjective ordering in the language of young children: An experimental investigation. *Journal of Child Language*, 1979, *6*, 253–278.

Ross, J. *The category squish: Endstation Hauptwort*. Chicago Linguistic Society, Eighth Regional Meeting, April 1972.

Rubin, D. The effectiveness of context before, after, and around a missing word. *Perception & Psychophysics*, 1976, *19*, 214–216.

Rubin, D. A unit analysis of prose memory. *Journal of Verbal Learning and Verbal Behavior*, 1978, *17*, 599–620.

Sachs, J. S. Recognition memory for syntactic and semantic aspects of connected discourse. *Perception and Psychophysics*, 1967, *2*, 437–442.

Scheffelin, M. Childrens' understanding of constraints upon adjective order. *Journal of Learning Disabilities*, 1971, *4*, 264–272.

Schieffelin, B. B. A developmental study of word order and case marking in an ergative language. *Papers and Reports on Child Language Development*, 1979, *17*, 30–40.

Schlesinger, I. M. *Production and comprehension of utterances*. Hillsdale, N.J.: Lawrence Erlbaum Associates, 1977.

Schwenk, M., & Danks, J. A developmental study of the pragmatic communication rule for prenominal adjective ordering. *Memory & Cognition*, 1974, *2*, 149–152.

Scollon, R. *Conversations with a one year old*. Honolulu: University of Hawaii Press, 1976.

Sechehaye, M. A. *Essai sur la structure logique de la phrase*. Paris: Champion, 1926.

Segalowitz, N., & Galang, R. Agent-patient word-order preference in the acquisition of Tagalog. *Journal of Child Language,* 1976, *5,* 47-64.

Sgall, P., Hajičova, E., & Benešova, E. *Topic, focus and generative semantics.* Kronberg, Germany: Scriptor Verlag, 1973.

Shattuck-Hufnagel, S. Speech errors as evidence for a serial-ordering mechanism in sentence production. In W. E. Cooper & E. C. T. Walker (Eds.), *Sentence processing: Psycholinguistic studies presented to Merrill Garrett.* Hillsdale, N.J.: Lawrence Erlbaum Associates, 1979.

Sheldon, A. On the role of parallel function in the acquisition of relative clauses in English. *Journal of Verbal Learning and Verbal Behavior,* 1974, *13,* 272-281.

Sheldon, A. The acquisition of relative clauses in French and English: Implications for language-learning universals. In F. Eckman (Ed.), *Current themes in linguistics.* Washington: Hemisphere Publishing, 1977.(a)

Sheldon, A. On strategies for processing relative clauses: A comparison of children and adults. *Journal of Psycholinguistic Research,* 1977, *6,* 305-318. (b)

Shiffrin, R. M., & Schneider, W. Controlled and automatic human information processing: II. Perceptual learning, automatic attending and a general theory. *Psychological Review,* 1977, *84,* 127-190.

Shipley, E., Smith, C., & Gleitman, L. A study in the acquisition of language: Free responses to commands. *Language,* 1969, *45,* 322-342.

Sinclair, H., & Bronckart, J. S. V. O. A linguistic universal? A study in developmental psycholinguistics. *Journal of Experimental Child Psychology,* 1972, *14,* 329-348.

Sinclair, A., Sinclair, H., & DeMarcellus, O. Young children's comprehension and production of passive sentences. *Archives de Psychologie,* 1971, *41,* 1-22.

Skinner, B. F. *Verbal behavior.* New York: Appleton-Century-Crofts, 1957.

Slobin, D. I. Grammatical transformations and sentence comprehension in childhood and adulthood. *Journal of Verbal Learning and Verbal Behavior,* 1966, *5,* 219-227.

Slobin, D. I., & Aksu, A. The acquisition of Turkish. In D. Slobin (Ed.), *The cross-cultural study of language development.* Hillsdale, N.J.: Lawrence Erlbaum, (in press).

Slobin, D. I. Cognitive prerequisites for the development of grammar. In C. A. Ferguson & D. I. Slobin (Eds.), *Studies of child language development.* New York: Holt, Rinehart, & Winston, 1973.

Slobin, D. I., & Welsh, C. A. Elicited imitation as a research tool in developmental psycholinguistics. In C. A. Ferguson & D. I. Slobin (Eds.), *Studies in child language development.* New York: Holt, Rinehart, & Winston, 1973.

Smith, C. S. An experimental approach to children's linguistic competence. In J. R. Hayes (Ed.), *Cognition and the development of language.* New York: Wiley, 1970.

Smoczyńska, M. Early syntactic development: Pivot look and pivot grammar. *Polish Psychological Bulletin,* 1976, *1,* 37-43.

Snyder, L. The early presuppositions and performanatives of normal and language disabled children. *Papers and Reports on Child Language Development,* 1976, *12,* 221-229.

Solan, L. The acquisition of tough movement. In H. Goodluck & L. Solan (Eds.), *Papers in the structure and development of child language (Occasional Papers in Linguistics* [Vol. 4]). Amherst, University of Massachusetts, 1978.

Solan, L. *Contrastive stress and children's interpretation of pronouns.* Unpublished manuscript, Washington, D.C., 1979.

Solan, L., & Roeper, T. Children's use of syntactic structure in interpreting relative clauses. In H. Goodluck & L. Solan (Eds.), *Papers in the structure and development of child language (Occasional Papers in Linguistics* [Vol. 4]). Amherst, University of Massachusetts, 1978.

Strohner, H., & Nelson, K. E. The young child's development of sentence comprehension: Influence of event probability, nonverbal context, syntactic form, and their strategies. *Child Development,* 1974, *45,* 567-576.

Suci, G., & Hamacher, J. Psychological dimensions of case in sentence processing: Action role and animateness. *International Journal of Psycholinguistics*, 1972, *1*, 34-48.

Sweet, H. *A new English grammar*. Oxford: Clarendon Press, 1898.

Talmy, L. The relation of grammar to cognition—a synopsis. In D. Waltz (Ed.), *Theoretical issues in natural language processing*. University of Illinois, 1978.

Tavakolian, S. The conjoined-clause analysis of relative clauses and other structure. In H. Goodluck and L. Solan (Eds.), *Papers in the structure and development of child language* (*Occasional Papers in Linguistics* [Vol. 4]). University of Massachusetts, 1978.

Turner, E., & Rommetveit, R. The acquisition of sentence voice and reversibility. *Child Development*, 1967, *38*, 649-660.

Turner, E., & Rommetveit, R. Focus of attention in recall of active and passive sentences. *Journal of Verbal Learning and Verbal Behavior*, 1968, *7*, 543-548.

van der Geest, T. Some interactional aspects of language acquisition. In C. Snow & C. Ferguson (Eds.), *Talking to children*. Cambridge, Eng.: Cambridge University Press, 1977.

Vygotsky, L. *Thought and language*. Cambridge, Mass.: M.I.T. Press, 1962. (Originally published, 1934).

Waddington, C. H. *The strategy of the genes*. New York: Macmillan, 1957.

Weir, R. H. *Language in the crib*. The Hague: Mouton, 1962.

Weisenburger, J. L. A choice of words: Two-year-old speech from a situational point of view. *Journal of Child Language*, 1976, *3*, 275-281.

Wetstone, H. S., & Friedlander, B. Z. The effect of word order on young children's response to simple questions and commands. *Child Development*, 1973, *44*, 734-740.

4

On the Importance of Syntax and the Logical Use of Evidence in Language Acquisition

Thomas Roeper
University of Massachusetts/Amherst

Two questions occur to the linguist who looks at the literature in language acquisition: (1) What is the relation between proposed nonformal child grammars and adult grammars? (2) What kind of evidence moves a child from an incorrect grammar to a correct grammar? Linguistic theory offers something of an answer to each question. The perspective that comes from outside linguistic theory offers a great deal of obscurity.

There is now a large literature in acquisition that lies outside transformal grammar (TG). Proposals range from pragmatic ones to cognitive to generative semantics ones. Many researchers favor a kind of "thematic" semantics. In fact, it seems reasonable to claim that early stages in acquisition should not be described in any sort of transformational syntax. The two-to-three word stage seems genuinely "primitive." A loose form-class grammar, together with powerful inference systems, should be able to account for everything (see Roeper, 1973). Nevertheless, as Steve Pinker (1979) has observed, the available data are so restricted that all of the proposed systems may be descriptively adequate. Thus, it might be impossible to discover which is correct.

If one defends a nontransformational system for child language, then an important question arises: Does the system hold for adult language? If so, then it is incumbent upon the purporter to show how the facts of adult language fit the primitive system. If one believes that the adult language is described by TG, then one must ask: How does the child shift from a primitive system to TG? This question can be regarded as more important than the exact nature of the primitive system.

The person who accepts linguistic theory as a description of adult competence has no transition to explain. The assumption that a child had the power of TG

137

should be the preferred hypothesis unless there is strong evidence to the contrary. For example, in this chapter, we show how a non-TG theory of relative-clause interpretation (parallel function) misses the subtle but essential role of syntax.

The second question confronts the theorist of any school. The question, once again, is: How does a child learn that his or her current grammar is incorrect and therefore progress to a better grammar?[1] The question is approachable within the framework of TG. The answer involves the claim that children may take steps in the progress of acquisition that are not directly open to observation. There can, of course, be little doubt that many steps in acquisition never appear in the surface of produced child speech. Therefore, a theory that can project a convincing and rational version of silent stages in acquisition, based on the logic of linguistic theory, is a strong one. Needless to say, we are far from being able to project more than fragments of that process.

We can illustrate the problem by contrasting the English and German auxiliary. In German, it is possible to have several modals at once. Thus, we find the equivalent of *Lee must should come (kommen sollen müssen)*. Such a sentence is ungrammatical in English. The English child hears:

1.a. Lee must come.
   b. Lee can come.
   c. Lee has come.

There are at least four grammars that are possible if we assume that the child has no difficulty with order:

2. G_1. Lee (can) (must) (have) come.

G_2. Lee $\left\{ \begin{array}{c} \text{can} \\ \text{must} \\ \text{have} \end{array} \right\}$ come.

G_3. Lee $\left\{ \begin{array}{c} \text{can} \\ \text{must} \end{array} \right\}$ (have) come.

G_4. Lee (can) $\left\{ \begin{array}{c} \text{have} \\ \text{must} \end{array} \right\}$ come.

How does the child choose G_3? In particular, how does the child know, having heard all the sentences in 1, that *Lee must can come* is ungrammatical. We cannot assume that the child receives "negative evidence" from an adult; that is,

---

[1]We are generalizing from what has been called the problem of "negative evidence" first discussed by Gold (1967), then by Wexler and Culicover (1980), and most recently Baker (1979), and Roeper (in press). Children have a more impoverished array of data available to them than the linguist because they do not receive information about what is ungrammatical. They must, therefore, infer what is excluded on the basis of positive evidence alone.

no one will tell the child it is ungrammatical. One might say that the child uses a frequency metric. If this were true, then the child could never learn that a six-part verb is grammatical because it occurs extremely rarely: *Lee must have had been being shot just before the police arrived.* Rarity of a form does not exclude it from the grammar. How, then, do we guarantee that a child knows that English is not German?

The answer lies in the order in which the formal devices of grammar are applied. Transformational grammar has the power to represent rules conjunctively or disjunctively. Parentheses represent conjunctive relations and braces represent exclusive relations. The grammars G_1–G_4 reveal that they can be mixed. Suppose we make the following assumption:

3. Children assume that all rules are disjunctively ordered unless they hear counterevidence.

In other words, children assume English (even if they are German) until they hear evidence that forces a conjunctive interpretation. If they did the reverse—assumed conjunctive ordering—they would never hear contrary evidence. Nothing will show that G_1 is wrong. But the sentence *Lee must have come.* immediately shows that G_2 is wrong. (See Baker, in press, for an analysis in this spirit that deals with many subtle aspects of auxiliaries.) Nothing will show that G_4 is wrong. Therefore, we must prevent the acquisition mechanism from projecting G_4 or G_1 until there is specific evidence in their behalf. G_3 is generated just when that evidence occurs that overturns the first grammar G_2. This will happen very rapidly in both English and German, but in different ways. In English, children learn that the modal is compatible with other auxiliaries (by parentheses) but disjunctively ordered with respect to other modals (by braces), and in German, they will receive evidence that other modals are compatible with each other. The disjunctive principle (3) guarantees that children will not project one of the incorrect grammars, although they are compatible with the evidence, until the appropriate evidence arrives. Such evidence may arrive so rapidly that a child will pass through the G_2 stage silently. In the most extreme case, a single sentence could cause a child to both generate G_2 and discard it in favor of G_3.

This is unlikely in real life because of another factor. In order for children to focus on the correct sentences that will advance their grammar, they must exclude 99% of the sentences in their daily environment. Under the assumption that children need particular input sentences to advance their grammar, most sentences will either already be generated by the current grammar or they will be too advanced for the current grammar. Thus, if a child is ready to hear a sentence with one auxiliary, a sentence with no auxiliary (*Lee runs*) gives no new information and a sentence with two auxiliaries (*Lee must have run*) gives too much information. Even when more than one option is possible, we believe that it is necessary for the acquisition mechanism to determine which sentence type will serve as input. Thus, between an auxiliary (*Lee can run*) and an adverb (*Lee runs quickly*), we expect the acquisition mechanism to make a choice. The choice will guarantee that incorrect but irrefutable grammars are not generated. The details of how this works remains a major task of acquisition research. It is also reasonable to assume that all of the sentence types children need to learn language are available on a daily basis and children must simply decide when to let them, individually, alter their grammar.

In effect, therefore, children determine the order of input of sentences into the acquisition mechanism. Aside from vocabulary, the minor preferences that adults exhibit in their use of various structures have at most a minor impact on which syntactic forms children learn first.

The claim that the acquisition mechanism ignores most of the input does not mean that children ignore the content of conversations. Children may work very hard to guess what every sentence means, but nonetheless not allow those sentences to cause a change in their grammar. Thus, when faced with an incoming sentence that does not fit their current grammar, children must either change their grammar to absorb the new sentence or infer the meaning of the sentence from the meaning of its words and content. (See Roeper, in press, for a discussion of how both inferences and triggers are used to advance the grammar.)

This approach follows what we can call *the principle of disconfirmability* (suggested by Edwin Williams, 1981). The principle establishes a logic of evidence that prevents a child from adopting a grammar that is incorrect but for which there is no counterevidence. It says that hypotheses are ordered so that the most easily disconfirmed occurs first. This principle allows us to extend a theory of acquisition into those aspects of grammar development that are never manifested in production.

What does acquisition evidence tell us?[2] Do children produce the forms ruled out by G_1? There are very few reported instances of children's uttering sentences like *Lee will can come.*, but they are not unknown.[3] There is a dialect double modal that occurs regularly—"Lee might could win"—but it does not generalize to other modals. This suggests that the rules are not written "initially" in terms of the category modal but in terms of specific lexical items. The rarity of these examples works in behalf of our hypothesis. However, there is a large class of double modal expressions that occur in one particular syntactic configuration (question), and seem to justify G_5:

4. Can I can come
    Is Tom is busy

---

[2]See Roeper (1972) for an extensive discussion of the notion that *copying* rules precede *deletion* rules. See also D. Fay (1978), Kuczaj (1976), Goodluck and Solan (1979), Valian, Mayer, and Erreich (in press), and references cited therein.

[3]Kuczaj (1976) introduces the notion of redundancy with respect to the acquisition of auxiliaries.

Whose is that is

G_5. NP AUX V $\rightarrow$ AUX NP AUX V

We cannot explain how children reject G_5 without a further principle. The fact that they may learn another rule (the standard one)—NP AUX $\rightarrow$ AUX NP (in which we have movement instead of copying)— does not necessarily show that the grammar must eliminate the rule G_5.

First, we should observe that the frequency of constructions like *Can I can sing* is low. It is arguable that such constructions are nothing more than speech errors. However, this does not dissolve the acquisition problem. They are clearly errors of a systematic kind that are generable by a rule. If they can be formulated as a rule, then we must ask how children would prevent their adoption in their grammar, once again mindful of the fact that there is no counterevidence for such a rule. In brief, if children heard such a sentence, or uttered it themselves, what prevents its adoption in the grammar?

What principle would lead a child to "unlearn" the double-auxiliary construction? If we expand a suggestion by Ken Wexler, we may have the answer. Wexler (personal communication) proposed that in the "unmarked case" there is only one surface structure for every deep structure. One could have several surface structures only if there was specific evidence. Thus, a child would adopt the hypothesis that there were two surface structures for indirect objects only with specific evidence for each verb. The existence of *I gave Lee the ball* and *I gave the ball to Lee.* does not generalize to *report* unless the child hears specific positive evidence. Therefore, a child can correctly learn *I reported the answer to Lee* without forming **I reported Lee the answer.* In order to be sensitive to particular verbs, such rules must be represented within the lexicon (where we must substitute for deep structure and surface structure with "base subcategorization frame" and "derived subcategorization frame"; see Roeper, in press, and Baker, 1979).

Note that the rules of syntax, in sharp contrast to the lexicon, require that children make generalizations that are not sensitive to particular verbs or other lexical items. Children must be able to generalize from one instance of a question *what did I see* to a rule that allows them to form questions with any transitive verb. (In syntax, we must apply the uniqueness relation between the triple deep structure, surface structure, and "logical form" [or semantic representation; see Chomsky, 1980]; then we will have the appropriate restriction.)

The uniqueness principle must now be related to the dynamics of acquisition. We assume that children apply the uniqueness principle until repeated evidence forces them to modify it for some constructions. Suppose a child briefly allows the construction *Aux NP Aux VP* as the form of yes/no questions. The rule is simpler to formulate as a *copying* rule than a *movement* rule. Then, the child hears the form *Can I sing* and knows from context that it has the same "meaning" or "logical form" as *Can I can sing*. This will drive out the form *Can I can sing* by application of the uniqueness principle. If the child kept hearing the double-aux form, he or she would eventually adopt the *marked* hypothesis that both forms are acceptable.

The notion of uniqueness appears to be the converse of redundancy. However, it is important to note that what we have excluded is redundant rules, defined on abstract structures, not redundancy in the surface of the language. The surface of the language tolerates considerable redundancy. For instance, there are languages in which plurality is marked on the determiner, adjective, and noun within a single phrase. English marks negation redundantly by having both *not* and *any* forms in a sentence. Therefore, we cannot appeal to an extragrammatical notion of redundancy to explain how a child prevents the projection of certain rules. We need instead a theoretically defined notion of uniqueness.

In the remainder of this chapter, we consider the problem of how children learn relative-clause constructions. The principle of disconfirmability plays an important role in that analysis.

THE PARALLEL-FUNCTION HYPOTHESIS

A series of researchers have reported systematic misinterpretations of object relative clauses. Amy Sheldon (1974) first reported that children between 3 and 5 consistently took object relatives as subject relatives in toy-moving tasks. For instance, when children were given a sentence of the form:

5. the rat hit the cat that jumped over the pig.

they consistently chose the rat as the subject of both *hit* and *jump*. Sheldon found that the interpretation changed when the noun in the relative clause changes roles:

6. the rat hit the cat that the pig jumped over.

The *cat* is chosen as the object of both *hit* and *jump over*. For these sentences, children allowed object readings. One notion covered both sets of results: *parallel function*. In 5, the rat is the subject of both *hit* and *jump over*. In 6, *cat* is the object of both *hit* and *jump over*. Nothing in the argument that we present shows that parallel function is or is not a part of the pragmatic preferences that a child exhibits. We argue that, if it exists, it functions entirely outside syntactic constraints and that only syntactic constraints permit an explanation of how relative clauses are acquired. In other words, a syntactic theory explains how the child moves from the wrong theory to the right theory.

A number of further studies have shown that the primary effect lies in the interpretation of postobject relative clauses as referring to subjects. Tavakolian found that 63% of the responses from 24 children evenly divided between ages 3 and 5 gave subject readings for the relative clause in sentences like number 5.[4] Only 19% of the answers were correct. With sentences like 6, she found that only 38% correctly took the second noun as object of both verbs *hit* and *jumped over*. It was especially interesting to note that 22% of the children incorrectly took the subject of the first clause to be the object of the second clause in direct violation of the parallel-function strategy. In other words, the *rat* hits the *cat* and gets *jumped* over by the *pig*. In sum, half of the parallel-function theory seems less well substantiated; parallelism with objects is doubtful.

Linguistic theory can explain the preference for subject interpretation by reference to a phrase-structure tree and a universal principle of control (see the references in Reinhard, 1976; Solan, 1978). This principle has broad support (but we refine and modify it later). If we attach the relative clause directly to the topmost node, then, following an interpretive principle, it can only refer to NP_1:

7.

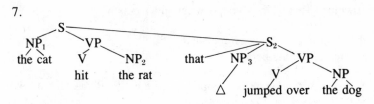

8. Universal: A missing NP cannot be higher on the tree than the NP that is its antecedent.[5]

(We modify this principle later.) It follows that the relative clause NP_3 can only have *cat* as subject. The adult language interpretation is produced by attaching the relative to NP_2 (the rat):

9.

We now have two explanations that can account for the facts. We have a pragmatic explanation, *parallel function,* and a syntactic explanation, which we can call the *structural misrepresentation hypothesis* (7 deviates from 9). How can one choose between them? One apparently involves more apparatus because

---

[4]See also de Villiers, Tager-Flusberg, and Hakuta (1976).

[5]This universal was proposed by Edwin Williams. It is now seen as a subpart of the c-command relation that governs anaphoric and transformational relations throughout grammar.

the structure of TG is involved. However, following our previous argument, failure to assume the presence of this apparatus requires that one explain its appearance at a later point in acquisition.

We decided to supplement our a priori reasoning with an experiment that would place the two theories in competition. What we sought was a syntactic context of sufficient subtlety that we would be able to pinpoint the differences between the two theories. We found such a context in the subcategorizations of the verb *put*. What follows is partially excerpted from a paper by L. Solan and T. Roeper (1978) that has not been widely circulated.

THE PUT EXPERIMENT

The verb *put* requires both a noun phrase and a prepositional phrase in its subcategorization. Thus, 10a is grammatical and 10b is not:

10a. the child put the book on the shelf.
  b. *the child put the book.

There is no limit to the length or complexity of the NP. It can take a relative clause:

11. the child put [$_{NP}$ the book that was under the bed] on the shelf.

It is impossible to interpret the relative clause as modifying the subject of the sentence. That is, *the child* cannot be interpreted as the one that was under the bed. It is possible, however, for a subject to relate to a discontinuous (extraposed) relative clause:

12a. the woman came in that was wearing a mink coat
  b. the child read the book who ate the sandwich.

An extraposed relative clause must be attached to the topmost S. The reason that the relative clause in a *put* sentence like 11 cannot relate to the subject is that it cannot be attached to the topmost S. Thus, 13 is possible, but not 14.

13.

14.*

```
        ___S₁___
    NP       VP_____PP
the child  V    NP      ___S₂      Prep    NP
         put the book    /  \       on   the shelf
                       that NP  VP
                            V    PP
                          Δ  was Prep    NP
                              under  the bed
```

The reason for the ungrammaticality of 14 lies in a fundamental aspect of universal phrase structure rules, which can be called the "no-tangle constraint": the lines in a tree may never cross. In 14, it is impossible to interpret the relative clause as being attached to the highest node in the tree without breaking the no-tangle constraint. It is fair to say that without the assumption of the no-tangle constraint, language would be unlearnable.

Let us now relate our two hypotheses to the *put* sentences:

1. The *parallell-function hypothesis* makes no reference to phrase structure. Therefore, the prediction is that children will allow *the child* to be the subject of both the matrix clause and the relative clauses.

2. *The structural-misrepresentation hypothesis* claims that it will be impossible for *the child* to be the subject of both the matrix and the relative clause. It makes no prediction about whether the relative clause will be interpreted with reference to the object.

There are two further assumptions that we need to make hypothesis 2 complete. First, we must assume that the children in the experiment know that *put* takes an obligatory prepositional phrase. Our pretest meets this requirement. Second, we must assume that relative clauses undergo "bound-variable" interpretation and do not behave like free pronouns. Thus, in a sentence like *John put the boy that he liked in the corner.* the *he* may refer to *John*. There is good evidence for the universal claim that relative clauses behave like bound variables (see Hirschbuhler, 1978). The gap in 14, therefore, cannot be interpreted as a free pronoun. As we see later, our results support this assumption.

Subjects

The subjects were 30 children attending several schools and day-care centers. Although we originally intended to test children between 3 and 5 years of age, no one under 4 completed the questionnaire; the subjects were all between 4 and 6 years old. The subjects were interviewed one at a time and were presented with a toy barn whose doors were open, a number of toy animals, a boy, and a girl.

Subcategorization Pretest

After a number of practice sentences in which the children became used to toys, we gave them the following sentence:

15. The dog put the turtle in the barn.

There were two turtles. One was already in the barn. If the child took the turtle outside the barn and put it into the barn, it was considered a correct response. If the child tried in some way to associate the task with the turtle already in the barn, then the response was considered incorrect. The incorrect response arises when the child takes *the turtle in the barn* to be a constituent. This is possible only if the child assumes that *put* does not take an obligatory PP, but rather the PP is part of the NP (the turtle). Only children who answered both of two sentences like 15 correctly were scored for the remainder of the questionnaire. But, because no subject who was able to finish the questionnaire failed to understand the subcategorization for *put*, this was not an issue. Only three children failed the pretest.

Test Sentences

Twenty sentences of the following four kinds were presented to the children:

16a. The boy put the dog_O $that_S$ kicked the horse in the barn.   (OS)
  b. The boy put the dog_O $that_O$ the horse kicked in the barn.   (OS)
  c. The boy pushed the dog_O $that_S$ kicked the horse.   (OS)
  d. The boy pushed the dog_O $that_O$ the horse kicked.   (OO)

The letters O and S represent the grammatical role of subject or object in the adult language. The *push* sentences provided a crucial contrast because they do not require an obligatory prepositional phrase. Therefore, they should permit top-S attachment of relative clauses. Two different questionnaires were used and the results were combined (see Solan & Roeper, 1978, for further details).

Results

There were 300 responses to *put* sentences and 300 to *push* sentences. Of these, 53 (18%) of the *put* responses were incorrect, and 64 (21%) of the *push* sentences were incorrect. That is, there was no significant difference in the relative difficulty of the two sentence types.

Half of the sentences were OS sentences, and the other half were OO sentences. Of the 300 OS responses, there were 59 errors (20%); there were 57 errors (19%) on the OO sentences. That there were no fewer OO errors than OS

TABLE 4.1
Number of Each Type of Structural Error
According to the Syntactic Structure of the
Sentence[a]

	S Attachment	Failure to Attach
Put	0 (0)	42 (14)
Push	40 (9)	6 (2)

[a] Numbers in parentheses indicate the number of children who made each type of error.

errors fails to support the parallel-function hypothesis. In gross measures, therefore, the sentences were all of roughly the same difficulty.

There were two kinds of errors that are pertinent to our analysis: *structural misrepresentation* (attachment to the topmost S) and *attachment failures* (the child asks "who kicked the horse" or just ignores the relative clause). Table 4.1 provides a breakdown of responses:

The relationship between structural errors and sentence type was found to be highly significant, as was the distribution of children making these errors ($p < .005$ in both cases). Thus, whether or not the child will commit either of these errors depends crucially on whether the main verb is *put* or *push*.

The contrast between OS and OO relative clauses proved nonexistent. The errors are evenly divided between them, as shown in table 4.2:

Chi-square analysis reveals no significant relation between errors and sentence types ($p < .10$ in both cases).

The strength of these results deserves emphasis. There were *no* children who disobeyed the no-tangle constraint and allowed the subject of the matrix sentence to control the relative clause in *put* sentences. Nothing in the parallel-function

TABLE 4.2
Number of Each Type of Structural Error
According to the Functional Relations of the
Sentence[a]

	S Attachment	Failure to Attach
OS	22 (10)	22 (7)
OO	20 (9)	24 (9)

[a] Numbers in parentheses indicate the number of children who made each type of error.

hypothesis predicts this result. By contrast, there were 40 instances with *push* sentences in which we obtained top-S attachment readings. The *put* sentences received 42 attachment failures, whereas the *push* sentences had only six. These cases are of particular interest and we return to them later.

The fact that the no-tangle constraint was obeyed 100% of the time differentiates this result from most of the results one finds in the acquisition literature. The explanation for the difference lies in the fact that the no-tangle constraint is different from linguistic rules. The passive, for example, will generally—but with exceptions—be comprehended by 5 year olds. But the passive represents a possible rule in universal grammar; it is optional in any particular language. The no-tangle constraint, by contrast, is a boundary condition on the projection of all syntactic rules. In this light, exceptionless results are to be expected.

These results establish that by the age of 4 children use structure in the representation of relative-clause sentences and obey both the no-tangle constraint and the c-command principle of control. There is no evidence that parallel function plays a role. If it plays a role, it clearly does not supplant the precise structural principles that children and adults follow. We find, in other words, that attributing adult principles to children enables us to predict the differential behavior of children in a fairly subtle syntactic contrast. It is in the subtle aspects of syntax that genuine principles emerge clearly.

TOPMOSTS IN THE GRAMMAR OF CHILDREN

What is the child's grammar that leads to the structural misrepresentation we have discovered? A straightforward projection of the facts into phrase structure rules leads us to posit recursion as part of the topmost S:

17. S → NP VP (S).

Although we believe that this claim is correct, the conclusion is not straightforward.

Variability

There are two features of the relative-clause behavior that must be examined. First, our results are essentially percentage results. The children should have provided 100% *failure to attach* for the *put* sentences and 100% *subject* interpretation for the *push* sentence-final relatives. This was not the case. All of the children gave some object-relative clause readings. We might attribute this variation to experimental noise, but that is an unhappy step when one is dealing with a deterministic system.

The second set of facts are these: In another experiment, Goodluck and Tavakolian (1979) found that an even higher proportion (66%) of correct object-relative sentences were provided when they used an *inanimate* object as the direct object in the subordinate clause:

18. the dog kicks the horse that knocks over *the fence.*

Results improved further when an intransitive relative clause was used:

19. the dog hits the horse that jumps up and down.

Here, the children were correct 76% of the time. The children were of the same age and performed similarly to those in the *put* experiment when given animate objects in the relative clause (see Goodluck & Tavakolian, 1979, for details).

These results suggest that a cognitive variable interacts with linguistic functioning. It is difficult to state what that cognitive variable is, but we can reason about it. When there are three animals to be manipulated, the child finds it easier to interpret the relative clause as a subject relative. Consequently, animacy makes greater cognitive demands, which forces the child to take the "earlier" of two linguistic alternatives. Object relativization interpretation is apparently more difficult. We have not stated a direct mechanical relation between the cognitive variable and the linguistic structure. Variation is what one expects when two systems that are not mechanically connected interact. A deterministic system is what one expects when there is a mechanical connection between two systems. These results are, therefore, consistent with a view of cognitive variables interacting with a grammatical system but not being a mechanical part of that system.

The Control Question

What, then, is the child's grammatical system? Is there any provision in linguistic theory with which we can state, using linguistic formalism, a grammar that permits variation in the interpretation of relative clauses? Recent work in the theory of control, which has reached a new level of refinement, suggests a way to account for our data. Our conclusions about the reality of structure in the child's grammar remain firm; however, the principle of control needs revision. That is, the "no-tangle" principle that we found to be present in the *put* experiment suggests the necessary presence of structure in children's grammars. However, the principle of control that says a relative clause can never be governed by an NP lower in the tree needs revision because we find that the children provide both subject and object control.

The first question to raise is this: Is there any evidence in the adult language that would lead a child to treat a sentence-final relative as an object relative? There is; it is possible to say:

20. Lee put *the coat* in the closet *that you wanted to wear*.

The relative clause clearly relates to the object and not the subject although it is not dominated by the object NP. It is outside the VP prepositional phrase, which means that it must be attached to the VP or higher. In the adult grammar, this relative is generally called "extraposed," although most recent accounts believe that it is generated sentence finally and "interpreted" to be the same as a relative generated under a subject or object NP.

In addition, Williams (1980) has argued that many structures previously regarded as controlled are sometimes uncontrolled. For instance, infinitivals are controlled in some circumstances (*I try to win*) in which no lexical subject is possible (**I try for Lee to win*), but not obligatorily controlled in others (*I want to win*) in which a lexical subject is possible (*I want for Lee to win*), but noncontrol is also possible (*I want to meet at six*). In this sentence, the implication is that several people will meet and not just I. (There are a number of stimulating and intricate arguments for which I refer the reader to Williams, 1980.)

If we now argue that relative clauses are uncontrolled,[6] then we must account for the fact that in the *put* sentences, they are always interpreted, if interpreted at all, as object relatives. Williams argues that an additional principle is needed: Structures (including sentences) directly dominated by an NP are always controlled by that NP.

Now the theory connects perfectly to the facts we have observed. Some of the children allowed sentence-final relatives (the *push* sentences) to refer to either subject or object. This follows if the relatives are attached to the topmost S. These children divided into two groups. When confronted with the *put* sentences, one group gave object interpretation because they were forced by the no-tangle restriction to put the relative under the object NP where it is uniquely controlled. The other group exhibited *failure-to-attach* behavior. There were 42 *failure-to-attach* responses and nine children who consistently responded in this way. These children got both subject- and object-relative interpretation from the topmost-S attachment on *push* sentences, but they were unable to attach relatives at all on the *put* sentences because their grammars did not contain an NP-S expansion in the phrase-structure rules. We see no other possible explanation for their variable behavior on the sentence-final relatives and their *failure-to-attach* behavior on the sentence-internal relatives.

The perspective of universal grammar offers further evidence to buttress our account. There are, apparently, languages in which one can have sentence-final

---

[6]The c-command principle itself is well-established in child grammars (See Solan (1978) and Goodluck (1978)). There may still be arguments for maintaining c-command for relative clause control as well (See Hsu (1981)). The crucial part of the argument is that extraposition from object position involves VP-attachment and not S-attachment. In that case the object still c-commands the relative clause although it does not dominate the relative clause.

relatives but they cannot occur internally (i.e., you never have *the person that was here left*). Therefore, they must be generated in sentence-final position and be connected via an interpretive rule to the sentence-medial position. The perspective of universal grammar invites us to ask what the principle of disconfirmability can contribute.

There are apparently two sets of languages in the world: those that have restrictive relatives exclusively attached to the topmost S, which we call *A*, and those that allow both topmost-S and NP–S structures, which we call *B* (see Cooper, 1975, and Keenan, 1977). Children who learn English must at some point decide that their language is of the *B* variety.

21A. $S \rightarrow NP\ VP\ (S)$
  B. $S \rightarrow NP\ VP\ (S)$
      $NP \rightarrow NP\ (S)$

Which grammar would a child choose first? The answer should be clear: *A*. If a child chose A, then a single sentence that contained a subject relative (*the person that I saw is here*) could move the child from grammar *A* to grammar *B*. However, if the child began with the assumption that *B* is correct, then it is very difficult to imagine what kind of evidence would prove that *A* is correct. All the sentences from the *A* grammar would simply reaffirm that S expanded to include a second S and they would not bear upon the NP expansion. The child could simply assume that NP expansions were rare in adult grammar and for that reason happened not to occur in the corpus examined. Therefore, there would be no way in which the child could disallow the expansion of *B* if that were his or her initial grammar. We are led by the principle of disconfirmability to propose that at some point, grammar *A* should be the grammar that the child adopts.

The prevalence of both subject and object-relative clauses in the adult language might lead us to expect that children pass through the topmost-S or *A*-grammar phase silently. That is, the first day that they allow a recursive S in their grammar, children immediately encounter evidence (a subject-relative clause) that indicates an S expansion at both the sentence and NP level. On the other hand, the evidence we have assembled suggests that children may in fact utilize grammar *A* for a period. This in turn illustrates our earlier claim that children ignore certain sentences for a period of time until they are ready to allow them to affect their grammars.

Extraction and Tree-Structure

We have thus far provided arguments in behalf of the topmost-S analysis from children's responses to *put* sentences and from language universals. Recent work by Yukio Otsu (in preparation) adds to our evidence from a new domain: extraction rules. Otsu contrasted the extraction of NP's from within PP's (22a) and from within S's (22b) (both under NP's in the adult grammar):

Here's a dog with a bandage. What did he hit the dog with?

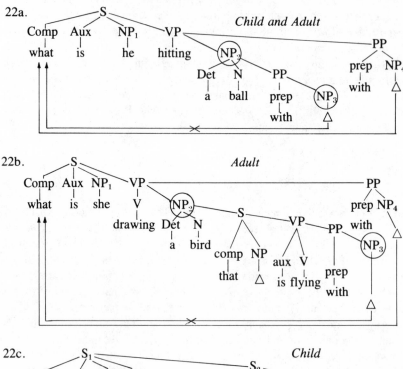

22a.

Child and Adult

22b.

Adult

22c.

Child

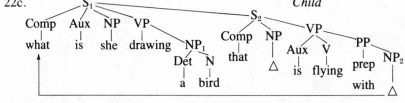

The experimental procedure, in brief, was this: Otsu gave individualized tests to children who were 3, 4, and 5. In each instance, the children were shown a picture. One of the pictures shows a boy using a bat to hit a dog with a bandage. Another picture shows a girl who is using a pen to draw a bird that is flying with long wings. The experimenter says to the child, "This is Susan. She is drawing a bird which is flying with long wings. What is she drawing a bird which is flying with?" or for the earlier sentence: "This is John. He is hitting a ball with a funny shape. What is he hitting a ball with?" The adult answer to both of these questions will not allow the object to be taken from the *with* phrase under the NP because it violates a basic principle of grammar called the A-over-A principle. This states that if an NP is under another NP, a transformation will always operate only on the higher NP. The *with* question can be interpreted to apply to a

PP that is attached to a higher VP and therefore the extraction of an NP is permitted. This is applicable even if no *with* has been mentioned before the question but it is inferred from the picture. So, an adult answer is "with a bat" and not "with a long tail."

One might have expected the children to take the lower NP and violate A-over-A on the pragmatic grounds that the only "with" mentioned involved the lower NP. The answers divided in just the fashion predicted by the topmost-S hypothesis. The children answered the NP–PP sentences correctly with "a bat," which was appropriate. When an S.was involved, the children gave the NP from the relative clause "with long wings." These results are explainable under the assumption that children always obey the A-over-A principle, but attach relative clauses to the topmost S. In 22a, one can see that a NP dominates the NP "a bandage"—namely, "a dog"—which is not therefore accessible to the transformation and *with* must be interpreted as an instrumental PP on the VP. In (22c), since S_2 is attached directly to S_1, no NP dominates NP_2. Therefore NP_2 is available for extraction. This provides further evidence in behalf of the topmost-S hypothesis.

These results are consistent with the general view that what children must do is justify the nodes in a syntactic tree, or, put differently, establish the phrase structure rules of their language. Everything else could be universal: The transformations and their constraints would require no learning. This view is compatible with evidentiary requirements. It is fairly easy to imagine the evidence needed to establish phrase-structure rules, but very difficult to imagine the evidence needed for constraints on transformations.

Further Evidence

The grammar *A* that we have proposed as the child's first grammar makes predictions that are more extensive than the evidence we have considered thus far. The rule S → NP VP (S) does not limit the sentence-final S to relative clauses but implies that all complex sentences will initially emerge in this fashion. In fact, there exists evidence that an impressive variety of complement clauses can be generated under the sentence-final S. S. Tavakolian (1977) found that with infinitive sentences, the same principle applies:

23. Infinitive: the lion tells the pig to jump over the horse. The lion both tells the pig and jumps over the horse. [Goodluck and Roeper (1979) found subject interpretations for -*ing* perception verb complements:]
24. Lee saw Sandy sitting in the chair (Lee sits in the chair).

In addition, there is evidence from children's interpretation of negatives (Phinney, 1981) that they interpret negatives as if they are attached to the topmost S. All of the children involved were in the same 3–5 age range.

THE DISTINCTION BETWEEN CONTEXT AND MECHANISM

Hamburger and Crain (this volume) show quite clearly that a number of contextual factors—which they call felicity conditions—facilitate the acquisition of relative clauses. For instance, children respond differently if different numbers of animals are involved in an experimental situation. Hamburger and Crain argue persuasively that acquisition theory must be sensitive to such factors. We can now ask where such felicity conditions connect to an acquisition device.

We outline three features of an acquisition mechanism (see Roeper, in press, for more discussion). The primary function of an acquisition mechanism is to add rules and specifications to a grammar. We can assume that the child begins with "core" grammar. The concept of "core" grammar remains programmatic and needs refinement, but it is conceptually clear. It consists of a set of universal assumptions plus a set of open parameters whose character is set by specific pieces of information. One parameter is what we have just discussed: alternative grammars A and B.

The assumption of "core" grammar is an abstraction but a necessary and not an arbitrary abstraction. It is abstract in the sense that the features of core grammar may themselves be instantiated by other mental or biological growth. Therefore, the principles of core grammar may have a biological substructure or a cognitive substructure, which itself is an appropriate object of study. It is a necessary abstraction in that any effort towards a reductionist account will miss generalizations and fail to provide the explanatory logic that the assumption of core grammar is able to provide. If core grammar itself is subject to maturational processes, then it is quite possible that only certain parts of core grammar provide open parameters for specification at certain stages. We illustrate this later.

A second function of an acquisition mechanism involves the exclusion of irrelevant sentences. Children must know or easily infer exactly what data is relevant to current hypotheses. If they do not, then two dangers arise: First, a child could analyze a certain sentence (or set of like structures) forever without being able to resolve ambiguities (as work in mathematical approaches to linguistics illustrates; see Wexler & Culicover, 1980). Second, if a child chose the wrong sentence, he or she would integrate it in his or her grammar in a way that made the next step in acquisition impossible (see Roeper, in press).

A third function of an acquisition mechanism is the pairing of triggers with grammatical principles. Triggers may come from within the grammar or from outside the grammar. The extragrammatical concept *thing* may be involved in triggering the grammatical concept *noun,* although in the adult language *noun* is defined abstractly and specifically not limited to things (e.g., *the dancing*). The grammatical fact about German that negatives appear at the end of clauses could be the inside trigger for the fact that German is verb final.

Here is where one argument of Hamburger and Crain applies. Let us suppose that the cognitive notion of *presuppostion* is a trigger for the syntactic structure of relative clauses. It signals to the child that *relatives* are different from other complements. There are certain contexts in which the notion of presupposition applies naturally, and these contexts, presumably, will be the first to elicit correct usage of relative clauses. Hamburger and Crain show that a sentence of the form *the rat hit the cat that pushed the dog* is most naturally understood if there are two cats. Under those circumstances, the relative clause serves to identify which cat got hit by linking that cat to the presuppositional relative clause.

Now, if a child fails to understand relative clauses properly when there is no obvious role for presupposition, should we credit the child with the adult knowledge of relative clauses? It is important to remember that presupposition is not a part of a syntactic definition. Phrase-structure rules cannot express the concept of presupposition. The reality of phrase-structure rules is reflected in the fact that the syntax of restrictive (presuppositional) relatives and nonrestrictive relatives is essentially the same. Therefore, adults can use relative clauses without a notion of presupposition. That is, the child forces the NP–S analysis in realizing, by presuppositional analysis, that it is the object that is required.

Strong hypotheses generally have a clarifying effect. Let us consider the strongest hypothesis: Children do not have an autonomous syntactic representation until they can interpret relative clauses when no presupposition is necessary. Thus, children first use the notion ''presupposition'' to identify relative clauses as a particular complement type. They interpret them with respect to whatever noun most naturally takes a presupposition as long as it is consistent with their syntactic rules. Our analysis suggests that both subject- and object-relative interpretation is acceptable for relatives attached to the topmost S. When both nouns take the presupposition equally well, a variety of other contextual and cognitive factors could come into play. This variation is what we predict from our formulation of relative-clause control as being partially open to nonsyntactic influences.

The use of presupposition as a trigger for relative clauses prepares the acquisition mechanism to be sensitive to a new syntactic trigger: sentences with subject relatives (*the person that I like is here*). These sentences cannot be generated with sentence-final relative-phrase structure. They therefore trigger a reanalysis of relatives as being generated in an NP–S phrase-structure expansion. This new expansion automatically becomes an option for object relatives as well.

There is an alternative hypothesis: The notion of presupposition could immediately trigger the NP–S analysis directly. This analysis has two potential problems: (1) for languages in which there is no NP–S rule, it would be difficult to state how the child would unlearn this analysis; (2) the acquisition mechanism would be required to undergo a decoupling of syntactic structure from semantic type because the NP–S structure also occurs with nonrestrictive relatives that are not presupposed.

We have not stated an algorithm for determining what is part of context and what should be formally described as part of grammar. The distinction should be clear, although its representation changes as theory is enriched. Context may never lend itself to formal representation, but this does not mean that grammatical theory cannot be formally represented, nor that we cannot determine specific points in grammar where extragrammatical factors will have an influence.

Parsing

We have discussed a number of factors that interact with an acquisition mechanism: pragmatic factors in experimental situations, cognitive factors that are sensitive to animacy, the principle of disconfirmability in language universals. Now we would like to introduce real-time factors. The child's capacity to acquire language must be responsive to real-time pressures or it will not succeed. If an initial grammar made requirements that overloaded memory, then although the grammar was present and the evidence was present, the child might be unable to make them connect. If grammar A were difficult to parse, acquisition might fail. In fact, grammar A appears to be very easy to parse; it involves a "flat" structure and no extra nodes. (See Frazier, 1978, for a definition of "minimal attachment"'that fits the facts under discussion fairly well.) This may be an accident with respect to the principle of disconfirmability, but it is probably not an accident in biological terms. Every organism must be so arranged that different systems favor each other's efficient operation. There is no logical connection between linguistic universals and parsing procedures, but there can be a biological one. Evolution may have brought about their compatibility. Until evolution took place, it is quite possible that an organism could have had grammatical ability, but a memory system that was inadequate to carry out that ability. Our brains may still retain many abilities that the recent evolution of upright posture has rendered unusable.

Therefore, we can argue that the fact that a child's grammar is consistent with a fairly undemanding parsing procedure is a prerequisite for acquisition. We have not thereby argued that a grammar is reducible to a parsing system or that any feature of "use" has some priority in biological terms over competence. The grammar is not derived from parsing strategies, nor parsing strategies from the grammar. Each, doubtless, has complex connections to other aspects of our biology, but without a biological explanation, we can only say that they are both independently necessary for language acquisition.

Conclusion

Our approach has been to give a role in acquisition to a diverse set of factors: linguistic, cognitive, processing, pragmatic. Our emphasis falls not upon defining each of these, but upon the specification of a mechanism that determines with exactitude how they interact. These factors are not all susceptible to precise definition. Similarly, the concept of "environment" in evolutionary theory cannot be fully defined. Nevertheless, genetic theory, which is partially sensitive to environment, can be formally defined and is therefore the focus of attention. Likewise, we believe that ''pragmatic'' factors and some aspects of ''cognitive'' factors will not receive a precise definition; nevertheless the growth of a grammar in a child's mind reveals in precise ways how they interact.

Our model of how they interact is incomplete, but it begins with the assumption that there is a pairing between specific ''triggers'' and specific ''decisions'' a child must make (or parameters) about particular features of his or her language. When those decisions have been made, and not before, the relevant universals in language appear. Thus, the relative-clause structure appears when the child hears a subject relative and this in turn follows the universal principles of control.

It should be apparent that as linguistic theory becomes refined, it provides increasingly subtle and illuminating insights into language acquisition.

ACKNOWLEDGMENTS

This research was supported in part by NIH grant HD09647 to T. Roeper and S. J. Keyser, and a grant from the Alfred P. Sloan Foundation. I would like to thank Edwin Williams for discussions of the major ideas in this chapter and Helen Goodluck, Ed Matthei, Yukio Otsu, Marianne Phinney, Larry Solan, and Susan Tavakolian whose research provided the background for much of what is discussed herein.

REFERENCES

Baker, C. L. Syntactic theory and the projection problem. *Linguistic Inquiry*, 1979, 10, 533–583.

Baker, C. L. Learnability and the English auxiliary system. In C. L. Baker & J. McCarthy (Eds.), *Proceedings of the logical problem of language acquisition*. M.I.T. Press Cambridge Mass. In press.

Chomsky, N. On binding. *Linguistic Inquiry* 11, 1980, 1–47.

Cooper, R. *Montatgues semantics theory and transformation syntax*. Doctorial dissertation, University of Massachusetts, 1975.

de Villiers, J. H. Tager-flusberg K. Hakuta & Cohen, M. Children's comprehension of relative clauses (mimeo) Havard University.

Fay, D. Transformation as mental operations: A reply to Kuczaj. *Journal of Children Language* 5 (1), 143–151.

Frazier, L. *On comprehending sentences: Syntactic parsing strategies*. Indiana University Linguistics Club Publications, 1978.

Gold, E. M. Language Identification in the limit. *Information and Control*, 1967, *16*, 447–474.

Goodluck, H. & Roeper, T. The acquisition of perception verb complements. In F. Eckman & A. Hastings (Eds), *Studies in the first and second language acquisition* Rowley Mass. Newbury House, 1979.

Goodluck, H. & Solan, L. Reply to Erreich, Valian, Winzemer. *Cognition*, 1979.

Goodluck, H. *Linguistic Principles in Children's grammar of Complement subject Interpretation* University of Massachusetts doctoral dissertation, 1978.

Goodluck, H. & Tavakolian, S. Parsing, Recursion, and the LAD (mimeo) University of Wisconsin, Madison, 1979.

Hirschbuler, P. *The Semantics and Syntax of Wh-Constructions*. Doctoral Dissertation University of Massachusetts, 1978.

Hsu, J. *The Development of Structural Principles Related to Complement Subject Interpretation*. Doctoral Dissertation CUNY, 1981.

Keenan, E. Noun phrase accesibility and universal grammar. *Linguisitics Inquiry* 1977, *8* (1) 63–101.

Kuczaj, S. Arguments against Hurfords aux copying rule. *Journal of Child Languages*, 1979, *3*, 423–427.

Phinney, M. The interpretation of negation in complex sentences. In S. Tavakolian (Eds.) *Linguistic theory and language acquisition*. Cambridge, Mass.: M.I.T. Press, in press.

Pinker, S. Formal models of language learning. *Cognition* 1979 7, 217–283.

Reinhard, T. The syntactic domain of anaphora. Doctorial dissertation, Cambridge, Mass. M.I.T. 1976.

Roeper, T. On the interpretation of one word utterances. *Chicago Linguistics Society*, 1973, 9, 545–556.

Roeper, T. In pursuit of a deductive model of language acquisition. In C. L. Baker & J. McCarthy (Eds.) *The logical problem of language acquisition*. Cambridge Mass. M.I.T. in press.

Roeper, T. *Approaches to a theory of language acquisition*. Doctorial dissertation, Harvard University, 1972.

Sheldon, A. The role of parallel function in the acquisition of relative clauses in English. *Journal of Verbal Learning and Verbal Behavior*, 1974, *13*, 272–281.

Solan, L. & Roeper, T. Children's use of Syntactic structure in interpreting relative clauses. In H. Goodluck & L. Solan (Eds.), *Papers in the structures and development of child language* (University of Massachusetts Occasional Papers in Linguistics, No. 4.) Amherst, Mass. 1978, 105–127.

Solan, L. *Anaphora in child language*. Doctorial dissertation, University of Massachusetts, 1978.

Tavakolian, S. *Structural principles in the acquisition of complex sentences*. Doctorial dissertation, University of Massuchusetts, 1977.

Tavakolian. S. Children's use of syntactic structure in interpreting relative clauses. In S. Tavakolian (Eds.) *Linguistic theory and language acquisition*. Cambridge, Mass. M.I.T. Press, 1981.

Valian, V., Mayer, J. W. & Erreich, A. A little linguistic model for learning syntax. In S. Tavakolian (Eds.) *Linguistic theory and language acquisition*. Cambridge, Mass M.I.T. Press, in press.

Wexler, K. & Culicover, P. *Formal principles of language acquisition*. Cambridge, Mass. M.I.T. Press, 1980.

Williams, E. S. Predication. *Linguistic Inquiry*. 1980, *11*, (1), 203–239.

Williams, E. Language acquisition, markedness, and phrase structure, in S. Tavakolian (ed.) *Language acquisition and linguistic theory*, M.I.T. Press, 1981.

5
Experimental Gambits in the Service of Language-Acquisition Theory: From the Fiffin Project to Operation Input Swap

Keith E. Nelson
Pennsylvania State University

The core concept for this chapter is "Experimental Language-Acquisition Studies." This means that the chapter examines research in which experimental control or manipulation of the input has been used so that some aspects of children's language learning might be revealed. In so doing, however, I occasionally cross the fuzzy border between experimental and observational work. As the first section of the chapter illustrates, one reason for relating observational and experimental evidence together is that when convergent patterns are obtained, they can be much more conclusive than extensive doses of either brand of evidence alone.

The first section also introduces the Fiffin Project, with data on syntax, discourse, and semantics. In line with the chapter title, the on-going Operation Input Swap comes next. After that, there is much more, presented with the twin goals of stimulating new experimental gambits and of providing a good sampling of completed studies and experimental work in progress. Initial vocabularies and comparison–discrepancy theories come next in this series of topics. Then, an extensive set of experimental semantic acquisition studies are reviewed. This leads to a consideration of carrier input as opposed to target input effects. The last section takes on a range of theoretical questions, including the roles of prototypes and the often-overlooked issue of individual differences.

CONVERGENT EXPERIMENTAL AND OBSERVATIONAL WORK ON SYNTAX AND DISCOURSE

Here, I would like to tell you about a perfect sample of children—perfect for telling us how input characteristics relate to children's syntactic and discourse growth. In fact, I report on a large sample, but not a perfect sample. In describing some of the answers this particular sample can and cannot provide, it is possible also to touch on a broader set of strategies for studying language acquisition than most investigators have so far employed. This section addresses first the number of different ways in which one sample my colleagues and I have examined can be helpful. Additional studies are also briefly reviewed. Then, we return to the following proposition: So far, investigations of input effects have been both too ambitious and not ambitious enough.

The Fiffin Sample

The children observed were seen first as 22 month olds in conversation with their mothers. Then, the complete sample of 25 dyads were observed again when the children were 27 month olds. The results reported here concern primarily how the children's language growth between 22 and 27 months can be accounted for. Unless otherwise noted, the results are outcomes that hold at a closely similar level both for the overall sample of 25 dyads *and* for a subsample of 19 dyads consisting of all mother–child pairs we were able to follow up when the children were 4½ years of age (see also Nelson, 1980a; Nelson & Bonvillian, 1978; Nelson, Denninger, Bonvillian, & Kaplan, 1979).

Now, I present and discuss in turn three major findings for this sample, named after the experimental "Fiffin" concept the children also acquired (discussed later with Semantic Gambits).

Finding Number One

This outcome was computed, like most analyses of relations between maternal input and child-language growth, in terms of a correlation between the mother's speech at point one (22 months for child) and the child's growth between point one and two (27 months). Mothers who tended to use many verbs rich in aux-iliaries at point one had children who advanced between point one and two relatively rapidly in terms of auxiliary use ($r = +.52$). This is true despite the fact that at point one the mother's use of auxiliaries was not "adjusted" to or correlated with the child's level of auxiliary use ($r = -.03$). Note that the direction of the effect, greater complexity of structure in input associated with more rapid advance in the child's language, runs contrary to much theorizing (cf. Snow, 1977). Of further interest is the specificity of the outcome—auxiliary verb use by the mother predicts auxiliary verb growth for the child.

Comment.   We hasten to comment that this result does not imply that high complexity in input *generally* will facilitate syntactic growth. It only suggests that for some constructions at some periods of growth, children may be able to process and use relatively high complexity levels; "fine tuning" in such instances appears less useful than display of a relatively full range of structural complexity. Contrasting examples, in which high complexity was not useful, were encountered when the analysis centered on complete input sentences rather than on auxiliary use in input. Consider the outcomes when mothers' "recasts" of children's preceding utterances were examined. *Simple* recasts were mothers' replies that maintained reference to the same basic meaning in the child's preceding utterance, with the recasting change limited to just one component—the subject, the verb, or the object. An example is the reply "Daddy is eating cake" to the utterance "Daddy is eating." *Complex* recasts involved structural changes in two or three of these components. The 22 month old's ability to analyze and make use of the structurally new information in recast replies, we reasoned, would be higher for the simpler recasts. A high proportion of simple recasts in mothers' replies, in fact, was correlated ($r = +.47$) with the children's rapid growth in mean length of utterance, but the mothers' use of a high proportion of *complex* recasts was negatively related to this measure of language growth ($r = -.41$).

Comment.   In analyzing the relationship between maternal auxiliaries and the child's growth between points one and two in auxiliaries, in *this* sample, the outcome is interpretable because the mother's auxiliary use at point one is *not* tied to the child's level of auxiliaries. This kind of *specific* look at variable relationships is likely to be more appropriate than attempts to statistically control for "overall" language level of the child in terms of utterance length (cf. Newport, Gleitman, & Gleitman, 1977). The problem in general with adjustments for "overall" level is that the adjustments work unequally for different areas of language growth. In this particular sample—and it is bound to vary across samples—the child's utterance length at point one is only very weakly correlated ($r = +.20$) concurrently with the child's complexity of auxiliaries. So, adjusting for utterance length would provide very little adjustment for auxiliary level. In other areas of syntax—noun phrases and questions, for example—the relationships to utterance length are different. The conclusion, then, is that part of what needs to be reported about each sample is the pattern of unadjusted correlations for all areas of syntactic growth. These data allow us to decide for any specific samples which of several interpretations are most reasonable for particular pairings of an input variable with a child-syntax–growth variable. For example, in area X of the child's progress, given a raw correlation with a maternal input variable, we may try to choose from the following possible conclusions: (1) the unadjusted correlation reflects the linkage between the input variable and the child's syntactic growth in area X; (2) the input variable in the sample is hopelessly confounded with the child's initial language level in area X; (3) after an appropriate, specific adjustment (typically not by an MLU adjustment), the input variable's linkage to the child's syntactic growth in area X can be assessed.

Finding Number Two

When a mother and child converse, it is also appropriate to ask what aspects of the *child's* replies to the mother at point one are associated with the child's subsequent syntactic progress. Few prior reports address this question. The strongest answer in our data assumes a negative form. The children at point one who showed *infrequent* reworking or recasting structurally of what their mothers said were the children whose utterance lengths increased most strongly in the 5 months following point one: $r = -.63$. A tentative interpretation is that when the child recasts what the adult has just said, this may often disrupt or interfere with the child's thorough analysis of the adult utterance.

Comment.   As in the case of Finding Number One on mother's and children's auxiliaries, it is important to check on whether the predictive variable for point-one-to-point-two growth is unconfounded with the child's initial level on the particular growth variable under examination—in this case, utterance length. The answer is that the children's initial utterance lengths are *not* associated with how much recasting of their mothers' utterances they show.

Comment.   We assume that this result—22 month olds who engage in relatively little recasting also showing relatively rapid progress in utterance lengths between 22 and 27 months—would not be seen in parallel form for very many other age periods. Instead, we assume that what the child does and what the mother does that make it easier for a child to attend to, process, and use conversational material in revising and improving his or her language systems will *shift as the child's age and language levels shift* (see also Nelson, 1977a, 1980a, 1980b.) To the extent that this holds true, it is imperative that we make efforts to restrict our boundaries for any sample to reasonably narrow ranges in terms of age and language levels.

Illustrations of the shifting meaning of the child's and the mother's language behavior as developmental periods shift are provided with this sample when additional data at age 4½ are also considered. The data show the following results for measures of *discourse* behavior as possible predictors of children's language growth:

1. Neither the child's tendency to change the mother's topic nor the mother's tendency to change the child's topic at 22 months significantly predicts syntactic growth between 22 and 27 months.

2. Similarly, a *joint* measure of discourse at 22 months is unrelated to syntactic growth between 22 and 27 months. The measure employed here was the

average number of speaker turns (C–M–C = three turns) pertaining to the same topic, a measure that clearly considers whether the topic is maintained but ignores the syntactic structure used by the mother and child.

3. Although this turn-taking measure is unrelated to early language growth, mother–child dyads with long topic chains at 22 months strongly tended to be dyads in which the children's communication skill at age 4½ years was high: $r = +.64$ (cf. Wells, 1980). In this case, the measure of 4½ year olds' communication skill was ability to generate a highly communicable, precise description of one picture within a set.

These findings, in conjunction with the other findings previously reviewed, suggest that fairly specific patterns of relationship may hold at particular age periods between input components and children's growth in areas related to such specific input.

Finding Number Three

Correlational data can be supplemented by intervention experiments and also by "natural experiments," which compare the circumstances that obtain when syntactic progress does or does not take place. Such a natural experiment occurred in the present project. The pattern observed was that between point one (22 months) and point two (27 months), some children acquired simple past-tense verbs but other children did not. Moreover, children who did acquire past-tense verbs during this period differed in terms of input from children who failed to show the acquisition: The former heard more past-tense verbs per session in their mothers' speech at point one than did the latter ($t = 2.65$, $p < .02$, means = 16.7 and 10.2). This result suggests that if parents are using a form but not with high frequency, then a modest increase in the availability of the form in input may facilitate the child's analysis of the form and the child's introduction of the form into productive speech.

OPERATION INPUT SWAP AND BEYOND: NEW EXPERIMENTAL BEGINNINGS ON DISCOURSE

Current data from many sources (cf. Gleason & Weintraub, 1978; Snow, 1977) indicates that to some degree, mothers "adjust" their conversational, semantic, and syntactic input to the immature level of their language-learning child. However, if mothers' speech adjustments are actually *responsive* to the child as language growth, it should be possible to demonstrate that mothers with children at language "level X" are prepared to rapidly adjust their input level up when the child moves to "level $X + 1$." We have begun Operation Input Swap to assess this possibility. As a start, we looked at the conversational behavior (videotaped) between a 28 month old with an MLU (in words) of 1.5 (longest = 6 words) and his mother, and then compared (on the same day) these conversations with those between this mother and a *more advanced* child with an MLU of 1.8 (longest = 7 words). The data reveal that on the first occasion of interaction with this new child, the mother was prepared in a number of ways to respond sensitively to the child's level of speech:

> her MLU jumped from 3.7 with her son to 4.6 with the new partner; particularly increased were utterances with nine or more words, from 2.7% to 9.9%; the longest utterance increased from 12 to 21 words; and the following conversational devices, completely lacking in this mother's speech with her son, were introduced— informational choice questions ("Was it a big boat or a little boat?"), complex affirmation ("a good idea."), and recasts of the child's 3–6 word utterances (*C*: "No. I do it." *M*: "Oh, you wanna do it?").

The next step, which will require more time, is to determine whether this mother and mothers like her succeed in influencing positively the advances of their *own children* in ways that are predictable from the sensitivity of their adjustments to children not their own. Ideally, in future investigations, it will be possible to assess each mother's conversational adjustments to several children at different levels as a predictor of her future linguistic behavior with her own child. Such experimental assessments are crucial to breaking the confounding between child–adult and adult–child influences. Similar assessments should also be very helpful in cases in which some therapeutic intervention procedures are needed to improve the quality of child–adult discourse (cf. Bonvillian & Nelson, 1981; Bonvillian, Nelson, & Rhyne, in press; Westerman & Havstad, 1981).

Concluding Remarks

Any particular sample of children and their conversational partners can be informative about *some* input-growth correlations, and it may include some "natural experiments" concerning the transition from absence to presence of a form in the child's system. But it is important not to be too ambitious in the sense of expecting one sample to provide interpretable data on all categories of input-growth relationships (cf. Brown, 1977).

On the other hand, there is room for greater ambition in several directions in how we examine possible language influences of caregiver on child and child on caregiver. First, sample selection—what we might call naturalistic design—can be refined. By intensively studying samples in which the initial ages of the children and the initial language behavior of child and caregiver represent somewhat constricted ranges, we can increase the chances of finding relatively straightforward, unconfounded associations between initial language behaviors and the child's language growth over time in specific areas of language. On a second level, we can study in concert more than one sample at a time—thus allowing selection of, say, a second sample that is informative about precisely those relationships that are clouded in a first sample. Finally, we can be more ambitious in looking for *experimental* evidence that may complement what naturalistic data seem to be telling us. When the child seems to be controlling the parent's language levels, can we test this out? As in Operation Input Swap, by pairing the child with *other* adults, and the parents with children not their own, we can at least come closer to knowing who is controlling whom (see also Gleason & Weintraub, 1978). And when the observational data seem to say that at a particular stage of syntactic growth the child requires certain forms of input for a next step, can we determine in complementary experimental work whether such forms really are necessary (cf. Shatz, 1980) and, if so, in what temporal, conversational patterns? So far, the one example of this sort of complementary work in the literature is the series of studies on recasts reported by Nelson and his colleagues (Nelson, 1977a, 1977b, 1980a, 1980b; Nelson, Carskaddon, & Bonvillian, 1973; Nelson & Denninger, 1977). The pattern of experimental and observational outcomes on recasts established not only that recasts can facilitate syntactic progress, but that the child's acquisition of *specific* question and verb forms is aided by recasts that carry those forms. Still, the precise roles (catalytic? sufficient? necessary and sufficient?) of various kinds of recasts and other contingent replies to the language-learner's utterances remain to be spelled out (Nelson, 1980a).

In my view, it is only through combining possibly convergent evidence from many angles, from a variety of differently constituted samples and different experimental procedures, that we can gain the data required for constructing a persuasive theory of how the child draws upon conversations to gradually construct mature syntactic and discourse systems. Another part of this strategy in theory construction should be to give more careful attention in experimental work to the internal structure of the rules and concepts the child acquires in language, a topic addressed later in this chapter in a section on prototypes and inferential foci.

POSSIBLE EXPERIMENTAL GAMBITS ON ACQUISITION OF AN INITIAL VOCABULARY AND AN INITIAL FUNCTIONAL STRATEGY

In 1973, Katherine Nelson presented evidence on 18 young children and their mothers that was suggestive of two major ideas. First, the child cognitively structures the world and then learns words to mark already acquired concepts, most of which have a strong association with change. "Thus, (according to K. Nelson, 1973) the words the child learns reflect the child's mode of structuring the world. Their properties are those of high salience to the child exhibited either through his own interactions or through their apparent changes [p. 33]." Data interpreted as supporting this notion are the mean percentage of words that label either actions (13%) or specific (14%) or general (51%) things (people, animals, objects, etc.) that generally either move or are moved by the child, as contrasted with words classified in such categories as attribute modifiers (1%), question words and other relational–functional words (2%), and social assertions such as "no" (4%). Second, despite these overall patterns, there are two *functional* hypotheses about the use of language which children and mothers may adopt: that language is primarily Referential (*R*) or that language is primarily an Expressive (*E*) tool. The *E* child as compared with the *R* child learns more general, descriptive nouns (61% versus 34%), fewer assertions and other social words (5% versus 11%), and fewer functional–relational words (1% versus 8%). In short (K. Nelson, 1973), "at an early point the child appears to act on one or another dominant hypothesis about the function of speech. This hypothesis appears to be drawn from his mother's use of the language, while in other cases it is independently derived. The mother's use of the language may also coincide with or conflict with the child's preverbal cognitive organization [p. 102]."

The correlational and descriptive data that support these ideas are intriguing, but they leave wide open the degree to which the child's initial vocabulary and initial theory of language use can be directly influenced by the semantic and conversational input of adults. On the basis of unpublished data of my own on the first 10 to 50 words acquired by 23 children (a total of 923 vocabulary entries, comparable with Katherine Nelson's 900), it seems not too rash to speculate that the lexical input for these children could have led to early acquisition of the following words, apparently missing or extremely rare in prior reports: words for static objects the child does not move or see move ("wall," "star," "stove," "radio"); "taboo" words ("Damn," "shit"); attribute labels such as "pink," "stinky," "two," and "super"); clothing items the child tends not to manipulate ("mittens," "diaper"); and functional–relationals not frequent in most English speech ("very," "could"). It may be that the child of about 12 to 24 months is conceptually prepared to deal with many more such words and that their frequencies in initial vocabularies could be shifted up dramatically if they were given greater salience in the linguistic input of the young child. Experimental intervention tests along these lines might wisely control independently (to the extent possible) the input frequencies of different major lexical categories and the input frequency of discourse devices that are primarily referential or expressive–social in nature. Investigations in this area would be particularly valuable if measures of the children's conceptual mastery and conceptual style outside language were also assessed.

GAMBITS IN THE SERVICE OF
COMPARISON–DISCREPANCY THEORIES

It has become commonplace in developmental theory to talk of the "match" or "discrepancy" between new cognitive structures and representational structures already in the child's cognitive repertoire (e.g., Hunt, 1961; Kagan, 1971; McCall & Kagan, 1970; Nelson, 1980b; Nelson et al., 1973; Piaget, 1970; Turiel, 1969; Vygotsky, in press). Unfortunately, however, it is not commonplace for evidence about "discrepancies" to be collected in a fashion detailed enough to guide theory.

If a developmental discrepancy theory is to be testable in a refined and interesting way, then five conditions need to be met for the experimental study of the child's acquisition of a new structure discrepant from already acquired structures:

1. Base-line information must support (though it cannot prove absolutely) the conclusion that the to-be-acquired structure is not yet in the child's system.
2. Care must be taken to see that variable activation of available structures from baseline to criterion is not confused with acquisition of a new structure.
3. The input providing the basis for the new structure can be readily discriminated from other input.
4. The child shows *specific responses* that indicate use of the new target structure rather than any other structure.
5. A metric of "distance" between old structures and the new structure, independent of response measures, is available.

Later, I argue that cognitive-discrepancy theory is essential to language-acquisition theory and that new experimental gambits are needed because no extant experiments satisfy (and few approach) the just cited conditions.

On Presumed Cognitive Bases and Processes in
Language Acquisition

Language and cognitive processes develop together, with rapid advances in both general areas for most children during their first four years of life. Language as a tool of thought can certainly contribute to basic steps forward in cognitive development, and many new concepts are brought to the child's attention through language. In short, in early development, language can influence cognition. But it is the other side of the coin that I feel requires more emphasis, the cognitive bases of language acquisition. There are many reasons for seeing a lot of cognitive skills in language, some of which are indicated in this passage (Nelson, 1977a):

In terms of individual differences, more and more observations are accumulating that demonstrate that there are many ways (involving physical, personality and cognitive dysfunction) to "go wrong" in language development, to fail to develop a full mastery of language. Increasingly there is evidence that successful paths of language acquisition also are highly varied. Children who use language fluently when they are 6-year-olds differ in the preceding developmental course, showing different rates, contrasting beginning steps, diverse strategies, and even different modes (speech, sign language, print). One implication of these findings is that there may be few fixed, language-specific abilities involved in language acquisition. Rather, general cognitive skills may underlie language acquisition and each child may use these skills to construct an initial, tentative language system that is idiosyncratic [p. 604].

Beyond this, there is correlational evidence that individual differences in language acquisition rates in both normal and retarded populations are tied to rates of cognitive development (Bates, Bretherton, Shore, & McNew, 1981; Lenneberg, 1967; Moore, Clark, Mael, Dawson Myers, Rajotte, & Stoel-Gammon, 1977; Nelson & Bonvillian, 1978). Moreover, when one considers what the child who acquires a particular piece of new linguistic structure must do—attend to, analyze, store, and retrieve the input and connect it to other information already in his or her linguistic system, and then monitor the new structure as it is produced in conversation—then it is easy to recognize the myriad cognitive skills relevant to learning syntax, discourse, phonology, and semantics. Therefore, we are going to continue to have difficulty in understanding *how* language acquisition proceeds until we have refined our models of cognitive advance. So, after a brief look at the question of prerequisites to language, we turn to a particular area of cognitive theorizing—discrepancy theory for the "prelinguistic" child.

Along with many other theorists, I find it highly probable that essential cognitive *prerequisites* for language are established in the "sensorimotor" period of development (Bates, 1976; Bloom & Lahey, 1978; Brown, 1973; Macnamara, 1972; Sinclair, 1969; Slobin, 1973), even though evidence of a persuasive sort by and large has not yet been gathered. To be certain of prerequisites, we must look for possible exceptional and "negative" instances in which a cognitive step has not been taken on time, even though language progressed (cf. Nelson, 1977a; Nelson & Bonvillian, 1978). An interesting pay-off from this strategy has been reported by Affolter (1980): For severely language delayed children given play and sensory training, she found that complex play and imitation (although regularly precedents to onset of genuine, complex language in normal children) were not necessary prerequistes to their language onset. Beyond such beginnings, there is much room for educationally and theoretically rich experimental initiatives concerning the sufficient, necessary, and necessary and sufficient cognitive associates of important language milestones.

Discrepancy Evidence and Theory for the "Prelinguistic" Child

In the first six months of development, many "tests" of discrepancy theories have been conducted. In most instances, the procedure has been to expose the child to respected presentations of one visual stimulus and then to compare the child's relative visual attention to yet another presentation of the original stimulus and to a new stimulus somehow discrepant from the original. One difficulty with tests conducted in this way is that different versions of discrepancy theory have been invoked (Cohen & Gelber, 1975):

> Most investigators have assumed that the more the test stimulus differs from the familiar one, the more the infant will attend. This assumption is not universally accepted, however. McCall (1971) proposed that infant attention can be best described by an inverted-U-shaped function based upon the degree of discrepancy from the familiar stimulus. . . . According to this "discrepancy hypothesis," infants should display maximum attention to a stimulus which offers an optimal amount of discrepancy—a stimulus which is sufficiently familiar that it can be assimilated but sufficiently novel that it provides some new information. Stimuli which are either too familiar or too novel should recruit little attention [p. 376].

A second, compound difficulty is that the majority of stimuli used have been arbitrary collections of objects and forms that bear no obvious relationship to important events or situations the child must learn to code and retrieve, and that for these stimuli as well as for various permutations of faces, the data across studies from 1971 to 1980 (McCall & Kennedy) do not approach consistent support of either of the preceding versions of discrepancy theory. Yet another difficulty, and a major one, is that the *degree* of discrepancy between a familiarized, arbitrary stimulus and a new probe stimulus has seldom been given adequate definition, as Thomas (1971) has noted. Finally, and the most damaging criticism to the infant visual-preference studies, is that the visual responses to all the stimuli, familiar or mildly descrepant, or highly novel, are *nonspecific*. The child's looking behavior towards a stimulus is at once the most easily elicited response for the 4- to 36-week-old subjects in these studies and also the most ambiguous. Novelty, meaningfulness, discrepancy, familiarity, or ease of scanning for a whole pattern or any of its subparts may be determinants of a particular visual fixation. Given such ambiguity on the response side, few inroads on a satisfactory theory of the child's interpretation and processing of discrepant stimuli can be expected. What is needed instead are selection of well-organized, well-defined, meaningful stimuli for repeated presentation in paradigms in which the possible responses can be specific indicators of whether and how both an original and a new stimulus are processed. Also, in the absence of any compelling data to the contrary, the question for a discrepancy comparison of cognitive change should *not* be focused on whether a moderately or maximally discrepant stimulus is the most "interesting" to a child; the question should rather be *how does the child deal with each level of discrepancy* from an originally interpreted stimulus? For 10 month olds—certainly young enough to lack productive labels for concepts—Husaim and Cohen (1980) have presented data on special animal-like stimulus concepts that deal in an interesting way with learning-set and generalization-set discrepancies. Specifically, they show that on the basis of stimulus similarities, the infants respond (head turns) most strongly to those new stimuli with "prototypical" values. Still to be worked out is the meaning of response generalization to these special "concepts" and the relations between an infant's ability to deal with such arrays outside and within the context of language acquisition.

One intriguiging question deserving experimental work is whether variations in child–adult discrepancy in the presyntactic period differentially "prepare" the child for onset of particular aspects of combinatorial speech. It appears that mothers and other input sources may use longer utterances to 6 month olds than to 8 month olds (Sherrod, Friedman, Crawley, Drake, & Devieux, 1977), possibly because of more feedback from the older infants. But the literature so far is silent on whether long or short utterances, simple or complex verbs, or a broad or narrow range of utterance types in the period from 6 months to the child's onset of two-word combinations matter to the child's ability to make an early or smooth beginning in syntax. Longitudinal work that manipulated such presyntactic input variations or that contrasted sharply different naturally occurring subsamples thus would be valuable.

Another area in which presyntactic discrepancy deserves attention concerns discrepancy effects on acquisition of major cognitive milestones. Here, I would first like to review a bit of my own work on input effects on object permanence acquisition and then relate this to rare events, discrepancies, and individual differences in both language and cognition.

A component of object permanence is the ability to predict future positions of moving objects by extrapolating from their trajectories. To understand how the child learns to do this reliably by about 12 months of age, we must have some analyses of situations in which the child progresses in his or her ability to deal with trajectory information. This was provided in an experiment (Nelson, 1971) in which 3 to 9 month olds were treated to the (usually) entertaining spectacle of a toy electric train that ran around most of an oval circuit in plain view, disappeared (with appropriate masking of sound cues) into a tunnel, and reappeared to continue additional laps. As Piaget (1954) and more recent investigators would expect, initial behavior by the infants was confined to looking away or to staring at the tunnel entrance after the train disappeared. But given a dozen or so repeated, regular presentations of the same input pattern, much appropriate anticipation of the train's reappearance at the exit developed. Similarly, when movement-disappearance-reappearance-movement input sequences were presented to a new sample of infants (Nelson, 1974), the infants progressed in using trajectory information to find and anticipate objects. Further, in this second study, generalization between different objects and spatiotemporal trajectories was produced. These observations are unusual in the sense that such *recurrent, well-structured* input examples are probably infrequent in the child's experience. Given such input, the infant shows progress in components of object permanence mastery within minutes. Overall acquisition of object permanence could well rest on a series of such learning encounters typically spread over many months, interspersed with a great deal of experience that the child cannot relate to object-permanence acquisition. A closely related idea is that *rare events* are involved here as in much of cognitive development—roughly stated, a little bit of well-structured, timely, attended-to input is often all that is needed for a child to make a cognitive advance. However, if we do not use experiments to demonstrate when the child can profit rapidly from selected input, then we may vastly underestimate the child's cognitive abilities; we may confuse lack of many appropriately structured input exemplars with a lack of ability to process these exemplars when they do occur.

Now these object-permanence studies have many points of connection with possible strategies for other investigations of language and cognition in young children. For instance, the sequential pattern in input invites responses by the child that are matched to the input—so that the requirement, previously discussed, for response specificity, can be met. In addition, the sequential nature of the appropriate response pattern provides a parallel not only to appropriate formation of sentences but also to the child's developing representation of many complex social and nonsocial events over time. It is my hunch that concentrating research effort on the child's developing sequentially organized behavior will be more productive for theoretical construction than concentration on various recognition responses infants make to isolated, static stimulus displays. Finally, there are at least four reasons for studying well specified input-cognitive-progress relations *together* with input-linguistic-progress relations:

1. Despite previously described cautions, *some* cognitive milestones will be firmly established in future research as prerequisities to linguistic advance.

2. As Nelson and Bonvillian (1973, 1978) have strongly argued, extensive *individual* differences occur in language acquisition and a good part of these appear attributable to differences in the *evidence patterns* children receive; such individual differences should be examined in relation to better descriptions of individual cognitive mastery pathways.

3. As one part of this accounting of individual differences, it may turn out that children at given language stages who—compared with their stage peers—

learn most easily from a relatively broad stage-input discrepancy are also children in nonlinguistic areas of cognition who also best process and use relatively wide discrepancies.

4. The feasibility of any general developmental discrepancy theory can only be determined by considering linguistic as well as nonlinguistic development, normative as well as atypical growth patterns, and frequent as well as infrequent input sets.

SEMANTIC GAMBITS

Initial Semantic Gambit: The Hedgehog Study

Input Control.   This study (Nelson & Bonvillian, 1973; completed, 1971) is apparently the first study on acquisition of multiple labels for a series of different concepts to control the frequency of exposure to *either* the concept exemplars or their semantic labels, and both were controlled. Ten children encountered six examples for each concept studied. The concepts chosen are well described by Leonard (1976):

> None of the objects nor their names were familiar to the children. Nonsense words were not employed, but when one inspects the names of the objects one does not get the impression that they represent everyday household words—"barrel," "bobber," "caboose," "canteen" "compass," "eyebolt," "handcuff," "hedgehog," "nozzle," "oiler," "pulley," "sifter," "silo," "sinker," "snorkel," and "whetstone" [p. 136].

Half the exemplars were named by the mothers and the remaining exemplars of each concept provided opportunities for the children to generalize the labels they learned.

The exposure of the objects and their names were controlled in frequency, but each mother was free to embed these labels in whatever particular sentences she chose. The children were initially 18 month olds. After participating in 10 to 14 sessions spaced about 2 weeks apart, they approached 24 months of age. It was our assumption that the properties of the input were "naturalistic" in the sense that what was to be learned about the "experimental" concepts and their labels shared important properties with the learning of many nonexperimental concepts: (1) mothers labeled some but not all (unlikely for most concepts for reasons of attention and endurance) of the exemplars the children encountered; (2) exemplars encountered by the child were spaced over weeks and months, so that considerable long-term memory was required before a concept and its label was mastered; (3) mothers made a conscious attempt to draw the child's attention to *some* of the exemplars of concepts and their labels, but mixed such input into a stream of more general conversation and nonverbal interaction; and (4) multiple concepts were in the process of acquisition—mothers did not single out a particular day as "hedgehog" day or "bobber" day—and the child's attentional, conceptual, and mnemonic processes were therefore required to deal with possible confusions between different concepts and different labels.

Memory. The ability of these 18–24 month olds to draw upon considerable memory of exemplars and their labels presented in sessions weeks or months previously is implied by these mean data on performance by the end of the study: 69% of the concepts were named and 35% of the total exemplars. Further, the potential high confusion between concepts was not realized—only 12% of the concepts were overgeneralized (see also Nelson & Nelson, 1978).

Learning Set Size and Structure. As each of the 16 concepts included three labeled exemplars, the one clear conclusion allowable is that three such exemplars can provide a sufficient base for the young child's acquisition of a more general semantic concept for which the label is extended to new exemplars that the child never hears named by adults. Information on learning sets with just one or two exemplars is considered in the Rabbit, the Rainbow, the Naete Et Alia, and the Fiffins-Plus gambits in the following sections.

A (Piece of the) Rainbow Gambit

Input Control. Bartlett and Carey (as reported in Carey, 1978) chose a piece of the color lexicon—olive—labeled it "chromium" (felt to be a rarer word in children's experience), and traced its acquisition in 14 nursery-school children. The children were not directly taught the name or given demonstrations of specific naming. Instead, a teacher first used the word in indirect labeling, as in the request "Bring me the chromium cup, not the red one, the chromium one." In addition, the report by Carey suggests that an uncontrolled amount of indirect and direct teaching took place in the classroom as peers interacted. Also, the children must have sometimes overheard "chromium" requests by the teacher that were not addressed to them. Next, a "test" was given 1 week after the original "chromium" requests had been introduced. This test provided an additional instance of input, as each child was asked to pick the "chromium one" from a set of six color chips. Finally, the children were tested 6 weeks after the word "chromium" entered their input. Although children had earlier called olive referents either brown or green, at this 6-week testing point, eight children had made a first step in "mapping" color names to olive referents—they now responded to olive with either "don't know" color answers or with a color name for which they had not yet acquired a stable meaning.

Memory.   If the only exposure to the word "chromium" for a child had been the teacher's original "chromium" request and the testing 1 week later on finding a "chromium" color, then these two labeling events might have carried in their impact across 5 weeks to influence the children's choices of labels in the final testing. For most of the eight children who had progressed, this meant that their original use of "green" to label olive referents had shifted to some uncertain response. However, because the labeling input, as argued immediately above, was not so neatly limited and because the actual exposure to label use may have varied across children, the actual carry over in memory could have ranged from 5 weeks to much less.

Learning Set Size and Structure.   The exemplars available in the experiment proper apparently were one olive color chip (used only in testing) and two continuously available objects, an olive cup and an olive tray. Each child heard others use the word "chromium" two or more times, saw the olive color chip twice, and saw the olive cup and tray a frequent but undetermined number of times.

Despite the many uncertainties about label and referent encounter patterns, Carey's conclusion that a process of "fast mapping" began soon after olive objects and their label "chromium" were introduced to the child appears sound. Following the experiment proper, the children were given a combination of additional input, ambiguous rather than direct feedback to their questions about "chromium," and testing across several months. Some of the children stuck to "green" as a label for olive objects despite all the new input. Others gradually progressed from comprehension control of "chromium" to productive use for olive referent. Within 18 weeks learning time, these latter children fully mapped "chromium" into their lexicon in a way that matched experimental adult input but that conflicted both with the naming behavior of some of their peers and with *most* adults. After all, in my rainbow, any olive tints are called "olive" or "green" and not "chromium." If any of the children encountered uses of "olive" or "chromium" at home or any place besides the study's nursery setting, the input structure uncertainties are even further compounded. In sum, this study shows us that within the rainbow of colors, children given a little new input rapidly began mapping a new label and a new referent color in relation to what they already knew about colors. But, we can precisely chart neither the input to each child nor how the child used it.

The Rabbit Gambit

Input Control.   This study was done "live": the initial exemplar was either a live rabbit (for half of the S's) or a live hamster. Controlled input presentation and testing were accomplished in one day with each of the children. With 10 infants at each of these age periods—9–11 months, 12–14 months, and 15–17 months—Oviatt (1979) has assembled experimental evidence on very early stages in concept acquisition.

The child heard the live exemplar (in a cage) named about 24 times, and was then tested for *comprehension*. Some clear evidence of comprehension emerged. For example, some children looked at or touched the rabbit when asked "where is the rabbit?" but looked at or touched a book when asked "where is the book?" Such comprehension for the original exemplar after the brief training increased sharply with age, from one of 10 children at 9-11 months to eight of 10 children at 15-17 months. When a subset of the children (21) were tested with similar questions for three new, inanimate exemplars (e.g., a drawing of a rabbit) as opposed to distractors, concept-appropriate "generalization" responses also increased with age.

Memory. The children credited with comprehension for the original exemplar all showed appropriate responses after delays of at least 3 minutes and 15 minutes following training. Overall, even after comprehension of generalization ememplars had been assessed, the child's memory was not taxed beyond 30-40 minutes.

Learning Set Size and Structure. Only one exemplar, either a rabbit or a hamster, constituted the learning set for each child. Improved comprehension of the new concept with increased age between 9 and 17 months was definitely indicated. However, the children gave virtually no appropriate productive labels (one child on one occasion said "rabbit") and sometimes produced inappropriate labels like "dog." This result, coupled with the open-ended response measures of looking and reaching, leaves us with few *distinctive* responses to tally as comprehension for the target concepts. Further contributions to the uncertainty are these two conditions when a generalization example was tested: There was just one distractor item present, and the original training animal was still in view and so could be used as a basis for perceptual matching to the generalization exemplar. Thus, we have to plead insufficient evidence concerning *how well* the children comprehended the verbal label for the concept "rabbit" or the concept "hamster." But after a single, very brief training on one exemplar, most 15-17 month olds and at least a few younger children appear to have made some progress in learning a concept and its name.

Picture Generalization Gambits

In 1962, Hochberg and Brooks (see Gibson, 1969) reported on one child who had been given no training in studying or labeling pictures but who, at 19 months, gave many appropriate verbal labels to drawings and pictures of previously encountered solid exemplars of concepts. We cannot determine from the research report either the learning set structure or the memory demands involved. But

Gibson (1969) may be correct in concluding that "differentiation of pictured objects is learned at the same time that distinctive features of the real objects are learned [p. 40]." Similar evidence of generalization by 12 to 27 month olds to pictures of concepts originally encountered through three-dimensional exemplars has been obtained in the "Rabbit" and "Fiffin" studies described in this chapter.

Camel to Zoo

Input Control. "Camel" (on wheels!), "cash register," "spinner" (from a child's board game), and "zoo animal" (a sort of composite with a giraffe's head) were the four "concepts" studied by Leonard (1976). The eight children observed were first presented one toy (named three times) for each concept when they variously were 17 to 24 months of age. In two to seven additional sessions spaced at least 1 month apart, each child again encountered the same set of four toys and heard each named three times.

Memory. The memory burden on the child cannot be judged from reports available. The only data reported are the child's *first* spontaneous uses, in two-word-or-longer utterances, of the label for each toy. It is likely that these name productions by the child followed by seconds or minutes the experimenter's prior use of the names in the same session, but some memory over 1 to 7 months cannot be ruled out.

Learning Set Size and Structure. As no generalization set was included and as each word was represented by one toy, when the child used "camel" or any of the other words we cannot tell whether the child knew the concept involved or only the label for a specific referent (this also applies to a related, single-subject report by Braine [1971] on acquisition of two labels). Nevertheless, Leonard's study provides interesting variation in the carrier sentences he used to introduce the new words. Eight sentence types were employed, including use of the target word for these semantic notions: nomination: "That is a camel"; place: "The camel is under the table"; object: "The camel is getting hit"; and instrument: "The camel is gonna get you." Variation in experimenter placement of the target word in subject or predicate position had little effect. But one overall conclusion of interest is that 22/24 of the children's uses of the words were restricted to semantic notions already detected in the child's system. When the experimenter used a target word semantically as "instrument," a notion absent for all children when they first used a target word, six of eight children still learned to label the toy. However, the sentences they produced worked the label into object, notice, or nomination roles. This kind of analysis of the relation between carrier sentence variation and the children's initial (and later) incorporations of target elements into their speech patterns deserves much more attention and elaboration in future work.

Lubniks: An In-Depth Assessment of Boundaries for Concepts

Input Control. With colleagues Marilyn Denninger, Sheila Katt Olewitz, and Gabriel Kovac, I launched a "Lubnik Study" that centrally concerned initial mastery of concepts followed by presentation of a *large* generalization set: about 500 exemplars. Two groups of children, 3 year olds and 5 year olds, saw four concepts in common. Some data on these concepts have been presented in Nelson and Nelson (1978) and Kogan (1976). For example, after mastery (4/6 or better accuracy) of a learning set of six exemplars for each concept, new, well-defined ("good") exemplars received the relevant concept name over 91% of the time by both age groups, but when the generalization exemplars lacked more than two defining features, the concept name was applied only 54% of the time by 3 year olds and 69% of the time by 5 year olds.

Here, it is appropriate to provide additional information on the 5 year olds (*n* = 7) that gives a better feel of the concepts involved and the children's concept-formation processes. In Fig. 5.1, the two top exemplars are "marlets," which fully satisfy the characteristics (e.g., a notch on either the left or right side) the experimenters chose as "defining." Fig. 5.2 and the remainder of Fig. 5.1 illustrate exemplars *not* satisfying the concept definition. Later in the chapter, the concept definitions in terms of prototypes, inferential focus, and child- rather

FIG. 5.1.   "Marlet" concept exemplars. The top two ("best") toys possess all the defining features. One defining feature is missing for each of the bottom two exemplars.

FIG. 5.2.   On the left are two examples of "marlets" that are "wrong" on two defining features. Each of the two toys on the right are "wrong" on at least three defining features.

than adult-defined features are discussed. But for the moment, notice simply that the marlets were defined according to the features shown in Figs. 5.1 and 5.2 and that in addition marlets and one other concept (weetoos) rounded out to six the number of concepts the 5 year olds acquired. For this full set, the rate of naming both appropriate or "good" (97%) exemplars and extremely poor (77%) generalization exemplars was higher than the rates already described for just four concepts. Analyses of variance and t-tests establish statistically reliable effects of two sorts when either four concepts or all concepts (six at age 5, seven at age 3) are analyzed for each age level: At both ages, an increasing number of defining features *not* satisfied by generalization exemplars (0 = best exemplars, one, two, or three or more) was related to decreased extension of the concept names, and older children named significantly *more* of the one-, two-, or three-or-more feature-wrong exemplars but named only slightly more of the well-defined exemplars.

Memory.   The learning set for each concept was acquired within 5 days, in three sessions. The generalization testing was spread over five or six sessions in 4 to 8 weeks, with no fewer than 4 days between any two successive sessions. As the experimenter *never* used the concept labels in any generalization session and as all children generalized the concept names they had initially acquired, both the 3 year olds and 5 year olds successfully carried both the concepts and their names across at least 4 weeks following acquisition. Even during the training sessions, the children were neither drilled nor corrected for errors, but instead were first exposed to the exemplars and their labels and then asked to do the naming themselves rather than waiting for the adult to provide the labels. The combination of the children's high performance and these procedural characteristics leaves us with the best demonstration so far that young children can rapidly form multiple concepts from a few exemplars and then carry these concepts in long-term memory and use them in a truly generalized way for identification of new, "good" exemplars.

Learning Set Size and Structure. The interesting structural variations primarily involve the relations between the six learning-set exemplars, all fully satisfactory exemplars in terms of all defining features, and the generalization exemplars—also good exemplars, or lacking one, two, three or more defining features. Again, see Figs. 5.1 and 5.2. To explore these relations, we confine our attention to the seven 5 year olds. For these children, one additional factor is of interest—whether the concept exemplars were flat, two-dimensional pictures attached to a background ("lubniks," as shown in Fig. 5.3; "anvils," see Nelson & Nelson, 1978; "oilers"; "cutters," another invented concept) or whether they were thin background-free toys that could be picked up and moved ("marlets" and "weetoos"). The latter elicited more naming at every level of concept exemplar, as Table 5.1 demonstrates. The children could tactually explore the marlets and weetoos, and this action-defined characteristic could have been, from the child's point of view, an additional *defining* characteristic of these concepts. If so, that would help explain the pattern of name generalization

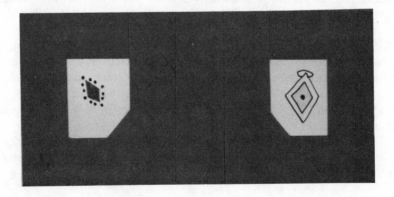

FIG. 5.3. The "lubnik" on the right satisfies all the defining features. The exemplar on the left is one of the "poorest" lubniks—it does not satisfy criteria for one internal dot, two borders, and one ring.

TABLE 5.1
Percentage of Exemplars 5 Year Olds Named with Only the
Relevant Experimenter-Provided Concept Label

	Number of Experimenter-Defined Essential Characteristics Present in Exemplar			
Concepts	All	−1	−2	−3 or More
Marlets and Weetoos	99	97	95	94
Remaining four concepts	95	93	82	69

seen in Table 5.1. Perhaps the children defined a marlet or weetoo as an object that possessed two features: *any one* of the defining characteristics we built into the concepts, plus the feature of manipulability.

"Action" Versus "Object" Concepts

Input Control.   Across 10 sessions in about 4 months, 12 children (initially 13 to 15 months of age) were exposed by Schwartz (1978) to eight "action" concepts (e.g., spinning actions) and labels (nonsense words), and eight "object" concepts (e.g., objects on a string, such as a yo-yo) and labels (also nonsense words). Four exemplar objects or particular action situations were used for each concept, and within concepts those exemplars (two) shown twice per session were named about half again as often as those (two) presented just once per session. Also, nonsense labels with sounds initially already within rather than outside the child's phonological production system were more easily acquired. Overall, though, the finding that Schwartz stresses is that "action" concepts were less easily acquired than "object" concepts, presumably because actions are more transient and thus harder to remember and because actions may be vehicles for organizing the world before they are targets themselves for categorization and labeling. If we take as the minimal criterion for concept acquisition that (excluding immediate imitations) naming of two exemplars occurred at least once, then 27% of the action concepts, but 79% of the object concepts, were acquired. When all available exemplars are considered, 36% were named by these young children.

Memory.   Memory requirements were very limited because all exemplars were presented and labeled by adults in each session.

Learning Set Size and Structure.   As all exemplars were adult labeled, the children who named two or more exemplars in a category may have learned only the *associations* between individual exemplars and the label; the data cannot decide this issue. The other limitation built into this study is that there is no close equation of familiarity of the objects and the actions intended as target concepts. Although labeled objects were presented with unlabeled actions accompanying them, and labeled actions were performed with unlabeled objects, this match on the "dynamics" of presentation does not ensure a fair test of learning action labels versus object labels. The problem is that many of the *objects* used to illustrate an action category, such as spinning or swaying, are likely to be familiar to a 13 month old and to have labels that the child can at least comprehend; this would seem true for objects such as balls and plastic rings and toy babies and trucks. In conclusion, this study illustrates label acquisition by 13 to 19 month olds, but leaves open the questions of whether concepts were acquired and whether under appropriately matched input conditions, object concepts are easier to master than action concepts (the latter question applies also to function-versus-form issues in acquiring and generalizing concepts; e.g., K. Nelson, 1978).

Naete Et Alia

Input Control. Six invented concepts with invented consonant-vowel-consonant-vowel names, such as "Naete," were introduced to kindergarten children (mean age about 5 years, 9 months) and undergraduates. Mervis and Pani (1980) report on two closely related experiments. In both, the subjects had a chance to demonstrate acquired production and comprehension mastery for four exemplars of each concept. Learning and testing were concentrated in a first study within a single day and in a second study within 5 consecutive days. The level of appropriate naming by the end of Study One and Study Two, respectively, averaged over 96% and 89% for adults and 80% and 57% for the kindergartners. These levels were reached without feedback. The children's performance, as described below, varied substantially in relation to the structure of the stimulus sets.

Memory. The exact memory requirements were not specified, but they ranged from less than 1 hour to a maximum of about 96 hours. For the most part, it appears that subjects progressed from initial learning to final generalization tests within 36 hours.

Learning Set Size and Structure. In Study One, the learning "set" was either one very "good" exemplar or one very "poor" exemplar. The two types led to directly contrary results in generalization for kindergartners. Poor exemplars in training led to most errors on good generalization exemplars, whereas good training exemplars resulted in most frequent errors on poor generalization exemplars. In Study Two, with a harder set of exposure conditions for the subjects, both adults and kindergartners were subject to the "good" versus "poor" exemplar manipulation. Good exemplars were defined here (in line with

Rosch, 1973, and Rosch & Mervis, 1975) as those with maximal within-category similarity and minimal extracategory similarity. In this second study, appropriate generalization was speeded if the experimenter named only the good exemplars rather than only poor exemplars or a mixture of good and poor exemplars. And for the kindergartners especially, the learning set of good exemplars only inclined the the children towards over- rather than undergeneralization errors.

The Fiffins-Plus Gambit

Input Control.   "Fiffins" plus 17 additional concepts were exposed along with the concept labels in learning sessions. The concepts were then tested in separate generalization sessions in which the children heard no adult naming of exemplars. The 25 children were initially 21 or 22 months old (Nelson & Bonvillian, 1978).

Memory.   Ten sessions were spaced about evenly across 5 months. Generalization testing took place in sessions three, six, and nine. Thus, when the children named generalization exemplars, they were recalling concept names used by adults in one or more sessions 2 or more weeks prior to the particular generalization session.

Learning Set Size and Structure.   For six concepts, the learning set was only one exemplar. Nevertheless, many of the children learned the concepts involved—they extended the concept names to one or more of the generalization exemplars available per concept, and showed appropriate comprehension responses.

For the concepts with learning sets of two exemplars each (six concepts) or four exemplars each (six concepts), the data are pooled. When naming of the adult-named learning sets are examined, the performance of these 21 to 27 month olds provides a comparison with Schwartz's subjects on object concepts (see the previous section, *"Action" Versus "Object" Concepts*). These older "Fiffin" children labeled 57% of the learning-set toys, whereas Schwartz's 12 to 19 month olds named just 36% of their four-exemplar learning sets. So, just as Oviatt's data (see the section, *The Rabbit Gambit*) suggest for comprehension, speed of mastering concept name production does reliably increase with age for young children. In addition, for each of these two- and four-exemplar concepts in the Fiffin Project, there were three additional, adult-unnamed, generalization exemplars. These were named at a 28% rate. "Hybrid" exemplars that included features from two concepts, but were quite "poor" exemplars for both concepts because defining features were absent, were given the concept names only 14% of the time. Examples of fiffins, lobsters, and fiffin–lobster hybrids are provided in Fig. 5.4 through 5.8.

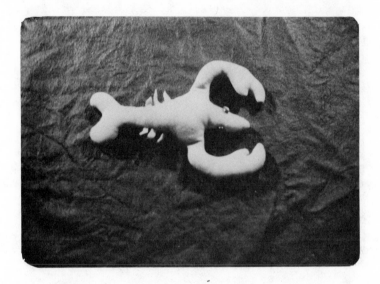

FIG. 5.4.   A "lobster" that satisfies all defining features.

FIG. 5.5.   A "fiffin" with all defining features (including loose beans inside).

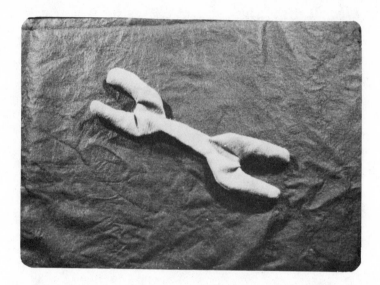

FIG. 5.6.   Another "fiffin" endowed with the full set of defining features.

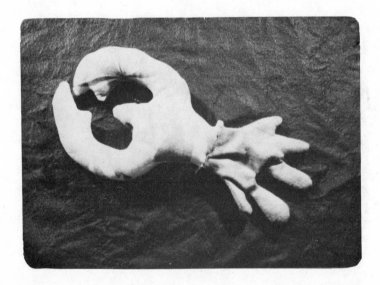

FIG. 5.7.   A hybrid between the concepts of "fiffin" and "lobster," with features of the latter more salient.

FIG. 5.8.   The "fiffin" features are more salient in this "fiffin–lobster" hybrid.

Mastery of the Fiffin concepts was also demonstrated in comprehension tests. The relation between comprehension and production varied extensively between children; four children unexpectedly demonstrated very clear superiority of production over comprehension, and others ranged from a mild production advantage to a strong comprehension advantage.

Other Recent Investigations

Ross, Nelson, Wetstone & Tanouye (1980) recently reported on a comparison of 20 month olds (13) given a single-exemplar learning set per concept and 20 month olds (10) given three exemplars per concept. Fast learners in the two groups generalized as extensively when given one as when given three exemplars (an advantage for slow learners) in acquisition. Generalization for both groups was tested with a new exemplar for each of five concepts. Adult-rated similarity levels predicted which generalization exemplars were most likely to be appropriately selected in comprehension tests of "mobol," "weedle," and other concept names. Learning and generalization sessions were completed within 2 months. Bates and Garrison (1980) looked at five-exemplar object concepts named "fiffins" and novel actions named "bloop" in 20 month olds. The name "fiffin" was presented (with appropriate exemplars) at least 10 times on 1 day and reasonable levels of comprehension were shown by the children four days later. The "bloop" actions were then presented and tested on the same testing day; 21 of 26 children showed some comprehension of "bloop" (a special sweeping motion with an object). In my own laboratory, we have again used "fiffins"—this time the original fiffins from Nelson and Bonvillian (1978)—and "lobsters" in a new test of concept acquisition. For both these concepts, only a single exemplar was presented in Session One; generalization was tested 2 weeks later and many of the 2½ to 3 year olds showed productive naming of two new exemplars for each concept at this point; nearly all those who did not were able, after hearing adult use of the names at the end of the 2-week test, to remember at least one of the concept names and extend it to appropriate new exemplars in a session 4 weeks after the original learning session. All three of these studies show rapid concept and name learning by 20 to 36 month olds.

Summary of Semantic Gambits

The gambits just reviewed conclusively demonstrate that 18 month olds to 6 year olds (also some 12 month olds) can learn to comprehend and produce some new labels for specific referents on the basis of brief, controlled exposure to referents and names. *Generalized concepts* applicable to numerous exemplars have also been observed under conditions in which the input history has been controlled and recorded, allowing the following conclusions for this age range: A *single referent* (a "rare event") as a learning-set exemplar can induce formation of a concept; at least some input information is carried in long-term memory across 1- to 8-week time periods; *no corrective feedback* is necessary to concept formation or appropriate, continued use of concept labels; if the child acquires a concept on the basis of one to six exemplars, the *less similar* a new exemplar to the learning set, the less likely it is to be named; when the history of exemplar and concept-label encounters have been recorded systematically, it appears that for the same concepts, *older children* as compared with younger children are likely to form *broader rather than narrower concepts*.

Two open issues are noteworthy. The first is developmental continuity. So far, only one study has followed up early experimental-concept acquisition. Nelson and Bonvillian (1978) found, for *new* concepts, that ease of concept acquisition and breadth of generalization were predicted for the Fiffin-Project children as 4½ year olds (cf. Table 5.2) from their performance in these areas as 2 year olds. The second issue concerns information-processing aspects of developmental theory. Still in the process of development (e.g., see the next section) are well-detailed descriptions of the memory and abstraction skills that allow the child to sometimes use one or a few instances of input to form a linguistic concept or rule that is then used over many weeks or months without further direct input. Deepening the puzzle, I would argue, is the observation that sometimes children not only capitalize on "rare events," but go on to internally reorganize certain concepts and rules in the absence of any further input— restructuring even for young children may occasionally occur when "no events" are externally provided.

TABLE 5.2
Percentage of "Appropriate" Category Responses to
Varied Exemplars After Training

Study and Learning Set	Naming after Learning Phase According to Exemplar Level			
	Best	Good	Poor	Poorest
Mervis and Pani (Study 1):				
One best exemplar (age 5)	100	100	97	72
One poorest exemplar (age 5)	68	62	48	97
Lubnik Study:				
Six best exemplars (age 5)	95	93	82	69
Six best exemplars (age 3)	91	83	69	54
Fiffin Project, 19 S's				
Observed at 2 and 5:				
One to four best exemplars of				
Fiffins, etc. (age 2)	49	—	—	14[a]
Four best exemplars of				
Lubniks, etc., learned in				
one session only (age 5)	68	54	49	46

[a] Naming of "hybrid" exemplars combining some features from each of two concepts.

DISENTANGLING TARGET CONSTRUCTIONS AND THEIR CARRIER INPUT

It is possible to imagine circumstances in which the child receives "pure " target constructions as input. A parent may present a new toy or picture and say "Lobster. Lobster. Lobster. . ." and only "Lobster" in the presence of the appropriate referent. Or, in focusing on the future-tense construction, an adult may say, as each of a series of blocks is slowly pushed over the edge of a table, "Will fall. Will Fall . . ." But far more typically, the child will receive the target construction embedded within at least a few different carriers, such as, "Now look at this lobster. Nice lobster. Do you see the lobster's claw? What will the lobster have for dinner?"

In the experimental semantic gambits just reviewed, it is clear that many different carriers have been used by the parents and experimenters in the process of providing verbal labels like "chromium," "fiffin," "rabbit," and so on. No investigator except Leonard (1976) has yet presented data on what effects, if any, carrier variations produce, and neither his variable data for the Camel-to-Zoo Study nor the combined pool of experiments allow any strong inferences. One hunch, though, is that *some* of the carriers make it very much easier for most children to attend to and analyze the target semantic terms. But which ones? Perhaps the simplest constructions would seem the most likely candidates, but there is no certainty that the child's attention will stray from the target as the overall utterance becomes complex. Moreover, another important factor may be whether the utterance invites and produces a clear-cut response from the child; utterances that succeed in this way may often be complex—"Wouldn't you like to pet the rabbit, dear?" In any event, the dimensions (and values) that matter for the positive, neutral, or negative effects of carrier utterance remain to be specified. Experimental manipulations of carriers should be undertaken to speed such specification. The outcomes will be useful in design of teaching procedures for the developmentally delayed as well as in theoretical descriptions of how the child at different developmental levels manages to successfully process new semantic input.

Similar experimental attempts to identify carrier effects will be appropriate for the areas of discourse and syntax acquisition. A beginning, of course, for syntax can be seen in the completed and projected research on recasts considered early in this chapter. Beyond the demonstration that broadly defined recasts can be an effective carrier for some targets (e.g., future-tense verbs), there is much room for determining which subtypes of recasts and other carriers are most effective and which are not only effective but necessary. And, given persuasive data on those questions, we may be able to go further and say *how* the most potent input elements engage the child's attention, memory, and analytic power.

ON TENTATIVE ABSTRACTED FOCI, PROTOTYPES, AND OTHER THEORETICAL ISSUES IN LANGUAGE ACQUISITION

It is necessary to take a closer look both at how experimenters have defined category structures and at the process of concept formation children may use. We use as springboards for this discussion the "prototype" experiments of Mervis and Pani along with the Fiffin and the Lubnik Studies. An essential point is that, with few exceptions, the *arbitrariness* of conceptual and semantic boundaries has been underemphasized.

An Apparent Exception to Arbitrariness: Color Prototypes

Rosch (1973) called attention to the tendency of adult subjects in many cultures to use the same "focal" or "prototypical" colors as best representatives and as best-remembered and best-labeled examples of colors such as red, green, and blue. This work is backed by prior and subsequent work that, in concert, is highly suggestive of the notion that there are perceptual constraints from infancy onward (Bornstein, Kessen, & Weiskopf, 1976) that lead the spectrum to be nonarbitrarily divided into categories. Although there is no solid experimental work on whether very rich or very impoverished exposure to focal as contrasted with nonfocal colors could shift the child's color concepts, the data in hand imply more constraints on color-category formation than in any other semantic domain yet given much analysis by psychologists.

Cautions on Prototypes and Family Resemblances

Outside the color domain, there may be too ready a tendency to also assume a preordained, nonarbitrary structure underlying semantic concepts. This is so despite the fact that Rosch and Mervis (1975) and other recent writers on prototypes and related conceptual structures (Palermo, 1978, this volume; Posner & Keele, 1968; Rips, Shoben, & Smith, 1973; Rosch, Mervis, Gray, Johnson, & Boyes-Braem, 1976) have often been careful to admit that we do not know the bases of *formation* for conceptual structures that are used by adults in consensual, consistent fashion. Thus, we know that "robin" is an excellent, typical example of "bird," whereas "chicken" is not, and also that "robin" has relatively high similarity (intracategory) to many other birds and low extracategory similarity to examples potentially confusable with birds. But we do *not* know whether such consensual aspects of animal categories arise from cognitive/perceptual constraints, from selective patterns of exposure to input exemplars prior to semantic labeling, to selective input patterns for the labels in conjunction with the category examples, or from a more complex mix of factors.

On such questions, experimental work in the mold of Mervis and Pani (1980) in the Naete Et Alia Study previously reviewed should be very valuable. However, the insights offered on concept and language learning will be greater when 1 to 3 year olds are examined rather than just 5 year olds and older language users. In addition, the Naete Et Alia Study illustrates that there are two arbitrary aspects of the categories used in nearly all semantic concept-acquisition studies—the concept boundaries are arbitrarily defined by adults (the investigators alone or with the help of other adult raters), and then the productions or comprehensions of labels for particular examples are arbitrarily classified as "error" or "correct." Mervis and Pani decide which four exemplars will represent "naetes," and then they count as an error any failure to use "naete" (and naete only) for one of these examples or the extension of Naete to other "concepts" they have assigned a different label. Of course, the experimenters can be consistent in their classification of responses as errors, but this does not change the conclusion that the experimenter-defined category boundaries are arbitrary and that the subjects or other experimenters may have very good reasons for drawing new boundaries.

Redefining the Naete-Et-Alia Conceptual Boundaries

The consistent evidence across both studies is that 5½ year olds' production and comprehension of an acquired name was more likely to match the experimenter-defined concept boundaries when the *best* rather than the *poorest* exemplar was the one exemplar the child heard labeled by an adult. The interpretation of concept learning offered by Mervis and Pani (1980) is that "... the generalization process based on similarity is the same regardless of the initially presented exemplar. It is simply the case that this process will be more accurate when based on good exemplars ... [p. 518]."

Although this conclusion may be valid, there is no Study-One data and no fully *independent* data from Study Two to directly back it up. In the latter, after the children have reached a high level of training with the names, they also are *given an explanation* of the kind of category structure involved in family-resemblance theory and are then asked to rate how "typical" exemplars are of their categories. Clearly, the difficulty in using the obtained data is that if the children understand the instructions given, then regardless of their prior categorization experience with these exemplars, they should do what they did in this study—rate the experimenter-defined "best" exemplar as most typical of a category. Another difficulty in data interpretation is that adult Study Two similarity rankings for all 24 exemplars, although roughly supporting the experimenter's perceptions, are not reported in absolute terms either across or within categories. Here, as in the case of natural-world concepts, we need to know how closely each concept approaches the "ideal" family-resemblance structure and also how much subjects' assessments of one category are affected by the other categories to which they are compared. Finally, and a point to which we return later, *similarity rankings and sortings by similarity are evidence of information the child may use in semantic categorization—but the child may ignore some available information in forming a concept and may use the same information in different ways in different concepts.*

For the Merivs and Pani data, when we look at the only data broken down by all four levels of goodness of exemplar—those from Study One, as shown in Table 5.2—it is easy to imagine that many of the children may have indeed formed different concepts when learning from a "best" versus "poor" concept exemplar. The key piece of data is that given the "poorest" exemplar as the learning set, only 48% of the "poor" exemplars received experimenter-defined categorization, Thus, for the concept N, the N-Poor exemplar probably was included in category N—if we stick to the evidence presented, comprehension of label N—by about half the children but not by the other half. Two possible categories formed, then, would be N-Best + N-Good + N-Poorest and N-Best + N-Good + N-Poor + N-Poorest. In addition, because there are important similarities between exemplars of N and exemplars of the "contrast" category (call it "O"), and because Mervis and Pani tell us some generalization "errors" occurred to O, several other possible categories could have been formed by children trained on the N-Poorest exemplar. N-Poorest + N-Poor + O-Poor and N-Poor + N-Poorest and N-Poorest + 0-Poor certainly would be reasonable categories for a child to form, given training only on Poorest exemplars for experimenter-defined categories in which the similarity distances between

Best and Poorest exemplars are quite large. Such child-defined categories that cross the experimenter-defined boundaries of concepts would be expected fairly frequently for any pair of highly similar categories. Again, if N and O are such a "contrast set," then the N-Poorest exemplar should have (projecting from family-resemblance theory) *more* similarity than does the N-Best exemplar to the exemplar just across the border—the O-Poorest exemplar.

Several category sortings done with varied instructions by the same children would help determine, along with detailed name-production and comprehension data, when the children match their labels to the same concept structures the experimenters designed and when the children are forming and labeling modified conceptual structures.

Redefining the Lubnik-Study Conceptual Boundaries

It only seems fair at this juncture to also reinterpret work that my colleagues and I have done. Table 5.2 shows that in our work, as well as in the Mervis and Pani study, a training set of Best exemplars leads to progressively less naming (and/or comprehension) as the generalization exemplars lose features of the Best Exemplars and thus enter Good, Poor, and Poorest status. The concepts in the Lubnik Study can thus be redefined comfortably as family-resemblance structures in which the Best exemplars are prototypes and in which the Poorest, Poor, and Good exemplars vary in their similarity to the prototype (and to each other) but still satisfy a *narrow* set of defining features. By reducing the number of defining features for each concept from about five to two, then all the namings shown in Table 5.2 for the Lubnik Study's Good and Poor exemplars move from the category of "errors" to fully appropriate concept meaning. At age 3, for example, the 69% rate of naming Poor exemplars shows 69% "correct" responses and 31% no response or overgeneralization. Moreover, much of the naming of the Poorest exemplars should be considered fully correct (depending on the exact number of defining features missing) when the concept is considered to be narrowly defined. What we are left with certainly fits with "family resemblance"—the Best exemplars are prototypical in the sense of showing maximal within-category similarity and minimal extracategory similarity to other exemplars.

Individual Differences. In the preceding redefinition of concepts in the Lubnik Study, we have still assumed that *each* child was working with the same final category, just as Mervis and Pani assumed for their study. However, I am certain that our data do not uniformly support that assumption. In short, different children appear to select from the available mix of features *different* combinations of features as defining features. With 508 generalization exemplars to analyze, the analyses have taken awhile, but should soon be complete. But, in any experimental study in which a *wide range* of exemplars is used per concept—just as in most concepts children acquire—I am willing to bet that in the 1 to 6 year age range children will show important individual differences in how they use available input in concept definition (see also Nelson & Bonvillian, 1973, 1978). One recent example of the importance of individual differences comes from observations of six handicapped children with negligible communication skills who were taught signs to label concept exemplars for categories such as "wrench" or "pitcher." Hupp and Mervis (1980) report that these children showed better final concept mastery when *only one* "good" exemplar was used in the initial learning set rather than the good exemplar plus two additional, appropriate, but less prototypical exemplars. This decidedly is not true in several other studies using normally progressing children, and the finding suggests that information-processing abilities as well as semantic strategies may affect what different children carry away from the same input (cf. Nelson & Denninger, 1980).

Another Look at Prototypes

When acquisition of concepts is at issue, concepts never before exposed to the child, these are two ways the notions of prototypes and family-resemblance structures could apply. First, "good" examples that possessed a substantial proportion of characteristic features would be favored for concept membership over "good" examples that possessed few of these characteristic features. But, in this Anvil–Lubnik project, "good" examples were almost always named, so there was no reasonable test possible of the effect of the original experimenter-defined characteristic features; still, as we have just seen, it is plausible to view the children's categorizations as family-resemblance concepts with a narrow set of defining features. Moreover, there is a second way in which approximations to prototypical structure could affect acquisition. That is, overgeneralizations of the names to examples that *lacked* a full set of defining features—either broadly or narrowly construed—might be guided or constrained by how many nondefining but characteristic features exemplars possessed. There are many further analyses to be done, but the data available so far say "yes" to this sort of prototype influence, at least in the case of anvils.

Anvils.   The six anvil exemplars comprising the training set establish both the defining and characteristic features. As the schematic anvil in Fig. 5.9 illustrates, good anvil exemplars are composed of four parts, a base D topped by A, B, and C. These anvils were visually rather than functionally defined. Defining characteristics were: Parts A and C match in color and internal-shape schemes; A adjoins B without overlap and A does not narrow to a single point on the left; C adjoins B without overlap and C narrows to a single point on the right; B, is four-sided, with straight or close to straight edges; D has a flat bottom, and tapers towards its top; and, shape and color differences ensure that A, B, C, and D all appear as distinct parts. The good exemplar pictured in Fig. 5.9 shows (within

TABLE 5.3
Percentage of Anvil
Exemplars Named as
Related to Numbers of
Characteristic and
Defining Features

	Of Four Characteristic Features Number Possessed by Given Exemplars	
Number of defining[a] features absent	0–3	4
2	77	90
3	59	77

[a] By original experimenter definition. If fewer features are held to be defining, the number of characteristic features increases, but the basic relationships shown in the table do not change.

the limitations of a black-and-white drawing) these defining features, as well as all four of the characteristic features for anvils: high contrast between B and D, high contrast between B versus A and C, no horizontal edges in Part C, and no overlap at the boundary between B and D.

Now for the prototypical breakdown when "anvil," after reaching criterion, was used in generalization sessions as a name for two classes of exemplars—those lacking two defining features and those lacking three defining features. As Table 5.3 indicates, for each class those anvil-like pictures with all of the *characteristic, prototypical* features were called "anvils" by the children more frequently than were examples with fewer such features (see also, Nelson & Denninger, 1980).

FIG. 5.9.   A "good" exemplar of an "anvil," with letters A–D identifying the four essential shape components.

Beyond Prototypes: Tentative Abstracted Foci (TAF)

Taken together, the preceding discussions establish that no developmental concept-acquisition study yet reported can be considered a strict test of a family-resemblance-and-prototype theory. Knowing adult perceptions or rankings of similarities within a set of exemplars is not equivalent to knowing the concept structures a child will form when presented with the exemplars and adult-assigned labels for one or more exemplar per experimenter-defined concept. To the extent that individual differences are widespread in the "focus" characteristics that control generalizations and overgeneralization for a concept, then the utility of "prototypes" declines.

Accordingly, I suggest that "foci" may be a more broadly applicable notion. The concept learner may form one or more foci that help to summarize the information relevant to a concept, and in each focus *both defining and characteristic* information (perceptual or functional) may be included. A "Best-Exemplar Focus" might be supplemented with a "Boundary-One–Exemplar Focus" and a "Boundary-Two–Exemplar Focus" (in a different area of the similarity space than Boundary One). These foci are *abstracted* from the available input, and for a considerable part of the acquisition phase, they are likely to be *tentative*—thus, the suggested acronym, TAF, for Tentative Abstracted Foci. The tentative nature of such foci also meshes well with the important, flexible shifts in concept meaning and use as development reaches a high level (Nelson & Nelson, 1978) and as context is varied (Ortony, Reynolds, & Arter, 1978; Palermo, 1978, this volume).

To trace the establishment by individual children of such Tentative Abstract Foci in different conceptual domains, we need new work that combines the best of the experiments to date—contrasting learning sets, large and varied generalizations sets, repeated measurements over time to see how the concept evolves, similarity rankings, multiple sortings into categories, and careful analyses of individual subjects.

CONCLUDING REMARKS

The notions of "prototypes" and of "Tentative Abstract Foci" are ones potentially applicable not only to semantic concepts but also to the concepts and rules of syntax, discourse, and phonology. By stressing the need to look at a theoretical level for common processes across these domains, I return in a way to the opening theme of "convergent research." One empirical example from syntax and a few broader theoretical notes serve this theme.

In decidedly convergent work, de Villiers (1980, this volume) has argued that the notion of family resemblance and prototypes may apply to syntactic structures such as those involved in passive and cleft ("It's the donkey that bit the pony.") sentences. And de Villiers has been able to demonstrate that preschool children's generalization patterns in the laboratory for such sentences, after the child observes modeling by an experimenter, are heavily influenced by the "prototypicality" of the action verbs involved. The children most often generalize the sentence forms when "good" rather than "poor" (e.g., "hit" versus "read") exemplars of action verbs can be employed. Further work along these lines, with extensions to home and other contexts, should prove exciting and valuable.

On the broad theoretical level, there are two general proposals relevant to much of the preceding discussion and specifically to cross-domain process commonalities. Both are presented in more detail in a paper on "Cognitive Pendulums" that Katherine Nelson and I published in 1978. The first is the idea that there are "pendulum shifts" in conceptualization style as the child develops, shifts that cut across, to some extent, the child's progress in many separate areas of linguistic and cognitive progress. A clear look at such tendencies can be obtained, however, only when control of the *evidence patterns* available to the child is achieved. In the area of learning new semantic concepts, it appears from experimental work of the sort reviewed here that tendencies toward relatively broad boundaries in new concepts may apply at around 4 or 5 years of age as contrasted with either 2 years or 9 years. These "pendulum swings" in the child's conceptualization style complicate interpretation of average performance as well as interpretation of the cutting edge of progress in each cognitive and linguistic subarea or "system."

At the same time, progress in each of the child's systems appears to fit well with a sequence of five stages. Individual children certainly vary in terms of which systems progress most rapidly, and the input available in each area no doubt contributes to such individual differences. Nevertheless, the following sequence is expected: Stage 1, Idiosyncratic First Steps—broad rules cooccur with rules of narrow scope; Stage 2, General Rule Stage—great breadth of rule application typical, in comparison with Stages 3, 4, and 5; Stage 3, Many Rule Stage—rapidly changing system, with many fairly narrow rules; Stage 4, Integration and Consolidation—stable and well-coordinated rules, which may be inflexibly applied; and, Stage 5, Flexible Extension—rule use monitored consciously and rules flexibly adapted for different contexts and purposes.

There are many implications of these system stages for the mastery of *new* concepts. How the child interprets a particular set of semantic input exemplars will be expected to vary by the child's semantic system stage level. Phrased in the theoretical terms just discussed, a Stage-2 child and a Stage-5 child will form different Tentative Foci or Prototypes and the boundaries of their concepts after exposure to the same input set will differ. Similar effects are to be expected for the phonological system and the discourse system, but the timing of Stage-2 achievement usually will not be coordinated between systems. Thus, to understand how a child of a given age is using semantic input, discourse input, syntactic input, or phonological input to acquire new rules or concepts will require a sensitive analysis of the child's stage level in each system. The wide variations expected are illustrated by a contrast between metaphoric/figurative language and phonology; flexible, conscious behavior that appears to fit Stage 5 emerges for most children by the late preschool period in phonology (Ferguson & Macken, in press) but only at adolescence in figurative language (Gardner, Winner, Bechhofer, & Wolf, 1978).

In thinking about system stages, individual differences, and prototypes or tentative foci, there is one additional distinction we should keep in mind. That is the distinction between concepts well established in a child's system and concepts in the process of acquisition. Evidence that a child uses prototypes or foci of a certain sort for the former by no means establishes that the same structures are applicable in concept acquisition. To test whether particular definitions of prototypes or foci accurately describe an early, intermediate, or late stage in acquisition of a new concept or rule, the tests should be varied enough to allow disproof as well as proof. For example, to test the role of family-resemblance structures in concept acquisition, it is necessary to compare how children deal with exemplar sets nicely matching versus very weakly matching a typical family-resemblance structure. Our completed experiments have opened up inviting theoretical territory, but they do not yet establish at which stages and in which contexts a child will use one kind of focus or prototype versus another. Moreover, as argued earlier, it is not even clear when just one rather than several foci may be employed. And for any one focus, there are many possible bases for the formation of the focus—mean values, modal values, most-salient values, pleasing or aesthetic values, biologically determined values, and the family-resemblance prototype. Once some clear, tentative concept and set of foci (one or more) are acquired by the child, the transition to a more complete and stable concept or rule that is well integrated with the other rules at the child's current system stage also requires a place in our theories (for related views, see Anglin, 1977; Bates et al., 1981; Clark & Clark, 1977; Maratsos & Chalkley, 1980; K. Nelson, 1978). So, there is no lack of open questions about language-acquisition and concept-acquisition processes in children. Especially when the entire range is considered between a child at Stage 1 in a system and the child, or the adult, who is operating at the flexible level of Stage 5 the diversities between individuals in their cognitive operations on new exemplar sets, in their tentative conceptual foci, may be rich enough to provoke a very long string of experimental gambits. My special recommendations for this series are presaged earlier—needed are convergent data from studies with clear records of input patterns, of long-term memory demands, and of stability or change in concepts and rules across new contexts and new developmental periods.

REFERENCES

Affolter, F. Manuscript, in press, and paper given at the Pennsylvania State University, 1980.

Anglin, J. M. *Word, object, and conceptual development*. New York: Norton, 1977.

Bates, E. *Language and context*. New York: Academic Press, 1976.

Bates, E., Bretherton, I., Shore, D., & McNew, S. Names, gestures, and objects: The role of context in the emergence of symbols. In K. E. Nelson (Ed.), *Children's language* (Vol. 4). New York: Gardner Press, 1981.

Bates, E., & Garrison, A. *Object naming at 20 months: Novel versus natural categories.* Paper presented at the International Conference on Infant Studies, New Haven, April 1980.

Bloom, L., & Lahey, M. *Language development and language disorders.* New York: Wiley, 1978.

Bonvillian, J. D., & Nelson, K. E. Exceptional cases of language development. In K. E. Nelson (Ed.), *Children's language, volume 3.* New York: Gardner Press, 1981.

Bonvillian, J. D., Nelson, K. E., & Rhyne, J. M. Sign language and autism. *Journal of Autism and Developmental Disorders,* in press.

Bornstein, M., Kessen, W., & Weiskopf, S. The categories of hue in infancy. *Science,* 1976, *191,* 201–202.

Braine, M. The acquisition of language in infant and child. In C. Reed (Ed.), *The learning of language.* New York: Appleton-Century-Crofts, 1971.

Brown, R. *A first language.* Cambridge, Mass.: Harvard University Press, 1973.

Brown, R. Introduction. In C. E. Snow & C. A. Ferguson (Eds.), *Talking to children.* London: Cambridge University Press, 1977.

Carey, S. The child as word learner. In M. Halle, J. Bresnan, G. A. Mutter (Eds.), *Linguistic theory and psychological reality.* Cambridge, Mass.: MIT Press, 1978.

Clark, H., & Clark, E. *Psychology and language.* New York: Harcourt, Brace, Jovanovich, 1977.

Cohen, L. B., & Gelber, E. R. Infant visual memory. In L. Cohen & P. Salapatek (Eds.), *Infant perception: From sensation to cognition.* New York: Academic Press, 1975.

de Villiers, J. G. The process of rule learning in child speech: A new look. In K. E. Nelson (Ed.), *Children's language* (Vol. 2). New York: Gardner Press (Wiley), 1980.

Ferguson, C., & Macken, M. The acquisition of phonology. In K. E. Nelson (Ed.), *Children's language* (Vol. 4). New York: Gardner Press, 1981.

Gardner, H., Winner, E., Bechhofer, R., & Wolf, D. The development of figurative language. In K. E. Nelson (Ed.), *Children's language* (Vol. 1). New York: Gardner Press (Wiley), 1978.

Gibson, E. J. *Principles of perceptual learning and development.* New York: Appleton-Century-Crofts, 1969.

Gleason, J. B., & Weintraub, S. Input language and the acquisition of communicative competence. In K. E. Nelson (Ed.), *Children's language* (Vol. 1). New York: Gardner Press (Wiley), 1978.

Hunt, J. M. *Intelligence and experience.* New York: Ronald Press, 1961.

Hupp, S. C., & Mervis, C. B. *Acquisition of basic level categories by profoundly handicapped children.* Unpublished manuscript, University of Illinois, 1980.

Husaim, J. S., & Cohen, L. B. *Infant learning of ill-defined categories.* Paper presented at the International Conference on Infant Studies, New Haven, April 1980.

Kagan, J. *Change and continuity in infancy.* New York: Wiley, 1971.

Kogan, N. *Cognitive styles in infancy and early childhood.* Hillsdale, N.J.: Lawrence Erlbaum Associates, 1976.

Lenneberg, E. H. *Biological foundations of language.* New York: Wiley, 1967.

Leonard, L. B. *Meaning in child language.* New York: Grune & Stratton, 1976.

Macnamara, J. The cognitive basis of language learning in infants. *Psychological Review,* 1972, *79,* 1–13.

Maratsos, M., & Chalkley, M. A. The internal language of children's syntax: The ontogenesis and representation of syntactic categories. *In* K. E. Nelson (Ed.), *Children's language* (Vol. 2). New York: Gardner Press (Wiley), 1980.

McCall, R. B. Attention in the infant: Avenue to the study of cognitive development. In D. N. Walcher & D. L. Peters (Eds.), *Early childhood: The development of self-regulatory mechanisms.* New York: Academic Press, 1971.

McCall, R. B., & Kagan, J. Individual differences in the distribution of attention to stimulus discrepancy. *Developmental Psychology,* 1970, *2,* 90–98.

McCall, R. B., & Kennedy, C. B. Attention of 4-month infants to discrepancy of babyishness. *Journal of Experimental Child Psychology,* 1980, *29,* 189–201.

Mervis, C. B., & Pani, J. R. Acquisition of basic object categories. *Cognitive Psychology*, 1980, *12*, 496–522.

Moore, K., Clark, D., Mael, M., Dawson Myers, G., Rajotte, P., & Stoel-Gammon, C. *The relationship between language and object permanence development: A study of Down's infants and children.* Paper presented to the Society for Research in Child Development, New Orleans, March 1977.

Nelson, K. Structure and strategy in learning to talk. *Monographs of the Society for Research in Child Development*, 1973, *38*, (Serial No. 149).

Nelson, K. Semantic development and the development of semantic memory. *In* K. E. Nelson (Ed.), *Children's language* (Vol. 1). New York: Gardner Press (Wiley), 1978.

Nelson, K. E. Accommodation of visual-tracking patterns in human infants to object movement patterns. *Journal of Experimental Child Psychology*, 1971, *12*, 182–196.

Nelson, K. E. Infants' short-term progress toward one component of object permanence. *Merrill-Palmer Quarterly*, 1974, *20*, 3–8.

Nelson, K. E. Aspects of language acquisition and use from age two to age twenty. *Journal of the American Academy of Child Psychiatry*, 1977, *16*, 584–607. (a) (Also reprinted in *Annual Progress in Child Psychiatry and Child Development* [Vol. 11], S. Chess & A. Thomas,[Eds.])

Nelson, K. E. Facilitating children's syntax acquisition. *Developmental Psychology*, 1977, *13*, 101–107. (b)

Nelson, K. E. Theories of the child's acquisition of syntax: A look at rare events and at necessary, catalytic, and irrelevant components of mother–child conversation. *Annals of the New York Academy of Sciences*, 1980, *345*, 45–67. (a)

Nelson, K. E. Toward a rare event cognitive comparison theory of syntax acquisition: Insights from work with recasts. In D. Ingram & P. S. Dale (Ed.), *Child language: An international perspective*. Baltimore, Md.: University Park Press, 1980.(b)

Nelson, K. E., & Bonvillian, J. D. Concepts and words in the two-year-old: Acquisition of concept names under controlled conditions, *Cognition*, 1973, *2*, 435–450.

Nelson, K. E., & Bonvillian, J. D. Early language development: Conceptual growth and related processes between 2 and 4½ years of age. In K. E. Nelson (Ed.), *Children's language* (Vol. 1). New York: Gardner Press (Wiley), 1978.

Nelson, K. E., Carskaddon, G., & Bonvillian, J. D. Syntax acquisition: Impact of experimental variation in adult verbal interaction with the child. *Child Development*, 1973, *44*, 497–504.

Nelson, K. E. & Denninger, M. *The shadow technique in the investigation of children's acquisition of new syntactic forms.* Unpublished manuscript, New School for Social Research, 1977.

Nelson, K. E., & Denninger, M. *Semantic concept acquisition and generalization at three age levels: Beyond prototypes.* Paper presented at the Boston University Conference on Language Development, October 1980.

Nelson, K. E., Denninger, M., Bonvillian, J. D., & Kaplan, B. J. *Maternal input adjustments and non-adjustments as related to children's linguistic advances and to language acquisition theories.* Unpublished manuscript, Pennsylvania State University, 1979.

Nelson, K. E. & Nelson, K. Cognitive pendulums and their linguistic realization. In K. E. Nelson (Ed.), *Children's language*, (Vol. 1). New York: Gardner Press (Wiley), 1978.

Newport, L., Gleitman, H., & Gleitman, L. Mother I'd rather do it myself: Some effects and non-effects of maternal speech style. In C. E. Snow & C. A. Ferguson, *Talking to children*. London: Cambridge University Press, 1977.

Ortony, A., Reynolds, R. E., & Arter, J. A. Metaphor: Theoretical and empirical research. *Psychological Bulletin*, 1978, *85*, 919–943.

Oviatt, S. L. *The development of language comprehension in infancy.* Doctoral dissertation, University of Toronto, 1979.

Palermo, D. S. *Psychology of language.* Glenview Ill.: Scott, Foresman, 1978.

Piaget, J. *The construction of reality in the child.* New York: Basic Books, 1954.

Piaget, J. Piaget's theory. In P. H. Mussen (Ed.), *Carmichael's manual of child psychology* (Vol. 1). New York: Wiley, 1970.

Posner, M. I., & Keele, S. W. On the genesis of abstract ideas. *Journal of Experimental Psychology*, 1968, *77*, 353-363.

Rips, L. J., Shoben, E. J., & Smith, E. E. Semantic distance and the verification of semantic relations. *Journal of Verbal Learning and Verbal Behavior*, 1973, *12*, 1-20.

Rosch, E. On the internal structure of perceptual and semantic categories. In T. E. Moore (Ed.), *Cognitive development and the acquisition of language*. New York: Academic Press, 1973.

Rosch, E., & Mervis, C. B. Family resemblances: Studies in the internal structure of categories. *Cognitive Psychology*, 1975, *7*, 573-605.

Rosch, E., Mervis, C. B., Gray, W. D., Johnson, D. M., & Boyes-Braem, P. Basic objects in natural categories. *Cognitive Psychology*, 1976, *8*, 382-439.

Ross, G., Nelson, D., Wetstone, H. & Tanonye *Concept acquisition at 20 months*. Unpublished manuscript, City University of New York, 1980.

Schwartz, R. G. *Words, objects, and actions in early lexical acquisition*. Doctoral dissertation, Memphis, State University, 1978.

Shatz, M. On mechanisms of language acquisition: Can features of the communicative environment account for development? In L. Gleitman & E. Wanner (Eds.), *Language acquisition: The state of the art*. Hillsdale, N. J.: Lawrence Erlbaum Associates, 1980.

Sherrod, K. B., Friedman, S., Crawley, S., Drake, D., & Devieux, J. Maternal language to prelinguistic infants: Syntactic aspects. *Child Development*, 1977, *48*, 1662-1665.

Sinclair, H. Developmental psycholinguistics. In D. Elkind & J. H. Flavell (Eds.), *Studies in cognitive development*. New York: Oxford University Press, 1969.

Slobin, D. Cognitive prerequisites for the development of grammar. In C. A. Ferguson & D. Slobin (Eds.), *Studies of child language development*. New York: Holt, Rinehart, & Winston, 1973.

Snow, C. E. Mothers' speech research: From input to interaction. In C. E. Snow & C. A. Ferguson (Eds.), *Talking to children*. London: Cambridge University Press, 1977.

Thomas, H. Discrepancy hypotheses: Methodological and theoretical considerations. *Psychological Review*, 1971, *78*, 249-259.

Turiel, E. Developmental processes in the child's moral thinking. In P. Mussen, J. Langer, & M. Covington (Eds.), *Trends and issues in developmental psychology*. New York: Holt, Rinehart, & Winston, 1969.

Vygotsky, L. S. The genesis of higher mental functions. In J. V. Wertsch (Ed.), *The concept of activity in Soviet psychology*. New York: Wiley, in press.

Wells, G. Apprenticeship in meaning. In K. E. Nelson (Ed.), *Children's language* (Vol. 2). New York: Gardner Press (Wiley), 1980.

Westerman, M. A., & Havstad, L. F. A pattern-oriented model of caretaker-child interaction, psychopathology, and control. In K. E. Nelson (Ed.), *Children's language* (Vol. 3). New York: Gardner Press, 1980.

6

The Development of Sentence Coordination

Helen Tager-Flusberg
University of Massachusetts/Boston

Jill de Villiers
Smith College

Kenji Hakuta
Yale University

INTRODUCTION

A fundamental issue that must be addressed in the study of child language is the relationship between linguistic theory and child-language data. There are at least three possibilities that can be identified in current thinking:

1. Data from the way children acquire language should be used as a gauge of linguistic theories; constraints can be set on possible theories of adult language by studying the process of language acquisition. Researchers of many different persuasions have adopted this approach (e.g. Bates, 1976; Bruner, 1975; Mc-Neill, 1970).

2. Child language is no more revealing about the nature of adult language than the wing movements of fledgling birds are to an account of adult bird flight. In both cases, there are such strong biological constraints on the final form that the preparatory attempts do not necessarily play a role in the end product (Chomsky, 1976). This extreme position has not been endorsed by developmental psycholinguists.

3. Linguistic theory provides information for the developmental psycholinguist about how to look at the development of language, what rules children are likely to need, and the hypotheses they might adopt as partial or whole solutions.

During the 1960's, this third approach was by far the most popular, especially in the debate involving the psychological reality of transformational rules. The fate of the simple "derivational theory of complexity" in accounting for adult performance is well known (see Fodor, Bever, & Garrett, 1974), but R. Brown (Brown & Herrnstein, 1975) proposed that in certain areas it may provide an apt description of the acquisition of knowledge rather than the use of it in comprehension or memory tasks by adults. The specific cases Brown had in mind were the acquisition of grammatical morphemes (Brown, 1973) and the development of tag questions (Brown & Hanlon, 1970), both of which seem to involve well-defined prerequisite knowledge. There are, unfortunately, numerous other instances in which the predictions of the derivational theory of complexity fail against data from child language (de Villiers & de Villiers, 1978; Maratsos, 1978).

Subsequent investigations of grammatical development have generally proceeded more independently, without particular linguistic theories guiding them. However, there are three general observations we have distilled from the current child-language literature, some paralleling changes in linguistic theory, which may once again lead to a closer relationship between the two disciplines (see Halle, Bresnan, & Miller, 1978).

1. *Structures may not have the same source in child language that they have in adult language.* Two examples from the current literature illustrate this general point. Ingram (1975) studied the relative clauses produced by children in telling stories, and found that children younger than age 5 or so produce a very limited variety of relative clauses that do not seem to require transformational rules, but instead could result from phrase-structure rules.

Horgan (1978) points to the large number of truncated passives in child speech and the paucity of full passives. She argues that the truncated forms are not plausibly derived from their corresponding full forms because they are grammatically distinct in many ways, and may instead be formed by analogy with predicate adjectives.

2. *Language is more closely tied to context for young children than for adults.* If an adult speaker were asked: Are the following two sentences identical in meaning?

> The dog bites the child.
> The child is bitten by the dog.

she or he would most probably say "yes" with a qualification that the sentences would be used in slightly different circumstances. In particular, choice of one or the other would depend on whether the child or the dog was the focus of attention in the discourse. Children apparently learn constructions such as the passive much more readily when it is presented to them as a motivated construction for highlighting certain topics (e.g., I. Brown, 1976). A reasonable generalization may be that children learn a variety of constructions to serve a variety of purposes in communication—that is, the formal differences among sentences are used to signal functional differences, or differences in the situation. The child at first may not be able to represent a sentence in isolation from the context in which it is used, and for this reason, may not be attuned to the purely structural similarities and differences among sentences. As a result, the abstract commonalities that linguists observe so readily among different sentence types considered out of context may be much less evident to the language-learning child. Several different investigators have postulated a reorganization of linguistic knowledge that might occur after the child's language is comparatively sophisticated (e.g., Bowerman, 1974; Ingram, 1975), and possibly even coincident with the emergence of metalinguistic awareness. Perhaps only at this point do the relations among sentence types become consolidated.

3. *There appear to be surface structure constraints in child speech and comprehension.* Children's comprehension of passive sentences (Bever, 1970) and relative-clause sentences (de Villiers, Tager-Flusberg, Hakuta, & Cohen, 1979) is characterized by a tendency to interpret noun-verb-noun sequences as agent-action-patient, and a difficulty with noncanonical sequences.

Hakuta (1979) presents evidence from Japanese children that sentence configuration is a major variable influencing comprehension of relative-clause structures, and that this is to a large extent independent of the direction of embedding (i.e., left branching versus center embedded). Children have difficulty comprehending sentences in which noun phrases are "stacked" in a row and this is also reflected in their avoidance of such structures in production tasks.[1]

The particular construction we have chosen to study, sentence coordination, is one of the major hallmarks of syntactic development, marking the beginning of recursivity in the child's language. In this chapter, we discuss the development of the earliest and most frequent form of sentence conjunction—namely, the use of "and" in coordinated phrases and sentences.

LINGUISTIC TREATMENT OF COORDINATION

There are two major forms of syntactic coordination with the conjunction *and*. In *sentential* coordination, both propositions appear in their entirety:

Eliza flew the coop and James had a fit.
and may contain redundant elements:

---

[1]There is renewed interest in more precise performance models for child language that would incorporate these constraints and make contact with the models proposed for adult-language comprehension and production—for example, Augmented Transition Network models (see Kaplan, 1972).

Eliza washed the dishes and Eliza flooded the kitchen.
The other form of a coordinated sentence, called *phrasal* coordination, contains no redundancy—for example:

James and Philip grew orchids.

In phrasal coordination, many different conjuncts are possible: subjects, as in the preceding example: predicates:

Eliza washed the dishes and flooded the kitchen;

objects:

James grows orchids and petunias,

and so on.

The two main questions within linguistics are:

1. What is the relationship between sentential and phrasal coordination?
2. How many different rules are required to account for the variety of conjoined structures?

Stockwell, Schachter, and Partee (1973) describe three alternative answers to question 1:

1. Phrasal conjunctions are derived from sentential structures in the base by a process called *conjunction reduction,* in which redundant elements are eliminated.
2. Phrasal conjunctions are generated directly in the base by phrase-structure rules.
3. Some phrasal conjunctions are generated directly in the base and others are the result of conjunction reduction.

Conjunction Reduction

In *Syntactic Structures* (1957), Chomsky defined conjunction in transformational terms:

If S_1 and S_2 are grammatical sentences, and S_1 differs from S_2 only in that X appears in S_1 where Y appears in S_2 (i.e. S_1 = .. X .. and S_2 = .. Y ..), and X and Y are constituents of the same types in S_1 and S_2, respectively, then S_3 is the result of replacing X by X + and + Y in S_1 (i.e. S_3 = .. X + and + Y ..) [p. 36].

Gleitman (1965) pointed out certain cases in which X and Y are not constituents, e.g.

I gave the girl a nickel and the boy a dime.

He took John home and Mary to the station.

Speakers appear to accept these sentences as grammatical, but according to Gleitman, they frequently recall them inexactly, often recalling a sentence that obeys Chomsky's generalization in having conjoined constituents. Certain other cases of nonconstituent conjunction are almost always rejected by native speakers e.g.

I want to know why John and when Mary are coming.

An intermediate set are marginally acceptable, including:

The man saw and the woman heard the shot fired.

Koutsoudas (1971) reported that French and Italian informants rejected sentences like this latter, except when the subjects were identical; thus:

*Jean a vu et Marie a frappe le chien.

(John saw and Mary hit the dog.)

Marie a vu et Marie a frappe le chien.

(Mary saw and Mary hit the dog.)

It is not clear whether these marginal cases require restrictions on the general schema of conjunction, or result from semantic anomalies or pecularities. Stockwell et al. (1973) propose the latter and believe the advantages that result from a general schema in which all conjunction is derived from a general rule outweigh the difficulties presented by the marginal cases.

Ross (1967) specified a constraint on the conjunction-reduction schema that involves the direction of deletion. If the identical elements are on the left branches of a deep-structure configuration, deletion occurs in a *forward* direction—that is, the second occurrence of the redundant element is deleted; so:

The psychologist solved the problem and the psychologist saved the day.

becomes:

The psychologist solved the problem and saved the day.

not:

*Solved the problem and the psychologist saved the day.

If the elements are on right branches, then deletion is *backward*—that is, the first occurence of the redundant element is deleted:

The psychologist solved the problem and the chimp solved the problem.

becomes:

The psychologist and the chimp solved the problem.

not:

*The psychologist solved the problem and the chimp.

Harries (1973) has subsequently argued that forward reduction is the more basic process on two grounds: backward reduction can be reanalyzed as forward reduction plus regrouping of the constituents, and forward reduction is much more common in the world's languages than is backward reduction.

Ross (1967) argued for two types of rules to derive conjoined structures. The first rule, called *gapping,* reduces coordinated sentences by deleting a verb in the forward direction, e.g.

John hit Harry, and Jim, Michael.

The second rule is conjunction reduction, which accounts for all other kinds of reduced coordinations and consists of several steps: (1) raising an identical constituent; (2) deleting all lower identical repetitions of the same constitutent; (3) pruning non-branching nodes; and (4) relabeling constituents to yield an A-over-A structure.

Even though conjunction reduction remains the most accepted way of dealing with coordinated structures in the standard transformational grammar, there is still debate about the number of separate rules that are needed within that schema. For example, Koutsoudas (1971) argues that gapping and conjunction reduction should be collapsed into a single rule, and the status of gapping remains controversial.

Phrasal Conjunction Basic

Wierzbicka (1967) argued on logico–semantic grounds that conjoined *NP*'s in subject position constitute a single semantic unit, the argument on which a predication is made. So
    John and Mary left.
does not contain two separate predicates, one about John and the other about Mary, but a single predication on the conjunct *John and Mary*. Wierzbicka suggests further that conjuncts of this sort must have some semantic denominator, because sentences such as:
    The people and tables are all here.
sound peculiar. This common denominator is the subject or argument.

Stockwell et al. (1973) extend this observation to *VP*'s, which also seem to require a common denominator if they are conjoined—for example,
    I sing and dance.
    ?I sing and analyze conjunction.
However, Stockwell et al. do not accept this as an argument that phrasal conjunction is generated in the base.

Dougherty (1967) points out the close behavioral similarity of plurals and conjoined *NP*'s, and argues that because plural *NP*'s are not derived from conjoined sentences, then neither are conjoined *NP*'s derived. Dougherty proposes that all conjunctions of full, single constituents are generated in the base. However, he does admit the need for derived conjunction in cases in which the surface conjuncts are not full, single constituents.

Stockwell et al. (1973) argue against Dougherty's proposal primarily on the grounds that constituents can be conjoined even though they appear at different points in the deep structure. For example, given a transformational account of passivization, the following sentence could not arise from phrasal conjunction in the base because the underlined *VP* would not exist in that form prior to passivization:
    The boy was unhappy and *was ignored by everyone*.
In the surface structure the *VP*'s are conjoined, but they could not be conjoined in the deep structure if the second *VP* is the result of applying a passive transformation.

There are a number of similar instances that illustrate the ramifications of proposing that phrasal conjunction is generated directly in the base, *if* one accepts the standard transformational account of other phenomena such as passivization, adjectival phrases, and so on. The implications for conjunction of adopting a different approach to passivization (e.g., Bresnan, 1978) have not yet been worked out. Furthermore, recent changes in the standard theory (e.g., Chomsky, 1977; Fiengo, 1977) have led to a drastic reduction in the number of transformational rules, and an increased reliance on base rules. The status of conjunction reduction remains unclear with these refinements, although some have argued for the complete elimination of conjunction reduction as well as all other transformations (e.g., Grosu, 1979; but cf. Chomsky & Lasnik, 1977; Williams, 1978).

Stockwell et al. see no conflict in Dougherty's second claim about the close similarity of plural *NP*'s and conjoined *NP*'s, because although they do not work it out in detail, they propose that plural *NP*'s also derive from conjoined sentences.

Gleitman (1965) suggested that sentential forms in which a noun phrase is repeated often lead informants to guess that two different referents were intended e.g.

A tall man observed the criminal and a tall man called the police.
When there is no repetition of *NP*'s, informants guess that a repetition of referent occurred:

A tall man observed the criminal and called the police.
With a pronoun replacing the second *NP,* judgments about the identity of the referent are mixed:

A tall man observed the criminal and he called the police.
Presumably, the effect can be manipulated further by changing the second article to a definite one e.g.

A tall man observed the criminal and the tall man called the police.

Nonetheless, the effect seems to be a general one that repetition in a sentential form leads informants to guess nonequivalence, not just for identity of *NP* referents but also for actions, e.g. for:

John jumped and Mary jumped.
versus:
John and Mary jumped.

informants believe the action was simultaneous in the latter case but not necessarily in the former. Jeremy (1978) confirmed this for adults and children as young as 4 years of age.

It is a question of debate whether these differences of intended meaning should be handled by allowing phrasal conjunction to derive from a separate source, or by calling it a question of surface-structure interpretation (Stockwell et al., 1973).

Some Phrasal Conjunction Necessary

The discrepancy in meaning between phrasal and sentential forms reaches its extreme for certain predicates discussed by Lakoff and Peters (1969)—for example, the lack of paraphrase between:

> Mary and John are a happy couple.
> *Mary is a happy couple and John is a happy couple.
> or:
> Mary and John are similar.
> *Mary is similar and John is similar.

Lakoff and Peters proposed that phrasal conjunctions like these be generated directly in the base because they could not be derived from sentential equivalents, but this is by no means undisputed (Stockwell et al., 1973).

The main purpose of our studies is to investigate how young children produce conjoined structures in speaking. We were interested in the claim that children must have mastered a rule such as conjunction reduction before they produce phrasal conjunctions, and searched for evidence that this was the case. We have also investigated whether children's conjunctions involve conjoining non-constituents, and whether gapped sentences occur or give children trouble—this is to see if children's schema for conjunction reduction might be restricted in ways that it is not for adults. We have looked for evidence that structures hypothesized to involve backward deletion might be more difficult or later to appear than structures involving forward deletion. Finally, we have searched for clues about how children interpret sentential and phrasal forms, to see if they regard them as synonymous or distinct in meaning.

We report data on coordinating conjunction in young children that reveal the following:

1. Children's earliest phrasal conjunctions are *not* plausibly derived by conjunction reduction, but are most likely generated by directly combining like constituents by phrase-structure rules.

2. There are subtle differences in meaning and use between phrasal and sentential forms that children recognize very early and conform to in speaking and possibly in understanding.

3. Certain configurations of elements in conjoined structures present more problems than others for children to produce and understand. The direction of deletion (forward or backward) is not perfectly correlated with this difficulty.

The criticism can always be raised that a failure to find evidence for the psychological reality of linguistic structures is due to the limitations of studying performance rather than competence. In recognition of the pitfalls of drawing conclusions from a single performance, we have explored four different methods of investigating the child's knowledge of the syntax of conjunction: longitudinal records of spontaneous speech, elicited production, elicited imitation, and act-out comprehension. The results of our studies complement one another in all important respects, but without the interlocking nature of the data, we could not argue our case. In a later section of the chapter, we return to the methodological issues that must be resolved in studying children's syntax.

SPONTANEOUS-SPEECH ANALYSIS

One of the richest sources of acquisition data comes from longitudinal studies of natural speech. Let us begin by describing coordination data from the spontaneous-speech protocols of Adam, Eve, and Sarah, collected by Roger Brown and his colleagues. The main focus of this study was to find out which forms of coordination were the earliest to develop, and how the different forms enter the child's speech over time.

First, we combed through all the transcripts for each child separately and noted down every utterance that contained an "and." Because of the large number of such utterances, we stopped at the point at which the mean length of utterance (MLU) was 4.25, the beginning of Stage V. We noticed that many of the earliest coordinations were simple *noun* + *noun* phrases, such as:

milkshake and poopoo (from Sarah: 28 months).
Fraser and Cromer (from Eve; 23 months).

We were, however, more interested in the well-formed coordinations that could be classified into the different syntactic types. Sentences containing *and then* of which there were very few, were excluded, and the remaining well-formed coordinations were divided into the following five categories: forward phrasals (*FP*), forward sententials (*FS*), backward phrasals (*BP*), backward sententials (*BS*), and sentential coordinations with no potential for deletion (*S*) e.g.

Why I going in front of it and de man's not home yet? (from Adam; 41 months)

A total of 360 sentences were categorized and the number and percentage of each of the five types from each child are shown in Table 6.1. For all three subjects, over half the coordinations were *FP*, most of these involving conjoined objects. For example:

He having carrots and peas (from Eve, 26 months).

The most interesting aspect of this longitudinal data is the developmental progression of the different types of coordination. For each monthly time period, we plotted the proportion of each of the four main types of coordination (*FP*, *FS*,

TABLE 6.1
Number and Percentage of Different Coordination Types in the
Spontaneous Speech of Adam, Eve, and Sarah

	FP	BP	FS	BS	S	Total
Adam						
(20 months)	113	7	27	14	26	187
%	60	4	14	8	14	
Sarah						
(17 months)	52	7	16	2	5	82
%	63	9	20	2	6	
Eve						
(7 months)	47	26	6	7	5	91
%	52	28	7	8	5	

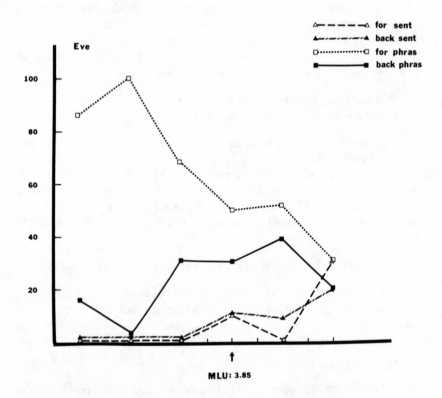

Fig. 6.1.   Graph showing the developmental course of the main forms of coordination in Eve's speech.

BP, BS) classified earlier, relative to the total number of such coordinations produced during that month. Thus, for each child, there is a graph depicting the development of the syntactic forms, and the degree to which each category dominates at different points during the acquisition of coordination. Figs. 6.1, 6.2, and 6.3 show the graphs from Eve, Sarah, and Adam, respectively.

The striking feature of the graphs from all the children is the almost exclusive use of *FP* forms in the early months. Sentential coordinations with or without potential deletion do not appear until midway through Stage IV, in which the MLU is around 3.80. Across the three subjects, there are 92 phrasal coordinations before the point where sententials begin to be produced. Even when the sententials do begin, there is still a preponderance of phrasal coordinations in the children's speech.

Another interesting finding from this spontaneous-speech data is that clearly the majority of coordinations produced are forward phrasals and sententials. There are, however, some differences among the three children. For Adam and Sarah, only 12% and 11% of their coordinations are backward forms, yet for Eve, the percentage is three times higher, 36%. Almost all the backward phrasals

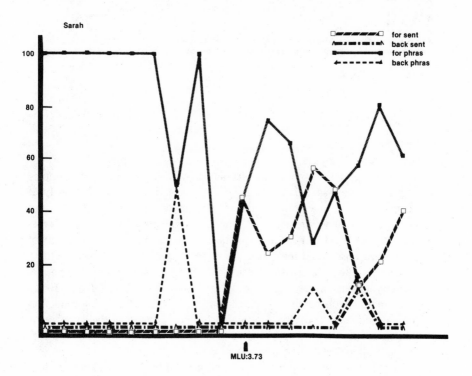

FIG. 6.2.   Graph showing the developmental course of the main forms of coordination in Sarah's speech.

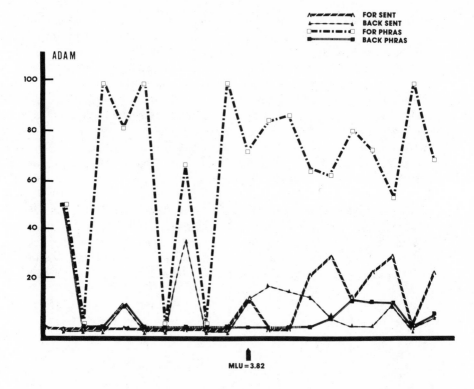

FIG. 6.3.   Graph showing the developmental course of the main forms of coordinated in Adam's speech.

involved conjoined subjects, and subjects are known to be either absent or very simple in child speech, which might account for why there are so few examples of backward phrasals in Adam's and Sarah's transcripts. Looking closely at Eve's conversations, one notices that she constantly speaks of "Fraser and Cromer"—the two experimenters who taped her spontaneous speech. Coordinations with "Fraser and Cromer" as the conjoined subject make up the majority of Eve's backward forms, and this particular coordination may well be a routine.

The main findings, then, from the longitudinal speech data are that phrasal coordinations appear earlier than sentential coordinations, and forward forms are much more frequent than backward forms. The conjunction-reduction hypothesis described previously, interpreted by the derivational theory of complexity, actually predicts the opposite: that sentential forms should develop earlier than phrasals because they are derivationally less complex.

Lust and Mervis (1980) report a cross-sectional study of spontaneous production of coordination in which they argue that their data support the standard theory, because sententials have primacy over phrasals. Their data are somewhat limited in that from 32 children ranging in age from 24 to 37 months, they collected only 68 examples of well-formed coordinations. Of these, the majority (40) they consider sentential, whereas they count only 28 phrasals. The main problem we have with Lust and Mervis' data is in the nature of the sentential coordinations they report. They include anaphoric reference, as in:

Some brown on my shirt and it was an accident.

Lust and Mervis also include various meaningless sentences that look like the child is just repeating himself or herself:

He sitting up and he sitting up.

Perhaps most problematic of all is the inclusion of sentences in which the child uses the same term but for two different referents, e.g.

That's a mama and that's a daddy.
There is a bigger boat and there's a truck.

(The preceding are all examples from Table 5.) Lust and Mervis argue that they did not have enough contextual information to decide on the issue of coreference in the sentential examples, but it seems highly likely that the child in such cases was pointing to two different things. A phrasal conjunction would be inappropriate in such circumstances, so it is misleading to present these sententials as an argument for the primacy of sententials over phrasals. In our study, these sentences were in the minority. In contrast, approximately one half of the sententials reported by Lust and Mervis appear to fall into this latter category. There remain too few cases to argue that children find it easier to produce sententials rather than phrasals.

Bloom, Lahey, Hood, Lifter, and Fiess (1980) reported the development of syntactic connectives in four children studied longitudinally, and found that phrasal conjunction emerged at the same time as sentential conjunction for three of the children, and earlier for the fourth subject. At this point, then, evidence in favor of the primacy of sententials over phrasals in development is equivocal.

Could this failure to support the conjunction-reduction hypothesis result from performance variables such as MLU limitations? For example, it has been argued that a length constraint is operating at the earliest stages of coordination production (cf. Lust & Mervis, 1980). Because the minimum length of well-formed sentential coordination is five words, compared to four in a phrasal coordination, this might explain why sentential forms do not appear until later stages. To check this possibility, we calculated the average length of Eve's phrasal coordinations, which were produced in the period before any sentential coordinations appeared. The MLU of these sentences was 6.40, higher than the five necessary for sentential coordination. Only 25% of these phrasals were four words or less in length. Thus, it does not appear that length alone is constraining the form of coordination at the earliest stages. This view is consistent with other findings in language acquisition (cf. Bloom, Miller, & Hood, 1975).

No linguistic theory offers an explanation for the earlier emergence of phrasal conjunctions and so we have explored three alternative interpretations for our longitudinal data.

A Syntactic Account

In previous papers (de Villiers, Tager-Flusberg, & Hakuta, 1976, 1977) we proposed that coordination develops in the following way: The earliest forms of conjunction in the child's speech are groupings of parts of speech, such as *noun + noun* phrases. These are then slotted into a sentence frame to produce a well-formed phrasal coordination. Over time, the conjoined parts of speech become more and more complex until ultimately, complete propositions are coordinated, yielding sentential coordinations. We argued that at this point the child has the option to conjoin phrases in phrasal coordination, or complete propositions in sentential coordination, and that perhaps the child then might indeed use deletion rules to derive phrasal coordinations from corresponding sentential forms.

In support of this argument, we find that all the early well-formed phrasal conjunctions involve the conjunction of simple constituents, such as subjects, objects, and predicates, but never nonconstituents. Furthermore, the variety of elements that are conjoined is much less than the variety of elements that would require reduction in the conjunction-reduction schema.

The Input to the Children

We explored the input provided by the children's mothers for clues about the process of coordination development (cf. de Villiers et al., 1977). We followed the same procedure described earlier. All the well-formed coordinations were categorized as *FP, BP, FS, BS,* or *S* (with no potential deletion). For all three mothers, the proportions of the different coordination types were very similar to those of their children. *FP*'s were the most frequent forms used and backward coordinations made up only a small proportion of the total sample. None of the children were imitating their mother's coordinations, nor was the specific content of the mother's and child's coordinations the same.

There exist a number of alternative explanations for this close matching of syntactic form in the input and child's speech. One possibility is that the parents and children are highly sensitive to the syntactic form of the coordinations in their conversations and either mother or child is responding to the forms each hears in the other's speech. Alternatively, the same contextual constraints operate on both mothers and children. For example, Jeremy (1978) found that events separated in time favor sentential forms, which are rare in the spontaneous-speech data. We know from other input studies that mothers tend to speak about events taking place in the "here and now" (Cross, 1977; Snow, 1971), which would perhaps favor phrasal coordination.

Contextual Constraints

The third possibility, then, is that the forms have different frequencies in child speech because the eliciting contexts have different frequencies. Let us consider separately the difference between forward versus backward forms, and phrasal versus sentential.

Forward Versus Backward. Forward phrasals were many times more frequent in the children's speech than backward phrasals. Consider what is conjoined in these sentences: Forward phrasals are predominantly object or predicate conjunctions, in which the children made reference to multiple toys or foodstuffs that they were acting upon. Backward phrasals are predominantly subject conjunctions, but the children's subjects were mostly self-referent and frequently pronominal (see also Limber, 1973). The children seemed to have little need to refer to multiple subjects, and only Eve used subject conjunction with any frequency. As we remarked earlier, she made frequent reference to "Fraser and Cromer", who, from Eve's perspective at least, always appeared together and engaged in the same activities.

Forward reduction has been argued to be more basic than backward reduction (Harries, 1973), and Lust (1977) used this to account for her subjects' superior imitation of forward phrasals than backward phrasals. If children had trouble with backward reduction, one would expect a high frequency of backward sententials—that is, forms that they failed to reduce—in their speech. As can be seen from our data, backward sententials were also quite rare, adding force to our contextual-frequency explanation of these data.

Sentential Versus Phrasal. As mentioned earlier, phrasal conjunction may be more frequent than sentential conjunction because the latter is used, for example, when events are separated in time and space (Jeremy, 1978), and those contexts are quite rare as topics for children's discourse. In discussing Lust and Mervis' data, we pointed out a second constraint on the production of phrasal conjunction versus sentential conjunction. Sentential conjunction is used when two identical NP's are not identical in reference, e.g.

John$_1$ went home and John$_2$ took a photograph.
could not be expressed as
John went home and took a photograph.
Similarly,
Jane went to school$_1$ and Sue went to school$_2$.
could not be expressed as:
Jane and Sue went to school.
Without implying something different.

Perhaps children reserve sentential conjunction for just such cases of nonidentical referents, and use phrasal conjunction for cases in which the NP referents are identical. It would be our guess that opportunities for sentential conjunction of this type would be quite rare except when the child is pointing and labeling different objects, as in:

There's one and *there's* another one.

or

That's mine and *that's* yours.

We are suggesting that phrasal and sentential conjunctions are not functionally equivalent but are used in different kinds of contexts. Jeremy (1978) demonstrated that 4 year olds, as well as adults, respect the contextual constraints she identified (see also Greenfield & Dent, 1979). This opens up the possibility that children as young as Adam, Eve, and Sarah were sensitive to the different conditions of use of sententials and phrasals, and to the extent that these conditions varied in frequency, so also did their use of the forms.

These interpretations remain speculations, however, because we do not know the context for every utterance, nor do we have control over the opportunities for producing the different forms in spontaneous-speech data. Without such data, we do not know whether young children could identify and respect the pragmatic constraints such as referential identity/nonidentity that might operate on coordination.

ELICITED PRODUCTION OF ENGLISH AND JAPANESE COORDINATIONS

There were two primary motives for conducting this study. First, we wanted to test our hypothesis that there were various contextual reasons why children produced few sentential coordinations. The specific constraint we had in mind in this study was the case in which there were two examples from the same class of referents. For example, a picture of a frog and a turtle watching a single television might tend to be described by a phrasal sentence; the same picture with the frog and the turtle watching their own respective television sets would set the stage for a sentential coordination. We refer to this variable of whether a single or double referent is pictured as the referential context. Our second reason for this production study was to control and equalize opportunities for producing backward forms of coordination, which rarely appeared in the spontaneous-speech samples.

The task involved asking children to describe a series of pictures presented to them in a portable slide viewer. In an earlier pilot study (de Villiers et al., 1977), we found this an extremely successful task in eliciting coordinations in young children when the slides depict compound events such as two animals doing something together, or one animal doing a number of things.

Thirteen different types of pictures were created for this experiment. One example of each is described in Table 6.2. Four examples of each type were

TABLE 6.2
List of Pictures Used in Elicited Production Study

1. *FP* (SVO + O) object conjoined/subject–verb reduced; single referent
   A rabbit holding an umbrella and a balloon.
2. *FS* (SVO + SVO); double referent
   A rabbit holding an umbrella and another rabbit holding a balloon.
3. *BP* (S + SVO) subject conjoined/verb–object reduced; single referent
   A frog and a turtle watching television.
4. *BS* (SVO + SVO); double referent
   A frog watching television and a turtle watching another television.
5. *FP* (SVO + VO) verb–object conjoined/subject reduced; single referent
   A rabbit riding a bike and flying a kite.
6. *FS* (SVO + SVO); double referent
   A rabbit riding a bike and another rabbit flying a kite.
7. *BP* (SV + SVO) subject–verb conjoined/object reduced; single referent
   A fox pulling and a cat pushing a wagon.
8. *BS* (SVO + SVO); double referent
   A fox pulling a wagon and a cat pushing another wagon.
9. *FBP* (SV + VO) verb conjoined/subject–object reduced; single referents
   A cat painting and driving a car.
10. *FP(BS)* (SVO + VO) verb–object conjoined/subject reduced; single agent
    A cat painting a car and driving another car.
11. *BP(FS)* (SV + SVO) subject–verb conjoined/object reduced; single object
    A cat painting and another cat driving a car.
12. *FBS* (SVO + SVO); double referents
    A cat driving a car and another cat painting another car.
13. *FP* (SVO + SO) gapping–verb reduced
    A horse eating a banana and a cow an apple.

drawn, giving a total of 52 pictures from which slides were made. These slides were divided into two sets of 26, with two examples of each type in each set. The sets were crossed with each other such that a picture used for a phrasal form in one set (single referent) had its corresponding sentential form, with the same lexical items, in the other set (two referents). Thus, Set *A* contained the picture described in example 1 in Table 6.2, whereas example 2 was in Set *B*.

Our sample for this study included a group of Japanese children as well as American children, because Japanese provided some interesting contrasts to English. Briefly, Japanese is a case-inflected language with a predominant subject–object–verb order. As in English, the subject-conjoined coordination could be described as a backward reduction (SØV + SOV), but the object-conjoined coordination is both backward and forward (SOV̸ + $OV).[2] Unlike English, in which the morpheme "and" is used in both phrasal and sentential coordinations, in Japanese, different morphemes are used. Because Japanese is not the primary focus of this chapter, however, we omit details of grammar

[2]Therefore, to make the terminology comparable across both languages, when necessary, we also refer to the sentences in terms of which elements are conjoined.

TABLE 6.3
Number and Percentage of Coordinated Sentences Produced by
American Children in the Elicited-Production Study

	Age Group		
	3	*4*	*5*
Number of children in group	18	14	17
Number of sentences containing ''and''	241	276	358
% of total number of sentences produced	53%	76%	81%

except when relevant for our discussion. The interested reader is referred to other sources on Japanese grammar (cf. Kuno, 1973).

Forty-nine American children participated in this study. There were 18 3 year olds, 14 4 year olds, and 17 5 year olds, balanced with respect to the between-subjects variables of sex and set of pictures they were shown. The Japanese sample consisted of 36 children from a day-care center in Tokyo. These subjects were distributed into three age groups: 3;6–4;5, 4;6–5;5, and 5;6–6;5, also balanced with respect to the between-subjects variables.

Children were shown the portable slide viewer and were told they would see some pictures in it. They were asked to describe to the experimenter, who could not see into the viewer, everything they saw happening in the slide. If a child was unwilling to offer a response, he or she was gently prompted. The slides were shown in random order, and the whole session, which lasted about 15 minutes, was taped. At no time was the child asked to use the word ''and.'' The tapes were later transcribed onto individual coding forms.

The scoring scheme used to code the sentences was quite elaborate, involving numerous categories. First, all sentences were excluded from further analysis if they did not contain the morpheme ''and.'' Table 6.3 shows the number of sentences that did contain ''and'' obtained from American children in each age group. Across all these subjects, about 70% of the responses contained ''and,'' showing the success of this task in yielding coordinated sentences.

We were most interested in the type of well-formed coordinations subjects produced for the different pictures. Well-formed was defined as the presence of at least one subject-noun phrase, verb, and object-noun phrase in each coordination, thus excluding sentences in which transitive verbs were expressed as intransitives; for example:

The owl and the bear are hammering.[3]

---

[3]In all, there were 72 such intransitives, or 8.2% of the total number of ''and'' sentences. The children were most likely to omit mention of the object for particular verbs such as *driving, painting,* and *hammering,* so that the distribution of intransitives was uneven across the pictures. Nonetheless, we subjected them to an identical analysis and the results on this subset of sentences are equivalent in essential respects to those on the full set discussed in the text.

Also, only sentences that conformed closely to a description of the relevant picture were considered.

The main categories used for classifying the sentences included:

		Example from English
1.	*FP* forward phrasal	A rabbit is holding a balloon and umbrella.
		(object conjoined)
2.	*FS* forward sentential	A rabbit is holding a balloon and a rabbit is holding an umbrella.
3.	*BP* backward phrasal	A raccoon and a pig is hitting a drum.
		(subject conjoined)
4.	*BS* backward sentential	A pig is playing a drum and a raccoon is playing a drum.
5.	*FBP* forward backward phrasal	A cat is painting and driving a car.
		(verb conjoined)
6.	*FBS* forward backward sentential	One cat is painting a car and one cat is driving a car.
7.	*G* Gapping	A cow is eating a banana and a horse an apple.
8.	*PRO* anaphoric reference	A fox is pulling a wagon and a kitty is pushing it.

First consider the English data from pictures 1 to 4 (see Table 6.2). These pictures were designed to elicit, ideally, *FP, FS, BP,* and *BS* coordination respectively, when the action is the same in both propositions.

The overall number of coordinations produced was lower for the backward coordinations (pictures 3 and 4) than for the forward ones: 72% compared to 83%. Looking closely, in fact, this was true for the 3's and 4's, but not for the 5 year olds. The younger children either ignored the second subject in the backward pictures or referred to two subjects collectively; for example;

They are watching TV (picture 3).
They are hammering nails (picture 4).

One cannot easily avoid using "and" in this way for the first two pictures.

The first concern with the data is whether children tend to use phrasal and sentential forms of coordination differentially with respect to the referential context. The summary data for the American sample appear in Table 6.4, represented as the percentage of phrasal forms used over the sum of phrasal and sentential forms. Thus, a low percentage indicates predominant usage of sententials. As can be readily seen, for the object-conjoined (forward) and the subject-conjoined (backward) pictures with single referential contexts, the descriptions

TABLE 6.4
Percentage Phrasals (over Phrasals Plus
Sententials) for American Children for
Pictures 1 to 8 in Elicited-Production Study

	Pictures 1 and 2 Object Conjoined Subj–Vb Reduced	Pictures 3 and 4 Subject Conjoined Vb–Obj Reduced
Referential Context		
Single	95% (52/58)	75% (30/40)
Double	11% (6/57)	27% (13/48)
	Pictures 5 and 6 Vb–Obj Conjoined Subject Reduced	Pictures 7 and 8 Subj–Vb Conjoined Object Reduced
Single	86% (25/29)	7% (2/27)
Double	5% (2/39)	3% (1/31)

were predominantly phrasal (95% and 75% respectively). But when there were two referents, the descriptions were primarily sentential in form. This effect was robust across the three age levels, with a slight tendency for the younger children to use more phrasal forms in describing the double referential pictures. Thus, the data so far support the notion that children differentially use the two forms of coordination depending on referential context.

The hypothesized effect of referential context was less striking for subject-conjoined (backward) sentences than for object-conjoined (forward) sentences. However, because the children produced approximately equal numbers of phrasal and sentential coordinations, it was not the case that sentential forms predominated. There was also an age effect: The younger children (3 year olds) showed slightly less sensitivity to referential context than the older subjects (4 and 5 year olds), 67% to 76%.

A similar analysis was carried out on the next four pictures, 5 to 8, which were also designed to elicit FP (verb–object conjoined), FS, BP (subject–verb conjoined), and BS coordination, respectively. These pictures illustrated the agent(s) doing two different actions to the object(s). The summary data are in the bottom half of Table 6.4.

For pictures 5 and 6, the data look much like the data presented earlier for pictures 1 and 2, with 86% phrasals on the single, and only 5% phrasals on the double referential contexts. But for pictures 7 and 8, very few phrasals were produced for either referential contexts (7% of single and 3% of double referential contexts). Picture 7, depicting two animals doing two different things to one object, thus did not elicit phrasals of the form SV + SVO. From the perspective of the conjunction hypothesis, this phrasal involves the conjunction of subject–

verb, which is not a true constituent, and the data indicate that the children are sensitive to this structural constraint.

A general difference between the data from this group of pictures and the sentences produced in response to the first four pictures is that there was a higher proportion of anaphoric references: 28 such responses compared to only 1.

The corresponding data for the sentences considered thus far for the Japanese children appear in Table 6.5. The children produced a large proportion of phrasal forms for the subject-(picture 3) and object-conjoined (picture 1) pictures with single referents (96% and 94% respectively). As in the English data, the senten-tials tend to cluster on the pictures with two referents, although less strongly so for the Japanese children. Across age, for subject-conjoined descriptions, 75% were phrasal, and for the object-conjoined descriptions, 24%. It should be em-phasized that for Japanese, phrasal forms in the double referential context are not incorrect, but rather in these contexts sentential forms become more likely. There was a strong age effect for the Japanese children, with the younger children heavily favoring phrasal forms. The preference for sentential forms on the double referential pictures is comparable to that of the English sample by the time the children are in the oldest age group. It is likely that the preference of the younger Japanese children to use the phrasal forms results from the fact that sentential coordination in Japanese requires a morphological change on the verb of the first sentence, which can be quite complex. Phrasal coordination does not require such a change, and younger children may in fact find this form easier to produce than sententials. One can conclude from this part of the Japanese data that the children almost categorically prefer the phrasal form in describing single ref-

TABLE 6.5
Percentage Phrasals (Over Phrasals plus
Sententials) for Japanese Children for
Pictures 1 to 8 in Elicited-Production Study

	Pictures 1 and 2 Object Conjoined Subj–Vb Reduced	Pictures 3 and 4 Subject Conjoined Vb–Obj Reduced
Referential Context		
Single	94% (51/54)	96% (49/51)
Double	24% (8/33)	75% (36/48)
	Pictures 5 and 6 Vb–Obj Conjoined Subject Reduced	Pictures 7 and 8 Subj–Vb Conjoined Object Reduced
Single	100% (41/41)	0% (0/15)
Double	25% (9/36)	0% (0/12)

erential pictures, and that sentential forms are produced with increasing frequency on the double referential pictures as the children grow older.

The data for the subject–verb (pictures 7 and 8) and the object–verb conjoined (pictures 5 and 6) pictures closely resemble the English data. For object–verb conjunctions, the data look similar to those just described, with a high preference for phrasals on the single referential pictures (100%) and a low preference on the double referential pictures (25%). Subject–verb is not a constituent in Japanese either, and this is respected by the Japanese children in that all sentences produced for pictures 7 and 8 were sentential, irrespective of the referential context. Thus, the Japanese data strongly corroborate the English result that referential context is an important factor in determining whether coordinations are phrasal or sentential, but that structural factors must be considered as well. Nonconstituents cannot be conjoined.

It is of some interest to note that there was a consistent difference within the double referential pictures across languages. A higher proportion of phrasals were produced on the subject-conjoined than on the object-conjoined items for both English and Japanese. The reason, we suspect, is psychological rather than linguistic. Our pictures by necessity had animate subjects, and mostly inanimate objects. A subject-conjoined, double referential picture might be that of an owl hammering a nail and a bear hammering another nail. An object-conjoined, double referential picture might be of a gorilla eating an apple and another gorilla eating a banana. Assuming that children see the distinction between animates as more psychologically significant than the distinction between inanimate objects, they would be more likely to collapse inanimates into a single term of reference, resulting in a phrasal form. This suggests yet another nonlinguistic constraint on the form of coordination that future investigation might elucidate by separating animacy and grammatical role.

Further analysis of the structural constraints on coordination can be performed by looking at differences between the various forms of single referential contexts. In the English data, a comparison of the subject-conjoined and the object-conjoined sentences shows that children produced a higher proportion of phrasals on the object-conjoined (95%) than on the subject-conjoined (75%) sentences. Notice that this trend is in the opposite direction from what was found for the double referential contexts, where there was a higher proportion of phrasals on the subject-conjoined pictures. Thus, we infer a structural constraint favoring the conjoining of objects over the conjoining of subjects. This result is to be expected given the combination of the surface configurational properties of the sentence and a left-to-right processing model. Because the constituent *subject + subject* by necessity appears at the beginning of the sentence, it must be planned in advance, whereas *object + object* can be formed by a process of concatenation at the end of the simple sentence without advance planning. The way to produce subject-conjoined sentences given failure to plan in advance is to use the sentential form, which accounts for why more sententials in fact appeared in the data.

We suggest that subject-conjoined sentences are more difficult to produce than object-conjoined sentences in the phrasal form because the former require conjoining of constituents in advance, whereas the latter, by nature of the left-to-right properties of the language, can be formed through concatenation.

The Japanese data, coded into the categories phrasal and sentential, show no difference between the subject-conjoined and object-conjoined descriptions. Ninety-six percent of the subject-conjoined sentences were phrasal, whereas 94% of the object-conjoined were phrasal. However, in this particular case, coding the data with respect to percent phrasal obscures an interesting fact: Of the 51 instances of phrasal coordination in the object-conjoined descriptions, 13, or 25%, of them took the form SOV + OV, when the same verb was repeated. Thus, in actuality, of the total number of relevant utterances for the object-conjoined pictures, only 70% (38/54) were of the form SO + OV. In the English data, a comparable analysis revealed that there were only three instances when the verb was repeated, resulting in SVO + VO. Thus, unlike American children who find the subject-conjoined form relatively more difficult than the object-conjoined form, Japanese children find the reverse.

The English and Japanese data are summarized graphically in Fig. 6.4. The American children, as mentioned earlier, use the sentential form in describing the subject-conjoined pictures more frequently than in the object-conjoined pictures. This was attributed to the S + SVO form's requiring advanced planning whereas SVO + O could be formed through concatenation. The SVO + VO option is rarely taken, because it is not a structurally motivated redundancy of the verb. The Japanese children, on the other hand, do not produce sentials for either

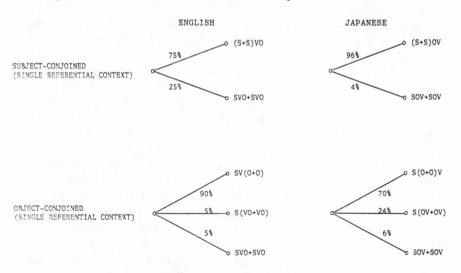

FIG. 6.4.   Percentage that various forms were used for subject- and object-conjoined descriptions, for English and Japanese samples.

subject-conjoined or for object-conjoined descriptions. For subject-conjunctions, even if they presumably require advanced planning, they almost categorically opt for the phrasal form. This may reflect the overall finding that Japanese children tend to use more phrasals. But for the object conjunctions, the SOV + OV option, whose analogous SVO + VO is not produced by American children, is quite frequently employed. The Japanese children seem to avoid constructions in which the conjoined constituent is placed in sentence-medial position, and to produce sentences by concatenation of OV + OV at the expense of repeating the verb. It is a structurally motivated redundancy.

But how can we be sure that the difference between the Japanese and American children reported here is the result of structural differences between the languages, and not simply the result of the Japanese children's more frequently repeating items in general? There are other sentences that can be compared in which the reverse prediction is made. When verbs are conjoined, as in the case of a cat driving and painting a car, the following forms are possible:

ENGLISH	SV + VO	sentence-internal conjunction
	SVO + VO	concatenation
JAPANESE	SOV + V	concatenation
	SOV + OV	concatenation

In this sentence, one would predict that the American children would choose the form involving concatenation, in which the object is repeated, avoiding sentence-internal conjunction. No such preference should be found for the Japanese children.

Pictures with this type of sentence as a target were used (see Table 6.2, picture 9), but with less success than the sentences we have been discussing earlier. It is difficult to depict a single agent performing two distinct actions to a single object, a highly improbable event. Nevertheless, we can try to milk the data, if only to see if it disconfirms the predictions. In the English data, there were seven sentences that took the form SVO + VO in which the object was repeated. In addition, there were six sentences in which the object was not repeated but in which there was an anaphoric pronoun, thus taking the form SVO + VPro. Finally. there were only three instances of complete phrasals, of the form SV + VO. One might summarize these data by saying that 19% (3/16) of the phrasals produced took the alternative of sentence-internal conjunction, whereas the reaminder (81%) were formed through concatenation. The Japanese data look even sparser. There were only seven sentences of relevance to this question, primarily because the particular lexical items chosen by the children did not conform well to our target. However, of the seven sentences produced, six involved no repetition of the object and took the form SOV + V. Thus, the data are consistent with the view that children favor sentence-final concatenation over conjunction internal to the sentence.

The response to the group of four pictures related to and including picture 9 (9, 10, 11, and 12) were not so easily categorized. For English, overall there were fewer coordinations—only 55%—as children tended to ignore parts of the pictures. There was also a high proportion of anaphora, an average of 11% PRO responses to each picture. Children often misinterpreted the pictures or chose to report irrelevant information. Sometimes, they used quite complex constructions (passives, embeddings, etc.) or long-winded descriptions, reflecting the trouble they had in understanding the event.

In more general terms, the data from the American children on these four pictures conform to the data obtained from the other pictures discussed. The pictures designed to elicit *FBP* (picture 9) and *FP* (picture 10) elicited almost no sentential responses ($n = 5$), whereas the other two pictures, the *BP* (picture 11, subject–verb conjoined) and *FBS* (picture 12) elicited primarily sentential coordinations ($n = 39$).

Finally, it is worth noting the results from the American children on picture 13, which showed two animals carrying out the same action on different objects. In English, this could elicit a phrasal coordination of the form SVO + SO, involving forward deletion of the verb, gapping. Ninety percent of the responses obtained contained the morpheme "and"; however, there were only two phrasal coordinations compared to 52 sententials (4%). Again, we find this is a phrasal form that the children avoid. Notice that this sentence cannot be derived by conjoining like parts of speech, which may explain its absence. We do not know what proportion of adult responses would be phrasal rather than sentential for these pictures.

The results of this study indicate that there are referential contexts that will differentially elicit phrasal versus sentential coordinations even for 3 year olds. The effect was more compelling when the animate subject was involved than when inanimate objects were the focus of attention. The effect was present in both English and Japanese, although Japanese children showed an overall preference for phrasal coordinations. Detailed comparison of key sentences revealed a preference for concatenation of final elements rather than sentence-internal conjunction in both languages.

Two types of phrasal coordination were not readily produced by English-speaking children. The first is a backward phrasal of the form SV + SVO, which can be described as backward object deletion, or conjunction of subject–verb. The second is the forward phrasal form SVO + SO, involving forward deletion of the verb (gapping). Both forms may be rare in adult spoken language. In addition, the first type involves conjunction of subject–verb, not a true constituent, and the second type cannot be derived by conjunction at all. This might explain their absence, if indeed children form coordinations by conjoining constituents rather than via conjunction reduction, as we proposed in earlier papers (de Villiers et al. 1976, 1977). We have no evidence supporting the view that sententials are more readily produced at any age than phrasal forms in this study.

ELICITED IMITATION STUDY

In order to assess the generality of our findings from the production studies described earlier, we also collected data on coordination processing in young children using two other performance measures: imitation and act-out comprehension. We investigated the same set of sentences that our production task had been designed to elicit (see Table 6.2).

Imitation of coordination has been the subject of a number of other studies on coordination development, notably Slobin and Welsh (1973) and Lust (1977). Both these studies report findings that are consistent with the standard theory of conjunction reduction. Sentential coordinations were imitated better than phrasal coordinations, and the error data showed that forward coordinations were more primary than backward coordinations (Lust, 1977). Our study on imitation was an attempt to replicate this earlier research utilizing a more extensive set of test sentences.

The subjects for this experiment included 13 3 year olds, 20 4 year olds, and 17 5 year olds, approximately half male and half female within each group.

Two similar sets of 18 sentences were constructed to control for lexical preference. All the sentences were of the basic SVO + SVO syntactic structure, exhausting all the well-formed forward, backward, sentential, and phrasal coordinations at all levels of redundancy, by which we mean the number of repeated items in a sentence. Table 6.6 gives examples of the 18 sentences used in this experiment. All the sentences were irreversible and proper names were used in subject position to ensure all the sentences were the same length—namely, 11 syllables.

Children were always tested individually. They were introduced to a parrot puppet who repeated everything spoken to it. They were asked to play the role of the puppet and all children readily agreed. Three practice trials were given when the subjects learned they were to imitate sentences spoken by the experimenter. Then, the 18 sentences from the assigned set were presented at a normal speaking rate, in random order. The session was tape recorded and later transcribed. The subjects in each age group were about equally divided between the two sets of sentences (sex was also balanced).

The subjects' responses were scored into the following categories: correct; incorrect; elaboration (when the response contained elements that had been deleted from the surface structure of the model sentence); or reduction (when the response had elements deleted that had been present in the model sentence).

The data were analyzed using a series of mixed-model ANOVAs. In all the ANOVAs, three between-subjects variables were specified: age, set, and sex. Different repeated-measures factors were tested in three separate ANOVA's because not all the factors were crossed with each other in the sentences because of grammatical restrictions. For the purposes of these analyses, elaboration and reduction responses were counted as incorrect, following Lust.

TABLE 6.6
List of Sentences Used in Elicited Imitation Study

1. *S* (SVO + SVO)
   Jim writes a letter and Jim writes a letter.
2. *S* (SVO + SVO)
   John ate a cookie and George rode a donkey.
3. *FS* (SVO + SVO) subject redundant
   Barry pushed a train and Barry pulled a truck.
4. *FS* (SVO + SVO) verb redundant
   Paula climbed a tree and Sally climbed a fence.
5. *FS* (SVO + SVO) subject–verb redundant
   Rosy flies a kite and Rosy flies a plane.
6. *BS* (SVO + SVO) object redundant
   Sammy wiped the floor and Billy swept the floor.
7. *BS* (SVO + SVO) verb–object redundant
   Judy sent a note and Philip sent a note.
8. *FBS* (SVO + SVO) subject–object redundant
   Roger washed a cup and Roger dropped a cup.
9. *FP* (SVO + VO) verb–object conjoined/subject reduced
   Joey played the piano and beat the drum.
10. *FP* (SVO + SO) gapping; verb reduced
    Bobby drank the milk and Jane the lemonade.
11. *FP* (SVO + VO) verb–object conjoined/subject reduced; verb redundant
    Susy bought a necklace and bought a bracelet.
12. *FP* (SVO + O) object conjoined/subject–verb reduced
    Marion chased the rabbit and the hamster.
13. *BP* (SV + SVO) subject–verb conjoined/object reduced
    Hilary made and Laurie wrapped a sandwich.
14. *BP* (SV + SVO) subject–verb conjoined/object reduced; verb redundant
    Charlie fixed and Tommy fixed the cabinet.
15. *BP* (S + SVO) subject conjoined/verb–object reduced
    Anthony and Melanie cooked a hotdog.
16. *BP/FS* (SV + SVO) subject–verb conjoined/object reduced; subject redundant
    Mickey rode and Mickey fed an elephant.
17. *FP/BS* (SVO + VO) verb–object conjoined/subject reduced; object redundant
    Stephen chased the balloon and hit the balloon.
18. *FBP* (SV + VO) verb conjoined/subject–object reduced
    Benjamin painted and drove a motorboat.

The first ANOVA tested *form*—sentential or phrasal; *direction*—forward or backward; and *scope* of redundancy/deletion—whether one element or two were redundant/deleted (sentences 3, 5, 6, 7, 9, 12, 13, 15). Age was the only significant between-subjects variable, $F (2,38) = 6.73$, $p < .01$, with 4 year olds imitating better than 3 year olds, and 5 year olds performing best of all. Neither form [$F (1,38) = .01$] nor direction [$F (1,38) = .02$] were significant; however, scope was highly significant [$F (1,38) = 36.15$ p $< .001$]. Overall, single-element redundancies/deletions were harder than double element (mean scores were .42 and .67 respectively). The only other significant result was the three-way interaction between form, direction, and scope [F (1,38) = 12.37, p < .01], which is difficult to interpret in the absence of strong main effects for two of these factors.

Lust (1977) reported an identical ANOVA carried out on data from sentences with the same syntactic structure. The only conflict between Lust's findings and ours is that form was a significant main effect in her ANOVA, sententials being easier than phrasals. We should point out that Lust's subjects were younger than ours, although 3 year olds participated in both these studies and neither found interactions of main effects with age. The only other difference between the studies lay in the particular lexical items used. Lust used some words like *Mommy* and *Daddy*, some animal names, and some given names. We chose all given names to minimize variation in salience. However, the given names undoubtedly also vary in their familiarity for individual children and some of the variation in imitation is due to memory problems caused by unfamiliar names. We introduced a minimal control for this problem by having two sets of sentences with different lexical items. However, it is still possible in either study that lexical differences accounted for a greater part of the variance than syntactic differences, because neither Lust's study nor ours considered sentences as a random variable (Clark, 1973). It is possible, then, that lexical variation was a factor obscuring or confounding the effects of syntactic form per se and creating the discrepancy in the results.

In a second ANOVA, form was tested again, along with single *constituents*—subject, verb, or object, which were either redundant or deleted (sentences 3, 4, 6, 9, 10, 13). Age was significant [F (2,38) = 3.93, p < .05], but sex and set were not. Neither form [F (1,38) = .27] nor constituent [F (2,76) = .82 were significant main effects; however, the interaction between them was at the 5% level [F (2,76) = 4.18] An inspection of the means for these sentences showed that for the sentences involving redundant/deleted *subjects,* the phrasal form (sentence 9) was superior to the sentential form (sentence 3), whereas for the redundant/deleted *object* sentences, the sentential form was superior (sentence 6) compared to the phrasal (sentence 13). The means obtained on the sentences involving a redundant or deleted verb (sentences 4 and 10) were about the same.

The last ANOVA examined various *sentence types* with two redundant/ deleted elements (*SV, VO,* or *SO*) and the number of actual *deletions*—none (sentential), 1, or 2 (complete phrasal) (sentences 5, 7, 8, 11, 12, 14, 15, 16/17, 18). Because the *SO* forward–backward sentence had two alternative one-deletion sentences, 16 or 17, two separate ANOVAs were conducted, once including sentence 16, once sentence 17. The results were virtually identical; therefore, we report the F *values* from the first ANOVA only. Once again, age was significant [F (2,38) = 8.91, p < .001], but not sex or set. Sentence type was not significant [F (2,76) = 1.09], but deletion was [F (2,76) = 9.21, p

< .001]. The means for the three deletion patterns—0, 1, or 2—were .69, .48, and .61, respectively. Although the difference between the sentential and complete phrasal coordinations was not significant, sentences with one element deleted were significantly poorer than either none or two (using the Scheffé test at .05 significance level). These one-element–deleted sentences (sentences 11, 14, and 16/17) sound rather unnatural, and many of the errors produced by subjects in all three age groups consisted of elaborations or reductions. Across these four sentences, there were 15 elaborations and 17 reductions, making up over 40% of these two responses obtained across all the sentences (see Table 6.7).

The two repeated-measures factors, sentence type and number of deletions, interacted significantly [F (4, 152) = 5.57, $p < .001$]. This interaction is probably due to the poor performance on sentence 18, a forward–backward phrasal, compared to the other two-deletion phrasal sentences.

Looking at Table 6.7, which shows the distribution of the elaboration and reduction responses, we confirm Lust's finding that there are no reductions on backward sententials. However, only 4% of the responses to all sentential forms were reduction errors, compared to 8% in Lust's data. Most of the elaboration errors on phrasal sentences occurred on the single-deletion sentences discussed earlier, and sentence 10, which involved gapping. Thirty-six percent of the responses to this sentence were elaborations.

The main findings from this experiment were that in imitation, there were no overall differences between sententials and phrasals, forward and backward forms. The sentences that were the hardest to imitate were the ones with scope of one deletion, or scope of two, with only one unit actually deleted:

e.g., 11. Susy bought a necklace and bought a bracelet.

Included in this group are those sentences that do not involve the conjunction of like constituents in their phrasal forms:

e.g., 13. Hilary made and Laurie wrapped a sandwich.

Despite our attempt to control for sentence length in syllables, it is evident that those phrasal sentences that are shorter in number of words were easier to imitate. Also easy were sentential forms with two redundant elements, despite their extra length in number of words:

TABLE 6.7
Number of Reduction and Elaboration Responses in
Elicited Imitation Study

	Sentence Type						
	FS	BS	FBS	FP	BP	FBP	Total
Reductions	7	0	5	10	8	0	30
Elaborations	0	0	0	39	5	4	48

e.g., 5. Rosy flies a kite and Rosy flies a plane.
Most difficult were sentences that were intermediate in word length with little redundancy:

e.g., 10. Bobby drank the milk and Jane the lemonade.
These latter include sentences that adults regard as questionably grammatical (Gleitman, 1965; Koutsoudas, 1971).

In contrast to our findings, Lust's study of elicited imitation of coordination did show a main effect of syntactic form, with sententials being easier to imitate than phrasals. One explanation for this difference could be the choice of sentences in both the studies. A major drawback of both Lust's experiment and our own is that neither of us considered language as a random variable (cf. Clark, 1973) and so we cannot rule out from either study confounding lexical factors. A second criticism against both imitation studies is in the choice of performance measure. In a recent paper, Hood and Lightbown (1977) point out that elicited imitation is a very complex task attended to in different ways by different children. As a performance measure, it assesses not only language processing, but memory factors, motivation, understanding of task requirements, among other nonlinguistic variables.

ACT-OUT COMPREHENSION STUDY

One task that has proven consistently more informative than elicited imitation is act-out comprehension. In the final study reported here, we investigated how children interpret coordinated sentences they hear. Specifically, the conjunction-reduction hypothesis would predict that sentential forms in which all the information is explicit in the surface form should receive a more correct interpretation than phrasal forms in which information has been deleted. However, if our earlier data are correct, children should have no more difficulty with phrasal than sentential forms, but may balk at certain constructions that involve the conjunction of nonconstituents.

The subjects for this experiment included 42 children, 14 in each of three age groups: 3's, 4's, and 5's. Half the children in each group were male, half female. None of these subjects had participated in the imitation experiment.

Two sets of 18 sentences were constructed using the same types of sentences employed in the imitation experiment. These sentences, however, were reversible in meaning, with assorted animals playing the roles of agent and patient. The length of the sentences ranged from 13 to 15 syllables. Table 6.8 lists one of the sets of sentences used in this study.

Each child was tested individually in separate sessions on both sets of sentences. First, the child was asked to name all the animals that were to be used in the experiment. Then, the child was told to act out on a small stage the event described by the experimenter. Three practice trials were given with simple

TABLE 6.8
List of Sentences Used in Act-Out Comprehension Study

---

1. S (SVO + SVO)
   The turtle bumped the zebra and the turtle bumped the zebra.
2. S (SVO + SVO)
   The elephant kissed the giraffe and the horse touched the turkey.
3. FS (SVO + SVO) subject redundant
   The sheep licked the gorilla and the sheep pushed the kangaroo.
4. FS (SVO + SVO) verb redundant
   The camel hit the elephant and the pig hit the turtle.
5. FS (SVO + SVO) subject-verb redundant
   The zebra kicked the turkey and the zebra kicked the camel.
6. BS (SVO + SVO) object redundant
   The gorilla touched the sheep and the kangaroo pushed the sheep.
7. BS (SVO + SVO) verb–object redundant
   The pig kicked the giraffe and the turkey kicked the giraffe.
8. FBS (SVO + SVO) subject-object redundant
   The horse kissed the turtle and the horse hit the turtle.
9. FP (SVO + VO) verb–object conjoined/subject reduced
   The gorilla bumped the camel and licked the zebra.
10. FP (SVO + SO) gapping; verb reduced
    The sheep patted the kangaroo and the pig the giraffe.
11. FP (SVO + VO) verb–object conjoined/subject reduced; verb redundant
    The elephant touched the horse and touched the turkey.
12. FP (SVO + O) object conjoined/subject-verb reduced
    The alligator patted the turtle and the horse.
13. BP (SV + SVO) subject-verb conjoined/object reduced
    The camel kissed and the pig bumped the kangaroo.
14. BP (SV + SVO) subject-verb conjoined/object reduced; verb redundant
    The sheep hit and the zebra hit the alligator.
15. BP (S + SVO) subject conjoined/verb–object reduced
    The gorilla and the elephant kicked the giraffe.
16. BP/FS (SV + SVO) subject-verb conjoined/object reduced; subject redundant
    The zebra pushed and the zebra licked the alligator.
17. FP/BS (SVO + VO) verb–object conjoined/subject reduced; object redundant
    The sheep touched the gorilla and pushed the gorilla.
18. FBP (SV + VO) verb conjoined/subject-object reduced
    The alligator patted and kissed the kangaroo.

---

noncoordinated sentences. Then, the 18 test sentences were presented in random order by one experimenter, while a second experimenter wrote down exactly what the child did. For each sentence, the experimenters selected the animals needed to act out the sentence and placed them on the stage. If less than three were needed, additional distractor animals were added, so that on each trial a minimum of three animals occupied the stage. The responses were coded as correct or incorrect. Because each child received both sets of sentences, for each sentence type, a maximum score of 2 could be obtained.

The data were analyzed using the same ANOVA models as in the imitation experiment. Age and sex were the two between-subject variables.

In the first ANOVA, there were three repeated-measures factors: *form* (sentential or phrasal), *direction* (forward or backward), and *scope* of redundancy/deletion (one or two). Age was significant at the 1% level [F (2,39) = 6.44]. As in the imitation experiment, only scope was significant among the repeated measures [F (1,39) = 89.94, p < .001]. Sentences with scope of two were understood better than sentences with scope of one. Scope interacted significantly with direction [F (1,39) = 24.17, p < .001] and form [F (1,39) = 8.46, p < .01], and also with direction and form [F (1,39) = 12.41, p < .01]. These interactions are explained by the selective poor performance on the backward single-scope coordinations of the form SVØ + SVO (sentences 6 and 13).

In the second ANOVA, *form* and *constituent* (S, V, or O) were the two repeated-measures factors analyzed. All three main effects were significant: age [F (2,39) = 5.37, p < .01], form [F (1,39) = 6.34, p < .05], and constituent [F (2,78) = 21.05, p < .001]. There were no significant interactions. Sentences with verb or object redundant/deleted were harder to understand than those in which the subject was redundant/deleted, particularly in their phrasal forms. The object-reduced sentence is of the form SV + SVO in which the child has difficulty capitalizing on an initial NVN clause corresponding to subject–verb–object. In fact, 62% of the errors made on this sentence included making the subject of the first clause act on the subject of the second clause—that is, taking the first NVN and interpreting it as agent–action–patient. The verb-deleted (gapping) sentence of the form SVO + SO was also very difficult to understand. Generally, the first clause was acted out correctly, but then children did not know what to do with the remaining two nouns. These two sentences, which were so poorly understood, correspond to the two phrasal forms children hardly ever produced, again pointing to a difficulty in processing these forms that do not involve conjunction of constituents.

The third and fourth ANOVA's tested *deletion* (none, 1, or 2) by sentence *type* (SV, VO, or SO) with sentence 16 and 17 as the one-deletion SO sentence respectively. Age was significant at the 1% level [F (2,39) = 5.36/5.49]. Deletion was significant in both ANOVA's [F (2,78) = 31.64, p < .001/F (2,78) = 4.94, p < .01]; however, sentence type was significant only when sentence 16 was included [F (2,78) = 6.65, p < .05], but not with sentence 17 [F (2,78) = .61]. The interaction between the two repeated-measures factors was highly significant (p < .001) in both ANOVA's [F (4,156) = 9.6/15.61]. As in the imitation experiment, the deletion effect is due to the fact that the sentences with one element deleted were worse than either the complete phrasals or sententials. The other significant effects were due to the relatively poor comprehension of sentence 16—which is also the object-reduced form SV + SVO—and sentence 18, SV + VO. Seventy-one percent of the errors on sentence 16 involved the intital clause, making the subject of the first clause act on a distractor object

TABLE 6.9
Proportion of correct
Responses Involving
Simultaneous Action in
Act-Out Comprehension
Study

	Sentence		
	15	14	7
3 year olds	55	40	21
4 year olds	63	42	20
5 year olds	68	33	25

rather on than the correct object. Although sentence 18 was comprehended better than sentence 16, children sometimes only acted out one of the two actions specified, or included a distractor animal as the object of the first clause (accounting for 70% of the errors on this sentence).

In general, these results closely support the findings from the other experiments we conducted. We found no overall effect of sentential or phrasal form, nor of backward or forward direction of deletion. Sentences that were difficult to understand were backward phrasals of the form SV + SVO, forward phrasals involving gapping of the form SVO + SO, and forward–backward phrasals, SV + VO. None of these forms were readily produced in the elicited-production experiment, and they were relatively difficult for children to imitate. Ardery (1979) has conducted a similar comprehension study, using the same act-out procedure, and with many of the same sentence types. Her results confirm our findings in every respect.

In the comprehension data, we also found evidence that phrasals were interpreted as meaning something different than corresponding sententials. For example, in the group of backward coordinations with scope of two—sentences 7, 14 (one deletion), and 15—we obtained two types of correct responses. In one, the two agents act on the object successively; in the other, they act simultaneously. Table 6.9 shows the proportion of *simultaneous* responses relative to the total number of correct responses for each of these sentences. It is clear that the complete phrasal (sentence 15) was most frequently interpreted as simultaneous action, whereas sententials (sentence 7) were primarily understood as successive action. This finding supports Jeremy's (1978) study on temporal constraints on coordination production. It was not possible to determine whether other groups of sentences were also interpreted differently depending on syntactic form, because one could not act out other sentences in different ways.

Unfortunately, we did not include in this experiment the possibility of interpreting two identical *NP*'s as being nonidentical reference. For example, for a sentence such as:

The giraffe kicked the elephant and the giraffe pushed the turtle.

we only had available a single giraffe, precluding the possibilty that the child could demonstrate to us the same contextual constraints as we discovered in the elicited-production study. The proper experiment on comprehension thus remains to be done.

PERFORMANCE VARIABLES

Before turning to the major conclusions of this chapter, we would like to address one important issue in child-language research—namely, the effects of different tasks on performance. In the course of our investigations into this particular area of syntactic development, we uncovered numerous methodological pitfalls in all the measures we used. Taking our studies as an example, it is worth describing these difficulties to illustrate the importance of adopting a varied methodology in research on child language.

Spontaneous-Speech Samples

The difficulties in drawing conclusions from spontaneous-speech data fall into three major categories:

1. Unless a transcript is richly supported with contextual notes, or videotape methods are used, it is often very difficult to study the referential context of the speech. In our study, we wanted to know not only which contexts produced which types of coordinated sentence (phrasal versus sentential), but also how contexts themselves varied in frequency. For example, did opportunities for subject conjunction occur quite often, but did the children avoid talking about them? Or, were opportunities for subject conjunction as rare as the sentences involving subject conjunction? Spontaneous speech is one of the richest sources of data on child language, offering no artificial constraints on the child's performance. Unfortunately, this lack of constraint means that the context is out of the control of the researcher, and a child's failure to produce some construction could result from either a lack of knowledge or a lack of opportunity.

2. Given a sample of spontaneous speech, how can one make inferences about the child's linguistic knowledge? We encountered two difficulties that are representative of this problem. First, we were sensitive to the criticism that children might have failed to produce sentential conjunctions because they had low MLU's. The argument was that although they derived phrasal conjunctions from an underlying sentential form, they never actualized sentential forms in speaking because of a length constraint. It is difficult to counter speculation of this type because any failure of the predictions of a theory could reasonably be

assigned to a performance deficit. In this particular case, we were able to show that the child's phrasal conjunctions were longer than the minimum needed to produce a sentential form. Thus, although in general the MLU was low, the absence of sentential coordinations was not due simply to a length constraint.

Second, there is the problem of the correct level of analysis for the sentences. It is tempting to borrow the terminology of adult linguistics and refer to sentences as involving "subject conjunction" or "deletion of the predicate," but these sentences are being produced at an age when there is very little evidence that the child *has* abstract grammatical categories like subject at all (Bowerman, 1973). Conjunction has been proposed as a reasonable test of whether or not sentence elements are constituents (Chomsky, 1957), but one can hardly apply that reasoning to the earliest forms that children produce, at least not without considerably more evidence than we have available. Thus, researchers in child language who are interested in syntactic development face a dilemma: either to start at the beginning of speech, justify categories and rules on conservative grounds as the evidence becomes available in the child's language, and gradually build from there; or to use the less conservative method and assign adult-like structural descriptions as early as possible.

3. Because of the time and effort involved in collecting transcripts of spontaneous speech, usually only a small number of children participate in such studies, particularly if they are longitudinal. Given the limited sample size, one might reasonably question how representative the data obtained would be for the population at large. Although in general there has been considerable consistency across different studies of spontaneous speech (e.g., Brown, 1973), with respect to the development of coordination, we found some important individual differences. Whereas our own data from Adam, Eve, and Sarah indicated the primacy of phrasal coordinations, Bloom et al. (1980) report that for some of their subjects sentential and phrasal forms entered their speech at the same time.

Elicited Production

This type of task has not been exploited to any great extent in developmental psycholinguistics, though it has the advantage over spontaneous speech that the experimenter can control the context and equalize opportunities for different types of constructions. The main difficulties with this methodology are as follows:

1. There are limits to what can be drawn or acted out successfully for the child to describe. Some of these limitations are relatively superficial; only certain events can be depicted clearly, thus limiting the semantic content of the pictures. In our study, we also found that some of our pictures were rather implausible, such as the one of a bear simultaneously painting and sawing a piece of wood. We struggled to draw pictures that would compel the child to use certain con-

structions, and discovered that the rarity of a construction in spontaneous speech was due to the implausibility of the event's ever occurring.

2. The second problem is more pervasive: Children vary in how much they will say under these circumstances. We had four warm-up slides in which we encouraged children to describe everything they saw, ideally in complete sentences. However, some children, especially the younger 3 year olds, persisted in saying the minimum until prompted. For example:

Child: "A bear."
E: "And what else?"
Child: "Wood."
E: "Anything else?"
Child: "Painting it."

and so forth, and these responses could not be counted. Motivational problems were quite rare in the population we tested; the reverse problem we encountered was a child's saying much more than we intended. For example:

Child: "Two elephants . . . one eating a apple and . . . two elephants, and one has pink on and one's . . . no, their pants, one's pants are blue and one's green and one of the coats . . . one is yellow and one is pink, and the gray, and one's eating a apple and riding a bike."

Elicited Imitation

Slobin and Welsh (1973) believed that elicited imitation was an excellent way of assessing a child's linguistic knowledge as the child appeared to filter sentences through his or her own grammar while still preserving the meaning. However, more recently, this method has come under attack for the following reasons:

1. Because the usual procedure is to present sentences in the absence of context, the data obtained could seriously underestimate what a child is capable of producing in a context in which the sentences might be plausible (Bloom, 1975). Elicited-imitation studies of constructions that are highly sensitive to contextual constraints, like coordination, would be especially vulnerable to such criticism.

2. Children may "parrot" sentences within their immediate memory span and hence appear to process sentences they could not themselves produce (Hood & Lightbown, 1977). It may be better to introduce a delay between presentation and imitation.

3. Length and redundancy of items are two factors known to influence short-term memory, yet they covary with some of the more interesting linguistic variables and thus may contaminate results. For example, in coordination, sentential forms are longer than corresponding phrasals. If one controls for length, then sentential forms have the advantage of more repeated items. Controlling for length in number of words is not possible without adding grammatical complexity—for example, including adjectives to the phrasal coordinations

(e.g., Lust, 1977)—but length in syllables may not be a psychologically real dimension. Fortunately, certain results that emerged in our study—namely, the difficulty of some types of sentences and the lack of a difference between backward and forward coordinations—cannot be explained away by appeal to differences in length or redundancy.

Act-Out Comprehension

We chose act-out comprehension in preference to picture-cued comprehension because the latter is much more restricted by the alternatives that can be presented. Nevertheless, there are problems with this method:

1. Even our task limited the kinds of interpretations a child could show us, as we pointed out earlier. Thus, we could not demonstrate whether children differentiated the meaning of sentential and phrasal coordinations with respect to referential context. Potentially, one could do so by adding duplicate animals; however this would increase the difficulty of the task considerably.

2. Perhaps the most serious shortcoming of this task is the restricted lexical variety in the sentences that can be used. Reversible sentences preclude a child from using semantic strategies of interpretation, and yet this may lead to a false picture of the child's interpretative strategies. Maratsos, Kuczaj, Fox, & Chalkley (1979) have shown that children who understand the passive voice with action verbs like *hit* or *push* fail to understand it with mental verbs like *know* or *remember*. The use of action verbs in comprehension tasks may thus overestimate the child's general comprehension of a construction.

Not one method currently used in child-language research is free of criticism. Even if the shortcomings just outlined *could* be eliminated, the data obtained from a single method would still only be a measure of one aspect of the child's linguistic performance, and not a clear reflection of underlying competence. To reduce the problems and limitations inherent in assessing performance, we advocate the use of diverse tasks whenever possible.

There are two major advantages in using several performance measures in child-language research: The first is that when there is overlap in the data from several experiments, this increases confidence in the results obtained. In the present study, for example, the imitation task produced results that were very close to those obtained from the comprehension task in most respects; the correlation between the difficulty ranking of the 18 sentence types used in the two tasks was .73. This occurred despite the lack of precise control over sentence length in the comprehension task, the extra requirements of acting out an event, and the fact that the sentences were irreversible for imitation and reversible for comprehension.

Secondly, different tasks will often produce complementary findings; thus, while the elicited-production study highlighted the importance of contextual variables in sentence coordination, the spontaneous-speech data illustrated the developmental course of sentence coordination.

THE DEVELOPMENT OF SENTENCE COORDINATION

The major question this chapter set out to answer is how sentence coordination develops in young children. Based on the data from four studies we described earlier, we propose the following model: Children in the age range we have studied, from 2 to 6 years old, process coordinated sentences in a relatively simple way, by directly conjoining like constituents in a sentence. In addition, certain psychological processing constraints operate within this model so that the site where the conjoined elements are placed affects the difficulty in producing different forms of coordination. Specifically, because spoken language is processed in a left-to-right manner, conjunction of elements at the end of a sentence is easiest, at the beginning is harder, and in the middle is hardest.

Our first piece of evidence in favor of this model comes from the spontaneous-speech data, which shows that phrasal and sentential forms of coordination are not derived from one another. In our study, phrasal coordinations were developmentally earlier than corresponding sentential forms. Bloom et al.'s data (1980) are in close agreement with our own, although in three of their subjects, phrasals and sententials appeared at about the same time, whereas in the fourth child, phrasals came in earlier. In addition, we found that the very earliest conjunctions to appear were not in well-formed sentences, but consisted of simple *noun + noun* or *verb + verb* phrases that probably form the basis for later phrasal coordinations. Although these data strongly indicate that in child language, phrasal and sentential coordinations have separate roots, we do not dismiss the possibility that for the adult, the different forms come from the same source (we return to this issue in a later section). As we pointed out in the Introduction, there are other examples in the literature that illustrate that syntactic structures may have different roots for children and adults.

The second piece of evidence in favor of this model is that very early on, children are sensitive to the different contextual constraints on the form of coordination. Thus, in the study of elicited production in English and Japanese, we found that even the youngest subjects respected referential identity/nonidentity as a powerful constraint on the use of phrasal or sentential form. Again, this argues for the separate roots of sentential and phrasal coordinations, as right from the start children consider that the different forms have different meanings.

The third piece of evidence comes from the kinds of sentences that the children in all the studies had the most difficulty with. The forms most rarely produced, correctly imitated and understood, were two phrasals of the form: SV + SVO and SVO + SO. The first type, a backward phrasal, involves, from the perspective of a conjunction model, the conjoining of subject and verb, as in:

The rabbit is holding and the cat is hitting the drum.

This type of sentence does not involve the conjunction of a true constituent and would therefore not be generated within a conjunction model. The second type of sentence cannot be described by conjunction. It can only be described in terms of deletion of the verb (gapping) as in:

The cow is eating the apple and the horse the banana.

Almost no examples of these types of sentences were found in the production data. They were also difficult to understand and imitate correctly.

The second part of our proposed model of the development of sentence coordination addresses the issue of processing constraints within a surface-structure model. Because in such a model, left-to-right processing of language is a central factor, the place in the sentence where the conjoined elements are situated will affect the difficulty of the sentence. Placing extra elements at the end of a sentence poses the least load, and requires the least advanced planning; thus, in English, object conjunctions of the form:

The rabbit is holding the umbrella and the balloon.

are the easiest phrasal coordinations to produce in the elicited-production task. There is also a preponderance of such sentences in the spontaneous-speech data, although as we pointed out earlier, this may be because there are more opportunities for such sentences rather than because of any syntactic constraints. In English, we found that these object conjunctions were more frequently produced in the phrasal form than subject conjunctions like:

The frog and the turtle are watching television.

Placing conjoined elements at the end of a sentence is perhaps easier than at the beginning. An alternative explanation might be that the grammatical role affects the processing difficulty; thus, objects may be easier to conjoin than subjects irrespective of their place in the sentence. We ruled out this explanation by looking at data from Japanese children in the elicited-production task. In Japanese, both object and subject conjunction are backward, but subjects are placed at the beginning of the sentence, whereas objects are placed in the middle. Japanese children found it easier to produce the subject-conjoined sentences rather than the object-conjoined, thus showing that it is not a question of grammatical role, but rather where the conjoined elements are placed. Furthermore, this Japanese data shows that placing conjoined elements in the middle of a sentence is harder than doing so at either end.

THE RELATION BETWEEN LINGUISTIC THEORY AND
CHILD LANGUAGE

In the first part of this chapter, we laid out the two major alternative linguistic models of sentence coordination. In the standard transformational theory, sentential and phrasal coordinations share a common deep structure, but phrasals are more complex, as they involve conjunction reduction in deriving their surface forms. In the second model, phrasal coordinations are not derived from sentential coordinations, but are generated directly by conjoining like elements.

Until recently, the conjunction-reduction model has enjoyed the greatest support among linguists (e.g., Stockwell et al., 1973) and psychologists (e.g., Lust, 1977, Lust & Mervis, 1980). However, as we pointed out earlier, with the changes now taking place in linguistic theory, the status of conjunction reduction is uncertain. The general trend has been towards reducing the transformational component and allowing for more direct generation of complex forms in the base. Although no one to our knowledge has recently worked out a detailed alternative to conjunction reduction within this new framework, the conjunction model originally proposed by Dougherty (1967, for one example) seems to correspond to the proposal that some phrasal forms would be generated in the base, rather than being derived from sententials via deletion and regrouping.

The model for the development of sentence coordination outlined earlier is compatible with Dougherty's conjunction model; we find that children only process well coordinations involving the conjunction of like constituents, and have the greatest difficulty with those phrasal coordinations that cannot be derived by conjunction. On the other hand, we have no data to support the conjunction-reduction schema; we do not find that children in the age range we studied derive phrasals from corresponding sententials, and sentential forms are not the earliest to appear in children's speech.

Clearly, at some point, the psychological data and linguistic theory must be compatible. At present, though there is a wealth of evidence from child-language data in favor of the conjunction model (see also Ardery, 1979; Bloom et al., 1980; Greenfield & Dent, 1979; Jeremy, 1978), the issue is still controversial among linguists. This asymmetry could be resolved in a number of ways.

One possibility would be that the conjunction-reduction schema is the correct model for the way adults process coordination. This would imply that at some point in development, a reorganization takes place in the child's linguistic system and there is a shift from phrase-structure rules for conjunction to conjunction reduction. We suggested this possibility in earlier papers (de Villiers et al., 1976, 1977); however, the evidence on which we based that argument now appears inadequate. Specifically, we argued that at about 4 years of age, it appeared that children were confusing sentential and phrasal forms in memory, and in the imitation task produced many elaborations and reduction errors. This coincided with the point when sententials appeared in the spontaneous-speech protocols.

We have now collected imitation data from more subjects and the 4 year olds look no different from the other children. Also, Bloom et al.'s (1980) spontaneous-speech data show that sententials can begin earlier than we originally thought. There are no comparable psycholinguistic data on coordination processing in older children or adults from the same performance measures that we have used with preschoolers. This means that there is no evidence to support the hypothesis of a syntactic reorganization in later childhood (see also Maratsos, 1978).

The alternative would be that the conjunction model is the correct description for both children's and adults' coordination processing. Given the evidence we have described in this chapter, this possibility appears the most parsimonious. Linguistic models that aim to achieve psychological reality can look towards data from child language to resolve theoretical conflicts. In the case of sentence coordination, the developmental research points to a close-to-the-surface model, with different forms of coordinated sentences being generated by phrase-structure rules rather than by conjunction reduction.

ACKNOWLEDGMENTS

The research described in this chapter was supported by Grant #BNS 73-09150 from the National Science Foundation to Dr. Roger Brown, Harvard University. We thank the following schools for their help in the completion of the studies: The Living and Learning Center, Waltham, Massachusetts; Harvard University Law School Day Care Center, Cambridge, Massachusetts; University of Minnesota Day Care Center, Minneapolis, Minnesota.

REFERENCES

Ardery, G. The development of coordinations in child language. *Journal of Verbal Learning and Verbal Behavior,* 1979, *18,* 745-756.

Bates, E. *Language and context: The acquisition of pragmatics.* New York: Academic Press, 1976.

Bever, T. The cognitive basis for linguistic structures. In J. R. Hayes (Ed.), *Cognition and the development of language.* New York: Wiley, 1970.

Bloom L., Miller, P. & Hood, L. Variation and reduction as aspects of competence in language development. In A. Pick (Ed.), *Minnesota symposium on child psychology.* Minneapolis: University of Minnesota Press, 1975.

Bloom, L., Lahey, M., Hood, L., Lifter, K., & Fiess, K. Complex sentences: Acquisition of syntactic connectives and the semantic relations they encode. *Journal of Child Language,* 1980, *7,* 235-261.

Bowerman, M. *Learning to talk: A cross-linguistic study of early syntactic development with special reference to Finnish.* Cambridge, England, Cambridge University Press, 1973.

Bowerman, M. Learning the structure of causative verbs: A study in the relationship of cognitive, semantic, and syntactic development. *Stanford Papers and Reports on Child Language Development,* 1974, *8* 142-178.

Bresnan, J. W. A realistic transformational grammar. In M. Halle, J. Bresnan, & G. A. Miller (Eds.), *Linguistic theory and psychological reality.* Cambridge, Mass. MIT Press, 1978.

Brown, I. Role of referent concreteness in the acquisition of passive sentence comprehension through abstract modelling. *Journal of Experimental Child Psychology,* 1976, *22,* 185-199.

Brown, R. *A first language.* Cambridge, Mass. Harvard University Press, 1973.

Brown, R., & Hanlon, C. Derivational complexity and the order of acquisition in child speech. In J. R. Hayes (Ed.), *Cognition and the development of language.* New York: Wiley, 1970.

Brown, R., & Herrnstein, R. *Psychology.* Boston: Little, Brown, 1975.

Bruner, J. From communication to language: A psychological perspective. *Cognition,* 1975, *3,* 255-287.

Chomsky, N. *Syntactic structures.* The Hague: Mouton, 1957.

Chomsky, N. *Reflections on language.* New York: Pantheon, 1976.

Chomsky, N. *Essays on form and interpretation.* New York: North-Holland, 1977.

Chomsky, N., & Lasnik, H. Filters and control. *Linguistic Inquiry,* 1977, *8,* 425-504.

Clark, H. H. The language-as-fixed-effect fallacy: A critique of language statistics in psychological research. *Journal of Verbal Learning and Verbal Behavior,* 1973, *12,* 335-359.

Cross, T. Mothers' speech adjustment: The contribution of selected child listener variables. In C. E. Snow & C. A. Ferguson (Eds.), *Talking to children: Language input and acquisition.* Cambridge, England, Cambridge University Press, 1977.

de Villiers, J., & de Villiers, P. *Language acquisition* Cambridge, Mass.: Harvard University Press, 1978.

de Villiers, J., Tager-Flusberg, H., & Hakuta, K. *The roots of coordination in child speech.* Paper presented at the First Annual Boston University Conference on Language Development, 1976.

de Villiers, J., Tager-Flusberg, H., & Hakuta, K. Deciding among theories of the development of coordination in child speech. *Stanford Papers and Reports on Child Language Development,* 1977, *13,* 118-125.

de Villiers, J., Tager-Flusberg, H., Hakuta, K., & Cohen, M. Children's comprehension of relative clauses. *Journal of Psycholinguistic Research,* 1979, *8,* 499-518.

Dougherty, R. A. *Coordination conjunction.* Unpublished paper, Massachusetts Institute of Technology, 1967.

Fiengo, R. W. On trace theory. *Linguistic Inquiry,* 1977, *8,* 35-62.

Fodor, J. A., Bever, T., & Garrett, M. *The psychology of language: An introduction to psycholinguistics and generative grammar.* New York: McGraw-Hill, 1974.

Gleitman, L. Coordinating conjunctions in English. *Language,* 1965, *41,* 260-293.

Greenfield, P., & Dent, C. *Syntax vs. pragmatics: A psychological account of coordinate structures in child language.* Paper presented at the Stanford Child Language Forum, April 1979.

Grosu, A. Review of N. Chomsky, Essays on Form and Interpretation (New York: North-Holland). *Journal of Linguistics,* 1979, *15,* 356-364.

Hakuta, K. *Comprehension and production of simple and complex sentences by Japanese children.* Unpublished doctoral dissertation, Harvard University, 1979.

Halle, M., Bresnan, J., & Miller, G. A. (Eds.). *Linguistic Theory and psychological reality,* Cambridge, Mass.: M.I.T. Press, 1978.

Harries, H. Coordination reduction. *Stanford University Working Papers on Language Universals,* 1973, *11,* 139-209.

Hood, L., & Lightbown, P. M. *What children do when asked to "say what I say": Does elicited imitation measure linguistic knowledge?* Paper presented at the Conference on Comprehension and Production of Speech and Language, University of Wisconsin—Milwaukee, 1977.

Horgan, D. The development of the full passive. *Journal of Child Language,* 1978, *5,* 65-80.

Ingram, D. If and when transformations are acquired by children. In D. P. Dato (Ed.), *Developmental psycholinguistics: Theory and application. 26th annual Georgetown University roundtable.* Washington, D.C.: Georgetown University Press, 1975.

Jeremy, R. J. Use of coordinate sentences with the conjunction "and" for describing temporal and locative relations between events. *Journal of Psycholinguistic Research,* 1978, *7,* 135–150.

Kaplan, R. Augmented transition networks as psychological models of sentence comprehension. *Artificial Intelligence,* 1972, *3,* 77–100.

Koutsoudas, A. Gapping, conjunction reduction, and coordinate deletion. *Foundations of Language,* 1971, *7,* 337–386.

Kuno, S. *The Structure of the Japanese Language:* Cambridge, Mass.: M.I.T. Press, 1973.

Lakoff, G., & Peters, S. Phrasal conjunction and symmetric predicates. In D. Reibel & S. Shane (Eds.), *Modern studies in English.* New York: Prentice-Hall, 1969.

Limber, J. The genesis of complex sentences. In T. E. Moore (Ed.), *Cognitive development and the acquisition of language.* New York: Academic Press, 1973.

Lust, B. Conjunction reduction in child language. *Journal of Child Language,* 1977, *4,* 257–287.

Lust, B. & Mervis, C. A. Development of coordination in the natural speech of young children. *Journal of Child Language,* 1980, *7,* 279–304.

Maratsos, M. New models in linguistics and language acquisition. In M. Halle, J. Bresnan, & G. A. Miller (Eds.), *Linguistic theory and psychological reality.* Cambridge, Mass.: M.I.T., 1978.

Maratsos, M., Kuczaj, S., Fox, D. M. & Chalkley, N. A. Some empirical studies in the acquisition of transformational relations: Passives, negatives, and the past tense. In W. A. Collins (Ed.), *Children's Language and Communication, Minnesota symposium on child psychology* (Vol. 12). New York: Harper & Row, 1979.

McNeill, D. *The acquisition of language: The study of developmental psycholinguistics.* New York: Harper & Row, 1970.

Ross, J. R. *Constraints on variables in syntax.* Unpublished doctoral dissertation, Massachusetts Institute of Technology, 1967.

Slobin, D. I., & Welsh, C. A. Elicited imitation as a research tool in developmental psycholinguistics. In C. A. Ferguson & D. I. Slobin (Eds.), *Studies of child language development.* New York: Holt, Rinehart, & Winston, 1973.

Snow, C. *Language acquisition and mothers' speech to children.* Unpublished doctoral dissertation, McGill University, 1971.

Stockwell, P., Schachter, P., & Partee, B. *The major syntactic structures of English.* New York: Holt, Rinehart, & Winston, 1973.

Wierzbicka, A. *Against conjunction reduction.* Unpublished paper, Massachusetts Institute of Technology, 1967.

Williams, E. Across-the-board rule application. *Linguistic Inquiry,* 1978, *9,* 31–43.

7 Relative Acquisition

Henry Hamburger
University of California, Irvine
and
National Science Foundation

Stephen Crain
University of Texas at Austin

OVERVIEW

A child can partially acquire a concept and/or the means to express it. One might then say that relative acquisition has taken place: relatively more than nothing, relatively less than everything. On the other hand, a child ultimately achieves full competence with respect to the relative clause. One might then say that relative acquisition has taken place. In these senses, the topic of this chapter is relative relative acquisition.

To clarify what is involved in the acquisition of relative clauses, we lay out a rather long list of their syntactic and semantic aspects. Although no one has denied that these could be acquired one by one, or at least in small groups, there has been very little study of such a possibility. This dearth of concern with the internal workings of a construction suggests a need to discuss both the rationale and the methodology for trying to study independently the acquisition of 'subrules' involved in relative clauses.

The acquisition of relative clauses has received considerable attention lately, and our debt to recent researchers for certain aspects of methodology is apparent. Nevertheless, we argue that certain methodological oversights and questionable orientations have led to a somewhat misleading picture of the course of acquisition. We propose new comprehension tasks and methods of eliciting production, both designed to remedy these alleged shortcomings.

245

Our experimental results substantially alter the current picture of the acquisition of relative clauses. We find considerably earlier acquisition than in previous work, with evidence coming from both the comprehension and the elicited-production tasks. More importantly, we have obtained some evidence for the kind of piecewise acquisition that we argue is crucial to an understanding of the acquisition process.

The remaining sections are organized as follows: In the first section, we offer some motivational remarks and lay out the promised steps along with a summary of our findings. The next section is a review of some relevant literature. The third section provides a bridge to our own work by pointing out those aspects of previous work that we propose to remedy. The fourth section is the heart of the chapter, a presentation of our own methodology and a fuller account of our experimental results.

INTRODUCTION: WHY STEPS AND WHAT STEPS?

Why Relative Acquisition?

Consider two assertions: (1) relative clauses play a central role in natural language; (2) documenting children's relative progress in the smallest possible steps can play a central role in the study of acquisition. If these two assertions are correct, our topic of relative relative acquisition deserves careful study. We therefore support each briefly.

Both the syntax and the semantics of the relative clause have commanded attention. Its syntax allows recursion, the basis of unlimited novelty in language. Indeed, it allows self-embedding, historically used to show the inadequacy of finite-state grammars and the need for at least context-free grammars to model natural language. Context-free grammars, in turn, have seemed awkward for dealing with another aspect of relatives, the "empty" noun phrase (e.g., the direct object of "want" in "That's what I want."). The relative clause has therefore figured prominently in arguments for transformational grammar.

On the semantic side, a key aspect of relative clauses is the assignment of a referent to the empty noun phrase. Considerable attention has recently been devoted to how well children perform this chore in comprehension (see references in the next section). One facet of the present study combines this referent-assignment task with recognition of another semantic aspect of some relative clauses: that they are presupposed rather than asserted. This very subtle aspect of human communication appears from the work reported below to be well-understood, implicitly, by a substantial majority of children at the surprisingly early age of 5. As a final comment on the semantics of relative clauses, it is worth noting that in Montague-type approaches the relative clause is a kind of quantification, involving the most complex kind of rule (see, e.g., Thomason, 1974).

Turning from relative clauses to relative (partial) acquisition, it may seem a mundane point that constructions can be learned in pieces. Nevertheless, we argue that previous work has not pursued this point assiduously enough. The result has been at the least a misleading view of the emergence of the relative clause. At worst, failure to look at minimal subrules can seriously bias the empirical question of whether child language is a rule-governed phenomenon (this point is developed in the section *Stepwise Tasks for Steps of Acquisition*).

Early Steps of Relative Acquisition

Mastering the relative clause requires a child to make several syntactic and semantic achievements. This subsection and the next describe 13 aspects to be acquired, along with evidence that some of them can be acquired independently of others. The presentation makes it clear that the entire process of mastering the relative clause is spread over a period of years. This subsection introduces the dissection process with reference to early "protorelatives" found in previous work. It is the aspects in the next subsection that directly underlie the rest of the chapter.

Exactly when acquisition of relatives begins is unclear. It is particularly difficult to pinpoint a child's first attempts at a protorelative, because our ideas about the young child's syntax, meaning, and the relation between them are all somewhat tentative. Nonetheless, it is important to try to piece the early evidence together if we are to gain insight into the acquisition process. To our knowledge, the earliest that anyone has claimed a child to be using a protorelative is at 24 months (Hamburger, 1980). Perhaps other comparable data will be forthcoming, now that the importance of this subject has been argued.

There are two aspects that we feel *must* be present for a construction to qualify as a protorelative, one syntactic and one semantic. In form, it is necessary to have at least a verb phrase within a noun phrase, and in meaning the *restrictive* relative clause places a restriction on the set referred to by the noun phrase. Early examples are utterances 1-3a, each ending in a noun phrase (signaled by an article or a genitive pronoun), which contains a verb phrase that restricts the referent set.

	Age	*Utterance*	*Referent*
1.	2;0	This my did it.	a painting
2.	2;2	That's a flush a toilet.	a toilet handle
3a.	2;4	Look-a my made . . .	a toy construction
3b.		Look-a wha I made.	

These utterances are from an intensive (8,000 utterances) year-long study of a 2-year-old child, Emily. That they reflect reasonably stable grammatical rules is argued at length in Hamburger (1980), where evidence is also given for Emily's deliberate use of *my* versus *I*. Utterance 1 is claimed to mean something like "This is my thing such that I did it." Utterance 2 differs from 1 with respect to the role of the referent noun phrase: In 1, it is the direct object, whereas in 2, it is not. The possible importance of this distinction is discussed in the work cited, but is not counted as a separate aspect here.

An important property of 3a that distinguishes it from the first two utterances is the absence of a direct object of the verb in the protorelative. Such empty noun phrase sites in adult relatives have by some linguists been attributed to *wh* movement, but here there is no overt *wh* word in the utterance. Interestingly enough, the *wh* word was supplied when this utterance was self-corrected to 3b. This event is an additional encouragement for interpreting 3a, and indirectly 1 and 2, as protorelatives. Some care must be taken with 3b itself, however, because unlike 1–3a, it is not supported by other similarly constructed utterances in the corpus near the same time.

The (proto)relative in 3b is further distinguished from 1–3a by containing a subject, making it look like an objectless *S* rather than an objectless *VP*. Another aspect of some relative clauses, manifested by none of those shown, is a head. In this particular corpus, utterances 4 and 5 are among the earliest relatives to have heads (this tardiness of heads is consistent with findings by Lust, 1979).

Age	*Utterance*	*Referent*
4. 2;7	Look at that noise . . . you're making again.	a car horn
5. 2;9	I want something that the cow(s) eat.	(uttered while playing with a cow, a horse, and an empty trough)

TABLE 7.1
Aspects of Early Relative Clause Exemplified by Utterances 1–5[a]

	1	*2*	*3a*	*3b*	*4*	*5*
A. Restricts referent set	X	X	X	(X)	X	X
B. *VP* or *S*, in an *NP*	X	X	X	(X)	X	S
C. Empty *NP* site			X	(X)	X	X
D. *S* (not *VP*), in an *NP*				(X)	X	X
E. Head included (optional)					X	X
F. *wh* word included				(X)		X

[a] X indicates that an utterance exhibits a particular property. Utterance 3b is a self-correction. The distribution of X's suggests that these aspects need not all be acquired at once.

The foregoing observations are summarized in Table 7.1. If the various aspects just discussed had been acquired entirely independently of each other, and if each one, once acquired, had been reliably present thereafter, it would be possible to construct a table with a triangular array of X's. Table 7.1 approximates such a case, but because it does not contain the whole corpus, much less the entire verbal output of the child, it can only be suggestive. Nevertheless, it is clear that the relative clause can, at least to some extent, be acquired in pieces.

Further Steps of Relative Acquisition

Several more aspects of relative clauses must ultimately be dealt with. Two that have received much attention are (continuing the lettering system of Table 7.1): G, the various sites (especially subject, object) for the whole complex noun phrase within the main clause; and H, the various sites possible for an unfilled noun phrase within the relative clause itself. Whatever the combination of these sites in a particular sentence, I, the relative clause must be attached properly with respect to the phrase structure of the sentence. An important approach that has yielded results in this latter area is that of Solan and Roeper (1978).

In addition to the foregoing structural matters, there are important semantic points that must be mastered. First, there is the much studied question of J construal, the assignment of the correct referent to an unfilled noun-phrase site. Then, there is the distinction between K restrictive versus nonrestrictive relative clauses. All of the examples in the previous section, as well as aspect A, restricting the referent set, had to do with restrictive relatives. Next, perhaps the most important for our purposes here, there is L, the distinction between what is asserted by a sentence and what it presupposes to be true. Finally comes M, felicity; it is felicitous to use a restrictive relative only when some restricting needs to be done.

The last three items are the focus of the rest of the chapter, so it is useful to comment further on them here. First, note that although *we* do not use nonrestrictive clauses to the children, there is nothing to stop *them* from using them, or from believing that we are doing so. The problems that arise from this circumstance interact with presupposition. On the other hand, it is by adhering to felicity conditions that we enable these effects to manifest themselves.

The restrictive relative clause, as noted earlier, restricts the set referred to. In the comprehension studies cited herein, there is typically a head noun that designates a set of physical objects (dog, fence, etc.), and there is a relative clause that restricts this set to fewer potential referents. For present purposes, we can regard this restriction as equivalent to the intersection operation acting on the semantic interpretations of the head noun and the relative clause (Quine, 1960). For example, the restrictive relative clause in 6a restricts the set designated by "ball," presumably the six balls displayed, to just the three balls that are striped. "The second" specifies the second element of this smaller set, ball 3. There is no superfluous verbiage here: The restrictive relative clause is an essential part of the specification of a particular ball. (For discussion of a related adjectival example, see Matthei, 1979.)

6.

1   2 3 4 5 6

a. Give me the second ball that is striped.

b. Give me the second ball, which is striped.

A nonrestrictive relative clause, on the other hand, serves as a comment about the noun phrase it modifies rather than as a restriction on the head noun. Thus, in 6b, the referent of "the second ball" can be determined without regard to the nonrestrictive relative clause. Here again, "ball" refers to the six on display, but now "the second" specifies a particular element of this larger original set, specifically ball 2. Because ball 2 is in fact striped, the comment (that it is striped) is true. That comment is, however, quite unnecessary unless the listener is expected for some reason to need the reassurance of a confirming comment. The question of gratuitous comments is taken up in the subsection *Conversational Maxims*.

This distinction between the two types of clauses can be reflected in phrase markers, invoking the principle of semantic compositionality (Partee, 1973). In this analysis, phrase marker (7a) is used for the restrictive case. The N and S nodes each correspond to a set, and the *Nom* node corresponds to the intersection of those two sets. If that intersection has one member (or one member that is somehow more prominent than others), then that member can be referred to by using "the" and making the head noun singular. In the nonrestrictive case, in phrase marker 7b, use of "the" and the singular is appropriate if there is only one element (or one prominent element) in the set corresponding to the N node (rather than the *Nom* node). What is consistent across the two cases is that the *Det* node (which dominates "the") is attached directly to the node corresponding to a set with one (prominent) element.

7a.   NP
     Det   Nom
       | /   \
       | N   S___
       | | _____
      the   cow   that stands
                    on the lion

7b.   NP
       /   \
      NP   S___
     / \   _____
   Det   N   ,which stands
    | | on the lion
   the cow

There has been little attention in the acquisition literature to the distinction between the two types of clause. Experiments have not been strong enough to ascertain which one the child's conceptualization resembles more. Tavakolian

(1978) notes that "there is no direct evidence that children interpret a restrictive relative clause as a restriction of the head noun rather than a nonrestrictive comment about it [p. 70]."

The distinction between presupposition and assertion is related to the two types of relative clause. In many cases (all cases of interest here), the *restrictive* relative is presupposed, rather than asserted. Thus, in a sentence like "The cow jumps over the horse that the dog kisses," there must exist some horse that the dog kisses. The listener should know of such a horse before the sentence is uttered. The speaker then asserts that some cow jumps over that horse.

We anticipated that at least some children might at some point in the course of acquisition make a point of acting out the presupposition before the assertion. This turns out to be the case (see the subsection *Results* under *Methodology and Results*). It also seemed to us that some children would, perhaps at a later stage, regard acting out the presupposition as unnecessary, on the grounds that it is not really what the sentence "says" (asserts). This also turns out to be correct (see the subsections *Rationale for Procedural Innovations* and *Results*).

On the other hand, such results are *not* to be expected in the case of *non*restrictive relatives. It is our contention that the results of de Villiers et al. (1979) confirm this point. Because (as explained later) their settings meet the felicity conditions only for nonrestrictives, their finding of no consistent order (in acting out the two clauses of a sentence) would appear to pertain to nonrestrictives, and not to restrictives.

LITERATURE REVIEW

One important property of relative clauses is that they allow self-embedding, a consequence of which is that the outer clause is interrupted. It was noted by Miller (1962) that sentences containing successively nested relatives are more difficult for adults to understand than are their right-branching counterparts. An information-processing explanation is that self-embedding requires orderly memory of return addresses. There is no reason to expect children to be exempt from such considerations. Indeed, Slobin (1966) proposed universal constraints that predict, for one thing, that a sentence in which the main clause is interrupted by a subordinate clause will be relatively difficult for children to process, *ceteris paribus*. Empirical support for this "Interruption Hypothesis" is found in the work of Menyuk (1969) and Slobin and Welsh (1973).

In a systematic test of the Interruption Hypothesis, Sheldon (1974) used restrictive relative clauses, as in 8, in a comprehension task with 3-, 4-, and 5-year-old children.

8a. *SS*: The dog that jumps over the pig bumps into the lion.
8b. *SO*: The lion that the horse bumps into jumps over the cat.
8c. *OS*: The pig bumps into the horse that jumps over the cat.
8d. *OO*: The dog stands on the horse that the giraffe jumps over.

As in Sheldon's terminology, S and O (in front of sentences 8) stand for subject and object (of verb or preposition). They identify, in order, the position of the matrix noun phrase that bears the relative clause and the position of the empty noun phrase inside the relative clause. For example, 8b is an SO (subject, object) relative clause because the subject of the matrix sentence bears a relative clause whose object is superficially empty. The Interruption Hypothesis predicts that the subject relatives (SS and SO) will be more difficult to understand than the object relatives.

The children's task was to act out sentences with toy animals. They did better on SS and OO relatives than on OS and SO relatives, disconfirming the Interruption Hypothesis, which predicts that SS and SO are the difficult ones. The inferior performance found for OS and SO relatives Sheldon explained by the "Parallel-Function Hypothesis." The idea is that sentences in which the same noun phrase is used with different, "nonparallel," grammatical functions in the two clauses (main and relative) will be more difficult to comprehend than sentences in which a noun phrase plays the same, "parallel," function in the two clauses.

Unexplained by this hypothesis is the fact that children do worse on OO than on SS relatives. In fact, for both types of object relatives, OO and OS, almost one third of the children interpreted the relative clause at the end of the sentence as modifying the subject of the main clause. To account for this response type, Sheldon turned to the rule "Extraposition from Noun Phrase" (Ross, 1967). Such extraposition can account for sentences like "A man entered the room who was smoking a cigar," in which the relative clause "who was smoking a cigar" has been moved away from its head noun "man." Sheldon hypothesized that this rule was readily invoked by children despite its infrequency of use by adults. For example, she claims that children interpret an OS relative like 9a as if it has the underlying form of an SS relative like 9b. Similarly, OO sentences could receive an SO interpretation.

9a. OS: The pig bumps into the horse *that jumps over the giraffe*.

9b. SS: The pig *that jumps over the giraffe* bumps into the horse.

On the basis of a subsequent experiment using a similar task and a greater variety of sentence types, Tavakolian (1978) argues against Sheldon's Parallel-Function and Extraposition Hypotheses. She notes that the Extraposition Hypothesis predicts no difficulty for SS and SO relatives, only for OS and OO. Therefore, SO relatives should be easier than OS relatives, because the Parallel-Function Hypothesis treats the two equally. However, SO relatives were interpreted incorrectly more often than OS relatives in the Sheldon study, and errors occurred with nearly equal frequency in Tavakolian's study.

In order to undermine the Parallel-Function Hypothesis, Tavakolian made a more detailed analysis of the incorrect responses and thereby established the importance of a particular error type in both her own and Sheldon's results. She attributed this response to the children's use of a set of rules needed anyway to explain children's correct interpretation of missing noun phrases in conjoined clauses, such as 10a:

1   2   3

10a. The sheep knocks down the rabbit *and* stands on the lion.

1   2   3

10b. The sheep knocks down the rabbit *that* stands on the lion.

CORRECT RESPONSES: 10a—(12,13)   10b—(12,23)

The nouns in 10a and 10b are numbered, as by Tavakolian, in order of occurrence. The response code (12,13) indicates that a child made animal 1 perform the action of the first clause on animal 2, which in turn was made to perform the action of the second clause on animal 3. Other sets of action are encoded similarly. It is the (12,13) response, which Tavakolian found was the most common for all four types of relative clause, that provides the focal point for her alternative analysis, which follows.

The Conjoined-Clause Analysis accounts for the (12,13) response in a two part argument. Syntactically, it assumes that a child's phrase structure rules are sharply limited with respect to recursion, but that the recursive rule $S \rightarrow S\,S$ is needed on independent grounds to assign structure to conjoined simplex sentences, such as 10a. A simple grammar including this rule then maps *all* strings of the form 11a into the labeled bracketing, 11b, ignoring the distinction between *that* and *and*.

1   2   3

11a. $NP \ldots V \ldots NP \ldots V \ldots NP$

11b. $[_S[_SNP \ldots [_{VP}V \ldots NP]]\ [_S\Delta \ldots [_{VP}V \ldots NP]]]$

The second step of the argument is that coreference is determined by a control principle of universal grammar: that a controller must c-command the missing noun phrase position. Only the subject noun phrase in the main clause of 11, by virtue of being directly attached to the S node, meets this requirement. Therefore, this subject noun phrase gets interpreted as coreferential to the missing noun phrase. On this reasoning, one would expect (12,13) responses for both 10a and 10b. Such a response is correct and typical for the sentence conjunction in 10a, whereas for 10b it is precisely the very frequent error that the Conjoined-Clause Analysis was designed to explain.

In Tavakolian's experiment, children produced the incorrect (12,13) response for 63% of the *OS* relatives. From cross-age comparisons, Tavakolian (1978) inferred that children continue to use this response to *OS* relatives even after they stop using it for *OO* and *SO* relatives. She attributed this to the fact that the order of elements in *OS* relatives is the same as the order specified by the conjoined clause analysis.

Both Sheldon and Tavakolian allow only a limited role for children's grammatical knowledge in explaining comprehension results, assigning considerable importance to general processing strategies. Tavakolian (1978) explicitly states, for example, that "the percentage of correct responses to SS relatives is not due to children's competence in relative clause formation [p. 59]." Even less grammar-oriented is Legum's (1975) intriguing explanation for the (12,13) response. Legum's idea is that once a child gets ahold of an animal, s/he tends to hang onto it. By this reasoning, known as the "Bird-in-Hand Strategy," there would be a tendency to use the same subject in each clause, skewing the response distribution towards (12,13) and possibly also (21,23).

Some recent studies have found that children around 4 years old can be diverted from the (12,13) response to *OS* relatives by careful selection of test sentences. Solan and Roeper (1978) found few errors with *OS* relatives like 12, in which, as Goodluck (1978) notes, the relative clause semantically combines more naturally with the object of the matrix sentence than with its subject (in the example, girls do not bite horses).

12. The girl pushed the cow that bit the horse.

In her own experiments, Goodluck reduced the number of animals from three to two by using an intransistive verb in the relative clause, as in 13. Like the semantic clue in 12, this change also sharply improved performance. Goodluck hypothesized that the earlier tasks with three different animals had presented too great a cognitive-processing burden. To investigate this hypothesis further, Goodluck used sentences like 14. In this sentence, there is no semantic clue because either animal could conceivably jump, but the total number of animals is reduced to two anyway.

13. The dog kicks the horse that jumps up and down.
14. The pig bumps into the sheep that jumps over the fence.

Four- and 5-year-old children produced a substantially reduced number of (12,13) responses to sentences like 13 and 14, in comparison to *OS* sentences like 8c. They responded correctly 76% of the time to sentences like 13 and 69% of the time to sentences like 14. As in earlier work, few (less than one half) of the responses were correct on traditional *OS* relatives with three animate noun phrases like 8c. On the basis of their recent findings, Goodluck and Tavakolian (1979) suggest a processing—rather than a competence—account of children's errors in relative clause interpretation.

These recent studies cast doubt on the various hypotheses. All of them—Parallel Function, Extraposition, Conjoined Clause, and Bird-in-Hand—are unresponsive to the choice of lexical item as in 12 and 14 and to the use of an intransitive verb as in 13. To the extent that children abandon the (12,13) response for these special subsets of *OS* relatives, theories explaining that response are undermined or at least in need of supplementation.

CRITICISM

A common thread runs through previous research on the restrictive relative clause: the conclusion that this construction is frequently misinterpreted by 5-year-old children. Mastery of a construction presumably includes its production as well as its comprehension. If, as might seem reasonable, comprehension were to precede meaningful production, then the age of mastery of the construction would be even later than 5.

In rather strong contrast, this chapter presents evidence that children around 3 years old have partial command of the restrictive relative clause and, typically, it is mastered by the age of 5. To demonstrate this early acquisition, we have devised new methods both in comprehension and in elicited production. These methods and their results are presented in the next section.

What went wrong in the previous experiments? Why did they not discern the degree of grammatical competence we claim exists in younger children? To help make our own findings plausible, we prepare the way, in this section, by suggesting strong but previously unmentioned reasons why children might have had difficulties interpreting restrictive relative clauses in previous studies. The three parts of this section deal with violation of conversational maxims, violation of felicity conditions, and mingling the study of acquisition with the study of youthful processing.

Conversational Maxims

One possible source of difficulty for children in previous comprehension studies is the violation of Conversational Maxims (Grice, 1975), specifically the Maxim of Manner, somewhat rephrased here as sentence 15. This subsection is a discussion of specific ways in which previously used tasks may have violated the various parts of the maxim.

    15. Manner: be perspicuous
       a. avoid obscurity (of expression)
       b. avoid ambiguity
       c. be brief (give only necessary information)
       d. be orderly
       (Note: c conflates Grice's maxims of Quantity and Quality.)

Use of the present tense with nonprogressive aspect, as in "The lion jumps... ,'' appears to run counter to submaxim 15a. This verb form, used by Sheldon (1974) and Tavakolian (1978), is normally used for definitions and recurrent events, but is unnatural, hence somewhat obscure, in the situation of the experiments. In ordinary adult conversational descriptions of on-going non-recurrent events, the progressive is preferred ("Look! The lion is jumping.") Perhaps the experimental setting makes it appropriate to use stage directions, but then one would expect the infinitive ("Make the lion jump."). For story telling, the past tense seems more natural (acting out a story that includes ". . . and then the lion jumped . . ."). These judgments are not absolute, but they do suggest that the form selected was more "obscure" than necessary.

The importance of maxim 15a in conversations involving children is im-plicitly underscored by research on parentese, which shows how people modify their speech for young children. Even nonparents and quite young children take into account the limitations of their listeners. For example, Meissner and Ap-thorp (1976) found that children as young as 3 resist pointing and resort to verbal descriptions when paired with a blindfolded listener. Thus, children have good reason to anticipate that what is said to them will be said nonobscurely.

Ambiguity, proscribed by maxim 15b, gives rise to processing difficulties for adults, according to various psycholinguistic studies (e.g., MacKay, 1966). Be-cause listeners apparently look for a single structure and interpretation and have difficulty when two are possible, it makes sense for a speaker to provide only one. If Sheldon is correct that children can extrapose from a noun phrase, then sentence 16a is ambiguous for them between the "correct" *OS* reading and an extraposed reading, as if 16a were derived from the deep structure underlying the *SS* relative (16b).

16a. The boy hit the man that saw the girl.
16b. The boy that saw the girl hit the man.

This criticism does not apply to Tavakolian (1978), who changed verb forms, possibly to eliminate this type of ambiguity. The ambiguity difficulty of sen-tences like 16a can be removed by providing a context that eliminates one of the readings, but (to our knowledge) this has not been done.

Ambiguity is also present in subject relatives like 16b (Sheldon, 1977). This string of words can be interpreted as a complex noun phrase (instead of a complete sentence) in which "that saw the girl hit the man" is a relative clause attached to the noun phrase, "the boy." This interpretation would actually be favored if children utilized the parsing strategy of "Late Closure" (Frazier, 1979). The ambiguity arises because the verb *to see* may take either an object noun phrase or a sentential complement, and the verb form "hit" is both a tensed form and the untensed form of *to hit*. (Replace "hit" by "push" or "pushed" to get the two readings.)

The maxim of brevity, 15c, is violated by all the relative clauses in the previous experiments because all those clauses provide redundant information with respect to the setting in which they are used. The restrictive relative is supposed to restrict the referent set, in the manner described earlier, but it doesn't in these experiments because only one possible referent is provided. For example, with only one horse available, the assertions of 17a and 17b are the same, so the relative clause in 17a provides unnecessary information, counter to the admonition 15c to be brief.

17a. The cow bumped the horse that tickled the cat.
17b. The cow bumped the horse.

More than speaker efficiency may be at stake. Suppose the listener has been understanding the sentence perfectly, right up through the head noun "horse." This word, prior to being modified by any relative clause, indicates the set of available horses, of which there is only one. Next, the listener gets a relative clause, with its implicit message to restrict, and hence diminish, the set of potential referents. But this instruction cannot be carried out in the context provided. We do not know what mental events are involved in trying but failing to carry out the implicit demands of such sentences, but the result may well be disruption of the young listener's attempt to use whatever grammatical competence she does have.

To circumvent these difficulties, one must devise a situation in which the relative clause is indeed needed to communicate what is to be done. Specifically, in terms of the preceding example, it suffices to make additional horses available. Then it is 17b that cannot rightly be carried out, because "the horse" demands a set with one (prominent) horse (Maratsos, 1976). Thus, in this revised environment, a relative clause is just what is needed after "horse" in 17a.

Orderliness, counseled by the final submaxim, is difficult to achieve, because language makes conflicting demands. There is a sense in which the presupposition is conceptually prior to the assertion of a sentence. The fact that this conceptual order is opposite to order of mention of the clauses in object-relative sentences (*OS* and *OO*) might be regarded as a lack of orderliness. However, to achieve reordering of mention would require using a passive main clause, itself a comparable source of disordering. We return to this point of order later (in the section Comprehension and Presupposition) and put it to methodological use.

Felicity Conditions

For a sentence (or other form of expression) to be appropriate and correctly interpretable, it must meet certain "felicity conditions." The idea of felicity conditions is closely related to that of conversational maxims. The maxims guide sentence choice, given a meaning and context, whereas the felicity conditions state, for a given sentence (on a particular reading), what should true of the context. In the earlier example, the maxim of brevity says that with one horse available, 17a, being redundant, is inappropriate. The felicity conditions of the relative clause, on the other hand, specify conditions under which 17a may be used, specifically that there should be more than one horse available. We believed that 4- and 5-year-old children might be sensitive to such felicity conditions, and would hence perform better if those conditions were met.

Ambiguous sentences will, in general, have different felicity conditions associated with different readings. For example, 16a, as noted, has both an *OS* reading and an *SS*-Extraposed reading. An OS relative requires two or more elements in the referent set for the noun of the direct object in the matrix sentence. On the other hand, for an extraposed *SS* relative, it is the noun in the subject noun phrase whose referent set must have at least two elements. By providing one of each animal type, previous experiments have been unbiased between the two correct readings, but only by failing to meet the felicity conditions of either.

Interestingly, the incorrect conjoined-clause interpretation fits felicitously in this environment of one-element sets. Replacing "that" in 17a by "and" yields the conjoined-clause interpretation (18), with no relative clause and hence no requirement for a multielement set.

18. ⟨The cow bumped the horse and (the cow) tickled the cat⟩

In this interpretation, each noun phrase consists simply of "the" plus a noun. For such a noun phrase, the felicity condition is a set with one (prominent) member, precisely what has typically been provided for the children. In this way, the experimental settings have been biased towards the incorrect conjoined-clause interpretation, meeting its felicity conditions but not those of the other interpretations.

The nonrestrictive relative clause, like the conjoined clause, permits a setting with one animal of each type. This construction is of particular interest because it is the only one that both fits the exact wording of the sentence given by the experimenter (not requiring "that" to be changed to "and") and also has its felicity conditions met by the settings typically provided. If children use this nonrestrictive interpretation, then even if they correctly comprehend and act out the subject–object relationships, they will not take the relative clause to be presupposed. As noted earlier, presupposition provides a basis on which to act out the relative clause before the main clause, but nonrestrictives, being merely comments, need not be acted out first.

This reasoning explains the results of de Villiers et al. (1979) who found that "no child consistently acted out the relative clause first [p. 514]." They attribute this to children's failure to notice the syntactic marker for embedding. However, since they did not meet the felicity conditions of the restrictive relative, the children were quite correct in not conforming to the demands of that construction. When we did provide an appropriate setting, by making more than one animal of a type available, many children did consistently act out the relative clause first or not at all. This topic receives further attention in the subsection *Rationale for Procedural Innovations*.

Felicity conditions, as discussed so far, stipulate that enough objects must be present in the experimental setting. One can ask equally whether providing *too many* objects of a type or providing extraneous types of objects can also violate some sort of felicity condition. Returning to 17a, for example, should there be a cat present or not? We have argued that "the cat" is not part of the asserted action. Having a cat present might therefore seem to undermine the idea that the horse's tickling of the cat is to be taken on faith as having occurred, rather than having to be acted out. On the other hand, if there were no cat in evidence (or at least in prior discourse), one might reasonably respond to 17a by saying "What cat?" since use of "the" (in "the cat" of 17a), even within a relative clause, presupposes knowledge by the listener of a lone or prominent member of a relevant set.

One way to reconcile these conflicting requirements might be to let the cat be visible but somehow less accessible than the other animals, but unfortunately this biases the experiment with respect to its original objectives. We are driven, therefore, to accepting the possibility that extraneous objects may be present (and equally accessible) so long as they do not explicitly violate any felicity conditions. This is consistent with the way things unavoidably are in ordinary discourse. To be sure that children realize that not all the animals need be used, one can include extra animals in practice trials. (Tavakolian did this, though she was not testing understanding of presupposition.)

Taking all these matters into consideration, the most reasonable display for a sentence with a relative clause (and in which each determiner is "the") consists of at least two objects of the type named by the head noun and one of each of the others. Thus, with sentence 17a, assuming that it is intended as an *OS* relative, we would present one cow, one cat, and a few horses.

On Patching Up

Some of the work in the Goodluck and Solan volume (1978) indicates an interest not only in the child's grammar but also in a set of processing mechanisms that the child uses to patch things up when the grammar is inadequate. An explicit statement of the patch-up orientation is given by Tavakolian (1978):

> Multiple-clause sentences are a challenge to children's *parsing strategies* and rules for interpreting missing elements [p. 39].
> Hypothesis A: When children are *uncertain* about the structure of a multiple-clause sentence, they *attempt* to parse the string as though it contained conjoined simplex sentences [p. 40].

Hypothesis B: (Where deep and surface structure differ), children will attempt the most direct projection of thematic relations . . . in a *complicated* sentence whose structure they are *uncertain* of [p. 42; emphasis added in each of the foregoing quotes].

Is this orientation appropriate for the study of acquisition? First note that simplicity is sacrificed when one tries to consider two things at once, in this case grammatical change (acquisition) and grammatical expedients. Ample compensation might accrue if the two were intimately connected, specifically if the results of the patching operations could potentially solidify into new rules. Those operations would then be essential to the mechanism of acquisition and would be of central concern. This, however, is not the interpretation placed upon them by Tavakolian. Indeed, to account for successful acquisition, one would need something more explicit than principles which say, in effect, "do the best you can using old structures (hypothesis A) and when in doubt proceed superficially (hypothesis B)." In sum, the approach could be important but so far lacks precision.

Now consider a lesser claim one might make for these hypotheses: Though not principles of acquisition, they account for quite real performance phenomena; therefore, even if they do clutter things up, ignoring them will lead to incorrect analyses. Thus, we would need studies directed at "partialing out" processing performance. In response, note that the patch-up operations are only brought into play when the child is confronted by something beyond her current ability. Therefore, by devising tasks (in the manner indicated in the subsection *Stepwise Tasks for Steps of Acquisition*) that reveal in greater detail what children *can* do rather than what they can't, we may be able to diminish or bypass the need for a patch-up approach.

It is interesting and useful to glance at some of the history of "can" versus "can't" studies of children. Gelman (1978) notes that although the Piagetian tradition in cognitive development has stressed "can't" studies, language-acquisition studies have taken a more positive approach. She discerns and praises a recent trend in cognitive studies toward the assessment of early partial success. Against such a background, it would be ironic to find language acquisitionists moving toward the study of incompetence.

One interpretation of this apparent interest in incorrectness is as a merging of two types of precaution in making sure the child is really as advanced as s/he may seem. To guard against crediting a child's utterances with being based on a sophisticated grammar when in fact they may be only routines or partially routinized, at least four sources of information have been drawn upon: (1) productivity (use of a word in various combinations); (2) intended meaning (assessed from linguistic context, situation, and child's actions); (3) erroneous utterances (because they presumably cannot be copied from adults); and (4) comprehension (constructing situations in which a clearly defined set of possible responses includes an incorrect one that accords with the experimenter's theory of a child).

The last two of these points apparently provide the motivation for studying comprehension errors. Still, they do not overcome the earlier comments about unnecessarily confounding acquisition with processing. We believe that the comprehension studies referred to herein have been useful principally for setting an upper bound on a child's competence, thereby providing a guide (but only a guide) in pursuing a more important goal, knowledge of actual competence.

Such knowledge is crucial if one accepts our view that the study of acquisition should be based on a series of competences. A child's competence at one time should be compared with her competence at another, slightly later, time with a view to determining changes in competence. (For details of one example of carrying out such a study, see Hamburger, 1980). Many such changes in competence from the same child and from other children constitute the input for theorizing about competence change and about a process that could both (1) bring about the competence-change types that are observed; and (2) be proved to converge, given appropriate linguistic (and associated situational) input, to an appropriate adult grammar.

METHODOLOGY AND RESULTS

Our search for the separate emergence of the various aspects of the relative clause involves comprehension tasks and elicited production, both reported later in this section. The evidence strongly indicates that certain aspects emerge considerably earlier than recent literature leads one to believe. The purpose of showing how early children learn things is not to see how clever they are, but to determine the course of their emerging competence. Theories of the dynamics of acquisition can then be examined for compatibility with this empirically ascertained sequence. The search for such a sequence hinges on the use of appropriate tasks. How to devise such tasks and some consequences of not doing so are explored in the opening subsection.

Stepwise Tasks for Steps of Acquisition

Ideally, one would like a comprehension task that a child can perform correctly if and only if s/he has mastered a single aspect under study. Then, the source of each error would be clear. A series of such tasks would make it possible to determine each child's course of acquisition. Alternatively, one might seek a task that demands mastery not only of the aspect under study but also of one or more easier aspects, ones that the child is presumed or known to have already acquired. This latter objective is less demanding on the experimenter but presents the temptation of presuming too freely about what is "easier." To get independent evidence of what is really easier, one needs a task requiring mastery of the easier but not the harder aspect.

The desirability in principle of pinpointed diagnostics is not controversial. However, it is not always appreciated that failure to find such tasks may have serious consequences for the kind of conclusions that one draws about the basic nature of language acquisition. Brown (1973) raises the theoretical point though he does not pursue the methodological question:

> It is true of all the grammatical morphemes in all three children that performance does not pass from total absence to reliable presence. There is always a considerable period . . . in which production-where-required is probabilistic. This is a fact that does not accord well with the notion that the acquisition of grammar is a matter of the acquisition of rules . . . One would expect rule acquisition to be sudden [p. 257].

With this statement appears a graph showing the fluctuating improvement over several months of the relative frequency with which a child supplies *ing* in contexts requiring it.

Given that adult language is rule governed, it might seem straightforward to assume that acquisition takes place rule by rule. The gradualism described by Brown sits uneasily with the notion of hypothesis formation, not to mention the triggering of innate structure. But gradualism may be only an artifact, if a particular rule turns out not to be a monolithic entity but a complex of several subrules, possibly depending on context as well. To be precise, suppose that a construction requires acquisition of two capabilities, *A* and *B,* but in certain contexts only draws upon *A*. Then, a child who has only *A* will use the construction reliably when only *A* is needed, otherwise not. In such a case, the relative frequency of correct responses is a function of the environment, not the child, and is therefore of sharply limited interest.

One possible problem with subrules is that too fine a subdivision can lead to insufficient data for each subrule, a remedy for which is to contrive specific test situations. Brown (1973) did find one case in which the rule-governed look emerged even without appeal to subrules: "One can, in the case of prepositions, identify a quite abrupt and continuous rise to criterion. Probably this is because the curves for *in* and *on* sum across *much less varied semantic and grammatical subrules* than do the curves for the other forms [p. 263–264; emphasis added]."

A rule or construction can be broken up on internal or external grounds. Internally, a construction may be decomposable into several syntactic and semantic aspects; such decomposition is our principal focus. It is, however, also of interest to look externally, asking whether a particular construction has been "acquired" only in a restricted context, and, if so, whether it is really appropriate to say that the construction has been acquired.

An external or contextual example is the observation that children tend to elaborate the direct-object noun phrase earlier than the subject noun phrase. This observation runs counter to the notion that if a child has a rule, say $NP \rightarrow Art +$ $(Adj) + N$, then one ought to expect its options to crop up at least occasionally wherever the grammar permits. It is presumably at least in part to examine such external effects that the investigators cited earlier concerned themselves with the distinction between the sentence types referred to as $SS, SO, OS,$ and OO.

Internally, a particular instance of a relative construction includes such aspects as presupposition and restriction of referent set, as already noted. The point is that one can try to test for these aspects outside of relative clauses. For example, presupposition is apparently required for appropriate interpretation of a (nonrelative) sentence like "Take the hat off the table," in which it is presupposed that a hat is already on the table. If a hat is available but not on the table, a child's response to this command could conceivably begin with the acting out of the presupposition—placing the hat *on* the table to set the stage—even though the presupposition is not referred to at all overtly. In such a case, one might well conclude that the child has some understanding of a certain aspect of relative clauses (namely, presupposition), even though that child might not be able to deal reliably with the relative clause itself.

In the work described in the next subsection, we have followed a variant of the strategy just sketched. Earlier experiments with restrictive relative clauses not only involve presupposition, as they must, but also draw upon an additional ability, the ability to suspend conversational maxims and felicity conditions. We have altered the circumstances to conform to those maxims and conditions, so that this extra ability is not required. If indeed children have mastered presupposition at the ages under study, but do not yet have the ability to suspend the maxims and conditions, then they will succeed at the new tasks despite having failed at the old ones.

Comprehension of Presupposition

Procedure. In general procedure, our comprehension experiments resemble previous work. Each child takes part individually in a single tape-recorded session. The experimenter places a number of objects in front of the child, whose task is to act out the sentence spoken by the experimenter. Practice on simple sentences ensures that the child understands the task. One practice trial is designed to make the child realize that it is not always necessary to move all available objects.

The major overt innovation in our experimental procedures has to do with the number of each type of object made available to the child for acting out a sentence. Previous researchers have invariably presented only one object of each type. To meet the felicity conditions, as discussed earlier, we present more than one object of the type referred to by the head of the relative clause—for example, three horses in addition to one duck and one pig with sentence 19:

1   2   3

19. The duck stands on the horse that jumps over the pig.

RESPONSE: 23,12

A second important procedural difference is that we observe not only what the children do but also the *order* in which their actions occur. A corresponding change in notation is called for. Retaining the order-of-mention numbering of animals (''1'' for the duck, etc., in sentence 19), let (*wx,yz*) stand for the response in which the child makes animal *w* act upon animal *x* and, *following that,* *y* upon *z*. (In the example here, (23,12) would mean that a child made the horse jump over the pig and then made the duck stand on the horse). Previous notation looks the same but ignores order so that (*wx,yz*) and (*yz,wx*) could refer to the same response. Also, the notation *A* will signify that only the assertion was enacted.

The test sentences did not include *SS, SO,* or *OO* relatives. Instead, the only relatives were of the *OS* variety; these made up one fourth of the sentences. Another quarter were conjoined-clause sentences and the remainder were unrelated items included to eliminate response bias. There were 40 sentences in all. Of the 10 *OS* relatives, five had animate referents for all three noun phrases. In the other five, either one of the noun phrases referred to an inanimate object or else the relative clause contained an intransitive verb. These sentences were included to determine whether having too many animals still would affect performance even when the felicity conditions were met. The 10 conjoined sentences served as matched pairs for the *OS* relatives. All verbs were in the past tense as in Solan and Roeper (1978), and Sheldon (1977), but unlike Tavakolian (1978) and Goodluck and Tavakolian (1979).

Eighteen children aged 3, 4, and 5 were tested in two nursery schools. All children spoke either standard or Black English as a first language. They come from a mixture of social backgrounds and income groups.

Rationale for Procedural Innovations.   We focused on *OS* relatives for two reasons. First, this type of relative clause had presented the most difficulty for children in all the previous studies. Therefore, these sentences provide the best opportunity to show the predicted improvement in children's responses that might result from meeting the felicity conditions. The difficulty of *OS* relatives also seemed to hold the promise of diverse responses that might indicate various stages of acquisition.

A second reason to focus on *OS* relatives is that they (as well as *OO* relatives) have an order-of-mention of clauses that is opposite to the conceptual order, presupposition followed by assertion. Before stating the methodological usefulness of this opposition of orders, let us clarify in what sense there is a conceptual order.

Informally, thinking about our own potential response to these tasks as adults, it occurred to us that an adult might well begin by acting out the clause that states what is presupposed, to set the stage for the assertion, and might only then proceed to act out the assertion itself. We were encouraged by the reaction of a 9 year old who performed a similar task in just such a way and, under minimal questioning, essentially explained the idea of presupposition in lay terms.

Even apart from the task of acting out, presupposition is conceptually prior to assertion. Suppose a listener tries to think through the meaning of a sentence like 19, binding noun phrases to specific animals (tokens, not types) as referents. It will not be possible for such a listener to finish processing the assertion without first processing the presupposition. It is in this sense that presupposition is conceptually prior to the assertion, even though it need not be temporally or causally prior.

The fact that this conceptual order is opposite to the order of mention of the corresponding items in OS and OO sentences may be a cause of poor performance on them. In any case, precisely because the orders are opposite, their effects can be distinguished. Young children often acted out clauses in order of mention in the temporal conjunction experiments of Clark (1970) and Coker (1978), apparently as a kind of default when they failed to pick up the relevant linguistic cues. If this occurred here, then use of OS sentences would permit us to discern whether and when children change from order-of-mention to presupposition–assertion order. Such a changeover would be a clear signal that relative clauses were being comprehended as such and not as conjoined clauses.

These concerns necessitate recording the order of the child's actions. The previous representation system, which ignored such order, was adequate as long as one looked only at the subject and object relations within each clause. The relationship between the clauses was recorded only implicitly via the shared noun phrase. (In example 19, "2" appears twice, because "the horse" is both object of the main clause and subject of the relative clause.) However, one of the principal points of interest about the relative construction is that it connects clauses. Therefore, it is of particular interest to investigate explicitly the semantic relationships between whole clauses.

This discussion of clausal order need not imply that both clauses must be acted out. A quite reasonable interpretation is that this task requires just the acting out of the assertion, the rationale being that what is presupposed should already have taken place. In fact, we would argue that if anything can be said to be the uniquely correct response to this task, this is it. If someone says, "Show me the pen you wrote your dissertation with," you do not sit down at your desk for 2 years and recreate it.

Accordingly, we hypothesized that relatively older children would give the assertion-only response, or, failing that, the presupposition-first response. Younger children, in contrast, would be expected to act out the clauses in random order or possibly in accord with some kind of order-of-mention criterion.

In this discussion of whole clauses, nothing has been said about whether the child is at least getting the correct subjects and objects within each clause. Mistakes on these latter matters are not directly our concern here, though it was our hope that performance on subjects and objects would improve, vis-a-vis previous results, because we had revised the situation to be consistent with the felicity conditions of the presupposition.

Results. The responses that are correct with respect to the within-clause actions for *OS* sentences are (12,23), (23,12), and the assertion-only response, *A*. These responses, which we call *wc* correct, comprise 79% of all responses (across ages and number of animal types) to all *OS* sentences. This represents a substantial improvement over even the most recent previous results and indeed a reversal of the early findings.

The 5 year olds in our experiment had no trouble dealing with three different types of animals; their responses were *wc* correct on 92% of such trials. The most closely corresponding result for Goodluck and Tavakolian (1979) is 60%, though this figure excludes *A* responses that may have occurred and gone unnoticed. Presumably, this difference in results arises from the procedural difference— namely our compliance with the felicity conditions. Though 4 year olds do less well, that age group also appears to benefit from (experimenter's) adherence to felicity conditions. Even with three types of animals, this group responds *wc* correctly 67% of the time versus 37% in the Goodluck–Tavakolian task (the latter figure again leaving out possible unnoticed *A* responses).

The present work confirms that performance improves when the number of animals is reduced from three to two. In that case, we get 97% and 83% for 5 and 4 year olds, compared to findings of 70% and 72% by Goodluck and Tavakolian for the two age groups. One way to summarize the data in these two paragraphs is to say that well over half the errors in the Goodluck–Tavakolian experiment are apparently attributable to unmet felicity conditions.

The clearest single finding is that 5 year olds really have mastered comprehension of the relative clause, at least in the *OS* case. Because this was the one of the worst cases in the early work, our 97% *wc*-correct figure strongly suggests that the previous failures in this age group were an experimental artifact. The Goodluck and Tavakolian procedural innovation (fewer animal types) allows one dramatic leap in performance and ours allows another.

In addition to improved performance, we were particularly interested in looking for stages of development, in accord with our general orientation as set out earlier in the chapter. A breakdown of the *wc*-correct responses by type and by age group appears in Table 7.2. The most prevalent response type for each age group is italicized in the table to stress that there are indeed different stages in the acquisition of relative clauses.

Three year olds clearly distinguished *OS* relatives from conjoined sentences, giving a (12,13) response to only 22% of *OS* relatives. The most frequent

TABLE 7.2
Within-Clause Correct Responses to *OS* Relatives

		Response Type			
		(12, 23)	*(23, 12)*	*A*	*Total of WC Correct*
Age	3 years	*42%*	27%	0%	69%
	4 years	18%	*43%*	13%	74%
	5 years	5%	35%	*55%*	95%

response in this age group was (12,23). This is the response that is correct within clauses but uses an order-of-mention strategy at the level of whole clauses. The 4 year olds, as a group, present a different picture. Their most frequent response is (23,12), correct within clauses and also exhibiting what we have said is the correct conceptual order, presupposition followed by assertion. For the 5 year olds, a majority of all responses consisted of a correct enactment of just the assertion.

Although we have already seen that even with three animate noun phrases the children do much better in these experiments than formerly, it is of interest to look at the effect of having one less type of animal to keep straight. For seven children, four of them 3 year olds and the rest 4's, this aspect did matter. As a group, these seven children had a majority response of (12,23), correct within clauses, but violating presupposition–assertion order. This group of children also made significantly more of the incorrect or questionable (12,13) responses with three animals than with two. These results are compatible with those of Goodluck and Tavakolian (1979) and suggest that the ability to keep track of three animals emerges towards the beginning of the period in which the linguistic abilities under study here are acquired. In contrast, the ability to overcome infelicitous settings is apparently acquired later, because infelicity alone (with no third animal type) trips up 5 year olds as a group about 30% of the time (Goodluck and Tavakolian's finding), whereas the third animal type alone (with felicity conditions met) brings about less than a 10% error rate (our finding).

Random Token Selection.   Our change in paraphernalia may seem to be a potential source of bias. Use of three animals of one type appears to favor that type as a response. Thus, in example 19, repeated here, the child has three horses to choose from, and only one duck and one pig.

19. The duck stands on the horse that jumps over the pig.

If a child were to choose randomly among these five tokens, then on each selection the probability of picking a horse would be 60% versus 20% for each of the other types. This interesting point requires discussion. (It was raised by members of the University of Massachusetts Linguistics Department at a presentation of some of these results.)

We do not consider this criticism damaging, for the following reasons: First, randomness is a very bad overall predictor. Next, even if the randomness argument is sharpened in the most favorable way, it explains only part of the observed changes. Finally, this sharpened version introduces new predictions that are manifestly false. These points will now be expanded.

There are three animal types that can be chosen as subject of the main clause, and either of the two that remain can be the object, yielding six combinations. Similar comments hold for the relative clause, for a total of 36 overall possible responses. Only a few of these occur more than 2% of the time. Therefore, overall randomness is ruled out.

Now suppose that random choice is presumed to operate only when a child is uncertain, and that the only point of uncertainty that arises for any child is how to fill the subject of the relative clause, the other three positions always being done correctly. Then the random choice, in terms of the older notation, would be between responses (12,13) and (12,23). Because we provide three tokens of animal #2 and only one of animal #1, the (12,23) response would then be chosen with probability ¾ under our procedure, assuming random token selection, rather than random type selection. In all previous procedures, this probability would be only ½. The number of observed errors would thus be cut from ½ ($= 1 - $ ½) of the instances of uncertainty to ¼ ($= 1 - $ ¾) of such instances, thereby cutting the number of observed errors in half.

For the 4 year olds, this prediction is at least superficially in accord with the results in the preceding subsection. However, we have ignored here the order in which these children act out the clauses. Recall that the predominent response among 4 year olds involves not only correct subject–object relations but also putting the two clauses in what we have called the correct conceptual order. Improvement in this clausal order cannot be explained by random token selection. Because previous work has not taken note of clause order, nothing further can be concluded.

For the 5 year olds, the predicted halving of the error rate is greatly exceeded. In this age group, our procedure cuts the error rate from 40% to 8% in the three-animal–type condition (vis-a-vis Goodluck and Tavakolian) and from 30% to 3% in the two-animal–type condition. Thus, for this age group, not half but 80% to 90% of the errors disappear. The random token model, therefore, cannot explain the extent of the improvement among 5 year olds.

The last few paragraphs, however, do not really get to the crux of the matter. The random token model predicts, absolutely erroneously, that when animal type #2 is chosen twice, as it very frequently is, it may be that two different tokens are used. Such a response could be denoted, say, (12,2'3) or (23, 12'). For example, in sentence 19, it is conceivable that a child might make the duck stand on one of the horses and then have a different horse jump over the pig. (Such a response may seem a little bizarre; we are only saying that it is predicted to occur fairly often by the random token hypothesis). If such responses were counted as incorrect, then random token selection, far from explaining our results, would actually predict worse results with our procedure than in previous experiments. Since in fact such responses almost never occur, counting them as errors would not affect our results. Finally, note that we *do* have the relevant data on this point: Because the younger children almost always act out both clauses, we generally can be sure that it is indeed the same token in each clause; as for the 5 year olds, their status is already clear from the earlier discussion.

In summary of this last point, it is simply not the case that children choose the relative-clause subject in 19 by random selection among the three horses and the duck. Rather, they limit their choice to the duck and one particular horse. For the younger children, we can directly observe when they use the same horse twice, whereas for the 5 year olds (for whom we can often observe only one clause), the random token hypothesis predicts far too many errors.

Elicited Production

Why Elicitation: Meaning–Utterance Pairs. To learn a language is to master a mapping between potential utterances and (associated) potential meanings. Such mastery has, at least overtly, two parts: comprehension and meaningful production. To decide which of these two parts to investigate, or whether it is worth the effort to examine both, let us briefly look at certain gaps intrinsic to the study of each.

To test a child's comprehension, one would like to input an utterance, u, and observe whether it is interpreted at all and, if so, to what interpretation, m, it is mapped. Unfortunately, direct observation of the child's interpretation is impossible, since it consists of brain activity. One must therefore deduce the interpretation from its use in guiding the child's response, r, to some task—say, acting out, picture selection, or question answering. In the case of acting out (used here and in all the studies cited), the experimenter codes the action into a response category, c.

An acting-out comprehension experiment, in sum, induces a mapping $u \rightarrow m \rightarrow r \rightarrow c$. The recorded data, however, consist only of (u,c) pairs. Since what one seeks is (u,m) pairs, it would be handy if there were a 1–1 mapping between m and c, and if one knew what it was. Our comprehension tasks move in the direction of establishing such a mapping.

Testing a child's ability to go in the other direction, from meaning to utterance, involves comparable though not identical difficulties. We do not examine the differences in detail here, but it is worth noting that, loosely speaking, experimental inputs are often easier to control finely than are a subject's responses. In the present context, let (m,u) be a correct meaning–utterance pair in the adult language. Then in a comprehension task, u is under our control, whereas in an elicited-production task, we hope to create a situation in which m is uniquely presented. If this contrast between the two types of experiment is correct, then each of the two can provide data of a form unavailable from the other: Comprehension tasks can yield pairs of the form (m',u), whereas elicitation can yield (m,u') pairs. Note that such pairs may be outside the adult mapping yet consistent with the child's current competence, hence not errors of performance. Therefore, patching up need not be involved.

In sum, elicited meaningful production can not only confirm the results of comprehension tasks, but may provide information that is unavailable from comprehension tasks. The converse is also true. These remarks hold whether or not the processes of comprehension and production are exact inverses of each other. If they are not, then there is all the more reason to study both processes.

Procedure. An elicitation experiment should set up a situation that heeds the felicity conditions and conversational maxims as they bear upon the following aspects of the subject's cognitive state:

20a. the subject's model (her mental representation of the situation and of the relevant background);
20b. the subject's model of the listener's model;
20c. the subject's understanding of what s/he is to get listener to do or understand.

To elicit relative clauses, these requirements can be met by using two identical animals along with information that distinguishes them. This information should be expressible by a relative clause and not by a simpler means of expression. The subject is to know which is the designated element of the pair, and is charged with conveying that information to an ostensibly uninformed listener. The exact setting and procedure are given in sentences 21 and 22:

21. Setting
   a. Three people: the subject, S, the experimenter, E, and a listener, L.
   b. Three objects: two identical, W_d and W, and one unique, Z (say, two walruses and a zebra). W_d is distinguished from W only by E's actions, including pointing at it.
22. Procedure
   a. Blindfold put on L.
   b. E makes W_d start acting on Z (say, by tickling).
   c. E tells S, "Tell L to pick up this one," indicating W_d.
   d. S responds.
   e. Blindfold taken off L.
   f. Action stops.

A typical response (at 22d) is a complex noun phrase or a sentence containing one—for example, 23a. This OS response is appropriate with procedure 22. To make the OO response in 23b appropriate, E merely performs the opposite action at 22b, making Z act on W_d. A passive like 23c would also then be appropriate. (A passive is also possible, but awkward, in the original case.)

23a. Pick up the walrus that is tickling the zebra.

23b. Pick up the walrus that the zebra is tickling.

23c. Pick up the walrus that is being tickled by the zebra.

It is quite clear to most 4 year olds that, with a blindfolded listener, pointing is useless. In this respect, the experiment is consistent with findings by Meissner and Apthorp (1976) and Blank (1975). If a subject does rely on gestures and deictics, L says, "I can't see. Please tell me." Also note that the need to distinguish two identical animals makes a relative clause essential. If the two differed, then an adjective or a prepositional phrase (e.g., the blue W; the W with a hat) might provide an adequate description.

Results.   The setting and procedure of 20 and 21 were used with each of 12 children. Of the seven 4 year olds, two of the youngest did not seem able to respond. Of the remaining 10 children, the five 4 year olds did not differ significantly, as a group, from the five 5 year olds. Among these 10 children, the average rate of OS-relative production was 72%.

In another production task, children were given mini-stories followed by a question, as in 24:

24. There were two brothers. One boy ate dinner and the other went to bed without dinner. Which boy was sad? (Typical response: "the one that didn't eat dinner.")

Eight such (mini-story,question) pairs were administered to five 4 year olds and five 5 year olds. The results were almost identical to those of the preceding task. Again, the two age groups did not differ significantly; here the rate of successful responses—full (headed) relative clauses—was 73%. Note that the question demands only a noun phrase, not a full sentence. (Requiring even less, only a relative clause without its head, is the sentence-completion task of Potts, Carlson, Cocking, & Copple [1979]. In that experiment, there was a comparable rate of successful response, 69%.)

Reliable elicitation of relative clauses from 4 year olds is thus possible. These results are compatible with the picture emerging from newer comprehension results, in particular those reported here. (However, these elicited relative clauses are for the most part not part of OS-relative sentences nor of sentences at all, just noun phrases.) In a way, this success in eliciting relative clauses from 4 year olds should come as no surprise, because spontaneous production of relatives, apparently in appropriate context, has been observed in children under 3 (Limber, 1973). Nevertheless, standard elicitation conditions, like those here, have two potential advantages over reliance on spontaneous production: readily replicable results and greater confidence and precision with respect to the meaning a child attaches to the relative clause.

SUMMARY

Piecewise acquisition of relative clauses begins early and lasts long. Its study can contribute importantly to an understanding of the acquisition process. Such contribution requires appropriate methodology and orientation. We have made explicit suggestions along these lines and have incorporated these suggestions into our work in an attempt to delineate a typical acquisition sequence. (However, potential pitfalls inhere in the cross-sectional approach; for discussion see Hamburger, 1980). The following picture emerges:

Key pieces of relative clauses have been observed independently of each other in the spontaneous production of 2 year olds. Many 3 year olds comprehend OS relatives well enough to bind referents correctly, though this ability has been masked in previous studies by requiring children to overcome infelicitous conditions, conditions appropriate only to a conjoined-clause interpretation. In 4 year olds, one often finds the additional ability to conform to conceptual order—that is, to act out presupposed matter before the assertion. Four year olds are also usually able to deal with three animal types. On the production side, one can reliably elicit relative clauses from most children of this age. Many 5 year olds evince further mastery, or at least consolidation, of relative-clause interpretation by suppressing enactment of the presupposition. The children in this age group were essentially impervious to three-animal complexities, but from previous work it appears that infelicity can still, at age 5, disrupt the process of relative comprehension.

This sequence is tentative and methodology-dependent. The long delay between spontaneous and elicited production, for example, suggests a need for improved elicitation techniques. In comprehension, one must, in some cases, compromise among competing demands made by the conversational maxims. Still, there has been good progress in the last few years. It is to be hoped that new tasks will be found that will continue the process of disaggregating relative acquisition.

REFERENCES

Blank, M. Eliciting verbalization from young children in experimental tasks: A methodological note. *Child Development*, 1978, *46*, 254–257.

Brown, R. *A first language: The early stages*. Cambridge, Mass.: Harvard University Press, 1973.

Clark, E. V. How young children describe events in time. In G. B. Flores d'Arcais & W. J. M. Levelt (Eds.), *Advances in psycholinguistics*. Amsterdam: North-Holland, 1970.

Coker, P. L. Syntactic and semantic factors in the acquisition of *before* and *after*. *Journal of Child Language*, 1978, *5*, 261–277.

de Villiers, J. G., Tager-Flusberg, H. B. T., Hakuta, K., & Cohen, M. Children's comprehension of relative clauses. *Journal of Psycholinguistic Research*, 1979, *8*, 499–518.

Flynn, S., & Lust, B. Acquisition of relative clauses: A study of development changes in their heads. Presented at the Linguistic Society of American Annual Meeting, Los Angeles, California, 1979.

Frazier, L. *On comprehending sentences: Syntactic parsing strategies*. Bloomington, Indiana: Indiana University Linguistic Club, 1979.

Gelman, R. Cognitive development. *Annual Review of Psychology*, 1978, *29*, 297–332.

Goodluck, H. *Linguistic principles in children's grammar of complement subject interpretation*. Unpublished doctoral dissertation, University of Massachusetts, Amherst, 1978.

Goodluck, H., & Solan, L. (Eds.). *Papers in the structure and development of child language*. University of Massachusetts Occasional Papers, Vol. 4. Linguistics Department, University of Massachusetts, Amherst, 1978.

Goodluck, H., & Tavakolian, S. Parsing, recursion, and the LAD. Presented at the Linguistic Society of America Summer Meeting, Salzburg, Austria, 1979.

Grice, H. P. Logic and conversation. In P. Cole & J. L. Morgan (Eds.), *Syntax and semantics, Vol. 3: Speech acts*. New York: Seminar Press, 1975.

Hamburger, H. A deletion ahead of its time. *Cognition*, 1980, *8*, 389–416.

Legum, S. Strategies in the acquisition of relative clauses. *Southwest Regional Laboratory Technical Note*, No. TN 2-75-10, 1975.

Limber, J. The genesis of complex sentences. In T. E. Moore (Ed.), *Cognitive development and the acquisition of language*. New York: Academic Press, 1973.

MacKay, D. C. To end ambiguous sentences. *Perception and Psychophysics*, 1966, *1*, 426–436.

Maratsos, M. *The use of definite and indefinite reference in young children*. London: Cambridge University Press, 1976.

Matthei, E. M. *The acquisition of prenominal modifier sequences: Stalking the second green ball*. Unpublished doctoral dissertation, University of Massachusetts, Amherst, 1979.

Meissner, J. A., & Apthrop, H. Nonegocentrism and communication mode switching in black pre-school children. *Developmental Psychology*, 1976, *12*, 245–249.

Menyuk, P. *Sentences children use*. Cambridge, Mass.: MIT Press, 1969.

Miller, G. Some psychological studies of grammar. *American Psychologist*, 1962, *17*, 748–762.

Partee, B. Some transformational extensions of Montague grammar. *Journal of Philosophical Logic*, 1973, *2*, 509–534.

Potts, M., Carlson, P., Cocking, R., & Copple, C. *Structure and development in child language*. Ithaca, N.Y.: Cornell University Press, 1979.

Quine, W. V. O. *Word and object*. Cambridge, Mass.: MIT Press, 1960.

Ross, J. *Constraints on variables in syntax*. Unpublished doctoral dissertation, Massachusetts Institute of Technology, 1967.

Sheldon, A. The role of parallel function in the acquisition of relative clauses in English. *Journal of Verbal Learning and Verbal Behavior*, 1974, *13*, 272–281.

Sheldon, A. On strategies for processing relative clauses: A comparison of children and adults. *Journal of Psycholinguistic Research*, 1977, *6* (4), 305–318.

Slobin, D. I. Grammatical transformations and sentence comprehension in childhood and adulthood. *Journal of Verbal Learning and Verbal Behavior*, 1966, *5*, 219–227.

Slobin, D. I., & Welsh, C. A. Elicited imitation as a research tool in developmental psycholinguistics. In C. Ferguson & D. I. Slobin (Eds.), *Studies of child language development*. New York: Holt, Rinehart, & Winston, 1973.

Solan, L., & Roeper, T. Children's use of syntactic structure in interpreting relative clauses. In H. Goodluck & L. Solan (Eds.), 1978.

Tavakolian, S. The conjoined-clause analysis of relative clauses and other structures. In H. Goodluck & L. Solan (Eds.), 1978.

Thomason, R. *Formal philosophy: Selected papers of Richard Montague*. New Haven, Conn.: Yale University Press, 1974.

8 Towards a Theory of Substantive Word-Meaning Acquisition

Jeff Greenberg
University of Kansas

Stan A. Kuczaj II
Southern Methodist University

In the present chapter, we attempt to provide a theoretical framework for the acquisition of the meaning of words that refer to objects (hereafter referred to as substantive words). Restricting the scope of the present chapter to substantive word meaning limits its theoretical import to a general theory of lexical-meaning acquisition. However, contemporary theories of lexical-meaning acquisition have been concerned primarily or solely with substantive word-meaning acquisition, and much of the following discussion is based on these theories. The concern here is with substantive word-meaning acquisition, not word-meaning acquisition per se. However, any general theory of lexical-meaning acquisition must account for substantive word-meaning acquisition and so a theory of the acquisition of the substantive word meaning should be integrable with a general theory of lexical-meaning acquisition.

Because the primary concern of this chapter is with the developmental relations between object concepts and object words, we need to consider both the end results of this developmental process or set of processes and how the child attains these results. We attempt to achieve this goal by dividing the remainder of the chapter into four main sections. The first section examines the end products of development: objects and object concepts and the relations between them. It also briefly explores the relations between objects and concepts and reference to such objects and object concepts. The second section considers requisite processes involved in concept formation and thereby substantive word-meaning acquisition. The third section summarizes several recent theories that have been formulated to account for early substantive word meaning-acquisition and critiques each of these theories in light of the conclusions drawn in the first two sections, other theoretical considerations, and some data from empirical research with children. Based on these examinations, the last section offers a hybrid theoretical approach to substantive word-meaning acquisition and suggestions for future research in this area.

OBJECTS AND CONCEPTS

In a psychological sense, an object is what a person perceives as the result of the immediate sensations that originate from the object. When a perceived object is made unavailable to a person's sense receptors, what remains (given the occurrence of whatever processes transfer experiential phenomena to short-term and long-term memory) is a memory of the object, which, following Nelson (1974), may be referred to as a concept of that particular object. The justification for this assertion is that the exact sensations resulting in the perception of the object at a particular time are available only once. If, during subsequent interpretations of perceived information concerning the world, a person experiences a sense of recognition—that is, if a person feels he or she is experiencing the *same* object, he or she is evincing concept-like knowledge of the object. This knowledge, having been derived from the initial experience with the object (and possibly altered by subsequent experiences), allows one to interpret the second (and subsequent) experience(s) with the object as bearing some crucial similarity to the first (and subsequent) experience(s) with the object. For our purposes, this ability rests on a concept of the object in question, hereafter referred to as a single-object concept (because it is concerned with only one object). The possession of such concepts implies that the possessor is capable of perceiving, storing, and organizing real-world invariants, perhaps because of a genetic predisposition to attend to such invariant information (see Gibson, 1969). The notion of perceptual and conceptual invariants is important because one's senses rarely, if ever, record two temporally disparate experiences as identical. Nonetheless, we are able to judge different experiences with the same object as experiences involving the same object even if there is not a one-to-one correspondence between the sensations resulting from the different experiences. This is made possible by the ability to attend to and utilize the perceptual invariants that underlie these identity decisions.

Our brief explication of the nature of object concepts has thus far focused on the simplest type of object concept—the ability to perceive two disparate perceptions of the same object as manifestations of the same object. Inclusion of this type of object concept is certainly necessary for any theory of substantive word reference, because such concepts underlie the use of terms such as proper nouns, which refer to particular objects. Obviously, in order to refer to a present particular object as an instance of a previously experienced object, one must be able to recognize the object when it is in one's immediate perceptual field. Single-object concepts allow such recognition. Moreover, language users sometimes wish to refer to nonpresent objects, and single-object concepts allow such reference to proper nouns.

Reference involving proper nouns, though important for any theory of reference, is less interesting than reference involving common nouns, because common nouns involve meaning as well as reference (see Russell, 1919, for an explication of why proper nouns involve reference but not meaning). Not surprisingly then, the object concepts needed for reference with common nouns differ from those necessary for reference with proper nouns. Reference with proper nouns entails object concepts that permit one to recognize various instances of an object as instances of the same object, whereas reference with common nouns involves object concepts that provide the basis for the decision that a particular object is an instance of a particular class of objects. In reference involving proper nouns, the crucial relation is that of *identity*—that is, deciding whether an object *is* a particular object. In reference involving common nouns, the crucial relation is one of *extension* or *inclusion*—that is, deciding whether an object is a member of a particular class of objects. (Bloom & Lahey, 1978, following Brown, 1958a), contrast *identity* with *equivalence*; identity is involved in decisions whether an object is an instance of a particular object and equivalence is involved in decisions whether an object is a particular *type* of object. We have chosen to use *extension* and *inclusion* rather than *equivalence* because the former terms denote the type of concept with which we are concerned better than does *equivalence*.) Because intension (the informational basis for deciding if an object is a member of a given class) determines extension, and because the object concepts underlying reference with common nouns must provide the basis for extension (that is, the decision whether an object is or is not a member of a particular class), such object concepts must contain intensional information. The nature of the intensional information underlying extensional decisions is a crucial problem for theories of concept formation and theories of reference, particularly concerning the development of reference to objects as class members. The ontogenesis of object concepts underlying reference with common nouns (hereafter referred to as object-class concepts) involves the ability to extract and recognize some important similarity among relatively disparate objects that are sufficiently alike to be members of the same class. However, determining exactly what is meant by "sufficiently alike" is problematic, because the objects of concern could be very similar (e.g., baseballs and softballs are types of balls) or quite different (e.g., Newfoundlands and Pekingese are types of dogs). Thus, object-class concepts are conceptually more complex than single-object concepts in two ways: (1) single-object concepts provide the basis for decisions about identity whereas object-class concepts prescribe for extensional decisions; (2) single-object concepts may be included in object-class concepts because the ability to recognize an object as a particular object would facilitate the development and use of object-class concepts. Therefore, although object-class concepts and single-object concepts are related to experience with objects in similar ways, the development of object-class concepts involves cognitive processes that are not necessary for the development of single-object concepts. Thus, object-class concepts may be viewed as cognitively more complex than single-object concepts.

The preceding discussion is significant because, as has been assumed by many theorists in word-meaning acquisition, substantive words are symbols for—that is, can be defined by—object concepts regardless of whether the words are attached to previously developed concepts or whether they instigate and guide the development of new concepts. Thus, the problem of substantive word-meaning acquisition is determining the nature of the concept(s) to which the word refers, as well as determining whether such words are primarily attached to already existing concepts or lead to the formation of new concepts. (Words may be defined by their conditions of application as well as by the concepts to which they refer [Nelson, 1979], but the conditions of application of a substantive word reduce to those instances when the expression and communication of the concept symbolized by the word is appropriate, which is dependent on the purpose of the speaker.)

CONCEPT STRUCTURE, CONCEPT FORMATION, AND IMPLICATIONS FOR THEORIES OF THE ACQUISITION OF SUBSTANTIVE WORD MEANING

The following discussion focuses on object-class concepts rather than single-object concepts. However, single-object concepts are considered (albeit briefly) in the subsequent discussion of substantive word-meaning acquisition. We initially consider two theoretical approaches to concept structure and concept formation: (1) a criterial feature-list approach; and (2) a prototype approach.

The criterial feature-list approach to concept structure and concept formation assumes that concepts consist of a list of defining features that determine the extension of the class (Bierwisch, 1967, 1970; Clark, 1973). Thus, the intension of a class consists of the defining features. However, this approach encounters two related difficulties. First, it is difficult to determine how many features are necessary to adequately define a concept. Second, it is difficult to specify which features are essential (that is, defining) for a particular concept. As Miller (1978) notes: "Essentialism has come under severe attack from several quarters. A psychologist who accepts (essentialism) accepts a responsibility to explain how children are able to sort out the essential from the accidental properties [p. 1002]."

As an example, consider the object-class concept of *dog*. A feature-list approach might define *dog* as the following list of features: + animate, + furry, + quadruped, + barks, + tail (which wags). One might argue that this list is too brief in that it does not specify all of the features that distinguish dogs from nondogs. For example, one might want to list the negative features that denote those attributes dogs lack (e.g., − horns), and those behaviors in which dogs do not engage (e.g., − moo). However, if one adopted this strategy, it is not clear where one would stop. After all, there are an infinite number of attributes that dogs do not possess and an infinite number of behaviors in which dogs do not engage. However, there are also a large number of attributes dogs do possess and a large number of behaviors in which dogs do engage. It is not clear how many of these attributes and features need to be included in the list of features that specify the intension and thereby determine the extension of *dog*. Moreover, it is not clear what features are essential to determine the extension of *dog*. A dog obviously must be animate, but this attribute certainly does not distinguish dogs from nondogs. Moreover, a dog that possessed only three legs (either through genetic defect or accident) would still be a dog, as would a dog that lacked fur, a dog that could not bark, and a dog that lacked a tail (or had a tail that would not wag). There simply do not appear to be any features that are criterial for *dog* that would accurately distinguish dogs from nondogs without inaccurately classifying some dogs as nondogs. A horse is not a dog, even though it is animate and a quadruped. A dog without fur is nonetheless a dog, albeit an atypical one. A dog that cannot bark is nonetheless a dog, albeit an atypical one. A dog that could moo like a cow would be classified as a dog that could moo like a cow. Newfoundlands and Pekingese are both types of dogs, though they bear less perceptual (and perhaps functional) similarity to one another than a Newfoundland does to a brown bear and a Pekingese does to a longhaired cat. The fact that there can be typical and atypical members of a class both in the sense of the atypical class members lacking one or more "criterial features" (a three-legged dog that cannot bark) and in the sense of the atypical class members bearing little resemblance to more prototypic class members (e.g., a Newfoundland and a Pekingese compared to a Collie or an Irish Setter) bring us to the other theoretical stance with which we are concerned, the prototype approach to object-class concept structure and concept formation.

Basically, the prototype view of object-class concepts supposes that exemplars of a concept differ in their status as exemplars. That is, simply being a member of a class does not entail equal status with other members of the class. There are "good" or "central" exemplars (prototypes); the status of other exemplars depends on their relation (i.e., similarity) to the prototypic exemplar(s). This notion of concept structure and concept formation is supported by various investigations of concept formation in experimental settings.

A number of studies using visual patterns (Franks & Bransford, 1972; Posner, 1969; Posner & Keele, 1968, 1970; Reed, 1972) have found that adult subjects exhibit a strong tendency to "recognize" the prototype (i.e., best exemplar) of a set of patterns presented as instances of a concept, even when they were not shown the prototype during testing but instead were shown only distortions of the prototypic exemplar of the concept. In fact, if the interval between pattern presentation and the recognition test was sufficiently long, the prototype appeared to be the best remembered instance of the concept even though it had not been previously presented as an instance of the concept. Although these studies were conducted in experimental settings and involved simple, two-dimensional representations, the results suggest that adults have a strong tendency to form some sort of prototypic representation for concepts (Posner, 1973). However, adults do not *equate* the prototype with the concept, because they often more readily recognize patterns they had actually seen as instances of a concept than they do novel instances, even though the novel instances may bear a closer resemblance to the prototype than do the experienced exemplers (Posner & Keele, 1968, 1970).

Thus, it appears that there exists a tendency on the part of adults to formulate an abstract prototype of a concept but also to retain information about experienced individual exemplars of the concept. The importance of the retained information about individual exemplars has been investigated by manipulating the variety of individual exemplars of a concept given to subjects. Appropriate classification of novel exemplars was better when instances of a concept varied insignificantly than when instances of a concept varied greatly, if only a meager amount of training was allowed. However, if a large number of instances was provided, the subjects who were shown the more varied instances applied the concept name more appropriately (Dukes & Bevan, 1967; Posner & Keele, 1968). Based on these findings, Posner (1973) posits that two processes may be involved:

> One involves learning the central tendency or prototype, and would be expected to occur more rapidly with small distortions . . . (the other) involves representing the boundaries of instances to which the concept might apply. Highly variable instances probably increase the difficulty of extracting a prototype, but if learning is sufficient to allow such extraction, the variability eases recognition of distorted patterns [p. 53.]

This view offers the complementary predictions that (1) when the exemplars of a concept are very similar, underextensions of the concept are more likely than overextensions; but (2) when the exemplars are very different, overextensions are more likely than are underextensions. These predictions have been confirmed experimentally with adults and the developmental implications could be examined by studying children's experiences with a word and its referents and the children's appropriate and inappropriate applications of the word (this is currently being examined in the laboratories of the second author).

The concept-formation research reviewed thus far indicates that knowledge of a central tendency and certain boundaries is the best description of what knowing a concept entails. Though the previously described research has typically involved abstract two-dimensional concepts, studies by Rosch (1973), Rosch and Mervis (1975), Anglin (1977), Mulford (1977), and McCloskey and Glucksberg (1979) have suggested that for many ''natural'' concepts—that is, concepts referred to by common nouns—certain instances are more central, ''good,'' or prototypic than others. This claim is based on data obtained from subjects' judgments of prototypicality or goodness of instances, and the easier recognition and more appropriate classification of some instances of a concept than others. This latter evidence might appear to be merely a function of the familiarity of a particular instance, but the judged ''goodness'' of an instance has been found to be a more important factor affecting differential recognition and classification of instances of a concept than mere familiarity of the instances (Anglin, 1977). Note that the basic structure of concepts considered here is holistic. The rationale for this assumption is well stated by Posner (1973):

> Taking the perceived object as the starting place, a person's analysis of it into attributes is a cognitive achievement of considerable complexity. Indeed the ability to describe the difference between objects by reference to a set of attributes is more difficult to acquire than the ability to discriminate the objects. It is easier to distinguish between dogs and cats than to say why they are different [p. 55].

An experiment by Hyman and Frost (1974) supported the predictions implicit in the preceding quotation, because their subjects exhibited knowledge of prototypes but very little knowledge of the attributes that they used to correctly classify instances as one or another concept. Undoubtedly, knowledge of criterial attributes would constitute a more complete understanding and analysis of a concept than the intuitive holistic (prototypic) type of concept adults seem predisposed to employ (at least concerning object concepts). However, the basic problem of attempting to adequately and accurately define a concept via a finite list of features has so far remained insoluble, and this failure must be taken into account when theories positing concept-formation processes for adults and/or children are formulated.

This does not mean that a prototype approach to concept structure and formation is necessarily incompatible with the notion of feature-list concept structure. As Rosch (1978) notes, the notion of prototypes per se does not entail any particular model of processes, structure, or learning. There are at least two types of prototype approaches to concept structure: one that utilizes the notion of features and one that emphasizes the holistic nature of prototypes. The former approach supposes an abstraction process that is utilized in concept formation and extension whereas the latter approach implies a process that is able to make holistic comparisons. Examples of the feature-list approach to prototype concept structure, formation, and process come from Rips, Shoben, and Smith (1973) and Clark and Clark (1977). Rips et al. suggest that there are two lists of features for each word—one list specifying the defining features and another specifying the features that determine whether a particular exemplar is prototypic or non-prototypic, and if non prototypic, exactly how nonprototypic the exemplar is (i.e., the conceptual distance between the nonprototypic exemplar and the concept's prototypic exemplars is specified by this second list of features). Clark and Clark argue that if a class has defining features, these features must be present in all exemplars of the class. But if a category lacks defining features, some sufficient number of shared features must be present in order to decide if an object is a member of a particular class. Following Rosch and Mervis (1975), Clark and Clark also suggest that the more features an object shares with the class prototype(s), the more central the object is to that class (i.e., the conceptual distance between an instance of a concept and that concept's prototype(s) is a function of the number of features the instance and the prototype(s) share). Because both Rip et al. and Clark and Clark utilize the notion of defining features, the problems associated with essentialism (particularly that of specifying what is meant by the notion of defining feature) become problems for these theories and so need to be resolved in order for these feature-list approaches to prototype concepts to be viewed as valid.

Brooks (1978) suggests a learning principle that implies the use of unanalyzed holistic memory representations of particular instances such that the formation of concepts occurs via the storage of particular experienced exemplars and the later comparison of novel instances to the stored holistic exemplars. This approach, though minimizing the abstraction of attributes, cannot rest solely on the storage of unanalyzed holistic representations because, as Rosch and Lloyd (1978) point out, each experience of an object involves some analysis and transformation if information about the object is to be stored in memory at all. The critical question then becomes determining the nature of the analyses and transformations of the information obtained and stored concerning the experienced object. As Rosch and Lloyd (1978) note: "What is required is a model of representation that allows for differing levels of analysis; at the minimum, we must allow for a type of representation that is sufficiently analyzed to be stored but not coded into criterial features [p. 76]."

So in spite of the supposed independence of a holistic-prototype approach from analyses of attributes (features) of a concept's exemplars, even a holistic approach to concept structure and formation involves at least the partial analysis of objects as attributes. This is necessitated because we do not compare objects to one another holistically but instead on the basis of shared attributes. However, this does not mean that we compare objects attribute by attribute. Instead, comparison can take place at a holistic level yet involve the comparison of attributes or sets of attributes. Such a holistic-comparison process may be facilitated by the highly correlational structure of attributes—some features frequently occur together (e.g., feathers and wings) whereas others do not (Rosch, Mervis, Gray, Johnson, & Boyes-Braem, 1976).

Attribute analyses of experienced objects is necessary for the structure of stored representations (concepts) as well as for the comparison of novel objects with stored representations. Rosch (1978) has suggested that the prototypic instances of concepts are those that contain the attributes most representative of exemplars of the concept and least representative of nonexemplars. Thus, even holistic prototypic accounts of concept structure, formation, and extension necessitate some analysis of concept iinstances into attributes. However, this does not in turn entail that these attributes are stored as defining features.

We have explored the nature of concepts as implied by concept-formation research using adult subjects. Before proceeding, guided by these findings, to examine the major theoretical constructs that have been developed concerning the acquisition of object word meaning in young children, a brief discussion of the relationship between the child's word-meaning acquisition and concept formation is in order. To recapitulate, there seems to be a consensus (to which we also ascribe) that common noun words are symbols for object-class concepts (e.g., the meaning of the word *chair* is the concept "chair"). From a developmental perspective, then, one issue that must be dealt with is whether the young child comes to view two disparate instances of the same concept as similar because the language the child is learning treats them as equivalent or if the young child maps prelinguistic concepts onto words that he or she hears used in the presence of instances of such concepts. The views of Bowerman (1975), Clark (1977), and Nelson (1978) seem to have converged on this issue, despite initial disagreements. Nelson (1973) at first took the strong stand that object words were attached only to already well-formed prelinguistic concepts, a position since modified to allow for the influence of object words on the development of at least some object concepts (Nelson, Rescorla, Gruendel, & Benedict, 1977). Clark (1973) originally emphasized the importance of object words in the formation of object concepts, but has since elaborated mechanisms for the mapping of words onto preexisting concepts (Clark, 1977). Essentially, Clark and Nelson have arrived at a position on the relationship between concept formation and word-meaning acquisition that Bowerman (1976) terms "interactionist," a theoretical stance that allows for numerous possible relationships between language and concept formation depending on the kinds of concepts involved and on the type of language input provided (see also Kuczaj & Lederberg, 1977). In this view, language input may influence the child's cognitive structuring from the beginning of his or her attempts to interpret language. Some concepts, though requiring of the child a nonlinguistic capacity for recognizing various similarities across experiences, start to develop primarily because others in the child's environment call attention to the possibility of grouping along certain lines by using the same word in different situations, thereby indicating some equivalence across these situations. (Of course, how the child establishes the appropriate equivalence relations is not well understood.) The interactionist position also recognizes that many concepts are partially or fully formed by the child before he or she attaches words to these concepts. In such cases, the problem is not how the child formulates concepts and thereby creates meaning for newly acquired words, but instead how the child decides that a particular word may be used to express a previously acquired meaning (concept). Thus, the two central problems concerning the developmental implications of the relations between object words and concepts are (1) how the child creates meaning for newly acquired substantive words for which he or she has not yet developed an object-class concept; and (2) how the child decides to use a particular newly acquired word to refer to a previously developed concept. This latter problem is compounded if the child has been using a previously acquired word to erroneously refer (or correctly refer, in the case of synonyms) to the concept. The problem then becomes one of determining how the child comes to replace old forms with new forms, a recurrent problem in the study of language acquisition (Kuczaj, 1977; Slobin, 1973; Werner & Kaplan, 1963).

THEORIES OF EARLY SUBSTANTIVE WORD-MEANING ACQUISITION

Theories of Analytic Concept-Formation Processes and Feature-List Concept Structures

Clark (1973) proposed a semantic-feature theory of object-class (common noun) word-meaning acquisition in young children. She theorized that the child initially associates an object word with the first object to which it is applied (thus, the child's initial attachment of meaning to a word might be viewed as based on a template of the object referred to by the word). Subsequently, upon experiencing differing instances to which the word is applied, the child abstracts one feature that each of the instances share, and the abstracted feature becomes the meaning (concept) expressed by the word. Then, gradually, with the experience of more and more varying instances and noninstances of the concept, the child adds more features until a set of features in a particular combination forms the "adult" concept that is expressed by the word. (The features abstracted earliest in the child's acquisition of object word meaning are thought to be derived from semantic primitives—that is, primitive perceptual categories—which reflect abstract properties such as shape, size, and movement to which the child is innately predisposed to attend; cf. Miller & Johnson-Laird, 1976.)

Clark's (1973) semantic-feature theory of lexical-meaning acquisition accords well with the data on early substantive word-meaning acquisition in the sense that children appear to gradually build the meaning of a word rather than acquiring it in toto (Clark, 1973; Kuczaj, 1975). This process might be accounted for in terms of the addition of semantic features in the course of the acquisition of the meaning of an object word. However, the theory is problematic in several respects. First, this analytic feature-list learning approach encounters a problem common to all feature (component) theories—namely, that most concepts (meanings) cannot be adequately (accurately) defined by a list of features, no matter how exhaustive the list. As noted earlier, the problem centers on false inclusion and/or exclusion of instances as members of the concept; for most concepts, it is difficult (impossible) to provide a list of features that would permit one to include only appropriate instances as members of the class but at the same time exclude all inappropriate instances as nonmembers of the class. Thus, the feature-list approach per se has yet to be demonstrated as a viable theory of meaning, certainly presenting a problem for a theory that incorporates this approach as a central part of the child's acquisition of word meaning (cf. Richards, 1979).

Another problem concerns the assumption that object concepts follow a general-to-specific developmental path, with general referring to an overly broad concept and specific referring to the "adult" concept. If this is true for single-object concepts, then a child who saw a beagle on two different occasions and in each instance heard it called *Rover* might be expected to initially conclude that *Rover* refers to "quadrupeds" or "furry creatures." In regards to object-class concepts, a child who saw a Newfoundland on one occasion, a terrier on another, and a Great Dane on another, and in each case heard the animal referred to as a *dog* might be expected to initially conclude that *dog* refers to "quadrupeds" or "furry creatures." Clark's assertion for this general-to-specific developmental pattern rests on the assumption that children initially choose one or perhaps two features as criterial and subsequently add more features as their experiences warrant. For any pair of disparate experiences concerning a given object or two objects from a given class, there are numerous relevant features (attributes) for the child to notice and remember, and there is no a priori reason why a child should initially extract only one (or two) features from the larger array, rather than some larger set of information, as intensional for the concept. Moreover, it is not clear what would determine which features the child comes to view as *criterial* or how the child could correct earlier inappropriate selections of features as criterial because the hypothesized process is restricted to the addition of new features (see Barrett, 1978, for further discussion of these problems with criterial feature-list approaches to substantive word meaning). More problems for the notion of immediate criterial feature abstraction come from the concept-formation research with adults, which demonstrated that the analysis of criterial features for concepts is an extremely complex ability that follows rather than precedes holistic (prototypic) knowledge of the concept (Hyman & Frost, 1974). Thus, Clark's (1973) model posits a pattern counter to that exhibited by adults.

Moreover, the initial stages of formation of single-object concepts and object-class concepts need not always be characterized by an overly broad concept that subsequently must be narrowed in order to accord with the "adult" concept. If the acquisition of at least some concepts is characterized by the initial formation of an overly narrow concept that would then need to be broadened with development, one would expect to observe underextensions (e.g., a child using the term *dog* to refer to only a particular dog) as well as overextensions (e.g., a child using the term *dog* to refer to dogs, sheep, cows, etc.) of early substantive word meaning; such has proven to be the case (Anglin, 1977; Reich, 1976).

One other aspect of Clark's theory is worth restating at this point because of the contrast it provides for Nelson's (1974) theory (discussed next). Clark suggests that although semantic features probably include information concerning dynamic and functional attributes of objects, static perceptual information is of central importance for the development of early object concepts, to the extent that children usually acquire such information first and thus use such information as criterial in regards to object concepts. This assertion follows from Clark's belief in the importance of primitive (universal) perceptual categories and contrasts with Nelson's functional-core hypothesis.

Nelson (1974, 1977) has asserted that the core of the child's concept of an object contains the child's comprehension of the object's "function"—that is, what the child can do with or to the object or what the object itself does. The process involved is one of whole elements being defined as holistic concepts in terms of the synthesis of their functional relationships (e.g., a "ball" is something that rolls, bounces, and that can be thrown). Following the formation of this functional core, the child expands the concept by attaching to it and organizing a set of identifying features (i.e., static perceptual attributes) that make possible recognition of novel instances of the concept without necessitating experience evincing the function of such instances. For the most part, Nelson's model holds that concepts are generalized (extended) on the basis of form, even though the concepts are initially formed on the basis of function. However, function is thought to be more important than form, in spite of form's influence on class extension, in that function is criterial. For instance, a round object that did not bounce might initially be classified as a ball by the child but after exploring the functional attributes of the object, the child would no longer classify it as a ball because of its inability to bounce. According to Nelson, then, the essential meaning of an object-class concept is derived from appropriate objects' functional relationships with the environment and the child.

Nelson's functional-core theory of early object word-meaning acquisition is problematic in several respects. Although she asserts that object concepts are first learned as unanalyzable wholes, she also maintains that only part of the information available to the child about an object is used to form this "holistic" concept. This unsatisfactorily results in the claim that the child formulates a "holistic" concept initially based solely on the function of objects and thereby independent of the perceptual attributes of the object. It is not clear in what sense a concept is holistic if perceptual attributes have been abstracted out of it. Thus, although Nelson has suggested a theory that appears to fit well with the previously discussed research on concept formation in adults, which indicated that the abstraction of particular criterial features of a concept follows rather than precedes the formation of a holistic concept, her supposition that the child uses only certain aspects of the available information to first form the holistic concept implies an initial concept-formation process dependent on differential attribute analyses, a notion that does not coincide well with the results of the investigations on adult concept-formation processes.

Interestingly, Nelson criticizes Clark's theory because of the latter's assumption of some abstract feature analysis and comparison process. However, Nelson's theory rests on the assumption that the child is capable of establishing functional equivalence across visual experiences, which presupposes some abstract functional analysis and comparison process (cf. Anglin, 1977), As Bowerman (1976) points out, kinds of shared functions are themselves categories, and Nelson ignores the need to account for the acquisition of such categories. Every roll and bounce is experienced uniquely, and thus a theory of abstraction or concept formation of "roll," "bounce," and so on, is necessary to make Nelson's account complete. Nelson's (1974) criticism of abstraction theory, that it presupposes what it is meant to explain (i.e., the principle by which common elements [in Nelson's theory, functions] are abstracted as common), also holds for her functional-core hypothesis. Even if one makes the questionable assumption that the functional qualities of an object can be separated from its general perceptual attributes, Nelson's theory is inconsistent in that it supposes that "holistic" concepts are acquired via the *synthesis* of abstract functional attributes, and so an analytical process is still prerequisite to the acquisition of the concepts. To compound matters, the analytic process is restricted to functional qualities, at least in the early part of the concept-formation process; it is not evident how or why an analytic process would preclude perceptual attributes, given the intimate relation between form and function (see the following discussion).

The original basis for Nelson's theory came from observations of children's early use of object words, which usually refer to objects that perform interesting actions or that the child can act upon (Nelson, 1973). Bowerman (1976) and Nelson (1973) found that concepts for objects with certain functions are more familiar to young children than concepts for immobile objects with less interesting functions (e.g., walls, sofas). Also, words having to do with changes of state (e.g., *dry, empty, dirty*) are better comprehended and produced by young children than words that refer to static attributes such as *rough, square,* and *black.* Thus, one could argue that functional relevance determines *which* word meanings children learn first, but the salience of objects that move or change state does not necessarily imply that the acquisition of the object concepts that underlie the use of the corresponding object words is based primarily on the functional attributes of the objects. Whether the functions of such objects as "Daddy," "dog," "ball," and "door" are viewed specifically enough by young children to allow conceptual discrimination among these mobile objects independent of static perceptual differences is unlikely, though undetermined, given what we view to be necessarily complementary relationships between functions and forms (e.g., a square ball would not roll). Rosch et al. (1976) have previously posited that form and function are inseparable (a conclusion supported by Bloom & Lahey, 1978). The research of Rosch et al. led them to assert that functional and perceptual attributes of objects are not unrelated factors but rather are different aspects of the same correlational structures of an object concept. In the view of Rosch et al., a concept of an object consists of the properties of the object that have been found to cooccur over a large number of instances; a variety of instances that do not share cooccurring properties will not be considered instances of the same concept. For most object concepts, function and form are both essential. If one were altered, so would be the other (as previously noted, a nonround ball would neither bounce nor roll). To us, this view seems intuitively more plausible than Nelson's hypothesis that function comprises the core aspect of object concepts, with perceptual attributes only being added secondarily in order to allow the identification of new instances that are removed from a functional context (see Bowerman, 1975, for a discussion of some data that fail to support Nelson's predictions).

Comparison of Clark's and Nelson's Theories.   Clark's notion of a concept is based on a list of semantic features and her hypothesized concept-formation process is analytic, based on the ability of the child to abstract and categorize certain perceptual attributes across a variety of experiences. The structure of concepts posited by Nelson also involves the initial synthesis of abstracted attributes (functional rather than perceptual, however) and the later abstraction of perceptual attributes. Although the approaches of Clark and Nelson have often been pitted against one another because of the differing influences of form (Clark) or function (Nelson) (e.g., Bowerman, 1975; Gentner, 1977; Gruendel, 1977; Nelson, 1974), the two theories share a feature-list vision of concept structure and both entail some type of analytic concept-formation process in young children. Thus, Nelson's theory, like Clark's, encounters difficulty in that most natural concepts cannot be adequately defined by feature lists. Also, because both theories involve criterial functional or perceptual features, each seems to predict strict, definite concept boundaries, whereas many natural concepts appear to have vague, fuzzy boundaries (Anderson, 1975; McCloskey & Glucksberg, 1979; Oden, 1975).

Prototype Approaches to Substantive Word-Meaning Acquisition

Anglin (1977) has formulated a theory of early object word-concept formation that consciously evinces an analogue of the prototype approach implied from the adult concept-formation research and that was inspired at least in part by Rosch (1973). Anglin hypothesized that children might initially define a category (i.e., a word) in terms of its central instances rather than in terms of abstract criterial attributes. In Anglin's view, object concepts are composed of intensional knowledge and extensional knowledge. In partial agreement with Nelson (1974), he asserts that the functional aspects of an object (for Anglin, particularly its use) comprise an important part of the child's intensional knowledge of an object concept. However, Anglin also recognizes that static perceptual properties are important components of a child's knowledge of an object concept, and are not necessarily secondary to functional properties. A basic difference between Anglin's view and those of Clark and Nelson is that, according to Anglin, although the young child possesses some knowledge of abstracted properties of objects, these properties are not necessarily used as criterial when the child classifies instances as members or nonmembers of a particular concept. Thus, Anglin is hypothesizing a lack of coordination between the intension of a concept and its extension (i.e., application) in the young child. In essence, this view holds that although upon reflection a child may be able to think of certain functional and/or perceptual attributes of a particular object concept, this ability may reflect knowledge of the attributes of a prototype or particular instances of a concept rather than a set of common features abstracted across all instances of the concept. Thus, even though the child can name attributes, he or she may not apply abstract attributes as criteria for concept membership. Anglin instead suggests that children's extensions often involve associative complexes whereby the child classifies objects in accordance with a nuclear object (prototype), and that such grouping is based not on any one criterion but rather on a number of different relevant links between the nuclear object and other objects. In this view, children, possibly due to cognitive constraints, do not formulate abstract criterial attributes that allow them to identify instances of concepts, but instead rely on a more primitive process, namely matching the novel instances to a prototype (note the influence of Posner, 1973). Anglin envisions the child's having a multimodal prototype that reflects properties such as movement, sound, texture, and shape, supplemented by information concerning specific instances of the concept (the amount of this type of information is limited by memory capacity), which assists the child in establishing at least fuzzy boundaries in regard to the concept's field of application.

According to Anglin, prototypes arise initially from whatever perceptual information the child retains from his or her first experience with an object named in his or her presence; however, the prototype may also incorporate previously gained knowledge the child possesses about such objects (thereby allowing for the influence of prelinguistic concept formation). As the child is exposed to more instances, the prototype becomes a more generalized conception—that is, a central tendency. The child at this point, based on an hypothesized innate tendency to generalize to objects that he or she perceives as similar to the stored prototype, may begin to spontaneously classify objects he or she encounters as instances or noninstances of the object concept. In addition to such classification, the child retains some information about specific instances of the concept, resulting in the fuzzy boundaries that limit concept extension.

Bowerman (1975) has criticized prototype theories of classification (i.e., extension of a concept) on two counts. At one level, Bowerman suggested that unanalyzable wholes cannot be used to compare with new instances in order to judge concept membership, a process that seems to necessitate comparison of "prototypic attributes" and the attributes of the novel objects. However, the adult concept-formation research demonstrates that a "matching to prototype" mechanism can be used to correctly classify new instances without conscious knowledge of the specific attributes incorporated in the prototype; such knowledge occurs subsequent to that concerning the prototypic whole. Admittedly, it is not clear how holistic comparison of a prototype with a novel object occurs. Nor is it clear how such comparison results in decisions that the novel object is or is not significantly similar to the prototype and thus is or is not a member of the class exemplified by the prototype. Although the comparison process most likely does not entail an attribute by attribute comparison, consideration of "attribute complexes" (cooccurring attributes) may be quite important for the extension of concepts that possess such associated attributes (see later discussion).

Bowerman's second criticism of prototype theories is the more serious of the two, and points to a flaw in Anglin's prototype theory in particular. Bowerman points out that some features may be more central, concept defining, or criterially used for concept classification than others. Matching potential instances to a single abstract prototype, as Anglin posits, cannot account for the greater centrality of particular features than others, because Anglin's theory predicts that the better the match between a novel instance and a prototype in terms of number of common features, the more likely the novel instance will be considered a member of the concept represented by the prototype. In other words, Anglin's theory emphasizes the number of features in common between a novel instance and a prototype, ignoring the problem of greater centrality of certain of the prototype's features.

Mulford (1977) has offered a prototype approach to early substantive word-meaning acquisition that differs from that offered by Anglin. Mulford hypothesizes that when a young child learns the meaning of a word, he or she first learns the characteristics of its prototypes (i.e., those referents that are prototypical) and then organizes his or her knowledge of instances of the concept expressed by the word based on the instances' prototypicality. Mulford proposes that the child must "recreate" the prototype by abstracting the characteristic attributes from the different referents of a term; she views this process as somewhat simplified because many object concepts are structured around significantly correlated *sets* of attributes (e.g., feathers and wings for the concept "bird"), a notion derived from Rosch et al. (1976). Because these sets of attributes are significantly correlated, Mulford suggests that they should be particularly salient to the child, and so should be associated with the concept (and the corresponding word's meaning) first and most reliably. Furthermore, instances of the concept that exhibit the greatest number of such features in common are the most prototypic and should be among the earliest learned instances of the concept. Presumably, from this beginning, the child further develops the concept structure based on the prototypicality of the experienced instances of the concept. Thus, an object-class concept is comprised of a hierarchy of iconic representations of experienced instances of the concept, based on their prototypicality, which is determined for each iconic representation by its degree of similarity to other instances that are included within the concept. This view of concepts leads to the interesting notion that the concept of a word never really becomes a rigid definition. To the contrary, even throughout adulthood, any given object-class concept may be modified by experiences with new instances that are judged to be exemplars of the concept. New instances that are assimilated within a concept may have an effect on the hierarchies of prototypicality, which is essential to the concept.

Mulford's concept-formation process is in opposition to that postulated by Anglin and suggested by the adult concept-formation research, in that Mulford's theory entails an initial analytic process and thus an initial common feature-based concept, only later replaced by a more holistic concept structure based on prototypes. However, Mulford's approach avoids the pitfalls of a simple feature-list concept structure by positing an initial set of correlated features (established after the first experience with an instance of an object class) that may be used to establish which instances are the best exemplars (most prototypic). Following this, the child's concept develops as a result of experience with various instances such that he or she now becomes capable of matching novel instances to prototypes, a process that Rosch has asserted is an efficient processing mechanism for concept classification (Rosch et al., 1976). Rosch states that prototypes (holistic representations of objects) enable one to use one's knowledge of the contingency structure of the environment without engaging in the laborious cognitive processes of continually computing and summing the validities of individual cues, because one decides on a probabilistic basis (derived from how well the new instance matches the prototypical class members) whether a new instance is a member of a particular class.

Mulford's theoretical stance also differs from Anglin's in that she posits internal representations of specific instances of a concept, particularly if these instances are prototypical, whereas Anglin postulates a single, more general abstract prototype for each concept. This prototype is not necessarily an internal representation of any single instance but instead is a composite consisting of the most common attributes found among all the instances of the concept (note that this notion of a prototype entails some sort of attribute abstraction process in order to produce the composite prototype). Anglin's view gains some support from the work of Posner and Keele (1968), who were able to demonstrate the development of an internal prototype that the adult subjects had never seen and that appeared to be a composite average of the instances the subjects had seen (though, of course, the two-dimensional prototype formation exhibited by Posner and Keele's subjects is a much simpler task than the multidimensional prototype-formation process posited by Anglin). Nonetheless, the prototype-formation process Mulford adopted from Rosch is superior to Anglin's in that the prototypes hypothesized by Rosch, which are the most representative real instance(s), contain information about the most common aspects (including functional information) of instances of the concept, whereas Anglin believes that functional information is not contained in a concept's prototype. (Anglin argued for this exclusion of functional information from prototypes because he assumed that functional information is not important for extension even though it may play a role in intension). Thus, Mulford, following Rosch, can explain the intension of a concept in terms of its prototype(s) function and form whereas Anglin cannot. Anglin's view necessitates separate (though probably not completely independent) information-accumulation and abstraction processes for extensional and intensional knowledge of a concept, an uncomfortable state of affairs for Anglin's theory because intension and extension are intimately related in that, certainly for the adult, the former would appear to prescribe the latter (see Miller, 1978, for a critical discussion of this assumption).

Another advantage of Mulford's approach over that of Anglin is that Rosch's idea of concept structure (which Mulford has adopted) is less vulnerable to Bowerman's (1976) argument that some attributes of objects will be more central (and thus more concept defining) than others for a particular concept. Rosch's probabilistic view allows that the importance of an attribute depends not only on whether it is exhibited by the internal holistic prototypic representations, but also on the frequency with which it cooccurs with other common attributes of the concept prototypes in all internally represented instances of the concept. The consistency with which it appears across all prototypic representations and the degree to which an attribute distinguishes instances from noninstances of a concept determine how central the attribute is. Thus, differential centrality of attributes common to prototypes of a concept is inherent in Rosch's model. For Anglin, an attribute either is or is not part of the single abstract prototype of a concept and so either is or is not central to the concept; there is no allowance for degrees of centrality.

Empirical Investigations: The Findings in Relation to the Theories

Much of the experimental research concerned with early object word-meaning acquisition in children has attempted to establish the primacy of either form or function as criterial for the application of newly acquired words to novel instances (Anderson, 1975; Gentner, 1977; Nelson, 1973, 1974, 1978; Prawat & Cancell, 1977). The results of such investigations do not unequivocally favor the primacy of form or the primacy of function, because children who are taught a new word to express a particular object concept either tend to generalize the use of the word to novel objects with a form similar to that of the training objects but with a novel function, or in other cases, to novel objects with a function similar to that of the training objects but with a different form. In addition to the equivocal nature of the results across investigations, the lack of a metric to equate the distance between forms and the distance between functions and the saliences of particular forms and functions entails that investigations pitting form against function will yield only singular findings and thereby fail to resolve the form–function controversy (Nelson, 1977).

The primary theoretical concern of the previously described research has been with contrasting Clark's semantic-feature theory and Nelson's functional-core theory. However, despite Clark's emphasis on form and Nelson's emphasis on function, the two theories share many commonalities, as noted earlier (cf. Mac-Namara, 1977 and Miller, 1978, for other discussions of the common aspects of both theories). The theories posited by Clark and Nelson both entail analytic concept-formation processes that are greatly dependent on the abstraction and organization of common elements across varying experiences. Moreover, both theories envision concept structure as sets or aggregates of these abstracted features. With respect to the processes and nature of children's early substantive word-meaning acquisition, the important contrast is between the feature-list ap-proach (shared by Clark and Nelson) and the prototype approach, which posits a holistic concept structure consisting of representations of particular instances (the prototype approach may or may not involve holistic concept structure; e.g., for Anglin, the prototype is an abstract image; for Rosch, a prototype is a representa-tion of a real instance). Thus the research pitting form versus function focuses on a relatively minor and, given the lack of success in establishing form or function as primary, in our opinion, unresolvable issue (i.e., the salience of particular object attributes), rather than discriminating between the two major types of concept structures (feature list versus prototype) and between the two major types of concept-formation processes (analytic versus holistic). For this reason, we do not attempt a study-by-study review of the literature on early object word-meaning acquisition in an attempt to resolve the form–function dispute (for specific treatments, see Anglin, 1977; Bowerman, 1975; Bowerman, 1976; Clark, 1977; Nelson, 1977), but we instead review more pertinent literature to determine whether the available data support the notion of an abstract feature-list concept structure or the notion of a prototypic concept structure.

Bowerman (1975) analyzed the nature of her children's word extensions. She found that some word extensions were apparently based on a particular percep-tual feature, which may be accounted for by any of the theoretical formulations of concern, although it appears to fit best with Clark's theoretical stance (Nelson would need to assume that such extensions resulted because the child used form to extend a concept based on a functional core). Bowerman also found that some words were used in a complexive fashion, wherein successive instances of a word (i.e., concept) do not necessarily share common features but do share at least one feature with a central or nuclear instance (i.e., a prototype). This finding is not unique among investigations of children's categorization/word extension (cf. Anglin, 1977; Bloom, 1973; Gruendel, 1977; Labov & Labov, 1974; Rescorla, 1976; Vygotsky, 1962). Such a finding, although consistent with a prototype view of concept structure, is clearly inconsistent with feature-list theories, which hold that acquired features are criterial in all decisions of concept membership. In associative complex categorizations (such as those posited by Rosch and her colleagues), no single feature is viewed as criterial; rather, sharing some similarity with a prototype of a concept determines whether an object will be considered an instance of the concept (of course, specifying what is meant by "some similarity" is a problem). Bowerman (1975) and many others (Anglin, 1977; Bloom, 1973; Clark, 1973, 1974; Gruendel, 1977; Nelson, 1974; Rescorla, 1976) have also looked at the overextensions of words by young children, and have exhibited a special concern with nature of the child's overly broad word meaning. A finding that appears again and again is that even though overextensions may be based on numerous types of similarities among instances, the vast majority of overextensions are based on perceptual similarity, particularly form. Both Clark and Nelson have attempted to account for this body of evidence in formulating their theories. The evidence provides no problem for Clark's theory, because overextensions in general, including those involving perceptual similarities, may be accounted for by assuming that the child has attached too few criterial features to the concepts underlying the use of the overextended words and thus is erroneously classifying too many objects as members of the concepts of concern. Such mistakes are gradually eliminated via the acquisition of new criterial features, which further restrict the classification of objects as members of particular object-class concepts.

Nelson (1974) has specifically relegated to perceptual attributes the role of identifiers of potential new instances of a concept. The final decision rests on the functional isomorphism between the new instance and the concept, so that although function is central for concept formation in Nelson's view, form provides the basis for extension of the concept. However, many of the perceptual overextensions cut across functional differences among the objects of concern (e.g., Eva, one of Bowerman's children, used *moon* to refer to both the moon and a grapefruit half), a phenomenon in apparent contradiction to Nelson's notion that functions comprise the essential core meaning of early concepts (cf. Bowerman, 1976).

However, there is some question concerning the interpretation of apparent overextensions. Nelson et al. (1977) have proposed that what have been termed overextensions may in fact be merely assertions of similarity between two objects, judgments of analogy rather than equivalence. Based on evidence that words that are overextended in production may not be overextended in comprehension (Gruendel, 1977; Huttenlocher, 1974; Thomson & Chapman, 1977),

Clark (1977) has made a similar argument, suggesting that children in the one-word stage (overextensions of object words are observed infrequently in older, more articulate children, Nelson et al., 1977) are applying words from their lexicon that best fit the context. In this view, then, children's overextensions are partial rather than complete. Inappropriate uses appear because the child applies the "overextended" words when there is a certain degree of overlap between what the child has perceived as their conditions of application and the properties of the objects to which he or she wishes to direct the listener's attention. In other words, Clark (1977) assumes that some overextensions result because of a communicative strategy employed by young children rather than as a result of too few features having been acquired in regards to a particular concept/meaning, a departure from her earlier interpretation (Clark, 1973). Anglin (1977), however, has reported overextensions by young children in comprehension, and one of the present authors has found instances of overextensions in both comprehension and production (Kuczaj, 1979), so the exact nature of children's early overextensions of object words is undetermined. We suspect that children do overextend words in production that they do not overextend in comprehension, but that they also overextend some words in both comprehension and production, so that any single interpretation of, or approach to, overextensions is inadequate. (Even if all or most overextensions are analogous uses of quasi-appropriate words, as suggested by Nelson and Clark, Nelson's functional-core hypothesis of lexical-meaning acquisition would not predict the rarity of occurrence of such analogistic assertions based on shared function as compared to the frequency of such assertions based on shared form. Opportunities for functionally based analogistic assertions are plentiful and children sometimes do make such errors [one of the children studied by Bowerman used *wastebasket* to refer to any place she dropped scraps of waste paper; Bowerman, 1976], yet perceptual similarities are referred to by children in overextensions much more than are functional similarities [regardless of whether the overextensions indicate perceived similarity or assumed equivalence].)

Although the preceding discussion has focused on the identity/similarity issue in regard to overextensions, the conditions that elicit overextensions, the type of words that are most commonly overextended, and the developmental pattern of appearance and disappearance of overextensions are more central to our discussion of theories of early object word-meaning acquisition and concept structure and formation in young children. Research pertinent to these topics is considered next.

Rescorla (1976) studied the overextensions of six 12 to 18 month olds and found that 33% of their early words were overextended. Rescorla classified these overextensions as categorical, analogical, or predicate statement. Categorical overextensions, which comprised 55% of all overextensions, involved the use of the overextended term to label an object close to the word's standard referents in some clear higher-order taxonomic category of adult usage (e.g., use of the term *baby* to refer to children in general). Predicate statement overextensions, which comprised 25% of all overextensions, involved an attempt by the child to convey some information about the relationship between the immediate referent and some absent person, object, property, and so on (e.g., use of the term *doll* to refer to the usual location of the absent doll—these sorts of overextensions have been labeled combinatorial productions by Greenfield & Smith, 1976, and association through contiguity by Anglin, 1977). Analogical overextensions, which comprised 19% of all overextensions, involved a comment on some similarity between the standard referent and the labeled referent (e.g., calling a centipede a *comb*). Overextensions were found to be based on perceptual similarity (229 cases), action or function similarity (87 cases), affective similarity (15 cases), or contextual association (47 cases). Rescorla also found generalization of substantive terms to occur in a chain-complex fashion and an associative-complex fashion. In a chain complex, a collection of referents is linked by some similarity between one object and another without any unifying or consistent features relating each object to a standard. An associative complex involves a collection of objects in which each object shares some similarity with a standard, but no single feature characterizes all examples (cf. Bloom, 1973; Bowerman, 1976; Brown, 1965; Vygotsky, 1962; Werner, 1948 for discussions of chain and associative complexes).

Gruendel (1977) investigated children's word-meaning acquisition patterns and found a developmental progression from a word's being used for a specific referent to its being used as the symbol for a general class of objects to be quite common (see also Nelson & Bonvillian, 1973). However, Anglin (1977) has found that some words are initially underextended (supporting Gruendel's finding) but other words are initially overextended. Anglin has hypothesized that relatively specific object words such as *flower*, which young children tend to overextend, follow a general to specific pattern of development towards matching the adult meaning, whereas more general object words such as *plant*, which children typically underextend, follow a specific to general pattern of development. The fact that children underextend object words is problematic for Clark's (1973) theory, which proposed that children gradually acquire criterial features to form the basis of a word's meaning such that the development of meaning should proceed from general to specific, so that although overextensions are predicted by Clark's theory, underextensions clearly are not, except perhaps for the latter phases of word-meaning acquisition when, in fact, no such underextensions have been observed. It is difficult to determine how well underextensions accord with the theories of Nelson, Anglin, and Mulford, primarily because each of their theories fails to specify the mechanisms of extension to the extent that particular predictions concerning the developmental patterns of word meaning extension may be generated (a fault that Clark's (1973) theory avoids). (However, Anglin [1977] did attempt to determine the types of instances that are most often underextended. He found that the instances most often excluded from concept mem bership by children were those that adults rated as peripheral members of the concept, whereas prototypic instances were virtually always recognized as instances of the concept [i.e., as referents of the word that symbolized the concept of which the objects are instances].)

TOWARDS A THEORY OF SUBSTANTIVE WORD-MEANING ACQUISITION

In this section, we attempt to outline a theory of substantive word-meaning acquisition. In so doing, we incorporate the hypotheses of other theorists; the result is a hybrid theoretical approach integrating notions from both feature-list and prototype advocates. Others have attempted such an integration (Clark & Clark, 1977; Rips et al., 1973), but our theoretical stance differs somewhat from these earlier attempts particularly in its developmental implications. We show that the theory we outline accords well with the available data on word underextension and overextension and we also specify a number of developmental predictions based on our theoretical position.

As discussed in the preceding two sections, it is quite difficult, if not impossible, to define substantive word meaning in terms of criterial features. We agree with Miller (1978) that meaning cannot be equated with criterial features. A dog need not bark, have four legs, a tail, and fur in order to be a dog, even though dogs *characteristically* possess these qualities. The very fact that we can talk of a class of objects as possessing certain characteristic features implies a concept structure and formation process based on the notion of prototypes (the prototype(s) of a concept are those objects that possess the most characteristic features). Although the theory developed by Rosch is not meant as a developmental theory (Rosch, 1978), like other work with prototype concept-formation processes and structure in adults, it provides a basis for a developmental theory using the notion of concept prototypes (see Mulford, 1977, and the discussion of her theory in the preceding section of this chapter).

Concept Structure and Formation in Children and Adults

As Rosch and Lloyd (1978) note, the main problem in concept-formation and concept-structure research and theorizing is how the child and adult are able to segment the environment so that nonidentical stimuli can be treated as equivalent. Prototype theoretical approaches to this problem assume that the stored mental representations used in a concept are highly specific (in respect to within-class variation), the similarity dimension is highly resolved, and a best-fit criterion is used to decide if a novel instance is or is not a member of a concept (Palmer, 1978). Still, it is not clear whether the matching of novel instances takes place holistically, feature by feature, or via some intermediate process.

We suggest that the object-class concepts of young children are characterized primarily by the storage and representation of particular examples of the concept, some of which are prototypic examples. Although we agree with Sinclair's (1970) assertion that the "organizing activity" on the part of the young child is crucial in concept formation, we do not believe that this organizing activity in the young child is primarily characterized by the abstraction and comparison of object attributes. Instead, the posited concept-formation process entails holistic representations and judgments as to whether an object is or is not a member of a particular class and analytic judgments as to how central (prototypic) a member of the object-class the object is. Such an holistically based comparison and concept-formation process is supported by the work of Brooks (1978), Shepp (1978), and Smith (in press). Shepp and Smith each suggest that attribute combinations that are perceived by older children and adults as separable are perceived by younger children as integral, implicating holistic processing in younger children and more analytic processing in older children and adults, a developmental difference to which we return shortly.

Thus, we suggest that the object-class concepts of young children are primarily characterized by the utilization of stored representations of particular instances (of varying degrees of prototypicality) rather than by the formation and utilization of abstract prototypes and/or specific attribute analysis and comparison. In this view, the child usually groups objects together on the basis of holistic similarity, utilizing both perceptual and functional information. During this phase of concept formation and utilization, the child would be as likely to underextend as overextend the concept because the holistic-comparison process will result in the child's including certain objects because of irrelevant similarities and excluding others because of irrelevant differences. For example, a child who has formed a concept of *dog* based on experience with Springer Spaniels and English Setters might view sheep as instances of the concept *dog* but Great Danes as noninstances of dogs. Thus, the child's early overextensions and underextensions of a substantive word's meaning will reflect the child's early experience with and decisions about concept exemplars, and the child's overextensions and underextensions will result from the child's concern with matching novel instances to his or her stored representations. Some of the information the child uses for class extension is appropriate but other information is unimportant. For example, the child who views a sheep as an instance of a dog but a Great Dane as a noninstance may have had no experience with large dogs and insufficient experience with sheep; the similarities between the child's memories of dogs and the Great Dane may become clearer with closer inspection and interaction with the animal (in conjunction with hearing the animal labeled as a *dog*). Such experience would also accentuate the differences between these memories and the sheep. With more experience, the child learns to use only appropriate intensional information, resulting in fewer and fewer overextensions and underextensions and a broadening of the class extension such that more and more disparate instances will be included in the class, grouped according to the similarity the novel disparate instances share with the prototypic instances. Thus, with development, the child's object-class concepts (e.g., *dog*) come to include more and more nonprototypic but correct instances (Newfoundlands, Pekingese) and to exclude noninstances (sheep) that bear more perceptual similarity to the earliest prototypic exemplars (Springer Spaniel, Collie) than do the nonprototypic exemplars. The child learns what is appropriate and inappropriate intensional information for a particular concept.

How, though, does the child learn to accurately extend object-class concepts? Consider the following hypothetical situation—the child has come to categorize Collies, Springer Spaniels, and sheep as exemplars of the object-class concept *dog*. How does the child learn to include Pekingese and Newfoundlands as instances of the concept dog and to exclude sheep, goats, and bears (the latter of which bear more similarity to Newfoundlands than do Pekingese and/or Collies)? There are two important environmental variables that influence the development of the child's extension of a substantive word: (1) experience with exemplars and nonexemplars; and (2) feedback about past and present decisions concerning a concept's extension. Obviously, the child needs to experience a variety of possible exemplars of a concept in order to both broaden and narrow the range of extension of the concept. However, experience with objects per se is not sufficient to produce a variation in the range of extension of a concept by the child. The child must somehow decide if a novel object is or is not an exemplar of a particular concept. Such decisions can result from the child's matching the novel instances to the concept prototypes (the first learned exemplars) and deciding on the basis of "closeness of fit" whether the concept can be extended to include this instance. However, this matching process would yield many errors of overextension and underextension. For example, Pekingese are less similar to Collies than are sheep, and so the child who views Collies as dogs might initially classify sheep as dogs and Pekingese as nondogs. However, sheep are similar to Collies only in their surface perceptual characteristics. Collies are treated and act more like Pekingese than like sheep. Thus, functional similarity may override perceptual similarity in the organization of a concept. Also, the role of feedback may be paramount in concept extension (cf. Anglin, 1977; Brown, 1958b). Two types of feedback are considered here—implicit feedback and explicit feedback.

Implicit feedback refers to the naming practices of others and the child's attention to these practices. Suppose a child has included sheep but not Pekingese as instances of dogs. If a child is to correct these errors because of implicit feedback, then he or she must pay attention to the naming practices of others and must notice that others do not refer to sheep as dogs and do refer to Pekingese as dogs. Thus, the child notices a conflict between his or her naming practices and those of others and resolves this conflict by eventually restructuring his or her concept of dog to exclude sheep and include Pekingese. (This notion of conflict resolution as a factor in conceptual growth is borrowed from the work of Piaget, e.g., 1954; see also Bower, 1974.) This same result can be brought about via explicit feedback—that is, others explicitly correcting or confirming the child's naming practices. Not only can implicit and explicit feedback result in the child's adding and eliminating objects as instances of a concept but such feedback can also result in the child's viewing a novel instance as a prototypic or nonprototypic instance. For example, the child who hears Pekingese referred to as "funny-looking dogs" and Collies as "nice dogs" might classify Pekingese as nonprototypic exemplars of the concept *dog* and Collies as prototypic or close to the prototypic dog(s).

In this view, the object-class concepts that underlie children's early use of substantive words are formulated by the child via the mental representation of the particular instances first experienced by the child in conjunction with the substantive word in question. These concepts are modified by the child, who matches novel instances to the concept prototype(s) and uses a "goodness of fit" criteria to decide class membership and the centrality of concept instances. Modification of concepts occurs because of experience with objects to which the concepts can be extended and implicit and explicit feedback about the child's extensional decisions. In addition to leading to modification of concept extension, feedback can result in the shifting of central instances to noncentral instances and vice versa, if the first exemplars a child attaches to a concept are not prototypic ones in the adult vernacular. Thus, early experience can result in the child's prototype(s) for a given concept differing from those of older children and adults, and feedback and experience can then result in these early prototypes' losing at least some of their status as central exemplars.

Two points about children's early object-class concepts need to be emphasized at this point. First, given the importance of experience with the instances that the child first views as exemplars of a concept, the initial prototype(s) children use in concept formation and extension will be variable—that is, different children will have different prototypes for the same (adult) concept, depending on their early experiences. Second, although perceptual characteristics are likely to be quite important in object-class concept extension, functional information is also quite important. In other words, the child will use whatever information he or she can in order to accurately extend a concept. Thus, the child who is learning to refine an extension of a term such as *dog* must learn that perceptual similarity is not a sufficient criterial factor, and that other factors (such as the role dogs have in relation to humans) are important in extensional decisions.

It is worth restating at this time that children (and adults) may extend concepts on the basis of some partial similarity between what they believe to be instances of the concept and novel instances. Moreover, the intensional partial similarity may vary from one instance to another, resulting in certain instances not sharing any similarity to certain other instances. Piaget (1955, 1962), Werner (1954), and Werner and Kaplan (1950, 1952) have reported that children are prone to such *syncretic reasoning* and Maratsos (1977) has argued convincingly that adults employ such reasoning. The phenomenon of syncretic reasoning results, according to Maratsos (1977), when "because of partial similarity of one situation to another, children may assume further similarities in an unjustified manner . . . there is an overattribution of further similarity of outcome or attribute on the basis of partial and often complex-like links [pp. 354-357]."

Thus, children will not always form concepts that are internally consistent and such categorization will be reflected in their referential use of substantive words (cf. Bowerman, 1975; Rescorla, 1976).

To this point, we have argued that children's early object-class concepts, which underlie their referential use of substantive words, are prototype-based concepts and that the prototypes of a particular concept are mental representations of particular instances that are experienced early and/or frequently in the concept-formation process. Moreover, the extension of the concept rests on a matching process that utilizes a variety of information (both perceptual and functional, though we suspect perceptual information is initially the most important, resulting in premature judgments of class membership and thus overextension and underextension errors).

A number of investigators have suggested that development results in both a restructuring and reanalysis of previously learned concepts and new formation processes involved in the learning of new object-class concepts (cf. Anglin, 1977; Kossan, 1979; Mansfield, 1977; Smith, in press). The general idea is that even if the young child's object-class concepts are characterized by the representations and organization of particular concept instances, the object-class concepts of older children and adults are best characterized by the formation of abstract prototypes (i.e., prototypes that do not correspond to any experienced concept instance but instead represent the attribute aggregates most commonly associated with instances of the concept). These abstract prototypes may be represented as feature sets (see also Clark & Clark, 1977; Tversky & Gati, 1978), given the greater analytic skills of older children and adults than younger children. We would like to argue, however, that it is not the case that only young children engage in holistic-concept–formation process, but that, to the contrary, holistic concepts are the prototypic object-class concept for both adults and children (see Boswell & Green, 1979, and McCloskey & Glucksberg, 1979, for supporting data and theorizing). Although we certainly do not agree with Berkeley (1957) that there are *no* abstract ideas, we would like to suggest that object-class concepts do not typically involve abstract feature lists, *though such concepts may be described in terms of such feature lists*. In fact, the capacity of theorists to describe object-class concepts in terms of abstract feature sets rests on the same analytic capabilities of the older child who can define and extend an object-class concept on the basis of an abstract feature (or function) or set of abstract features in an experimental context (Smith, in press). Younger children apparently lack the necessary analytic skills or perhaps the ability to recognize that the skills are appropriate for the experimental tasks. In spite of the increasing analytic skills of the developing child, we suggest that the object-class concept-formation processes remain basically the same—that is, holistic. Thus, although the conceptual capabilities of older children and adults are broader (more varied) than those of younger children, the basic type of object-class formation process involves the representation of particular instances (note that the representation is what is holistic—we are not suggesting that the child stores exact copies of individual objects, but we are instead positing that the representations the child creates are holistic in nature) and the structural organization of such instances. So, although the older child and adult may employ nonholistic representations and abstract concept-formation processes, the typical concept-formation process involves holistic representations. The types of formation processes used by older children and adults may depend on the interrelations of the stimulus properties that are relevant for the object-class concept (see Garner, 1976) and the task. The greater adaptability of older children and adults than younger children (in terms of conceptual-processing skills) will result in greater likelihood of success on tasks that necessitate analytic skills. This is not to say that young children lack analytic skills altogether, because the child's acquisition of syntax necessitates some sort of analytic skills. But the young child's analytic skill repertoire is significantly smaller (and perhaps more constrained) than that of the older child and adult. Also, the object-class concepts about which we have been concerned here involve holistic processing and organizational skills rather than abstract analytical processing and organizational skills. More specifically, the object-class concepts involve both holistic processing and representation and analytic processing. Individual instances are stored holistically, though the created and stored representations are not exact duplicates of the individual objects. Thus, prototypic structure is achieved by relating particular representations relative to one another according to how well they accord with the concept prototype(s) and with one another. It may be that a well-developed concept structure entails highly prototypic exemplars that are not very similar to each other but each of which is quite similar to many other instances of the concept. For example, mockingbird and eagle both appear to be prototypic birds. Such a concept structure is illustrated in the following diagram:

Concept Prototypicality of Bird Exemplars

Low	*High*
certain other song birds — — — — — — — — — — — — — — —	mockingbird
certain other birds of prey — — — — — — — — — — — — — — — —	eagle

However, even the prototypic exemplars in this structure may reflect prototypic structure themselves. For example, if eagles are viewed as prototypic birds (of prey), there will be "good" instances and "bad" instances of eagles.

Similarly, if hummingbirds are viewed as nonprototypic birds, there will be "good" instances and "bad" instances of hummingbirds.

We are arguing, then, that the representations used in object-class concepts are holistic in nature, such that representations of individual instances are involved. However, the concept structure involves analytic processing, and the relation of prototypic and nonprototypic instances to one another will be determined by the similarity (perceptual/functional) the instances have to one another. Such similarity decisions rest on nonholistic (i.e., analytic) processes. Although identity decisions may rest on holistic processing, similarity decisions necessitate some sort of analytic processing. Thus, we are suggesting that the object-class concepts of the child and adult depend on holistic representations and nonholistic comparison processes (though identity decisions may be made holistically). The analytic skills of the child improve with age, leading to better comparison decisions and more refined concept structures (e.g., Smith, in press). A study by Boswell and Green (1979) supports the notion that in spite of the increasing analytic skills of the developing child, the child's representations remain holistic rather than changing to abstract feature lists. The children in Boswell and Green's study (ranging in age from 47 to 71 months) were exposed to a concept-learning task and were then shown new concept instances, including novel abstract prototypic instances. The children did view the novel prototypic instances as concept instances, demonstrating the generality of the learned concepts. However, the children were able to recognize that they had *not* been previously exposed to the novel prototypic instances, which indicates that they had not formulated an abstract prototype based on their previous experiences with concept instances. These findings support the notion that children can productively employ concept structures based on holistic and nonabstract representations of individual instances.

Different sorts of object-class concepts may necessitate different acquisitional processes. Horton and Markman (1979) have contrasted basic categories with superordinate categories. Basic categories (e.g., *dog*) carry much information and are distinguishable from one another; they share considerable perceptual and/or functional information with one another but not with members of other basic categories. Superordinate categories (e.g., *animal*) are very general and inclusive, with less perceptual and/or functional similarity among members than is so for basic categories. Horton and Markman suggest that experience with individual instances is sufficient for the acquisition of basic categories, whereas intensional information (linguistically conveyed) is necessary for the acquisition of superordinate categories. In other words, the acquisition of basic-level object-class concepts involves holistic processing whereas the acquisition of superordinate object-class concepts involves analytic processing. Not surprisingly, then, basic-level object-class concepts have been found to be easier and earlier acquisitions than superordinate object-class concepts (Horton & Markman, 1979; Rosch et al., 1976). Still, it should not be assumed that superordinate object-class concepts do not possess holistic prototypic structure. Just as there are prototypic collies and prototypic dogs, there are also prototypic animals, vehicles, and so on. Thus, both subordinate and superordinate object-class concepts are compatible with the notion of holistic prototypic concept structure and analytic comparison processes.

Overextensions and Underextensions

Children should initially engage in more reference with proper names rather than correct (i.e., nonunderextended) reference with common nouns because the former require single-object concepts whereas the latter require object-class concepts. In single-object concepts, the child must recognize that a particular instance of an object is in fact an instance of the object represented by the single-object concept. A single experience with an object is sufficient to produce a single-object concept (though formation of such concepts will not always result from a single experience with an object). Thus, a minimal amount of experience is necessary for the child to learn the extension of a proper noun. This same minimal amount of experience could result in the child's underextending a substantive word that refers to an object-class concept because the child could view it as a proper noun. In other words, a single experience with an object and its corresponding word could result in correct reference for proper nouns and underextended use for common nouns because a single experience with an object can only result in the formation of a single-object concept. The formation of an object-class concept requires experience with at least two objects that the child might view as exemplars of an object-class concept (this might occur because the child has heard the same term being used to refer to each of the objects or because of the natural spontaneous categorization behavior of the child).

Because at least one experience with two different concept instances is required for the formation of an object-class concept, overextensions of substantive words should not occur without a minimum of one experience with two different concept instances because object-class concepts underlie the overextended referential use of a substantive word. Underextended referential use of a term can result from a single experience with a single object because single-object concepts are all that is necessary to result in underextensions (underextensions may result from overly narrow object-class concepts as well as from single-object concepts). Thus, the experiential base of underextensions differs from that of overextensions in regard to the minimally sufficient amount of experience with concept instance(s).

Of course, underextensions and overextensions differ in terms of the type of processing engaged in by the child, as well as in terms of the minimally sufficient amount of experience. As noted by Kuczaj and Lederberg (1977), the *internal context* is as important as the *external context*. Internal context refers to what the child contributes to his or her interpretation of a given experience (this is a factor of the child's predispositions and past experiences), whereas external context refers to the situation in which a child encounters a term. Thus, identical external contexts may result in varying acquisition patterns due to children's providing different internal contexts (Bowerman, 1975; Kuczaj & Lederberg, 1977). We now consider how the child's predispositions and past experiences interact to result in underextended and overextended referential use of substantive words.

Although much of the theorizing on early substantive word-meaning acquisition has focused on overextensions, a number of investigators have reported evidence for underextended referential use of substantive words (Anglin, 1977; Bloch, 1921; Bloom, 1973; Reich, 1976). The typical developmental pattern is evidently one in which the child goes from underextended referential use of a term to more general, perhaps overextended, referential use. Bloom (1973) reports a three-stage sequence: (1) unsystematic overextensions; (2) underextensions; and (3) systematic overextensions. In fact, there are two types of underextension: (1) extreme underextension—the child treats a common noun as a proper noun; and (2) relative overextension—the child treats a common noun as a common noun, but applies it to an overly narrow set of objects. Extreme underextension results when a single-object concept underlies the child's use of a term. Relative overextension results when the object-class concept underlying the referential use of a term is overly narrow, most likely because the child's experience with concept exemplars has involved exemplars that bear a great deal of similarity to one another. The result is an overly specific object-class concept (cf. Anglin, 1977; Posner, 1973).

There seems to be little doubt that children overextend substantive words (Bloom, 1973; Clark, 1973; Gruendel, 1977; Rescorla, 1976). Various authors have classified overextensions in various ways, as the following (nonexhaustive) list illustrates: (1) unsystematic and systematic overextensions (Bloom, 1973); (2) pure overextensions, in which the child views one or more properties as essential for extension of the word (Clark & Clark, 1977); (3) mixed overextensions, in which the child may use a number of properties but none are essential (Bowerman, 1976; Clark & Clark, 1977); (4) chaining overextensions, in which the meaning of the word is loosely defined and changes each time the child attempts to use it (Bloom & Lahey, 1978); and (5) holistic-association overextensions, in which overextensions occur on the basis of some holistic-comparison process (Bloom & Lahey, 1978). Although the aforementioned types of overextension errors are not mutually exclusive, it is clear that the term *overextension* covers a multitude of overgeneralization sins. However, each of these overextension types can be accounted for by the prototype account of substantive word-meaning acquisition outlined earlier. Holistic-association overextensions are obviously within the realm of the prototype theory. Unsystematic overextensions, mised overextensions, and chaining overextensions can be explained by the notion of syncretic reasoning and so are also compatible with the notion of prototype-based substantive word meaning (because syncretic reasoning can involve inaccurate comparison of new instances to prototypes as well as inaccurate comparison of object and event attributes). Systematic and pure overextensions are also accountable within the framework of a prototype theory of early substantive word meaning in that such overextensions can be said to involve some type of systematic but overgeneral comparison of new instances to concept prototypes.

As noted earlier, experience with exemplars of a concept that share a great deal of similarity should lead to underextensions. Experience with unsimilar exemplars of a concept should lead to overextension errors because it results in an overly broad concept. Thus, the occurrence of underextension and overextension errors is a function of the similarity (or lack of similarity) of what one perceives to be members of a particular concept.

Moreover, the child's overextension errors can provide a clue to whether the child is attaching a newly acquired word to a previously formed concept or is formulating a concept for the newly acquired word. If the child makes overextension errors immediately following the acquisition of a word, this would indicate that the child is attaching the word to a previously formulated concept (and one that is overextended insofar as correct referential use of the newly learned word is concerned). If, however, the child makes overextension errors only after some time, it is likely that the child is formulating a concept to which he or she can attach the word. Of course, in both cases, the concepts will be continually refined during the course of development.

Conclusions and Summary

We have argued that early substantive word-meaning acquisition is best characterized as a process entailing the attachment of substantive words to single-object concepts and object-class concepts. These concepts are thought to be prototype-based concepts, involving the development of holistic representations and the organization of actually experienced particular instances. Later development results in a restructuring of the concept. In fact, the actual prototypes, as well as the nature of the representation of the prototypes, may change with development, depending on the relation between the child's initial and subsequent experience with concept exemplars.

According to this view, the child's early prototypes will be based primarily on perceptual (form) information but will also utilize functional information for concept extension. Therefore, the child's referential use of substantive words will reflect this concern with form *and* function, though for early use, form will be the dominant factor in extension. Not only is correct extension of a word likely to reflect both form and function information, but such is also likely to be the case for both underextended and overextended word use. However, we expect that although overextensions involve both form and function information (though information about form is overextended much more often than information about function), underextensions will invariably involve perceptual attributes.

We would like to make one last point concerning substantive word-meaning underextensions and overextensions. Although certain words will not be overextended or underextended, other words will be overextended, others underextended, and others both underextended and overextended. For most words in the latter category, the developmental sequence will involve underextensions appearing first, then disappearing, after which overextensions will appear. However, some words may be underextended and overextended at the same time. Such underextensions/overextensions combinations reflect object-class concepts that are simultaneously too narrow and too broad (for example, the child who views sheep as instances of *dog* but Newfoundlands as noninstances of *dog*). The developmental pattern exhibited in a child's referential extension of a particular substantive word is a function of the child's categorization predispositions, experience with various concept instances and noninstances, and the child's interpretation and organization of these experiences. Experience will determine the initial prototype(s) of a concept, subsequent changes in the status of the initial prototype(s), and perhaps the emergence of new prototypes for an earlier-learned concept. Experience will also influence patterns of underextension, overextension, and correct extension of object-class concepts, and thereby the child's referential use of the substantive words that represent these concepts in the child's native tongue. Moreover, experience will interact with categorizing predispositions to determine whether variant or invariant acquisition patterns will be observed in different children acquiring the same term(s).

As we conclude our discussions, we would like to suggest future directions of research, which we suspect would prove to be quite fruitful. Investigations of the influence of experience on subsequent underextension, overextension, and appropriate extension would undoubtedly increase our understanding of the acquisition of appropriate object concepts for words. Also, to better understand the processes underlying the development of concept structure, studies examining the relationship between children's judgments of the "goodness" of various exemplars of a particular concept and their prior experience with the exemplars would be useful. Further, if it could be determined which exemplars are most central to one of a child's concepts, the child could be exposed to novel exemplars, differing along a variety of dimensions, to find out if and how the child's hierarchy of prototypicality for a given concept could be altered. It seems clear to us that studies such as these, and others that assess the concept structures of children of varying ages and the factors that determine the hierarchy of prototypicality of particular concepts, are needed in order to better account for the phenomenon of object word-meaning acquisition .

REFERENCES

Anderson, E. Cups and glasses: Learning that boundaries are vague. *Journal of Child Language*, 1975, *2*, 79-103.

Anglin, J. *Word, object, and conceptual development*. New York: Norton, 1977.

Barrett, M. Lexical development and overextension in child language. *Journal of Child Language*, 1978, *5*, 205-220.

Berkeley, G. *A treatise concerning the principles of human knowledge*. New York: Bobbs-Merrill, 1957.

Bierwisch, M. Some semantic universals of German adjectivals. *Foundations of Language*, 1967, *3*, 1-36.

Bierwisch, M. Semantics. In J. Lyons (Ed.), *New horizons in linguistics*. Middlesex, Eng.: Penguin Books, 1970.

Bloch, O. Les premiers stades du language de l'enfant. *Journal de Psychologie*, 1921, *18*, 693-712.

Bloom, L. *One word at a time: The use of single word utterances before syntax*. The Hague: Mouton, 1973.

Bloom, L., & Lahey, M. *Language development and language disorders*. New York: Wiley, 1978.

Boswell, D. R., & Green, H. *Children's abstraction and recognition of visual concepts*. Paper presented at the Biennial Meeting of the Society for Research in Child Development, San Francisco, March 1979.

Bower, T. *Development in infancy*. San Francisco: Freeman, 1974.

Bowerman, M. *The acquisition of word meaning: An investigation of some current conflicts*. Paper presented at the Third International Child Language Symposium, London, 1975.

Bowerman, M. Semantic factors in the acquisition of rules for word use and sentence construction. In D. Morehead & A. Morehead (Eds.), *Normal and deficient child language*. Baltimore: University Park Press, 1976.

Brooks, L. Nonanalytic concept formation and memory for instances. In E. Rosch & B. Lloyd (Eds.), *Cognition and categorization*. Hillsdale, N.J.: Lawrence Erlbaum Associates, 1978.

Brown, R. *Words and things*. New York: Free Press, 1958. (a)

Brown, R. How shall a thing be called? *Psychological Review*, 1958, *65*, 14-21. (b)

Brown, R. *Social Psychology*. New York: Free Press, 1965.

Clark, E. What's in a word? On the child's acquisition of semantics in his first language. In T. Moore (Ed.), *Cognitive development and the acquisition of language*. New York: Academic Press, 1973.

Clark, E. Some aspects of the conceptual basis for first language acquisition. In R. Schiefelbusch & R. L. Lloyd (Eds.), *Language perspectives: Acquisition, retardation and intervention*. Baltimore: University Park Press, 1974.

Clark, E. Strategies and the mapping problem in first language acquisition. In J. MacNamara (Ed.), *Language learning and thought*. New York: Academic Press, 1977.

Clark, H., & Clark, E. *Psychology and language*. New York: Harcourt, Brace, Jovanovich, 1977.

Dukes, W., & Bevan, W. Stimulus variation and repetition in the acquisition of naming responses. *Journal of Experimental Psychology*, 1967, *74*, 178-181.

Franks, J., & Bransford, J. Abstraction of visual patterns. *Journal of Experimental Psychology*, 1972, *90*, 65-74.

Garner, W. Interaction of stimulus dimensions in concept and choice processes. *Cognitive Psychology*, 1976, *8*, 98-123.

Gentner, D. *On relational meaning: The acquisition of verb meaning*. Paper presented at the Biennial Meeting of the Society for Research in Child Development, New Orleans, March 1977.

Gibson, E. *Principles of perceptual learning and development*. New York: Appleton-Century-Crofts, 1969.

Greenfield, P., & Smith, J. *The structure of communication in early language development.* New York: Academic Press, 1976.

Gruendel, J. Referential extension in early language development. *Child Development,* 1977, *48,* 1567–1576.

Horton, M., & Markman, E. *Children's acquisition of basic and superordinate level categories from intensional and extensional information.* Paper presented at the Biennial Meeting of the Society for Research in Child Development, San Francisco, March 1979.

Huttenlocher, J. The origins of language comprehension. In R. Solso (Ed.), *Theories in cognitive psychology.* Hillsdale, N.J.: Lawrence Erlbaum Associates, 1974.

Hyman, R., & Frost, N. Gradients and schema in pattern recognition. In P. Rabbitt (Ed.), *Attention and performance.* New York: Academic Press, 1974.

Kossan, N. *Developmental differences in concept acquisition strategies.* Paper presented at the Biennial Meeting of the Society for Research in Child Development, San Francisco, March 1979.

Kuczaj, S. On the acquisition of a semantic system. *Journal of Verbal Learning and Verbal Behavior,* 1975, *14,* 340–358.

Kuczaj, S. *Old and new forms, old and new meanings: The form–function hypotheses revisited.* Paper presented at the Biennial Meeting of the Society for Research in Child Development, New Orleans, March 1977.

Kuczaj, S. *Children's overextensions in comprehension and production: Support for a prototype theory of object word meaning acquisition.* Paper presented at the Biennial Meeting of the Society for Research in Child Development, San Francisco, March 1979.

Kuczaj, S., & Lederberg, A. Height, age, and function: Differing influences on children's comprehension of "younger" and "older." *Journal of Child Language,* 1977, *4,* 395–416.

Labov, W., & Labov, T. *The grammar of "eat" and "mama."* Paper presented at the Annual Meeting of the Linguistic Society of America, New York, 1974.

MacNamara, J. *Language learning and thought.* New York: Academic Press, 1977.

Mansfield, A. Semantic organization in the young child: Evidence for the development of semantic future systems. *Journal of Experimental Child Psychology,* 1977, *23,* 57–77.

Maratsos, M. Disorganization in thought and word. In R. Shaw & J. Bransford (Eds.), *Perceiving, acting, and knowing.* Hillsdale, N.J.: Lawrence Erlbaum Associates, 1977.

McCloskey, M., & Glucksberg, S. Decision processes in verifying category membership statements: Implications for models of semantic memory. *Cognitive Psychology,* 1979, *11,* 1–37.

Miller, G. Comments on the acquisition of word meaning. *Child Development,* 1978, *49,* 999–1004.

Miller, G., & Johnson-Laird, P. *Language and perception.* Cambridge, Mass.: Harvard University Press, 1976.

Mulford, R. *Prototypicality and the development of categorization.* Paper presented at the Boston University Child Language Conference, 1977.

Nelson, K. Structure and strategy in learning to talk. *Monographs of the Society for Research in Child Development,* 1973, *38*(No. 149).

Nelson, K. Concept, word, and sentence: Interrelations in acquisition and development. *Psychology Review,* 1974, *81,* 269–285.

Nelson, K. The conceptual basis for naming. In J. MacNamara (Ed.), *Language learning and thought.* New York: Academic Press, 1977.

Nelson, K. Semantic development and the development of semantic memory. In K. E. Nelson (Ed.) *Children's Language, Vol. 1.* New York: Gardner Press, Inc., 1978.

Nelson, K. Explorations in the development of a functional semantic system. In W. Collins (Ed.), *The Minnesota symposia on child psychology,* Vol. 12: *Children's language and communication.* Hillsdale, N.J.: Lawrence Erlbaum Associates, 1979.

Nelson, K. E., & Bonvillian, J. Concepts and words in the 18-month-old: acquiring concept names under controlled conditions. *Cognition,* 1973, *2,* 435–450.

Nelson, K., Rescorla, L., Gruendel, J., & Benedict, H. *Early lexicons: What do they mean?* Paper presented at the Biennial Meeting of the Society for Research in Child Development, New Orleans, March 1977.

Oden, G. Fuzziness in semantic memory: Choosing exemplars of subjective categories. *Memory and Cognition*, 1975, *5*, 198-204.

Palmer, S. Fundamental aspects of cognitive representation. In E. Rosch & B. Lloyd (Eds.), *Cognition and categorization*. Hillsdale, N.J.: Lawrence Erlbaum Associates, 1978.

Piaget, J. *Origins of intelligence*. New York: Basic Books, 1954.

Piaget, J. *The construction of reality in the child*. London: Routledge and Kegan Paul, 1955.

Piaget, J. *Play, dreams and imitation*. New York: Norton, 1962.

Posner, M. Abstraction and the process of recognition. In G. Bower & J. Spence (Eds.), *The psychology of learning motivation*. New York: Academic Press, 1969.

Posner, M. *Cognition: An introduction*. Glenview, Ill.: Scott, Foresman, 1973.

Posner, M., & Keele, S. On the genesis of abstract ideas. *Journal of Experimental Psychology*, 1968, *77*, 353-363.

Posner, M., & Keele, S. Retention of abstract ideas. *Journal of Experimental Psychology*, 1970, *83*, 304-308.

Prawat, R., & Cancell, A. Semantic retrieval in young children as a function of type of meaning. *Developmental Psychology*, 1977, *13*, 354-358.

Reed, S. Pattern recognition and categorization. *Cognitive Psychology*, 1972, *3*, 382-407.

Reich, P. The early acquisition of word meaning. *Journal of Child Language*, 1976, *3*, 117-124.

Rescorla, L. *Concept formation in early word learning*. Unpublished doctoral dissertation, Yale University, 1976.

Richards, M. Sorting out what's in a word from what's not: Evaluating Clark's semantic features acquisition theory. *Journal of Experimental Child Psychology*, 1979, *27*, 1-47.

Rips, L., Shoben, E., & Smith, E. Semantic distance and the verification of semantic relations. *Journal of Verbal Learning and Verbal Behavior*, 1973, *12*, 1-10.

Rosch, E. On the internal structure of perceptual and semantic categories. In T. Moore (Ed.), *Cognition and the acquisition of language*. New York: Academic Press, 1973.

Rosch, E. Principles of categorization. In E. Rosch & B. Lloyd (Eds.), *Cognition and categorization*. Hillsdale, N.J.: Lawrence Erlbaum Associates, 1978.

Rosch, E., & Lloyd, B. *Cognition and categorization*. Hillsdale, N.J.: Lawrence Erlbaum Associates, 1978.

Rosch, E., & Mervis, C. Family resemblances: Studies in the internal structure of categories. *Cognitive Psychology*, 1975, *7*, 573-605.

Rosch, E., Mervis, C., Gray, W., Johnson, D., & Boyes-Braem, P. Basic objects in natural categories. *Cognitive Psychology*, 1976, *8*, 382-439.

Russell, B. *Introduction to mathematical philosophy*. London: George Allen, 1919.

Shepp, B. From perceived similarity to dimensional structure: A new hypothesis about perspective development. In E. Rosch & B. Lloyd (Eds.), *Cognition and categorization*. Hillsdale, N.J.: Lawrence Erlbaum Associates, 1978.

Sinclair, H. The transition from sensor-motor behavior to symbolic activity. *Interchange*, 1970, *1*, 119-126.

Slobin, D. Cognitive prerequisites for the development of grammar. In C. Ferguson & D. Slobin (Eds.), *Studies of child language development*. New York: Holt, Rinehart, & Winson, 1973.

Smith, L. Perceptual development and category generalization. *Child Development*, in press.

Thomson, J., & Chapman, R. Who is "daddy" revisited: The status of two-year-olds' overextended words in use and comprehension. *Journal of Child Language*, 1977, *4*, 359-376.

Tversky, A., & Gati, I. Studies of similarity. In E. Rosch & B. Lloyd (Eds.), *Cognition and categorization*. Hillsdale, N.J.: Lawrence Erlbaum Associates, 1978.

Vygotsky, L. *Thought and language*. Cambridge, Mass.: M.I.T. Press, 1962.

Werner, H. *Comparative psychology of mental development*. Chicago: Follett, 1948.

Werner, H. Change of meaning: A study of semantic processes through the experimental method. *Journal of General Psychology*, 1954, *50*, 181–208.

Werner, H., & Kaplan, B. *Symbol formation*. New York: Wiley, 1963.

Werner, H., & Kaplan, E. Development of word meaning through verbal context: An experimental study. *Journal of Psychology*, 1950, *29*, 251–257.

Werner, H., & Kaplan, E. The acquisition of word meanings: A developmental study. *Monograph of the Society for Research in Child Development*, 1952, *15*.

9 Distinguishing Between Prototypes: The Early Acquisition of the Meaning of Object Names

Martyn D. Barrett
Roehampton Institute

INTRODUCTION

Imre Lakatos (1970) once observed that the history of science has been and should be a history of competing theories, and that the sooner such competition begins, the more auspicious are the prospects for scientific progress. Lakatos would thus presumably have approved of the current state of research into the early acquisition of the meaning of object names by children, for no less than four distinct theoretical positions have been advanced in the recent literature on this topic: the semantic-feature hypothesis (Clark, 1973, 1975), the functional-core hypothesis (Nelson, 1974, 1977), the prototype hypothesis (Bowerman, 1978), and the contrastive hypothesis (Barrett, 1978).

The first of these four theories to be proposed was the semantic-feature hypothesis (Clark, 1973). This hypothesis postulates that the meaning of a word is composed of semantic features (e.g., "four-legged," "barks," etc. compose the meaning of the word *dog*), that word being applied to label any object that possesses those features: the semantic-feature hypothesis, therefore, postulates that the child acquires the meaning of a word by gradually acquiring individual semantic features and by adding them to the lexical entry for that word. In her initial statement of this hypothesis, Clark (1973) further suggested that these semantic features are organized hierarchically with respect to their generality, with the most general semantic features being acquired earliest by the child (e.g., "four-legged" would be acquired before "barks"); Clark also suggested that the earliest semantic features to be acquired are derived from an encoding of the perceptual attributes of referents.

From these initial postulates, Clark was able to make certain predictions about the course of early lexical development. If a child initially acquires only the more general semantic features for a particular word, then it would be predicted that this word will be overextended with respect to the adult lexicon when first acquired by that child (e.g., the word *dog* would be used to label all four-legged animals and not only dogs if the single semantic feature "four-legged" has been acquired for this word). Furthermore, if these initial semantic features have been derived from an encoding of the perceptual attributes of referents, then it would also be predicted that the objects to which an overextended word is applied will have certain perceptual features in common with the original objects by reference to which the meaning of the word was first acquired.

The diary data at first seemed to confirm both of these two predictions; Clark (1973) presents a wealth of examples drawn from the existing literature to support the contention that young children frequently overextend the names of objects and that these overextensions are based upon the perceptual similarities between objects. However, more recent studies have tended to throw considerable doubt upon the empirical adequacy of the semantic-feature hypothesis. First, it has been pointed out by Reich (1976) that underextension, as well as overextension, occurs in early lexical development, suggesting that it need not be the most general semantic features that are acquired earliest by the child. And second, Barrett (1978) has shown that overextension is not such a common phenomenon as the semantic-feature hypothesis predicts. For example, one child, Hildegard (observed by Leopold, 1939, 1949), only overextended 20 words out of a total number of well over 300 words that she acquired during her first 2 years. The semantic-feature hypothesis, however, predicts that the meanings of many and maybe all words will be overextended when they are first acquired (see Clark, 1973). Although Clark has subsequently modified her initial statement of the semantic-feature hypothesis (see, for example, Clark, 1975, where she introduces the possibility of overextensions being based upon functional, as well as perceptual, similarities between objects), it is difficult to see how this hypothesis can explain either the existence of extensional errors other than overextension or the relative paucity of overextensions in early child language.

The second theory that was proposed as an explanation of the early acquisition of the meaning of object names was the functional-core hypothesis (Nelson, 1974). This hypothesis suggests that objects are initially assigned to concepts by the child on the basis of their functional relationships (i.e., on the basis of what the child can do with those objects or on the basis of what those objects themselves can do). It is also hypothesized that the child then analyzes the objects that have been included within a particular concept on functional grounds, in order to obtain a hierarchy of attributes that facilitates the identification of new instances of the concept. At the top of this hierarchy is a functional core that defines the functional relationships into which an object must be able to enter in order to be included as an instance of that concept. The features that describe the perceptual attributes of concept instances are represented lower down in the hierarchy. Finally, the functional-core hypothesis postulates that a word is then attached to the concept that has been formed in this way (although it has been suggested in a more recent paper by Nelson, Rescorla, Gruendel, & Benedict, 1978, that words can be attached to concepts at any point in the concept-formation process).

The priority that the functional-core hypothesis attributes to functional relations in the formation of lexical categories is motivated by the finding (Nelson, 1973) that the vast majority of the earliest object names to be acquired by children typically refer to objects that either possess a high degree of mobility (e.g., animals, vehicles, etc.) or that the child acts upon in some way (e.g., toys, foodstuffs, etc.). Thus, the functional-core hypothesis, by postulating that objects are initially assigned to concepts on the basis of their dynamic, functional properties, can explain this early selectivity of referents.

However, the functional-core hypothesis has difficulty in accounting for some of the other phenomena that characterize early lexical development. First, this hypothesis does not provide a very adequate explanation of the phenomenon of overextension. If the functional core of a concept defines the functional relationships into which an object must be able to enter in order to be included as an instance of that concept, then it would be predicted that all the objects that are labeled by a particular word will have certain functional relationships in common with one another. Recent studies, however, have shown this prediction to be false (e.g., Barrett, 1979; Bowerman, 1978); some overextensions are based upon a single perceptual feature, and the manifest functional differences between objects are totally ignored by the child in the process. Hildegard, for example, used the word *ball* to label an observatory dome, an overextension that ignores all the possible functional information about balls that Hildegard might have acquired. It is perhaps for this reason that Nelson (1977) modified her original view, suggesting that although lexical categories are initially formed on the basis of function, new instances are identified on the basis of form. However, this formulation fares little better than the original statement. It has been found that although some overextensions can occur solely on the basis of form, other overextensions can occur solely on the basis of the shared functions of objects (see Barrett, 1979). For example, Hildegard used the word *bobby pin* to refer to any pin, irrespective of form, that was used in her hair. As a result of these criticisms, Nelson (1979) has recently modified the functional-core hypothesis again, suggesting that children may use language for many communicative functions, including statements of similarity as well as identify; thus, the preceding examples could be explained as cases of the child's asserting an analogical relationship between balls and observatory domes and between bobby pins and other types of hair pin. But the major problem here is that the distinction between analogical and other types of overextension is based solely upon adult judgments rather than upon any empirical data (see Nelson et al., 1978), thus enabling the concept of an analogical overextension to be used as a post hoc explanation for all instances of overextension that appear to refute the functional-core hypothesis, effectively insulating this hypothesis against even the possibility of refutation through observations of overextension.

However, there is a second phenomenon for which the functional-core hypothesis fails to provide any explanation—namely, the systematic subdivision of semantic fields (see Barrett, 1978). For example, Leopold (1949) reports that Hildegard initially used the word *cookie* to refer to cookies, crackers, and cakes; she later acquired the word *cracker* to refer to crackers, at which point the extension of *cookie* was partially rescinded in the direction of standard usage. Finally, she acquired the word *cake,* which cut down the extension of *cookie* again. The functional-core hypothesis, however, fails to provide any explanation of these systematic developments within semantic fields (see, for example, Nelson, 1979, where these developments are discussed but no explanation of them is offered).

A theory that seems to provide a far more adequate explanation of the extensional errors that are made by children than either the semantic-feature hypothesis or the functional-core hypothesis is the prototype hypothesis as developed by Bowerman (1978). Bowerman points out that children hear particular words modeled most frequently in connection with only one referent or a small group of highly similar referents; she therefore argues that children will later begin to produce these words themselves only in connection with these prototypical referents (i.e., these words will be underextended). At a later stage, however, they begin to extend these words to novel referents that share one or more features with these prototypes. Bowerman further suggests that these shared features do not necessarily function in a criterial way; consequently, although every referent will have one or more features in common with the prototype, they need not all possess the same conjunctive set of features; they will only be linked by a family resemblance instead.

In support of this hypothesis, Bowerman (1978) describes a variety of the overextensions that were produced by her own two children to show that the objects that are named by a word are indeed only linked by a family resemblance and not by criterial features. Furthermore, the evidence obtained from several other children also supports this prediction (Barrett, 1979). But although the prototype hypothesis can thus explain the data on extensional errors in a relatively simple and coherent manner, this hypothesis nevertheless fails to account for the systematic developments that occur within semantic fields (such as those in the example from Leopold [1949], which was described earlier).

Indeed, it was precisely in order to account for these previously unexplained developments within semantic fields that the contrastive hypothesis was originally proposed (see Barrett, 1978). This hypothesis disputes the assumption (made by the semantic-feature, functional-core, and prototype hypotheses) that it is sufficient for the child merely to abstract features from the referents of a word in order to delimit the extension of that word. Instead, it is suggested that the child must abstract the contrasting features that distinguish the referents of that word from the referents of other words within the same semantic field in order for the child to be able to exclude incorrect referents from the extension of that word (see Barrett, 1978, for a detailed discussion of the reasons for this suggestion). Consequently, this hypothesis postulates that the acquisition of the meaning of an object name occurs in the following way: The word is first assigned by the child to a semantic field on the basis of the general invariant attributes shared by the referents of that word; the child then compares the referents of the word with the referents of the other words already assigned to the same semantic field on similar grounds. The features (either perceptual or functional) that distinguish these referents from one another are abstracted and stored in the lexicon as the meaning of that word.

This hypothesis predicts that a word will not be overextended to label an object for which the child has already acquired a more appropriate name. This is because if the appropriate name for an object is in fact known (i.e., the referents of that word have been differentiated from the referents of the other words in the same semantic field), then the use of an inappropriate name for that object should not occur; instead, overextension should only occur in those instances in which the more appropriate name for the object to be labeled has yet to be acquired. This prediction was confirmed (see Barrett, 1978). The contrastive hypothesis further predicts that semantic fields will be systematically subdivided by the nonoverlapping extensions of related words during the course of early lexical development, and overextended words will be used to label objects that are not yet included within the extensions of underextended words. Evidence to support this prediction is also provided by Barrett (1978). The empirical adequacy of this theory, however, has also been recently challenged. Nelson (1979) has argued that the contrastive hypothesis predicts that the meaning of a word can only be acquired by reference to both positive and negative referential instances, yet evidence is available (e.g., from Bowerman, 1978, and from K. E. Nelson & Bonvillian, 1978) that the child can in fact learn the meaning of an object name from a single positive referent.[1]

---

[1]Nelson (1979) also argues that the contrastive hypothesis is reducible to the semantic-feature hypothesis, contrary to the claims of Barrett (1978). This question is, of course, ultimately a matter of interpretation. In Barrett (1978), several phenomena are discussed that cannot be explained by the semantic-feature hypothesis but that can be explained by the contrastive hypothesis (e.g., the relative rarity of overextension, the existence of extensional errors other than overextension, the discriminative selection of negative features by the child, etc.). It is the explanation of these phenomena that should be regarded as the issue of importance, and not whether the contrastive hypothesis can or cannot be interpreted as a variant of the semantic-feature hypothesis.

Nelson (1979) additionally charges Barrett (1978) with committing the analytic fallacy—that is, using logical analysis to describe a system and then applying this analysis to explain the development of that system in substitution for developmental observation. However, careful reference to Barrett (1978) will show that logical analysis was not used there as a substitute for developmental observation, but was used instead to suggest a hypothesis that generated an empirical prediction that was

Research into the early acquisition of the meanings of object names would thus appear to be in a highly problematical situation at present. Previous studies have certainly made considerable progress in identifying the phenomena that characterize early lexical development; there is, however, no single theory available that can plausibly account for all of these phenomena. Thus, there is now considerable evidence to support all of the following observational statements:

1. The earliest object names to be acquired typically refer either to objects that possess a high degree of mobility or to objects that the child manipulates in some way (Nelson, 1973).

2. The meaning of an object name can be acquired from a single referent (Bowerman, 1978; K. E. Nelson & Bonvillian, 1978).

3. Children sometimes (but not always) overextend or underextend the meanings of object names (Barrett, 1978; Reich 1976).

4. Object names are not usually overextended to label objects for which the child has already acquired more appropriate names (Barrett, 1978).

5. The objects to which an overextended object name is applied need only have a single feature in common with the initial referents of that word (Barrett, 1979; Bowerman, 1978).

6. Semantic fields are sometimes systematically subdivided by children during the course of early lexical development (Barrett, 1978).

But, as has been seen, each of the four theories that have been proposed until now can only account for some of the foregoing phenomena. Thus, the semantic-feature hypothesis fails to account for observation 3; the functional-core hypothesis fails to account for observations 4, 5, and 6; the prototype hypothesis fails to account for observations 4 and 6; and the contrastive hypothesis fails to account for observation 2. The fundamental problem currently facing the study of the early acquisition of the meanings of object names would therefore seem to be the absence of any single coherent theoretical framework that can explain all of these phenomena. Consequently, in the following section of this chapter, we propose an outline of a new theory of the early acquisition of the meanings of object names, in an attempt to account in a nonselective way for the phenomena previously listed; the presentation of this outline is then followed by a more detailed discussion of the available data, in the course of which the finer details of the theory being proposed are elucidated.

---

potentially falsifiable. Developmental data were therefore used to ascertain whether or not the data refuted the prediction. Finding that the prediction was not refuted, it was concluded that the hypothesis that had generated the prediction was consistent with the developmental data and, indeed, could explain an aspect of those data that had not previously been explained explicitly by any of the available theories of early lexical development. It was thus precisely the developmental data that were regarded as crucial to the contrastive hypothesis. Logical analysis was simply used to suggest the initial hypothesis.

A BRIEF OUTLINE OF THE THEORY

The theory proposed here can be viewed as an integration of the two hypotheses previously developed by Bowerman (1978) and Barrett (1978)—that is, the prototype and the contrastive hypotheses. This theory postulates that the following four component processes underlie the acquisition and the development of the meaning of an object name:

1. *The initial acquisition of the word together with a prototypical referent for that word.* It is hypothesized that the child first acquires the meaning of an object name in the form of a prototypical referent. This could be a result of the adults in the environment of the child using the word most frequently in connection with just one referent or a small group of highly similar referents, as suggested by Bowerman (1978). Alternatively, the child might develop a word of an idiosyncratic phonological form to refer to an object for which no name is readily available in the linguistic environment but that is nevertheless salient for the child. In either case, the net result would be the initial representation of the meaning of that word in the form of a prototypical referent.

2. *A preliminary identification of the attributes that characterize the prototypical referent of the word.* Once a protypical referent has been acquired for a word, it is hypothesized that the child then identifies some of the more salient features of that prototype. Thus, at this stage, the meaning of the word is represented in the form of a prototypical referent and a small set of basic features.

3. *The allocation of the word to a particular semantic field on the basis of these previously identified features.* Having identified some of the more salient features of the prototypical referent, it is hypothesized that the child then groups that word with other words (which he or she has already acquired) whose prototypical referents possess features that are similar to the identified features of the prototypical referent of the newly acquired word. These common features therefore function, in effect, as a definition of the semantic field to which the word is assigned.

4. *The identification of the features that distinguish the prototypical referent from the prototypical referents of the other words within the same semantic field.* Finally, it is hypothesized that the child then compares the prototypical referent of the word with the prototypical referents of the other words in the same semantic field, and identifies those features that distinguish these prototypes from one another. Thus, by the end of this final stage, the meaning of the word is represented in the lexicon of the child in terms of a prototypical referent, a set of features that serve to define the semantic field to which that word belongs, and a set of features that differentiate the prototypical referent of that word from the prototypical referents of the other words within the same semantic field.

A RECONSIDERATION OF THE DATA

Having briefly outlined this theory, it is now possible to return to the observations that were mentioned in the Introduction to this chapter in order to ascertain how this theory can account for these observations. The first of the observations drew attention to the fact that the earliest object names to be acquired typically refer either to objects that possess a high degree of mobility or to objects that the child manipulates in some way (Nelson, 1973). Now, this finding can be explained by positing that, at the outset of language acquisition, the child simply names those objects to which he or she attends the most. It is well established that infants pay more attention to moving objects than to stationary objects (see, for example, Kagan, 1970), and it is not unreasonable to suppose that the young child also pays more attention to the objects that he or she manipulates in some way than to objects that he or she does not manipulate. Consequently, the finding that children generally label dynamic or manipulable objects during the early stages of lexical development is explicable on the current theory by postulating that the earliest prototypical referents are selected by the child because of their salience for that child.

The second observation mentioned in the Introduction was that the meaning of an object name can be acquired as a result of the child's hearing that word modeled in connection with just a single referent. The evidence for this observation comes both from naturalistic studies (Bowerman, 1978) and from experimental studies (K. E. Nelson & Bonvillian, 1978). This observation is explained on the current theory by postulating that the meaning of an object name is initially represented by means of a prototypical referent; thus, the single exemplar that is labeled with a word could subsequently function as the prototypical referent of that word.

The third observation drew attention to the fact that children sometimes (but not always) overextend or underextend the meanings of object names. The present theory suggests that overextension and underextension are explicable by reference to different underlying processes. Thus, it would be expected that underextension could occur if the child initially uses a word only to refer to the prototypical referent and not to refer to any other object. By contrast, it would be expected that overextension could occur only after the child has performed the preliminary identification of the features that characterize the prototypical referent, after which the child may begin to extend the word to novel referents on the basis that these new referents possess features that are similar to the identified features of the prototypical referent.[2]

The fourth observation—namely, that object names are not usually overextended to label objects for which the child has already acquired more appro-

---

[2]Other possible sources of overextension and underextension are discussed later, in connection with the fourth and sixth observations.

priate names—is a direct prediction of the fourth component process postulated by the current theory. If the child has already acquired a more appropriate name for an object, then this theory would suggest that the child has compared the prototypical referent of this name with the prototypical referents of the other words in the same semantic field, and has identified the features that distinguish these referents from one another. It therefore follows that these other words should not then be overextended to label the objects that fall within the extension of that name, because the extensions of these other words have been differentiated from the extension of that name. The data previously reported by Barrett (1978, 1979) is reproduced here in Tables 9.1–9.4, in order to examine this prediction in detail.

Table 9.1 contains all the overextensions of object names that were produced by Hildegard (as reported by Leopold, 1939, 1949) during her first 2 years of life. The words that this child overextended are given in the first column of Table 9.1, and the objects to which she applied these words are given in the second column, together with her age at the time that she produced each overextension. The third column shows the words that would have been more appropriate for naming the objects to which the overextended word was instead applied, together with the age of Hildegard at the time when she acquired these more appropriate words. From an inspection of this table, it can be seen that in only one instance was a word (*ball*) overextended to label an object for which a more appropriate name had already been acquired (*beads*), and then this word was conjoined with the more appropriate name for that object.[3]

Tables 9.2 and 9.3 contain the overextensions that were produced by two other children, Tina and Emily, who were regularly observed by the present author for a period of 9 months during their second year of life (see Barrett, 1979). Because these observations are drawn from video-recording sessions that took place for half an hour once every 2 weeks, these data are more equivocal than those reported by Leopold, and represent only a sample of the total linguistic productions of these two children. Nevertheless, there is again only one exception to the general prediction that words will not be overextended to label objects for which the child has already acquired more appropriate names—namely, Tina's use of the word *Mummy* when addressing Annette and Martyn (this exception stems from Tina's use of *Mummy* as a general term to request an action from the person addressed, a usage that is discussed in detail in Barrett, 1979). Table 9.4 contains a fourth source of data (taken from Lewis, 1951) against which this prediction can be tested. Again, these data contain only one instance of an overextension ([*ti:*], which was used to name a horse) subsequent to the acquisition of the more appropriate word ([*hɔʃ*]). This overextension occurred

---

[3]The most plausible explanation of the use of *ball–beads* is that Hildegard was trying to draw attention to the spherical shape of the bead by using the compound, one of the features composing the meaning of the word *ball* apparently being "spherical" (see Table 9.5).

TABLE 9.1
Overextensions Produced by Hildegard as Reported
by Leopold (1939, 1949)[a]

Lexical Item	Initial and Subsequent Referents	More Appropriate Lexical Item
Papa	Father/grandfather/mother (1;0); any man (1;2)	Mama (1;3) Mann (1;5)
Mann	Pictures of adults (1;5); any adult (1;6)	Frau (1;7)
Baby	Self/other children (1;2)	Boy (1;8)
Boy	Any child (1;8)	—
Ball	Balls (1;0); balloon/ball of yarn (1;4); observatory dome (1;8); balls of tin foil and paper (called *paper-ball*)/marbles/ovoid ball (called *egg-ball*)/a spherical bead (called *ball-beads*) (1;11)	Balloon (1;10) Beads (1;9)
Tick-tock	Square watch (0;11); other clocks and watches/round gas meter (1;0); fire hose wound on spool (1;2); bathroom scales (1;3); machine with disk-shaped dial (1;4); a round eraser (1;9)	—
Taschentuch	Handkerchief/napkin (1;10)	—
Bobby pin	A particular type of pin used in the child's hair/any shaped hairpin (1;7)	—
Sch	Locomotive game with toy bricks (1;0); real trains and cars/pictures of cars/toy wheelbarrow/old-fashioned carriages/riding motions (1;4)	Auto (1;5) Choo-choo (1;7) Wheelbarrow (1;11) Ride (1;8)
Auto	Pictures of cars (1;5); real cars (1;8); Bradyscope/airplane (called *piep-piep Auto*, literally *bird car*) (1;9); electric mangle (1;10)	Airplane (1;11)
Choo-choo	Trains (1;7); Bradyscope (1;9); airplane/wheelbarrow (1;10); streetcar/a trunk (1;11)	Airplane (1;11) Streetcar (1;11) Wheelbarrow (1;11)
Wheel	A wheelbarrow wheel (1;8); a wheelbarrow (1;10); toy wagon/a ring (1;11)	Wheelbarrow (1;11)
[ʔaʔa]	Dogs (1;0); pictures of dogs (1;1); cows (1;2)	Dog (1;11)
Wauwau	Dogs (1;1); stone lion (1;1); horses (bronze book-ends)/toy dog/soft slippers with face (1;3); fur-clad man in poster (1;4); porcelain elephant (1;6); picture of sloth (1;8); cake lamb (1;9)	Mann (1;5) Shoe (1;6) Cake (1;9) Hottey (horse) (1;10) Dog (1;11)
Boat	Toy sailboat (1;10); airship (1;11)	—
Oil	Cod-liver oil (1;6); all other oily preparations used on child (1;6)	—
Milkbottle	Milkbottles (1;10); bottle containing white toothpowder (1;10)	—
Cake	Candy (1;6); real cakes and sand cakes (1;9)	Candy (1;10)
Cookie	Cookies/crackers/cakes (1;6)	Cracker (1;7) Cake (1;6)
Candy	Candy (1;10); cherries/anything sweet (1;11)	—

[a] Reproduced from Barrett, 1978, by permission of Cambridge University Press. Note that the age of the child at the time of overextension and at the time of acquisition of the more appropriate word is given in parentheses in years and months.

TABLE 9.2
Overextensions Produced by Tina as Reported by Barrett (1979)[a]

Lexical Item	Initial and Subsequent Referents	More Appropriate Lexical Item
Mummy	Mother (1;5;1); Annette (1;7;10) (1;10;2); Martyn (1;8;21) (1;9;4) (1;10;2)	Nettie (1;11;0) Martyn (1;9;18)
Robert	Robert/Martyn (1;7;24)	Martyn (1;9;18)
Car	Toy cars/toy bus (1;7;24)	Bus (1;7;24)[b]
Bus	Toy bus (1;7;24); toy truck (1;8;21)	—
Doggie	Dogs (1;7;24); toy horse (1;8;21)	Horse (1;8;21)[b]
Book	Books/videotape box (1;9;4)	Box (1;10;2)
Horse	Horses (1;8;21); picture of cow (1;9;18)	Cow (1;9;18)[b]
Hat	Hats[c]; bucket on Tina's head (1;10;2)	—
Teeth	Toothbrush (1;11;0)	—
Chair	Chairs[c]; bench (1;11;0)	—
Pencils	Pencils[c]; picture of pen (1;11;0)	—
Monkey	Toy monkey (1;11;0); picture of tortoise (1;11;14)	—
Duck	Toy duck (1;10;2); picture of penguin (1;11;14)	—

[a] The age of the child at the time of overextension and at the time of acquisition of the more appropriate word is given in parentheses in years, months, and days.

[b] These instances were all repetitions of an adult's correction of the overextension.

[c] These uses of the word were not observed during recording sessions, but were reported by the mother.

TABLE 9.3
Overextensions Produced by Emily as Reported by Barrett (1979)[a]

Lexical Item	Initial and Subsequent Referents	More Appropriate Lexical Item
Teddy	Teddy (1;4;6); toy panda (1;5;5) (1;7;14) (1;8;26) (1;10;8) (1;10;22)	—
Baby	Babies[b]; pictures of children (1;6;2); doll (1;11;19)	Girl (1;8;26)
Judy	Judy[b]; pictures of women (1;6;2) (1;8;26)	—
Daddy	Daddy[b]; pictures of men (1;6;2)	Man (1;9;9)
Car	Cars (1;6;2); motorbike (1;6;15) (1;7;0); box Emily is sitting in (1;9;24)	—
Cat	Cats (1;4;6); picture of rabbit (1;6;15); picture of puma (1;9;9)	Rabbit (1;7;0)
Chair	chairs/sofa/large floor cushion (1;7;28)	—
Girl	Girls (1;8;26); dolls (1;8;26) (1;9;24) (1;10;8) (1;11;5) (2;0;2)	—
Mama	Grandmother (1;9;24); Martyn (1;11;5)	Martyn (2;0;2)

[a] The age of the child at the time of overextension and at the time of acquisition of the more appropriate word is given in parentheses in years, months, and days.

[b] These uses of the word were not observed during recording sessions, but were reported by the mother.

TABLE 9.4
Overextensions of Words Used to Refer to Animals Produced by K
as Reported by Lewis (1951)[a]

Age of Child	Cat	Cow	Horse	Large Dog	Small Dog	Toy Dog
	→ ti:[b]					
1;9;11					ti:	
1;10;18		→ ti:				
1;11;1						gɔgi ←
1;11;2					gɔgi ←	
1;11;24			→ ti:			
1;11;25			→ hɔʃ			
1;11;26			(ti:)			
1;11;27	→ puʃi					
2;0;10				→ hɔʃ		
2;0;20		→ muka		gɔgi ←		
Vocabulary at end of period	puʃi	muka	hɔʃ	(bigi) gɔgi	gɔgi	gɔgi
Adult equivalent	Pussy	Moo-cow	Horse	(big) Doggie	Doggie	Doggie

[a] Reproduced from Barrett, 1978, by permission of Cambridge University Press. Note that the age of the child is given in years, months, and days.

[b] In this table, → indicates the introduction of a word and ⊥ indicates that a word ceases to be used.

only 1 day after that on which the more appropriate word had been acquired. Note that the general pattern of these results, which have been derived from naturalistic studies, is in accordance with the results that were obtained by K. E. Nelson and Bonvillian (1973) in an experimental study on early word usage. These authors found that 90% of all the words that were taught to a sample of children in an experimental setting came to acquire extensions that were mutually exclusive of one another.

According to the present theory, the majority of overextensions result from the child's extending a word to label novel referents on the basis that these new referents possess some of the same features that characterize the prototypical referent of that word. However, the data reported in Tables 9.1–9.4 also suggest that a minority of overextensions can occur for reasons other than the common features that are possessed by the different referents of the word. Thus, for example, Tina's overextension of the word *mummy* seemed to be based not on the common features possessed by her mother and by Annette and Martyn, but rather on her usage of this word as a general term for requesting actions from the person addressed. Similarly, Tina's use of the word *teeth* to label a toothbrush (see Table 9.2) was perhaps based on an associative (rather than featural) link between toothbrushes and teeth, whereas Emily's use of *Mama* to label Martyn (see Table 9.3) appeared to stem from the phonetic similarity of the initial syllables in the names for her grandmother and for Martyn. And finally, Hildegard's use of *choo-choo* to label a traveling trunk (see Table 9.1) also seems to be most plausibly explained on an associative basis. Leopold (1949) suggests that she used this word because the sight of the trunk recalled to Hildegard her traveling experiences by association. Grieve and Hoogenraad (1977) have outlined several other nonfeatural strategies that might lead children into producing overextensions, and it is perhaps these nonfeatural strategies that led to the remaining 10% of the words in the study by K. E. Nelson and Bonvillian (1973) not possessing mutually exclusive extensions. Nevertheless, the general prediction that words are not usually overextended to label objects for which the child has already acquired more appropriate names does seem to be upheld by the developmental data, in spite of these exceptions to this general prediction.

Turning now to the fifth observation mentioned in the Introduction (namely, that the objects to which an overextended object name is applied need only have a single feature in common with the initial referents of that word), the data in Tables 9.1–9.3 can be analyzed further in order to demonstrate in detail how the present theory accounts for this observation. Such an analysis is presented in Tables 9.5–9.7 (which follow the pattern of analysis previously adopted by Bowerman, 1978, to facilitate comparison). In these tables, column one lists the overextended words (excluding those previously discussed that did not seem to possess a featural basis), whereas column two suggests possible prototypical referents for these words. As it is hypothesized that the overextension of these words is based upon an identification of the features of these prototypes, some of the features of these prototypes are suggested in column three. In column four, the objects to which the object name was overextended are given, together with the features that these objects have in common with the prototypical referent.

From these analyses, several important points emerge. First, it can be seen from these tables that the features hypothesized to be derived by the child from the prototypical referent can be of two types: those that encode perceptual information about referents, and those that encode functional information about referents. For example, Tina's overextension of the word *book* to label a videotape box indicates that the features that she had derived from the prototype for this word included perceptually based information about the cuboidal shape of the prototype (see Table 9.6). However, Emily's overextension of the word *chair* to label a large floor cushion upon which people sat suggests that the features that this child had derived from the prototypical referent for the word included information about the function of the prototype (see Table 9.7).

The second point to emerge from these analyses is that in order for an object to be labeled with a word, that object does not have to possess all the features that have been abstracted from the prototype, but need only possess one of these features (thus providing additional evidence for the fifth observation mentioned in the Introduction). For example, Hildegard's various uses of the word *ball* suggest that at least two different features ("spherical" and "used for throw-

TABLE 9.5
Analysis of Overextensions Presented in Table 9.1

Lexical Item	Possible Prototype	Features of Prototype	Overextensions and Their Featural Bases
Papa	Father	a. Adult male	Grandfather, men (a)
		b. Caregiver	Mother (b)
Mann	Man	a. Adult	Women (a)
		b. Male	
Baby	Self	a. Human	Children (a, b)
		b. Small	
Boy	Boy	a. Human	Children (a, b)
		b. Small	
Ball	Ball	a. Spherical	Balloon, marbles, observatory
		b. Used for throwing	dome, bead, ball of yarn (a)
			Ovoid, tin foil, and paper balls (b)
Tick-tock	Square watch	a. Square	Round watches (b)
		b. Has dial	
	Round watch	a. Round	Fire hose, eraser (a)
		b. Has dial	Scales, machine with Dial (b)
			Gas meter (a, b)
Taschentuch	Handkerchief	a. Cloth	Napkins (a, b)
		b. Used for wiping self	
Bobby pin	Bobby pin	a. Special shape	Any shaped hair pin (b)
		b. Used in hair	
Sch	Locomotive game	a. Uses bricks	Trains (b)
		b. Accompanied by *sch* sounds	
	Train	a. Has wheels	Cars, carriages (a, b)
		b. Moves people	Wheelbarrow (a)
			Riding motions (b)
Auto	Picture of car	a. Has wheels	Real cars (a, b)
		b. On road	
	Car	a. Machine	Bradyscope, electric
		b. Has wheels	mangle (a)
		c. Moves	Airplane (a, c)
		d. On road	
Choo-choo	Train	a. Machine	Bradyscope (a)
		b. Has wheels	Airplane (a, c)
		c. Moves	Wheelbarrow (b)
		d. On rails	Streetcar (a, b, c, d)
Wheel	Wheel	a. Round	Ring (a)
	Wheelbarrow	a. Has wheels	Toy wagon (a, b)
		b. Using for conveying objects	
[ʔaʔa]	Dog	a. Animal	Cow (a, b)
		b. Four legs	
Wauwau	Dog	a. Animal	Lion, horses, sloth, elephant,
		b. Four legs	lamb (a, b)
		c. Furry	Slippers (d)
		d. Has face	Fur-clad man (c, d)

TABLE 9.5—*Continued*

Lexical Item	Possible Prototype	Features of Prototype	Overextensions and their Featural Bases
Boat	Toy boat	a. Has hull b. Used in play	Airship (a)
Oil	Cod-liver oil	a. Oily b. Used on self	Oils used on self (a, b)
Milkbottle	Milkbottle	a. Bottle b. Contains white substance	Bottle of toothpowder (a, b)
Cake	Candy	a. Edible b. Sweet c. Small and compact	Cake (a, b, c) Sand cakes (c)
Cookie	Cookie	a. Edible b. Small c. Flat	Crackers (a, b, c) Cakes (a)
Candy	Candy	a. Edible b. Sweet	Sweet foods (a, b)

TABLE 9.6
Analysis of Overextensions Presented in Table 9.2

Lexical Item	Possible Prototype	Features of Prototype	Overextensions and their Featural Bases
Robert	Robert	a Adult b. Male	Martyn (a, b)
Car	Toy car	a. Has wheels b. Used in play	Toy bus (a, b)
Bus	Toy bus	a. Has wheels b. Used in play	Toy truck (a, b)
Doggie	Dog	a. Animal b. Four legs	Toy horse (a, b)
Book	Book	a. Cuboid b. Has pages	Videotape box (a)
Horse	Horse	a. Animal b. Four legs	Picture of cow (a, b)
Hat	Hat	a. Made of cloth b. Worn on head	Bucket on head (b)
Chair	Chair	a. Has flat surface b. Used for sitting on	Bench (a, b)
Pencils	Pencil	a. Long b. Thin c. Used for writing	Picture of pen (a, b)
Monkey	Toy monkey	a. Animal b. Has fur c. Used in play	Picture of tortoise (a)
Duck	Toy duck	a. Bird b. Used in play	Picture of penguin (a)

TABLE 9.7
Analysis of Overextensions Presented in Table 9.3

Lexical Item	Possible Prototype	Features of Prototype	Overextensions and their Featural Bases
Teddy	Toy teddy	a. Cuddly b. Used in play	Toy panda (a, b)
Baby	Baby	a. Human b. Small	Pictures of children (a, b) Doll (a, b)
Judy	Judy	a. Adult b. Female	Pictures of women (a, b)
Daddy	Father	a. Adult b. Male c. Caregiver	Pictures of men (a, b)
Car	Car	a. Has wheels b. On road c. Can be sat inside	Motorbike (a, b) Box (c)
Cat	Cat	a. Animal b. Four legs	Picture of rabbit (a, b) Picture of puma (a, b)
Chair	Chair	a. Has flat surface b. Used for sitting on	Sofa (a, b) Floor cushion (b)
Girl	Girl	a. Human form b. Small	Dolls (a, b)

ing'') had been derived by the child from the prototypical referent for this word. However, an observatory dome and a crumpled piece of tin foil that was used as a ball were both called *ball* even though each only possessed one of these two features (see Table 9.5). It therefore appears that the features that are derived from the prototype are not necessarily criterial in nature, and that the objects that fall within the extension of a word may indeed only be linked by a family resemblance instead, as suggested by Bowerman (1978).

Third, the analyses shown in Tables 9.5–9.7 suggest that the prototypical referent of a word can be changed by the child. For example, Hildegard's use of the word *tick-tock,* which she initially learned by reference to a square watch but which she later used to refer to round objects (the fire hose wound on a spool and the eraser), suggests that the initial prototype of a square watch was later exchanged for that of a round watch; similarly, *sch,* which she originally learned in the context of a locomotive game with toy bricks but which she later used to refer to various forms of transport and to riding motions, suggests that the initial prototype of the game was later exchanged for that of a real train (see Table 9.5).

Turning now to the sixth observation mentioned in the Introduction (that semantic fields are sometimes systematically subdivided during the course of early lexical development), the manner in which the current theory accounts for this observation can be illustrated in detail here by reference to the data displayed in Table 9.4, which concern one child's lexical development in a single semantic field—namely, that of four-legged animals. At 1;9;11, this child possessed only one word [ti:], initially learned by reference to a cat, to refer to four-legged animals. Because this word was used to label not only cats, but also small dogs, cows, and horses, it appears that the child derived a feature such as "four legged" in the preliminary identification of the features of the prototype, and then extended the word to label novel referents on the basis of this feature. At 1;11;1, the word [gɔgi] was acquired by reference to a toy dog. It is therefore hypothesized that the child first performed a preliminary analysis of the features that characterized this prototypical referent, deriving the features "four legged" in the process. Consequently, the child grouped this word with [ti:] in the semantic field that was now defined by means of this general feature. At 1;11;2, the child then compared the prototypical referent for [ti:] with the prototypical referent for [gɔgi] and identified the features that distinguish cats from toy dogs (e.g., the differences between their bodily configurations). These features were then stored in the lexicon as the meanings of [ti:] and [gɔgi], with the result that, after this time, small dogs were no longer called [ti:]. The next acquisition was that of the word [hɔʃ], which occurred by reference to a horse, at 1;11;25/26; again it is hypothesized that the child performed a preliminary analysis of the general features of the prototypical referent, identified the features "four legged," and consequently allocated this word to the semantic field already containing [ti:] and [gɔgi] on the basis of this feature. The child then compared the prototype for [hɔʃ] with the prototypes for [ti:] and [gɔgi], and identified the features that distinguish horses from cats and dogs (e.g., "large" versus "small," "hoofed" versus "not hoofed," etc.), storing these features in the lexicon as the meanings of [hɔʃ], [ti:] and [gɔgi]; consequently, after this time, horses were no longer called [ti:]. Sometime before 1;11;27, the prototypical referent for [ti:] was probably changed from a cat to a cow, because at 1;11;27, the child acquired the word [puʃi] to refer to cats (replacing [ti:] in this context), but continued to use [ti:] for referring to cows. Again it is hypothesized that a prototypical referent for [puʃi] was acquired, its general features identified, and the word assigned to this semantic field on the basis of the feature "four legged." The prototype for [puʃi] was then compared with the prototypes for [ti:], [gɔgi], and [hɔʃ], the features distinguishing cats from other animals thus being stored in the lexicon as the meaning of [puʃi]. The extension of this word was consequently differentiated from the extensions of the other words, and the word [ti:] was thus no longer used to refer to cats. At 2;0;10, the child began to call large dogs [hɔʃ], presumably because they shared the feature "large" with the prototype of [hɔʃ]; at 2;0;20, however, the features that distinguished between the prototypes for [hɔʃ] and [gɔgi] were reassessed, with the result that large dogs were then included in the extension of [gɔgi] rather than [hɔʃ]. And finally, also at 2;0;20, [ti:] was dropped altogether and was replaced by [muka] for referring to cows.

From this description, it is apparent that, according to the present theory, a word could be underextended in the lexicon of a child for either one of two different reasons. First, the child might initially use a word only to refer to the prototypical referent and not to refer to any other referents (if he or she has not yet performed the preliminary identification of the features that characterize the prototypical referent), with the result that the word is underextended with respect to the adult lexicon. An example of this type of underextension, involving the word *shoe,* is discussed in detail by Reich (1976), who reports that his son, Adam, initially only included shoes that were in his mother's closet within the extension of this word. Alternatively, underextension could occur if the child fails to correctly identify the features that, in the adult lexicon, differentiate between the referents of two different words; in this case, therefore, one of the words might be overextended while the other is underextended (their extensions nevertheless being mutually exclusive). An example of this second type of under-extension, involving the word [gɔ gi], was discussed earlier, and it was seen that the word [hɔʃ] was overextended to label large dogs that were, as yet, not included within the extension of [gɔ gi] owing to an incorrect identification (from the point of view of the adult language) of the features distinguishing between the prototypes for [hɔʃ] and [gɔ gi]; the subsequent development of the meanings of these two words therefore consisted of a reevaluation of the features that distinguished between the prototypes for these words.

It should also be apparent that, according to the present theory, a featurally based overextension could occur for either one of two different reasons. First, a word could be overextended because the child has incorrectly identified the features that, in the adult lexicon, differentiate between the referents of two different words (the converse of the explanation given earlier for the second type of underextension). An example of this type of extensional error is therefore the overextension of [hɔʃ], as previously described, to label large dogs. Alternatively, overextension could occur because the child does not yet possess an appropriate name for an object that he or she wishes to label; in order to refer to that object, therefore, the child deliberately overextends that word in his or her lexicon whose prototype has the most features in common with that object. An example of this second type of overextension, again taken from Table 9.4, is the overextension of the word [ti:] to refer not only to cats but also to small dogs, cows, and horses (in spite of the manifest differences between these various objects) until more appropriate words had been acquired for labeling these objects.

If this is the case, however, then it would be predicted that in the first type of overextension, the child would not be aware that he or she is incorrectly labeling the objects (as the semantic field is well divided here by the mutually exclusive extensions of related words). However, in the second type of overextension, it would be predicted that the child realizes that the word is being applied to inappropriate objects but, because he or she lacks a more appropriate word, he or she persists in the overextension. Consequently, it would be predicted by the current theory that if children are tested for their comprehension of words that they spontaneously overextend in production by being asked to identify the correct referent from an array of possible referents, two patterns of results should arise. In some cases, these children should be unable to identify the correct referent of a word that they overextend in production and should overextend that word even in comprehension. In other cases, however, these children should be able to identify the correct referent of a word even though they consistently overextend that word in production. Thomson and Chapman (1975), who conducted an experiment of this type, found precisely this twofold result. For example, one child, who overextended *cow* in production to label horses as well as cows, showed no preference between pictures of a horse and of a cow when asked to identify the referent of this word. Another child, however, who overextended *apple* in production to refer to cherries, tomatoes, etc., was nevertheless able to consistently identify the correct referent for this word.

Finally, it can be noted here that the latter situation, in which an extensional asymmetry exists (i.e., when an overextension occurs in production but not in comprehension), offers a solution to the problem of identifying analogical overextensions, a problem that was raised in the Introduction. It was seen there that Nelson (1979) uses the concept of an analogical overextension as a post hoc explanation of extensional errors that cannot otherwise be explained by the functional-core hypothesis. This explanation is unsatisfactory because analogical overextensions are identified by Nelson not on the basis of empirical data but on the basis of adult intuitions instead. However, the preceding discussion suggests that if the child overextends a word to label an object in production but does not overextend the word to label that object in comprehension, then this particular overextension should be interpreted as a statement of similarity (between the prototype and the object) and not as a statement of identity (i.e., the child understands that the object does not in fact fall within the extension of that word). Thus, the use of comprehension data can be regarded as a principal, nonarbitrary method of establishing which overextensions that are produced by a child are in fact analogical overextensions, thus avoiding the use of this concept as a general post hoc explanation of those overextensions that cannot otherwise be explained by a particular theory.

CONCLUSIONS

At the beginning of the Introduction to this chapter, the view of Lakatos (1970), that theoretical controversy engenders scientific progress, was mentioned. This view would certainly seem to be borne out by the past decade of research into early lexical development. Although none of the four competing theories previously proposed have provided an adequate explanation of the early acquisition of the meanings of object names, each of these four theories has nevertheless made a significant contribution to the understanding of early lexical development. Thus, the semantic-feature hypothesis highlighted overextension as an important source of data, and the utility of a featural analysis of such errors. The functional-core hypothesis, however, redressed the bias towards the notion of perceptually based features that was present in the semantic-feature hypothesis, by attributing a major role to the functions of referents in the formation of lexical categories. The prototype hypothesis, however, served to demonstrate the fundamental incapacity of both the semantic-feature and the functional-core hypotheses to provide an adequate explanation of the extensional errors that are made by children during early lexical development, and also drew attention to the utility of the concept of a prototypical referent (and the features that characterize this prototype) in explaining the nature of these errors. And finally, the contrastive hypothesis, by disputing the assumption made by the other three theories that the meanings of words can be acquired in isolation from one another, served to highlight the systematic developments that occur within semantic fields. However, as was seen in the Introduction, in spite of the considerable progress made by these four theories, each of them can only account for a subset of the phenomena that characterize early lexical development.

Consequently, an alternative theory has been proposed in this chapter in an attempt to account in a more comprehensive manner for the data that are currently available on the early acquisition of the meanings of object names. This theory draws upon the more significant contributions made by the four previous theories; it postulates that the meaning of an object name is first acquired in the form of a prototypical referent, and that the child then performs a preliminary identification of the features (either functional or perceptual) that characterize this prototypical referent. It is hypothesized that the word is then assigned to a semantic field on the basis of these initial features, and that the child then identifies the features that differentiate the prototypical referent from the prototypical referents of the other words in the same semantic field.

Thus, this theory suggests that, during the earliest stage of lexical development, a word is likely to be underextended with respect to the adult lexicon, because the child initially uses that word only to refer to the prototypical referent. As soon as some of the more salient features of the prototype are identified, however, the word will then be overextended to label new referents for which the child has not yet acquired more appropriate names, on the basis that these new referents have certain features in common with the prototypical referent of that word. As new words are assigned to the same semantic field, however, the existing overextensions will be gradually rescinded as these new words take over the overextended domains. Consequently, as lexical development proceeds, the child comes to make fewer extensional errors because the semantic field becomes progressively subdivided by the extensions of newly acquired words (the extensional errors made at this later stage of development are most likely to arise from an incorrect identification of the features that differentiate the referents of related words).

It has been seen that this theory can account not only for the six observations that were listed in the Introduction to this chapter, but also for the data that have been obtained in studies of lexical comprehension by young children. It is thus hoped that this chapter has served to elucidate the range of phenomena that have been identified during the last decade ef research into early lexical development by providing a more general and comprehensive theoretical perspective than has hitherto been available from which these various phenomena may be interpreted.

REFERENCES

Barrett, M. D. Lexical development and overextension in child language. *Journal of Child Language,* 1978, *5,* 205-219.

Barrett, M. D. *Semantic development during the single-word stage of language acquisition.* Unpublished doctoral thesis, University of Sussex, 1979.

Bowerman, M. The acquisition of word meaning: An investigation into some current conflicts. In N. Waterson & C. Snow (Eds.), *The development of communication.* New York: Wiley, 1978.

Clark, E. V. What's in a word? On the child's acquisition of semantics in his first language. In T. E. Moore (Ed.), *Cognitive development and the acquisition of language.* New York: Academic Press, 1973.

Clark, E. V. Knowledge, context, and strategy in the acquisition of meaning. In D. P. Dato (Ed.), *Developmental psycholinguistics: Theory and applications. Georgetown University Round Table on Languages and Linguistics 1975.* Washington, D.C.: Goergetown University Press, 1975.

Grieve, R., & Hoogenraad, R. Using language if you don't have much. In R. J. Wales & E. Walker (Eds.), *New approaches to language mechanisms.* Amsterdam: North Holland, 1977.

Kagan, J. The determinants of attention in the infant. *American Scientist,* 1970, *58,* 298-306.

Lakatos, I. Falsification and the methodology of scientific research programmes. In I. Lakatos & A. Musgrave (Eds.), *Criticism and the growth of knowledge.* Cambridge, Eng.: Cambridge University Press, 1970.

Leopold, W. F. *Speech development of a bilingual child: A linguist's record. Volume 1: Vocabulary growth in the first two years.* Evanston, Ill.: Northwestern University Press, 1939.

Leopold, W. F. *Speech development of a bilingual child: A linguist's record. Volume 3: Grammar and general problems in the first two years.* Evanston, Ill.: Northwestern University Press, 1949.

Lewis, M. M. *Infant speech: A study of the beginnings of language.* London: Routledge and Kegan Paul, 1951.

Nelson, K. Structure and strategy in learning to talk. *Monographs of the Society for Research in Child Development,* 1973, *38*(Serial No. 149).

Nelson, K. Concept, word, and sentence: Interrelations in acquisition and development. *Psychological Review,* 1974, *81,* 267-285.

Nelson, K. The conceptual basis for naming. In J. Macnamara (Ed.), *Language learning and thought.* New York: Academic Press, 1977.

Nelson, K. Features, contrasts and the FCH: Some comments on Barrett's lexical development hypothesis. *Journal of Child Language,* 1979, *6,* 139-146.

Nelson, K., Rescorla, L., Gruendel, J., & Benedict, H. Early lexicons: What do they mean? *Child Development,* 1978, *49,* 960-968.

Nelson, K. E., & Bonvillian, J. D. Concepts and words in the two-year-old: Acquisition of concept names under controlled conditions. *Cognition,* 1973, *2,* 435-450.

Nelson, K. E., & Bonvillian, J. D. Early language development: Conceptual growth and related processes between 2 and 4½ years of age. In K. E. Nelson (Ed.), *Children's language* (Vol. 1). New York: Gardner Press, 1978.

Reich, P. A. The early acquisition of word meaning. *Journal of Child Language,* 1976, *3,* 117–123.

Thomson, J., & Chapman, R. Who is daddy? The status of two-year-olds' overextended words in use and comprehension. *Papers and Reports on Child Language Development, Stanford University,* 1975, *10,* 59–68.

10 Theoretical Issues in Semantic Development

David S. Palermo
Pennsylvania State University

> *But although our knowledge begins with experience, it does not follow that it arises from experience. For it is quite possible that even our empirical experience is a compound of that which we receive through impressions, and of that which our own faculty of knowledge (initiated by sensuous impressions), supplies from itself, a supplement which we do not distinguish from that raw material, until long practice has roused our attention and rendered us capable of separating one from the other.*
> —Kant, I. Supplement 4, p. 1. Trans. by Max Muller
> from Vol. 1, Kant's *Critique of Pure Reason.*

In previous discussions of theoretical issues related to semantic development, I have focused upon the necessity to account for the holistic or synthetic nature of the meanings of words for the child acquiring the language. That synthetic theoretical orientation has been placed in contrast to a componential, or analytic, account that focuses upon the building of complete meanings through the process of adding elements or features. It would appear that there is little point in restating the arguments relating to the weaknesses of the analytic approach to semantic development here. The problems with the latter approach have been carefully detailed by several persons elsewhere (e.g., Anglin, 1977; Nelson, 1974; Palermo, 1978a, 1978b). The major disadvantage, however, of rejecting a componential or feature theoretical approach to semantic development lies in the lack of a comparable heuristically simple conceptual structure for dealing with the synthetic nature of meaning. We have no clear and precise way to talk about conceptual wholes and the relations among those whole units. In short, we have no theory that allows us to identify the variables of importance and how those variables relate to each other. Without such a theory, it is difficult to give an account of how the child acquires a meaningful interpretation of the world that makes it possible to interpret that world and to talk about the objects and events in it. In the present chapter I hope to further develop a theory of semantic development and to suggest some lines of research that may lead to additional elaboration of the theory.

My concerns here are with questions raised in the quotation from Kant that introduces this chapter. Kant points to the relation between organism and experience and the variables that enter into the interpretation of experience by the organism. The problem is how we make sense of, or give meaning to, our experiences. Notice that the issue is one of giving meaning to our experiences, not deriving meaning from our experiences. The meanings are not out there in the real world waiting to be discovered but, rather, they are in the person who encounters the real world and imposes a meaning upon it. To say that a person provides the meaning is not, however, to say that the objects and events of reality have no structure that influences the organism that assigns the meaning to them. As has been pointed out by others e.g., (MacNamara, in press; Piaget, 1969)., there are important distinctions between perception and meaning. The point is that even though it is structured, the real world is ambiguous and the meaning is assigned to objects and events by the person and is not given by, nor picked up from, information that is in the external world.

Subsidiary to the larger question of how we assign meaning are questions related to how we establish similarities that allow for categories or classes and thereby make distinctions that separate classes or categories. What are the dimensions that we are capable of discriminating, dimensions we are likely to use for discrimination, and dimensions we are likely to ignore as we formulate classes? How does it happen, for example, that we classify static objects as a category distinct from moving objects rather than basing our classification system on some other basis that cuts across the static–dynamic dimension? Equally important, we know little about the basis of our conceptualizing of the relations among classes. It is not at all clear, for example, why we should classify some plants or animals as more closely related than others. There is no obvious reason that chihuahua and St. Bernard are considered to be in the same class but chihuahua and kitten, for example, are in different classes. One cannot appeal to our scientific knowledge of the biological relations among these animals as the basis for these classifications because the classifications of such taxonomic categories by people unaware of the science of biology reveal similar systems of relations (Berlin, Breedlove, & Raven, 1973).

The last question, subsidiary to the previous two questions and upon which this chapter is supposed to focus, has to do with how we develop the ability to convey our classifications or categories and the relations among those categories to other persons. How do we transfer the ideas in one mind to another mind in the meaningful manner that we call communication? Looked at in light of the previous questions, it becomes clear that language is but a tool that makes it possible for people to convey concepts and relations among concepts to other people. Language acquisition, then, is the learning of the use of a tool for communicating what is already known in the form of concepts and concept relations.

THE STRUCTURE OF CONCEPTS

It is assumed here that the child, as the adult, uses words to represent concepts and relations among those concepts. Words represent concepts and relations for which objects and events are exemplars. The concepts and relations are abstract and specified in terms of a set of differentially weighted, context-sensitive rules. The rules that specify the structure of the concepts and relations allow one to classify particular exemplars of those concepts and relations that are encountered in the real world. The particulars in the real world may vary in terms of their exemplariness of the abstract categories. Some will be classified as good or prototypic, others poor or peripheral, and still others as nonmembers of the class or relation in any particular context. The structures are, therefore, assumed to be of two types: those that are specified by the set of rules underlying what we usually refer to as nouns in the language and those that are specified by the rules underlying what we usually refer to as verbs[1] in the language. Thus, there are category or class structures and relational structures, the latter serving the function of relating the former.

The nature of the rules that establish the structure of a concept is difficult to specify because the rules form a part of the tacit knowledge system of the conceptualizer. At this point, we have less understanding of these rules than of syntactic rules, for example, which also form a part of the tacit knowledge system. We do not know, for example, what rules we use to decide that arm chairs, rockers, Chippendale chairs, and bean-bag chairs are all members of the category *chair* whereas tables, stools, and rocks are members of other categories. It may be possible, however, to understand more clearly the structure of a concept, be it relational or categorical, by examining the relations among the set of exemplars encompassed by that concept. One way to think of those relations is in terms of a spherical metaphor. The tacit rules specify those exemplars that fall within the category and those that fall outside the category in any particular context. In addition, the rules specify the relative position of the exemplars within the conceptual space defining the category. In most cases of natural categories, some exemplars are more central to the meaning of the conept

---

[1]Obviously, many adjectives and adverbs are used to convey relational meanings. It is assumed that these linguistic forms are closely related to verbs, as many linguists since Plato have noted (Lyons, 1969).

whereas others are more peripheral. Thus, the rules identify the prototypicality of a particular exemplar and they also specify the relative similarity or position of the exemplars in the spherical space. Prototypes stand at the center of the sphere whereas other exemplars are positioned in the infinite number of directions emanating from the central core. Thus, the tacit rules for any concept determine the basis for deciding whether any particular object or event in the real world is to be included in the conceptual category, establish the prototypicality of that exemplar with respect to the conceptual category, and specify the similarity relations among exemplars within the category.

Although those advocating prototype theories (e.g., Nelson, 1974; Palermo, 1978a, 1978b; Rosch, 1973, 1975) have tended to emphasize the holistic nature of the conceptual meaning derived within specific contexts, Rosch and Mervis (1975) have suggested that the problem of similarity among exemplars may be handled within the framework of family resemblance that they borrowed from Wittgenstein (1953). Although there are no defining sets of features for a concept that determine whether a particular exemplar is a representative of that concept, exemplars of a concept do have some attributes in common (as opposed to distinctive features) so that there is a family resemblance among them. Some exemplars are more prototypic of a concept in that they may be characterized as having more attributes in common with other exemplars of the concept whereas other exemplars have fewer common attributes and are, therefore, more peripheral to the concept. It should be noted that the idea of partially accounting for the relations among exemplars of a conceptual category in terms of family resemblance allows for a similarity metric that not only relates prototypic exemplars to peripheral exemplars but also helps to account for relations among peripheral exemplars where close similarities and vast differences may exist depending on the positions in the spherical space of the peripheral exemplars. For example, the difference between chihuahuas and St. Bernards is large whereas those between malamutes and elkhounds or salukis and greyhounds is small, although all of these pairs might be considered peripheral exemplars of the dog category. Rosch and Mervis (1975) have demonstrated in several contexts how the relations among meanings of prototypic and peripheral exemplars may be, in part, a function of attribute overlap of the exemplars.

The principle of family resemblance not only helps to account for the relations among exemplars of a class but also has the advantage of making clearer another aspect of prototype theory that has been problematic for feature theories. If a set of criterial features define a category as feature theorists have suggested, then all exemplars of the category must have all of the criterial features and, therefore, should be equally representative of the category. As previously suggested, and as several investigators have demonstrated empirically (e.g., Andersen, 1975; Labov, 1973; Rosch, 1975), this is not the case for most natural categories. Rather, almost any object or event may be categorized as an exemplar of almost any conceptual category if the context focuses upon an aspect of the exemplar that is relevant to the concept (Palermo, 1978a). For example, there are many exemplars of the concept *furniture* ranging from those close to the core meaning (e.g., chair or table) to those more pheripheral to the core meaning (e.g., rug or lamp). Seldom would rocks or logs be considered as a part of the furniture category, but they could be considered furniture in the context of a campfire where people were sitting on logs and placing their food on rocks. Thus, the meaning of furniture may be extended to include logs and rocks in appropriate contexts, although logs and rocks would not be considered close to the core meaning, or prototypic exemplars, of the furniture category. The focus on the functional aspects of rocks and logs in this context permits this extension of the concept meaning to these exemplars. Similar extensions based upon perceptual, affective, social, or other aspects of exemplars could be constructed as well, as is often done in the case of figurative uses of language. Consider the following mundane examples as instances of such extensions: ''The basketball player is a tower among ordinary people.''; ''The teacher is a dirty rat.''; and ''That person is a social butterfly.'' Such focusing, or foregrounding, points to the need for recognizing the context-sensitive nature of conceptual rules that take into account the relative salience and/or weighting of different attributes of exemplars of a concept yielding different meanings for those exemplars in varying contexts.

In discussing a prototype semantic theory, I have suggested elsewhere (Palermo, 1978a, 1978b) that there may be other contextually determined effects on the rules defining the meaning of a concept. Context may lead to transformations of the rules or the generation of new rules that change the relations among exemplars of the concept—that is, the relative positions of exemplars encompassed by a concept may vary in the semantic space defined by the concept. Thus, the core meaning of the concept *furniture* might be expected to shift in the context specified by ''living-room'' furniture, ''bedroom'' furniture, or ''kitchen'' furniture. Even though some shifting in meaning would be expected as a function of contextual variations, if it should be the case that the meaning of a concept, such as *furniture,* were to change completely as a function of context, then a prototype theory of meaning cannot account for the commonality of meaning across contexts. Each new context would require a new prototypic structure analogous to the theoretical need for a new set of features required of feature theories faced with the same problem. Both the stability and the variation in the meaning of words and their conceptual referents is something that needs to be taken into consideration.

A recent set of experiments conducted in our laboratory bears on this question (MacKenzie & Palermo, 1980). The question of concern related to the stability of the normative data collected by Rosch (1975) establishing the prototypical structure of sets of exemplars for several conceptual categories. Rosch established the category norms in the context of the category name alone. In addition, she demonstrated that exemplars close to the core meaning of the concept, defined in terms of the normative data, are classified faster as members of the conceptual category than are peripheral exemplars (Rosch, 1975). Our efforts focused upon the effects of contextual manipulation on the category structures reflected in the relations among the exemplars identified on the basis of the normative data. For example, it is known from Rosch's norms that "table" is a prototypic exemplar of the category *furniture* and "rug" is a peripheral exemplar. It is also known from Rosch's experiments that it takes less time to classify prototypic exemplars as members of the category than peripheral exemplars. If the normative data do reflect the conceptual structure of the categories, and that structure is not ephemeral, then it should be the case that performance affected by that structure will reflect the same relationships among the exemplars of a concept regardless of the context in which the concept is used. In terms of the furniture exemplar, the prototypic exemplar "table" and the peripheral exemplar "rug" should maintain their relative positions in the *furniture* concept regardless of the context in which furniture may occur.

After demonstrating the replicability of Rosch's (1975) findings that classification time is relatively faster for prototypic exemplars of conceptual categories than peripheral exemplars in a linguistically barren context and in the context of the category name, the category names were placed in adjectival and sentential contexts designed to be appropriate for the prototypic or the peripheral exemplars of the concepts. The relative classification time for exemplars varying in normative prototypicality were compared and used as a basis for inferring the effect of context on the structure of the categories. For example, subjects were required to decide whether the normatively prototypic exemplars "apple" and "pear," and the normatively peripheral exemplars "coconut" and "date," are members of the category *fruit* in the contexts:

1. He climbed the orchard tree to pick the ripe /fruit/.
2. He climbed the palm tree to pick the tropical /fruit/.

The context of the first sentence was designed to be appropriate for the prototypic, but inappropriate for the peripheral, exemplars whereas the second sentence was appropriate to the peripheral exemplars and inappropriate to the prototypic exemplars. Preliminary research established that prototypic exemplars were, in fact, called to mind in the first context and peripheral exemplars in the second context.

The results indicated that in the sentence contexts appropriate to the prototypic exemplars, those exemplars were classified more rapidly than peripheral exemplars, as expected. The sentence contexts appropriate to peripheral exemplars led to slower classification of good exemplars and faster classification of poor exemplars, relative to the other contexts, but there was no reversal in classification speed of prototypic and peripheral exemplars. In both contexts, classification of prototypic exemplars was faster. There was no evidence that peripheral became prototypic nor that protytypic became peripheral exemplars when the context was deliberately constructed to be appropriate for peripheral exemplars and inappropriate for prototypic exemplars. The same results were obtained when the category labels were presented in the context of a modifying adjective (e.g., living-room furniture and kitchen furniture).

These experiments provide evidence that the tacit rules used to classify common objects of the real world into categories and to specify their structural relations are sensitive to contextual manipulations but, at the same time, the classification and the structural relations remain relatively stable regardless of the context in which those semantic categories occur. The effort in these experiments was directed to providing contexts in which exemplars, ordinarily considered peripheral to the meaning of a category, might be considered central, or prototypical, whereas normatively prototypical exemplars might be considered as peripheral. Insofar as the task and categories used were sensitive to structural changes in the meanings of the categories due to contextual modifications, the experiments reflected changes only in the relative positions of exemplars of a category with respect to each other and failed to show absolute changes in the relations among exemplars. The contextual manipulations expanded or contracted the structural distances among exemplars but the results provided no evidence that the basic categorical structure was modified. Contexts designed as appropriate to prototypic exemplars of a category yielded results that suggested a topological expansion of the semantic space whereas contexts designed as appropriate to peripheral exemplars of a category yielded results that suggested a topological contraction of the semantic space as reflected in the differences in response speeds between prototypic and peripheral exemplars in the two contexts. In short, contextual changes led to changes in topological relations among exemplars but no exemplars that were peripheral in one context became prototypical in another, or vice versa.

Both the stability and the variability in meaning that are reflected in the results of these experiments are important to any theory of semantics. The problem for those concerned with these issues, regardless of their theoretical approach, is the two-horned dilemma that words, or other linguistically meaningful units, are used to convey different meanings in different contexts and yet maintain some, as yet poorly specified, commonality of meaning across contexts. The theoretical problem centers around the need to account for both the *commonality* and the *variability* that are readily apparent in the modifications in meaning that occur when contexts are changed, as in the experiments just described, as well as others (e.g., Barclay, Bransford, Franks, McCarrell, & Nitsch, 1974). Perhaps more important, we need to account for the seemingly broader commonality-variability problem evident in the figurative use of language. It is clear, for example, that when Shelley wrote in *Prometheus Unbound* that "My soul is an enchanted boat," the meaning conveyed by the phrase both preserves the basic structure of the meanings of the words involved while, at the same time, modifying them in an as yet unspecifiable but, presumably, rule-governed way that may be understood by others who also have a tacit knowledge of those rules. To say that the meanings of the words are fixed to certain readings is to say that Shelley's phrase is an anomaly or is meaningless, which is absurd. On the other hand, to argue that words may convey any and all meanings would suggest that Shelley could have substituted "dog," for example, in the phrase and conveyed the same meaning, which is equally absurd. The particular words used by Shelley were selected both because of the stable aspects of their meaning and because of the variable aspects of their meaning, which allowed them to be brought together in that phrase to generate a specific meaning appropriate to the concepts the author wished to convey in that context. Tacit knowledge of the rules underlying the concepts and the relations into which those concepts may enter make it possible both for the creation and the understanding of a metaphor such as that created by Shelley.

Another apsect of conceptual structure implied in the discussion to this point should be made explicit. Most natural categories have no well-defined boundaries, a point made most clearly by Rosch (1973). The meaning of a concept is best exemplified by some objects or events encountered in the real world, but boundaries that specify what belongs within the conceptual category and what should be excluded appear to be fuzzy because they are strongly influenced by context. Furthermore, as Rosch and Mervis (1975) have shown, peripheral exemplars are more likely to be classed in more than one category. The fuzzy boundaries of different conceptual categories may overlap, as, for example, Labov (1973) and Andersen (1975) demonstrated, and may be included within other larger categories as in the case of hierarchical relations. The core meaning of a concept is specified by the rules that define the abstract concept, but what counts as an exemplar of that concept will vary, as well the relation of the exemplars to the core meaning as a function of context. It would appear that the rules that define what exemplars may be included in the category are themselves generative of other rules dependent on the context, so that exemplars included in one context are excluded in other contexts.[2] The nature of the rules that specify the structure of any natural concept and how those rules are modified by contextual constraints are, unfortunately, not specifiable at this point.

Some significant subset of the rules specifying the structure of concepts is surely naturally determined in the sense that the human organism classifies in particular ways as, for example, Rosch (1973) has reported for colors and geometric forms, and Berlin et al. (1973) have reported for taxonomic classes. The basis for forming classes appears to include at least functional, perceptual,

---

[2]Weimer (personal communication) 1980 argues that boundaries of concepts are never fuzzy. Boundaries appear to be fuzzy because some exemplars are counted in the class in some contexts and out of the class in other contexts. The result is that across contexts the concept boundaries appear to be fuzzy. Weimer's point is that the rules defining a concept generate rules appropriate to contexts specifying exactly what are to be counted as exemplars in any particular context.

social, and affective dimensions, but we have little guidance at this point as to the nature of these abstract dimensions or the rules into which these dimensions enter as variables. There are hints coming from a variety of sources, however, as researchers are beginning to look at the manner in which infants and young children categorize the world about them. Consider, for example, the recent research and theoretical account provided by Haith (1978, 1980) of infant visual behavior. Haith has suggested that newborn infants follow a specified set of rules that guide visual-search activity. According to Haith, the basic rule, or principle, governing the infant's scanning is to maximize visual–cortical firing rate. He proposes an Ambient Scan Routine and an Inspection Scan Routine. The first facilitates the detection of visual stimuli and the second generates eye movements that maximize visual–cortical firing rate. With these two principles, Haith accounts for scanning in darkness and formless light fields, fixation of edges and bars, crossing of edges, scanning of stimuli with varying edge density, acquisition of accommodation, and binocular convergence, as well as speculations about later visual activity as maturational development occurs.

Even though Haith's theory deals with perception rather than cognition as such, his approach suggests the beginnings of principles that underlie classificatory dimensions and that will play a part in subsequent cognitive development. It might also be noted that Haith points out that the natural movements of the eyes are on a horizontal plane. This natural biological characteristic of the organism makes it more probable that the infant's initial perceptual classes will be divided on the basis of vertical contours because the scanning patterns are more likely to encounter vertical than horizontal contours. It is not that the infant cannot scan vertically, only that it is more natural to scan horizontally, and this biological characteristic influences the infant's perceptual experience. It seems very likely that there are many other naturally determined constraints on the perceptual differentiations made by the infant. Recent research has demonstrated, for example, that infants have an innate capacity for shape constancy (Schwartz & Day, 1979), and other research concerned with infant visual capacities assume a natural ability to distinguish figure from ground. Other aspects of the innate organization of perception are currently being explored in research with infants (cf. Cohen & Salapatek, 1975).

In the auditory realm, we now have impressive evidence of the natural classificatory capabilities of the infant on dimensions that are relevant to speech (e.g., Eimas, Siqueland, Jusczyk, & Vigorito, 1971; Molfese, Freeman, & Palermo, 1975; Trehub, 1973). Again, at least some of these classificatory abilities appear to be based upon the biological characteristics of the organism (Molfese & Molfese, 1979). Similar research on the gustatory and olfactory senses yields indications of natural dimensions demarking classes there, too (e.g., Crook & Lipsitt, 1976; Rieser, Yonas, & Wikner, 1976).

There are less well-documented indications of natural relational concepts, too. Chang and Trehub (1977) have demonstrated relational processing of auditory stimuli at 5 months. Certainly, aspects of movement are naturally conceptualized relations, regardless of conclusions about object permanence (Moore, Borton, & Darby, 1978), whereas it would seem that static relations are less likely to prove natural. MacNamara (1972) has argued that this should be the case, and Nelson (1973, 1975) has provided evidence that children's early meanings in many instances may be closely tied to function and to changing aspects of referents as opposed to static attributes of those referents. One might also expect that process verbs would appear before state verbs in the acquisition process; Brown's (1973) data seem to support that hypothesis. There must be many as yet unknown natural dimensions forming the basis of relational-concept formation that are common to most humans. Certainly, there are individual differences but, as MacNamara (1972) has pointed out, the child seldom forms bizarre concepts, indicating that there must be some constraints on what is classed together. Further research specifically oriented to establishing what those constraints are, both in infancy and at later maturational developmental periods, should prove helpful in expanding our understanding of the perceptual systems and their relation to the rules and structure of the abstract conceptual system.

Acquired concepts presumably derive from or are induced from objects and events classified, in part, on the basis of natural dimensions in complex interrelations with distinctions acquired perforce the child's interactions with his or her environment. In the latter case, a distinction may be made between those concepts that are based upon the tradition of rules and practices that are the culture into which the child is born and those specifically or deliberately learned distinctions (Hayek, 1978). It is clear that certain classes (e.g., colors and animals) are naturally categorized because humans are biologically constructed as they are, but other categories may be formed in addition to the natural categories. The categories of *furniture* and *sport,* for example, are not likely candidates for natural categories. They are, however, likely to be formed on the basis of some abstract dimensions that are natural—some that are culturally acquired and some that are deliberately learned. Those dimensions, in turn, are related by natural and acquired relational rules, allowing us to generate which exemplars belong to the categories furniture and sport and where in our conceptual space for each category the exemplars fall. Finally, it should be noted that although some bases for forming conceptual categories may be more natural than others, it is clear that seemingly unnatural classes can be formed with deliberate effort as, for example, the classes required in relating spoken to written or printed language are required in learning to read. The letter–sound relations are clearly unnatural as is obvious from the fact that establishing the relation between print and the conceptual system requires conscious effort. The relation between speech sounds and the conceptual system is much more natural, and yet culturally acquired; witness the fact that children learn different languages in different speech communities at about the same rate. The abstract dimensions and rules that compose the conceptual system, therefore, emerge from biological, cultural, and rational sources.

It should be noted that the sense of words—that is, the conceptual structure that the words represent—in the case of at least some natural categories must be known to the child and adult alike as a function of the nature of the organism. The commonality in meaning for these words is assured by the commonality of the biological organism that assures commonality in the conceptual structure. As has been demonstrated (Mervis, Catlin, & Rosch, 1975), for example, the child's prototype of a natural color concept is the same as that of an adult, although the boundaries of the color concept may differ for the two age groups. In the case of words representing acquired concepts, however, the commonality of meaning is a function of the commonality of the abstracting characteristics of the organism and the particular exemplars and context experienced by the individual organism. There is, therefore, likely to be greater variability in the sense, or meaning, of words representing acquired concepts than words representing natural concepts.

Some research is beginning to appear in the literature exploring the development of what might be viewed as acquired concepts. In the case of the concept of *human face* or *dog,* for example, it might be expected that the concept structure might initially be a function of the faces or dogs with which the child comes into contact in terms of particular exemplars, pictures of exemplars, and verbal input from others about exemplars of the concepts. Cohen and his colleagues, for instance, have recently demonstrated that infants as young as 30 weeks of age form prototypically structured concepts of human faces based upon several varying exemplars (Cohen & Strauss, 1979; Strauss, 1979). Strauss interprets his research as indicating that the infant uses some sort of averaging procedure over experienced exemplars to form a prototype for the category *human face*. This hypothesis that infants register each exemplar and compute a running average, however, seems to be a rather simplistic account of what is surely a much more complicated process. At least two factors argue against Strauss' hypothesis. First, Schwartz and Day (1979) have shown, using the habituation technique, that 8-week-old infants have shape constancy—that is, different orientations of the same object are categorized by the child as the same object. If the averaging hypothesis were correct, it would be impossible to establish shape constancy because the infants would average the various retinal images of any particular shape viewed from different perspectives and respond differentially to the averaged retinal image than to retinal images that differ markedly from the average. The infants, however, habituated to one version of the shape and treated all others as the same shape—that is, they showed evidence of knowing the relations among the shapes rather than averaging all the exemplars presented. Schwartz and Day's experiments, incidentally, provide strong support for the innate abstract classificatory capacities of the infant—that is, exemplars with the same perceptual relations are classed as the same shape.

The second type of evidence arguing against the averaging hypothesis is provided by K. E. Nelson and Bonvillian (1978), who have shown that children may form concepts on the basis of a single exemplar. They presented children with a single exemplar of a new concept and found that that single positive exemplar resulted in generalization of the concept to similar objects. It is not necessary to have a number of different exemplars to form a concept. Thus, even though the Cohen and Strauss' (1979) and Strauss' (1979) experiments are of considerable interest in demonstrating the conceptual abilities of very young infants and the prototypic structure of those conceptual categories, a theoretical account of those results in terms of either feature averaging or feature frequency (Goldman & Homa, 1977) seems unsatisfactory.

In any case, at least some of the child's acquired concepts are likely to be different from those of an adult, resulting in overextending or underextending the use of words associated with those concepts to exemplars that adults might exclude or include. Both overextension and underextension should be anticipated in early language acquisition because the child's concepts may be, at least in part, a function of the particulars the child encounters. Note, however, that the child's concept is not an incomplete version of the adult concept but, rather, it is a complete concept that may be different from an adult's with respect to the abstract rules defining the concept, especially with respect to the boundaries and relations with other categories. Thus, children may not, in the case of the dog concept, for example, draw the line between wolves and dogs that an adult might. Similarly, the child may not have the concept that dogs are in a category of animals that bite when teased. Given some minimal experience with dogs, however, the child is quite capable of forming the concept *dog* much as the adult does. Three year olds with whom we have worked had no difficulty at all identifying some 300 plus breeds as exemplars of the category *dog* distinct from other animals. Most concepts of child and adult, both natural and acquired, are likely to be the same. It is only the number of conceptual classes, their relations, and the recognition and use of these classes and relations that are likely to differ from child to adult and from individual to individual.

In summary, the following can be said about the conceptual system:

1. Concepts are defined in terms of a tacitly known set of rules that identify abstract categories and the basis for relating categories to each other.

2. The tacit rules, in turn, provide a basis for classifying exemplars encountered in the real world as members or nonmembers of the category.

3. Concrete exemplars of the abstract category vary with respect to how well they fit the conceptual specification for the category.

4. The structural relations among exemplars of an abstract category may be conceived metaphorically as spherically shaped. Prototypic exemplars are located at the core of the sphere whereas poor exemplars are towards the surface or periphery of the spherical semantic space.

5. What counts as an exemplar of a category is contextually related. Thus, the boundaries of concepts appear fuzzy in the sense that some exemplars are counted as members of the category in some contexts but not in other contexts,

and the topological relations among exemplars in the spherical conceptual space will vary with context. In short, the rules defining a conceptual category are generative in that they may create rules appropriate to specific contexts.

6. Concepts are both natural and acquired. More appropriately, concepts are relatively natural and relatively acquired in the sense that some are determined primarily by the biological structure of the organism, others are acquired rather naturally in the cultural mileau, and others are acquired by rational effort devoted to dimensions and rules that are less related to the biological nature of the organism. Different animals and different maturational levels of the same animal may conceptualize differently. Natural concepts provide a common base for conceptualization across individuals within a species. Culturally acquired concepts provide a common base for conceptualization across individuals within social groups of a species.

7. Acquired concepts are based upon rules for combining natural dimensions for making distinctions and acquired bases for making distinctions. Acquired categories, therefore, vary across individuals and the exemplars included within those categories vary as a function of individual differences in the rules for forming the abstract classes.

8. Words in particular, and language in general, are used to communicate the conceptual system in terms of the particulars, or exemplars, encountered in the world of the language user.

THE MEANING OF EXPERIENCE

Up to this point, we have been discussing the subsidiary question of how we classify. Let us turn now to the larger question of how we make sense of, or give meaning to, our experiences. One thing that has become particularly clear in the wake of Chomsky's influence on psychology is the pervasiveness of ambiguity. Until fairly recently, most psychologists have treated ambiguity as a curiosity exemplified in visual phenomena such as the Nekker Cube, the vase–face figure, and the Ames rooms. Chomsky added sentences to the psychologist's list of ambiguous curiosities. More important, of course, Chomsky pointed to the necessity of making a distinction between the surface or exemplary level of a phenomenon and the abstract or deep structural level of that phenomenon in accounting for the meaning of such ambiguous sentences (Chomsky, 1957). As Weimer (1973, 1974; see also Hayek, 1969) points out, Chomsky focused upon the primacy of the abstract.

It has taken some time for psychologists to accept the implications of ambiguity for a theory of the mind. Many assumed that Chomsky treated ambiguity as a special case too, albeit requiring drastic changes in scientific conceptualizations and research approaches to the study of mind. That interpretation led to the study of ambiguity as a particular type of phenomenon, a class of sentences that required separate analyses in contrast to apparently unambiguous sentences. Recent work by psychologists has now made it clear that ambiguity is the rule rather than the exception. The work of Bransford and his colleagues (e.g., Bransford & McCarrell, 1974), for example, has made it evident that almost any visual or verbal stimulus (and surely any other stimulus) may be interpreted in more than one meaningful way. In short, all surface-structure phenomena are ambiguous.

Given a world of stimuli all of which are ambiguous with respect to their meaning, and given that we as individuals are very seldom confused by, nor even aware of, that ambiguity, the question immediately arises as to why we fail to note the ambiguity. Some theorists (e.g., Jenkins, 1977; Ortony, Reynolds, & Arter, 1978; Ortony, Schallert, Reynolds, & Antos, 1978) have argued that the context of a sentence or some other stimulus acts to disambiguate the sentence or stimulus. In its simplest form, the argument is that the ambiguity of a sentence, for example, is eliminated by the sentences that precede or follow the ambiguous sentence in question. The problem with this account seems obvious. The sentences that precede or follow an ambiguous sentence are themselves ambiguous. There is no way, in principle, that something that is itself ambiguous can act to disambiguate another ambiguity.[3]

Given this state of affairs, that the surface form of one sentence cannot disambiguate the surface form of another sentence, even when the independent deep-structure forms of those sentences are examined, the meanings of the sentences must be related at some more abstract level. Furthermore, the sentences must be related to the ambiguous context in which they occur, and those contexts must be related to the contexts in which they occur, and so on. It seems clear that the only manner in which a sentence, or any other stimulus, can become meaningful—that is, unambiguous—is from the meaning placed upon it by the person who is interpreting the sentence or stimulus. The disambiguation must come from the person and cannot come from the stimulus or stimuli that form the context for the stimulus. The constraints upon meaning—that is, what determines the particular meaning selected from the many possible meanings—must come from within the person and not from the stimuli without. In short, persons must have some sort of basis for making a judgment about the meaning of the stimuli about them. They must have a conceptual framework that makes it possible to place a meaningful and, therefore, unambiguous interpretation upon those events that occur in their environment. They must have some sort of theory about the world that allows them to interpret what goes on about them in a systematic way (Weimer, 1973).

---

[3]In making this point on another occasion, it was pointed out to me that the sentence, $a + b = 12$ is ambiguous, and that the additional sentence, $a = 4$ completely disambiguates the prior sentence. Although the example is clear, the disambiguation rests upon the presupposition of a theory of arithmetic, which is precisely the point to follow.

By a theory of the world, I mean a set of rules used by the person to interpret the events, objects, and relations with which that person comes into contact internally and externally in everyday living. The theory is what one uses to make sense of one's senses. The theory of the world each of us has allows us to place single meanings upon specific empirical experiences that have an indeterminant number of possible meanings. Furthermore, that theory allows us to construct a systematic integration of those empirical experiences.

By systematic, I do not necessarily mean logically consistent. Individuals will develop schemata, or theories, over limited domains that may not necessarily be logically consistent with schemata that they have developed in other limited domains. The overall theory of the world of an individual may either provide rules that allow for inconsistencies of schemata in different domains or the schemata will be changed when inconsistencies between schemata and the total theory become apparent to the person. Such changes may occur via social interactions, as Piaget (e.g., Piaget & Inhelder, 1969) has noted, by the person's inability to meaningfully interpret events within the framework of the theory in hand, or by maturational changes in the biological organism that may lead to spontaneous internal reorganization of the conceptual system. The lack of a totally logical system is evidenced at all levels of human development and in many related spheres of cognition. Piaget has referred to a part of what is implied here in his concept of horizontal decalage, although I believe that the lack of logical consistency is broader than implied in his presentations. For example, the social-psychological phenomenon of prejudice fits nicely with the conception presented here. Prejudice within this framework is conceived as an exception in the way one interprets the meaning of the behaviors of some identifiable group. The rules for conceptualizing people in general are suspended for some specified group for whom another set of rules is applied.

The general theoretical position taken here, however, is not unlike that proposed by Piaget and others. As Piaget has formulated his position, the child, through interactions with the world, develops abstract intellectual structures that allow that child to make sense of the intellectual problems and challenges with which he or she is faced. Those structures change with the interactions in which the child engages with the world and, thus, the meanings placed upon the events, objects, and relations faced by the child change. The meaning of a ball, the modification of the shape of an object, or the relation of sticks graded in size to a child in the sensory-motor stage is not the same as the meaning of those same objects, events, and relations at the concrete-operations or formal-operations stages. At each level, the child's theory of the world has changed. As Piaget describes it, the cognitive structures that define the stages are modified or developed through the child's interactions with the environment. Although Piaget discusses the evolving nature of cognitive structures and processes, he tends to focus attention on the organism–environment interaction in the development of the child's theory and he deemphasizes the direct effects of the hereditarily determined biological structures on the cognitive processes (Piaget, 1971, 1977). I feel that the evidence today suggests some rather direct biological constraints on cognitive processes. Furthermore, it seems likely that some of those biological constraints may be directly related to maturational changes that occur in the developing child and that account for the transitions in the child's theory of the world that are associated with the stages proposed in Piaget's theory.

There are other theorists who have also taken positions similar to that outlined here. Beck (1976), for example, has suggested that the clinical syndrome of depression is a product of a particular theory of the world. A depressed person views the world as a negative place in which to exist and most events that occur in the life of the depressed person are interpreted—that is, given meaning—as negatively related to the person. The depressed person's theory includes a view of the self as incompetent to deal with the misfortunes of life. Finally, the depressed person's theory of the future includes little hope for change in the present state of affairs. The same events interpreted by one person as hopeful, encouraging, or inconsequential are interpreted within the theoretical framework of the depressed person as discouraging and the outlook futile. Beck's behavioristically oriented therapeutic techniques are cognitively directed to changing the depressed patient's theory so that different meanings are imposed upon the same events in reality.

Still another theorist with a similar approach was Kurt Lewin (1946). Lewin argued that the goals, motivations or forces, valences, and conceptualizations of the relations of the self with the environment are given meaning in terms of the individual's theory, represented at any particular moment by the person's phenomenological life space. Two persons with the same external goals will view them differently, according to Lewin, as a function of the structure of each individual's life space. Lewin provided a comprehensive account of the developmental changes in the life space. At the time Lewin proposed his theory, he received a hostile reception from his behavioristic colleagues because he could not operationalize what he meant by the life space. Although operationalism is no longer as strong a requirement today, theory is. We need a way of conceptualizing the phenomenological world of the person to allow something more than after-the-fact accounts of the cognitive processes.

In all these theories, and some others as well, the theoretical concern is with the abstract mental structures (and, to a lesser extent with processes) that are used by the developing child to give meaning to the concrete individual objects, events, and relations that make up the experiences of the child. Those objects, events, and relations are indefinitely ambiguous in and of themselves with respect to their possible meanings. Each theorist, explicitly or implicitly, has proposed that the individual person constructs the meaning of experience in terms of a theory held by that individual. In order to disambiguate our experiences, we must have a theory of how the world is constructed and how it operates. The theory we hold permits us to interpret or disambiguate the empirical experience in a meaningful way. In fact, the theory gives us such a clear view of the world that we seldom notice ambiguity. For the most part, ambiguity only becomes apparent when two persons see the world differently because they hold different theories about aspects of the world. Note also that our theories of the world, yours and mine, are theories of how the world ought to be and not how it is (Proffitt, 1976). That is, we make certain assumptions about the world and predicate other aspects of our theory based upon those assumptions. We make decisions, judgments, and act according to our theories of how we expect the world to be. On those occasions when we err, we are faced with the fact that our theory, as all other theories, is fallible.

It must be that we have some sort of theory of the world from at least the time of birth. Otherwise, the world of the infant would be the blooming, buzzing confusion suggested by James. Furthermore, without a theory, the behavior of the infant with respect to the world would be in a similar random state. That neither of these states appears to be the case makes it clear that some organizational principles are available, allowing the infant to interpret and respond to the world in a meaningful way insofar as the infant is concerned. Children's conceptions, or theories, of the world certainly change with age, but they always have a theory that provides the organization or meaningful integration of the environment and their behavior with respect to that environment. The child, as the adult, has a set of rules establishing abstract concepts and organizing those concepts in abstract relations that provide for the interpretation of concrete events and responses to those events. The theory is a grammar of the world and the person's relations to that world.

Accepting the idea that a theory of the world allows us to interpret our particular empirical experiences—that is, give them meaning—we are faced immediately with at least two general types of questions. The first concerns the source of the theories we possess. How is a theory developed? This is the ontogenetic question of how a particular person develops a particular theory. More broadly, however, the question is an evolutionary one pertaining to the way in which the human has evolved and the commonalities in the species that are reflected in the commonalities in the theories of individual members of the species.

The second question relates to how two persons can communicate, given that they may not necessarily have the same theory of the world. Although there are species commonalities, there are, too, individual differences in both biological composition and in empirical experience. The biological and empirical similarities will make for common theories whereas the individual variations will lead to different theories. How do we overcome the latter for the purposes of communication? The ontogenetic or evolutionary question and the communication question, as already implied, are inevitably related. We begin by looking at the second question and then turn to the first.

The basic assumption of our theories of the world is that the world is meaningful. We assume without question that the world can be rendered coherent, regular, and predictable. The world is dependable and it can be understood. Obviously, there are some matters that we admit that we cannot understand, but we make the assumption that there is some principle, some structure, some sort of organization even if we cannot comprehend it at the moment. Despite our conscious lack of knowledge, we are forced to deal with our environment and we do so within the framework of our conceptualization of it (see Martin, in press, for a somewhat different position).

Given the assumption of a meaningful world, it follows that when we talk with other people, we assume that some meaning can be given to that empirical experience. When we try to interact or communicate with others—people, animals, plants, or even objects—we believe that it will be possible to impose some meaning on that experience. In the language case, at least, we assume a contractual relation between ourself and the person with whom we are communicating. That agreement involves the commitment to be meaningful, to make sense, to be relevant, and to tell the truth. Grice (1975) has discussed this relationship between speakers in terms of conversational implicatures. Proffitt and his colleagues (Cutting & Proffitt, 1979; Proffitt, 1976) have spoken of contractualism in the broader perspective of perceptual modes and other experiential relations. The point is that all empirical experiences including those involving language assume meaning and, therefore, it is up to the receiver of the message to assign a meaning to them. Thus, for example, when we encounter Shelley's phrase, "My soul is an enchanted boat," we do not throw up our hands in disgust. Instead, assuming Shelley was abiding by the contract to make sense, we create a meaning for the phrase and proceed. In fact, given the contractual assumptions made in communication situations, we give meaning where none may have been intended. Boswell (1977), for example, has shown that people can readily interpret metaphors created from a random selection of nouns randomly assigned to the syntactic frame, "A ——— is a ———." Furthermore, graduate students in English could not differentiate metaphors created in this way from metaphors created and used by noted poets. Metaphors from both sources were judged as equally difficult. These findings point up both the importance of the contractual assumptions between communicators, and the theoretical position that the meaning of an utterance or written statement is imposed or created by the person interpreting it and does not reside in the statement per se.

There are times, however, when the rules or contractual assumptions in communications appear to have been disregarded. When we encounter such situations, we usually ask questions about words used, interpretations of sentences, presuppositions, and implications. In such conversational situations, one speaker stops the flow of the conversation to ask, "How are you using the word X?"; "Are you assuming Y?"; "What is implied by Z?" and so on. Upon clarification—that is, once meaning has been agreed upon or at least stated more clearly—the conversation proceeds. When we cannot clarify the meaning by questioning, as in the case of a book or a lecture, often we will leave the field. It is too much work to provide a meaning and we put the book away or turn off the lecturer. Children often do this to parents, teachers, and other adults. In fact, when adults are communicating with children, one might expect ambiguity to prevail. But such ambiguity would only occur when the adult or child does not take into account the different theory of the other person. As is now well documented, that seldom occurs because the adult takes the child's theory into account as do older children when talking to younger children (Slobin, 1975).

Sometimes, however, our theory is so different from the communicator's theory that communication is very difficult. At such times, the conceptual referents of words differ, assumptions about the world differ, and communication breaks down badly because the two persons have conceptualized the world in seemingly irreconcilable ways. People from different cultures often have such problems. In the scientific community, Kuhn (1970) and more recently Weimer (1979) have argued that two scientists with different paradigmatic views of their discipline have this kind of communication problem.

At still other times, communication is so bizarre as to cause us to define the other person as psychotic. But, in general, we have no reason to question the contractual arrangement in communication situations. We assign meaning to our empirical experiences within the framework of our own theory. The fact that we assign meanings does not, however, guarantee that the meaning the speaker assigns and the meaning the listener assigns are the same. It seems unlikely that the two are ever exactly the same. We are not, after all, identically programmed robots. There is, however, considerable overlap between meanings of speaker and listener in most cases. Consideration of the commonality of meaning for two persons leads to the ontogenetic and/or evolutionary developmental question that we raised earlier.

The fulfillment of the contractual arrangements assumed in our ambiguous environment are made possible by the commonalities in the theories of the world that are held by different people. Those commonalities within a species are here assumed to be based at one level upon the commonalities that must exist in the biological structures of the organisms involved. In the same sense that dogs can communicate with dogs, birds with birds, and chimps with chimps, humans communicate with humans because each species has a biological commonality that forms a part of the basis for the theory of the world held by that species. The genetic characteristics of humans passed from one generation to the next and set in motion for the individual at the time of conception establish part of the sensory equipment, central nervous system, glandular, muscular, and other biological characteristics that underlie the common structure we, as humans, will impose upon our world. That common biological structure establishes, in part, the manner in which we will be predisposed to classify and to relate given any empirical experience. The biological structure constrains the theory we will develop.

There are some empirical experiences that cannot be classified because the biological organism cannot sense them. Ultraviolet light and high-frequency sounds are examples of sensory stimuli of which we are not aware, but some of which we know of because of machines and the responses of other animals. There are some stimuli that the human prefers to classify in one way rather than another, although when forced to, the human can classify the same stimuli in many ways. The recent child literature on classification has provided a number of examples here (e.g., Nelson, 1977; Smiley & Brown, 1979). The point is that there are natural ways of classifying, or conceptualizing, or theorizing about the world. As human beings, we have an increasingly ordered set of natural conceptualizing rule systems in common from the point of conception. The natural conceptual base has evolved over time as the evolution of humanity has taken place.

At a second, and not entirely independent, level, the commonalities in our theories of the world are made possible by the commonalities in the culture in which societal members are immersed. The cultural commonalities, too, have evolved over time as the evolution of society has taken place. The cultural characteristics of a society are passed from one generation to the next and establish, among other things, particular languages and the rules and practices of conduct and custom that govern the conceptualization of interactions among humans in groups (Campbell, 1975; Hayek, 1952, 1978).

Thus, the child has a theory of the world from the very beginning. The child has an abstract classification system, presumably prototypic in structure, and a system of relating the abstract classes. In short, there is a conceptual framework with which the child can understand the particulars of the world. That conceptual framework, or theory, is a system of rules for making judgments about what is and what ought to be.

Once the child becomes capable of language, he or she contracts with others to talk about how to talk about the world that the child already knows or understands in terms of the theory of the world he or she possesses. The child knows the meaning because he or she has a theory. What the child must learn is not the meanings of words but, rather, what words are used to convey the meanings that the child already knows. Language acquisition, in this view, is a matter of determining the contractually agreed-upon language mechanisms people in a particular language community ordinarily use in talking about the concepts and relations among concepts that are natural to people.

As suggested earlier, the child already has a concept of, for example, dog that allows the classification of chahauhau and St. Bernard. What the child needs to learn is that in English (if that is the language of the community) the word "dog" is used when one wishes to communicate that concept. The concept of dog is not as rich in relations for the child as for the adult in the sense that the child does not know that teasing dogs leads to biting or that dogs have a particular phylogenetic status among animals. The child does know, however, how to classify in terms of fur, bark, weight, ears, animateness, and so on. The child has a concept of dog that is a synthesis used to identify particular exemplars of dogs, to separate dogs from other conceptual categories, and, in turn, that concept allows for an analysis of the concept in terms of some of the attributes of dog.

In summary, the human organism organizes its empirical experiences in terms of a cognitive system that encompasses and provides a structure for the concepts and relations used to give meaning to individual events encountered in those empirical experiences. The cognitive system has been referred to here as a theory of the world. The theory of each individual makes it possible for the individual to create a meaning for the empirical experience and thus avoid the inherent ambiguity of that experience. The very fact of communication among individuals makes it clear that individuals share a commonality in their theories of the world. The commonality of theory is assumed to derive from the sameness of the genetic and cultural endowment passed from one generation to the next and manifest in the biological systems of individual organisms and societal systems of groups within a species. The variations in theory are assumed to derive from individual differences in biological and cultural endowment and to the particular empirical experiences of individuals.

Children's cognitive development reflects the maturational changes in the biological system and the modification of the theoretical system of the child brought about by failure to confirm the theory with respect to the way things ought to be in the empirical experience. Thus, the biologically established abstract dimensions and relations are organized and reorganized in terms of the biological changes that have their effects upon the theory at any moment of development, and the failure of that naturally determined theory to account for the actual experiences viewed from the perspective of that theory.

METAPHOR AND THE CONCEPTUAL SYSTEM

In the third, and last, section of this chapter, I would like to consider briefly the potential in the study of metaphor for the elucidation of some of the theoretical issues considered in the previous sections. The enigmatic nature of metaphor created by relating exemplars of two diverse conceptual categories to generate a new relation or meaning may be a key to the understanding of the abstract, tacit conceptual system. Although it may seem improbable that we might use metaphor as a key to unlocking the mysteries of the mind in light of its continued enigmatic status after such a long intellectual history, we shall see that there are reasons for being optimistic.

Metaphor, as every introduction to the topic relates, has received the attention of scholars from the time of Aristotle. Since that time, we find that many other philosophers have struggled to account for the nature of the metaphoric form of figurative language. In addition, metaphor has drawn the attention of poets, linguists, anthropologists, and psychologists, among others. Actually, Aristotle was concerned with metaphor less as a philosophical problem and more as a pedagogical tool. He considered metaphor rather narrowly as a rhetorical and poetic device used to infuse liveliness, vividness, pleasantness, clearness, charm, and a distinctive style into one's communication. Aristotle assumed this linguistic ability to be natural and otherwise acquired only by long practice. Although others since Aristotle have viewed metaphor primarily as a linguistic device (e.g., Beardsley, 1962), some have suggested that metaphor is more a reflection of thought in language (e.g., Richards, 1936; Wheelwright, 1962), and others have argued that metaphor is basic to all cognitive processes (e.g., Cassirer, 1946). As Cassirer has suggested, perception of reality is a construction of humans and metaphor is a construction on that construction. It is the latter point of view that suggests the importance of metaphor in understanding the cognitive processes of humans.

Regardless of the breadth of scope assumed to be encompassed by metaphor, there is general agreement that a metaphor is composed of a tenor or subject, a vehicle or object, and a ground or relation that allows the tenor and vehicle to come together in a meaningful way (Richards, 1936). It is, of course, the unstated ground relating tenor and vehicle that is the riddle of metaphor. The issue concerns the manner in which one person can create a relationship between two distinct concepts and, without stating the relationship explicitly, communicate that relationship to another person. There is no surface-strcuture hint in a metaphor as to the underlying meaning that is conveyed by bringing together the disparate conceptual domains of the tenor and vehicle that form the metaphor. Three major accounts of the nature of the relationship have been offered. The first, offered initially by Aristotle, is that there is a resemblance between tenor and vehicle. Understanding a metaphor, by this account, involves determining the similarity dimension relating the two parts. The second account is that metaphor creates thoughts of two different things together and the meaning derives from their interaction. It is not the similarity of one part to the other, but the interaction of the two parts that yields the meaning (Black, 1962, 1979; Richards, 1936). By interaction is meant the selection of properties of the vehicle meaning, construction of implications for the tenor from those meaning properties, and a reciprocal change in the vehicle as a result of the construction for the tenor (Black, 1979). Finally, the third account suggests that the meaning emerges from the whole metaphor as a unit rather than some kind of composition of the separate parts (Beardsley, 1962; Cassirer, 1946; Perrine, 1971; Wheelwright, 1962). From the latter perspective, metaphor is composed of two elements, tenor and vehicle, each of which has its own conceptual sphere, but the very bringing together of those elements into a metaphor creates a new conceptual sphere that cannot be broken down into its elements without losing the concept that is the metaphor.

As several investigators of metaphor have noted, in order to understand metaphor, we need a comprehensive theory of semantics or meaning because metaphor is only a part of a larger problem. As Black (1962) has indicated, such a theory will have to encompass pragmatics and context as well as language itself. Cassirer (1946) and Verbrugge (in press) add that the theory will have to account for artistic metaphor as well as linguistic metaphor. Furthermore, others have noted that other forms of figurative language such as simile, proverb, hyperbole, oxymoron, and even riddles are not basically different from metaphor and, therefore, must be encompassed by the theory.

Careful consideration of metaphor reveals the inherent complexities for any theory. To begin, linguistic metaphors are created in at least two forms: A is B and $A:B$ is $C:D$. The latter form, called the proportional metaphor, is often considered superior to the simple metaphor as a rhetorical or poetic device. In addition to the analogy inherent in the proportional metaphor, it is further complicated by the fact that often, some parts of the proportional metaphor do not appear in the surface form (e.g., Billboards are warts on the landscape.). Such ommissions require creation of the full proportion as well as the ground in the process of comprehension. Simple metaphors are considered by some writers as simpler than proportional metaphors, but others have argued that simple metaphors are really proportional metaphors with two elements of the proportion omitted. For example, "The man is a fox." should be understood as something like "The man is clever as the fox is sly."

On another level, several students of metaphor have noted the necessity of taking into account the nature of the tenor and the vehicle in the metaphoric relationship and the frame of reference in which the metaphor itself is created. Barfield (1928), for example, has argued that the poet's metaphors create relations between objects and other objects, between objects and feelings, and between objects and ideas. Upton (1961), also moving away from a consideration of the words per se in the metaphor, argues for a consideration of the frame of reference of the speaker and listener in the understanding of metaphor. He suggests that the logical, sensory, and affective point of view of the creator of the metaphor must be captured by the comprehender to obtain the meaning.

Others have taken the position that in order to fully understand metaphor, one must know the etymological history of the words involved (e.g., Barfield, 1928). The meaning of a metaphor from this perspective involves not only the current meanings of the words, but also aspects of the historical meanings each word brings to the metaphor. Many historical linguists, approaching the problem of metaphor from yet another perspective, have argued that shifts in the meanings of words have been initiated through the creation of metaphors (e.g., Sturtevant, 1917; Ullman, 1957). As particular metaphors capture the imagination of the language community, they are passed from one generation to the next as a part of the culture. In the process, the metaphors change from interesting creations, to dead metaphors, to words with new meanings. Tracing the history of particular words in the metaphor through this history, there is an initial meaning for the word, followed by a polysemous stage when both new and old meanings are available, to a final stage in which only the new meaning is used (e.g., sharp tongue). Because metaphoric creations are unpredictable, the expanding and shifting semantic space encompassed by words is difficult to anticipate. Several linguists, however, have suggested that at least some of the changes attributable to metaphor are based upon universal semantic relations (Fernandez, 1972; Upton, 1961; Williams, 1976). There is some evidence that the same metaphors have appeared in widely different cultural linguistic groups providing support for this hypothesis (Dezso, 1979).

From an anthropological perspective, it has been argued that metaphors have social–behavioral influences in different cultures. Conceptions of people, for example, may be created in either an adorning or disparaging manner by metaphor. Particular grounds used to relate tenor and vehicle, however, are related to the culture in which the persons exist (Fernandez, 1972). At the same time, Dickey (1968), among others, has noted that because metaphor involves the mind of the individual, it is necessary to take into account the history that that particular mind brings to each word in a metaphor, and therefore, to the metaphor itself. Dickey is, therefore, recognizing idiosyncratic as well as general meanings for metaphors. The universal nature of some metaphoric creations, the cultural influences on others, and the individual creativity involved in still others reveals the complexity of the problem with which any theory of meaning must deal.

Although there are a number of hypotheses advanced to account for metaphor, it is viewed by most psychologists as a special case that, when encountered in a linguistic environment, creates a tension in the comprehender because literal processing routines cannot be applied to achieve meaning. The distinction between literal and nonliteral statements, it is assumed, requires a separate conceptualization of the nonliteral metaphor. Most psychologists have taken positions that are variations on the theme that metaphor can best be understood in terms of similarity and analogy (e.g., Miller, 1979; Ortony, 1979; Sternberg, Tourangeau, & Nigro, 1979). Metaphor is conceived as a disguised simile that at base is an analogy of the form A is similar to B as C is similar to D. The basic problem is to establish similarity metrics for the A–B and C–D relations (e.g., Tversky, 1977) and the processes or rules for forming the analogy involved. The difficulty with this approach is in many ways the same as the difficulties in analyzing the meaning of a word in terms of the compontential features of which it is composed. The meaning of the metaphor is assumed to be the sum of the parts, albeit complicated by similarity and analogy relations as well as the, often unspecified, need to create some of the assumed parts of the analogy that are frequently omitted from the surface form of the metaphor.

Two points may be noted here. First, there does seem to be some, at least qualitative, difference between sentences that are clear cases of what are called literal sentences and clear cases of metaphor. For example, the sentence "Billboards are signs on the landscape." is literal in the sense that it provides a piece of information that may be evaluated in terms of its truth or falsity. On the other hand, "Billboards are warts on the landscape." is a metaphor that engenders generation of its meaning rather than its truth. It is conceivable that the difference between the strategies engendered by the two types of statements may be important to our understanding of sentences, in general, and metaphor, in particular, although to my knowledge no one has scrutinized the question. It might also be noted in this context that metaphors never involve negatives. They are always assertions, which, of course, is not true of clear cases of literal statements.

Second, even though it is obvious that the meaning of a metaphor, as any sentence, is constrained by the components of which it is composed, it does not follow that the meaning of any sentence, metaphoric or otherwise, can be derived from an analysis of those components. As is the case with a word, a metaphor is a unit and must be analyzed as such. A componential analysis presupposes a knowledge of the object being analyzed and the sum of the components does not, in itself, yield the object. It is, of course, possible, and may be fruitful for some purposes, to analyze the metaphoric unit into components, just as it is possible to analyze words into features. Such analyses, however, are at different levels dealing with different units and, as a result, cannot be used to explain questions about processing, for example, at other levels of analysis.

In this context, it is worthwhile to recognize that a metaphor is composed of at least two words set in a kind of equivalence relation (i.e., X is Y). The two words, in turn, are exemplars of conceptual categories. It is, therefore, the case that the creation of a metaphor brings together two diverse or unrelated classes and subsumes them under a higher level concept in which the two no longer are exemplars but, rather, are merged as a new conceptualization. This being the case, it may be useful to examine the dimensional structure and the rules used to generate the exemplars of those conceptual categories. The rules of any category will not only generate the exemplars of the category but the transformations of the category structure, given a particular context. In the case of metaphor, we have a tenor in the context of a vehicle undergoing transformations in conceptual structure. We might anticipate that the position of the tenor and vehicle in their respective conceptual structures would influence the meaning of the metaphor (Sternberg et al., 1979). Prototypic exemplars of a concept might, for example, affect metaphor meaning differently than peripheral exemplars. More important, perhaps, is the system of interrelationships between tenor and vehicle brought about by the metaphor (Verbrugge, in press; Verbrugge & McCarrell, 1977). The vehicle influences the conceptualization of the tenor via some transformational rules analogous, in some ways, to the syntactic embedding of one sentence into another. In both cases, the matrix and embedded portions of the whole undergo changes themselves and at the same time impose constraints upon the nature of the final product that emerges as a result of those transformational rules.

The importance of metaphor lies in the potential that the study of metaphor processing holds for revealing the characteristics of the abstract dimensions and rules used in creating a meaning for them. If we think of metaphor as the creation of a new meaning from the merging of two unrelated meanings, we can begin to ask questions about the nature of the emergent meaning in terms of the constraints imposed by the unrelated meanings, the context in which the metaphor is created, the developmental characteristics of the person creating or comprehending the meaning and, most important, the characteristics of the abstract dimensions and generative rules used to achieve the meaning.

Given the metaphors, "My uncle is a pretty summer." or "Love is a dressed-up doll."—the first a randomly selected set of words placed in a metaphoric syntactic frame and the second from Keat's *Modern Love* (Boswell, 1977)—we can begin to look for the answers to how they are interpreted. We can ask about what meanings emerge from these metaphors. How are the concepts of "uncle" and "love" expanded or transformed by their merging with "pretty summer" and "dressed-up doll"? Do those meanings vary as a function of larger contexts in which they are embedded? What cultural variations affect the meanings? What meaning changes occur as a child grows conceptually? Are there commonalities across persons regardless of age, culture, and context? Are there commonalities within cultures and individuals that differ across cultures and individuals? We can study individuals as they reveal meanings of the same metaphors in different settings and of commonalities of meanings across individuals in the same contexts. We can identify persons with apparently different theories of the world and establish their meanings for particular metaphors. We can establish the structure of the concepts for the words used in the metaphors and their influences on the emergent meaning of the metaphor. Research in this area has only begun to scratch the surface of the potential insights available here (cf. Gardner, Winner, Bechhofer, & Wolf, 1978; Hoffman, 1980; Pollio, Barlow, Fine, & Pollio, 1977; Verbrugge, in press).

SUMMARY

In summary, I have attempted here to elaborate a theory of the structure of concepts, to advance a theory of how a child develops a framework within which to impose meaning on experience, and to illustrate how the investigation of metaphor may be an empirical entree to an examination of the theory advanced. It has been suggested that the biological organism is structured in a way that constrains the manner in which the world is explored and predisposes the organism to a conceptual system with prototypically organized concepts. Those concepts, in turn, are related to each other within the framework of a continually changing theoretical system, which allows the child to understand the environmental experiences that he or she encounters. Such an approach places the emphasis upon the abstract system of rules, mostly tacit in nature, that, within any particular context, define the meaning of any experience for the person. By implication, any empirical approach to the study of language acquisition and, more broadly, the cognitive development of the child must focus upon the abstract if we are to gain an understanding of the problem Kant raised concerning the relation of the raw material of experience and our faculty of knowledge.

ACKNOWLEDGMENTS

I would like to thank James E. Martin and Walter B. Weimer for their critical readings of portions of this chapter. They stimulated further thinking, modification of some ideas, and correction of others. They can not, however, be held responsible for problems that may remain.

REFERENCES

Andersen, E. S. Cups and glasses: Learning that boundaries are vague. *Journal of Child Language,* 1975, *2,* 79–104.

Anglin, J. M. *Word, object, and conceptual development.* New York: Norton, 1977.

Barclay, R. J., Bransford, J. D., Franks, J. J., McCarrell, N. S., & Nitsch, K. Comprehension and semantic flexibility. *Journal of Verbal Learning and Verbal Behavior,* 1974, *13,* 471–481.

Barfield, O. *Poetic diction.* London: Faber & Faber, 1928.

Beardsley, M. The metaphorical twist. *Philosophy and Phenomenological Research,* 1962, *22,* 293–307.

Beck, A. T. *Cognitive therapy and the emotional disorders.* New York: International Universities Press, 1976.

Berlin, B., Breedlove, D. E., & Raven, P. H. General principles of classification and nomenclature in folk biology. *American Anthropologist,* 1973, *75,* 214–242.

Black, M. *Models and metaphors: Studies in language and philosophy.* Ithaca, N.Y.: Cornell University Press, 1962.

Black, M. More about metaphor. In A. Ortony (Ed.), *Metaphor and thought.* Cambridge, Eng.: Cambridge University Press, 1979.

Boswell, D. A. *Metaphoric processing in maturity.* Unpublished doctoral dissertation, Pennsylvania State University, 1977.

Bransford, J. D., & McCarrell, N. S. A sketch of a cognitive approach to comprehension: Some thoughts about understanding what it means to comprehend. In W. B. Weimer & D. S. Palermo (Eds.), *Cognition and the symbolic processes.* Hillsdale, N.J.: Lawrence Erlbaum Associates, 1974.

Brown, R. W. *A first language: The early stages.* Cambridge, Mass.: Harvard University Press, 1973.

Campbell, D. T. On the conflicts between biological and social evolution and between psychology and moral tradition. *American Psychologist,* 1975, *30,* 1103–1126.

Cassirer, E. *Language and myth.* New York: Harper & Brothers, 1946.

Chang, H. W., & Trehub, S. E. Auditory processing of relational information by young infants. *Journal of Experimental Child Psychology,* 1977, *24,* 324–331.

Chomsky, N. *Syntactic structures.* The Hague: Mouton, 1957.

Cohen, L. B., & Salapatek, P. *Infant perception: From sensation to cognition* (Vols. 1 & 2). New York: Academic Press, 1975.

Cohen, L., & Strauss, M. S. Concept acquisition in the human infant. *Child Development,* 1979, *50,* 419–424.

Crook, C. K., & Lipsitt, L. P. Neonatal nutritive sucking: Effects of taste stimulation upon sucking rhythm and heart rate. *Child Development,* 1976, *47,* 518–522.

Cutting, J. E., & Proffitt, D. R. *Modes and mechanisms in the perception of speech and other events.* Unpublished paper, 1979.

Dezso, B. *Prospectus on metaphor comprehension and comparison.* Unpublished paper, 1979.

Dickey, J. *Metaphor as pure adventure* (a lecture delivered at the Library of Congress, 1967). Washington, D.C.: Library of Congress, 1968.

Eimas, P. D., Siqueland, E. R., Jusczyk, P., & Vigorito, J. M. Speech perception in infants. *Science*, 1971, *171*, 303–306.

Fernandez, J. Persuasions and performances: Of the beast in everybody and the metaphors in every man. *Daedalus*, 1972, *101*, 39–60.

Gardner, H., Winner, E., Bechhofer, R., & Wolf, D. The development of figurative language. In K. Nelson (Ed.), *Children's language (Vol. 1)*. New York: Gardner Press, 1978.

Goldman, D., & Homa, D. Integrative and metric properties of abstracted information as a function of category discriminability, instance variability, and experience. *Journal of Experimental Psychology: Human Learning and Memory*, 1977, *3*, 375–385.

Grice, H. P. Logic and conversation. In P. Cole & J. L. Morgan (Eds.), *Syntax and semantics. Volume 3: Speech acts*. New York: Academic Press, 1975.

Haith, M. M. Visual competence in early infancy. In R. Held, H. Leibowitz, & H. L. Teuber (Eds.), *Handbook of sensory physiology* (Vol. 8). Berlin: Springer-Verlag, 1978.

Haith, M. M. *Rules that babies look by*. Hillsdale, N.J.: Lawrence Erlbaum Associates, 1980.

Hayek, F. A. *The sensory order. An inquiry into the foundations of theoretical psychology*. Chicago: University of Chicago Press, 1952.

Hayek, F. A. The primacy of the abstract. In A. Koestler & J. R. Smythies (Eds.), *Beyond Reductionism*. New York: Macmillan, 1969.

Hayek, F. A. *The three sources of human values* (L. T. Hobhouse Memorial Trust Lecture). London: London School of Economics and Political Science, 1978.

Hoffman, R. R. Metaphor in science. In R. P. Honeck & R. R. Hoffman (Eds.), *Cognitive psychology and figurative language*. Hillsdale, N.J.: Lawrence Erlbaum Associates, 1980.

Jenkins, J. J. Remember that old theory of memory? Well, forget it! In R. Shaw & J. D. Bransford (Eds.), *Perceiving, acting, and knowing*. Hillsdale, N.J.: Lawrence Erlbaum Associates, 1977.

Kuhn, T. S. *The structure of scientific revolutions*. Chicago, Ill.: University of Chicago Press, 1970.

Labov, W. The boundaries of words and their meanings. In C. J. N. Bailey & R. W. Shuy (Eds.), *New ways of analyzing variation in English*. Washington, D.C.: Georgetown University Press, 1973.

Lewin, K. Behavior and development as a function of the total situation. In L. Carmichael (Ed.), *Manual of child psychology*. New York: Wiley, 1946.

Lyons, J. *Introduction to theoretical linguistics*. Cambridge, Eng.: Cambridge University Press, 1969.

MacKenzie, D. L., & Palermo, D. S. The effect of context on semantic categorization. Unpublished paper, 1980.

MacNamara, J. Cognitive basis of language learning in infants. *Psychological Review*, 1972, *79*, 1–13.

MacNamara, J. *Concepts and words: Some cautionary observations*. In W. B. Weimer & D. S. Palermo (Eds.), *Cognition and the symbolic processes* (Vol. 2). Hillsdale, N.J.: Lawrence Erlbaum Associates, in press.

Martin, J. E. Presentationalism: An essay toward self-reflexive psychological theory. In W. B. Weimer & D. S. Palermo (Eds.), *Cognition and the symbolic processes* (Vol. 2). Hillsdale, N.J.: Lawrence Erlbaum Associates, in press.

Mervis, C. B., Catlin, J., & Rosch, E. Development of the structure of color categories. *Developmental Psychology*, 1975, *11*, 54–60.

Miller, G. A. Images and models, similes, and metaphors. In A. Ortony (Ed.), *Metaphor and thought*. Cambridge, Eng.: Cambridge University Press, 1979.

Molfese, D. L., Freeman, R. B., Jr., & Palermo, D. S. The ontogeny of brain lateralization for speech and nonspeech stimuli. *Brain and Language*, 1975, *2*, 356–368.

Molfese, D. L., & Molfese, V. Infant speech perceptions: Learned or innate. In H. A. Whitaker & H. Whitaker (Eds.), *Advances in neurolinguistics* (Vol. 4). New York: Academic Press, 1979.

Moore, M. K., Borton, R., & Darby, B. L. Visual tracking in young infants: Evidence for object identity or object permanence. *Journal of Experimental Child Psychology*, 1978, *25*, 183–198.

Nelson, K. Structure and strategy in learning to talk. *Monographs of the Society for Research in Child Development*, 1973, *38*(Nos. 1–2), 1–135.

Nelson, K. Concept, word, and sentence: Interrelations in acquisition and development. *Psychological Review*, 1974, *81*, 267–285.

Nelson, K. The nominal shift in semantic–syntactic development. *Cognitive Psychology*, 1975, *7*, 461–479.

Nelson, K. The conceptual basis for naming. In J. MacNamara (Ed.), *Language, learning, and thought*. New York: Academic Press, 1977.

Nelson, K. E., & Bonvillian, J. D. Early language development: Conceptual growth and related processes between 2 and 4½ years of age. In K. E. Nelson (Ed.), *Children's language*. New York: Gardner Press, 1978.

Ortony, A. The role of similarity in similes and metaphors. In A. Ortony (Ed.), *Metaphor and thought*. Cambridge, Eng.: Cambridge University Press, 1979.

Ortony, A., Reynolds, R. E., & Arter, J. Metaphor: Theoretical and empirical research. *Psychological Bulletin*, 1978, *18*, 919–943.

Ortony, A., Schallert, D. L., Reynolds, R. E., & Antos, S. J. Interpreting metaphors and idioms: Some effects of context on comprehension. *Journal of Verbal Learning and Verbal Behavior*, 1978, *17*, 465–477.

Palermo, D. S. *Psychology of language*. Glencove, Ill.: Scott, Foresman, 1978. (a)

Palermo, D. S. Semantics and language acquisition: Some theoretical considerations. In R. N. Campbell & P. T. Smith (Eds.), *Recent advances in the psychology of language: Formal and experimental approaches* (NATO Conference Series), 1978, *4B*, 45–54. (b)

Perrine, L. Psychological forms of metaphor. *College English*, 1971, *33*, 125–138.

Piaget, J. *The mechanisms of perception*. New York: Basic Books, 1969.

Piaget, J. *Biology and knowledge*. Chicago, Ill.: University of Chicago Press, 1971.

Piaget, J. Chance and dialectic in biological epistemology: A critical analysis of Jacques Monod's theses. In W. F. Overton & J. McCarthy Gallagher (Eds.), *Knowledge and development* (Vol. 1). New York: Plenum Press, 1977.

Piaget, J., & Inhelder, B. *The psychology of the child*. New York: Basic Books, 1969.

Pollio, H. R., Barlow, J., Fine, H. J., & Pollio, M. *The poetics of growth: Figurative language in psychotherapy and education*. Hillsdale, N.J.: Lawrence Erlbaum Associates, 1977.

Proffitt, D. R. *Demonstrations to investigate the meaning of everyday experience*. Unpublished doctoral dissertation, Pennsylvania State University, 1976.

Richards, I. A. *The philosophy of rhetoric*. Oxford: Oxford University Press, 1936.

Rieser, J., Yonas, A., & Wikner, K. Radical localization of odors by human newborns. *Child Development*, 1976, *47*, 856–859.

Rosch, E. On the internal structure of perceptual and semantic categories. In T. E. Moore (Ed.), *Cognitive development and the acquisition of language*. New York: Academic Press, 1973.

Rosch, E. Cognitive representation of semantic categories. *Journal of Experimental Psychology*, 1975, *104*, 192–233.

Rosch, E., & Mervis, C. B. Family resemblances: Studies in the internal structure of categories. *Cognitive Psychology*, 1975, *7*, 573–605.

Schwartz, M., & Day, R. H. Visual shape perception in early infancy. *Monographs of the Society for Research in Child Development*, 1979, *44*(7, Serial No. 182).

Slobin, D. I. On the nature of talk to children. In E. H. Lenneberg & E. Lenneberg (Eds.), *Foundations of language development* (Vol. 1). New York: Academic Press, 1975.

Smiley, S. S., & Brown, A. L. Conceptual preference for thematic or taxonomic relations: A nonmonotonic age trend from preschool to old age. *Journal of Experimental Child Psychology,* 1979, *28,* 249–257.

Sternberg, R. J., Tourangeau, R., & Nigro, G. Metaphor, induction, and social policy: The convergence of macroscopic and microscopic views. In A. Ortony (Ed.), *Metaphor and thought.* Cambridge, Eng.: Cambridge University Press, 1979.

Strauss, M. S. Abstraction of prototypical information by adults and 10-month-old infants. *Journal of Experimental Psychology: Human Learning and Memory,* 1979, *5,* 618–632.

Sturtevant, E. H. *Linguistic change.* Chicago, Ill.: University of Chicago Press, 1917.

Trehub, S. E. Infants' sensitivity to vowel and tonal contrasts. *Developmental Psychology,* 1973, *9,* 91–96.

Tversky, A. Features of similarity. *Psychological Review,* 1977, *84,* 327–352.

Ullmann, S. *The principles of semantics* (2nd ed.). London: Basil & Blackwell, 1957.

Upton, A. W. *Design for thinking: A first book in semantics.* Stanford, Calif.: Stanford University Press, 1961.

Verbrugge, R. R. The primacy of metaphor in development. *New Directions for Child Development,* in press.

Verbrugge, R. R., & McCarrell, N. S. Metaphoric comprehension: Studies in reminding and resembling. *Cognitive Psychology,* 1977, *9,* 494–533.

Weimer, W. B. Psycholinguistics and Plato's paradoxes of the Meno. *American Psychologist,* 1973, *28,* 15–33.

Weimer, W. B. Overview of a cognitive conspiracy: Reflections on the volume. In W. B. Weimer & D. S. Palermo (Eds.), *Cognitions and the symbolic processes.* Hillsdale, N.J.: Lawrence Erlbaum Associates, 1974.

Weimer, W. B. A conceptual framework for cognitive psychology: Motor theories of the mind. In R. Shaw, & J. D. Bransford (Eds.), *Perceiving, acting, and knowing.* Hillsdale, N.J.: Lawrence Erlbaum Associates, 1977.

Weimer, W. B. *Notes on the methodology of scientific research.* Hillsdale, N.J.: Lawrence Erlbaum Associates, 1979.

Weimer, W. B. Personal communication, 1980.

Wheelwright, P. E. *Metaphor and reality.* Bloomington, Ind.: Indiana University Press, 1962.

Williams, J. M. Synaesthetic adjectives: A possible law of semantic change. *Language,* 1976, *52,* 461–478.

Wittgenstein, L. *Philosophical investigations.* New York: Macmillan, 1953.

11 Empiricism and Learning to Mean

Meredith Martin Richards
University of Louisville

Bertrand Russell argued that a word is a series of occurrences, and what it denotes is an idea abstracted from the series of occurrences. In his lectures on mind (1921), Russell defined a word as a series of particular occurrences bound together and recognizable as instances of the same word by similarities of articulation, movement, and sound. The meaning (referent) of the word, like the word itself, is not something unique and particular, but a set of occurrences bound together by causal laws that make the occurrences taken together constitute what we call one person, thing, class of things, or quality of things. Each particular occurrence of the thing, person, and so on, is as a rule much more brief and less complex than the person or thing itself; we do not give separate names or designations to each such particular, but rather call the idea gained from the whole of such occurrences by the name of the person or thing, class of things, or quality. Thus, meaning comes to be empirically known from experience with a series of particular instances, none of which, by itself, is sufficiently complete, complex, or self-containing as to be definitive.

Russell was attempting to harmonize two divergent scientific developments of the time—the increasing materialism of psychology and the increasing antimaterialism of physics. Whereas psychologists under the influence of Watson considered mental events to be material events and therefore externally observable, physicists under the influence of Einstein had come to think of matter itself as constructed of immaterial events that could not be directly observed. Russell sought to show that the referent of a word is not an immutable part of the material world, but an internal state of knowledge gained from experience with the world in its many mutable and changing states.

EXPERIENCE: THE NEGLECTED VARIABLE

Even though contemporary investigators might be concerned with the psychological definition of Russell's notion of an "idea," few would disagree with his position that meaning is drawn from repeated experience with particular instances of a word in its various contexts of usage. This premise should be basic to the study of word-meaning acquisition. However, I would argue that we have given inadequate attention to the role of experience in our studies of semantic development. Instead, our inquiry has been limited to the progressive stages of acquisition of definitional meaning characterized as a formal, logical, and a priori system.

We typically begin our investigations by presupposing the end product of acquisition to be the definitional structure of the word as a competent adult would know it, and try to understand the progressive stages of approximation to this goal through which the child passes. Although acknowledging on a theoretical level that the child must look for what is "out there" to achieve understanding of the conditions of reference of a word, in practice we fall back upon the definitional structure of the word to describe the acquisition process, disregarding what actually is "out there" and how the child interacts with it to achieve this structure. We suppose that, by tracing a series of intermediate approximations to an adult meaning, we understand the stages of meaning the child achieves, and thus have understood the acquisition process itself. The nature of the input from linguistic and extralinguistic experience, the unique shape that such experience takes in the language and culture surrounding the child, and the ways in which such experience shapes the child's developing conceptions of meaning, play little or no practical part in our investigations. We typically do not systematically assess the structure of the environment, either in terms of its intrinsic properties—that is, the information of a logical and extralogical sort that it provides about word meaning—or in terms of the interactive process of adaptation to that environment through which the child accomplishes the task of learning to mean.

In this chapter, I trace the roots of this neglect in terms of our history and current paradigms, and then illustrate how attention to certain experiental variables helps to clarify what we know or should know about the acquisition process. I limit my focus to variables present in the situations in which words are used that contribute to the child's understanding of what the word refers to. I do not deal with the role of cultural variance or invariance in early experience, or with an analysis of interaction between children and their caretakers. Both of these are extremely important sources of experience contributing to language acquisition, but the point of this chapter is somewhat removed from either issue.

The neglect of the role of experience in semantic development research has arisen from two sources, one methodological, the other historical.

Methodological Constraints on our Inquiry

As in all fields of science, our methods are at once our servants and our masters. They are our servants because they help us accomplish our purposes; if they fail to do so, we discard them and find alternative methods. They are our masters because each method carries with it certain limiting assumptions, and to accept the method and what it does for us, we must accept its limiting assumptions.

In the case of meaning acquisition, our method of investigation has consisted largely of the observation of errors of interpretation (comprehension) and their changing patterns with age. Through the analysis of errors, we have acquired valuable information about the ontogenesis of meaning, described in terms of an orderly progression of increasingly mature (i.e., "accurate") semantic representations, which we identify with different stages.

The use of error data has structured both our procedures of inquiry and the form of our knowledge through its own limiting assumptions. An error can only be defined with respect to an agreed-upon "correct" or "standard" definition that delimits the range of acceptable interpretations. The first limiting assumption in the error approach is, therefore: (1) that the meaning of a word can be described in a unique and exact "correct" way. The second assumption arises when we take this description to be the goal of meaning acquisition, hence: (2) the task for the child is to "solve for" this unique and exact definition through successive refinement of less exact or inaccurate notions of what the word means. Thus, we define the goal of acquisition in terms of a formal product, and conceptualize the acquisition process in terms of a succession of increasingly accurate stages towards the acquisition of that product.

Historical Constraints on our Inquiry

The second type of constraint on our approach to the study of semantic development follows from the intellectual background of the field. Contemporary interest in child language acquisition is the stepchild of Chomskyian rationalism. Chomsky's compelling arguments for the innate origins of syntactic knowledge variously challenged and inspired a generation of psychologists, accustomed to thinking about language in terms of verbal associations and its acquisition in terms of conditioning, to undertake painstaking longitudinal studies of the acquisition of syntax. Eventually, through both naturalistic and experimental study, a large volume of data on the ontogenesis of grammar was collected. Interest in semantic development emerged as a "second wave" against the background of intense interest in child language that Chomsky generated. Both linguists and psycholinguists began to question Chomsky's theory on the basis of its neglect of semantics. As the importance of the semantic component was increasingly recognized, studies of the nature of semantic representation and its development in the child began to proliferate.

The prevailing assumptions of the Chomskyian approach to syntactic development identify a "paradigm" (Kuhn, 1962). The product of acquisition is competence in the rules of grammar that govern performance in such areas as passivization, reflexivization, coordination, compounding, embedding, etc. The goal (end state) for the child can be specified a priori with great precision as a result of linquistic analysis of the structural characteristics of the language. The developmental questions of interest are: What are the ages and stages of progression in approaching competence in these rules, how are these stages related to the relative complexity of the rules themselves, and how do stages of grammar development correspond to other aspects of cognitive growth?

The Rationalist View of Syntactic Development.   In the early days of Chomskyian rationalism, the rules to be acquired were thought to be transformational, and the child's adaptation to them was a matter of matching innate knowledge of universal grammar to its local manifestations in the rules of the language being acquired. Rather than being a straightforward mirror of experience, the child's competence was thought to develop through a process of hypothesis testing (McNeill, 1970), in which the form of the hypotheses was determined by specifically linguistic, a priori knowledge that the child brings innately to the task. Chomsky's theory provided a powerful counterforce to the empiricist paradigm that had dominated linguistics, in the tradition of Bloomfield, and psychology, in the tradition of Watson, Skinner, Hull, and others, for many decades (Katz & Bever, 1977). The paradigm shift that Chomsky's theory stimulated was heralded by many prominent social scientists (e.g., Bever, 1968, Garrett & Fodor, 1968; Jenkins, 1968; Miller, 1965; Palermo, 1971). Chomsky's impact was due in large measure to a series of compelling observations that he made about language acquisition. It is useful to review these observations; even though not all have withstood the test of subsequent research, they nevertheless shaped the theoretical consciousness of two generations of language-development researchers:

1. *The nature of competence:* The grammar of a language consists of an intricately interwoven system of abstract rules that, once acquired, are capable of being applied recursively and creatively to enable the user to generate and understand a potentially infinite number of novel, well-formed sentences of indefinite length. Through the use of these rules, competent speakers are able to distinguish grammatically well-formed from ill-formed sentences, recognize ambiguities, paraphrases, synonymity relationships, and so forth. These rules are not apparent in the surface structure of the language, but instead make up an abstract system for mapping meaning (deep structure) onto sentences.

2. *Linguistic universals:* Certain very general principles of grammatical structure are present in all human languages.

3. *Acquisition universals:* Similar developmental patterns in the early stages of acquisition show up in all the world's languages, despite the widest possible variation in culture, environment, and individual intelligence.

4. *Degenerate sample:* The linguistic environment to which children are exposed is vernacular speech, which is often truncated, interrupted, colloquial, and otherwise less then fully grammatical, providing an impoverished and degenerate learning environment.

5. *Inferential nature of acquisition:* At no time during the crucial years of acquisition are children overtly instructed in the rules of grammar. To the contrary, grammar instruction in the school years typically occurs well after the child has acquired the competence necessary to perform the just-named linguistic operations. Acquisition is therefore inferential rather than instructed, and the rules of grammar are acquired through observation rather than overt rehearsal.

6. *Age of acquisition:* Grammatical competence is acquired at an age far younger than that at which most other complex cognitive capabilities are acquired.

Researchers, most notably McNeill (1970) and Brown, Cazden, and Bellugi (1968), quickly added data showing a lack of correlation between the simple frequency with which a given grammatical form occurs in the language and its order of acquisition relative to other forms, and demonstrating that neither practice nor overt reinforcement were necessary for given forms to be acquired.

Thus, the weight of evidence at the time argued strongly against the empiricist view of a naive organism learning verbal responses that mirror the surface features of the environment through classical principles of association, frequency, reinforcement, and feedback. Grammar acquisition was seen as a series of internal changes occurring within the child as Language Acquisition Device (Chomsky, 1965). The question of interest to investigators was how changes in the child's linguistic performance reflected the changing internal states of competence that mark stages in the acquisition process. The role of the environment was thought to be important only in the broad and trivial sense of providing the general corpus of data necessary to allow the child to make, test, and refine inferences about rules. This, in essence, was a strongly rationalist position.

I would argue that these broad underlying assumptions have been adopted almost without modification by semantic-development researchers as a result of their robustness and embeddedness in the broader discipline of language acquisition. Yet, they seem to me to be quite out of place in the semantic subfield of the discipline.

Differences between Semantics and Syntax. Chomsky was careful to limit the generality of his observations to the acquisition of syntax—a sound restriction, because there seems to be little convergence between the basic principles of semantics and its acquisition and those for syntax. Unlike syntax, the semantic code of a language consists of a very large number of independent, arbitrary connections between sound and meaning. The connection between a word and its meaning may be one-to-one, one-to-many (polysemy), or sometimes many-to-one (synonymy), but in no case is it mediated by abstract principles that govern the general nature of such connections. No set of rules can be learned from which one can generate all possible words or understand their meanings. Meaning is simply a learned connection between sound and its referent, and, as such, it is a sensitive map of environmental coding and usage. The use of words is not, for the most part, a creative exercise in which basic rules are applied in novel instances. Although speakers do make heavy use of figurative expressions (up to 9.5 million novel figurative expressions in a lifetime, according to an estimate by Pollio, Barlow, Fine, & Pollio, 1977), seldom are new words actually invented by a speaker to serve a particular communicative need on a particular speaking occasion.

Thus, in terms of the nature of what the child acquires, semantics is a vast pool of discrete information that must be learned piece by piece—a process involving entirely different mechanisms of learning than those required for a system of rules. This is not to say that there are no organizing structures, concepts, or features underlying the meaning of related sets of words—meaning is surely systematic, as memory itself is systematic. Yet these structures are not generative rules that regulate complex, serially organized behaviors, as do rules of syntax. They are organizing principles for an information network that permit deployment of the information with precision so that a user can produce the appropriate word on a particular speaking occasion or access the appropriate meaning on a particular listening occasion.

Also unlike syntax, the process of learning to mean is never complete— people continue to learn new words and new meanings throughout their lives, although the pace of learning varies from an estimated nine new words a day between the ages of 1½ and 6 (Carey, 1978) to perhaps that many new words a year during later adulthood. The early accelerated pace of semantic learning is aided by considerable overt instruction from the linguistic community. That adults and older children conscientiously instruct the younger child in word meaning has been recognized for some time (e.g., Brown, 1958/1970), as has the universal readiness of young children to ask questions about meaning (McNeill, 1970). Yet, one notion carried over from the study of grammar acquisition is that learning to mean is largely an inferential process—that is, the child observes the regular conditions of application that appear to be present whenever a particular word is used, and through a process of inference, comes to associate these with the meaning of the word. Learning is seen as occurring in a passive environment in which information about meaning is implicit and not directly available on the surface. This is a basic assumption in contemporary theories of semantic development (e.g., E. V. Clark, 1973b), and it neglects the role of an actively instructive language environment. Surely, much information about meaning is directly *communicated* to the child.

Finally, the question of universals offers little parallel between the domains of syntax and semantics. On the one hand, anthropologists have documented the widest possible variation in semantic coding for such universal aspects of human experience as kinship relations and color terminology. On the other hand, some researchers support the existence of universal dimensions of affective meaning (Osgood, May, & Miron, 1975) and of universal "focal instances" of attributes and "basic-level" objects in semantic categorization (Rosch, 1977). Although the former claim is well documented, the latter remains somewhat speculative. On the acquisition side, it is safe to say that nothing exists in semantics to parallel the data supporting universal stages of syntactic development.

In summary, the contemporary study of semantic development has been unduly limited by presuppositions about the representation of what is acquired and the nature of the acquisition process, which, although appropriate to the study of syntactic development, seem far less appropriate to semantics.

NEORATIONALISM: THE COGNITIVE-DEVELOPMENT APPROACH

Recently, many investigators have proposed cognitivist explanations for the relative order of acquisition of linguistic categories, structures, and distinctions. These relate the child's unfolding linguistic skills to more general, underlying, and prerequisite cognitive skills that determine the course of acquisition. This neorationalist theory of language development differs from the pure nativism of Chomskyian theory in that it places the rationalist burden upon the developing system of the higher processes in general, rather than specifically upon language. Cognition is seen as the mediator between inheritance and language; linguistic universals exist because of universal structures of thought, which are innate. Language is one of many types of perceptual input that the child must make sense of, and the child applies to it the same organizing principles applied to any other type of perceived input. Thus, language development receives its form and direction from more general developments in perception/cognition, which are both phylogenetically and ontogenetically prior to language.

Investigators applying this view to syntax have worked largely within a Piagetian theoretical framework, performing logical analyses of the similarities between early intellectual structures and early or base-level syntax (Edwards, 1974; McNeill, 1974; Mehrabian & Williams, 1971; Sinclair, 1971), or correlating linguistic competence with performance on specialized cognitive tasks (Beilin, 1975; Ferreiro & Sinclair, 1971). Other investigators have approached the question from non-Piagetian points of view (Bever, 1970; Bruner, 1975; Slobin, 1973).

The semantic equivalent of the neorationalist approach has not been so clearly articulated but is nevertheless a strong theoretical current in the contemporary literature. It is generally assumed that particular terms, referent categories, or semantic features are acquired relatively late because their acquisition must await the prior development of the perceptual distinctions or cognitive structures onto which the linguistic code is mapped. There are two distinct branches to the cognitivist view in semantic development.

Vocabulary and Cognitive Growth

The assumption that the direction of vocabulary growth reveals directly the direction of cognitive development is one branch of the cognitivist view. This assumption underlies the intense interest that has been shown in whether vocabulary growth proceeds from the concrete to the abstract, or vice versa. Early studies (e.g., International Kindergarten Union, 1928) tended to report that children use concrete words like *banana* and *apple* before they use the more abstract category label *fruit*. Children's word associations (Entwisle, 1966; Entwisle, Forsyth, & Muuss, 1964; Ervin, 1961) are also governed by concrete functional or perceptual similarities, rather than by semantic similarities that reveal higher levels of abstraction. The observation that vocabulary acquisition proceeds from the subordinate to the superordinate referent categories could be taken as evidence that cognitive structures develop from the particular to the general through a process of induction. After an initial primitive period of accumulation of particulars, the child draws on abstract similarities to group and organize the particulars into more general categories. It has recently been reported, however, that vocabulary development often proceeds from the more general or abstract to the particular (Anglin, 1977; Rosch, 1975). Children tend to learn the general name for *bugs* before they learn to use particular bug labels like *fly, bee,* etc. This observation could be taken as evidence that cognitive growth is characterized by increasing differentiation of an initially gross and overgeneralized division of the world into more finely grained subdivisions.

The difficulty with either conclusion is that, although each may be valid up to a point, the assumption that vocabulary growth follows cognitive growth fails to take into account the explicit and implicit structure of what is taught by the environment. Roger Brown (1958/1970) put the matter strongly:

> . . . the sequence in which words are acquired is set by adults rather than children, and may ultimately be determined by the utility of the various categorizations. This will sometimes result in a movement of vocabulary toward higher abstraction and sometimes in a movement toward greater concreteness. The cognitive development of the child may nevertheless always take the direction of increasing differentiation or concreteness . . . the sequence in which words are acquired is not determined by the cognitive preferences of children so much as by the naming practices of adults. [p. 13].

Brown suggests that adults provide the child with the name of a thing at just that level of generality or particularity that represents the level of usual utility in the adult world. A coin is called a *dime* rather than *coin* or *money* because of the functional utility of distinguishing a dime from a nickel, quarter, etc. A utensil is called a *spoon*, but not *plastic spoon* or *clean spoon*, because its level of utility is that of a large class of spoons that perform functions different from those of knives and forks but that need not usually be distinguished from other spoons. A piece of fruit, on the other hand, will be called *apple* or *banana* because the usual level of utility is to distinguish one type of fruit from another, rather than a fruit from, say, a piece of meat or bread. Frequently, the names provided by parents to children anticipate the functional structure of the child's world as distinct from the adult's. Both flies and bees may be called *bugs*—a general category of small, moving things that are not to be touched, played with, or eaten—a highly utilitarian category for the curious and investigative 2 year old!

Brown, then, believes that children's vocabulary development is a very direct reflection of the naming practices of adults, which are influenced by the frequency with which various names have been applied to things in the experience of the adult, and the functional utility of the name in the linguistic community or particular situation. Attempts to infer directions of cognitive growth from directions of vocabulary growth generally fail to take account of the powerful influence of direct instruction in naming things. They assume a structured child in an unstructured universe. The important point of Brown's analysis is this: *The experience from which the child learns to mean is highly structured.* The naming practices of adults are structured by psychological principles that we as a field have generally ignored because we have consistently downplayed the role of experience in semantic development.

An analysis of the influence of experience on learning to mean would have to start with an ecological survey of the names adults typically give to things in instructing children. Such a survey would have to be done normatively for different parent/child populations: parents of different sex, socioeconomic status, and cultural backgrounds with children of different ages and sex. As Brown notes, simple word-frequency counts will not suffice, because they do not reflect the particular names given to particular referents by the linguistic community, but only the overall frequency of usage of words in the (usually written) corpus. And, in particular, they do not represent the special case of adult speech specifically directed to children.

Relative Complexity and Order of Acquisition

The second branch of cognitivist explanations is through the analysis of the relative cognitive complexity of different terms. When investigators observe a high degree of apparent consistency in the acquisition patterns for a set of words, the usual explanation is in terms of cognitive structures that interact with the linguistic environment to limit the interpretations that can occur at given stages of development. These cognitive structures are typically not further specified or elaborated, except to say that they exist and exert an influence upon acquisition. Following an analysis of the semantic structure of the terms in the adult lexicon, it is proposed that some terms are logically more complex than others, require greater elaboration of subordinated semantic features than others, or encode concepts that are logically contingent upon others. It is then predicted that the more complex, elaborated, or logically contingent terms will be acquired later than those that are less complex, elaborated, or logically restricted. When these predictions are borne out by the data, it is taken as evidence to support both the a priori semantic analysis and the notion of relative complexity governing the acquisition sequence. The opposite direction of reasoning is also sometimes taken: A post-hoc analysis of semantic structure is undertaken to explain the relative order of acquisition, which is already known. The validity of either approach rests upon the assumption that the semantic complexity of the terms reflects directly their relative cognitive complexity for acquisition. The child must acquire the requisite cognitive skills to process information of a more complex, elaborated, or logically contingent sort before complex terms can be understood.

The cognitive complexity/cognitive skills explanation encounters several difficulties, the most serious of which is that it begs the question. The relationship of semantic complexity to cognitive complexity is not demonstrated; it is assumed. It is the correlation of semantic complexity to order of acquisition that is demonstrated. Cognitive complexity is an intervening variable that is given no independent definition or operations of measurement. In grammar-acquisition research, neorationalist theorists have taken pains to specify the psychological nature of the prerequisite cognitive structures, and some have undertaken to measure them. But in meaning-acquisition research, these underlying skills are defined by the nature of meaning itself and have no validity or characteristics independent of the adult definitional structure. Only a few attempts to independently demonstrate a relationship between nonlinguistic measures of cognitive complexity and the order of acquisition of terms have been made. For example, Klatzky, Clark, and Macken (1973) found that nonsense names for short objects were harder for young children to learn than nonsense names for long objects, independent evidence for their hypothesis that *short* is acquired later than its antonym *long* because it requires a more complex level of cognition.

A second difficulty with the cognitive complexity/cognitive skills explanation is that the validity of the semantic analysis that the investigator imposes upon the terms is assumed. Yet, the philosophical and linguistic analyses that we construct as adults may have little or no validity as representations of the knowledge children acquire in learning the meaning of a word. The representation of a word's meaning, as construed by a literate, highly educated adult, may be highly artificial and bear little correspondence to the concept of the word held by children (or by less-literate adults). Furthermore, it would always be possible to find an alternative logical representation of meaning such that any given acquisition order could be justified.

In short, as researchers in word-meaning acquisition, we often find ourselves in the position of inferring cognitive readiness factors that we have neither measured nor independently defined from semantic analyses of adult meaning that have no necessary validity, and supporting our reasoning by order of acquisition data, which merely begs the question. We have gotten into this uncomfortable position, I believe, by disregarding the contribution of experience in word-meaning acquisition. If we assume that what the environment contributes to language learning is either (1) very little; (2) trivial and uninteresting; or (3) irregular, unsystematic, and highly variable (i.e., unstructured), we cannot look to experiential variables to explain consistent patterns of word-meaning acquisition. Instead, we invoke organizing structures that emanate from the inner environment of the child rather than from the outer environment of experience.

THE EMPIRICIST APPROACH

An alternative to either the rationalist or neorationalist explanations for the order in which semantic distinctions are acquired is the empirical hypothesis that those distinctions reflect the structure of the child's experience with the world. As described by Broadbent (1973), the empiricist view is that:

> ... our processes of thought reflect very largely the particular structure and dynamics of the world in which we happen to find ourselves. Such a view does not of course play down the extraordinary endowment that our nervous system provides; but it does say that the brain is remarkable in its ability to adjust to different experiences, rather than being remarkable by having an inherent structure through which it is able to handle the world. We are unusual in the efficiency of our learning, not in the pre-established organization of our thinking [p. 187].

A succinct version of the empiricist hypothesis has also been stated by Simon (1969): "A man, viewed as a behaving system, is quite simple. The apparent complexity of his behavior over time is largely a reflection of the complexity of the environment in which he finds himself [p. 25]." According to Simon, there are only a few "intrinsic" characteristics of the inner environment that limit human cognitive adaptation to the structure of the outer environment.

Structure in the Language-Learning Environment

Is there a chaotic semantic universe "out there" in which different children undergo differences of experience so great that—should acquisition depend solely on learning in the absence of internally imposed structure—there would be no consistency in what is learned? Brown's dissertation on the naming practices of adults argues against this "contextual chaos" assumption. More compelling, however, is the inescapable fact that the linguistic community shares conventions of word usage that allow its members to communicate effectively. There is a tremendous amount of redundancy in what children in different environments experience in their exposure to word meaning through conventional word usage.

Words have meaning precisely because they occur in linguistic and nonlinguistic contexts having constant properties that are contingently related to the use of the word. The meaning of a word does not wholly change in different contexts, nor from one speaker to another. Meaning is a predictable selector of the contexts in which a word occurs. Given this perspective, one might well ask, how could there *fail* to be enormous overlap in what children from different environments within the same language community experience about the usage of a word?

From this perspective, we conclude that the covert and indirect instruction that children receive by simply listening to the language around them is also highly structured. The context of language learning is neither chaotic nor unsystematic. Yet, as a field of research, we have not generally tried to find representations of those redundancies of word usage that contribute to the process of learning to mean. We have only attempted to account for the proportion of the variance in the learning process that is contributed by the child and by the apparent complexity of definitional meaning. We have not accounted for, nor attempted to account for, the proportion contributed by the structure of the language-learning environment.

In making the point that models of word-meaning acquisition should take less account of the formal structure of definitional meaning and more account of the structure of the information from the environment, I am identifying closely with what artificial-intelligence and procedural-semantics researchers (e.g., Clippinger, 1977; Minsky, 1968; Simon, 1969; Winograd, 1972) have been saying for some time about modeling complex psychological processes. They point to the danger of isolating these processes from the environments in which they occur and studying them sui generis in terms of formal, logical systems. Developmentally, they point to Piaget's theory as an example of such a model. Piaget identifies intelligence with the presence or absence of certain structures and operations, providing what Clippinger (1977) calls a "static taxonomic" conception of cognitive development. On the practical side, comparative researchers attempting to identify sources of cultural influence on cognitive development point out that, even though organism–environment interaction is a central concept in his theory, Piaget has never specified the nature of these interactive processes nor made them the object of empirical study (Greenfield, 1976). According to Clippinger, (1977), cognitive development could better be assessed in terms of the organism's general regulatory capacity, which "requires a model that is able to represent the environments with which the model interacts [p. 149]."

Representing the Language-Learning Environment

How can experience constrain the process of learning to mean? To put it differently, how can we represent those features of the environment that structure the process of learning to mean, either independently or in interaction with those structures that are contributed by the child?

Initially, we must consider the nature of the child's experience with the multiple senses and uses of a given term; experience with a term is rarely limited to a single, semantically exclusive sense. Most terms are polysemous—that is, there are several meanings, some of which are semantically related, but some of which are distinct enough to result in usage of the term in quite different contexts. Some of these contexts may contain contrasting elements, which could delay acquisition of any particular sense. In addition, terms often occur in idioms and metaphors that distort their meaning in some substantial way. Thus, one representation of the environment is in terms of the relative frequency of occurrence of a word in each of its different senses, idioms, and vernacular uses.

Another representation is in terms of the relative salience or surface availability of the reference conditions for a word in the perceptual environment. It is probable that some words pose more problems to learning than others because their criterial conditions occur more subtly in the context or are buried beneath more salient but noncriterial contextual conditions. There may be noncriterial conditions that are highly variable and act to obscure from the child the contextual regularities that must be observed.

Another representation of the environment is in terms of the cumulative history of experience with a word. Recall Russell's (1921) claim that the child must accumulate knowledge from a complex history of experience with a word before its meaning can be thoroughly known. Words are used repeatedly, and the child accumulates knowledge about meaning from repetitions. Subsequent knowledge may either reinforce and reinstate that gained from previous uses, or conflict with it in ways that appear to disconfirm knowledge previously gained.

We explore these possible ways in which experience can pattern learning in the following sections, in which I discuss the acquisition of several sets of terms by reference to the structure provided by experience with their everyday usage by the language community.

ACQUISITION OF DUAL SPATIAL/TEMPORAL REFERENCE TERMS

The Cognitivist Hypothesis

An hypothesis recently proposed by H. Clark (1973) to explain the order of acquisition of terms of reference to space and time exemplifies the cognitivist approach to the acquisition of meaning. Clark agrues that the human concept of time is actually a spatial metaphor. Children spontaneously gain knowledge of physical space as a result of early perceptual and motor experience. Time is learned by analogy to this fundamental, cognitively prior, perceptual model of physical space. Linguistic references to time are merely metaphoric extensions of the dimensional semantics of space. Because temporal cognition is contingently dependent on the prior development of spatial cognition, the cognitivist hypothesis predicts that acquisition of linguistic references to time must await the prior acquisition of linguistic references to space. According to H. Clark (1973): "In general, therefore, spatial expressions should appear before time expressions, and in particular, each term that can be used both spatially and temporally should be acquired in its spatial sense first [p. 57]."

Some empirical evidence appears to support Clark's assertion. Records of early speech (e.g., Bellugi & Brown, 1964; Bloom, 1970) contain frequent references to spatial locations and relationships between objects in the child's world (e.g., *sweater chair*; Bloom, 1970), whereas few references to time appear this early (Cromer, 1968). Children do not appear to regularly use temporal terms until age 4½ or older. By age 5, comprehension of certain spatial terms is very good (E. V. Clark, 1973a; Grieve, Hoogenraad, & Murray, 1977; Harris & Strommen, 1972; Kuczaj & Maratsos, 1975; Tanz, 1980; Wilcox & Palermo, 1974), whereas comprehension of temporal terms such as *before–after, until–then,* and *early–late* is largely inaccurate (see Richards, 1979, for a review of this literature).

The problem with inferring a cognitive basis for this apparent asymmetry is that we have not taken account of the teaching function of structured experience in shaping the course of acquisition. We simply do not know the relative frequency or selective use of various references to space and time that may occur in the verbal environment of the child. It may be that adults selectively talk about spatial matters to children in a way that they do not selectively talk about time.

The Empiricist Hypothesis

Some English terms that can refer to relationships in both time or space are *before–after, first–last, beginning–end, initial–final, ahead–behind,* and *precede–follow*. Linda Hawpe and I questioned whether all these terms actually undergo the uniform space-before-time order of acquisition Clark describes. There are major differences in the natural language contexts in which these dual space/time reference terms typically occur. Some of these terms are dominated by the spatial dimension of meaning and others by the temporal dimension. *Before–after*, for example, appear to be dominantly temporal: They occur in the language as temporal adverbs ("I have been there before"), temporal prepositions with an object ("I left before you"), and temporal conjunctions introducing a full clause ("I left before you arrived"). But in spatial usage they occur only as prepositions ("I stand before the court"), never as adverbs (*"I stand before") or conjunctions introducing a clause (*"I stand before the court convenes"). English dictionaries tend to list the temporal sense of these terms first, as if it is the more central or core dimension of reference.

In contrast, *ahead–behind* seem to be dominantly spatial. There are few instances of their use in purely temporal reference—for example, "I am ahead in my work," "Do your math homework ahead of your spelling" (but not "behind your spelling"). Most temporal uses strongly imply a front/back relationship in space—for example, "I ran ahead," "I fell behind," "I lagged behind the others," "I arrived ahead of the crowd," so that a strong sense of advancing forward or lagging behind spatially invades the temporal denotation of these words. Further, the noun *time* is often affixed to these adverbs as a marking device for temporal usage ("ahead of time," "behind time"), indicating that they are primarily spatial and carry temporal meaning as a secondary sense.

There are some terms that do not seem to be strongly biased in either direction—for example, *first–last*. Historically and derivationally, their origins are temporal: *First* originally meant earliest (Fowler, 1965), the stem word for *last* is *late* (Evans & Evans, 1957; Fowler, 1965), and *first* and *last* are superlatives to the comparatives *former* and *latter* (*Oxford English Dictionary*). However, contemporary usage seems to have broadened to refer generally to anything in a series. Thus, there is no clearly dominant dimension of reference for these terms.

On this basis, we have good reason to expect less uniformity of acquisition of the spatial and temporal senses of these terms than Clark's hypothesis allows. If children experience a term most frequently and in a wider variety of temporal than spatial contexts, they are more likely to learn the temporal meaning earlier, and vice versa. This is the empiricist hypothesis regarding the acquisition of these terms. It assumes that constraints upon the order of acquisition of the spatial and temporal senses of these terms derive from external rather than internal sources.

Metaphysics and the Consciousness of Time.   Is it necessary for humans to conceptualize time as a spatial dimension? Many theorists (e.g., Jaynes, 1976; Miller & Johnson-Laird, 1976; Piaget, 1969) have thought so. In contrast, Navon (1978) argues for the opposite order of conceptual dominance, in which variations in spatial location are ordered on the time dimension, rather than the other way around.

The 19th century philosopher Bergson (1889/1910) criticized the spatialization of time in metaphysics as a misrepresentation of real concrete time (durée), which is grasped by and belongs only to inner consciousness. James (1890/1950) regarded time as an impression given by the senses, much like color, depth, and other psychophysical phenomena. Boring (1933/1963) considered time ("protensity") to be one of the five dimensions of consciousness, in no way different or more abstract from other dimensions such as "extensity" and "intensity," all of which have their psychophysiological correlates. Both psychologists explain the perception of time in terms of duration and change of events, and memory traces. Miller (1977) suggests that a primitive notion of time may be innate, due to the infant's sensitivity to changes, successions of impressions, or the innate faculty of memory. Without further empirical evidence, it is reasonable to expect that children can be conscious of time and the sequentiality of events from a very early point in development. If so, there is no necessary reason why their understanding of references to time must await the formalization of time as a geometric dimension.

An Experimental Test of Two Viewpoints

We have, then, two very different views about the acquisition of linguistic references to time and space. For terms that can refer to relationships in either dimension, Clark's hypothesis predicts that tests of comprehension on each dimension will reveal a uniform superiority on the spatial dimension. The empiricist would rely upon the notion of the linguistically dominant dimension to make separate predictions for each term. For *before–after,* the empiricist prediction is for earlier temporal than spatial understanding; for *ahead–behind,* it is for earlier spatial than temporal understanding; for *first–last,* there is no clear prediction. But it seemed likely that understanding of the temporal meaning would arise first.

We tested children's comprehension of each of these word pairs in reference to (1) serial events (temporal); (2) a linear alignment of objects in space (spatial); and (3) a linear alignment of objects determining a serial order of events (spatial–temporal) (Richards & Hawpe, 1981). The latter task represents a significant domain of usage in which there is a correlation between spatial location and temporal order (as in lining up to enter the school cafeteria). Tasks *b* and *c* used Sesame Street characters who could be placed in line in individual slots on a platform; by rotating the platform, the characters could appear in any orientation, either perpendicular or parallel to the child's left–right body axis. The child placed two characters into slots with respect to two other characters (already in line) on each set of two trials. For spatial–temporal tasks, the line formed on one side of a temporal goal—a bus that the characters were shown to board one at a time after having been lined up. Other versions of tasks *b* and *c* used geometric shapes having no intrinsic fronts or backs, but this feature of the study is not of immediate interest. Thus, tasks *b* and *c* each included several subtasks in which the type and orientation of the objects were varied.

For task *a*, the child pushed two buttons picturing Sesame Street characters in the instructed sequence. Each button caused the corresponding character to pop up out of a house mounted behind the buttons. The buttons were interchangeable so that any combination of characters could be used on a given trial.

To illustrate how these tasks correspond to different senses of the terms, consider instructions for each task containing the term *before*:

1. *Spatial:* "Put Ernie *before* Big Bird."
2. *Spatial–Temporal:* "Put Ernie so he gets on the bus *before* Big Bird."
3. *Temporal:* "Push Ernie *before* you push Big Bird."

We did try alternative instructions for the spatial–temporal task that omitted reference to the temporal event ("Put Ernie *before* Big Bird") and found no behavioral differences. Temporal task instructions counterbalanced the order of mention of the responses with their correct order of execution; in addition, the essential elements of the instruction were repeated ("Remember, Ernie *before* Big Bird") to eliminate the problem of failure to remember sequential responses sometimes reported by other investigators (see Richards, 1979).

Subjects were 150 4;0–6;11 year olds from Louisville, Kentucky, area schools. Each word-pair experiment was conducted with two samples, one of 5 year olds and the other either 4 or 6 year olds, depending on the word pair. Different samples were used for each word pair. Each subject performed all three tasks with a word pair so that cross-task comparisons could be made within subjects.

Results.   To compare performance across the three tasks, a standard criterion of mature performance was established for each subtask in the experiment as 7 out of 8 (87.5%) correct responses. Table 11.1 shows the percentage of mature scores on all subtasks within a task area for each word pair. Table 11.2 shows the results of two-way repeated-measures analyses of variance with age and task as main effects. Post-hoc comparisons between tasks are also shown.

TABLE 11.1
Percent of Subjects Meeting the Mature Criterion on all Sub-Tasks
Within Major Tasks With Each Word Pair

Word Pair	Age	Task		
		Spatial	*Spatial–Temporal*	*Temporal*
Before–After	5	0	10	30
	6	10	45	45
	$\bar{X}$	5	27.5	37.5
First–Last	4	7.5	10	17.5
	5	30	47.5	62.5
	$\bar{X}$	18.75	28.75	40
Ahead–Behind	5	33	13.33	0
	6	80	80	66.67
	$\bar{X}$	56.5	46.67	33.34

TABLE 11.2
Significant Analysis of Variance Statistics
on Cross-Task Comparison for Each Word Pair

	Before–After
Age	$F\,(1,\,38)^{a} = 4.55^{b}$
Task	$F\,(2,\,76) = 6.6$
Post-Hoc Comparisons:	
Spatial < Spatial–Temporal	$F\,(1,\,38) = 9.68$
Spatial < Temporal	$F\,(1,\,38) = 7.81$

	First–Last
Age	$F\,(1,\,78) = 21.76$
Task	$F\,(2,\,156) = 7.21$
Post-Hoc Comparisons:	
Spatial < Temporal	$F\,(1,\,78) = 12.1$
Spatial–Temporal < Temporal	$F\,(1,\,78) = 8.9$

	Ahead–Behind
Age	$F\,(1,\,28) = 23.76$
Task	$F\,(2,\,56) = 17.49$
Post-Hoc Comparisons:	
Spatial > Temporal	$F\,(1,\,28) = 17.4$
Spatial–Temporal > Temporal	$F\,(1,\,28) = 14.5$

[a] All F ratios reported are significant at .01 level, unless otherwise indicated.

[b] $p < .05$.

With *before–after*, both age groups were significantly worse on the spatial task than on either the spatial–temporal or temporal task, with no significant difference between the latter tasks. With *first–last*, both age groups were significantly better on the temporal task than on either of the other two, with no significant difference between spatial and spatial–temporal tasks. With *ahead–behind*, both age groups were significantly worse on the temporal task than on either spatial or spatial–temporal, with no significant difference between the latter two. With all word pairs, there is a significant difference between age groups, but both groups show the same pattern of task differences—there are no age-by-task interactions.

Survey of Adult Meaning. Although our intuitions and linguistic analysis indicated that the word pairs differ in their dominant dimension of reference in natural language usage, this claim required empirical verification. Spontaneous definitions of the six words were obtained from adult informants. We assumed that a language user providing a spontaneous description of the meaning of a word will as a rule supply the most accessible of several entries for that word from the subjective lexicon. We further assumed that the most accessible entry is the dominant sense of the word—that is, the sense most often intended when the word is used. Sixty University of Louisville students in four different classes supplied definitions for each of two words. Each subject received one semantically positive and one negative term, but never antonyms from the same word pair. The resulting 120 definitions were classified as *spatial, temporal,* or *ambiguous* if it mentioned either both spatial and temporal dimensions or neither one unambiguously. Our own classifications underwent blind reliability checks by two naive adults. Table 11.3 shows the frequency of each type of dimensional classification made for each word.

Definitions of *before* and *after* were predominantly temporal—for example, *before:* "Occurring prior to a given fixed time"; *after:* "Time reference meaning action following another." In contrast, *ahead* and *behind* definitions were predominantly spatial—for example, *ahead:* "Location of object in relation to a fixed point or speaker"; *behind:* "In the rear of." Definitions of *first* and *last* were most often ambiguous, containing dimensionally ambiguous paraphrases, such as "beginning" or "end." When a reference dimension was given, it was most often temporal—for example, *first:* "Initial in occurrence or presentation."

Conclusion. These results provide compelling support for the empiricist hypothesis. There is no evidence for a cognitivist principle favoring the uniform earlier acquisition of the spatial sense of these terms, nor is there a consistent trend in the other direction. Rather, the order of acquisition appears to be a function of the linguistic community's differing patterns of usage of the terms in their different senses.

TABLE 11.3
Frequency of Dimensional Reference
Obtained for Each Word in Adult-Usage Survey

| Word | *Dimensional Reference* | | |
	Temporal	*Spatial*	*Ambiguous*
Before	12	2	6
After	11	0	9
(T)	(23)	(2)	(15)
First	7	2	11
Last	6	5	9
(T)	(13)	(7)	(20)
Ahead	1	11	8
Behind	0	14	6
(T)	(1)	(25)	(14)

A clear majority of the survey informants gave explicitly temporal definitions for *before* and *after*, indicating a dominantly temporal meaning of these terms. The children's comprehension of these words indicated greater facility at an earlier age with their temporal than with their spatial sense. In contrast, most informants gave explicitly spatial definitions for *ahead* and *behind*, indicating a dominantly spatial meaning of these terms. Children's comprehension performance indicated that acquisition of the spatial sense of these terms is prior to their temporal sense. Fewer informants committed themselves unambiguously to a single reference dimension for *first* and *last;* of those who did, about twice as many gave temporal as gave spatial definitions. This indicates a slight bias favoring temporal usage (which is supported by historical and derivational evidence). Comprehension-task results indicate that the temporal meaning of *first–last* is acquired earlier than the spatial meaning.

These results demonstrate what might be called an empiricist principle: *When a term has more than one sense or dimension of reference in the language, the sense or dimension acquired first is in general the one that occurs most frequently in everyday contexts of usage of the term.*

We recognize that the child is not a tabula rasa but is a complex developing organism. It is reasonable to expect interactions among developing cognitive and linguistic systems. However, when the frequency principle correctly predicts the course of acquisition, there is no reason to invoke stronger assumptions of cognitive prerequisites.

Some Additional Findings.   Another finding of this study was that *first–last* are acquired much earlier than the other word pairs, despite the fact that in the temporal dimension, all three word pairs share the same hierarchy of semantic features (E. V. Clark, 1971). Yet the data for 5 year olds in Table 11.1 show appreciably higher percentages of mature responding for the *first–last* pair; a sample of 6 year olds performed so perfectly with these words that we chose to move downward rather than upward on the age scale for our second sample.

The difference between *first–last* and the other word pairs became clear from analyzing the strategies that immature responders used on the spatial and spatial–temporal tasks. A strategy is a consistent pattern of responding across all trials of a subtask. For *before–after* and *ahead–behind*, the preferred strategy was to place the movable figures either on the same or on opposite sides of the fixed figures on every set of two trials, regardless of instructions. For *first–last*, it was to place the movable object at one end of the line—always the same end—regardless of the instruction. The stimulus configurations allowed for either internal or endpoint placements of the movable objects in either case, but the children chose endpoints with *first–last* and internal positions with the other words, indicating that some learning has taken place in the absence of full comprehension with all the terms involved. The difference is that, by age 5, children have mapped *first–last* onto the correct endpoints but have largely not mapped the other terms onto their correct internal locations. In our view, this is because there is a difference between how *first–last* map onto the perceptual contexts in which they occur. Experience with *first* and *last* is always cumulative; as superlatives, they refer to fixed, unchanging positions in a series of objects or events. The other terms are not absolute in this sense. Whereas "X before Y" refers to an unchanging location of X *relative* to Y, Y's absolute location in the series may change on different occasions and so, therefore, will X's. If absolute location is more salient than relative location for the young child, the variability of absolute location across repeated experiences with a word could delay acquisition. This exemplifies a second empiricist principle of word-meaning acquisition: *When a word refers to features of the world that are fixed and do not shift or change on different utterance occasions, that word will be easier to acquire than one that has similar semantic features but for which noncriterial aspects of the reference context are subject to change across different occasions.*

The second principle assumes that the child initially looks for fixed, unchanging features of the world when inferring the reference conditions of a word. When salient features of the reference context shift across recurrent experiences with the word, it is more difficult to apprehend those features that do not change (e.g., the front-to-back relationship of X to Y) in the midst of those that do (e.g., the absolute location of X and Y).

A third, broader empiricist principle would be: *When subsequent experience with a term reliably reinforces the knowledge gained from prior experience, the term will be easier to acquire than when recurrent experiences do not reliably overlap informationally.*

These principles explain another finding of our study—namely, that comprehension of *first* is significantly better than *last* in temporal and spatial-temporal contexts. There are at least two asymmetries of usage for *first* and *last* that go beyond their linguistic status as semantic opposites. *First* is antonymic to both the comparative *second* and the superlative *last*, and as a consequence probably occurs more frequently than either of its separate antonyms. In either degree, however, *first* means "initial"—its meaning does not change from comparative to superlative usage. *Last*, on the other hand, occurs *very* frequently in an idiomatic sense meaning "most recent" or "latest," as in *last night, last Tuesday, my last letter, our last conversation, my last lecture*, etc. In this sense, *last* does not exclude future occurrences—that is, it does not mean "final" but only "last up to the present time."

From an empiricist standpoint, *first* should be easier to acquire than *last* because the multiple uses of *first* converge in meaning, whereas those for *last* do not; different experiences with *last* will not necessarily reinforce and verify each other in terms of knowledge gained. Some will have the sense of "most recent but not final'' whereas others will have the sense of ''final.'' It may even be that *last* is acquired earlier in its idiomatic sense of ''most recent'' rather than its antonymic sense of ''final''—our data cannot tell us this, however, because we were only testing for the latter sense.

Summary.   What we have learned from this study is that by going beyond the definitional similarities among a set of terms and considering their differences in patterns of usage, we can predict their respective order and patterns of acquisition more accurately. We have simply considered how and in what frequencies the child is most likely to experience these terms in their different dimensions of reference and predicted from it which dimension is most likely to be learned earlier for that word.

Failure to consider the patterning of information that is implicit in word usage not only may lead to incorrect predictions about the order of acquisition, and so on, but, more importantly, it may in the long run prove more difficult to pin down and verify cognitivist explanations for this order than empiricist ones. We can gain knowledge of the structure of the language-learning environment through methods that are considerably simpler than those required to learn about the inner environment of the child. This is not to say that the inner environment is not an important contributor to development. But when knowledge of the outer environment predicts behavior and its development accurately, we should make a minimum of assumptions about the inner environment. In semantic-development research, we have tended to opt for the harder task when the simpler one might serve us better.

THE ACQUISITION OF EPISTEMOLOGICAL TERMS

One consequence of defining the goal of semantic acquisition in terms of ''correct'' adult definitional structures is that whole stages of development may be either missed or misunderstood because they are incompatible with our tests for these structures. Melissa Brown and I recently encountered this problem in our investigation of children's understanding of the terms *to know* and *to guess.* Although our interest in this issue has broadened considerably, our initial concern was with separating the linguistic and the logical components of a test item from a battery of cognitive tests developed by Engelmann and Bereiter. A colleague at the University of Louisville has been testing Head-Start children with this battery for some years, and reports that literally all of these preschoolers miss the following question: A picture of three boxes is shown. The child is told that there is a ball in one of them. Pointing to one box, the tester says, ''It's *not* in this one. Do you know where the ball is? Don't guess.''

All the children immediately guess—often before the words ''don't guess'' can be spoken. This response is defined as a failure to understand the probabilistic nature of the problem, hence a failure of logic. However, the children's problem on this item might be linguistic rather than conceptual, so we set out to understand why they seem to interpret this question about knowing as an invitation to guess.

Epistemological terms and all terms referring to subjective states are developmentally interesting because they entail understanding the content of "other minds" in order to understand what people mean. There is great potential for misunderstanding between children and adults in this domain; what an adult means may be entirely different from what the child understands. Obviously, there is a difference between what the tester means by the question "Do you know . . . " and what the child understands it to mean when he or she guesses, rather than answering "no."

Elementary-school teachers often report a common classroom interaction: The teacher asks who knows something, only to find that the first eager child called upon is obviously guessing. Several studies of children's interactions with parents and teachers (Olson & Hildyard, 1978; Shatz, 1978; Sinclair & Coulthard, 1975) have reported that children often interpret adults' interrogatives and declaratives as imperatives—that is, a call for compliance, rather than assent or dissent.

What Does it Mean to "Know"?

The distinction between "knowledge" and "simple belief" occupied philosophers from Plato to Kant. Contemporary epistemologists are generally agreed on the definition of knowledge as *justified true belief* (Hamlyn, 1967) as distinguished from beliefs that are untrue and/or arrived at through invalid logical premises or inferences. However, our interest is in the semantic intent when people use the terms *know* and *guess;* we suspect it is far less rigorous than the truth and logic conditions that the philosopher imposes. Our second question is: What information is available to the child about the semantic intent of these terms when they are used in everyday contexts?

In everyday dialogue, we often assert that we "know" something when, in fact, this knowledge may not be objectively true. If we were to restrict the application of the verb *to know* to only cases of justified true belief, we could rarely be said to know anything at all (Ayer, 1956). The more commonly intended meaning is the sense of *subjective certainty*—that is, we have an internal representation of reality that we consider to be accurate with a high probability. We may acknowledge that this representation could prove false. It is not a semantic anomaly to say that we "thought we knew" a particular fact (e.g., the author of a book), but our "knowledge" turned out to be wrong.

This sense of *know* is most clearly the opposite of *guess.* It is quite acceptable to say about this sense of knowing: "Do you *know* that my socks are in the laundry, or are you just *guessing?*" When called upon to make a declaration concerning an event about which we have little or no information, the sense of subjective certainty is lacking, and we say that we are *guessing*—that is, we withhold the "right to be sure" (Ayer, 1956).

Subjective certainty develops as a result of the acquisition of information, either through direct experience, or through a communication act by another individual. Austin (1961) and Searle (1969) considered knowledge in the pragmatic sense of what goes on between speakers and listeners when one of them says, "I know." By telling someone we "know" something, we persuade that person to believe that the statement is true (a perlocutionary act). Rather than applying logical and truth criteria to what is asserted, the listener tends to accept what is claimed on the basis of the *license to believe* issued (as an illocutionary act) in performing the speech act.

A second commonly intended sense of *know* is that of acquaintance or familiarity. In this sense, *guess* is not the opposite of *know*. It is not acceptable to ask, for example, "Do you know my neighbor, Betsy Jones, or are you just guessing?"

A third frequently intended sense of *know* explicitly equates knowing with being correct, as when, upon hearing thunder and the first drops of rain, we exclaim (in exasperation), "I just knew it was going to rain today and ruin our picnic!" What is asserted is that a speculation or conjecture turned out to be correct. In this sense, *guess* is a synonym rather than an antonym of *know*, because a frequently intended sense of *guess* is also to "conjecture correctly" (*Webster's Third New International Dictionary of the English Language, Unabridged*, 1976), as in guessing riddles, or "guessing someone's age the first time." Hence, there are frequent references to both *know* and *guess* in the vernacular that equate both terms with the objectively correct outcome of a conjecture, rather than subjective certainty based upon prior information.

Thus, there are four common senses of what it means to *know*: (1) justified true belief, which implies a *know/believe* opposition; (2) subjective certainty, which implies a *know/guess* opposition; (3) acquaintance or familiarity, which implies a *know/do not know* but not a *know/guess* opposition; and (4) correct conjecture, which implies a *know/guess* synonymity. Investigators studying the acquisition of *know* and related epistemological terms have focused on a single meaning, and as a consequence have sometimes interpreted results with respect to one meaning that might more appropriately be considered in light of another.

Previous Developmental Studies

Johnson and Maratsos (1977) investigated 3 and 4 year olds' understanding of the mental verbs *think* and *know*. Their subjects were told stories about a "hider" putting a toy under one box and then tricking a "seeker" into believing that it was under another box. Following each of four stories, the child was asked a series of questions about the seeker and then about the hider—in particular:

Where each would look to find the toy, and whether each *thinks* or *knows* about the box it is under. The correct answers were defined as those that distinguish *knowing* the truth from *thinking* something that is false—that is, the sense of knowledge as justified true belief.

About half of the 3 year olds were eliminated from further questioning when they "failed" the initial question about where the seeker would look by indicating where the hider actually put the toy rather than where the seeker was told it was. The remaining 3 year olds either responded randomly or not at all on the subsequent questions. However, about 80% of the 4 year olds made the correct distinction—they said that the seeker *thinks* whereas the hider *knows*. Johnson and Maratsos concluded that 4 year olds understand that thinking can be false whereas knowing presupposes truth, and furthermore that they show no tendency to "confuse mental events with external events [p. 1747]."

In a similar study, Macnamara, Baker, and Olson (1976) also employed the definition of justified true belief to define correct responses to questions about knowing in situations in which one person tricked another into believing something false. Their 4-year-old subjects were more or less unable to answer the questions about *knowing,* although they successfully answered similar questions about *forgetting* and *pretending.* The authors concluded that the propositional logic involved in questions about *knowing* is more complex than that for the other epistemological terms.

The difficulty with these studies is that they presuppose one definition of knowing and fail to consider that children may be responding according to other conceptions of the term. By explicitly contrasting *know* with *think* (one of Johnson & Maratsos' questions used the disjunctive *or*—"Does the seeker think it's under the box or does he know it's under the box?"—in effect setting up the terms as mutually exclusive), they failed to allow for the possibility that these terms might not be regarded as opposites by the subject. Whereas *believe* may be regarded as the opposite of *know* in the sense of 1 described earlier, *think* does not seem to fit the opposite sense of "lack of truth" or "lack of knowledge." (*Think,* in fact, is derived from the Latin *tongere,* which means *to know.*) Furthermore, the story situations constructed by these experimenters implicate an everyday sense of *know* different from the philosophical definition—that of subjective certainty by virtue of a license to believe what another person tells us (even though it may be false). Although we have no reason to expect that any of the children were responding according to the latter sense, we cannot say for sure that they were not. There is simply no option for the child to respond according to another sense and be judged to have a mature understanding of what it means to *know.*

Miscione, Marvin, O'Brien, and Greenberg (1978) studied 3-7 year olds' understanding of *know* and *guess* in an investigation similar to our own. The experimenter (1) hid a shape in a box; (2) asked the child to pick the box he or she *thought* contained the shape; and (3) asked the child whether he or she *knew* or was *guessing* the location of the shape. Five conditions were differentiated according to whether or not the child watched the experimenter hide the ball, and whether the *know/guess* question was asked before or after the child was informed of the outcome of his or her choice. The children were asked (tense depending on condition), "Are you *guessing* that the shape is in this box, or do you *know* that the shape is in this box?" The ordering of the *know* and *guess* clauses was randomly distributed over trials.

There were four apparent stages towards the understanding of *know* as subjective certainty (i.e., prior information) and *guess* as lack of certainty (no prior information). At the earliest stage, children prior to age 4 do not respond systematically to either term. The second stage is a period of outcome dependency in which *knowing* is equated with positive outcome (correct choice) and *guessing* with negative outcome (incorrect choice). After a transition period, children reach mature understanding, around age 5½. By posing their question as a disjunctive choice between the two terms, Miscione et al. also treated *know* and *guess* as mutually exclusive.

The Present Investigation

In our study (Brown, 1979; Richards & Brown, 1981), we set no preconditions on the correct definition of *knowing*. Which of the numerous senses children learn first should be a function of their experiences with everyday discourse. In particular, children initially may learn that sense of *know* that refers to the most salient, externally available features of the contexts in which it is used. If a term refers to a tangible aspect of external experience, it is more likely to be understood in that sense than in one referring to an intangible aspect of the subjective experience of the speaker. Thus, we felt that children would acquire the sense of *know* as correct conjecture earlier than the sense of subjective certainty, because the former involves an externally observable outcome. In this sense, *know* and *guess* are not semantic opposites; thus, it was important to allow both to be used differentially, rather than treat them as mutually exclusive.

We conducted two different studies, the first with 120 4–10 year olds, the second with 60 5, 7, and 9 year olds, representing a nearly even distribution of Black and White middle-class school children. Only the results of the second study, which refined and extended those of the first, are reported here. A game was played in which the child hid a ball in one of two boxes and two adult assistants had to guess where it was. Under "no-observer" conditions, both adults turned away and covered their eyes while the ball was hidden; under "observer" conditions, one adult watched while the child hid the ball, and the other adult turned away as before. After hiding the ball, the child was asked whether either player "knows where to find the ball." The players then guessed the ball's location. The child was asked another series of questions, either before or after the outcome had been revealed to the players (although the child always knew the outcome): "Was either of them guessing where to find the ball?"; (if "yes") "Who was guessing?"; (if only one player indicated) "Was (other player) guessing, too?" Then: "Did either of them know where to find the ball?"; (if yes) "Who knew?"; (if only one player indicated) "Did (other player) know, too?" The pattern of correct/incorrect guesses by the adults was systematically varied over trials under each condition so that either one or both player(s) was correct or incorrect on a single trial. The experimenter never used epistemological terms during the experiment except in the questions (a violation of normal speaking habits that required considerable practice to master).

Results. The results indicate that the younger children shifted between two senses of *know* during the experiment. The response that neither player knew or the observer knew (depending on the condition) was given before guessing took place, whereas the response that the player who was correct (or both players, if both were correct) knew was given after the guessing took place. This shift is clearly attributable to the effects of outcome, because the only difference between the two questions was that one preceded the outcome whereas the other followed it. A greater shift occurred under "no-observer" conditions than with a "correct" observer, but more than half of the 5 and 7 year olds still responded in accordance with outcome rather than prior information in the postguessing questions. On trials in which the observer made the wrong choice, thus confronting children with a conflict between prior information and outcome, the greatest shifting to the outcome-dependent response took place. In contrast, most 9 year olds stuck with the "neither" knew or "observer only" knew responses, regardless of outcome, on the postguessing question, indicating greater confidence in the prior-information sense over the outcome sense at this age.

We conclude that the 5 and 7 year olds are aware of both prior-information (i. e., subjective-certainty) and correct-conjecture interpretations of *know,* and that they are quite capable of switching from one to the other when the context changes. Under most conditions, shifting to the correct-outcome interpretation is incompatible with the prior-information interpretation, yet these children see no apparent inconsistency in saying that no one knew prior to guessing and the correct player knew after guessing, or that the observer knew prior to guessing and the nonobserver knew after guessing.

In contrast, 10 adults run in the first experiment consistently chose the prior-information interpretation and did not change their response as a result of the outcome—at least, not most of the time. On a few occasions, adults would "slip" and say that the correct player knew; then they would immediately correct themselves, saying, "Well, he didn't actually *know,* he just guessed correctly." This was their way of saying that the player did not know in the subjective-certainty sense, but did know in the sense of correct conjecture. Trying to be consistent within the experimental context, they chose the subjective-certainty interpretation as correct.

Perhaps our most interesting results involved the development of *guess*. By asking the *know/guess* questions separately, we allowed the possibility that the terms are differentially related to the experimental variables.

At the youngest age, *guessing* was not distinguished from *knowing,* and was clearly not perceived as its opposite. The 5 year olds predominantly attributed guessing to the *same* player(s) to whom they attributed knowing— that is, the correct player(s). This result was stable across both "observer" and "no-observer" conditions. Only later were the terms treated as opposites; about half of the 7 year olds were positive outcome dependent with *know* and negative outcome dependent with *guess*. That is, *knowing* was attributed to the correct player(s) and *guessing* to the incorrect player(s). The remaining 7 year olds were positive outcome dependent on both terms. Although most 9 year olds retained the prior-information sense of *know* following the outcome, about 20% fell back on the negative-outcome interpretation of *guess*. This and other results pointed to an asymmetry of development of *know* and *guess* in the sense of subjective certainty, another indication that these terms do not initially develop as opposites.

Thus, the primary difference between older and younger subjects was in whether they felt constrained to use a single sense of *know* consistently in the experimental context. Even the youngest children seem to have acquired the sense of *know* in relation to prior information, as judged by their responses on the preguessing question. Yet they were so susceptible to the effects of a visible outcome that they shifted to a second, incompatible sense of *know* that related it to positive outcome. Children did not differentiate between *know* and *guess* in this sense until later (age 7 or beyond), when they began to treat them as opposite but still outcome-dependent terms. Older subjects were no longer influenced by the presence of a tangible outcome to shift their interpretations of *know* away from the prior-information sense appropriate to the preguessing context.

Summary.   There are a variety of intended meanings of *know* for the child to learn. Apparently, they have learned at least two of these by age 5. Contrary to our hypothesis, the sense of correct conjecture, which alludes to external rather than internal denotative events, is not necessarily learned first, but it is the *preferred* sense in contexts in which there is a tangible correct outcome. It is preferred at the expense of a consistent interpretation of *know* as related to prior information.

The verbal environment of the child is rich and varied, and children adapt to it by developing a rich and varied lexicon. Seldom does a term occur "unidimensionally" in the language in a single, semantically exclusive sense. Investigators of children's semantic development should consider possible multiple lexical entries for a term in planning their investigations and interpreting their results.

By focusing on a single "correct" sense, investigators may limit their ability to interpret stages of acquisition and the ways in which children interact with different contexts to interpret different meanings.

By defining the prior information sense of *know* as singularly "correct," Miscione et al. (1978) accepted its corollary that *guess* is the opposite of *know*, and thus posed their questions in the disjunctive. Thus, they could not discover the early stage of synonymy of these terms, nor chart the asymmetries in their development. By setting no preconditions on the goal of acquisition, we were able to observe these important developments.

CONCLUDING REMARKS

Prior to the 1960's, psycholinguistic research was dominated by the concepts and methods of empirical psychology. Several revolutionary developments in the late 1950's and throughout the 1960's led to greater emphasis on cognitive factors: These included the emergence of computer models, the success of generative grammar, and the acceptance of the developmental views of Piaget. Additionally, a number of traditional problems had proved intractable in terms of learning theory.

Several of Chomsky's (1959) criticisms of psychological approaches were well taken. We cannot limit ourselves to the traditional principles of even the most advanced learning theories and hope to explain the production and comprehension of language. Other concepts and principles are necessary. Chomsky himself developed many of them for the acquisition of syntax. However, the message of this episode in the history of psychology should be not "reject and ignore the traditional principles of empirical psychology" but rather, "if and when traditional concepts and principles fail, new ones should be developed. However, standard types of explanation should be tried first. There is a rich conceptual and methodological heritage in psychology that should not be ignored.

Research in semantic development has adopted rationalist assumptions or neorationalist concepts and theories without first testing the appropriateness of empiricist principles. Empiricism provides an approach to the problem of learning to mean in which the child is seen as adapting to a complex but structured and redundant environment. This approach requires representing the language-learning environment and assessing its effects upon learning. We have examined several cases in which empirical principles provide better predictions and explanations of experimental findings than the congitivist accounts.

Semantics is of the world, and semantic development necessarily reflects the child's experiences in the world. Therefore, empiricist principles should in general do very well in accounting for the acquisition of meaning.

REFERENCES

Anglin, J. *Word, object, and conceptual development*. New York: Norton, 1977.

Austin, J. Other minds. In *Philosophical papers*. London: Oxford University Press, 1961.

Ayer, A. J. *The problem of knowledge*. New York: Saint Martin's Press, 1956.

Beilin, H. (Ed.). *Studies in the cognitive basis of language development*. New York: Academic Press, 1975.

Bellugi, U., & Brown, R. (Eds.). The acquisition of language. *Monographs of the Society for Research in Child Development*, 1964, *29* (No. 92).

Bergson, H. *Time and free will*. (Trans. by F. L. Pogson from original French edition, 1889). London: S. Sonnenschein & Co., Lim.; New York: Macmillan Co., 1910.

Bever, T. G. Associations to stimulus–response theories of language. In T. R. Dixon & D. L. Horton (Eds.), *Verbal behavior and general behavior theory*. Englewood Cliffs, N.J.: Prentice-Hall, 1968.

Bever, T. G. The cognitive basis for linguistic structures. In J. R. Hayes (Ed.), *Cognition and the development of language*. New York: Wiley, 1970.

Bloom, L. *Language development: Form and function in emerging grammars*. Cambridge, Mass.: M.I.T. Press, 1970.

Boring, E. G. *The physical dimensions of consciousness*. New York: Dover, 1963. (Originally published, 1933.)

Broadbent, D. E. *In defence of empirical psychology*. London: Methuen, 1973.

Brown, M. L. *Epistemology in the young child: To guess (and be right) is to know*. Unpublished masters thesis, University of Louisville, 1979.

Brown, R. How shall a thing be called? In *Psycholinguistics: Selected papers by Roger Brown*. New York: Free Press, 1970. (Originally published in *Psychological Review*, 1958, *65*, 14–21.)

Brown, R., Cazden, C., & Bellugi, U. The child's grammar from I to III. In J. P. Hill (Ed.), *The 1967 Minnesota symposium on child psychology*. Minneapolis: University of Minnesota Press, 1968.

Bruner, J. The ontogenesis of speech acts. *Journal of Child Language*, 1975, *2*, 1–19.

Carey, S. The child as word learner. In M. Halle, J. Bresnan, & G. A. Miller (Eds.), *Linguistic theory and psychological reality*. Cambridge, Mass.: M.I.T. Press, 1978.

Chomsky, N. Review of Skinner's verbal behavior. *Language*, 1959, *35*, 26–58.

Chomsky, N. *Aspects of the theory of syntax*. Cambridge, Mass.: M.I.T. Press, 1965.

Clark, E. V. On the acquisition of the meaning of *before* and *after*. *Journal of Verbal Learning and Verbal Behavior*, 1971, *10*, 266–275.

Clark, E. V. Non-linguistic strategies and the acquisition of word meaning. *Cognition*, 1973, *2*, 161–182. (a)

Clark, E. V. What's in a word? On the child's acquisition of semantics in his first language. In T. Moore (Ed.), *Cognitive development and the acquisition of language*. New York: Academic Press, 1973. (b)

Clark, H. Space, time, semantics and the child. In T. Moore (Ed.), *Cognitive development and the acquisition of language*. New York: Academic Press, 1973.

Clippinger, J. H., Jr. *Meaning and discourse analysis: A computer model of psychoanalytic speech and cognition*. Baltimore, Md.: Johns Hopkins Press, 1977.

Cromer, R. F. *Development of temporal reference during the acquisition of language*. Unpublished doctoral dissertation, Harvard University, 1968.

Edwards, D. Sensorimotor intelligence and semantic relations in early child grammar. *Cognition*, 1974, *4*, 395–434.

Entwisle, D. R. *Word associations of young children*. Baltimore, Md.: Johns Hopkins Press, 1966.

Entwisle, D., Forsyth, D. F., & Muuss, R. The syntagmatic–paradigmatic shift in children's word associations. *Journal of Verbal Learning and Verbal Behavior*, 1964, *3*, 19–29.

Ervin, S. Changes with age in the verbal determinants of word association. *American Journal of Psychology*, 1961, *74*, 361-372.

Evans, B., & Evans, C. *A dictionary of contemporary American usage*. New York: Random House, 1957.

Ferreiro, E., & Sinclair, H. Temporal relationships in language. *International Journal of Psychology*, 1971, *6*, 39-47.

Fowler, H. W. *A dictionary of modern English usage* (Rev. ed.). Oxford: Oxford University Press, 1965.

Garrett, M., & Fodor, J. A. Psychological theories and linguistic constructs. In T. R. Dixon & D. L. Horton (Eds.), *Verbal behavior and general behavior theory*. Englewood Cliffs, N.J.: Prentice-Hall, 1968.

Greenfield, P. M. Cross-cultural research and Piagetian theory: Paradox and progress. In K. F. Riegel & J. A. Meacham (Eds.), *The developing individual in a changing world*. The Hague: Mouton, 1976.

Grieve, R., Hoogenraad, R., & Murray, D. On the young child's use of lexis and syntax in understanding locative instructions. *Cognition*, 1977, *5*, 235-250.

Hamlyn, D. W. History of epistemology. In P. Edwards (Ed.), *The encyclopedia of philosophy* (Vol. 3). New York: Free Press, 1967.

Harris, L. J., & Strommen, E. A. The role of front-back features in children's "front," "back," and "beside" placements of objects. *Merrill-Palmer Quarterly*, 1972, *18*, 259-271.

International Kindergarten Union. A study of the vocabulary of children before entering the first grade. Baltimore, Md.: Williams & Wilkins, 1928.

James, W. *The principles of psychology* (Vol. 1). New York: Dover, 1950. (Originally published, 1890).

Jaynes, J. *The origins of consciousness in the breakdown of the bicameral mind*. Boston: Houghton Mifflin, 1976.

Jenkins, J. J. A challenge to psychological theorists. In T. R. Dixon & D. L. Horton (Eds.), *Verbal behavior and general behavior theory*. Englewood Cliffs, N.J.: Prentice-Hall, 1968.

Johnson, C. N., & Maratsos, M. P. Early comprehension of mental verbs: Think and know. *Child Development*, 1977, *48*, 1743-1747.

Katz, J. J., & Bever, T. G. The fall and rise of empiricism. In T. G. Bever, J. J. Katz, & D. T. Langendoen, *An integrated theory of linguistic ability*. Sussex, Eng.: Harvester Press, 1977.

Klatzky, R. L., Clark, E. V., & Macken, M. Asymmetries in the acquisition of polar adjectives: Linguistic or conceptual? *Journal of Experimental Child Psychology*, 1973, *16*, 32-46.

Kuczaj, S. A., II, & Maratsos, M. P. On the acquisition of *front, back,* and *side. Child Development*, 1975, *46*, 202-210.

Kuhn, T. *The structure of scientific revolutions*. Chicago: University of Chicago Press, 1962.

Macnamara, J., Baker, E., & Olson, C. L. Four year olds' understanding of *pretend, forget,* and *know:* Evidence for propositional operations. *Child Development*, 1976, *47*, 62-70.

McNeill, D. *The acquisition of language: The study of developmental psycholinguistics*. New York: Harper & Row, 1970.

McNeill, D. *Semiotic extension*. Institute for Advanced Study, Princeton, Paper presented at the Loyola Symposium on Cognition, Chicago, Illinois, April 1974.

Mehrabian, A., & Williams, M. Piagetian measures of cognitive development for children up to age two. *Journal of Psycholinguistic Research*, 1971, *1*, 113-126.

Miller, G. A. Some preliminaries to psycholinguistics. *American Psychologist*, 1965, *20*, 15-20.

Miller, G. A. *Spontaneous apprentices: Children and language*. New York: Seabury Press, 1977.

Miller, G. A., & Johnson-Laird, P. N. *Language and perception*. Cambridge, Mass.: Harvard University Press, 1976.

Minsky, M. (Ed.). *Semantic information processing*. Cambridge, Mass.: M.I.T. Press, 1968.

Miscione, J. L., Marvin, R. S., O'Brien, R. G., & Greenberg, M. T. A developmental study of preschool children's understanding of the words "know" and "guess." *Child Development,* 1978, *49,* 1107–1113.

Navon, D. On a conceptual hierarchy of time, space, and other dimensions. *Cognition,* 1978, *6,* 223–228.

Olson, D. R., & Hildyard, A. *Assent and compliance in children's language comprehension: Knowing and doing.* Paper based on earlier version prepared for TINLAP-2. Urbana, Ill.: University of Illinois, July 1978. (Available from D. R. Olson, Ontario Institute for Studies in Education, Ontario, Canada, M5S 1V6).

Osgood, C. E., May, W., & Miron, M. *Cross-cultural universals of affective meaning.* Urbana, Ill.: University of Illinois Press, 1975.

Palermo, D. S. Is a scientific revolution taking place in psychology? *Science Studies,* 1971, *1,* 135–155.

Piaget, J. *The child's conception of time.* London: Routledge & Kegan Paul, 1969.

Pollio, H. R., Barlow, J. M., Fine, H. J., & Pollio, M. R. *Psychology and the poetics of growth: Figurative language in psychology, psychotherapy, and education.* Hillsdale, N.J.: Lawrence Erlbaum Associates, 1977.

Richards, M. M. Sorting out what's in a word from what's not: Evaluating Clark's semantic features acquisition theory. *Journal of Experimental Child Psychology,* 1979, *27,* 1–47.

Richards, M. M., & Brown, M. L. Acquiring different senses of the verb *to know.* Paper presented at the 1981 Biennial meetings of the Society for Research in Child Development. Boston, Mass., April, 1981.

Richards, M. M., & Hawpe, L. S. Contrasting patterns in the acquisition of spatial/temporal terms. *Journal of Experimental Child Psychology,* 1981.

Rosch, E. Cognitive representation of semantic categories. *Journal of Experimental Psychology: General,* 1975, *104,* 192–233.

Rosch, E. Human categorization. In N. Warren (Ed.), *Studies in cross-cultural psychology.* New York: Academic Press, 1977.

Russell, B. *The analysis of mind.* London: George Allen & Unwin, 1921.

Searle, J. R. *Speech acts: An essay in the philosophy of language.* London: Cambridge University Press, 1969.

Shatz, M. Children's comprehension of their mothers' question–directives. *Journal of Child Language,* 1978, *5,* 39–46.

Simon, H. A. *The sciences of the artificial.* Cambridge, Mass.: M.I.T. Press, 1969.

Sinclair, J., & Coulthard, R. M. *Towards an analysis of discourse: The English used by teachers and pupils.* London: Oxford University Press, 1975.

Sinclair, H. Sensorimotor action patterns as a condition for the acquisition of snytax. In R. Huxley & E. Ingram (Eds.), *Language acquisition: Models and methods.* New York: Academic Press, 1971.

Slobin, D. I. Cognitive prerequisites for the development of grammar. In C. A. Ferguson & D. I. Slobin (Eds.), *Studies of child language development.* New York: Holt, Rinehart, & Winston, 1973.

Tanz, C. Studies in the acquisition of deictic expressions. *Cambridge Studies in Linguistics, 26.* Cambridge: Cambridge University Press, 1980.

Wilcox, S., & Palermo, D. S. "In," "on," and "under" revisited. *Cognition,* 1974, *3,* 245–254.

Winograd, T. Understanding natural language. *Cognitive Psychology,* 1972, *3*(No. 1).

12 A Functional Analysis of Meaning

Grover J. Whitehurst
State University of New York at Stony Brook

Jurgen Kedesdy
State University of New York at Stony Brook

Thomas G. White
Gettysburg College

To take seriously much of the last 25 years' literature on language acquisition is to imagine a universal child, primed to learn his or her native tongue with lightning-like rapidity and in lock-step stages, immune from vagaries of environment, and operating through uniquely linguistic processes. The model for the science that has emerged from this work is astronomy: The investigator observes, describes, and tries to develop a rule that will be consistent with the accumulated observations.

This chapter cuts across the grain of this theoretical and research tradition. Our working assumption is that language is learned, that the processes at work are in large part shared in the acquisition of all complex skills, linguistic and nonlinguistic, and that theories of learning and the research methods of experimental psychology are relevant. We label our approach *functional* because we are interested in the relations among variables (see Zimmerman & Whitehurst, 1979).

In our view, then, a functional analysis of meaning is a specification of variables that affect the ability to use language in a manner that would be described as meaningful by the social community. A complete functional analysis would require a list of all the characteristics of language that relate to social judgments of meaningfulness and knowledge of all the variables that affect the ability to produce these characteristics, as well as knowledge of how these two aspects are related. Obviously, a complete functional analysis is impossible to formulate at this time (but not in principle).

We offer here some demonstrations of a functional analysis that follow from a theoretical analysis of semantic development by Whitehurst (1979). That paper is an attempt to describe in speculative terms some of the variables that might relate to a child's knowledge of word–referent relations and word–word relations. That is, how does a child come to learn to relate words to things and words to other words?

The present chapter focuses exclusively on word–thing, or referential, relations. We do so with the awareness that this represents but a subset of the domain of semantic development and perhaps the simplest subset at that. On the other hand, we cannot hope to understand complicated issues of sense and communication if we do not have a grasp of basic labeling. To restrict the analysis still further, we are interested here in the labeling practices of adults as they affect the labeling practices of children. Two separate semantic phenomena are examined. The first is the child's initial acquisition of basic object labels; the second and more developmentally advanced is the child's acquisition of labels for classes of objects and things.

THE ORIGINAL WORD GAME

One of the problems of child language, in its most basic formulation, is how children first make sense of, and learn from, the presumably undifferentiated stream of language that envelopes them. Although this problem has important phonetic and syntactic aspects, we are concerned here with a subset of the semantic aspect: how children come to learn the names of things.

It is generally acknowledged that many of the child's first terms of reference are learned in the context of what Brown (1958b) has called the original word game. The game is apparently simple:

> The tutor names things in accordance with the semantic customs of the community. The player forms hypotheses about the categorical nature of the things named. He tests his hypotheses by trying to name new things correctly. The tutor compares the player's utterances with his own anticipations of such utterances and, in this way, checks the accuracy of fit between his own categories and those of the player. He improves the fit by correction [p. 194].

The child, in playing the original word game, has two sources of information at his or her disposal: (1) the tutor's naming of things; (2) feedback for his or her own utterances. The first operation assures that something is learned, the second assures its validity. We are, in this section, solely concerned with the first process, the initial connecting of words and things.

Word-referent learning is a matter of learning the relationships between two sets of stimuli; the child's job is to learn what goes with what. Whitehurst (1979) has argued that the acquisition of word-referent relationships occurs largely through observational learning. In observational learning, according to Whitehurst (1979), "aspects of the context, form, and/or outcome of a model's behavior influence corresponding dimensions of an observer's behavior [p. 126]." Applied to lexical acquistion, the modeled response is, of course, the word and the context is the referent. It is important to emphasize that observational learning is *not* limited to the responses of the model, does *not* require an overt response from the learner at the time of learning and, the learner's overt response need not mimic that of the model. Observational learning of word-referent relationships, then, is not limited to instances in which children imitate adult verbalizations. The learning of verbal relationships may be indexed by a variety of responses. The child may demonstrate "spontaneous" use of the word, may respond appropriately when asked the name of a referent, or may indicate comprehension by pointing to the referent when asked to do so.

A Critique of Ostensive Definitions

Parental labeling is, of course, a kind of ostensive definition, and the present enterprise might be characterized as a functional analysis of observational learning via ostensive definition. The validity of ostensive definition has recently come under criticism by Bruner (1975) and his comments, because of their theoretical implications, merit some rebutal. Bruner begins his attack by reviving and elaborating some of Wittgenstein's (1953) arguments.

Wittgenstein's "demolition" (Bruner's term) of ostensive definition amounts to a puzzlement about how we can learn the connection between words and things when, in the simple act of naming, the feature or features of the object that control naming are not specified. When a tutor labels an object "dog," is it furriness, four-leggedness, cold-snoutedness, a tendency to bark, or some combination of those features, or countless others, that is being named? An ostensive definition, says Wittgenstein (1953), "can be variously interpreted in *every* case [p. 14e]." According to Wittgenstein, we mistakenly imagine first-language learning to be "as if the child came into a strange country and did not understand the language of the country; that is, as if it already had a language, only not this one [p. 16e]."

It is, of course, true that a child with *no* prior knowledge whatsoever would at best sense only undifferentiated streams of sounds and things and thus could not profit from ostensive definition. Wittgenstein's point is that the child must already know the conventions of the language game, must know what language is used for, before he or she can learn from ostensive definition. Bruner reiterates Wittgenstein's argument for similar reasons: He wants to stress the need for an understanding of the child's prelinguistic communication skills.

In this argument, and in much of his recent work, Bruner is concerned with establishing the preconditions of effective word–referent learning. What must the child know before he or she can learn from ostensive definition and how does he or she come to know it? Two of the devices Bruner mentions serve as an illustration. One necessary precursor to ostensive definition is joint attention to the referent to be named. Studies by Collis and Schaffer (1975) and Scaife and Bruner (1975) show that interaction between mother and child involves a mutual following of line of regard: Mothers look at what infants look at and infants as early as 4 months of age tend to track their mother's gaze. It is interesting to know that this occurs; it would be even more interesting to know why.

Another mechanism that assures joint attention is "marking" an object by touching or shaking it. Kaye (1976) has shown that mothers will use this technique to induce their child to take an object from behind a transparent barrier. Bruner (1975) comments on this process: "They not only mark the object, but evoke the action either by a process of tempting—putting the object nearer and at the edge of the barrier—or by modelling the behavior themselves. The marking involves a combination of 'highlighting' features and exaggerating the structure of the acts to be performed [p. 270]."

A mutual following of line of regard and the development of reciprocal marking, then, are elements of a "language prior to language," which may well be necessary before the child can learn from ostensive definitions. But, although even the simplest forms of learning often have preconditions (a rat learning to press a bar must first learn where the food is), these preconditions do not invalidate the principles that govern subsequent learning.

Bruner (1975) continues his criticism of ostensive definition by linking it with associative theories of reference:

> Moreover, associative theories of naming or reference are beleaguered by the presupposition that uttering a sound or making a gesture in the presence of a referent somehow evokes a nascent or innate recognition in the child that the name is associated with some features of something that is at focus of the child's attention, so that any concatenation of sign and referent is as likely as any other to be learned, and that is plainly not so [p. 268].

We are, of course, proposing a kind of associative theory of reference but one that is not, we think, beleaguered by the presuppositions Bruner complains of. Far from presupposing that "any concatenation of sign and referent is as likely as any other to be learned," we are interested in developing a model that might account for which word–referent relations are most likely to be learned. Indeed, it is difficult to imagine an associative theory that would not be interested in such a question.

Types of Associative Theories: S–S versus S–R

The observational learning of word–referent relationships is clearly a kind of associative learning. Because the history of associative theories of language has been long and, it now appears, not especially fruitful, we would like to emphasize briefly some of the fundamental differences between the present approach and earlier ones. The associative models of language that are now largely discredited are Hullian-derived, stimulus–response (S–R) models, and they can be distinguished from the present approach in terms of their proposed mechanisms.

There are, of course, numerous forms of S–R theory, the form of the theory usually being an adaptation to the research paradigm in which the theory presumes to do its explaining. The central tenet of all S–R theories, however, is that responses get connected to stimuli. For Pavlov, conditioned stimuli get connected to responses when the stimuli are followed by the unconditioned stimulus. For Thorndike, instrumental responses are connected to environmental stimuli when the responses are followed by reward. An example of one application of S–R theory is succinctly described by Asch (1968):

> Classical associationism was mentalistic. The shift to a systematically behavioristic position signaled the abandonment of reference to mental facts and the treatment of learning purely as changes of behavior. It also marked the conceptualization of associations as stimulus–response connections, a shift that coincided with the presumably more fundamental phenomena of conditioning. The paired associate method, which was increasingly favored as a result of this conceptualization, illustrates the S–R way of looking at the facts of learning. Given a list consisting of pairs of terms to be memorized by the method of anticipation, the first member was described as the stimulus, the second member as the response, and the connection between them as one of conditioning. Errors during learning were thought of in terms of stimulus generalization, their dissappearance as a consequence of differentiation, and interference between successive tasks as effects of extinction [p. 219].

It is not our intention to evaluate the adequacy of such mechanisms in the interpretation of verbal learning, only to stress that behavioral theories of association were essentially theories of *response* learning.

Observational learning theory, on the other hand, conceptualizes word–referent learning as the acquisition of stimulus–stimulus (S–S) relationships. As such, it is more closely related to current theories of classical conditioning (Rescorla, 1975, 1978) than to traditional behavioral analyses of verbal learning and semantic conditioning. In the more recent view, classical conditioning is regarded as a paradigm in which organisms learn the relation between events, not a transfer of response from one stimulus to another (Rescorla, 1978):

We view Pavlovian conditioning as the learning of relations among environmental events which occur outside the organism's control. As a result of the environment arranging a relation between two stimulus events, the organism undergoes learning which in turn is reflected by a change in its behavior. Typically one event (the conditioned stimulus (CS)) is initially neutral and one (the unconditioned stimulus(US)) is initially potent, and typically the change in behavior observed is a modification of the response to the CS. But from the present viewpoint *the essential feature is that the organism learns about interevent relations* [p. 15, italics added].

As should be clear from our discussion of S-R versus S-S mechanisms, we are sympathetic to an account that likens word–referent relations to the relations studied in classical conditioning, but we believe that it is relationships and not responses that are learned. Furthermore, we do not view meaning as a response (or corporeal entity of any kind). "Meaning" is best used as a label for the set of activities that constitute meaningful use of language. Meaningful language use incorporates and reflects a harmonious blending of semantic, syntactic, and pragmatic skills. Observational learning is only a single factor in the acquisition of those skills (and so is not the sole determinant of "meaning") but it is a critical one.

Word–Referent Contiguity

If lexical acquisition is a form of S-S learning, a number of potential variables immediately suggest themselves. The child's job of learning what goes with what should be strongly affected by the ease with which the relation between words and things can be detected. Whitehurst (1979) has called this the *transparency* factor and suggested that contiguity and reliability might be major determinants of transparency. Let us consider contiguity (Whitehurst, 1979):

Temporal contiguity as related to adults' speech concerns the delay between the time at which an adult uses a word and the time when the referent is perceptually available for the learner. The temporal contiguity dimension starts at simultaneity and moves in both directions on a time line from the adult's utterance, depending on whether the adult is speaking of the present, describing the past, or predicting the future [p. 126].

If temporal contiguity is important (as virtually any associative theory would insist), children should acquire early terms of reference more readily from adults who limit references to present events than from adults who talk primarily about the past or future. The word game is, of course, played almost exclusively in the present; parents rarely use incidents from the past or future during deliberate lexical tutoring. There is by now a large body of evidence showing that mothers' speech is tailored to the capacities of their children (Phillips, 1973; Snow, 1972) and part of this accommodation consists of limiting discussion to the here and now. The studies by Collis and Schaffer (1975) and Scaife and Bruner (1975), as well as a host of studies cited by Bruner (1975) as evidence of "indicating" procedures, may be regarded as evidence for the development of mechanisms that assure word–referent contiguity.

Even though these descriptive studies point to the importance of word–referent contiguity in early lexical acquisition, there are no experimental studies that straight forwardly assess the role of temporal contiguity. The following study was designed to remedy that deficit. The study manipulates word–referent contiguity in a relatively natural setting (a day-care center) in which 2 year olds have the opportunity to learn novel terms of reference. The contiguous (present) condition, in which words and referents are presented simultaneously, is contrasted with two noncontiguous conditions, in which words and referents are separated by a brief interval of time. In the past condition, referents precede words; in the future condition, words precede referents.

Six children, ages 2;1–2;8, from an infant day-care center located in an academic community served as subjects. The experiment was conducted in a room that was visually but not acoustically isolated from the rest of the day-care center. The experimental context was one in which the experimenter occasionally produced initially novel referents from a box and labeled them for the child.

Children were encouraged to sit next to the experimenter while objects were removed from the box. Children seldom sat attentively throughout an entire session. They would often roam about the room. hide under cots, and climb on the experimenter's back. The experimenter and the box of referents followed the child throughout the child's peregrinations to assure spatial contiguity between referent and child.

Children learned the names for 15 novel objects (see Table 12.1) under three different contiguity conditions. In the present condition, words and referents were presented simultaneously (e.g., "Look, Sandy, see the wick."). In the past condition, a delay of about 10 seconds intervened between the presentation and removal of an object and its labeling (e.g., "Sandy, that was a wick."). In the future condition, labeling of objects occurred 10 seconds prior to their presentation (e.g., "The next thing is the wick.").

Each child was exposed to each condition and the order of conditions was counterbalanced across children. Five novel word–referent relations were presented in each condition. Each novel referent was produced three times per session and was labeled three times on each occasion. Thus, each session contained 15 novel trials. The criteria for the onset of a trial were an intertrial interval of about 10 seconds and the child's visual contact with the referent. There were three sessions per condition, resulting in each referent being presented a total of nine times and labeled 27 times. Also included in each session were trials on which familiar referents (e.g., dog, ball, fish) were presented and labeled.

TABLE 12.1
Objects and Labels for a Study of Contiguity

Word	Description of Referent
WAND	A red and white striped stick with a silver star afixed at one end.
PAD	A knee pad.
HOE	A small, 6″ hoe.
MUFF	A piece of brown fur.
NIB	A nib.
PUMP	A small bicycle pump.
WICK	A fluffy yellow pipe cleaner.
BOW	A green bow.
GAUGE	A presta valve tire gauge.
CLIP	A large paper clip.
PUCK	An orange hockey puck.
MAP	A map.
HUB	A buffer wheel from an electric drill set.
NET	A small fish net.
TUBE	A vacuum tube.

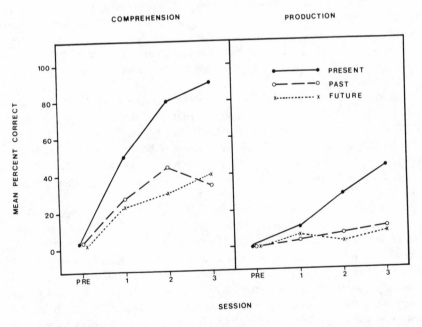

FIG. 12.1. Percentage correct comprehension and production responses in present-, past-, and future-tense conditions.

The first session of each condition was preceded by a pretest and every session was concluded with a posttest. Both tests had a comprehension and production component. In the production test, children were asked to name referents as they were presented one at a time (e.g., "What's this, Sandy? Do you know what this is?"). Comprehension was assessed by asking the child to pick a referent from an array of the referents for that condition (e.g., "Where's the wick, Sandy? Can you find the wick?"). The child's responses in both tests were scored either "correct," "incorrect," or "no answer." Finally, spontaneous imitations of both novel and familiar words was recorded throughout the experiment.

Both production and comprehension measures indicate more rapid acquisition of word–referent relations in the contiguous (present) condition than in either of the noncontiguous (past and future) conditions. Fig. 12.1 shows the mean acquisition functions. A one-factor ANOVA with repeated measures on the mean third-session scores of each condition confirms that comprehension ($F = 7.44$, $df = 2, 10, P < .05$) and production ($F = 5.97$, $df = 2, 10, P < .05$) in the present condition are significantly greater than in the past and future conditions. An analysis of linear trend indicates that comprehension of word–referent relations in the present condition increases significantly as a function of sessions ($F = 5.81$, $df = 1, 15, P < .05$), whereas the increase in production scores across sessions is marginally significant ($F = 4.42$, $df = 1, 15, P < .10$). There were no significant nonlinear components in either case. Neither comprehension nor production scores in either the past or future conditions shows a significant linear (or nonlinear) increase as a function of sessions.

The proportion of trials on which at least one spontaneous imitation occurred was .43, .30, and .26 for the present, past, and future conditions respectively. The relatively higher proportion of imitations in the present condition did not achieve statistical significance ($F = 2.4$, $df = 2, 10, P > .05$). There is a good deal of variation in the degree to which children spontaneously imitated. S7, for instance, imitated very little, whereas S8 imitated on almost 80% of the trials in the present condition. S8 also tended to imitate each of the three labels on each trial whereas multiple imitations per trial were very rare for other subjects.

There is little relationship between spontaneous imitation during training and subsequent measures of acquisition. The Pearson product-moment correlation coefficients calculated between all words for all subjects ($N = 90$) and the total number of correct comprehensions and productions is .14. Correlation coefficients calculated separately for present, past, and future conditions ($N = 30$) are .06, .10, and .14 respectively. The number of imitations per word, therefore, is not related to the acquisition of that word in any condition.

These data indicate that word–referent contiguity is an important feature of the adult labeling that occurs during the original word game. A word–referent interstimulus interval of as little as 10 seconds significantly retards both the comprehension and production of new referential relationships. Although this outcome is not surprising, neither is it trivial. The present procedures applied to adult subjects would not reveal such differences. Ostensive definitions seem to work over rather long intervals for adults. When we ask, "Who was that person I saw you with last week?", the answer is likely to establish a referential relationship. Or when X informs us, "I will show you my Mondrian tommorrow," we will be able to label X's painting appropriately on the following day.

One is tempted to ascribe such differences between children and adults to the ability to remember or anticipate. But 2-year old children have little trouble remembering things for 10 seconds. The children in the present study were able to relate incidents that happened to them several days in the past and to anticipate events of importance (e.g., "Grandma's coming.") several days in advance.

Nor are the present results usefully interpreted as due to differences in "attention." Visual contact with the referent was criterial for trial onset and it is difficult to imagine why auditory attention to the words should differ across conditions. It is more plausible to assume that children attend equally to words and referents across conditions, but attended differentially to their relationship. But this is merely a restatement of the importance of contiguity.

The finding that immediate imitation during training is uncorrelated with subsequent comprehension or production is largely in accord with previous reports. The debate about the function of imitation has often depended on a distinction between imitative and spontaneous utterances. Unfortunately, this distinction is controversial (Whitehurst & Vasta, 1975). Are productions after long (how long?) delays imitations or spontaneous utterances? Do verbal episodes that intervene between modeling and subsequent productions disqualify those productions as imitations? Spontaneous utterances are (weakly) defined as those utterances that are not imitative, but their determinants are left unspecified. Interpretation of the present study is limited to immediate copying and therefore avoids this troublesome distinction. Almost all of the imitations in the present study were immediate and the setting occasions for subsequent demonstrations of lexical acquisition are well specified. In this respect, the present results are most comparable to those obtained in Leonard, Schwartz, Fogler, Newhoff, and Wilcox (1979, Experiment 3), where imitation was found to be unrelated to subsequent naming in a task very similar to our production test. Our finding that immediate imitation is also unrelated to subsequent comprehension strengthens the conclusion that imitation, narrowly defined, does not facilitate lexical acquisition.

If immediate imitation does not facilitate acquisition of new lexical items, what does it do for those children who imitate? Leonard et al. (1979) propose that imitation enables young speakers to encode novel and informative referents. If that were the case, one might expect the number of imitations to be highest in the first of our three sessions in each condition. We found, however, that imitations were evenly distributed across the three sessions. Our imitation data seems most consistent with the view that imitation serves a more general pragmatic–communicative function, perhaps that of assuring the continuation of the word game.

Word-Referent Informativeness

Even though contiguity has been a variable of central importance in association theory, there is by now a substantial body of evidence that questions the necessity and sufficiency of temporal contiguity in the formation of associations. Rescorla (1967), for instance, has argued that classical conditioning depends on a contingency between the CS and US, not merely a pairing of those events. In this view, conditioning will occur only to the degree that CS predicts or carries information about the US for the learning. The informativeness of a CS is at least partially a function of the probability with which it precedes the US. In the conventional classical conditioning experiment, each CS is followed by US; thus, the probability of a US, given a CS, is 1.0. If, however, the number of CS-US pairings is held constant and additional unpaired CS or US are added to the session, the informativeness of the CS will be degraded, gradually approaching .0 as the extra events are increased. Thus, it is not enough to know how many times a CS and US are paired; one must know in addition the number of times they are unpaired.

We may then ask, in the pursuit of our analogy between classical conditioning and early lexical acquisition, whether word-referent informativeness plays a role in the original language game. The importance of information variables has not gone unnoticed by students of child language. Greenfield and Smith (1976), for instance, have argued that information, defined as uncertainty reduction, is a major determinant of what children in the one-word stage choose to say. Uncertainty reduction is a broad and vague definition of information that needs to be tightened before careful analytic work may proceed.

In the study described next, we manipulated word-referent informativeness by varying the correlation between words and things. In the perfect correlation condition, five words and things are paired, whereas in the two imperfect correlation conditions either extra words or extra things dilute the word-referent correlation—that is, the degree to which the referent is predicted by the word. We predicted that lexical acquisition in the two imperfect correlation conditions would be retarded relative to lexical acquisition in the perfect correlation condition.

Six new children, ages 1;10-2;5 were chosen from the same day-care center. The experimental setting and 15 referents were the same as those described in the previous study. The experimenter again produced novel referents from a box and labeled them for the child, but during the course of this study, the referents were given to the child and after roughly 5 seconds, the child was encouraged to give the referent to another, relatively inconspicuous adult who returned the object to the box.

In the perfect condition, children were presented with five referents and each referent was labeled once (e.g., "See the nib.") The extra-word and extra-thing conditions each had five word-referent pairings as well as 10 additional stimuli (words or referents respectively) from the same class as the paired stimuli. For instance, in the extra-word condition, "nib" might have been paired with its appropriate referent and might also have occurred unpaired on two randomly determined occasions. In the extra-thing condition, on the other hand, the nib itself would be presented on two extra occasions.

Each condition was in effect for five sessions and the order of conditions was counterbalanced across the six children. Pre- and posttest measures were the same as those in the contiguity study.

Acquisition of word–referent relationships was more rapid in the perfect correlation condition than in either of the imperfect correlation conditions. A one-factor ANOVA with repeated measures on the fifth-session scores of each condition shows a significant treatment effect on the comprehension measure ($F = 4.51$, $df = 2, 10$, $P < .05$), but not on the production measure ($F = 2.28$, $df = 2, 10$, $P > .05$).

Figure 12.2 shows the total number of productions and comprehensions for each condition across five sessions. Lexical acquisition in the perfect condition clearly outstrips that in either of the imperfect correlation conditions. The difference between the extra-thing condition and the extra-word condition does not appear to be large. An exception is the number of productions in the extra-thing condition, which is twice that in the extra-word condition and nearly equal to the perfect condition. This effect, however, is due largely to the performance of one

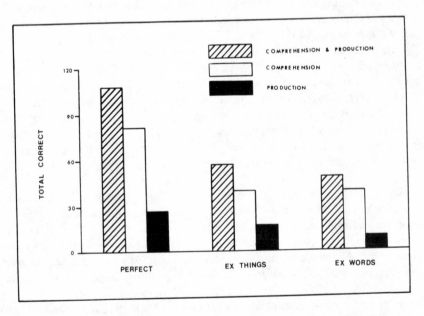

FIG. 12.2.   Total number of correct comprehensions and productions across five sessions.

subject. Perhaps more representative is the median number of productions, 5, 2, and 1, in the perfect, extra-thing, and extra-word conditions respectively.

The present findings confirm the general importance of information variables in early language development. Although previous studies suggest that referent informativeness plays a role in determining what children will say (Greenfield & Smith, 1976) and which lexical items they will imitate (Leonard et al., 1979), these data extend those findings by showing that word–referent informativeness is also an important acquisition variable.

The present data are also consistent with the classical conditioning analysis of word–referent relationships that we have outlined previously. Our extra-word condition is, of course, analogous to the partial reinforcement paradigm in classical conditioning in which some portion of the conditioned stimuli in each session are unreinforced. The typical result of a partial reinforcement procedure in classical conditioning is a lower rate of acquisition relative to consistent reinforcement (Mackintosh, 1974), an outcome that is in accordance with the retarded acquisition in the extra-word condition.

The second way to degrade CS–US correlation is to add extra US as, analogously, we added extra referents in our extra-thing condition. This procedure has been less frequently studied, but conditioned-suppression studies by Rescorla (1967) and a number of autoshaping studies (Hearst & Jenkins, 1974) have demonstrated the efficacy of such manipulations in retarding the acquisition of CS–US relationships.

Finally, even though acquisition in the perfect condition is superior to both extra-word and extra-thing conditions, there is virtually no difference between the two imperfect correlation conditions. This is exactly the outcome that would be expected by a correlation-based theory of association because the addition of extra events (words and/or things) should have equal effects on the degree of word–referent correlation.

Referent Value

Learning the relation between two events depends on the characteristics of those events as well as their temporal and predictive relationship. In classical conditioning, the salience of the CS and intensity of the US have both been shown to be variables of importance. Analogously, characteristics of the word and referent should influence their associability.

The role of referent characteristics in lexical acquisition has been investigated by Nelson (1973b), who obtained lists of the first words produced by 18 children. When the first 50 words were divided into categories on the basis of referent type, the following categories were represented most frequently: food, animals, clothes, toys, and vehicles, in that order of frequency. Nelson (1973b) argued that:

frequency of personal experience, exposure to words, strength of need or desire cannot apparently explain the selection of these words. They are personal, selective, and for the most part action related. It is apparent that children learn the names of the things they can act on as well as things that act themselves . . . With very few exceptions all the words listed are terms applying to the manipulable or movable objects . . . The common attribute of all the most frequent early referents is that they have salient properties of change [p. 33].

Thus, for Nelson, a major determinant of lexical-acquisition order is the activity or manipulability of the referents that the child first learns to label. We call this the "activity hypothesis."

The activity hypothesis has received partial experimental support from an observational learning study by Stewart and Hamilton (1976). The words modeled by adults in this study were novel (French) and were associated with five categories of referent type: edible, self-activating, manipulable, passive, and no-referent control. Recognition and spontaneous-imitation scores were found to be highly related to referent type, with foods commanding by far the greatest number of imitations, followed by self-activating, manipulable, passive, and no-referent scores, in that order.

In spite of such confirmation, there are a number of problems with the activity hypothesis. First, the class of things that are active *or* manipulable is very large indeed. So large that one is hard pressed to think of any referent that could not, a priori, belong to that class. This vitiates the predictive power of the hypothesis. For instance, what within Nelson's hypothesis accounts for the difference between the food and the manipulable categories in the Stewart and Hamilton (1976) study? Secondly, the hypothesis does not fit, even post hoc, Nelson's data as well as one would like. Rain is highly motile but never mentioned. Doors are conspicuous in both movement and manipulability, but "door" is used by only three of the 18 children. Pictures of animals, rather than live animals, often controlled animal references, and pictures are neither active nor manipulable in any important sense. Finally, the activity hypothesis does not speak to individual differences. What accounts for the variations that occur across children in the typical sequence of words acquired?

Whitehurst (1979) has suggested an alternative approach to the analysis of referent characteristics in which the important dimension is the referent's value to the child ("value" is defined as the child's preference for the referent; a measure of preference is described shortly). Value is therefore not a property of referents per se, but the relation between referents and the child. Thus, although "activity" may be a property of referents that endears them to some children some of the time, there may well be other, independent properties (such as novelty, perceptual salience, or the relation of an object to some other valued object or activity) that determines momentary referent value.

We call this alternative conception the "preference hypothesis." It differs in at least two important respects from the activity hypothesis. First, the preference hypothesis claims to *predict* the behavior of an *individual* child; although individuals may have common preferences, no commonality is assumed. Secondly, preferences are not assumed to be stable across time and situation. Referent value as preference is relative to the value of other referents and may fluctuate as a function of other variables, such as deprivation. A simple prediction is that a child would be more likely to learn the word "pear" after having taken one bite of a pear than after having consumed 10 pears, given that relative deprivation affects value.

It is important to note that both the preference hypothesis and activity hypothesis are incomplete causal analyses. The activity hypothesis does not address the issue of why activity is an important dimension of referent value. The preference hypothesis does not speak to the issue of why any dimension, including activity, might be of value to the child.

The purpose of the following study is to develop an empirical scale of value for a set of referents and to determine the relationship between a referent's value on that scale and the rapidity with which the label for that referent is acquired. Two procedurally independent scales are created to increase confidence in the validity of each measure of value.

The first is based on the relative amount of time a child spends playing with a referent. This measure is derived from a theory of value proposed by Premack (1971), which has the following principal features: (1) organisms can order any environmental event on a scale of value; (2) the value that an organism assigns to an event can be measured by the probability that the organism will respond to that event; and (3) this probability can be estimated from response duration. Thus, we assume that the amount of time a child spends playing with a referent, relative to time spent playing with other members of the set, is a measure of the child's preference for that referent.

The second measure of referent value is a simple paired-choice procedure in which children are asked to state their preferences for a referent when given a choice between two referents.

Six children, ages 2;2–3;1 were again selected from the day-care center. Four of them had previously participated in the word–referent contiguity study. One subject ultimately proved uncooperative and was replaced.

Five new referents were selected on the basis of three criteria: (1) they were referents for which the subjects had not learned names; (2) they had one-syllable names; and (3) they represented a relatively wide range of presumed value to children of the present age group.

Subjects were informed that they would have the opportunity to "play with some new toys," that they could play with each toy for a while but only with one toy at a time. Each child was then given a pretest to verify his or her naiveté with respect to the names of the five referents. The test included a production component in which children were shown a referent and were asked to name it (e.g., "What's this? Do you know what this is?"), as well as a comprehension component in which children were asked to select a particular referent from the array of five referents (e.g., "Can you find the bolt? Where's the bolt?"). Answers were scored either "correct," "incorrect," or "no answer."

As previously noted, there were two measures of referent value, the first based on time spent playing with each referent, the second based on a paired-choice procedure in which a child was asked which pair of referents he or she liked best.

After both measures of value had been taken, children were given training with word–referent relations. Each of the five referents was produced three times for a total of 15 trials per session. The child's visual contact with the referent defined trial onset and the referent was labeled three times during each session (e.g., "Look, Sandy, this is the punch."). There were three labeling sessions and a test of production and comprehension, identical to the pretest, followed each session.

Children differentially allocated time to each of the five referents, enabling the construction of an empirical scale of value for each child. The correlation between time-allocation measures (total time spent with each referent in both sessions) with the total number of correct productions and comprehensions was generally high, the mean correlation coefficient for the six subjects being .64. Individual correlation coefficients were .18, .61, .75, .98, and .67.

Children generally responded appropriately to the paired-choice test, enabling the construction of a second scale of value that could be compared with the time-allocation scale. The two scales were generally highly related, Kendall rank-order correlations between scales for each child being .84, .80, 1.0, .95, .80, and .60.

The present results indicate that it is possible to create an empirical scale of referent value for individual children and that there is a strong positive correlation between the value of a referent and the rapidity with which words are associated with their referents for most children. The strong positive correlations between time-allocation and paired-choice measures lend credence to the validity of those measures.

The correlation of our measures of value with lexical acquisition does not, of course, rule out alternative interpretations of referent value. In particular, the present results, are not necessarily incompatible with Nelson's activity hypothesis. Even though none of the present referents were self-activating, all of them, with the exception of the brain, could be acted upon meaningfully. The top could be twirled, the punch could punch, the cube could be rattled, the bolt could have its nuts adjusted. Of course, in order for the present data to be fully consistent with the activity hypothesis, one would have to assume that these referents *varied* on the activity dimension, the punch being most manipulable and the brain the least so. Although this may have some intuitive validity, it is, of course, post-hoc speculation and does not, moreover, account for the individual differences in preference observed in the present data.

LABELING OF CLASSES AND UNDEREXTENSION

Another semantic phenomenon, underextension of labels for classes, can be approached within the functional framework proposed by Whitehurst (1979). An underextension is a failure to include appropriate instances under a semantic label—for example, failing to understand that a chicken is a bird.

Consider first *typicality,* a related phenomenon that refers to the fact that some members of semantic categories are judged as more typical or representative than others, with category members forming a graded series from most to least typical. Thus, when Rosch (1975) asked college students to rate the degree to which members of common superordinate categories fit their idea or image of a category, ratings for the various category members not only differed sharply, but also showed high agreement across subjects. To illustrate, a robin was judged as a better, more representative example of the category *bird* than a pigeon, and a pigeon was deemed more bird-like than a duck or an ostrich.

Given adult typicality judgments, we might expect to find that children's semantic concepts initially comprise typical instances and only later come to include atypical or peripheral instances. This hypothesis is supported by several recent studies (Anglin, 1977; Carson & Abrahamson, 1976; White, 1979).

In the White (1979) study, adult typicality ratings were used to select two typical and two atypical instances of each of six categories. Color slides of these items plus noninstances were presented one at a time to 3- to 5-year-old children, and for each slide the child was asked, "Is this a bird?", or "Is this an animal?", or "Is this food?", and so on, depending on the item. If the child answered "yes," the experimenter said, "What kind?": and if the child answered "no," the experimenter asked, "What is it?" The results showed reliably fewer *underextensions* ("no" responses) for typical than for atypical instances (see Table 12.2). For example, a robin was likely to be included in the child's concept of *bird* whereas a chicken was not. As in Anglin's (1977) study, the atypical instances that resulted in errors of underextension were nonetheless apt to be identified with a specific, subordinate name (e.g., *chicken*).

Naming Practices and Underextension

Our suggestion is that underextension in young children reflects differential modeling frequency—namely, the more frequent occurrences of superordinate concept names (hereafter called *superordinates*) with typical events than with atypical ones in adult speech to children. Such differential modeling frequency could arise in either of two conceptually separate ways.

TABLE 12.2
Proportion of Underextension Responses for Typical and Atypical
Instances by Category

	Bird		Animal		Clothing	
Typical instances	Robin	.00	Horse	.10	Shirt	.00
	Blue jay	.00	Cow	.15	Pants	.10
Atypical instances	Turkey	.70	Starfish	.75	Mittens	.65
	Chicken	.45	Spider	.45	Boots	.70
	Plant		Food		Furniture	
Typical instances	Bean seedling	.10	Meat	.05	Table	.25
	Fern	.10	Peas	.05	Couch	.05
Atypical instances	Cactus	.45	Ketchup	.65	Lamp	.55
	Tree	.80	Candy cane	.40	Television	.60

According to an *event-frequency* account, nonverbal cultural practices or other natural influences conspire to make certain objects more prevalent in the child's world than others; consequently and for no other reason, these objects are more apt to be labeled with a superordinate. For example, oranges and apples, which are the two most typical fruits in Rosch's (1975) rankings, may often be present in our homes because they are available throughout the year, whereas watermelon is eaten in season and such delicacies as pomegranate are plainly hard to find in the local supermarket. If such circumstances are the norm, they would be sufficient to produce a greater likelihood of an adult's labeling an orange *fruit* than labeling a watermelon *fruit* when a child is present. This account assumes that adult naming practices are unsystematic with respect to typical versus atypical members of a category. The prediction would be that, given a set of referential events belonging to a category, a child listener, and an adult labeler, there will be some probability that the concept name will be used for each event, and this probability will not differ for typical and atypical events.

The second way differential modeling frequency could arise is *systematic naming practices*. This hypothesis can be stated as follows: (1) adults describe objects belonging to a category with both superordinate and subordinate terms; (2) in child-directed speech, parents occasionally or often label typical category events with a superordinate rather than a subordinate name; (3) parents show a strong preference for subordinates when labeling atypical category events for a child. For example, a mother may say "See the bird" when a sparrow is in the backyard but "See the duck" when a duck is seen at the park with her child. Based on a naming-practices hypothesis, we would expect adults to be more likely to use a superordinate when labeling typical category events than when naming atypical events for a child. Notice that this prediction differs from the expectation deduced from an event-frequency account.

But why would parents use a superordinate for some referents but choose a more specific subordinate name for others? Why would a mother name a sparrow *bird* but a duck *duck* for her child?

Roger Brown (1958b) suggests that parents initially provide children with names that "anticipate the functional structure of the child's world [p. 16]." By this, Brown means that objects are named in accordance with the nonlinguistic equivalences and differences that the young child needs to observe in dealing with the objects. For instance, there are certain actions that are generally appropriate for a child to take towards birds: The child should observe them from a distance and revel in their capacity for flight and song but not try to approach them too closely. Thus, a mother may name a particular sparrow *bird* as a means of encouraging her child to behave in an equivalent manner towards sparrows, robins, blue jays, and other creatures called *bird*. Use of the word *bird* instead of *sparrow* does not prepare the child to discriminate sparrows and robins, but a 2 year old need not appreciate such subtle differences; rather, what is important is that the child treat all of the things that have been called *bird* with due respect for their frailty and ferality. A duck, on the other hand, is unique in that the child's treatment of it should be different from birds in general: The child can approach it and even feed it by hand without fear that it will fly away or peck. So, the duck is named with a specific name that distinguishes it from other birds.

The argument, then, is that typical category events are apt to be named with a superordinate because they constitute a "functional core" of events that the child can or should relate to in the same way (cf. Nelson, 1973a, 1974). Atypical events, however, are not labeled with a superordinate because they fall outside of the functional core—that is, atypical events are associated with different actions on the child's part.

The following study was designed to determine whether parents are, in fact, more likely to use a superordinate when labeling typical category events than when labeling atypical events. To provide a reasonable test of this hypothesis, it was necessary to get superordinates to occur.

One variable besides typicality that may affect the likelihood of a parent's using a superordinate to refer to events is the context in which the events are embedded. But, which contexts should produce superordinates? Here, Brown's (1958a, 1958b) suggestion that parents name objects so as to encourage the child to take appropriate action towards them is of considerable help. It predicts, for instance, that if a child is playing with food, a mother will be apt to say, "Eat your food; don't play with it." because that is presumably the course of action she wants her child to take towards all things that are called *food*—not merely the lasagne that happens to be on the plate at the moment.

Another variable that may influence parental usage of superordinates is plurality, the presence of more than one member of a category. It seems intuitively clear that a pile containing shirts and slacks should be called *clothes* or *clothing*, whereas a shirt is called *shirt*.

However, neither plurality nor special contextual circumstances may be *necessary* for production of superordinates for some categories, such as *plant* or *bird*. For example, one can easily imagine a mother using the word *bird* when her child sees a solitary robin and asks, "What's that?"

In the present study, plurality was combined with selected contexts in an effort to maximize occurrence of superordinate terms as item typicality, the variable of major interest, was being manipulated. A simple naming condition was included in the study to test for possible category differences and to show that parents have both specific and general terms of reference for particular items.

Mothers of preschool children named color slides of the previously used instances of six categories (see Table 12.2). The mothers' children were present during the naming. In a simple-naming condition, each instance of each category was presented alone, and mothers were asked to respond when the child asked what it was. In a contextual-naming condition, slides comprised of two instances of the same category were presented, and the experimenter described an imaginary situational context to accompany each slide. All mothers received a typical pair (e.g., robin–blue jay), an atypical pair (chicken–turkey), and a mixed-typicality pair (robin–turkey) for each of the six categories. The following contexts were used and the mothers were asked in each case what they would say:

1. Birds: _____ (child's name) sees these.
2. Animals: These are on the page of a book _____ has brought you.
3. Plants: _____ points to these.
4. Food: _____ is playing with these.
5. Clothing: You want _____ to wear these.
6. Furniture: _____ is marking on these with a crayon.

Mothers' responses were tape recorded and transcribed and later scored in the following manner. For contextual naming, each recorded statement was assigned to one of four mutually exclusive, exhaustive categories of reference: (1) *collective,* if a superordinate name was used to refer to both of the paired items, either simultaneously or in sequence; (2) *distinctive,* if a superordinate name referred to one item and a subordinate name or demonstrative pronoun referred to the other item; (3) *specific,* if no superordinate and at least one subordinate name occurred; and (4) *indefinite,* if neither a superordinate nor a subordinate name was used. Examples of these types of reference are presented in Table 12.3. For simple naming, responses were scored as subordinate if a subordinate name only was used, or as superordinate if a superordinate name only was produced.

In the simple-naming condition, superordinates occurred with a reasonably high frequency for the *bird* and *plant* categories only, as expected. Mothers used the word *bird* to refer to a typical bird on 18 occasions, whereas only one trial involving an atypical bird resulted in *bird;* and, 37 of 39 occurrences of *plant*

TABLE 12.3
Examples of Types of Reference by Mothers During
Contextual Naming

Collective:
"Don't play with your *food*."
"See the pretty *plants*."
"These are the *clothes* Mommy wants you to wear."
"There are two *birds*; one's a blue jay and one's a robin."
"Don't write on the *furniture*."

Distinctive:
"That's a blue *birdie*, and that's a turkey like you saw at the turkey farm."
"This is a cactus like we have in the house—it's spiny. This is a small *plant*."

Specific:
"That's a tree and a cactus; one grows in the desert, one in the yard."
"You can play with the candy cane, but don't play with the bottle."
"Look at the horse. See the cow—we saw lots of those in Pennsylvania."
"Put on your boots and gloves; it's slushy and cold outside."

Indefinite:
"Don't mark on anything but your coloring books."

---

were associated with a typical instance of the *plant* category. In the contextual-naming condition, mothers were much more likely to use a superordinate name when referring to paired typical instances than when referring to paired atypical instances. As Table 12.4 shows, the proportion of collective (superordinate) references for typical pairs was indeed four times the proportion for atypical pairs, a highly significant difference. Notice also that distinctive references were produced for about 20% of the mixed-typicality pairs. All of these distinctive references consisted of labeling the typical instance with a superordinate and the atypical instance with a subordinate name, even though the instances were juxtaposed.

TABLE 12.4
Mean Proportion of Types of Reference by Mothers to Paired Items of
Differing Typicality

	Type of Reference			
	Superordinate		*Nonsuperordinate*	
	Collective	*Distinctive*	*Specific*	*Indefinite*
Typical Pairs	.52	.03	.39	.06
Mixed-Typicality Pairs	.24	.19	.49	.08
Atypical Pairs	.12	.03	.77	.08

These results provide strong support for the view that parental naming practices are systematic: When mothers use a superordinate name, they are much more likely to do so for typical category events than for atypical events. Thus, it is likely that a turkey will be named *turkey,* whereas a robin has a high probability of being named *bird* for a child; mothers tend to label a tree *tree,* but a fern is apt to be labeled *plant;* boots and mittens are usually called *boots* and *mittens,* whereas a shirt and pants may be called *clothes;* and, whereas meat and peas are termed *food, candy* and *ketchup* are the terms mothers generally apply to candy and ketchup. There are two implications. First, typical category events are likely to be involved in most of the superordinate-referent relations parents model for thier children. Second, young children's comprehension of a word like *food* is apt to be underextended by adult standards because it will not be applied to events that are physically dissimilar to the (typical) ones that have served as the basis for original word learning (Whitehurst, 1979).

Effects of Modeling on Underextension

Current discussions of underextension and typicality focus on abstracted prototypes or category structures (Anglin, 1977; de Villiers & de Villiers, 1978; Rosch & Mervis, 1975; Rosch, Simpson, & Miller, 1976). For example, if a child fails to apply the term *bird* to a duck, a prototype explanation would cite that item's distance from an abstracted *bird* category prototype, whereas Rosch's theory, presupposing a *bird* category (i.e., acquisition of the word *bird*), would simply say that a duck shares too few attributes with other birds. These explanations substantialize category structure and are based on research that may be inconsistent with children's semantic learning in the normal environment. In most studies of prototypicality, subjects see a number of category instances and receive as much training on atypical items (or items dissimilar to the category prototype) as on typical items (items resembling the prototype); therefore, modeling frequencies are high and equal for all category instances. But semantic concepts may arise from a single instance (Zimmerman, 1979) and probably reflect differential modeling frequency—namely, the more frequent occurrence of concept names with typical than with atypical instances. Additionally, these approaches neglect the role played by names that are subordinate to the concept name itself.

The alternative view presented here departs from the preceding approach in two ways. The first is that underextension and typicality are regarded as the product of differential modeling frequency that derives from systematic naming practices. This argument looks solid considering the results of the naming-practices study; however, that study does not demonstrate a causal relation between naming and superordinate extension or typicality and also does not tell us what would happen if modeling of concept name–atypical referent relations were predominant over modeling of concept name–typical reference relations. Such a reversed modeling condition ought to result in more underextensions for *typical* items, thus challenging structural accounts directly.

To say that concept names are more likely to occur with typical than with atypical events is an oversimplification. As the naming-practices study indicates, adults use subordinate names (e.g., *duck*) instead of an available superordinate (*bird*) when referring to atypical events, whereas for typical events, the opposite is ture. This brings us to the second point of departure—namely, consideration of the role played by the learning of subordinate names. It is suggested that if an adult has modeled a superordinate concept name for typical events and modeled subordinate names for atypical events, then the atypical events will have a higher probability of being excluded from the superordinate semantic class than they would otherwise have. This effect is not predicted by approaches that emphasize category structure and ignore naming practices.

The following study assessed the effects of four word–referent modeling conditions on kindergarten children's comprehension of a superordinate term. The modeling conditions varied the proportion of presentations of structurally typical or atypical items that resulted in a superordinate versus subordinate names so as to make the theoretical points just discussed.

Children, informed that the task was a naming game, saw slides of paired items including 45 pairs of items from one of two training categories and five pairs from a contrast category. An adult model made one of three types of statements each time a pair of items was presented. On superordinate trials, the model used the appropriate superordinate name but no subordinate name: "Here are two gokems; both of these are a gokem." The child was asked to repeat what the model had said. On subordinate trials, the model used the relevant subordinate name for each of the two items but no superordinate: "This is a sud and this is a zumap." The child was asked to point to one of the items—for example, "Which is the zumap?" On look trials, the adult simply said, "Look at these." Look trials equated simple frequency of exposure to items qua items, both across training conditions and within categories. Each presentation of a pair of items from the contrast category was a superordinate trial. For training-category pairs, the proportion of trial types varied with modeling conditions and item typicality as described next:

1. *Typical modeling with subordinates.* In this condition, nine presentations of a typical pair were superordinate trials and six were subordinate trials; one of the presentations of an atypical pair was a superordinate trial and 14 were subordinate trials; and, all 15 presentations of a medium-typicality pair were look trials. Thus, the superordinate term occurred more frequently with pairs of typical items than with pairs of atypical items, and subordinate names occurred on all remaining presentations of a typical or an atypical pair.

2. *Atypical modeling.* Here, the superordinate occurred more frequently with atypical pairs than with typical pairs, and subordinate names were used on the

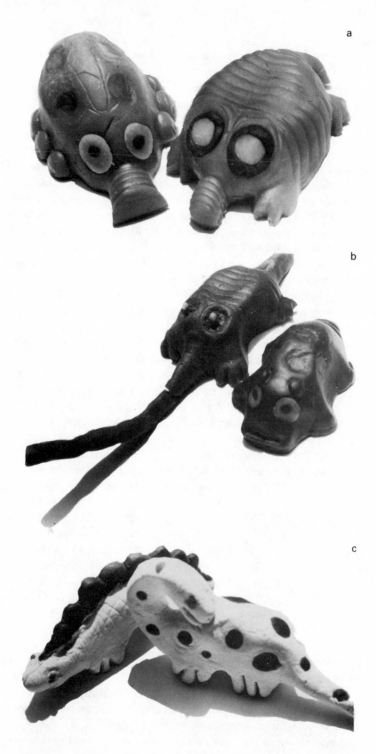

FIG. 12.3.   Examples of stimulus materials: (*a*) typical items; (*b*) atypical items; (*c*) contrast-category items.

remaining trials. Specifically, one of the presentations of a typical pair was a superordinate trial and 14 were subordinate trials; nine presentations of an atypical pair were superordinate trails and six were subordinate trials; and all 15 presentations of medium-typicality pairs were look trials.

3. *Typical modeling without subordinates.* This condition was the same as 1, except that no subordinate names were used. All trials that did not result in a superordinate were look trials.

4. *Control.* In this condition, cooccurrences of the superordinate with typical and atypical pairs were equal. Thus, for both typical and atypical pairs, five presentations were superordinate trials and 10 were subordinate trials. Medium-typicality pairs were look trials.

Stimulus materials used in the modeling conditions were color slides of fictitious animals made from Play Doh and commercially available molds (see Fig. 12.3). The creatures varied principally along two dimensions, form and color. In terms of these dimensions, the items belonging to each category were similar to, or had attributes in common with, other members of the category to varying degrees; the items had differing degrees of "family resemblance" (Rosch & Mervis, 1975). Table 12.5 shows the metric that was used to determine similarity and to operationalize typicality. The similarity scores in the table are based on weighting each attribute according to the number of items in the category that possess it and summing these weights across attributes. For example, the second item in Category A receives a score of five because the attribute (form A) occurs three times in the category and the attribute (orange) occurs twice in the category. Items 1–3, which have the highest similarity scores, are considered to be high-typicality items, whereas items 7–9, with the lowest similarity scores, are considered low-typicality items.

Immediately after training, all subjects received a test of superordinate extension, typicality judgments, and a test for comprehension of subordinate names, in that order. For superordinate extension, the child was shown each of the three typical and three atypical members of the training category (training items), each of the three typical and three atypical members of the category that was not used in training (transfer items), and the three members of the contrast category. For each item, the child was asked, for example, "Is this a gokem?" "No" answers for training items were followed by the question, "What is it?"

Typicality judgments were made for all of the nine possible pairs of a typical and an atypical member of the training category. The pair of items was shown, and the child was asked to point to the item that was "most like a gokem."

To test comprehension of subordinate names, pairs of items were presented, and the child was asked to point to the item that was an X, where X was a subordinate name. For subjects in both typical modeling groups, test stimuli consisted of the three possible pairs of atypical members of the training category; for subjects in the atypical modeling group, test stimuli were the three possible

TABLE 12.5
Training and Test Stimuli Used in Modeling Study

Training Category A

Item	Name	Form	Color	Similarity Score	Typicality
1	Bal	A	Red	6	High
2	Polef	A	Orange	5	High
3	Hum	B	Red	5	High
4	—	A	Yellow	4	Medium
5	—	B	Orange	4	Medium
6	—	C	Red	4	Medium
7	Lar	D	Green	2	Low
8	Zumap	E	Blue	2	Low
9	Sud	F	Violet	2	Low

Training Category B

Item	Name	Form	Color	Similarity Score	Typicality
1	Byssus	A	Red	6	High
2	Mel	A	Orange	5	High
3	Par	B	Red	5	High
4	—	A	Yellow	4	Medium
5	—	B	Orange	4	Medium
6	—	F	Red	4	Medium
7	Fem	D	Blue	2	Low
8	Neglan	E	Green	2	Low
9	Led	C	Violet	2	Low

Contrast Category

Item	Name	Form	Color	Similarity Score	Typicality
1	—	G	White	4	High
2	—	G	Lavender	3	Low
3	—	H	White	3	Low

typical pairs from the training category; and, for subjects in the control condition, test stimuli were either three typical pairs or three atypical pairs.

Results of the experiment are summarized in Table 12.6. Consider first the upper part of the table, which shows the proportion of underextension responses as a function of item typicality and modeling conditions.

For training items, the typical modeling with subordinates condition resulted in reliably fewer underextensions for structurally typical than for structurally atypical instances, whereas subjects receiving atypical modeling displayed significantly more underextensions for *typical* items than for atypical ones, as expected; atypical modeling thus resulted in a reversal of typicality effects. However, for transfer items, atypical modeling yielded an approximately equal number of underextensions for typical and atypical instances; atypical modeling thus eliminated typicality effects but did not reverse them.

The hypothesis that typical modeling with subordinate names would produce more underextensions for atypical instances than typical modeling without subordinate names was confirmed for tranfer items. For training items, the difference between typical modeling with and without subordinates was marginally significant.

The middle part of Table 12.6 shows the results of the typicality-judgment task. It is apparent that both subjects in the control condition and subjects exposed to typical modeling with subordinates selected typical instances more often than subjects receiving atypical modeling. These expected differences are statistically significant.

TABLE 12.6
Effects of Modeling Conditions

Modeling Condition					
	Proportion of "No" Responses				
	Training Items		Transfer Items		Contrast Items
	Typical	Atypical	Typical	Atypical	
Typical with subordinates	.24	.85	.24	.88	.73
Atypical	.67	.24	.55	.48	.55
Typical without subordinates	.03	.58	.03	.55	.88
Control	.18	.73	.30	.79	.45
	Proportion of Choices of Typical Instances				
Typical with subordinates	.90				
Atypical	.48				
Typical without subordinates	.75				
Control	.84				
	Comprehension of Subordinate Names[a]				
Typical with subordinates	.85				
Atypical	.64				
Typical without subordinates	.36				
Control	.45				

[a] Proportion correct.

Finally, as revealed in the lower portion of Table 12.6, subjects in the typical modeling with subordinate-names condition displayed reasonably good comprehension of subordinate names. Their performance was reliably better than that of subjects in the typical modeling without subordinates condition, who had no basis for answering the questions and who thus provide an appropriate comparison.

In this experiment, underextensions and typicality judgments were shown to be a function of not only structural typicality, defined as interitem similarity, but also modeling frequency. As anticipated, subjects receiving typical modeling extended a superordinate name to typical but not atypical category instances and also judged typical instances as typical. Yet children who observed an adult model describing structurally atypical events with a superordinate term were subsequently more likely to apply the superordinate to atypical events than to typical ones, and they were also less apt to judge typical instances as typical than children in the control condition; they failed to show the usual typicality effects. Because category structure and event frequency were held constant for the typical and atypical modeling groups, it seems that structural typicality is insufficient as an explanation of typicality effects. Rather, the critical determinant of superordinate extension and typicality judgments appears to be the attributes of events that are correlated with a superordinate in adult speech to children.

A subordinate-name effect was also demonstrated: Children were more likely to limit extension of a superordinate to typical instances when atypical instances were labeled with specific names than when they were not. This finding suggests that extension of a superordinate name by a child is jointly determined by modeling of superordinate-referent relations and learning of subordinate names via modeling or other learning processes.

One way of explaining the subordinate-name effect would be to assume that availability of another, dominant name interferes with comprehension of the relation between a superordinate and a referent. In other words, the child says that an object is not an X (superordinate) because to the child it is more of a Y (subordinate). This hypothesis is consistent with the fact that children's underextensions are usually accompanied by production of an appropriate subordinate name.

The alternative interpretation of the subordinate-name effect is discrimination learning. It is well established that discrimination of a conceptual class is influenced by noninstances as well as the instances to which the learner is exposed, and all modern formulations of concept learning include such an assumption (e.g., Medin & Schaffer, 1978). The discrimination-learning view would maintain that labeling atypical items with subordinate names made them function as noninstances affecting the superordinate concept that was learned, even though the atypical items shared a number of attributes with typical items and were much more similar to typical items than to contrast category items. This interpretation draws some support from the finding that typical modeling with subordinates resulted in more underextensions than typical modeling without subordinates for transfer items as well as training items. However, it is possible that subordinate names were generalizing to transfer items. Thus, these data indicate that learning of subordinate names affects superordinate extension, but they do not tell us how.

Based on the naming practices observed previously, the typical modeling-with-subordinates condition of this study is an appropriate natural environment analogue. Because it resulted in a high proportion of underextensions for atypical instances, the view that underextension is due primarily to observational learning of superordinate–typical referent relations is supported.

The atypical-modeling condition data prove that it is possible to reverse at least one kind of typicality effect, fewer underextensions for typical than for atypical instances, when modeling frequency is greater for atypical instances. This result contrasts with the findings of Rosch et al. (1976, Experiment 2), who obtained ordinary typicality effects when subjects received more training on atypical instances than on typical instances, and it calls into question Rosch et al.'s (1976) conclusion that "structural typicality is a robust phenomenon whose effects remain even under conditions in which frequency is inversely related to structure [p. 498]."

SUMMARY AND CONCLUSION

We have presented the results of several experiments that have isolated variables functioning in children's word learning. Our analysis of the original word game showed that early labeling can be seen as a type of observational learning in which the child forms associations between words and things. Placing word–referent learning in the context of modern theories of classical conditioning led to hypotheses that contiguity, informativeness, and referent value would be important variables. All were; children acquired new words more easily when word and referent were presented simultaneously, when word and referent occurred together exclusively, and when the referent was a preferred object.

A second series of studies examined the role of parental labeling in the acquisition and use of superordinate labels by older children. Preschool children often underextend class labels, applying them to typical members of a category but not extending them to atypical members of the same category. This was shown to be consistent with the labeling practices of mothers, who model subordinate labels for atypical members of categories although modeling superordinate labels for typical members of categories. This relationship was tested experimentally in an analogue study in which children were exposed to modeling of various ratios of superordinate and subordinate labels for artificially constructed categories of objects. As predicted, a reversal of the usual typicality effect was obtained: Children who observed a model describing structurally atypical events with a superordinate term were subsequently more likely to apply the superordinate to atypical events than to typical ones.

These studies are important in themselves in what they tell us about the conditions of semantic development. They also demonstrate the utility of a functional analysis of meaning. Such an analysis treats meaning as a dimension of behavior and searches for variables that affect that dimension. We argue that there are many utilities of such an approach for those interested in the acquisition of language. Perhaps the most important is the possibility of building on and relating to research and theory on learning of other skills. The research results we have presented show strong parallels between the conditions affecting vocabulary acquisition and those that affect learning in both simple animal learning tasks (Rescorla, 1978) and in other complex human skills (Rosenthal & Zimmerman, 1978). If there are such commonalities across tasks and species, we should opt for a scientific vocabulary that allows for crosstalk. No doubt language acquisition is unique in several respects. But it is also an expression of general learning processes about which psychology already knows something. A functional analysis can benefit from that knowledge and expand it, while at the same time providing data that should be useful to other varieties of theoretical effort in semantic development.

REFERENCES

Anglin, J. W. *Word, object, and conceptual development.* New York, Norton, 1977.

Asch, S. The doctrinal tyranny of associationism: Or what is wrong with rote learning. In T. R. Dixon & D. L. Horton (Eds.), *Verbal behavior and general behavior theory.* Englewood Cliffs N.J.: Prentice-Hall, 1968.

Brown, R. How shall a thing be called? *Psychological Review,* 1958, *65,* 14-21. (a)

Brown, R. *Words and things.* New York: Free Press, 1958. (b)

Bruner, J. S. From communication to language: A psychological perspective. *Cognition,* 1975, *3,* 255-287.

Carson, M. T., & Abrahamson, A. Some members are more equal than others: The effect of semantic typicality on class-inclusion performance. *Child Development,* 1976, *47,* 1186-1190.

Collis, G. M., & Schaffer, H. R. Synchronization of visual attention in mother–infant pairs. *Journal of Child Psychology and Psychiatry,* 1975, *16,* 315-320.

de Villiers, J. G., & de Villiers, P. A. *Language acquisition.* Cambridge, Mass.: Harvard University Press, 1978.

Greenfield, P. M., & Smith, J. H. *The structure of communication in early language development.* New York: Academic Press, 1976.

Hearst, E., & Jenkins, H. M. *Sign-Tracking: The stimulus-reinforcer relation and directed action.* Austin, Texas: Psychonomic Society, 1974.

Kaye, K. Infants' effects upon their mothers' teaching strategies. In J. C. Glidwell (Ed.), *The social context of learning and development.* New York: Harcourt, Brace, Jovanovich, 1976.

Leonard, L., Schwartz, R., Fogler, M., Newhoff, M., & Wilcox, M. Children's imitations of lexical items. *Child Development,* 1979, *50,* 19-27.

Mackintosh, N. J. *The psychology of animal learning.* New York: Academic Press, 1974.

Medin, D. L., & Schaffer, M. M. Context theory of classification learning. *Psychological Review,* 1978, *85,* 207–238.

Nelson, K. Some evidence for the cognitive primacy of categorization and its functional basis. *Merrill-Palmer Quarterly of Behavior and Development,* 1973, *19,* 21–39. (a)

Nelson, K. Structure and strategy in learning to talk. *Monographs of the Society for Research in Child Development,* 1973, *38*(Nos. 1–2). (b)

Nelson, K. Concept, word, and sentence: Interrelations in acquisition and development. *Psychological Review,* 1974, *81,* 267–285.

Phillips, J. R. Syntax and vocabulary of mother's speech to young children: Age and sex comparisons. *Child Development,* 1973, *44,* 182–185.

Premack, D. Catching up with common sense or two sides of a generalization: Reinforcement and punsihment. In R. Glaser (Ed.), *The nature of reinforcement.* New York: Academic Press, 1971.

Rescorla, R. A. Pavlovian excitatory and inhibitory conditioning. In W. K. Estes (Ed.), *Handbook of learning and cognitive processes* (Vol. 2). Hillsdale N.J.: Lawrence Erlbaum Associates, 1975.

Rescorla, R. A. Pavlovian conditioning and its proper control procedures. *Psychological Review,* 1967, *74,* 71–80.

Rescorla, R. A. Some implications of a cognitive perspective on Pavlovian conditioning. In S. H. Hulse, H. Fowler, W. Honig (Eds.), *Cognitive processes in animal behavior.* Hillsdale N.J.: Lawrence Erlbaum Associates, 1978.

Rosch, E. Cognitive representations of semantic categories. *Journal of Experimental Psychology: General,* 1975, *104,* 192–233.

Rosch, E., & Mervis, C. B. Family resemblances; Studies in the internal structure of categories. *Cognitive Psychology,* 1975, *7,* 573–605.

Rosch, E., Simpson, C., & Miller, R. S. Structural bases of typicality effects. *Journal of Experimental Psychology: Human Perception and Performance,* 1976, *2,* 491–502.

Rosenthal, T. L., & Zimmerman, B. J. *Social learning and cognition.* New York: Academic Press, 1978.

Scaife, M., & Bruner, J. S. The capacity for joint visual attention in the infant. *Nature,* 1975, *5489,* 265–266.

Snow, C. Mother's speech to children learning language. *Child Development,* 1972, *43,* 549–565.

Stewart, C. M., & Hamilton, M. L. Imitation as a learning strategy in the acquisition of vocabulary. *Journal of Experimental Child Psychology.* 1976, *21,* 380–392.

White, T. G. Naming practices, typicality, and underextension in child language. Unpublished doctoral dissertation, State University of New York at Stony Brook, 1979.

Whitehurst, G. J. Meaning and semantics. In G. J. Whitehurst & B. J. Zimmerman (Eds.), *The functions of language and cognition.* New York: Academic Press, 1979.

Whitehurst, G. J., & Vasta, R. Is language acquired through imitation? *Journal of Psycholinguistic Research,* 1975, *4,* 37–59.

Wittgenstein, L. *Philosophical investigations,* New York: Macmillan, 1953.

Zimmerman, B. J. Concepts and classification, In G. J. Whitehurst & B. J. Zimmerman (Eds.), *The functions of language and cognition.* New York: Academic Press, 1979.

Zimmerman, B. J., & Whitehurst, G. J. Structure and function: A comparison of two views of the development of language and cognition. In G. J. Whitehurst & B. J. Zimmerman (Eds.), The *functions of language and cognition.* New York: Academic Press, 1979.

13 Beyond the Definition Given: On the Growth of Connotation

Kenneth R. Livingston
Vassar College

Attempts to understand the development of semantic systems have thus far been confined almost exclusively to the study of the growth of intension and extension of terms, with very little attention given to aspects of meaning that are characterized colloquially as connotative. Traditionally, in the fields of linguistics and philosophy of language, connotation has meant the intensional aspects of meaning, and has been distinguished from denotation, or the extensional aspects of meaning. For the prupuses of this chapter, however, I intend to revert to the more colloquial distinction between these terms—that is, denotative meaning as used here refers to both intensional and extensional meanings, whereas connotative meaning is identified with the psychological associates to a term, apart from its intension and extension. In particular, these psychological associates often have an affective component, and are not themselves easy to articulate precisely.

Having mapped out the realm of meaning in this, more colloquial, way makes clearer the gap that currently exists in our understanding of the growth of semantic systems. In spite of the time and effort devoted to an elucidation of the growth of word meanings by developmental psychologists (e.g., Anglin, 1977, 1978; Clark, 1973, 1978; Nelson, 1974, 1979), and the considerable increase in our understanding of the process of semantic development that has resulted from this effort, there are certain limitations to research of this sort so long as its focus remains exclusively upon meaning in the narrow dictionary sense. After all, language operates in the context of a larger cognitive system (Bates, 1976), and that larger system incorporates more than extensional lists of category instances and intensional lists of features or properties. Is it really possible to appreciate and understand meaning, even of terms referring to concrete objects, without incorporating into our models components designed to capture significant aspects of this larger system? The answer depends in part on what one designates as the proper purview of the analysis of meaning, but given a broadly *psychological* perspective, the question becomes rhetorical. What is needed is an extension of the study of meaning into the realm of word sense, as Vygotsky (1962) used the term, or connotation as defined in the opening of this chapter. The study presented here made use of the semantic differential as the instrument of this extension. Although it does not sample all aspects of sense or connotation as these terms are used here, it does at least tap aspects of meaning not systematically captured by more conventional methods. In particular, it is one avenue to the study of connotative, especially affective, associations such as those represented by the bipolar adjectives of the semantic differential.

By administering the semantic differential to children from 5–10 years of age and appropriately analyzing the data, it becomes possible to examine changes with age in the differentiation and organization of connotative meanings. These can be analyzed in relation to changes with age in denotative meaning structures in a within-subject design. Two patterns of relationship between the two data sets are possible, given the constraint of information from prior research on the growth of natural language concepts (e.g., *furniture, tools, animals, living things*, etc.). This research suggests that certain general principles operate in the growth of these concepts—namely, that they become larger, more differentiated, and hierarchically organized with age (Anglin, 1977; Inhelder & Piaget, 1964). Werner (1957) has suggested that in addition to their application to the development of semantics, the principles of differentiation and hierarchical integration apply generally to the developmental process. Others have recently suggested, more specifically, that the growth of affective systems seems to be describable in part as a matter of increasing differentiation (Decarie, 1978; Saarni, 1978). To the extent that connotation as measured by the semantic differential includes at least some affective component, and is subject to development, it is reasonable to expect to see differentiation of meaning, as measured by the semantic differential, with increasing age. Put another way, the connotative distinctiveness of members of a class—for example, *animals*—should increase with age, in parallel with the increasing differentiation and hierarchical organization of the class and its meaning as measured in more conventional ways.

The other possibility, of course, is that connotative meaning becomes less differentiated with increasing age, in inverse relation to the pattern observed using conventional measures of the growth of meaning. This possibility is offered as a logical alternative, although there is no body of research or theory that would directly suggest it. Anecdotally, it does seem that the "big, bad wolf" of childhood is a less fearsome creature in adulthood, and the "big, brown cow" perhaps less benign. This would suggest less connotative differentiation of these two members of the class *animals,* but the suggestion is less compelling on the face of it than the argument of parallel increases in connotative and denotative differentiation. It was the latter pattern, therefore, that was expected.

In the pages that follow, details of procedures and results are presented, followed by two discussions. The first discussion is of the results in particular, and attempts to give a reasonable account of them. There follows a more general discussion, in which a case is made for the inclusion of connotation in studies of developing semantic systems.

METHOD

Seventy-two children from a private school in Cambridge, Massachusetts, took part in the study. There were 24 children in each of three age groups (5, 7, and 10 year olds), and equal numbers of boys and girls were included at each age level. The children worked on a number of tasks, in addition to those described here, which are not discussed in this chapter.

The children were asked to recall as many instances of each of two categories (*animals* and *living things*) as possible. The items were recorded in the order of their recall. In addition, each child was asked to rate two sets of five words (randomly drawn from a larger pool of words) on six semantic differential scales shown to be highly salient for school-aged children (diVesta, 1966). The six scales used were "good/bad," "beautiful/ugly," "strong/weak," "heavy/light," "fast/slow," and "sharp/dull." Prior to the task, the experimenter made certain that each child knew all pairs of opposites. Ratings were made on a 7-point scale, represented as boxes along the middle portion of a board approximately 7.5 cm by 700 cm. The words representing the poles of the scales (e.g., good and bad) were written on cards and placed at opposite ends of the board, with the placement accompanied by a spoken indication of which word went on each end. The child made a rating by placing a disk in the appropriate box on the board. The youngest group, and those older children who seemed to have difficulty with the task, were taken through the rating process in two steps. First, they were asked whether "a bear is good, bad, or in between," and if the response was "good" or "bad," the children were asked to discriminate among the three degrees of "good" or "bad." All children went through a series of trial ratings until the procedure was properly understood and consistently followed.

The sets of items rated on the semantic differential scales were designed to represent the categories *animals* and *living things,* but because the categories were nested, the distinction reduced to the inclusion of exactly one nonanimal (e.g., tree, daisy, etc.) in the *living-things* set. Two different rating sessions were used to avoid fatiguing the youngest children, and in order to parallel the two semantic-recall sessions each of which did request a different list from the child.

The four tasks, two semantic differential and two semantic recall, were administered on four separate occasions, at least one day apart, with appropriate systematic controls for order effects. No evidence of such effects was found in the data, and they are not discussed further.

RESULTS

The first task in examining these data is to show the existence of increased differentiation of the concepts studied. The most obvious and straightforward indicator of semantic differentiation of a category is an increase in the number of instances comprising the category. An age (3) by sex (2) ANOVA on number of items retrieved in the recall task revealed the expected main effects for age for both categories: $F(2, 71) = 8.81$, $p = .001$ for *animals; F(2, 71) = 13.54, p = .001* for *living things*. In the *living-things* condition, an age by sex interaction just reached statistical significance: $F(2, 71) = 3.22$, $p = .05$. An examination of Table 13.1 reveals a greater increase in the number of items recalled by boys than by girls between the ages of 7 and 10 years in both conditions, but the difference reached significance only when the children were recalling *living things*. The origins of this last pattern are unclear, but given the unrobust nature of the trend, factors such as motivation for the task, sampling anomalies, and a number of other possible explanations cannot be ruled out. The important finding is that differentiation of the category, as measured by semantic recall, does increase with age.

An increase in number recalled is one index of an increase in differentiation, but an examination of the instances themselves suggested the fact more strongly. It seemed clear that the young child's "bear" became the 10 year old's "grizzly bear, black bear, polar bear," and so on, and much of the increase in recall appeared to be the result of such differentiation of subcategories already known to the child. Furthermore, the order of the older child's recall suggested an increasingly hierarchical organization of the more differentiated set. The problem was to quantify, and thus to document, this shift.

Taxonomists have, of course, devoted considerable effort to the construction of a hierarchical system for the classification of living things, and the decision

TABLE 13.1
Age by Sex Breakdown of the Mean Number of Items Recalled in Both
the *Animals* and *Living Things* Conditions

	Animals		Living Things	
Age	*Male*	*Female*	*Male*	*Female*
5	25.50	24.33	25.42	27.58
7	36.92	36.75	38.75	41.25
10	55.33	38.67	63.67	43.33

TABLE 13.2
Observed and Expected Frequencies of Ordered Pairs of Items
Recalled in Semantic Recall by Age and Level of Taxonomic System
Had in Common (Animals Condition)

Age	Living	Phylum	Class	Order	Family	Genus	N's
5	105	156	178	78	26	36	572
	(66)	(155)	(188)	(114)	(36)	(29)	
7	83	239	305	124	49	48	868
	(101)	(235)	(285)	(173)	(55)	(44)	
10	107	295	355	305	86	46	1104
	(128)	(299)	(364)	(220)	(70)	(56)	
N's	295	690	838	507	161	130	2544

was made to use this system as the standard referent against which to evaluate the children's recall. This is obviously a somewhat arbitrary point of reference in some respects. The modern biologist's taxonomy does not correspond at all points to the taxonomies of lay adults, being based as it is in many cases on nonmorphological criteria for classification. However, the use of this system for analysis is conservative in that the likely noncorrespondence in specific instances would not be expected to systematically increase estimates of hierarchical organization, but would rather tend to decrease them. Nor is there any reason to expect a differential bias for any one age group as a result of this choice of a standard for comparison.

All of the items recalled by the children were identified as to their place in the taxonomic system, and each item in the set recalled by a child was compared with those recalled immediately before and after it in order to determine the lowest level of commonality for those two items in the system. For example, "dog" and "cat" refer to animals in different families but they are both members of the suborder *Fissipedia,* or terrestrial carnivores. If these instances were recalled contiguously, the child would be marked as having produced a pair of instances sharing a common suborder designation. In this way, all ordered, contiguous pairs of items for all 72 children and for both conditions were scored into 13 categories ranging from "common entity" at the most global level, to "common species" at the most specific. The 13 categories were collapsed for ease of interpretation (results of data analyses are not altered in any significant way by this manipulation) into six categories for *animals* and seven for *living things.* The resulting tables (see Tables 13.2 and 13.3) show frequency of pairings at each level of the hierarchy for each age group. Figures in parentheses indicate expected frequencies. For the *animals* condition, $\chi^2 = 177.35$, $df = 10$, $p < .001$; for *living things,* $\chi^2 = 457.54$, $df = 12$, $p < .001$. These are very straightforward findings. As the tables show, older children are more likely to recall items contiguously that are more immediately related according to the

TABLE 13.3
Observed and Expected Frequencies of Ordered Pairs of Items
Recalled in Semantic Recall by Age and Level of Taxonomic System
Had in Common (Living-Things Condition)

Age	Entity	Living	Phylum	Class	Order	Family	Genus	N's
5	104	139	102	178	52	16	27	618
	(28)	(145)	(134)	(179)	(91)	(37)	(28)	
7	10	219	244	255	111	61	39	839
	(38)	(197)	(182)	(243)	(123)	(51)	(38)	
10	10	279	242	352	236	87	56	1252
	(57)	(294)	(272)	(363)	(184)	(76)	(56)	
N's	124	637	588	785	399	164	122	2709

taxonomy, whereas younger children are more likely to recall items on the basis of different principles that seem to produce retrieval of items related only at the more general levels of the taxonomy. In the case of *living things,* the relationship is often one not involving the adult concept of "alive" at all, which accounts for the relatively large number of items in the category labeled "entity" for 5 year olds in Table 13.3. The lack of any age difference in the last category, "genus," is the result of the inclusion here of any differentiation on the basis of sex alone, such as might be scored if, for example, "cow" and "bull" were recalled contiguously. This was a more common pairing for younger than for older children, which washes out the tendency for older children to produce more contiguous recall at the level of shared genus than younger children. Chi-squares would have been even larger without this effect.

In conclusion, the semantic-recall data support the expectation of increased differentiation and hierarchical organization of the concepts *animals* and *living things* with increasing age (Anglin, 1977; Inhelder & Piaget, 1964). The discovery that these principles, especially hierarchical organization, seem to hold for a task as unstructured as semantic recall is an interesting extension of previous work on this phenomenon, but the crucial issue concerns whether the principles can be shown to apply to the realm of connotation as measured by the semantic differential.

The selection of scales for use in the semantic-differential task was obviously designed to encourage the use of three dimensions (evaluation, potency, activity) traditionally found to operate in the judgments of adults and children (Osgood, Suci, & Tannenbaum, 1957). In order to be certain that these were the dimensions used by the children, however, data from the semantic differential were first factor analyzed (principle factoring with iterations) and rotated (varimax) to determine factor structure. As expected, the three factors traditionally found did emerge, although the order of emergence was activity, potency, evaluation, and not the reverse of that sequence, which is the more usual finding when a larger

TABLE 13.4
Mean Semantic Distances at Each Age Level
and for Both Rating Sessions, Computed in
Original 7-Point Scale Units

	Age		
	5	*7*	*10*
Animals session	4.15	3.53	3.07
Living-things session	4.70	4.18	3.90

and more diverse group of concepts is rated on a longer list of scales. The three dimensions did, however, account for approximately 72% of the variance.

Once the presence of the three dimensions had been demonstrated, the child's ratings of each item on the six dimensions were reduced to ratings on the three dimensions by averaging the ratings on the two scales that contributed to each dimension. Each item could then be plotted in a three-dimensional semantic space. The next step was to produce some index of the connotative distinctiveness of the set rated for each child. This was accomplished by using the generalized distance formula from solid geometry (Osgood et al., 1957) to calculate the distance between all possible pairs of items rated. Items that were responded to differently on the dimensions measured here should be further apart in the semantic space; those rated similarly should be closer together for a set of items of any size. The mean distance between all possible pairs of instances was computed to reflect the overall degree of connotative distinctiveness of those items. Large values, representing greater dispersion of items in the semantic space, reflect relatively greater distinctiveness and differentiation than small values.

Table 13.4 contains the mean distance scores for each group for the two rating sessions. These mean distance scores were submitted to an age (3) by sex (2) ANOVA for both rating sessions and for data from the two sessions combined. The results of this analysis could not have been more contradictory to the original hypothesis. Although the main effect of age was significant for both sets of items rated—$F(2, 66) = 7.60$, $p = .001$ for the *animals* session; $F(2, 66) = 3.79$, $p = .037$ for the *living things* session)—and for the combined data from both sessions—$F(2, 66) = 14.01$, $p < .001$—the direction of the age differences was the *reverse* of that predicted.[1] Mean interitem distance in the semantic space

---

[1] For the mean distance scores in the *animals* condition, there was also a marginally significant main effect for sex—$F(1, 66) = 3.88$, $p = .05$—with females rating items in a less connotatively distinct way than males. Because this effect is not even remotely present when the larger sample of items from the combined rating sessions is analyzed and no meaningful interpretation of this sex difference is possible, the effect is not treated any further.

decreased with increasing age, suggesting that instances of the nested categories *animals/living things* become *less* connotatively distinct at the same time that the category is becoming more differentiated and hierarchically organized.

DISCUSSION OF RESULTS

These results are puzzling at best, because there is no extant conceptual framework that would account for them. Before attempting to construct one, however, it is important to exclude simple procedural or methodological explanations of this surprising effect.

One possibility is that the instrument itself is inappropriate for children in this age range. However, it has been used successfully with children as young as 8 years (diVesta, 1966), making only the data from the 5 year olds in the present sample suspect. Because no procedural difficulties were encountered and because the data from the 5-year-old children fit the trend that exists from 7–10 years, there is no evidence to support a simple inappropriateness explanation.

The possibility that the subset of instances rated was somehow peculiar and contributed to the findings is remote because the five items were randomly sampled from a larger pool for each subject, and is further inconsistent with the clear replication of the results for the two different rating sessions. Nor is there evidence of any unusual or rigid rating system by one age group compared to another. There were no zero-point or extreme-score response sets, and the youngest children obviously were not using a restricted range of the scales, as indicated by the mean distance scores themselves.

One could argue that the pattern is the result of age changes in response to the semantic differential scales themselves. Such an argument would have it that the bipolar adjectives that define each scale are understood differently by the children at different ages. As children get older, this argument goes, the meanings of these adjectives are more consensual for the group and the apparent decrease in connotative differentiation is really an indication of increased similarity of response to the scales themselves. This may be the case, but it cannot explain the pattern of data observed here. The results are based on the analysis of means for *each* child, which means that the pattern observed is a within- and not a between-subject result.

More problematic than any of these explanations is the possibility that the restricted set of scales along which the ratings were done may not sample the most salient dimensions for the children themselves, having been selected specifically in order to provoke the use of the evaluation, potency, and activity dimensions traditionally discovered in work with older children and adults. This seems an unlikely explanation of the particular pattern of results obtained, however, because the three dimensions mentioned and the scales selected to tap them have been shown to be appropriate for work with children as young as 8 years, as already pointed out. In order to salvage the original hypothesis, the suggestion that the scales used were not salient for the children would have to further imply that the use of more salient sclaes would result in evidence of greater differentiation. Yet, when the scales were used with children of an age known to be responsive to those sclaes, the data show decreasing differentiation. The argument might have been used to question the results had the original hypothesis been affirmed by the data, but not to account for the pattern that actually did emerge. Furthermore, this last point is generally applicable to any argument based on questioning the nature of the attribute structure implicit in the scales used. That is not to say that there are no limitations to these data and the methods used to collect them. Obviously, there are limitations of range of ages sampled, of concepts explored, and of the methods used to explore them. There is, however, no reason to discard the data themselves on these grounds. Given that this is the case, and having found no simple account of the phenomenon observed here, it remains only to revise the original hypothesis.

It is best to begin with a recognition that the results of this study are paradoxical. As the child's experience with instances of the categories increases, and a more differentiated meaning structure develops, the connotative distinctiveness of words referring to the same set of instances is gradually diminished. The first question one must answer is whether these findings can be generalized beyond this specific study. One certainly would not want to make this claim without first empirically demonstrating the same pattern for other concepts and different samples of children. Nor do I think the hypothesis that such generality exists is likely to bear up, for the simple reason that the connotation of terms is learned, as is denotation, and the circumstances of the learning can be expected to have something to do with final outcome. It seems highly unlikely that this pattern should hold for all categories, any more than the reverse pattern originally hypothesized. More probable is that the developmental pattern is specific to those categories that are experienced by children in a particular way. Consider, for purposes of clarification, the following explanation of the pattern observed here.

With few exceptions, the contemporary American child's exposure to animals occurs via books and television, supplemented by an occasional safari to the local zoo. The child's relationship to instances of the category *animals* and their associated names is thus generally homogenous, and more to the point, the experience is affectively fairly neutral, at least in a direct personal sense. The lion cannot really kill, the snake slithers behind thick glass, and someone else holds the cuddly koala bear, if anyone does at all. To the extent that the child's functional relationship, in personal form, is important for the growth of word connotation, then a homogenous set of experiences can be expected to produce a more nearly homogenous set of connotations for the associated words. Thus, as was the case here, differentiation of the extension of a term like "animals" does not imply increasing distinctiveness of word connotation or sense. The two *may* covary, but the relationship is not one of necessity.

This argument relates in provocative ways to Katherine Nelson's notion of a "functional core" around which terms of reference develop in the earliest phases of language acquisition (Nelson, 1974, 1979). In this conception of meaning, this functional core determines meaning without ultimately being defining in and of itself. Nelson is speaking, of course, of much younger children, with vocabularies of 50 words or so, and not, like the subjects in the present study, experienced language users. Nevertheless, the hypothesis proposed here for the development of word connotation is strongly analogous in that the child's functional relationship to named category instances is seen as determining the character of the word's connotations without itself defining the connotation. As in the case of denotative meaning, connotative meaning may be extended, once it has been established, to new terms, or may modify the intended or heard effect of old ones, on the basis of principles other than those by which it was established.

If the explanation of the data presented is in fact accurate, then there should be a measureable difference between urban and rural children, at least with respect to certain categories and their instances. The connotative distinctiveness of animals to which the farm-dwelling child is exposed should increase, whereas that of more exotic beasts decreases. The same pattern should hold for other categories when groups of children can be identified who are likely to have different experiences with the instances. This hypothesis is now under study in a paradigm similar to that reported here.

There is one important qualification to the arguments just presented that must be made before proceeding to a discussion of general issues. The hypothesis offered to account for the data does not encompass the fact that the connotative distinctiveness of the terms for the youngest children is as great as it is. After all, they would seem to be even less likely to have had personal interactions with lions, snakes, and koala bears than the older children, yet these terms are more connotatively distinct for them.

In order to preserve the hypothesized explanation for the data from the present study, it is necessary to remember that it is the terms that have connotations, not the instances themselves. Therefore, it is the occasion of the use of the term, whether its referent is also immediately present or not, that is crucial to the development of connotation. As the urban child grows older, these occasions become quite homogenous at a functional level for the class of living things. The child can now read books, visit the zoo, and so forth, and in these contexts encounters animal names. The younger child's encounters are of a different quality, in spite of being equally indirect. Informal observation of the occasions of use of animal terms by adults working in a nursery-school setting suggests that adults accompany their use of animal names (usually in the context of reading or telling stories) with exaggerated intonation, and, somewhat less consistently, exaggerated facial expression and other gestures. There is certainly a body of data showing the tendency of adults to use exaggerated intonation when speaking to younger children (Berko Gleason, 1973; Garnica, 1977), and even some evidence of the usefulness of this manipulation for increasing the child's capacity to process sentences (Bonvillian, Raeburn, & Horan, 1979). It seems reasonable to hypothesize that the connotative distinctiveness of animal names among the youngest group in this study is the result of hearing and learning about these words in a context that includes highly salient, nonverbal, affectively loaded cues on which basis connotative distinctions are established. The more limited hypothesis that such cues *can* systematically alter connotation is also currently under investigation in pilot work involving a combination of observational and laboratory approaches.

But there are larger issues here that go beyond the unexpected findings that led to all this further hypothesizing, and it is to these issues that I would like to speak in concluding this chapter.

GENERAL DISCUSSION

If a randomly selected group of adults is asked what the word *socialism* means, the range of replies is sufficient to make one wonder whether everyone heard the same word. The answers tend to locate the referent in the realm of politics and/or economics, but that minimal consensus is as good as it gets. Is socialism the same as communism? Does it necessarily involve government (what's government?)? Are equity, individualism, or freedom relevant descriptive dimensions? Asked where in the world one might find socialism, and where it is not found, people again give surprisingly diverse answers, in spite of a few high-frequency responses in each category. One even finds an occasional reflective sort who will suggest that socialism is an abstraction that has no concrete manifestation.

The wonderful thing about the lack of consensus as to the extension of the concept *socialism,* and the lack of precision in the expression of a definition for the term, is that they in no way prevent people from using the word, quite unself-consciously, in conversation. Furthermore, the use of the term is often associated with very definite attitudes and feelings about which many people can say a great deal, in spite of their inability to give a clear definition. It would seem that people may know a great deal else about socialism than its definition, even when they cannot define it.

The word "socialism" is not, of course, alone in having these characteristics. Many other words could no doubt be shown to have the same status in adult language. In fact, having a *sense* of a word, including an appreciation of its connotative meaning, sufficient for use of the word without knowing what it means in a precise denotative way, may characterize a greater proportion of the adult's lexicon than is generally assumed. From a developmental perspective, the interesting thing is that the sorts of answers one receives when one asks an adult about socialism in order to come to this hypothesis are not unlike the responses one gets upon asking young children to sort a set of objects or pictures into groups of things that go together, or a group of 5 year olds to define words referring to class names (cf. Anglin, 1977). Indeed, George Miller (1978) has suggested that there may be interesting similarities between, for example, the adult's understanding of the word *cancer* and the 2 year old's grasp of *doggie*. In both cases, the extension of the term is not stable, nor is intension a matter of precise understanding, yet the word can be used to some effect in communication. For the child, such usage will result in additional information that further identifies the appropriate conditions of use for the term (e.g., "No, that's a cat!"), and for the adult who has occasion to use the word "cancer" in a relevant setting, such as medical school, a similar process can be observed. According to the hypothesis outlined earlier, for the child learning animal names, the occasions of use include a variety of information, some of which may be nonverbal and provocative of affective responses. Similarly, the medical student learns to differentiate the concept *cancer* denotatively, but also connotatively. Some cancers are less predictive of death, or in other ways imply different probabilities for negative outcomes, and so would be expected to develop connotations that distinguish them from other cancers.

In both of these examples, the degree of differentiation of meaning that utlimately results is a function of the relationship of speaker to the context of communication. Developmentally, whether the development occurs at age 3 or at age 23, further differentiation of the meaning of a term in the lexicon will occur to the extent that such differentiation has functional significance in the context of communication. Clark's (1978) contention that early-language acquisition must be viewed as a process with a goal—namely, to communicate—is certainly consistent with this argument. But if the data presented here are any indication, differentiation of meaning involves more than increasing denotative specificity.

It is certainly *possible* to increase denotative differentiation without a corresponding increase in the connotative distinctiveness of the same set of terms, as the data presented here surely show. Indeed, it may be a common phenomenon in Western systems of education where learning often proceeds in contexts that are, for a diverse group of concepts, functionally homogenous. But there is nothing necessary about this pattern, any more than it is necessary, as originally hypothesized, that connotative distinctiveness must increase in parallel with increased denotative differentiation. The relationship between these two components of meaning, it is argued, will in fact determine characteristics of the full meaning of the term, especially as regards its perlocutionary force in the context of communication. Furthermore, meaning will be shared by speaker and hearer in this context to the extent that knowledge of both denotation and connotation is shared. The degree of such mutuality will be related to the extent that developmental histories of association with the term by the participants in the communication are similar. Shared meaning is thus not a matter of shared experience of word–concept or word–object pairings, but as a matter of *person*–word–concept or *person*–word–object relationships that are more or less similar. Only by understanding the relationship of the language user to the occasions of use can this level of meaning be properly analyzed.

There are, of course, a great many assumptions about the nature of meaning in the preceding discourse that must go unexamined here simply because they would require a digression into issues in the philosophy of language far beyond the scope of this chapter. However, I do feel compelled to make one or two remarks in this direction before drawing to a close.

The distinction drawn here between denotation and connotation is one of convenience. I assume that the meaning of a term is effectively a whole on most occasions of its use, and not the simple addition of distinct components (cf. Bates & Rankin, 1979). Assuming further that the relationship of denotation to connotation is an interactive one, especially over the course of the development of a term, it is still possible to analyze their relative contributions to the growth of meaning. For example, the variability between people in the meaning intended or understood when a word occurs may be a function of its connotation in adulthood when during early word acquisition it is a function of variation in denotation (Bates & Rankin, 1979; Clark, 1978; Nelson, Rescorla, Gruendel, and Benedict, 1978). Bates and Rankin's (1979) rare and provocative foray into the realm of connotative meaning indicates that in the case of learning size inflections in Italian, children first learn the inflection the meaning of which carries least connotation among adults. Only by adulthood is there evidence of interindividual variability in connotation of various inflections, as the children themselves give no indication of distinguishing the forms on the basis of connotation.

The interesting questions concern the principles by which this developmental pattern might be explained, which is, of course, a matter for further empirical study. However, the general arguments made earlier might be profitably applied here as well. By focusing on the larger context of use of a term, as described by the person–word–object or person–word–concept relationship, interesting hypotheses emerge. For example, late emergence of connotative distinctiveness of size inflections in Italian might result because it is difficult to provide clear, consistent nonverbal and affective cues in association with the use of these forms. Because of their relative nature, size inflections can be and are used in reference to a much wider range of phenomena than are, for example, the names of animals. This would be likely to lessen the consistency of cues that could provide the basis for the development of connotative distinctiveness of the forms. The same inconsistency might also account for the variability between users of the forms in the connotations intended and understood. Only by including the person in the context containing the word–concept or word–object relationship in a functional way are such predictions possible, and are complete models of meaning likely to be realized.

I take the inclusion of person–word–concept relationships, in addition to person–word–object relationships, to be fundamental to a full understanding of the growth of meaning because any semantic theory must consider that people develop the capacity to learn new words from hearing sentences containing other words, in the absence of anything concrete to which they might refer (Putnam, 1977). Among the words used to convey meanings of new words are those that describe dimensions of meaning independent of denotative meaning, and among these are precisely those words that make up the scales of the semantic differential: "good/bad," "strong/weak," and so on. The data presented here presupposed an appreciation of these dimensions for the children studied, but the question of the origins of meaning of *these* terms is a legitimate and important one. Deese (1973) has argued that the affective distinctions carried by these bipolar adjectives are inherent in cognitive structures onto which the terms are mapped. For example, the dimension "high/low" carries the same positive/negative implication in many languages. The argument is, as Deese acknowledges, a very Kantian one, involving a sort of categorical imperative that, as described, breaks down traditional, analytic distinctions between affect, cognition, and language in an intriguing and possibly useful way. Just how useful is a matter for further analysis and empirical study, but the idea is definitely intriguing if one considers the possibility that bipolar structures like the ones Deese describes could provide an inherent basis for early affective distinctions (good/bad) between perceptual events (high/low) such that new terms are attached to those events carrying more information than simple description would allow.

In any case, a theory of the development of connotation will probably have to include some explanation for the origins of these sorts of bipolar dimensions in order to account for the fact that ultimately people are able to learn some meaning for terms like "socialism" or "injustice" or "capitalism," including connotations, from sentences containing those words and in the absence of concrete manifestations of their referents.

This chapter has been primarily concerned with the growth of connotations of noun-like words, but the introduction of adjectival dimensions and sentences in the preceding paragraphs calls for a brief comment on connotation as it applies to other parts of speech and to problems of syntax. The Bates and Rankin (1979) study mentioned earlier offers a preliminary look at connotation and the growth of the adjective lexicon. Indeed, much of the available data that bear on connotation revolve around adjectival forms involving, as they do in so many cases, attribute structures like those captured by the semantic-differential scales (Deese, 1973; Osgood, et al., 1957; Saltz, Dunin-Markiewicz, & Rourke, 1975). In fact, much of the burden in language for conveying connotative meaning no doubt falls on adjectives and related forms. But connotation is an element of meaning in other forms as well. The work by Loftus and colleagues (Loftus & Palmer, 1974; Loftus & Zanni, 1975) showing that recall of events is affected by essentially connotative distinctions between verbs having a similar propositional form (e.g., hit, bumped, smashed, etc.) suggests interesting possibilities for the study of verb connotation, and places such study in the larger cognitive context of representation in momory as well. Nor are the issues confined to matters of single words. They encompass syntax as well, as indicated by Johnson's (1967) demonstration that use of the passive voice in English results in ratings of lower activity and potency on the semantic differential than active forms of the same sentence. The implication, of course, is that it is *not* the same sentence, and that this statement is true beyond the obvious differences in surface structure. At least, it is not the same sentence for the hearer, and one must question whether it is the same for speakers as well. Here is an ideal point of convergence for the study of developing semantic–syntactic relationships, one that arises out of the intent to systematically include connotation in the analysis of meaning.

This discussion has ranged rather widely, and strayed some distance from the data that provoked it, but not, I hope, without effect. It has been my intention to suggest the need to go beyond definition in the attempt to understand the development of semantics. The addition of new variables to any explanatory system is always problematic, and it may be more than usually so in this case. Connotation is itself a fuzzy concept; it introduces greater interindividual variability and complexity into the language equation, but perhaps it is necessary for a proper understanding of it. Vygotsky (1962) probably put it best, given the constraint of a single sentence, some half century ago:

> The dictionary meaning of a word is no more than a stone in the edifice of sense, no more than a potentiality that finds diversified realization in speech [p. 146].

ACKNOWLEDGMENTS

Work on the data presented here was begun while the author was a graduate student at Harvard University. The material is based in part on a paper presented at the Biennial Meeting of the Society for Research in Child Development, San Francisco, March 1979. My thanks to Jerome Kagan for his encouragement and support during the development and execution of this project. My thanks as well to David Kelley for his comments on an earlier draft, and to John Bonvillian and Jan Krueger for their thoughtful contributions to the final draft.

REFERENCES

Anglin, J. M. *Word, object, and conceptual development*. New York: Norton, 1977.

Anglin, J. M. From reference to meaning. *Child Development*, 1978, *49*, 969–976.

Bates, E. *Language and context*. New York: Academic Press, 1976.

Bates, E., & Rankin, J. Morphological development in Italian: Connotation and denotation, *Journal of Child Language*, 1979, *6*, 29–52.

Berko Gleason, J. Code switching in children's language. In T. E. Moore (Ed.), *Cognitive development and the acquisition of language*. New York: Academic Press, 1973.

Bonvillian, J. D., Raeburn, V. P., & Horan, E. A. Talking to children: The effects of rate, intonation, and length on children's sentence imitation. *Journal of Child Language*, 1979, *6*, 459–467.

Clark, E. V. What's in a word? On the child's acquisition of semantics in his first language. In T. E. Moore (Ed.), *Cognitive development and the acquisition of language.* New York: Academic Press, 1973.

Clark, E. V. Strategies for communicating. *Child Development,* 1978, *49,* 953–959.

Decarie, T. G. Affect development and cognition in Peagetian context. In M. Lewis & L. A. Rosenblum (Eds.), *The development of affect.* New York: Plenum Press, 1978.

Deese, J. Cognitive structure and affect in language. In P. Pliner, L. Krames, & T. Alloway (Eds.), *Communication and affect: Language and thought.* New York: Academic Press, 1973.

diVesta, F. J. A developmental study of the semantic structure of children. *Journal of Verbal Learning and Verbal Behavior,* 1966, *5,* 249–259.

Garnica, O. K. Some prosodic and paralinguistic features of speech to young children. In C. E. Snow & C. A. Ferguson (Eds.), *Talking to children: Language input and acquisition.* Cambridge, Eng.: Cambridge University Press, 1977.

Inhelder, B., & Piaget, J. *The early growth of logical thinking.* New York: Norton, 1964.

Johnson, M. G. Syntactic position and rated meaning. *Journal of Verbal Learning and Verbal Behavior,* 1967, *6,* 240–246.

Loftus, E. F., & Palmer, J. C. Reconstruction of automobile destruction: An example of the interaction between language and memory. *Journal of Verbal Learning and Verbal Behavior,* 1974, *13,* 585–589.

Loftus, E. F., & Zanni, G. Eyewitness testimony: The influence of the wording of a question. *Bulletin of the Psychonomic Society,* 1975, *5,* 86–88.

Miller, G. A. The acquisition of word meaning. *Child Development,* 1978, *49,* 999–1004.

Nelson, K. Concept, word and sentence: Interrelations in acquisition and development. *Psychological Review,* 1974, *81,* 267–285.

Nelson, K. Explorations in the development of a functional semantic system. In W. A. Collins (Ed.), *Minnesota symposium on child psychology* (Vol. 12). Hillsdale, N.J.: Lawrence Erlbaum Associates, 1979.

Nelson, K., Rescorla, L., Gruendel, J., & Benedict, H. Early lexicons: What do they mean? *Child Development,* 1978, *49,* 960–968.

Osgood, C., Suci, G., & Tannenbaum, P. *The measurement of meaning.* Urbana: University of Illinois Press, 1957.

Putnam. H. Is semantics possible? In S. P. Schwartz (Ed.), *Naming, necessity, and natural kinds.* Ithaca, N.Y.: Cornell University Press, 1977.

Saarni, C. Cognitive and communicative features of emotional experience, or do you show what you think you feel? In M. Lewis & L. A. Rosenblum (Eds.), *The development of affect.* New York: Plenum Press, 1978.

Saltz, E., Dunin-Markiewicz, A., & Rourke, D. The development of natural language concepts. II. Developmental changes in attribute structure. *Child Development,* 1975, *46,* 913–921.

Vygotsky, L. *Thought and language.* Cambridge, Mass.: M.I.T. Press, 1962.

Werner, H. The concept of development from a comparative and organismic point of view. In D. B. Harris (Ed.), *The concept of development,* 1957.

14 Acquisition of Mental Verbs and the Concept of Mind

Carl Nils Johnson
University of Pittsburgh

The study of lexical acquisition has contributed greatly to our understanding of the nature of human representation. This is particularly true with respect to representation of the physical world. Considerable research has focused on children's acquisition of "basic object" categories (see the chapters by Barrett and Palmero, this volume), and spatial–temporal relations (cf. Clark & Clark, 1977). In contrast, comparatively little attention has focused on children's representation of the mental world. One might suppose that this would be addressed as part of the now extensive study of children's knowledge about mental states and processes—that is, their social and metacognitions (Brown, 1978; Flavell, 1978b; Shantz, 1975). However, such research has been little concerned with how mental acts are ordinarily represented.

The cognitive-developmental literature includes numerous studies of how children make inferences about the feelings, perceptions, and motives of others, but few on how they ordinarily represent feelings, perceptions, and motives. Research has also dealt with children's knowledge about variables that affect cognitive performances of memory, comprehension, and attention, but not with their ordinary concepts of the cognitive acts themselves (see also Wellman, 1981). The present chapter stems from the author's belief that much could be gained from an integration of the study of metacognition with a more detailed study of the semantics of ordinary mental terms. The cognitive literature provides an indication of processes that may underlie lexical acquisition. A study of semantics provides an inroad into the structure of representation.

The goal here is to provide a general outline of the acquisition of representations in the mental domain. Two basic problems are considered, following lines of the author's research. The first concerns children's acquisition of mental verbs. The focus in this case is on a set of verbs that distinguish particularly cognitive acts or relations. The second concerns children's acquisition of the concept of "mind." This has to do with more general categorical distinctions between mental and nonmental phenomena. It is argued that these two concerns reflect fundamentally different kinds of representations with different patterns of acquisition. A preliminary framework for these considerations is provided by some old, but apt, ideas of John Locke.

SOME OLD IDEAS

In his *Essay on Human Understanding,* John Locke (1690) gave considerable attention to the nature and development of "ideas" about the mental world. His discussion is relevant in two respects. First, it provides a common-sense description of ordinary meanings of mental terms. Second, Locke's perspective on the development of such ideas corresponds to contemporary views, especially with respect to the cognitive basis of acquisition.

Locke (1690) argues that all ideas come from two sources, either from sensation of the physical world or the mind's reflection on its own operations. In both cases, Locke describes two levels of cognitive complexity. There are simple ideas, unreflectively occurring in the operation on simple ideas. And there are complex ideas, derived from the mind's reflective operation on simple ideas. Locke discusses complex ideas of space, time, number, and relations in the physical domain, and "modes of thinking" in the mental.

Locke uses the term thinking to refer to cognitive activities generally, including perception, contemplation, memories, ideas, expectancies, and the like. The particular instances are regarded as modes of the general class of mental operations. Hence, modes of thinking are defined in two respects. They are similarly defined as aspects of the general class of mental activities, or attributes of mind, but differently defined from one another. Locke (1690) provides the following examples of such distinctions:

> ... the perception which actually accompanies and is annexed to any impression on the body, made by an external object, being distinct from all other modification of *thinking,* furnishes the mind with a distinct *idea,* which we call *sensation;* which is, as it were, the actual entrance of any *idea* into the understanding by the senses. The same *idea,* when it again recurs without the operation of the like object on the external sensory, is *remembrance:* If it be sought after by the mind, and with pain and endeavour found, and brought into view, 'tis *recollection:* If it be held there long under attentive consideration, 'tis *contemplation:* When *ideas* float in our mind, without any reflection or regard of the understanding, it is that which the *French* call *reverie;* our language has scarce a name for it: When the *ideas* that offer themselves (for as I have observed in another place, whilst we are awake,

there will always be a train of *ideas* succeeding one another in our minds), are taken notice of, and, as it were, registered in the memory, it is *attention:* When the mind with great earnestness and of choice, fixes its view on any *idea,* considers it on all sides, and will not be called off by the ordinary solicitation of other *ideas,* it is that we call *intention* or *study* . . . [Book 2, Chapter 19]

Locke makes it clear that these modes of thinking are not distinguished by differences between unreflective mental experiences (simple ideas), nor by descriptions of externally perceived phenomena. Rather, these are complex ideas derived from the mind's reflection on its own operations. More specifically, the preceding quotation provides examples of two bases on which mental ideas are distinguished: one with regard to the derivation of the mental state (whether from sensation or memory), the other with regard to the degree and kind of attentive consideration.

Locke's position corresponds to current developmental theorizing. Piaget (1970) similarly distinguishes between two sources of knowledge—that from the physical world, and that from the mind's reflection on its own operations. Current descriptions of metacognition (cf. Brown, 1978; Flavell, 1978b) also distinguish between two levels of cognition, one of simple unreflective operations, the other of reflective knowledge about such operations. More generally, developmentalists have long noted the formal similarities between "complex ideas" of space, time, number, and relations.

Developmental research has, of course, added considerable substance and detail to Locke's speculations. But, it has skirted examination of ordinary mental concepts and the semantics of mental terms. There have been occasional studies of isolated concepts of mental phenomena, especially children's concepts of dreams (Kohlberg, 1969; Laurendeau & Pinard, 1962; Piaget, 1929), but nothing approximating a description of a broader domain of lexical terms. In this regard, Locke's description raises two problems for developmental consideration. One is how children come to understand the characteristics of different modes of thinking as described by ordinary mental verbs. The other is how children come to understand that differing modes are similarly attributes of mind. These two problems are separately addressed in the empirical considerations that follow.

MODES OF THINKING

Background

How do children come to distinguish between the different modes of thinking, as expressed by ordinary mental verbs? The focus in this section is on the development of children's understanding of verbs such as think, know, remember, and guess. The preliminary question is, what do such terms describe?

According to Locke (1690), mental verbs describe mental operations. But things are not as simple as they first appear. Take, for example, the statement, "Lee remembers where the hat is." This statement could describe a cognitive act whereby Lee locates the hat based on prior knowledge of its location. But this is a very abstract description of Lee's mental operations. It does not describe the particular processes Lee used to remember, nor whether Lee was even aware of remembering. Further, instead of describing Lee's actual memory performance, the same statement could be used to describe Lee's potential ability to remember, or a conscious state of having a memory in mind. The point is that the term *remember* does not necessarily specify any particular conscious state or mental operation at all.

What the term remember does specify is a general kind of cognitive basis of a person's actual or potential performance. To say that "Lee remembers where the hat is" ordinarily presumes that Lee can, at least potentially, designate the actual location of the hat and that such a performance is based on prior information about its location. In comparison, the term *know* is even less cognitively specific. Lee's knowing where the hat is could be based on memory, or equally on present perception or inference. In turn, the term *think* is least cognitively specific, merely indicating the presence of some cognitive operation without specifying anything about it.

These remarks are not inconsistent with Locke's position, as is evident from Locke's own analysis of modes of thinking previously cited. However, they qualify the sense in which mental verbs can be said to describe mental operations. It is accurate to say that such verbs commonly describe general kinds of applications of cognition or thinking, but not to say that such verbs describe the particular processes that are employed in such acts. With respect to the metacognitive literature (e.g., Wellman, 1981), mental acts such as remembering, attending, or comprehending refer to general kinds of applications of cognition, as distinct from specifying the strategies, operations, or other variables affecting particular performances of such acts.

There remains a further qualification of the meanings of mental verbs. Given that such verbs are commonly used to distinguish kinds of applications of thinking, there remain other uses that do not necessarily describe anything strictly mental at all. Urmson (1963), for example, discusses a wide variety of "parenthetical" uses of "mental" verbs. Such uses are said to modify the meaning of statements rather than to describe a person's psychological state. Urmson argues, for example, that terms such as *know, believe,* and *guess* are used to signal the degree of reliability of statements, rather than anything necessarily mental. In this sense, a statement such as "I believe it will rain" may function in a manner similar to "It will probably rain," signaling the likelihood of rain rather than describing any actual state of mind.

Uses of the sort described by Urmson (1963) cannot be dismissed as mere exceptions. Rather, there is reason to suspect that mental uses of terms are derived from more primitive nonmental uses. Sellars (1956), for one, argues that because language is intersubjective, categories of thinking must at bottom be semantic categories pertaining to overt uses of language. In a similar vein, Toulmin (1960) describes a logical stratification of concepts whereby descriptions of private states such as choosing and wanting are derivative from more primitive overt expressions. These arguments have an obvious developmental translation. Toulmin argues that children may first understand semantic uses of terms with respect to overt behaviors, and only later acquire an understanding of more complex mental implications. Limber (1973) has similarly hypothesized that young children may have a kind of parenthetical understanding of mental verbs before abstracting their strictly cognitive implications.

These considerations lead to an alternative to the Lockean thesis: Children first acquire a simple interpretation of mental verbs with respect to overt acts and uses of language and only subsequently develop a more reflective understanding of the verbs as definitively mental descriptions. This model of development is consistent with considerable evidence that social cognition proceeds from knowledge about overt acts and behaviors towards knowledge about inner mental processes and states (Flavell, 1978a; Shantz, 1975). It is also consistent with arguments that children's early word meanings are based primarily on perceptual information (Gentner, 1978).

This model predicts that young children's interpretations of mental terms will be characterized by both misapprehensions and limited appropriate uses. In the first case, it predicts that young children will be ignorant of the distinctly mental implications of terms and/or confuse mental with overt events or behavior. Such is the traditional characterization of young children's egocentrism (cf. Piaget, 1929). On the other hand, given that mental terms have some primitive use with respect to overt behaviors or uses of language, young children may exhibit considerable understanding of such uses.

An especially clear case of early primitive uses can be derived from research on visual role taking. Flavell (1978a) has described two levels of such skills that imply a change from interpreting terms of perception with respect to overt behavior towards understanding more distinctly mental implications. He argues that, at a simple level, very young children can judge whether or not a person sees an object by interpreting "seeing" as a kind of overt act, a visual contact, like touching. Only at a second, more complex level, do children recognize that people can have different views of the same object and hence interpret seeing (Flavell, 1978a) "more like an internal image than like an external action [p. 48]."

This sort of developmental sequence may be characteristic of terms, like those of perception, that map fairly directly onto overtly perceptible acts. The questions here, however, have to do with terms of a different order. Terms such as *think, know,* or *remember* are abstract in the very sense that their uses do not readily map onto any particular sensory or behavioral act.

The field of terms examined here represents the next step in a cognitive hierarchy, and is commonly used to distinguish states of knowing rather than immediate perception. To put it simply, whereas statements about perception describe particular sensory relations of a subject to perceptible objects of sense, statements about knowing describe general types of cognitive relations of a subject to facts, propositions, or performances. Terms used in this latter respect commonly indicate something about the presence, absence, degree, or type of a person's knowledge basis. In this sense, *know* indicates some rational or empirical basis, *remember* describes a more particular basis in prior apprehension, and *guess* distinguishes the comparative lack of any knowledge basis. *Think,* in this respect, indicates a tentative basis, where *forget* indicates the lack of one kind of knowing (i.e., memory).

It would be a mistake to assume that the terms described only function in this limited epistemic sense. Uses of such terms are notably various. Nevertheless, the epistemic distinctions provide a means for examining a system of semantic comparisons, and for determining the developmental steps in the criteria children use in ascribing knowledge states to themselves and others. The development of children's interpretations of these "modes of knowing" is described in three sections as follows: First is an examination of the general performance characteristics of 4-year-olds' interpretations of cognitive states. Second is an examination of particular patterns in the acquisition of three sets of semantically related verbs. Third is a discussion of children's earliest uses of mental verbs.

The Performance of 4 Year Olds

One basic question is whether young children interpret epistemic terms with respect to a person's knowledge basis as distinct from behavioral performance. Several recent studies have examined this using simple object-location tasks (Johnson & Wellman, 1980, Miscione, Marvin, O'Brien, & Greenberg, 1978; Wellman & Johnson, 1979). Such tasks involve the subject, or the character in a story, in conditions of hiding and finding an object in one of several possible locations. Two conditions can be varied: the subject's or story character's *prior information*—whether or not the person sees where the object is initially hidden—and his or her *present performance*—whether or not the judgment about the location of the hidden object proves correct or incorrect. As shown in Table 14.1, combinations of these conditions present distinct cases of mental states. Know and remember are represented by the combination of having prior information and presently demonstrating this knowledge; forget is represented by a failure in performance, but only on condition of having prior information. Guess is represented by performance in the absence of any knowledge basis, regardless of outcome.

Under these conditions, 4 year olds have typically been found to judge mental states strictly with respect to performance, ignoring knowledge basis. Miscione

TABLE 14.1
Representation of Cognitive States in
Hidden-Object Tasks

	Present Performance	
Prior Information	Correct	Incorrect
Present	Know/Remember	Forget
Absent	Guess (right)	Guess (wrong)

et al. (1978) found children stating that they knew the location of an object when their performance was correct, even when lacking any knowledge basis (i.e., when they simply guess right). Similarly, Wellman and Johnson (1979) found children stating that a story character remembered when the character correctly judged the location of a hidden object, and forgot when incorrect, regardless of the knowledge basis of these performances.

These limitations were further evident in a study by Johnson and Wellman (1980) of the terms know, remember, and guess. Using other variations of the hidden-object paradigm, results showed 4 year olds to completely confuse conditions of knowing, remembering, and guessing. For example, in conditions where children were given immediately *present information* of an object's location (e.g., the object was presently in sight), children stated that they not only knew the object's location, but also guessed and remembered its location. Thus, children failed to discriminate present knowledge from remembering, as well as guessing from knowing.

One way to interpret these results is in terms of a traditional referential model. This model assumes that children, being ignorant of internal processes, initially interpret mental states as referring to external states. Miscione et al. (1978) adopt this explanation as follows: "Limited to thinking in terms of the external appearance of things, children initially hypothesize that 'know' and 'guess' refer to external, perceivable aspects of situations [p. 1113]." This model, however, turns out to be wholly inadequate on two grounds. In the first place, the investigations described earlier do not test what children think mental states refer to; they test how children ascribe mental verbs to themselves and others. If such ascriptions refer to something, it is an abstract relation between a subject and the "accuracy," or truth condition of performance, not to "perceivable aspects of situations." One might try to salvage the referential model by arguing that children interpret mental verbs strictly with respect to "external" truth conditions of performance. However, this too is inadequate. Evidence, reported as follows, clearly indicates that young children do not make any simple equation between terms and external performances. They readily ascribe mental states to persons on grounds quite apart from any immediately perceptible performance.

There are contexts in which young children appropriately interpret cognitive states with respect to a person's prior information. In simple role-taking studies, Mossler, Marvin, and Greenberg (1976) reported that 4 year olds are capable of distinguishing what different people presently know according to whether or not a person initially heard given information. The same investigators (Marvin, Greenberg, & Mossler, 1976) reported that children of the same age were able to determine who had a secret depending on who initially saw a given event. In another study, Johnson and Maratsos (1977) found 4 year olds to be capable of distinguishing a character who was misinformed and hence thought something false from one who was correctly informed and hence knew the truth.

This evidence indicates that the performance of 4 year olds is context dependent. In conditions in which present performance is salient, children tend to ignore prior information conditions, but when the latter conditions are salient, children tend to make judgments on that basis. Given that present performance is generally more salient than prior information, it might be suggested that, relatively speaking, young children do interpret mental terms on the basis of salient "external perceivable aspects of situations." However, this too is misleading. It overlooks the fact that young children not only have salient external perceptions, they also have salient mental states that occur apart from or at odds with immediate perception. In this sense, there are situations in which children should interpret mental terms on the basis of their salient mental state in contrast to external perception. Demonstrating this, Johnson and Wellman (1980) set up a trick condition in which a subject's expectancy was violated in fact. Subjects were first shown where an object was being hidden, giving them initial knowledge of its location. Then, unbeknownst to the subjects, the object was moved elsewhere. Hence, the subjects' subsequent performance in locating the object, based on their prior information, turned out to be in error. In this case, 4 year olds based their judgments about their mental state on their salient expectancy as to the object's location, rather than on the perceived outcome of their performance.

These results point out that 4 year olds variably interpret mental terms with respect to any of three factors commonly associated with cognitive acts: prior information conditions, present states of mind, and present performances. In a given context, children interpret epistemic states according to the single most salient factor. On this basis, they can in many cases make accurate distinctions about whether or not a person has a given knowledge state. However, by focusing on a single factor, children are unable to distinguish different cognitive states with respect to the same event. Thus, for example, children are unaware that the same present performance (locating a hidden object) could be differently due to either remembering the object's location, or knowing through present information, or merely guessing with no knowledge at all. Only during the early school years do children typically become capable of weighing two aspects of a situation and hence discriminating between different cognitive states with respect to the same performance (Johnson & Wellman, 1980).

This pattern of development has been similarly described with regard to role-taking skills generally. Young children are reportedly capable of making inferences about the mental states of others if this can be done by focusing on single aspects of a situation, but only subsequently are they able to make inferences that involve simultaneous consideration of multiple aspects of a situation (Lyons-Ruth, 1978; Urberg & Docherty, 1976). For example, 4 year olds have been found to distinguish the motive of another when information about motive is salient, but otherwise focus on the consequences of acts. Only during the early school years are children typically capable of simultaneously weighing intentions and consequences and thus consistently distinguishing between intended and unintended acts (Keasey, 1978).

This description of development is part of a more general model of acquisition. In this, the differentiation of subjective from objective, at whatever level, is defined by the development of awareness that different subjective acts can operate on the same objective state. This applies to awareness that the same judgment could be due to different cognitive bases (remembering, guessing, knowing) or that the same act could be due to different intentional bases. At different levels, it also applies to awareness that the same object could be viewed from different visual perspectives (Flavell, 1978a), or that the same object could be acted upon by different action schemes (Piaget, 1952).

The development in these cases is commonly described as the coordination of actions or relations. Beginning with isolated actions or relations, there develops, through coordination, more complex and differentiated meanings. This relational model of acquisition contrasts to a referential model whereby development proceeds from "external" to "internal." The evidence described earlier indicates that children do not begin by interpreting mental verbs as describing external states and later interpret them as describing internal ones. Rather, children initially interpret terms with regard to acts or relations that are not differentiated as either internal or external. This fits well with the Lockean model. Young children acquire simple ideas of how mental verbs are used in talking about relations between subjects and conditions such as prior information, present states of mind, and outcomes of performance. Later, by coordinating these simple ideas, children discern the more complex cognitive meanings. Understanding of these complex ideas is derived from reflections on human acts, rather than from sensations of external things.

Patterns of Acquisition

The evidence described earlier indicates that young children can discriminate the presence or absence of a cognitive state, but leaves doubt about their ability to discriminate different types of cognitive states. By focusing on single aspects of situations, children failed to distinguish whether a given state was a case of remembering, knowing, or guessing (Johnson & Wellman, 1980). Remaining questions concern when and how children make such discriminations. Evidence reviewed in this section not only details the subsequent patterns of development, but also indicates that even young children have some discriminate understanding of the cognitive meanings of different mental verbs.

Children's acquisition of three sets of semantically related terms are considered here. The first set, *know–think–guess,* provides a means for assessing the hypothesis that children acquire a modifying use of mental verbs with respect to the truth of statements, before acquiring an understanding of their distinctive cognitive implications. The second set of terms, *remember–forget,* provides a look at the acquisition of an abstract pair of antonyms. The third set, *know–remember,* leads to an examination of children's developing discrimination of different types of knowing.

Know–Think–Guess.   One hypothesis about mental-verb acquisition, mentioned previously, is that children acquire a sense of modifying uses of mental verbs before they understand their distinctively cognitive descriptions (Limber, 1973). In this regard, a distinction can be made between modifying and cognitive uses of the terms know, think, and guess. First, in Urmson's (1963) sense, these terms have "parenthetical" uses in modifying the reliability of statements. Thus, know indicates a reliable statement whereas think and guess indicate increasing unreliability. From this standpoint, children might initially acquire a sense of the relative association of these different terms to the truth of the statements. This contrasts to understanding the distinctive cognitive implications of the terms— namely, that know implies a knowledge basis, whereas guess distinguishes the lack of such a basis.

There is some evidence that young children do have an early sense of the relative relation of these terms to the truth of assertions. Using the hidden-object paradigm described earlier, Miscione et al. (1978) reported that, when given a forced choice, 4 year olds associated know with assertions that proved to be true (i.e., judgments about the hidden object's location that proved correct), whereas they associated guess with assertions that proved to be false. Also using a forced-choice task, Johnson and Maratsos (1977) similarly found 4 year olds to differentially associate *know* with true assertions and *think* with false ones. In a more naturalistic context, Shatz and Gelman (1977) reported 4 year olds using *think* to modify their assertions when talking to adults.

Johnson and Wellman (1980) have further outlined a development from modifying uses to cognitive meanings of the terms know and guess. They describe three steps in this development, based on children's performances in the hidden-object paradigm. First, at age 4, children typically associate both know and guess with assertions that are true (i.e., assertions about the location of an object that prove correct), but in a forced-choice situation, they discriminate know as relatively more associated with truth. Second, by 5 years of age, children exhibit a more discrete sense of the truth relatedness of the terms. The term guess is freely ascribed regardless of the truth of the assertion, whereas know is still restricted to assertions that are true. Children at this point, however, still fail to distinguish the cognitive meanings of guess from know. Know is associated with any true assertion, even when based on merely guessing right, and guess is associated with any assertion whatsoever, even if based on obvious knowledge. Understanding of the contrasting cognitive meanings of the terms occurs as the final step in this development.

This evidence offers some confirmation that young children have a sense of the degree to which mental terms are related to the truth of assertions. However, there is a major stumbling block to the argument that modifying uses generally precede cognitive meanings. Specifically, children's early sense of modifying uses, as described earlier, in no way approximates the complexity of Urmson's (1963) description of modifying uses. In Urmson's sense, modifying the reliability of statements entails an assessment of the probability and evidence indicating that a statement is true. In other words, it requires an assessment of the truth of a statement before the fact, not just the relation of terms to the truth of statements after the fact. Assessing the truth of a statement appears no less complex than assessing the cognitive basis of a person's state of knowing. In fact, young children have traditionally been described as equally ignorant of both the cognitive basis of their knowing and the evidential or probabilistic basis of truth (cf. Piaget & Inhelder, 1975). From this standpoint, it seems likely that just as young children have a partial sense of modifying uses, they also have a partial sense of cognitive meanings.

A primary example of early cognitive meaning is children's awareness of the cognitive basis of their knowing. By simply questioning 3 and 4 year olds about what they know and how they know it, the author (Johnson, 1980a) has found children to readily explain that what they knew stemmed from being taught or told. In other words, young children have some sense that how one knows is related to how one found out. This must be compared with other evidence that indicates that young children are largely ignorant of the basis of their knowing. As discussed previously, young children commonly focus on the outcome of their judgment, ignoring its knowledge base. Similarly, Piaget (1928) long ago demonstrated that young children are ignorant of how they know things (e.g., claiming they "always knew" the word brain), resulting in confusion between subjective belief, conjecture, and objective fact (e.g., claiming they "always knew" that the moon is made of gold). The contrast between this ignorance and other instances of understanding apparently rests on three factors. First, children are presumably more familiar with sources of certain kinds of knowledge than others—for example, sources from explicit teaching rather than incidental acquisition. Second, young children are undoubtedly aware of sources of their knowledge in particular instances, even while remaining ignorant that knowing in general necessarily implies having some ratinal or empirical basis. Finally, children can apparently comprehend that questions about one's knowing are appropriately answered with descriptions about how one "found out"—that is, descriptions of one's informational experiences—yet still have poorly established criteria for what constitutes an adequate knowledge base.

Other evidence of early partial understanding of cognitive meanings appears in young children's association of different mental terms to different types of cognitive expressions. In the same study cited earlier, the author (Johnson, 1980a) asked children to give examples of both things they knew and things they thought. Children were encouraged to provide as many examples in each case as possible. The question here is whether children associated different kinds of statements with thinking versus knowing. It should first be noted that this was not an easy task for these children. A number of them could provide no examples on request and only a few children provided more than one. These children could apparently use the terms, but often had little sense of their meaning out of context. On the other hand, the examples that children did generate of thinking versus knowing represented very different types of cognitive phenomena. Examples of thinking distinctly included comments about dreams and preferences whereas examples of knowing were primarily statements of fact or know how. In this sense, children exhibited a distinction between subjective states and objective fact or ability.

Particularly intriguing in this context were children's associations of thinking with dreaming. Five of 23 subjects made such an association. This can be compared to Kohlberg's (1969) evidence that children do not understand the relation between thought and dreams until several years later. There is no contradiction here, because young children in the present study could not in any way explain how thinking and dreaming were related. In fact, they typically denied the relationship when explicitly asked if dreams were like thoughts. Nonetheless, at a more primitive level, these children exhibited some understanding of a relation between these cognitive phenomena. Comparable evidence can be found in children's substitutions in spontaneous speech. For example, a child just 3 years old was noted to reply as follows when asked "What was on your mind?": "Nothin, 'cept I dreamed, uh, I thinked about something at Greggy's house." This and other substitutions in this child's speech (e.g., between think and decide) indicate an early sense of relations between different "modes of thinking."

It is no accident that these examples of early knowledge of cognitive meanings have focused on the terms know and think, rather than guess. This appears because the cognitive meaning of guess is essentially negative, denoting the lack of a knowledge basis. In this respect, the meaning of guess appears dependent on a contrasting understanding of know. As noted previously, Johnson and Wellman (1980) found this understanding to be a comparatively late development. Up until the early school years, children exhibited no awareness that know and guess have opposing cognitive implications. Thus, even though young children exhibit a partial understanding of the cognitive meaning of know, a fuller understanding of know as related to guess represents a later semantic acquisition. This acquisition appears to occur more or less simultaneously for the two terms. Know is understood as necessarily involving some knowledge basis just as guess is understood as indicating a comparative lack of such a basis. As Kuczaj (1975) has suggested, simultaneous acquisition is likely when a core part of the meaning of terms is the relation they bear on each other. In the present case, children appear to be acquiring a sense of guess as used to indicate not knowing, and vice versa. Such a relation is expressed in ordinary statements like "I don't know, I'm just guessing."

In sum, there is no general support for the hypothesis that modifying uses of mental verbs precedes the acquisition of cognitive meanings. Modifying the probability that a statement is true appears to be conceptually no less complex than understanding the cognitive basis of a statement. Young children not only exhibit partial understanding of modifying uses, but also of cognitive meanings. In the latter case, children have early partial knowledge of both objective uses of know and subjective uses of think. They understand that know is related to how one found out, even though not comprehending the general epistemic implications of the term. And, they associate think with dreams and preferences, even though they are unable to conceptualize these relations. The acquisition of guess is an exception to the case of early knowledge of cognitive meanings. Lacking any simple association to a cognitive act, the negative epistemic use of guess is acquired as part of a later-developing semantic system.

Remember-Forget.   The terms remember and forget present another kind of semantic contrast. These terms can be described as referring to positive versus negative performances of the same cognitive type—that is, memory. Wellman and Johnson (1979) examined the development of this understanding using four simple stories about a character in hidden-object conditions (see Table 14.1). To correctly interpret these stories, children had to recognize that even though remember and forget differ in their performance implications, both terms commonly imply having prior information. In other words, stories in which a character had no prior information represented conditions of guessing right and wrong, not remembering and forgetting.

There were three steps in children's acquisition of this mature understanding. Older 4 year olds discriminated the terms on the basis of present performance alone, interpreting correct performance as remember and incorrect as forget. By age 5, the majority of children understood that remember entails prior information, and were able to distinguish remembering from guessing right. Children this age, however, did not understand that forget also entails having prior information. Understanding the full meaning of forget appeared as a much later step, not well developed even among 7 year olds.

The curious result is the comparatively late development in understanding the cognitive meaning of forget. On the surface, this might be explained by considering forget to be the semantically more complex, negatively marked term. However, a more convincing explanation lies in examining problems of interpretation in ordinary contexts of use (cf. Kuczaj & Lederberg, 1977). One factor is that the term forget is commonly used in unintentional contexts. In this respect, forget does not strictly mean not remember. For example, on arriving at work and noting the absence of my wallet, I am likely to explain, "I forgot my wallet." It would be strange to say "I did not remember my wallet" because I was not intentionally trying to remember it. On the other hand, if I am intentionally, but unsuccessfully, trying to find my wallet, the explanation is more likely to be "I cannot remember where I put it" (not "I forgot my wallet"). The point is that forget is typically used to indicate an unintentional failure in performance whereas not remember is used to indicate a failure in an intentional effort to remember. Presumably, the cognitive meaning of terms is more apparent in intentional than unintentional contexts. On this basis, it can be hypothesized that children will discern the cognitive meaning of both remember and not remember before forget.

Acquisition of the term forget is in one sense comparable to the acquisition of guess, as described earlier. Both terms have negative implications, the cognitive meanings of which are acquired relatively late. Initial interpretations of these terms appear to be uniquely lacking in cognitive meaning. In the present case, young children use forget to describe any failure or inability to produce an expected performance. This appears in spontaneous misuse of the term. The author has commonly found young children to respond "I forgot" to indicate their inability to respond to a question, regardless of the fact that they obviously had no prior knowledge of the answer.

Know-Remember.   It has been argued (Flavell, 1971) that memory is a kind of "applied cognition [p. 273]," a kind of knowing in specific, as distinct from knowing in general (Piaget & Inhelder, 1973; Tulving, 1972). Such distinctions are reflected in the ordinary meanings of the terms know and remember. The term *know* designates an epistemic basis in general, which includes inference, deduction, and present apprehension, as well as memory. The term remember, in contrast, designates a particular kind of epistemic basis—that is, memory. The question, then, is when do children distinguish remembering in particular from more general instances of nonremembered knowing?

To examine this, Johnson and Wellman (1980) included two variants of the basic hidden-object paradigm. Children were presented with two boxes, one that was transparent, the other opaque. In one condition, a hiding sequence was feined, with an object "hidden" under the transparent box. Hence, children were provided with knowledge (present sight) of the object's location that was distinctly not based on memory. In the second condition, using the same two boxes, the object was hidden under the opaque box. In this case, children again had knowledge of the object's location, this time by inference (if not under the transparent box, it must be under the opaque one), as distinct from memory. Following each of these conditions, subjects were asked where the object was located and, based on their judgment, whether they knew it was there and whether they remembered it was there. Results showed that young children completely confused *remember* with these conditions of knowing. Only in the early grade-school years did children regularly distinguish remember as distinctly entailing prior knowledge.

On the surface, this suggests that young children have little discriminate sense of what it means to remember. But here again, it appears that young children have some sense of relative, rather than categorical, differences between the terms. Forced-choice tasks are particularly useful in exposing this early discriminate understanding. Johnson and Wellman (1980) employed this method, asking children to categorize statements as either "something you know" or "something you remember." Results of this task indicated that even 4 year olds understood that remember is associated with statements about their own past experiences, whereas know is more associated with statements based on inference (i.e., inferences about the experience of another, or prediction about the future).

Another approach to children's distinctive understanding of remember can be derived from recent metamemory research. A number of studies have focused on what's been called the "differentiation hypotheses." This tests whether children differentially respond to instructions to remember given items versus instructions merely to look at such items. Evidence from such studies suggests that even preschoolers have acquired some sense of different performance demands of remembering versus looking (Flavell, 1978a).

This technique of eliciting differential responses has further potential in revealing more subtle conceptual distinctions between cognitive terms. For example, the author (Johnson, 1980a) recently engaged 3 and 4 year olds in a kind of differential retrieval task. Rather than examining children's responses to requests for task performances, this study examined children's responses to requests for different types of cognitive information. Children were first shown a series of pictures of animals on separate cards. These pictures were casually labeled and discussed with the child who was then told, "Now let's turn these pictures over." The pictures were turned face down and then children were asked one of two questions: "What do you remember about the pictures?" or "What do you think about the pictures?" Results showed that even 3 year olds responded differentially to these questions. When asked what they remembered, children typically named the pictures; when asked what they thought, children more frequently commented about the pictures or expressed their preferences. These results are comparable to the evidence discussed previously on children's differential responses to requests for examples of what they thought versus knew.

The results here again confirm that young children have a sense of different kinds of mental statements associated with different mental verbs.

Understanding Before Age Four

The research reviewed so far has focused mostly on the performance of children 4 years old and older. It should be emphasized in this respect that the patterns of performance of 4 year olds have often not been found in younger children. The performance of 3 year olds, and even young 4 year olds, has been found lacking in the regularities that are evident in the performance of older 4 year olds (Johnson & Maratsos, 1977; Miscione et al. 1978; Wellman & Johnson, 1979). But certainly children are beginning to use mental terms well before their fourth year. The question is, what characterizes such beginnings?

There is little evidence on children's early uses of mental verbs. However, there is good reason to suppose that the acquisition is consistent with a more general pattern of semantic development. As outlined by Bowerman (1978), Carey (1978), and Kuczaj (1975), children often begin with an understanding of appropriate uses of individual words in particular contexts, and only subsequently isolate features that organize a number of words across a broader lexical domain. From this standpoint, one would predict that children begin with some appropriate uses of mental terms in limited contexts. Hence, the performances of 4 year olds, previously described, represent later efforts of children to understand features that organize a broader domain of epistemic distinctions.

There is evidence to suggest that early uses of mental terms reflect a beginning ability to talk about the thoughts or intentions of persons as distinguished from immediate perception. In his early work, Piaget (1926) argued that beginning uses of mental verbs coincide with a more global developmental change, characterized by a broad range of emerging language skills that involve consciousness of a plane of reality distinct from immediate perception. This includes uses of mental terms, meaning *to think* or *to believe*, to distinguish what is imagined (or expected) from what is perceived. It also includes the use of *why* questions regarding the intentions of others, the first lies, beliefs about the future, and complex syntax with the rudiments of formulated reason.

The point here is that uses of mental verbs to talk about distinctly nonperceived phenomena is well within the competence of young children. Support for Piaget's contention is particularly evident in a recent investigation of children's why questions. Consistent with Piaget's contention, Hood and Bloom (1979) have suggested that children's first use of why questions, commonly occurring before 3 years of age, represents the development of an ability to refer to the intentions of self and others, as distinct from referring to immediately perceptible actions or states. In other words, in asking why of another person's actions, children are taking into account the distinctly nonperceptible intentions of another.

If young children are aware of the "intentions" of others, as Piaget (1926) suggests, this is a qualified sense. Although young children can refer to the mental states of themselves and others, they apparently know little of their categorically mental quality. In other words, the fact that children are aware that there is more to the world than their immediate perception does not imply that they have much understanding of what this is. An illustration of this was kindly provided by a 3-year-old friend of the author's who spontaneously made a "think" game. This game required one person to think of something ("you think something") while the other tried to guess what it was. Turns were taken, and the thoughts were limited to references to objects in the immediate environment (e.g., thinking about a ball). In playing this game, it was obvious that this child had some sense of a world of possible "thoughts," and that another's "thought" was not directly perceptible, but rather must be guessed. Yet, when it was her turn to think of something, it was clear that she played the game with no particular thought in mind. She simply evaluated the various guesses as to her "thought," and chose one for her own. Thus, this child had some notion of "thoughts" as distinct from immediate perception, yet little notion of them as something distinctly held in mind.

Summary

The following pattern of development has been outlined: First, by 3 years of age and often before, children are able to use mental terms in restricted contexts to talk about phenomena that are distinct from immediate perception. At this point, children are aware that there is something beyond what is immediately present, but they have little concept of what this is. Subsequently, the period between 4 and 5 years of age is characterized by attempts to isolate features that organize the broader domain of epistemic verbs. This includes partial understanding of the cognitive meanings that distinguish uses of terms such as remember, think, and know. Finally, during the early school years, children develop a more structured semantic system. This is evident in a more definitive sense of the cognitive meanings that include contrasting relations between positive and negative terms, such as know–guess, remember–forget.

This pattern of acquisition is at odds with a referential model of development, described as proceeding from "external" to "internal." Children do not first interpret mental verbs as referring to external acts and later interpret them as referring to internal ones. Even very young children attribute mental predicates to themselves and others apart from any immediately perceptible act. It is more accurate to say that children begin with an understanding of the verbs with respect to uses of language. Young children know something about how the terms are used, but only later acquire understanding of their distinctly mental descriptions. Yet, this too must be qualified. Children do not first acquire modifying uses with respect to language and only later acquire uses that refer to cognitive acts or states. Rather, they exhibit considerable early partial knowledge of cognitive meanings.

The findings here are consistent with the general argument, made by Gentner (1978), that verbs are more accurately described as having relational rather than referential meaning. In this sense, children initially discern how mental verbs are used in relational contexts and only later conceptualized the mental "things" to which they refer. However, the development described here is largely at odds with Gentner's model of verb acquisition. Gentner argues that children's early interpretations of verb meanings are based on perceptual information. For example, children are said to understand the perceptible action involved in "mix" before acquiring its functional meaning, indicating a change of state. This model simply does not apply to verbs such as think, know, and guess. These verbs cannot be interpreted in terms of any simple perceptible acts. Yet, children do acquire knowledge of their meanings at an early age.

Gentner (1978) also argues that verbs are typically acquired by the accretion of semantic components. This model has limited relevance to the acquisitions described here. It may be applied to the "negative" terms, guess and forget, which exhibit something of a step-like development from behavioral to cognitive meanings. However, it does not apply to the terms think, know, and remember, which are characterized by early partial knowledge of cognitive meanings. In the latter cases, development is more accurately described by a model of coordinating separate components, rather than adding new ones. Young children acquire a global sense of multiple components associated with uses of these verbs. These components are subsequently differentiated and integrated in the formation of more definitive meanings.

The application of these different models of development appears to depend on whether particular verbs map onto perceptible components in ordinary use. To the extent that verb meanings overlap with concretely perceptible components, children acquire such meanings early. But to the extent that verbs are used in various contexts, lacking consistent perceptual components, children first acquire a more global sense of these relational meanings. Thus, it is not an invariate principle of cognition that leads children to interpret words in terms of externally perceptible features. Rather, interpretations are dependent on particular uses of terms. This is consistent with considerable evidence that there is no single model that predicts the sequence of semantic acquisition. Rather, patterns of acquisition are individually determined with respect to the context of interpretation (Carey, 1978; Kuczaj & Lederberg, 1977).

Of course, this represents only a preliminary sketch of early acquisition. Evidence here has focused on a limited set of relatively concrete contexts of use (e.g., knowledge of spatial location). In this respect, it seems likely that there are more abstract meanings of the verbs that are acquired later. Such meanings may be acquired in a sequential order, more consistent with Gentner's (1978) model. The research reported here has also dealt little with variability in individual patterns of acquisition or with early natural use. Further investigation will undoubtedly provide a more complex picture of development.

ATTRIBUTES OF MIND

Background

We have examined how children come to distinguish mental verbs, or "modes of thinking." The second question is how they come to understand that differing modes are similarly mental, or attributes of mind. This concerns the development of general categories that structure the broader domain of mental concepts.

The issues in this case are more closely related to traditional studies of children's concepts of thoughts and dreams (Kohlberg, 1969; Laurendeau & Pinard, 1962; Piaget, 1929). It is important to emphasize that these studies were not concerned with children's understanding of the distinctive meanings of mental terms, but rather with children's developing categorization of mental phenomena as mental. This division must be carefully drawn because it has been the source of considerable confusion. For example, the traditional evidence purports to show that children confuse mental with material acts or events—dreams with seeing, thoughts with speaking. But this certainly does not imply that children are interpreting *dream* to mean *see* or *think* to mean *say*. The evidence reviewed previously leaves little doubt that even young preschoolers are quite capable of making appropriate distinctions between uses of these verbs. The problem is that they have not developed a means to categorize these differences—that is, a means to make reference to distinctly mental "objects." Thus, when Piaget (1926) concludes that "until age 11, to think is to speak [p. 60]," he is not arguing that children up to this age believe thinking means speaking, but rather that they have not yet abstracted a distinctive characteristic of mental acts—namely, their immateriality—which places thinking in a logically discrete category from speaking.

It is here that the referential model of development becomes applicable. The argument is that children's initial referential categories are tied to concrete, perceptible features of the world. Only subsequently can children interpret mental "objects" as categorically distinct from their material counterparts.

The problem with the traditional studies of children's concepts of mental phenomena is that they have largely missed the point. They have been limited to isolated demonstrations of confusions about particular mental phenomena, and have only indirectly assessed children's categorizations. This neglects a fundamental question: What is the underlying conceptual structure that organizes the broader domain of concepts about the mental world?

The concerns here are related to Keil's recent (1979) consideration of the development of children's "ontological" categories. The assumption is that there are basic ways in which children come to classify entities of the world. This includes categories such as physical objects, events, and abstract objects. The present description of children's acquisition of the concept of mind in many ways corroborates Keil's more general description of the acquisition of ontological categories. However, the research reported here was developed independently and employs different methods towards a more particular analysis of the ontological category of mind.

The present work is also comparable to Broughton's (1978) studies of children's philosophical concepts—their developing epistemology, metaphysics, or ontology. This is much involved with children's concept of mind. However, the goals and methods of Broughton's work are divergent from ones adopted here. Broughton's goal is to describe "ideal types" in children's philosophizing, by means of children's responses to open-ended interviews. The goal here, in contrast, is to describe the structure of children's ordinary concepts, by means of children's category judgments.

The present approach is suggested in the work of John Locke (1690). Part of the meaning of complex mental ideas is that they are conceived as commonly being attributes of mind. The question, then, is, what are the classes of phenomena that children attribute to the mind? The purpose is to determine the conceptual bases on which children make such attributions, their understanding of what makes mental phenomena "mental," and how this develops.

An Early Concept of Mind

One problem in studying the concept of mind in young children is that they are often unfamiliar with the term *mind*. However, there is considerable familiarity with another term that is commonly used to refer to the locus of distinctly mental activity, *brain*. This reflects ordinary uses of the term in expressions such as "use your brain" or "she's brainy." The focus here is not on children's scientific concepts of the brain as a physiological organ, but rather their ordinary concepts of it as a mind-like entity.

The first thing to note is that if children are simply asked about what the brain is used for, they typically describe its role in *thinking* ("it helps you think"), including other references to other characteristically cognitive activities, such as remembering or intellectual task performance. Johnson and Wellman (in press) found such responses to appear in the later preschool years. Between 3 and 5 years of age, there was a development from general ignorance of the brain's function to general reportings of this distinctly mental role. There were notably few references to physiological functions, and those that occurred were typically marked by confusion (e.g., the function of the brain was confused with that of the lungs or heart). Some time ago, Nagy (1953) reported comparable results in a study of children's understanding of body functions. Based on a sample of 4–7 year olds, Nagy concluded that children primarily interpreted the brain to be an organ of intellect.

Although this data provides a first impression of children's notion of the brain, it does not provide a general picture of what children judge to be the broader extent and limits of the brain's function. To examine this, Johnson and Wellman (in press) asked children to make judgments about the brain's role in a wide variety of activities. Two versions of the task were employed. In one, children were asked, "Do you need your brain to . . . ?"; in the other, "Suppose you didn't have a brain, could you still . . . ?" The items for judgment were selected to include typical "mental" operations (think, remember, dream, be smart), intellectual tasks (read, count . . .), as well as a broad spectrum of psychological processes and states including sensations (see, hear . . .), simple behaviors (walk, wiggle toes . . .), feelings (sad, surprised . . .), as well as involuntary responses (sneeze, breathe . . .). The results of three studies of this type have consistently indicated that by 5 or 6 years of age, children's judgments fall on a predictable scale. At the top of this scale, the brain is consistently regarded as essential for the class of strictly mental operations, and frequently for intellectual task performances. Intermediate on the scale are feelings, and at the bottom, the brain is judged as essentially unnecessary for simple behaviors, sensation, and involuntary acts.

The question is, what explains this pattern of judgments? Of course, children are presumably picking up an ordinary use of the term brain, as an organ used for intellectual performances. But how do children come to distinguish the extent on limits of such performances? One major factor appears to be that thinking and related mental acts are commonly dissociable from any one particular external organ of sense or behavior. Thus, the brain was judged to be unnecessary for particular sensations (see, hear . . .) and behaviors (walk, wriggle toes . . .) that were distinctly associated with external organs. Supporting this, children commonly explained that only the eyes were needed in order to see, the legs in order to walk, and so on. This does not explain, however, why children tended to associate the brain with performances such as reading and telling a story, which are respectively associated with the eyes and mouth. In this regard, it appears that young children are acquiring a sense of a set of tasks that require especially intentional applications of cognition, or the conscious using of one's brain. The combination of these two factors explains why feelings represent an ambiguous class—they are dissociable from external organs, but not distinctly characterized by the quality of thinking.

The argument that children are interpreting mental acts as dissociable from external organs rests in part on the assumption that children understand that the brain is distinctly internal. In this respect, Johnson and Wellman (in press) tested children on a variety of tasks that included judgments as to whether the brain is inside, whether the brain can be directly seen, and whether a doll (with various head parts) has a brain. Results were consistent. Three year olds were generally ignorant about the brain, whereas by 5 years old, most children knew it to be located in the head of real persons. Hence, during the same period that children are distinguishing a class of mental acts associated with the brain, they are also distinguishing the brain as an internal body part.

These results indicate that by the late preschool or early school years, children have acquired a general means of conceptualizing mental acts. These acts are characterized by "thinking," which can be dissociated from external behavior or sensation, or applied intentionally in cognitive acts. This understanding is represented in children's concept of brain as a body part with its own faculty, spatially and functionally dissociated from external body parts. Thus, the brain is conceived as "used to think," just as eyes are "used to see" or legs, "used to walk." This representation appears to be a natural extension of children's earlier understanding of external body parts and their functions. The task young children are confronted with is determining how mental acts are different from other behaviors ascribed to persons. Their initial solution is to categorize human action with respect to human body parts and their functions. Importantly, this solution is not only applied to early concepts of brain but also to initial concepts of mind in essentially the same manner as brain. Both are judged to be internal body parts with the faculty of thinking. Thus, the early concept of brain is indeed a concept of mind.

The performance of 5 and 6 year olds described here is a marked contrast to Broughton's (1978) characterization of children of the same age. Based on preliminary interview data of 4-7 year olds, Broughton (1978) comes to the following conclusion:

> The term mind is not used spontaneously but is assimilated under "brain." This in turn tends to be grossly identified with the head, the anatomical source of bodily movement. Weakly defined and poorly delimited, mental and physical show little differentiation, either in terms of spatial segregation or visibility/invisibility [pp. 82-83].

Except for the statement that the term mind is assimilated under "brain," this characterization is entirely at odds with the findings reported here. The Johnson and Wellman (in press) study clearly demonstrates a "spatial segregation" that Broughton reports as absent. In fact, even the performance of 3 year olds in the Johnson and Wellman research could not be characterized in Broughton's terms. Three year olds appeared to be ignorant, rather than confused, about the brain, and there was no evidence, at this or any age, that the brain was associated with anatomical movement.

The discrepancy between these findings could be due to a number of factors. One is Broughton's (1978) admittedly preliminary sampling. However, a more intriguing possibility is that the differences are to an extent real, and reflect something about the effects of different methods on children's performance. The suggestion is that traditional interview techniques, with questions such as "What is a brain?" or "What is a thought?", lead children to respond in terms of what the brain or thoughts are like. Lacking a concrete idea of what these things are, children resort to metaphors. In this sense, children can hardly be faulted for responses that the brain is your head, or thoughts are like speaking. Children may respond to interview questions by noting similarities, yet be discriminate when asked for more strictly categorical judgments. Thus, if asked to make comparative judgments about the head and brain, or thinking and talking, children who otherwise focus on similarities may now focus on differences. Children have otherwise been noted to overextend the use of words to point out similarities, even though being well aware of differences (Nelson, Rescorla, Gruendel, & Benedict, 1978). From this standpoint, the period from 4–7 years of age can be regarded as a transitional one in sorting out distinctive attributes of mind.

Later Concepts of Mind

The concept of brain as mental organ, located inside the head, marks the acquisition of one part of the ordinary meaning of mind. Mental acts are commonly located in the head (e.g., "It's all in your head."), and in this sense, brain and mind are commonly used synonymously to refer to the source of mental acts. Yet, this is only part of the full meaning of mind. In mature understanding, the mind is commonly distinguished as an immaterial construct, and thus differentiated from the material brain.

Distinctions between the mind and brain on the basis of their comparative materiality will be referred to as the *ontological* aspect of these concepts. A second aspect has to do with what the mind and brain are conceived as doing— that is, their *functional* implications. Here again, children's initial representation appears as a part of the broader adult meaning. The brain is commonly referred to as the sources of peculiarly mental acts, typically thinking and related modes, as distinct from simple behaviors, sensations, and feelings. This is one of the ordinary meanings of brain (i.e., "Use your brain.") and one of the ordinary meanings of mental in the sense of referring to "higher" cognitive functions (cf. Webster's dictionary). However, in the broader sense, mental functions, or attributes of mind, include the full range of subjective states, including sensations and feelings. Contrastingly, the adult understanding of brain includes functions that are distinctly physiological. The remaining issue, then, has to do with the development of a mind–body distinction with respect to children's differentiation of the ontological status and functions of mind and brain.

Johnson and Wellman (in press) examined this development in a study of children in first, third, fifth, and ninth grades. To test children's ontological distinction between mind and brain, children were asked whether they could see or touch the brain if a person's head was opened up, and contrastingly, if they could see or touch the mind under this condition. Results indicated a marked development between first and fifth grade. First graders judged the mind and brain to be equally visible and tangible entities in the head, whereas fifth graders typically distinguished the mind as intangible and invisible.

This developing ontological distinction is paralleled by functional distinctions. This is evident in a study employing a variant of the method just described. Children were asked to make judgments about their ability to perform various functions (sensations, behaviors, mental acts, etc.) in two conditions: supposing that one did not have a brain, and separately, supposing that one did not have a mind. First graders in these conditions similarly judged the mind and brain to be only necessary for the restricted set of mental acts, as previously described. In contrast, by fifth grade, children regarded the brain as necessary for a much broader array of functions, notably including sensation and behavior. The mind, in contrast, remained restricted in its function to more distinctly mental acts.

This would suggest that a mature understanding of mind and brain is appearing among fifth graders, between 10 and 12 years old. However, it turns out that interpretations of children this age still contrasted in revealing ways with those of older subjects. In the first place, although children this age regarded the brain as functioning throughout voluntary behavior and sensation, they rarely regarded the brain as functioning in strictly involuntary behaviors. This was true even among children who had explicit school instruction about the brain's involuntary functions. In the second place, children's explanations about the function of the brain were typically couched in mentalistic terms. Although these explanations indicated a definite sense of the physical connectedness of the brain to peripheral behavior and sensation, even mentioning nerve connections, these relations are typically explained by statements such as the brain "tells you what to do," "thinks what you're seeing," "helps you know where your feet are going," or "sends messages." Children rarely provided strictly physiological explanations of the brain's function.

This tentatively suggests that the fifth graders are not so much distinguishing the brain's physiological functions from the mind's mental operations, but that, rather, they are distinguishing the brain as a special kind of mental operator. Broughton (1978), from his interviews of 8–12 year olds, has suggested the type of operational distinction children may be making: "While the mind and brain share in thinking and deciding, there is a tendency to see the mind as imagining and dreaming, and the brain as having a more executive function [p. 85]."

To further examine this "tendency," the author (Johnson, 1980b) recently asked fifth graders and college juniors to make judgments about a new selection of operations. Because the purpose here was to examine a tendency to distinguish types of mental operations, subjects were asked to differentially judge examples of such types of operations as either being what the "mind mostly does" or what the "brain mostly does." The results were consistent with Broughton's suggestion. At fifth grade, children distinguished the brain as mostly "directing what you do,'' ''controlling the body,'' and ''helping see and hear,'' whereas the mind was regarded as mostly ''dreaming'' and ''imagining.'' Equally associated with mind and brain were items such as thinking, deciding, making plans, and solving problems. Feeling items were somewhat more associated with mind but not consistently so.

College juniors performed in a very different manner on this task than fifth graders. Whereas fifth graders judged ''directing what you do'' as mostly the brain's operation, college students distinctly judged this as mostly the mind's operation. Moreover, whereas fifth graders generally attributed mental operations (think, decide, make plans, feelings, etc.) equally to the mind and brain, college students overwhelmingly attributed all these operations to mind. The brain was judged to be more associated only with items with clearly bodily referents (i.e., ''controlling the body'' and ''helping see and hear'').

This evidence indicates that the mind–brain distinctions drawn by 10–12 year olds are not of the same order as those drawn by adults. Particularly, these children are not drawing a distinction between self-control (''describing what you do'') and bodily regulation (''controls body''). Rather, they are drawing a distinction between the brain's pervasive function in outward control of the body-self (control of arms, legs, eyes) versus the mind's inward fantasy (imagination, dreams). In contrast, the college juniors are distinguishing a more general class of mental predicates (mind) from those referring to distinctly physiological functions (brain).

These results can be interpreted as reflecting two levels in conceptions of the subjectivity of mind. At the first level, appearing among 10–12 year olds, children acquire a limited notion of subjectivity, typically characterized by acts of imagination or fantasy. This reflects the ordinary use of the term mind in statements like ''It's all in your mind.'' At a second level, the notion of subjectivity is extended to include all functions of the subjective self.

This interpretation is further supported by a corresponding development in conceptions of the ontological status of mind. As described earlier, fifth graders in the Johnson and Wellman (in press) study typically judged the mind to be invisible and intangible. Their explanations for this immateriality were typically that the mind is ''just a thought'' or ''it's what you think.'' Such responses are consistent with their views of the mind as distinctly associated with ''unreal'' imaginings or dreams. However, this evidence only indicates that children can distinguish the mind negatively, with respect to a single order of material reality. The remaining question is whether children can distinguish the mind positively, with respect to two orders of reality—the mental and physical.

This question can be addressed by examining the conceptual relations children draw between the mind and other mental constructs versus the brain and physical organs. In this respect, the author (Johnson, 1980b) asked fifth graders and college juniors about how the mind, and the brain, are related to concepts of self, soul, nerves, and organs. For example, contrasting questions were asked about whether the mind is like the self and whether the brain is like the self; whether the mind has nerves and whether the brain has nerves. Questions of this sort were designed to test understanding of the mind as related to the mental constructs of self and soul, as distinct from the brain as related to physical organs and nerves. Results showed that fifth graders had little sense of these broader conceptual relations. Few children expressed any sense of a relation between the mind and the subjective self. Similarly, the mind and soul were commonly judged to be different things (the soul being what goes to heaven), with their only commonality being their invisibility. Children often judged the mind to have nerves (perhaps in the metaphoric sense of "nervous") and somewhat less often to be an organ. This is not to say that there were no glimpses of greater sophistication among children this age; there were. But conceptions were a far cry from those of college juniors who evidenced pervasive understanding of the brain as distinctly an organ with nerves, and the mind as integrally related to the soul and subjective self.

In summary, the 10–12-year-old period appears to be a second turning point in the development of the concept of mind. During this period, children interpret the mind in terms of prototypically subjective acts of thought—namely, dreams and imagination. In this, the mind is equated with thought itself, and thus distinguished from physical reality. Only subsequently does there develop a concept of mind as an abstract object, comparable to the subjective self, to which is attributed the broader range of subjective acts and experiences.

Discussion

The development described in this section proceeds from concrete-physical to abstract-mental categories. Children first distinguish the mind as an internal physical thing and only later distinguish it as an abstract, immaterial object. In this respect, the development follows the traditional model of children's acquisition of mental concepts. Children have typically been reported to distinguish mental phenomena, such as dreams and thoughts, first as being internal things and later as being immaterial (Kohlberg, 1969; Laurendeau & Pinard, 1962; Piaget, 1926). However, because of methodological limitations and a narrow investigation of phenomena, these studies have neglected broader considerations about the development of reference to the world of mind.

In the first place, it is important to define the phenomena being studied. Pertinently, the world of mental phenomena, or mind, is largely defined negatively. "Mind" is distinguished as not external and not material. Thus, the very notion of reference to mental "things" appears to be derived from a more basic concept of reference to externally perceptible things. Children only gradually differentiate an alternate world of mind. This is not to say that children initially use mental terms to talk about physical things. The point is that children initially lack any concrete idea of what sorts of things mental terms refer to.

Lacking any other idea of what a mental term could refer to, young children, when asked to designate what a thought, dream, or mind is, will search for some relevant, externally perceptible referent. However, very early in development children exhibit some sense of the distinctive qualities of mental referents. For example, they may associate dreams with particularly ephemeral phenomena such as clouds, or characterize thoughts as a kind of inner voice, or mind as an internal body part. In this, children draw from their knowledge of other referents to distinguish peculiar attributes of mental phenomena. In the traditional interview situation, the exhibition of this partial knowledge depends on the creative spontaneity of the child. In the item-judgment tasks employed here, children's distinctive knowledge is likely to be more consistently revealed.

Development of the concept of mind is characterized by the application of old forms of reference to a new content. In this sense, it is metaphoric, reflecting children's changing characterizations of what the mind is like. In the late pre-school and early school years, children conceive the brain and mind to be like an internal body part with distinctly mental faculties. Thus, the mind and brain are modeled after more basic knowledge of reference to external body parts and things that are "inside," hidden from external perception. Between ages 10 and 12, children interpret the mind to be like a thought, associated particularly with dreams and imagination. In this case, the mind is modeled after reference to mental phenomena that are distinctly "unreal." Only during the adolescent years is the mind interpreted as an abstract entity unto itself, comparable to the "self" or "soul."

This development is comparable to Keil's (1979) description of the acquisition of ontological categories. Keil argues that categories of "objects" are differentiated "out of" one another. In this regard, he describes how mental phenomena such as secrets, dreams, and ideas are gradually differentiated as being nonphysical. This is based on grade-school children's judgments of anomalous sentences. In the early school years, Keil found that children judged everything to have properties of physical objects. Thus, for example, young children found nothing anomalous about sentences such as "The idea was heavy." or "Recess was tall." Subsequently, the category of events was differentiated out of the physical-object category. Hence, the preceding sentences were judged to be anomalous, and *idea* was interpreted as an event, such that "The idea was an hour long." was judged to be "O.K." Finally, in a third step, *idea* was differentiated as an abstract object, judged to be something "thought of" but lacking temporal properties.

This development similarly marks a sequence whereby mental phenomena are interpreted with respect to other types of referents. Children begin by interpreting mental phenomena in terms of a basic understanding of concrete physical referents. Subsequently, concepts, like ideas, are interpreted as events, and thus differentiated from physical objects. Finally, mental phenomena are differentiated as abstract objects in themselves, characterized solely by the property of being objects of thought. Keil's description thus follows the general lines of the developmental model proposed here. However, it leaves out more concrete issues regarding the differentiation of the world of mind.

Children apparently distinguish the nonphysical character of particular mental referents such as *idea* before they distinguish the general immateriality of mind. Keil's (1979) data indicate that by 7 or 8 years of age, a majority of children distinguish ideas as events lacking physical properties. Kohlberg (1969) also reports that by age 7, children are typically distinguishing dreams as immaterial. In contrast, only several years later do children typically distinguish the mind as immaterial. More importantly, it appears that early distinctions of "unreal" mental events, such as dreams, underlie the later understanding of the unreality of the mind. This is suggested by 10- and 12-year-old children's associations of the mind particularly with the functions of dreaming and imagining, as well as characterizing the mind as "just a thought." Thus, the mind is interpreted as like an idea or object of thought.

The development of conceptions of the kind of thing the mind is, ontologically, are basically a reflection of conceptions of what it purportedly does. In this respect, certain acts of mind are more basic or central to the concept than others. The case is similar to categories in the physical domain (cf. Rosch & Mervis, 1975), but here the "basic objects" are not physical things, but rather mental acts. Dreaming and imagining appear to centrally characterize the mind by age 10 to 12. Such phenomena concretely represent the "unreality" of mind. They are prototypical examples of the division between thought and things, marking instances where thinking is demonstrably at odds with reality. Piaget (1929) noted that the deceptive quality of dreams leads children to differentiate this phenomenon from physical referents before similar distinctions are drawn between thought and things or names and things. The suggestion here is that phenomena such as dreams hence more centrally characterize the immaterial quality of mind.

Whereas dreaming and imagining particularly characterize the unreality of the mental world, thinking more generally characterizes its function. Thinking and related cognitive modes appeared at the heart of early conceptions of mind and brain. As a cognitive faculty, dissociable from bodily or worldly involvement, thinking is apparently more central to the ordinary concept of mind/brain than sensing, behaving, or feeling. This core conception of mental function has a long history. It is apparent in Locke's (1690) description of modes of thinking, described earlier, as well as in the more recent history of psychology. In 19th century psychology, thinking was regarded as a faculty of mind, distinct from feeling, sensing, and willing. Subsequently, the study of thinking has similarly been treated as a separate discipline from other subjects such as emotion, perception, and motivation (Candland, 1977). It has taken a long time to undermine the notion of thinking as a separate faculty of mind and arrive at a conception of cognition as integral to the whole human psyche.

A remaining consideration is how successive interpretations of mind are related to one another. One model is that of a logically ordered addition of features. Kohlberg (1969) has suggested such a model with respect to the differentiation of mental events. As Kohlberg explains: "It is apparent that the differentiation of the immaterial from material presupposes the inside–outside distinction since all immaterial events are inside the body (but not vice versa [p. 359]." This "logic," however, is suspect. It is not at all self-evident that all immaterial events are necessarily inside the body. In fact, it could be just as well argued that this is logically contradictory. If an event is immaterial, how can it retain the physical property of spatial location? The same "logic" applies to the concept of mind: If the mind is not a material thing, then, strictly speaking, it cannot have the physical property of spatial location.

These two "logics" suggest alternate models of development. One implies that earlier conceptions of mind as internal are logically integrated with later conceptions of the mind as immaterial. The other suggests that the later conception of mind would supercede earlier conceptions. In fact, each model seems partially true. The author has found high-school and adult subjects who radically distinguish the mind as having no spatial location, explaining that it is "nowhere." Yet, more commonly the mind is considered as a kind of immaterial entity located somewhere in the brain. This, of course, raises the classical mind–body problem. Descartes, too, sought to locate the mind somewhere in the brain, and the logic of this position has remained in debate (cf. Globus, Maxwell, & Savodnik, 1976). The point here is that the relation of sequential interpretations of mind appears more like a juggling of different concepts than a logically discrete addition or subtraction of features. This is consistent with considerable other evidence of the logically loose relations that characterize ordinary concepts (Maratsos, 1977; Rosch & Mervis, 1975). More specifically, it is consistent with a view that the concept of mind is primarily based on concepts of what it does, rather than what it is. Knowledge of acts of mind precede knowledge of its "essence," which remains fundamentally ill-defined.

The fact that mind–body distinctions are ill-defined does not make them any less natural or universal. There has been a tendency to belittle such distinctions as being merely an arbitrary product of modern thinking. However, there is good reason to suspect that the problem is much older and more basic to human conception (see Popper & Eccles, 1977). Although this goes beyond the scope of this chapter, note that the acquisitions described here reflect very fundamental conceptions about human action. It is difficult to imagine any culture that does not refer to human acts—thoughts, intentions, memories—that are not externally perceptible. On this basis, it is natural to conceive an internal ground for such acts, a faculty of mind internal to the person. Moreover, this ground is commonly extended to distinguish the character of human action generally. In this case, the subjective basis of human action—mind, character, soul—is distinguished from mere bodily attributes.

CONCLUSION

Two developments have been outlined in this chapter: the acquisition of distinctive meanings of mental verbs and the development of distinctive reference to the world of mind. These considerations have presented a contrasting picture. Children do not initially interpret verb meanings strictly with reference to perceptible features, yet they do regard mental terms as having physical referents. These differences represent a fundamental asymmetry in children's acquisition of concepts in the physical and mental domains. Put simply, concepts of the mental domain are basically relational in meaning whereas those in the physical domain are basically referential. Mental terms are fundamentally used in relating mental predicates to subjects, whereas basic-object terms assume noun roles referring to concrete things. On these grounds, young children quite naturally apply old forms to new contents. Thus, children will apply their basic knowledge of reference in assuming mental terms also have physical referents (traditionally called "realism"). On the other hand, they will also apply their basic knowledge of mental predicates to physical objects (animism). This does not imply that children lack an awareness of differences between physical objects and mental statements. Children obviously have a basic sense of such differences, evident in their early use of language. Children's first references are to concrete externally perceptible objects, just as their first questions about causal relations concern psychological causes (Hood & Bloom, 1979). Confusions are not apparent at these basic levels of use, but rather occur later in reflection on these uses to derive secondary concepts of distinctly mental "objects" on the one hand and distinctly physicalistic predicates on the other.

Although different patterns have been described in the acquisition of mental verbs and the concept of mind, these developments are not unconnected. As described previously, the acquisition of meanings of mental verbs involves understanding that the same particular behavior or event could be due to different cognitive bases—for example, that a correct judgment could be equally due to knowing, remembering, or guessing. Thus, the development of relational meanings of mental verbs entails differentiating mental descriptions from external performance. Not surprisingly, children acquire these descriptive meanings of mental verbs at about the same time that they are distinguishing an internal faculty of mind (ages 4–7 years). Yet, the relation between these two developments is certainly not direct. Children could be well aware of particular mental descriptions without integrating this understanding with a concept of mind. Children might also acquire the descriptive meanings of mental verbs simultaneously with a concept of mind, or even acquire partial understanding of a mental faculty (e.g., "using one's brain") before acquiring other mental descriptors. There is, however, one restriction on possible sequences. An integrated concept of mind must entail some understanding of particularly mental acts. In this respect, concepts of what the mind is are basically a reflection of what it does.

There is a more general way of looking at relational versus referential meaning in the mental domain. The development of reference to mental phenomena should be marked by a change from the use of mental terms in attributing mental predicates to subjects towards attributing properties to mental "objects" themselves. In other words, children's ordinary comments about mental phenomena should be an indication of awareness of distinctively mental referents. Flavell (1978a) has suggested this with regard to the development of knowledge about visual perception. He argues that children's ability to qualify, or make "comments" about the "topic" of visual perception (e.g., that something is hard/easy to see, clear/unclear) indicates an understanding of the distinctly subjective quality of such perception—that is, that persons can have different subjective views of the same object. This argument deserves more general attention. Children come to talk about mental phenomena in all kinds of interesting ways that presumably reflect basic developmental changes. For example, one would predict that talk about the qualities of particular objects of thought, memory, and so on (e.g., that some particular idea is "just pretend" or "hard" to remember), would precede understanding of attributes of mental acts generally (e.g., that thoughts are "just in your mind"). The acquisition of metaphoric qualifiers also deserves attention. Metaphors are commonly used in talk about mental states. We say that thinking is clear, mixed up, or fuzzy; that attention is focused or wandering, that the mind grasps, holds, or is lost. As argued earlier, children's characterizations of mind can be regarded as largely metaphoric. The question is, when do children use what kinds of metaphors and what do they understand about their metaphoric quality?

Children's comments about mental phenomena is amenable naturalistic and experimental study. In the latter case, methods described earlier and otherwise by Keil (1979) seem promising. These commonly involve eliciting children's judgments about the appropriateness of selected attributes to the description of mental phenomena. Such methods could be extended to more thoroughly map out children's understanding of the distinctive properties of mental things.

The purpose of this chapter has been to outline a field of inquiry, regarding new approaches, theoretical problems, and developmental patterns. The research presented marks some initial steps into an extremely rich and fascinating area. It is curious that so little research has focused on such a fundamental set of representations. Perhaps this reflects assumptions that representation of the physical world is more basic, that concepts of mind are more arbitrary, less tied to the bedrock of "reality." Such assumptions, however, are not viable. Talk about mental phenomena certainly plays a central role in human social interaction and there is every reason to suggest that there are basic ways in which mental acts are represented. The time seems ripe for a major advance in understanding the structure and development of such representations. Such an advance promises to integrate very old ideas with new methods of inquiry.

ACKNOWLEDGMENTS

I wish to thank Henry Wellman as a collaborator on much of the research reported here as well as for comments on an earlier version of this chapter.

REFERENCES

Bowerman, M. Systematizing semantic knowledge: Changes over time in the child's organization of work meaning. *Child Development,* 1978, *49,* 977-987.

Broughton, J. Development of concepts of self, mind, reality, and knowledge. In W. Damon (Ed.), *New directions for child development* (No. 1). San Francisco: Jossey-Bass, 1978.

Brown, A. L. Metacognitive development and reading. In R. J. Spiro, B. Bruce, & W. F. Brewer (Eds.), *Theoretical issues in reading comprehension.* Hillsdale, N.J.: Lawrence Erlbaum Associates, 1978.

Candland, D. K. Persistent problems of emotion. In D. K. Candland, J. P. Fell, E. Keen, A. I. Leshner, R. M. Tarpy, & R. Plutchik (Eds.) *Emotion,* Bellmont, Calif.: Wadsworth, 1977.

Carey, S. The child as work learner. In M. Halle, J. Bresnan, & G. A. Miller (Eds.), *Linguistic theory and psychological reality.* Cambridge, Mass.: M.I.T. Press, 1978.

Clark, H. H., & Clark, E. V. *Psychology and language: An introduction to psycholinguistics.* New York: Harcourt, Brace, Jovanovich, 1977.

Flavell, J. H. First discussant's comments: What is memory development the development of? *Human Development,* 1971, *14,* 272-278.

Flavell, J. H. The development of knowledge about visual perception. In C. B. Keasey (Ed.), *Nebraska symposium on motivation.* Lincoln: University of Nebraska Press, 1978. (a)

Flavell, J. H. Metacognitive development. In J. M. Scandura & C. J. Brainerd (Eds.), *Structural/ process theories of complex human behavior.* Alphen a.a. Rijn, The Netherlands: Sijtnoff & Woordhoff, 1978. (b)

Gentner, D. On relational meaning: The acquisition of verb meaning. *Child Development,* 1978, *49,* 988-998.

Globus, G. G., Maxwell, G., & Savodnik, I. *Consciousness and the brain.* New York & London: Plenum Press, 1976.

Hood, L., & Bloom, L. What, when and how about why: A longitudinal study of early expressions of causality. *Monographs of the Society for Research in Child Development,* 1979, *6,* 1-47.

Johnson, C. N. *Early subjective-objective distinctions in response to requests to remember, think and know.* Manuscript submitted for publication, 1980. (a)

Johnson, C. N. *Development of the concept of mind: Distinguishing attributes of "mind" and "brain."* Manuscript in preparation, 1980. (b)

Johnson, C. N., & Maratsos, M. Early comprehension of mental verbs: Think and know. *Child Development,* 1977, *48,* 1743-1747.

Johnson, C. N., & Wellman, H. M. Children's developing conceptions of the mind and brain. *Child Development,* in press.

Johnson, C. N., & Wellman, H. M. Children's developing understanding of mental verbs: "Remember", "know", and "guess". *Child Development*, 1980, *51*, 1095-1102.

Keasey, C. B. Children's developing awareness and usage of intentionality and motives. In C. B. Keasey (Ed.), *Nebraska symposium on motivation* (Vol. 25). Lincoln: University of Nebraska Press, 1978.

Keil, F. C. *Semantic and conceptual development: An ontological perspective*. Cambridge, Mass.: Harvard University Press, 1979.

Kohlberg, L. Stage and sequence: The cognitive developmental approach to socialization. In D. A. Goslin (Ed.), *Handbook of socialization theory and research*. New York: Rand McNally, 1969.

Kuczaj, S. A. On the acquisition of a semantic system. *Journal of Verbal Learning and Behavior*, 1975, *14*, 340-358.

Kuczaj, S. A., & Lederberg, A. R. Height, age and function: Differing influences on children's comprehension of "younger" and "older." *Journal of Child Language*, 1977, *4*, 395-416.

Laurendeau, M., & Pinard, A. *Causal thinking in the child*. New York: International Universities Press, 1962.

Limber, J. The genesis of complex syntax. In T. E. Moore (Ed.), *Cognitive development and the acquisition of language*. New York: Academic Press, 1973.

Locke, J. *An essay on human understanding*. London, 1690.

Lyons-Ruth, K. Moral and personal value judgments of preschool children. *Child Development*, 1978, *49*, 1197-1207.

Maratsos, M. Disorganization in thought and word. In R. Shaw & J. Bransford (Eds.), *Perceiving, acting, and knowing: Toward an ecological psychology*. Hillsdale, N.J.: Lawrence Erlbaum Associates, 1977.

Marvin, R. S., Greenberg, M. T., & Mossler, D. G. The early development of conceptual perspective taking: Distinguishing among multiple perspectives. *Child Development*, 1976, *47*, 511-514.

Miscione, J. L., Marvin, R. S., O'Brien, R. G., & Greenberg, M. T. A developmental study of preschool children's understanding of the words "know" and "guess." *Child Development*, 1978, *49*, 1107-1113.

Mossler, D. G., Marvin, R. S., & Greenberg, M. T. Conceptual perspective taking in 2- to 6-year-old children. *Developmental Psychology*, 1976, *12*, 85-86.

Nagy, M. H. Children's conceptions of some bodily functions. *Journal of Genetic Psychology*, 1953, *22*, 359-378.

Nelson, K., Rescorla, L., Gruendel, J., & Benedict, H. Early lexicons: What do they mean? *Child Development*, 1978, *49*, 960-968.

Piaget, J. *The language and thought of the child*. London: Routledge & Kegan Paul, 1926.

Piaget, J. *Judgment and reasoning in the child*. New York: Harcourt, Brace, 1928.

Piaget, J. *The child's conception of the world*. New York: Harcourt, Brace, Jovanovich, 1929.

Piaget, J. *The origins of intelligence in children*. New York: International Universities Press, 1952.

Piaget, J. Piaget's theory. In P. H. Mussen (Ed.), *Carmichael's manual of child psychology* (Vol. 1). New York: Wiley, 1970.

Piaget, J., & Inhelder, B. *Memory and intelligence*. New York: Basic Books, 1973.

Piaget, J., & Inhelder, B. *The origin of the idea of chance in children*. New York: Norton, 1975.

Popper, K. R., & Eccles, J. C. *The self and its brain*. New York: Springer International, 1977.

Rosch, E., & Mervis, C. Family resemblances: Studies in the internal structure of categories. *Cognitive Psychology*, 1975, *7*, 573-605.

Sellars, W. Empiricism and the philosophy of mind. In H. Feigl & M. Scriven (Eds.), *Minnesota studies in the philosophy of science* (Vol. 1). Minneapolis: University of Minnesota Press, 1956.

Shantz, C. U. The development of social cognition. In E. M. Hetherington (Ed.), *Review of child development research* (Vol. 5). Chicago: University of Chicago Press, 1975.

Shatz, M., & Gelman, R. Beyond syntax: The influence of conversational constraints on speech modifications. In C. E. Snow & C. A. Ferguson (Eds.), *Talking to children, language input & acquisition*, Cambridge, Eng.: Cambridge University Press, 1977.

Toulmin, S. Concept formation in philosophy and psychology. In S. Hook (Ed.), *Dimensions of mind*. New York: New York University Press, 1960.

Tulving, E. Episodic and semantic memory. In E. Tulving & W. Donaldson (Eds.), *Organization of memory*. New York: Academic Press, 1972.

Urberg, K. A., & Docherty, E. M. The development of role-taking skills in young children. *Developmental Psychology*, 1976, *12*, 198–203.

Urmson, J. O. Parenthetical verbs. In C. E. Caton (Ed.), *Philosophy and ordinary language*. Urbana: University of Illinois Press, 1963.

Wellman, H. M. The child's theory of mind: The development of conceptions of cognition. In S. R. Yussen (Ed.), *The growth of insight in the child*. New York: Academic Press, 1981.

Wellman, H. M., & Johnson, C. N. Understanding of mental processes: A developmental study of "remember" and "forget." *Child Development*, 1979, *50*, 79–88.

Author Index

Subject Index